Yeats's Worlds

Yeats's Worlds

Ireland, England
and the Poetic Imagination

David Pierce

With contemporary photographs by Dan Harper

Yale University Press
New Haven and London
1995

For Graham Martin in London
and for Eileen and Frank Buckley in Dublin

Set in Sabon by Best-set Typesetter Ltd, Hong Kong
Printed and bound in Hong Kong through World Print Ltd

Library of Congress Cataloging-in-Publication Data

Pierce, David.
Yeat's Worlds/David Pierce: with contemporary
photographs by Dan Harper.
p.   cm.
Includes bibliographical references (p.) and index.
ISBN 0–300–06323–7
1. Yeats, W. B. (William Butler), 1865–1939—Homes and haunts—
England.   2. Yeats, W. B. (William Butler), 1865–1939—Homes and
haunts—Ireland.   3. Yeats, W. B. (William Butler), 1865–1939—
Knowledge—England.   4. Yeats, W. B. (William Butler), 1865–1939—
Knowledge—Ireland.   5. Poets, Irish—19th century—Biography.
6. Poets, Irish—20th century—Biography.   7. Poets, Irish—English—
Biography.   8. England—Intellectual life.   9. Ireland—
Intellectual life.   10. England—In literature.   11. Ireland—In
literature. I. Title. PR5906.P54 1995 821'.8—dc20 95–2457 CIP

A catalogue record for this book is available from
the British Library.

Photograph Credits. Dan Harper: 11, 13, 18 (both), 19 (top), 20, 27 (top), 37 (bottom), 50 (top), 189 (top left and
bottom), 145 (left), 230, 236 (top right), 268.   Anne Butler Yeats: 16, 19 (bottom), 57 (top), 65, 87, 97, 136 (top),
163 (bottom), 209, 233 (top right), 241 (bottom).   Michael Butler Yeats: xiv, 9, 132, 211 (right), 245, 261 (top
right).   Rex Roberts: 9 (both), 34, 105, 169 (bottom), 200 (both), 202, 208, 212, 256 (top).   Colin Smythe: 144
(bottom), 153, 236 (bottom), 237, 238 (bottom), 250, 252, 256 (bottom), 262 (top right).   Jean Townsend: 30, 37
(top), 226 (right).   Diana Adams: 261 (top left).   Anna MacBride-White: 198.   David Pierce: 40 (top), 189 (top
right), 246, 262 (bottom).   Pyms Gallery, London: 65 (top), 254 (bottom), 264.   The Savile Club: 181.
Kilmainham Gaol: 216 (top).   Pat Walsh, Black Swan Books, Connecticut: 218.   The Brotherton Library, the
University of Leeds: 127, 178.   The John Rylands University Library of Manchester: 144 (top), 146, 148.   The
Bodleian Library, the University of Oxford: 129, 213.   National Bank of Ireland: 141.   Special Collections,
Margaret Clapp Library, Wellesley College, Massachusetts: 151.   Henry W. and Albert A. Berg Collection, the
New York Public Library, Astor, Lenox, and Tilden Foundations: 26, 110, 139, 163 (top).   The William Butler
Yeats Microfilmed Manuscripts Collection, Special Collection Department, the Frank Melville Jr Memorial Library,
State University of New York at Stony Brook: 46, 57 (bottom), 59, 92, 195, 232, 239.   The Beinecke Rare Book
and Manuscript Library, Yale University: 135 (bottom left), 155, 169 (top), 171, 175, 231, 233 (left), 234, 266.

Frontispiece: Yeats with his very long fine hands. From Arthur Symons, *Studies in Prose and Verse*
(1904).

Contents

Acknowledgements

I would like to thank A. P. Watt Ltd on behalf of Michael B. Yeats and Anne B. Yeats for their various permissions and for their kindness and hospitality; Anne B. Yeats for permission to reproduce illustrations by Jack B. Yeats and material from her father's library at Dalkey; Roy Foster for permission to use unpublished manuscript material; Oxford University Press and John Kelly for permission to use excerpts from previously unpublished letters by W. B. Yeats, copyright © 1995 by Michael B. Yeats and Anne B. Yeats; Ann Saddlemyer for helpful advice with regard to George Yeats's correspondence. I am also indebted to the Council of Trustees of the National Library of Ireland for permission to cite extracts from Yeats's writings in their possession, and to the Board of Trinity College, Dublin for permission to cite extracts from the correspondence of Thomas MacGreevy and George Yeats. I am especially grateful to Valerie Eliot for permission to reproduce an unpublished (and previously unknown) letter of her husband, T. S. Eliot; Margaret Farrington and Elizabeth Ryan for permission to use material from the unpublished correspondence of Thomas MacGreevy; the eighth Duke of Wellington for permission to cite from the correspondence of Lady Gerald Wellesley. I am also grateful to: the Houghton Library, Harvard University for permission to cite from the correspondence of Allan Wade and Dorothy Wellesley; the Beinecke Rare Book and Manuscript Library, Yale University for permission to cite from the Olga Rudge Papers; the Frank Melville Jr Memorial Library, State University of New York for permission to cite from the William Butler Yeats Microfilmed Manuscript Collection; the New York Public Library for permission to cite from the work and correspondence of John Quinn, William Butler Yeats, John Butler Yeats, Lady Gregory; the Margaret Clapp Library, Wellesley College, Massachusetts for permission to use material from their Special Collections; the John Rylands University Library of Manchester for permission to cite from the correspondence of Annie Horniman; the Brotherton Library, University of Leeds for permission to cite from the correspondence of William Butler Yeats, John Butler Yeats, Lily Yeats, and Edmund Gosse. Grateful acknowledgement is given to New Directions Publishing Corporation and Faber and Faber Ltd for permission to quote from the following copyrighted works of Ezra Pound: *The Cantos* (Copyright © 1934, 1937, 1940, 1948, 1956, 1959, 1962, 1963, 1963, 1966, and 1968 by Ezra Pound), *Ezra Pound and Dorothy Shakespear* (Copyright © 1976, 1984 by the Trustees of the Ezra Pound Literary Property Trust). Previously unpublished material by Ezra Pound Copyright © 1995 by the Trustees of the Ezra Pound Literary Property Trust; used by permission of Faber and Faber and New Directions Publishing Corporation, agents. For rights to cite from Yeats's published work in the United States, I am grateful to Simon & Schuster for extracts from, firstly, *The Variorum Edition of the Poems of W. B. Yeats*, edited by Peter Allt and Russell K. Alspach, copyright © 1924,

1928, 1933, 1934 by Macmillan Publishing Company, renewed 1952, 1956, 1961, 1962 by Bertha Georgie Yeats; copyright © 1940 by Georgie Yeats, renewed 1958 by Bertha Georgie Yeats, Michael Butler Yeats, and Anne Yeats. And, secondly, *The Variorum Edition of the Plays of W. B. Yeats*, edited by Russell K. Alspach, copyright © 1921, 1934 by Macmillan Publishing Company, renewed 1949, 1962 by Bertha Georgie Yeats; copyright © 1940 by George Yeats, renewed by Bertha Georgie Yeats, Michael Butler Yeats, and Anne Yeats.

Among those I am specifically indebted to are Timothy Webb of Bristol University, George Watson of Aberdeen University, and Graham Martin, who kindly agreed to comment on the manuscript. I would like to record my debt of gratitude to Dan Harper of Aptos, California, for his photographs, and to the following: in my own College, the Principal for supporting my research and in particular for granting me a sabbatical; the Librarian and her staff; colleagues for their patience. Elsewhere in Britain: the Librarian and staff, the Brotherton Library, the University of Leeds; Dave Whiteley and Gordon Fraser in the Photographic Department, the University of York; Anthony Garrett Anderson and Peter Giles, Archivist, the Savile Club, London; Alan Hobart, Pyms Gallery, London; Dr Bruni de la Motte; Dr W. J. McCormack; Eva Reichmann; Dr Boger, The Chantry House, Steyning, Sussex; Lord Patrick Gibson, Penns in the Rocks, Groombridge, Sussex; the antiquarian booksellers in York, especially Peter Miller, Nigel Wallace, and George Ramsden; the York Bibliographical Society, the University of Leeds James Joyce Research Group, and the Second International Conference on Word and Image held in Zurich in August 1990, who kindly listened to lectures on Yeats as this book was taking shape in my head. Colin Smythe was particularly responsive to requests. A grant from the British Academy enabled me to consult material in the United States. I am, as ever, especially grateful to those individuals associated with the production of this book, including my editor at Yale Robert Baldock, Candida Brazil, Patty Rennie, Fiona Screen, Alice Mackrell for the index and to Otto Bohlmann whose 'light editing' made significant improvements to the text.

In the United States: Evert Volkersz, Curator, and Diane Englot, Instructional Support, at Stony Brook, New York; Ruth R. Rogers and Jill Triplet, Librarian and her assistant in Special Collections, Wellesley College; Lesley Morris, the Houghton Library; Vincent Giroud and Patricia Willis, Curators; the Beinecke Rare Book and Manuscript Library; Wayne Furman, Curator, the New York Public Library; Patience-Anne Lenk, former Librarian, Colby College, Maine; George Mills Harper; the photographer Diana Adams of Fairfax, Virginia; Pat Walsh, Black Swan Books, Connecticut; Dr Joe Schork and Betsy Boehne, the University of Massachusetts, Boston, for their kind hospitality. In Canada: Jean Townsend, as kind as ever.

In Ireland: Catherine Fahy, Assistant Keeper, Department of Manuscripts, the National Library of Ireland; Stuart O Seanóir, Assistant Librarian, Trinity College, Dublin; John Tooran, Kilmainham Gaol, Dublin; Anna MacBride-White; Rex Roberts; the Central Bank of Ireland, Dublin; Peter Costello; Dr Tim O'Neill.

My warmest thanks as ever go to Mary Eagleton and Matt Eagleton-Pierce.

Every effort has been made to ascertain and acknowledge ownership of illustrative material; any errors, absences, or oversights will be rectified at the earliest opportunity.

Abbreviations

A	*Autobiographies* (London: Macmillan, 1955).
AV [A]	*A Critical Edition of Yeats's* A Vision *(1925)*, ed. George Mills Harper and Walter Kelly Hood (London: Macmillan, 1978).
AV [B]	*A Vision* (1937; repr. London: Macmillan, 1962).
CT	*The Celtic Twilight* (London: A. H. Bullen, 1902).
DWL	*Letters on Poetry from W. B. Yeats to Dorothy Wellesley* (1940; repr. London: Oxford University Press, 1964).
E & I	*Essays and Introductions* (London: Macmillan, 1961).
Ex	*Explorations* (London: Macmillan, 1962).
L	*Letters of W. B. Yeats,*' ed. Allan Wade (London: Rupert Hart-Davis, 1954).
LGJ 1	*Lady Gregory's Journals, Volume I: Books One to Twenty-Nine, 10 October 1916 – 24 February 1925,* ed. Daniel Murphy (Gerrards Cross: Colin Smythe; New York: Oxford University Press, 1978).
LGJ 2	*Lady Gregory's Journals, Volume II: Books Thirty to Forty-Four, 21 February 1925 – 9 May 1932,* ed. Daniel Murphy (Gerrards Cross: Colin Smythe, 1987).
L [K]	*The Collected Letters of W. B. Yeats,* vol. 1, 1865–1895, ed. John Kelly (Oxford: Oxford University Press, 1986).
L [K] 3	*The Collected Letters of W. B. Yeats,* vol. 3, 1901–1904, ed. John Kelly and Ronald Schuchard (Oxford: Clarendon Press, 1994).
LS	*J. B. Yeats: Letters to his Son W. B. Yeats and Others, 1869–1922,* ed. Joseph Hone (London: Faber and Faber, 1944).
M	*Mythologies* (New York: Macmillan, 1959).
Mem	*Memoirs,* ed. Denis Donoghue (New York: Macmillan, 1973).
MGY	*The Gonne-Yeats Letters, 1893–1938,* ed. Anna MacBride White and A. N. Jeffares (London: Pimlico, 1993).
R or *Reveries*	*Reveries over Childhood and Youth* (London: Macmillan, 1916).
SB	*The Speckled Bird,* ed. William H. O'Donnell (Toronto: McClelland and Stewart, 1976).
SR	*The Secret Rose* (London: Lawrence and Bullen, 1897).
UP 1	*Uncollected Prose by W. B. Yeats,* vol. 1, ed. John P. Frayne (New York: Columbia University Press, 1970).
UP 2	*Uncollected Prose by W. B. Yeats,* vol. 2, ed. John P. Frayne and Colton Johnson (London: Macmillan, 1975).
VP	*The Variorum Edition of the Poems of W. B. Yeats,* ed. Peter Allt and Russell K. Alspach (New York: Macmillan, 1957, repr. 1971).
VPl	*The Variorum Edition of the Plays of W. B. Yeats,* ed. Russell K. Alspach (London: Macmillan, 1966, repr. 1979).
Y & TSM	*W. B. Yeats and T. Sturge Moore: Their Correspondence, 1901–1937,* ed. Ursula Bridge (London: Routledge and Kegan Paul, 1953; repr. Westport, Conn.: Greenwood Press, 1978).
YVP 1	George Mills Harper *et al.* (eds), *Yeats's 'Vision' Papers,* vol. 1, *The Automatic Script: 5 November 1917–18 June 1918* (London: Macmillan, 1992).

YVP 2	George Mills Harper *et al.* (eds), *Yeats's 'Vision' Papers*, vol. 2, *The Automatic Script: 25 June 1918–29 March 1920* (London: Macmillan, 1992).
YVP 3	George Mills Harper *et al.* (eds), *Yeats's 'Vision' Papers*, vol. 3, *Sleep and Dream Notebooks, Vision Notebooks 1 and 2, Card File* (London: Macmillan, 1992).
BERG	Henry W. and Albert A. Berg Collection, the New York Public Library, Astor, Lenox, and Tilden Foundations.
NLI	The National Library of Ireland.
QUINN	John Quinn Memorial Collection, Rare Books and Manuscript Division, the New York Public Library, Astor, Lenox, and Tilden Foundations.
SUNY Stony Brook	The William Butler Yeats Microfilmed Manuscripts Collection, Special Collections Department, the Frank Melville Jr Memorial Library, State University of New York at Stony Brook.
TCD	Trinity College, Dublin.
Yale	The Beinecke Rare Book and Manuscript Library, Yale University.

A Note on the Text

In transcribing Yeats's handwriting I have kept to a minimum the use of ⟨*sic*⟩, preferring instead that the reader gain a more direct appreciation of the vagaries of Yeats's spelling.

(?)   indicates a query in my reading of a transcription.
⟨?⟩   indicates an omission in my transcription of an illegible word or phrase.
*   after the first appearance of a person's name indicates a brief biographical sketch in the Appendix.

Introduction

Henry Nevinson said of Yeats: 'You have only to shake him and all manner of beautiful things tumble out.'[1] With this in mind I have consciously sought to make this book both beautiful to the eye and challenging to the intellect. The format is similar to my companion volume *James Joyce's Ireland*, published by Yale University Press in 1992, a mixture, that is, of history, biography, and critical discussion, supplemented by a range of illustrative material, including contemporary photographs by Dan Harper. This is a provisional study, for until the full correspondence and the new authorised biographies of Yeats and George Yeats are available, any picture which relies on a biographical reading of Yeats necessarily must be incomplete. In my guide to Yeats criticism, published by Bristol Classical Press in 1989, I suggested: 'Future readers of Yeats, especially when they possess what should be the definitive works, will marvel both at our ignorance and our achievement.'[2] I see no reason to alter this verdict. Here in this book, in my attempt to recreate the contexts for the reception of Yeats's work and to dwell on aspects in the Yeats story that have received relatively little attention, I have made as much use of unpublished correspondence and manuscript material as was permitted. From libraries in Ireland, Britain, and the United States, I have also assembled a range of less familiar items, such as newspaper reports, minutes of meetings Yeats attended, theatre brochures, postcards, notes, and jottings.

In highlighting Yeats's English contexts my aim has been to redress certain Irish claims to exclusivity and in the process to widen discussion about the nature of Anglo-Irish literary relations in the modern period. For much of his life Yeats lived in England: from 1887 and for most of the 1890s he was in London, first at Bedford Park, later at The Temple; from 1898 to 1918 he lived at Woburn Buildings near St Pancras; from 1918 until 1922, Oxford was his base; in the 1920s and 1930s when in London he frequently stayed at the Savile Club in Piccadilly (later, in Brook Street); in the 1930s he spent not an inconsiderable amount of time in Sussex at the homes of Lady Dorothy Wellesley and Edith Shackleton Heald. He was a seasoned clubman, and was delighted to be elected in 1917 to the male-only Savile Club and in 1937 to the Athenæum. He mixed in fashionable upper-middle-class English circles and could count among his friends and acquaintances those with titles such as Lady Ottoline Morrell, Lady Elizabeth Pelham, and Lady Cunard, those with influence, such as John Masefield and Edmund Gosse, and those with power, such as Augustine Birrell, who was Chief Secretary to Ireland from 1907 to 1916. He dined with Asquith at 10 Downing Street during the First World War, was a guest at Blenheim, Renishaw Hall, and Garsington Manor in the 1920s, and for his United States lecture tour in 1932 was lent a car by Henry Ford and driven by the same chauffeurs who acted for Churchill. He married an upper-middle-class woman from South Kensington, whose assets he shrewdly observed at the time were a little above his income. When he died, he did so outside Ireland and was surrounded by his English wife, the first Director of Talks at the BBC, an Australian poet and music critic who in part identified himself as English, and by the wife of the seventh Duke of Wellington. In many respects, his chief influences in literature were also English: William Blake (for whom Yeats invented an Irish lineage) and William Morris – and not far behind were Spenser, Shakespeare, Shelley, and Rossetti. In retrospect, it was right that early commentators insisted on his Irishness, but now the time seems propitious for a different kind of evaluation which also pays homage not so much to his Englishness as to his English contexts.

For ease of reference, I have kept to a chronological path; the first four chapters deal with Yeats in the nineteenth century, the second four with Yeats in the twentieth century. My first three chapters also introduce topics or strands other than biography or chronology, such as Yeats's Anglo-Irishness, Yeats and landscape, Yeats and the occult, Yeats and cultural nationalism. In this way Yeats emerges as a more complex figure against several overlapping contexts and backgrounds. Each of the chapters betrays a particular emphasis: the importance of Sligo and family to Yeats in chapter 1; the female-centredness of Yeats's interest in the occult and oral tradition in chapter 2; Yeats's debt (or otherwise) to the Irish tradition in the nineteenth century in chapter 3; the significance of 1890s London and the aesthetic movement in chapter 4; Yeats's involvement in the Abbey Theatre and the return to the people as signalled by Synge and his brother Jack B. Yeats in chapter 5; the context of the First World War for understanding Yeats in the years which witnessed a developing friendship with Pound, 'Easter 1916', and his marriage to Georgina Hyde-Lees. In the final two chapters I concentrate on Yeats's response to the emergence of the new Ireland in the 1920s and his attitudes, both personal and political, to a changed and changing world in the 1930s.

My argument is as much to do with texture as thesis, but by returning to the original contexts and reception of his work I have given an indication of my critical colours. Whether as a young man anticipating his future development or retrospectively arranging it, Yeats had the uncanny knack of making it look as if his life fell out according to a consciously conceived pattern. In puncturing holes in such a theory of continuity, my intention has been not to undermine Yeats's reputation but rather to establish a more faithful record. Ironically, when it came to the relationship between life and art, Yeats insisted on discontinuity, thereby demonstrating his ties were closer to Modernism than Romanticism. But, to my mind, the man who sat down to breakfast and the man who wrote verse shared more than Yeats imagined. Defining such a relationship requires of the critic a subtlety that is both dependent on and suspicious of reflectionist theories. It is also important not to lose the writer in the man or adopt a shallow form of contrastive analysis whereby the emperor is stripped of his clothes. In writing this study my concern throughout has been to point up connections, to disturb the living stream, and, if anything, to underline the significance of Yeats's achievement when set against his turbulent life.

When I was introduced to Yeats as an undergraduate in the 1960s, it was assumed that Yeats wrote nothing but verse and that whenever a woman was mentioned in a poem the reference must be to Maud Gonne. To redress such an imbalance I have included discussion of the full range of Yeats's writing and stressed the roles played by other women: Lady Gregory, Florence Farr, Olivia Shakespear, Annie Horniman, Iseult Gonne, and, in particular, George Yeats. I devote a significant proportion of the book to Yeats's wife, for having read her unpublished correspondence, I now believe she is central to any reassessment of Yeats: in chapter 2 I examine the automatic writing sessions she conducted with Yeats after 1917; in chapter 6 I consider the period leading up to her marriage with Yeats; in chapter 7 I reflect on her role as wife of an Irish Senator and Nobel Prize Winner and on the part she played in keeping Yeats in Ireland. Her presence (and humour) can be felt throughout, and I have chosen to end the book with her.

'Memory Harbour' (1900), by Jack B. Yeats. Yeats used this illustration opposite the title page of *Reveries*. 'When I look at my brother's picture, houses and anchored ship and distant lighthouse all set close together as in some old map, I recognize in the blue-coated man with the mass of white shirt the pilot I went fishing with, and I am full of disquiet and of excitement, and I am melancholy because I have not made more and better verses' (*R* 96). According to Lily Yeats, the pilot is Michael Gillen, whose duty it was to negotiate larger craft up to Sligo Creek.

1

Yeats and Sligo

BETWEEN EXTREMITIES

William Butler Yeats, 'Willie' or 'WB' as he was known to family and friends, was born in Dublin on 13 June 1865.[1] It would be hard to imagine a more fitting sign of the zodiac for 'Doubbllinnbbayyates', the label he wears in *Finnegans Wake* (1939), than Gemini, the twins. As he was later to confess to Dorothy Wellesley* in 1937: 'I begin to see things double – doubled in history, world history, personal history' (*DWL* 135). In his *Almanack* for June 1865, Partridge might have had Yeats in his sights: 'Another opposition! aye, and an unusually inauspicious one, because of the agents in the zodiacal misunderstanding. Jupiter and the Sun, the two great benign influences, pulling in opposite directions.'[2] Man and Mask, Dove or Swan, Self and Anti-Self – these are some of the dialectical terms used by critics when discussing Yeats. He comes down to us from the Golden Age of Modernism, in the robes of a Nobel Prize Winner, as someone who 'swerved in naught,/Something to perfection brought' (*VP* 577). But, in reality, Yeats, with his 'habit of vacillation',[3] is the troubled and troubling artist who spent a long time seeing, or hoping to see, things double.

> Between extremities
> Man runs his course;
> A brand, or flaming breath,
> Comes to destroy
> All those antinomies
> Of day and night;
> The body calls it death,
> The heart remorse.
> But if these be right
> What is joy?
> (*VP* 499–500)

As is apparent from these opening lines of 'Vacillation', Yeats touches a vein of rich suggestiveness by means that are both direct and elusive. Life is summed up in terms invented by the ancient Greeks and sanctioned by the Church: between day and night, good and evil, knowledge and ignorance, the intellect and the heart. Contrary to expectation, the use of the general Latinate word *antinomies*, carefully positioned to reverberate against the equally abstract word *extremities*, prompts all sorts of association. In converting borders into opposites, Yeats brings into dialectical play

1

co-ordinates which are spatially separate and distinct. Given that he knew no Latin or Greek, his choice of vocabulary is, on reflection, invariably precise. It is not 'oppositions' or 'contrasts' or 'antitheses', but a word associated with philosophy and the law: anti-nomia; against the law; or, following Kant, a 'contradiction between conclusions that seem equally logical, reasonable, or necessary' (OED). As if this were not complicated enough, Yeats introduces the dynamic image of the brand or flaming breath, an image that initially draws on and then detaches itself from the Pentecostal flame and the sexually charged Blakean heritage of 'crimson joy'. If death and remorse constitute life's horizons, the question Yeats asks is not Where can joy be found? but the more fundamental, arresting thought: What is joy? There seems little room here for the power of love to triumph – if, that is, we ignore the title, 'Vacillation'.

Throughout his life Yeats's own horoscope was often cast, but perhaps none was more apposite for beginning this book than the one outlined in the 1890s by a collaborator of his uncle George Pollexfen,* who was 'unacquainted with the subject':

> Saturn is most in the ascendant, Mercury is trine to ascendant, Saturn and Herschel are both trine to the moon, and Jupiter sextile to the moon. The personal appearance of the native is thus described: 'Dry and cold, a dark swarthy complexion, black hair and dark eyes . . . thin nose inclined to bend down over the lips, nostrils closed, chin long and rather large . . . head held slightly forward in stooping.' In matters of the mind the native is 'profound in imagination, reserved, patient, melancholy, in arguing and disputing grave and austere in manner . . . a lover of all honest sciences, and a searcher into, and delighter in, strange studies and novelties . . . very imaginative, subject to see visions, and dream dreams'.[4]

The accuracy of this is uncanny. 'No one could say', recalls 'John Eglinton',* 'he was without humour, but it was a saturnine humour, and he was certainly not one who suffered gladly the numerous people he considered fools.'[5] 'Yeats looks just what I expected,' declared Martin Ross when she met him at Coole Park. 'A cross between a Dominie Sampson and a starved R.C. curate – in seedy black clothes – with a large black bow at the root of his long naked throat.'[6]

As to Yeats's swarthy looks, these too were often commented on by contemporaries. According to Stephen MacKenna, his face was 'dark, very dark: Spanish looking . . . weird . . . something uncanny in that thin dark face crowned with a downfalling mane of dark hair and lit with the lambent light of those dark dreaming eyes'.[7] George Moore's* portrait of him in Evelyn Innes (1898) as Ulick Dean suggests that it 'was his eyes that gave its sombre ecstatic character to his face'.[8] In 1899 another commentator noted his 'rather narrow face, with eyes rather close, and the left eye looking a little outwards; clean-shaved, showing blue-black to match his suit; very much the poet all through his nature'.[9]

The first meeting Yeats attended of the Southwark Irish Literary Club in March 1888 made a similar impression on the first historian of the Irish Literary Revival, W. P. Ryan: 'In appearance he was tall, slight, and mystic of the mystical. His face was not so much dreamy as haunting: a little weird even – so that really if one were to meet him on an Irish mountain in the moonlight he would assuredly hasten away to the nearest fireside with a story of a new and genial ghost which had crossed his path. He spoke in a hushed, musical eerie tone: a tone which had constant suggestions of the faery world, of somebody "in them" (that is, in the councils of the fairies), as we say in Ireland.'[10] When Oliver St John Gogarty* spoke at Wellesley College, Massachusetts, in October 1939, he confessed that Yeats's personal appearance was 'something almost eerie': 'He was dark, with hawklike features, and very beautiful hands; he seemed to be between the human and the superhuman. "Sometimes I really believed he was a fairy king," Dr Gogarty said. The great poet was modest, aloof, sensitive, often disillusioned; one was conscious of the mystical strain in the man.'[11]

Wilfrid Gibson recalled his first meeting with Yeats in a Holborn teashop and listening to him 'pouring/A stream of scintillating eloquence/In his broad-vowelled brogue'.[12] At a reception held for him in the rooms of the Irish Literary Society in New York in March 1904, comment was passed on his 'attractive naivety in his unsual somewhat stiff gestures, in his disconcerting lapses into mood, in his ingeniously disarranged clothes'.[13] According to Maurice Bowra, 'Yeats was not in the least "cosy". His genius for words was an obstacle between you and easy intimacy.'[14] He spoke with a marked Irish brogue, and his choice of words was as striking as his sentences were well fashioned. For Max Beerbohm, whom he first met in the winter of 1893, Yeats was *une âme auguste*: 'His benign aloofness from whatever company I saw him in, whether he were inspired with language or silence, made everyone else seem rather cheap.'[15] As for comment on changes in Yeats's appearance, no-one was more discerning than Beerbohm, who in 1914 remarked:

> As years went by, the visual aspect of Yeats changed a little. His face grew gradually fuller in outline, and the sharp angles of his figure were smoothed away; and his hands – those hands which in his silences lay folded downward across his breast, but left each other and came forth and, as it were, stroked the air to and fro while he talked – those very long, fine hands did seem to have lost something of their insubstantiality. His dignity and his charm were as they always had been. But I found it less easy to draw caricatures of him. He seemed to have become subtly less like himself.[16]

In keeping with Gaelic verse, there was a tendency in Yeats 'to slur the stress and to avoid emphatic rhythms'.[17] Indeed, the experience of reading his verse is not unlike consuming heady wine, for, as Robert Lynd remarked in 1909, Yeats is 'the poet of intoxication'.[18] Yeats followed Blake in recognising that 'The Man who never in his Mind & Thoughts travel'd to Heaven Is No Artist.'[19] He lacks the integrity of Hardy, the intellectual certainty of Shaw, or the peculiarly compelling voice of Kipling, but for anyone interested in understanding or tracing the often bumpy transition from the nineteenth to the twentieth century, whether in thought or literature, there are few better models than the 'strong enchanter',[20] the Nietzschean poet who never stopped remaking himself. His work constitutes at once a form of intellectual wrestling and an engagement of the heart. In his best poetry there is a holding down of emotion, a pressure below the surface of words, the achievement of a 'powerful and passionate syntax' (*E & I* 522).[21] As John Masefield* claimed for his friend of forty years:

> No man in all this time has given more hope
> Or set alight such energy in souls.
> There was no rush-wick in an earthen saucer
> Half-filled with tallow, but he made it burn
> With something of a light for somebody.[22]

The course of Yeats's eventful life, which ran from 1865 to 1939, coincided with momentous events in the public arena: the beginning of the end of the British Empire, the fall of feudalism in Ireland, the renewed struggle for mastery in Europe, the widespread collapse of cultural optimism, and the difficult birth of modernity. Yeats began as a dream-led Victorian and ended as a scornful modern. As one acerbic Irish journalist observed in 1902, Yeats 'dreams dreams and gets things on his nerves'.[23] From the outset we need, therefore, a method of inquiry sufficiently agile both to appreciate and to contextualise his work, for he was, as George Bornstein suggests, 'perhaps the most complex mind of our century, and one cannot fully come to grips with him through any single approach'.[24]

When Clifton Fadiman reviewed Joseph Hone's biography of Yeats in the *New Yorker* in February 1943 he drew attention to the frame of two wars, the American Civil War and the Second World War: 'Yeats was born in the year of Appomatox and died January 28, 1939, in the first year of Germany's First War Against Mankind.'[25] In March 1904, in an interview with a reporter on the *Daily Chronicle* after his American tour, Yeats provocatively 'insisted all along on the idea of Ireland as being a "mother country"'.[26] In retrospect, the year of Yeats's birth can be read in terms either of coincidence or of doubles. In April 1865, within weeks of Lincoln's assassination, the American Civil War ended, at the close of which 'the Irish in America had wakened to a sense of power and a hope of vengeance'.[27] In September of the same year in Dublin, Yeats's later mentor John O'Leary* and Jeremiah O'Donovan Rossa were arrested for being members of an illegal secret society, the American-financed Irish Republican Brotherhood (IRB), an organisation that Yeats was to join, probably in 1886.[28] In London the hit play that summer, replete with the seditious song 'The Wearing of the Green', was Dion Boucicault's *Arrah-na-Pogue*, with Boucicault himself in the title role of Shaun the Post.[29]

Irishman Yeats was born the same year as India-born Kipling, one a severe critic, the other a tormented apologist of empire. With the publication of John Henry Newman's *The Dream of Gerontius*, Algernon Swinburne's *Atalanta in Calydon*, and Lewis Carroll's *Alice in Wonderland*, the mid-Victorian imagination was in full flight. Yeats, meanwhile, the 'backward-looking' philosopher who found some of his deepest inspiration in thinking about the body, was betrayed into life by the Porphyrean 'honey of generation', uncertain, as he later imagines it in 'Among School Children', of his 'setting forth':

> What youthful mother, a shape upon her lap
> Honey of generation had betrayed,
> And that must sleep, shriek, struggle to escape
> As recollection or the drug decide,
> Would think her son, did she but see that shape
> With sixty or more winters on its head,
> A compensation for the pang of his birth,
> Or the uncertainty of his setting forth.
>
> (*VP* 444)

In the 1930s when Eglinton, who sat next to Yeats at high school in Dublin, embarked on his recollections of the poet, he immediately pitched into a discussion of his Anglo-Irishness:

Yeats's boyhood was passed in the great peace of Queen Victoria and amid all the social and spiritual conditions prevailing throughout her realms, especially perhaps among the Anglo-Irish, who in addition to the universal feeling of stability, enjoyed a special sense of 'possessing the earth', a sublimation of the old Ascendancy feeling – a sense in the retrospect almost one of blessedness, but soon, alas! to engender in the spirit of the youth a vague restlessness. I have read that there was something like it in the Southern States of North America before the abolition of slavery, when families, even without actual wealth, passed on from one generation to another the inheritance of privileged leisure. The Yeats family, members of a little patriarchal community of traders in the enchanting county of Sligo, were likewise born into a natural sense of aristocracy, and the poet, though his father was an impoverished artist, acquired a strong feeling of superiority – which has not been altogether serviceable to him as a national poet – to all phases of human activity except 'the arts'.[30]

Though not strictly speaking one of their number, Yeats identified with the Anglo-Irish and in effect – though they would not have recognised this – sang their swan-song as a social class. In this he was alone among members of his immediate family. His father John Butler Yeats* spoke of 'a plebian ⟨*sic*⟩ pride';[31] his brother Jack* identified with the common people; Yeats's sister Lollie* came to regret the Yeatsian inheritance and her involvement in the Cuala Press. 'No Yeats has ever made money as far as I can find out,' she laments in a letter of April 1934. 'If I was to begin all over again – never never would I touch anything even touching art or literature – here am I having *worked hard* since I was 19 – & I do not make an income as big as a worker in a laundry gets.'[32]

The contexts for Yeats's work stem from but are not confined or reducible to the colonial encounter between Britain and Ireland. In the context of Anglo-Ireland, Yeats's general stance often looks highly political, but against the background of Irish Ireland it can often seem depoliticised or even anti-political. In his Introduction to *A Book of Irish Verse* (1895), Yeats caustically remarks that Trinity College, Dublin, 'desires to be English, has been the mother of many verse-writers and of few poets; and this can only be because she has set herself against the national genius, and taught her children to imitate alien styles and choose out alien themes, for it is not possible to believe that the educated Irishman is alone prosaic and uninventive'.[33] But his disparagement of English influence in Ireland is not always particularly enlightened. In a lecture delivered at Wellesley College in November 1903, he spoke in terms markedly different, for example, from Joyce:* 'Deprecating mention was made of the kind of literature sent to Ireland by England – everything with the Union jack tied round its neck – the cheap story, the music hall song, never the Milton and Shakespeare.'[34]

As for Yeats's feelings towards England itself, these were suitably double-edged, but one attitude stood out. Like his fellow-Irishman Shaw, he never felt any sense of inferiority towards England and never assumed he was the colonialist or she the mother country. After all, the English ate dogfish, put marmalade in their porridge, kissed at railway stations, and disclosed their affairs to strangers (*R* 60–62). 'Every one I knew well in Sligo despised Nationalists and Catholics, but all disliked England with a prejudice that had come down perhaps from the days of the Irish Parliament' (*R* 59). Again, it is Eglinton who fine-tunes the distinction: 'A dislike of England, curiously combined with a preference for the society of English people, was fostered among the Anglo-Irish during the great Victorian peace.'[35] Although (or perhaps it is because) he occupied a hyphenated position, Yeats betrayed no insecurity in such matters. As Arland Ussher suggests, Yeats 'enjoys his "antinomies" too much to wish to "transcend" them'.[36] When the Gaelic Society of TCD proposed in the autumn of 1914 to celebrate the birth of Thomas Davis, they invited to speak, as representing the various currents of

5

Irish intellectual life, Yeats, Pearse, and Thomas Kettle. J. P. Mahaffy the Provost took exception to Pearse being invited, and the meeting was moved to the Antient Concert Rooms. Yeats defended Pearse's right to speak but made his position clear: 'He knew only vaguely what Mr Pearse had written about politics, but if it was some sort of anti-Englishism he was as vehemently opposed to the politics of Mr Pearse as he was to the Unionism of Dr Mahaffy.'[37]

Yeats's view of Englishness is bound up with his sense of Irishness; his sense of Irishness is bound up with his view of Englishness, and in this he was no different from his contemporaries. His one-time confidante Katharine Tynan* once declared: 'We are an eternally contradictory people, and none of us can prognosticate exactly what we shall feel, what do, under given circumstances; whereas the Englishman is simple. He has no mysteries. Once you know him, you can pretty well tell what he will say, what feel, and do under given circumstances. You have a formula for him: you have no formula for the Irish.'[38] Susan Mitchell, who came from an Ascendancy background and who stayed with the Yeats family in Bedford Park, pointed out that Irish Protestants have two inheritances: '(O)ne is Foxe's "Book of Martyrs", the other is the history of their country. One tells of martyrdoms to Rome, the other of martyrdoms to England.'[39]

Such attitudes caution us against being too free in our characterisation of Anglo-Irish relations in terms of sister countries or of colonial relations; they also remind us of the dangers of uncritically accepting stereotypes. In a different but related context, John Wilson Foster has pointed out that 'London if truth be told is not for Ulster Protestants their capital, as it wasn't for Joyce's Dubliners.'[40] According to Gogarty, 'Yeats always regarded England as a foreign country though he resided there frequently and had many friends there. . . . He was impatient of England, a country so largely composed of bourgeois. To him the bourgeois mind was a "middle-class" mind. . . . When Yeats heard that in Russia Lenin had declared religion to be the "opium of the masses", Yeats remarked, "In England H. G. Wells is the opium of the middle classes." '[41] Like Kipling, Yeats saw England as a political nation and almost never distinguished 'England' or 'English' from 'Britain' or 'British'.[42] It was English, not British, commercialism that he attacked. Perhaps Scottish friends and admirers such as 'Fiona Macleod' (William Sharp), Cornish friends like Arthur Symons,* and Welsh friends like Lionel Johnson* (before his mystical transformation into an Irishman), found common cause in Yeats's anti-English, pro-Celtic stance. And he impressed his closest American friend, Ezra Pound,* with memorable attacks on the host country: 'England is the only country where a man will lie without being paid for it.'[43]

Of course, from today's perspective, Yeats's version of Englishness looks both familiar and dated, but there is more to it than this. Yeats went to school in Hammersmith, lived for more than half his life in London, and travelled throughout the country both on lecture tours and with the Abbey Theatre, but his understanding of Britain is almost entirely confined to stereotypes learnt in childhood and to images derived from his reading of English literature. He shows little appreciation of English landscape, little interest in regional differences, and no concern with the Yeatses' possible Yorkshire origins or the Pollexfens' origins in Devon.[44] In his construction of an earthly paradise, he insisted on a wedge not a tension between the country and the city, and made no room in his mind for imagining England an adopted country. The power of the metropolis was also stronger than he supposed: in one of his early letters to Tynan from London he refers to Sligo as 'down at' not 'across' or 'over in': 'Down at Sligo one sees the whole world in a days walk' (L [K] 153).[45]

6

Unlike Jack, Yeats spent most of his childhood away from Sligo. However, the two years he was there, between the ages of seven and nine, were, according to his father's biographer, 'among the most impressionable of his life',[46] and ensured that Sligo became for ever associated in his mind as a place of return, of nostalgia, of contrast. In the words of one of his Pollexfen cousins, 'Sligo was our paradise',[47] or, as his down-to-earth brother once boasted, Sligo was a 'fine deep broad country', 'where all the rogues come from'.[48] Sligo provided a break from the demands of living, whether economic or social, as in November 1894: 'I had not solved the difficulty of living. I went to Sligo and spent six months there with my uncle at Thornhill' (*Mem* 75). While he was a child and young man growing up in London, Sligo was rarely out of Yeats's head: 'I remember when I was nine or ten years old walking along Kensington High Street so full of love for the fields and roads of Sligo that I longed – a strange sentiment for a child – for earth from a road there that I might kiss it' (*A* 472). In a letter to Tynan written from Rosses Point in August 1887, again it is the earth – not the people – that is uppermost in his mind: 'It is a wonderfully beautiful day the air is full of trembling light. The very feel of the familiar Sligo earth puts me in good spirits. I should like to live here always not out of liking for the people so much as for the earth and the sky here, though I like the people too' (*L [K]* 33).

Interestingly, his most celebrated poem, 'The Lake Isle of Innisfree', owes its inspiration to 'homesick' thoughts of Sligo from abroad in 'hateful' London – but again the thought is 'unpeopled': 'I had still the ambition, formed in Sligo in my teens, of living in imitation of Thoreau on Innisfree, a little island in Lough Gill, and when walking through Fleet Street very homesick I heard a little tinkle of water and saw a fountain in

J. B. Yeats's mid-Victorian sketch of the poet's youthful mother, Susan Pollexfen. With her tied bonnet, closely wrapped, folded shawl, deep-set eyes, and passive face, Mrs Yeats looks not unlike a pre-Raphaelite Irish colleen. 'She would spend hours listening to stories or telling stories . . . of her own Sligo girlhood; and it was always assumed between her and us that Sligo was more beautiful than other places. I can see now that she had great depth of feeling, that she was her father's daughter' (*R* 54). Perhaps with his own case in mind, Yeats remarked in the *All Ireland Review* in April 1903: '(H)as it not been said that a man of genius takes the most after his mother?'

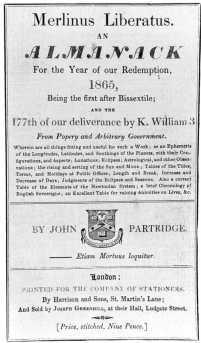

Partridge's *Almanack* for 1865 was concerned as much with ideology as astrology. The month before Yeats was born, Partridge lamented not secular tyranny but priestly dominion and gross superstition in Ireland, yet 'a sign of promise at length bursts out, and that for our emerald sister – Ireland'. Yeats also lamented the role of the Catholic Church in Ireland but never relinquished his belief in the fairies.

a shop-window which balanced a little ball upon its jet, and began to remember lake water. From the sudden remembrance came my poem *Innisfree*, my first lyric with anything in its rhythm of my own music' (A 153).[49]

In his semi-autobiographical novel *John Sherman* (1891), Yeats explores at some length his acute feelings for Sligo, at once 'the place that has really influenced my life most' (L [K] 195) and 'the lonliest place in the world' (L [K] 41), as he describes it in letters to Tynan in his early twenties. The protagonist Sherman is confronted with a choice: remain in Sligo and marry homely Mary Carton (modelled on Tynan) or depart for London and court disaster with the capricious Margaret Leland (modelled on Laura Armstrong). His clerical friend Howard taunts him to go: 'Sherman, how do you stand this place – you who have thoughts above mere eating and sleeping and are not always grinding at the stubble mill? Here everybody lives in the eighteenth century – the squalid century.'[50] The alternative case is put by an old woman on board the cattle-boat for Liverpool: 'Why are ye goin' among them savages in London, Misther John? Why don't ye stay among your own people – for what have we in this life but a mouthful of air?'[51] The plot, which turns on this tension inside Sherman, permits us glimpses of what Sligo meant to Yeats, perhaps best summarised as a mixture of personal recognition by the people, a rich use of language, an essentially folkloric way of looking at the world, and a bulwark against the levelling tide of an English way of life.

On one of Sherman's returns to Sligo from London, the emigration theme is again arrayed in Yeatsian colours:

As he went through the streets his heart went out to every familiar place and sight: the rows of tumble-down thatched cottages; the slated roofs of the shops; the women selling gooseberries; the river bridge; the high walls of the garden where it was said the gardener used to see the ghost of a former owner in the shape of a rabbit; the street corner no child would pass at nightfall for fear of the headless soldier; the deserted flour-store; the

8

Two pencil sketches by J. B. Yeats of Willie reading, one with his mother, about 1875.

Sketches by the Yeats children on holiday in Branscombe, Devon, 1879.

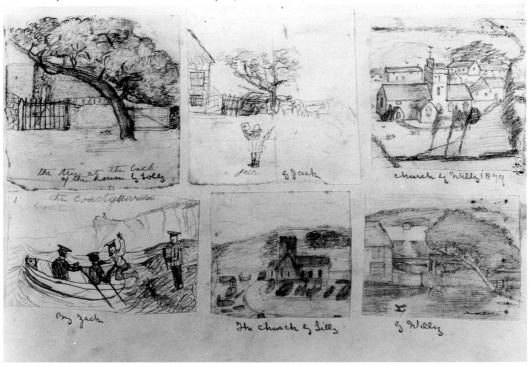

wharves covered with grass. All these he watched with Celtic devotion, that devotion carried to the ends of the world by the Celtic exiles, and since old time surrounding their journeyings with rumour of plaintive songs.[52]

In spite of the conventional description, a genuine note is being attempted here. On returning to Sligo (Ballah in the novel), Sherman/Yeats's mixed feelings of emptiness and longing for his native area resurface. On the one hand, Sligo unites people through memory, captured by the recorder-narrator through the use of such formulaic expressions as 'it was said' and 'no child would pass'. On the other hand, the homely image of thatched cottages is offset by the adjective 'tumble-down'; the flour-store is deserted; the wharves unused. Sligo is empty, but it is peopled with ghosts, in this case the ghost of a former owner in the shape of a rabbit and that of the headless soldier. To Yeats, the fears of the unknown in childhood become the ground of belief in adulthood; in this way nothing is ever quite forsaken. Sherman's thoughts take a different course at this point as he sentimentalises in 1890s fashion about the 'Celtic exiles'. But the direction of such a passage is towards the occult-inspired, literal idea of absence as presence.

The journey from Sligo to Liverpool was conducted on board a ship of his grandfather's Sligo Steam Navigation Company. When Yeats arrived at the Clarence Basin in Liverpool from the Godolphin School in Hammersmith, he felt immediately at home among Sligo people. 'I waited for this voyage always with excitement and boasted to other boys about it, and when I was a little boy had walked with my feet apart as I had seen sailors walk' (*R* 91). In Sligo, as his aunt in time-honoured colonial fashion declared (with Yeats's father in mind): 'Here you are somebody. There ⟨in London⟩ you will be nobody at all' (*R* 46). Yeats's father believed otherwise: 'The Irishman is, boy and man, a detached personality.'[53] When Sherman returned again to Sligo, '⟨H⟩e was occasionally recognised and greeted, and, as before, went on without knowing, his eyes full of unintelligent sadness because the mind was making merry afar.'[54] The three symbols of Sherman's life betray Yeats's incurable sense of isolation: 'the garden, the book, and the letter'[55] – in other words, his love of outdoor things, his meditative frame of mind, and his anxieties. In his 1915 study of the poet, Hone, who was himself a Southern Unionist, fastens onto this aspect of Yeats's personality, and he links it with the poet's Anglo-Irishness: 'Anglo-Irish writers have owed much to the fact that they are of a race without a myth, a people, therefore, that is easily capable of an excessive mental detachment.'[56]

William Pollexfen (1811–92)

The frame which surrounds the first volume of Yeats's autobiography, *Reveries over Childhood and Youth*, is supplied by the figure of his grandfather William Pollexfen. On the opening page the poet confesses that he confused his grandfather with God, and associated him with feelings of misery and loneliness:

> Some of my misery was loneliness and some of it fear of old William Pollexfen my grandfather. He was never unkind, and I cannot remember that he ever spoke harshly to me, but it was the custom to fear and admire him. . . . He had a violent temper and kept a hatchet at his bedside for burglars and would knock a man down instead of going to law, and I once saw him hunt a group of men with a horsewhip. He had no relation for he was an only child and, being solitary and silent, he had few friends.
>
> (*R* 4–6)

Merville, the house rich in association and memory for Yeats, is now part of a large convent, and its separate architectural identity has disappeared. When Yeats was a child, in front of the house was a little flagstaff, and every day he would fly a red flag with a Union Jack in the corner.

At the end of the volume – the year is 1892 – Yeats returns to Sligo for his grandmother's funeral and watches his grandfather dying. Ironically for a first-person narrative, *Reveries* casts Yeats as the shadowy outsider, passively observing events from a distance. But one image, which reappears four decades later in *Purgatory* (1938) to give that play a more particular historical underpinning, suggests that powerful forces were at work both inside Yeats himself and in the wider world: 'Before he was dead, old servants of that house where there had never been noise or disorder began their small pilferings, and after his death there was a quarrel over the disposition of certain mantel-piece ornaments of no value' (R 212).

Purgatory is concerned with 'dreaming back', with what for Yeats was the ethical issue of how one generation relives, and thereby relieves, the transgressions of another.[57] The stage setting, which consists of a bare tree and a ruined house, creates an atmosphere supernaturally charged and threatening. When the old man commands the young boy to 'study that house', Yeats seems to have in mind his grandfather's Merville and Lady Gregory's* Coole Park:

> I saw it fifty years ago
> Before the thunder bolt had riven it,
> Green leaves, ripe leaves, leaves thick as butter,
> Fat, greasy life. Stand there and look
> Because there is somebody in that house.
>
> (*VPl* 1042)

11

At the end of his life, Yeats's childhood memories form the basis for an impassioned outcry against the collapse in modern Ireland of the Big House and eighteenth-century landed values. With the transfer of land under the Wyndham Acts to tenant farmers in the last two decades of the nineteenth century, a thunderbolt, long associated perhaps in Yeats's mind with the death of his grandfather and the image of pilfering servants, had indeed riven the Old Order. But even when the stakes are high, as they are in this play, not everything points in a single direction. The image of life as fat and greasy suggests two separate counter-thoughts. Firstly, perhaps the landed interests in Ireland were ripe for a fall and incapable of reformation; secondly, such an exaggerated image seems designed to offer those in purgatory a way of suppressing their envy of the living.

Romance, which is more often than not associated in Yeats with aristocratic versus bourgeois values, was the quality above all others that Yeats as a child admired in his grandfather:

> He had great physical strength and had the reputation of never ordering a man to do anything he would not do himself. He owned many sailing ships and once, when a captain just come to anchor at Rosses Point reported something wrong with the rudder, had sent a messenger to say 'Send a man down to find out what's wrong.' 'The crew all refuse' was the answer. 'Go down yourself' was my grandfather's order, and when that was not obeyed, he dived from the main deck, all the neighbourhood lined along the pebbles of the shore. He came up with his skin torn but well informed about the rudder.
>
> (R 5–6)

Tynan recognised the importance of the Pollexfen romance for all the Yeats children: 'I am sure that Sligo and the Pollexfens' ships, and the wharves and quays and tarry ropes and warehouses, all contributed largely to the shaping of W. B. Yeats. The Pollexfens and romances were synonymous to the minds of the Yeats boys and girls as they grew.'[58]

William Pollexfen came from a landed family which owned Kitley Manor, Yealmpton, in Devon. For whatever reason, at the age of twelve he ran away to sea. In his twenties he found himself in Sligo married to the daughter of his cousin Elizabeth Pollexfen Middleton and joint owner with William Middleton of a shipping firm, the Sligo Steam Navigation Company, and a milling firm 'Middleton and Pollexfen', which traded in coal, maize, and other goods between Sligo, Liverpool, Spain, Portugal, and America. The business prospered, and in 1867 William regained a little of his landed status by purchasing Merville, a big house on the edge of Sligo complete with sixty acres and fine views of Ben Bulben. Whatever he privately felt or aspired to, or whatever his grandson fondly imagined about having blood that 'has not passed through any huckster's loins' (VP 269), Pollexfen was a small-town merchant whose legacy extended into the 1920s. Indeed, in Kilgannon's 1926 survey of Sligo, a whole section is devoted to 'Messrs. Pollexfen and Co., Limited'.[59]

Pollexfen's past may have contained romance, but any lingering gestures towards aristocratic recklessness were overturned by the market place, replaced by a depressive melancholia and, after 1880, by declining economic fortunes. The Pollexfens looked down on their Middleton relatives, who were comfortably established in Ireland, had business acumen, and mixed well with the locals. But they would never attain the landed-gentry status of, say, the Gore-Booths, who owned the estate at Lissadell nearby. Nevertheless, perched on top of his warehouse on the corner of Wine Street and Adelaide Street, the uncommunicative William Pollexfen must have been extremely satisfied to observe his ships on the river Garrogue bearing goods to and from his several

In 1885 Yeats's grandparents were forced to sell Merville, and they moved here to Charlemont House overlooking the harbour, marked Ardmore House on the map of Sligo Town. It was here that Yeats wrestled with 'that savage greybeard Oison' (*L [K]* 40). His struggle was rewarded: two years later *The Wanderings of Oisin*, his first volume of verse, was published. Charlemont is now a nursing home.

warehouses in Sligo Town.[60] His commercial empire was short-lived, and when his last son died in 1929, there were no more Pollexfens to continue the association with Sligo.

However, by the 1920s, Arthur Jackson, who married Alice Pollexfen and joined the firm in the 1880s, was a noted Sligo entrepreneur. According to Kilgannon, '⟨W⟩ere it not for the enterprise of such men as Senator Arthur Jackson and a few others who believe in investing their capital in Irish industries instead of British securities, industrial employment in Sligo would be practically nil.'[61] In 1909 Jackson established basic slag mills at the Quayside in Sligo, which produced an excellent fertiliser known as 'The Anchor Brand'. Yeats the poet complained bitterly against English commercialism, but he seemed not to connect this with the Pollexfen side of his family. Indeed, the valuing of nature in his verse stands in marked contrast with his family's efforts to control nature. Ironically, in the 1920s, both he and an in-law were appointed to the Irish Senate, one on account of his artistic, the other on account of his commercial success.

The Extended Family

In the space of nineteen years, from 1838 to 1857, William and Elizabeth Pollexfen had twelve children, eleven of whom survived childhood. As will become apparent in the next chapter, Yeats was especially fond of his uncle George, the astrologer who lived at Thornhill in Sligo. On the Middleton side of the family Yeats used to visit his cousin George, the son of William Middleton. In the summer months George lived in Elsinore Lodge, a smuggler's house at Rosses Point, and in winter at Ballysodare, where the family owned some flour mills. 'It was through the Middletons perhaps that I got my

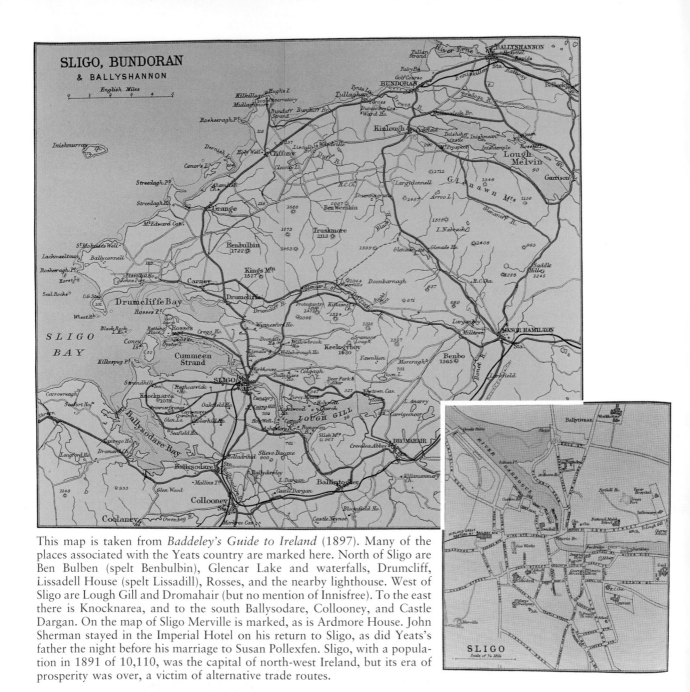

This map is taken from *Baddeley's Guide to Ireland* (1897). Many of the places associated with the Yeats country are marked here. North of Sligo are Ben Bulben (spelt Benbulbin), Glencar Lake and waterfalls, Drumcliff, Lissadell House (spelt Lissadill), Rosses, and the nearby lighthouse. West of Sligo are Lough Gill and Dromahair (but no mention of Innisfree). To the east there is Knocknarea, and to the south Ballysodare, Collooney, and Castle Dargan. On the map of Sligo Merville is marked, as is Ardmore House. John Sherman stayed in the Imperial Hotel on his return to Sligo, as did Yeats's father the night before his marriage to Susan Pollexfen. Sligo, with a population in 1891 of 10,110, was the capital of north-west Ireland, but its era of prosperity was over, a victim of alternative trade routes.

interest in country stories and certainly the first faery stories that I heard were in the cottages about their houses' (*R* 24). It was also the Middletons who were responsible for a drunken moment in Yeats's childhood when, after a stormy day on board a yacht, Willie was given some raw whisky and driven home from Rosses Point crying out to every passer-by that he was drunk. On his red pony Yeats would also ride to Castle Dargan (see left-centre at the bottom of the map of Sligo, Bundoran, and Ballyshannon above), where lived a 'brawling squireen, married to one of my Middleton cousins' (*R* 99). 'It was, I dare say', in a remark reminiscent of Somerville and Ross, 'the last household where I could have found the reckless Ireland of a hundred years ago in final degradation' (*R* 99).[62]

14

Members of the Yeats family also lived nearby. At Rathbroughan, not far from the centre of Sligo, lived his great-uncle Mat Yeats (1819–85) and his big family of boys. Six miles from Sligo under the slopes of Ben Bulben lived his great-aunt Mary (Micky) (1821–91), whose father was John Yeats, Rector of Drumcliff. Micky, who lived in a 'little square, two-storied house covered with creepers', was a 'spare, high-coloured, elderly woman and had the oldest-looking cat I had ever seen' (R 29–30). She was full of family history and possessed a little James the First cream jug with the Yeats motto and crest. Yeats discovered that one of his great-uncles chased the United Irishmen for a fortnight before being caught himself and hanged. A great-grandfather, on the other hand, was a friend of Robert Emmet; another great-uncle, Governor of Penang. 'I am delighted with all that joins my life to those who had power in Ireland' (R 35).

If social class played a part in the tensions between the Pollexfens and the Middletons, it did so as well between the Yeatses and the Pollexfens. 'I do not think any of these ⟨Yeatses⟩ liked the Pollexfens, who were well off and seemed to them purse-proud, whereas they themselves had come down in the world' (R 32). In this the son was reflecting the views of his father, who had once told him: 'You must do everything well . . . that the Pollexfens respect, though you must do other things also' (R 97). 'In Ireland,' his father was to inform an American audience three thousand miles from his Pollexfen in-laws, 'we are still medieval, and think that how to live is more important than how to get a living'.[63]

Yeats's family in Sligo, then, dramatised exemplary and opposing attitudes to life; they also laid by primary material for later use in his writing. It was his father who once remarked in an essay contrasting English and Irish family and schooling, no doubt with Willie in mind: '⟨B⟩ehind the Irish boy is the drama of a full home life.'[64] Perhaps all of

Rosses Point in an Edwardian postcard. According to the 1897 *Baddeley's Guide to Ireland*, Rosses Point is 'as quaint and tidy a little village as you wish to see – 'Sligo-super-Mare' – with four nice little hotels – or rather inns – and an abundance of trimly thatched, scrupulously white-washed cottages'. According to Yeats, 'Drumcliff and Rosses were, are, and ever shall be, please Heaven! places of unearthly resort' (*CT* 92).

Ross's Point   Co. Sligo

15

'The Metal Man' by Jack B. Yeats. This is a close-up of the figure in 'Memory Harbour'. Jack was brought up in his grandparents' house and, as Yeats – perhaps with envy – recalls in *Reveries*, 'had partly taken my place in my grandmother's affections'. Jack went to the local school, where he was always bottom of his class. 'My grandmother did not mind that, for she said, "He is too kindhearted to pass the other boys." He spent his free hours going here and there with crowds of little boys, sons of pilots and sailors, as their well-liked leader, arranging donkey races or driving donkeys tandem. . . . ⟨I⟩n half the pictures he paints today I recognise faces that I have met at Rosses or the Sligo quays' (*R* 128–9). 'The metal man' on the pedestal, pointing to where the water is deep enough for ships, can still be seen at Rosses Point.

Yeats's major ideas, as he suggests almost casually in *The Trembling of the Veil*, were forged in the family workshop: 'I am persuaded that our intellects at twenty contain all the truths we shall ever find' (*A* 189). Through the Middletons he was introduced to fairy tales and folklore and to a form of recklessness he was to associate with the Ascendancy. Through Micky Yeats came contact with his family lineage and the dynastic theme which began to preoccupy him after 1909. The Pollexfens gave him a conscience, an 'outlandish name meaning a solitary bird from a marsh',[65] and a sense of life as a hard-won struggle.

The family as such, and by extension his circle of friends, assumed an important subject for his verse. The early 1900s witnessed on the one hand his disillusionment with the Abbey Theatre and Irish nationalism and, on the other hand, the departure of his father in 1907 to the United States. George Pollexfen died in 1910, his brother Alfred in 1916. During all these years, especially from 1909 to 1916, as middle age approached, the theme of family matured in his mind. He dedicated the citizen-oriented volume *Responsibilities* (1914) to his family, and sought their pardon:

> *Pardon that for a barren passion's sake,*
> *Although I have come close on forty-nine,*
> *I have no child, I have nothing but a book,*
> *Nothing but that to prove your blood and mine.*
> (*VP* 270)

When Alfred Pollexfen died, the society magazine the *Sphere* on 18 August 1917 carried his tribute to the whole Pollexfen family:

16

IN MEMORY.

By W. B. YEATS

Five and twenty years have gone
Since old William Pollexfen
Laid his strong bones down in death,
By his wife Elizabeth,
In the grey stone tomb he made.
Some five years ago they laid
In that tomb by him and her,
His son George, the astrologer,
And Masons drove from miles away
To scatter the Acacia spray
Upon a melancholy man
Who had ended where his breath began.

Many a son and daughter lies
Far from the customary skies,

The Mall and Eade's grammar school,
In London or in Liverpool;
But where is laid the sailor John?
That so many lands had known:
Quiet lands or unquiet seas
Where the Indians trade or Japanese.
He never found his rest ashore
Moping for one voyage more.
Where have they laid the sailor John?

And yesterday the youngest son,
A humorous, unambitious man,
Was buried near the astrologer;

And are we now in the tenth year?
Since he, who had been contented long,
A nobody in a great throng,
Decided he would journey home,
Now that his fiftieth year had come,
And "Mr. Alfred" be again
Upon the lips of common men
Who carried in their memory
His childhood and his family.

At all these death-beds women heard
A visionary white sea-bird
Lamenting that a man should die:
And with that cry I have raised my cry.

In the 1930s Yeats returned again to the dynastic theme, but now 'blood' – as illustrated in a poem such as 'Are You Content?' – acquires more insidious meanings. In testamentary fashion the poet chisels the family names. Adjectives are restricted to an essentially honorific function, and, by this stage in the memorialising process, William Pollexfen is simply 'that notable man'. But it is difficult not to notice in the first stanza the scars of his flirtation with eugenics:[66]

> I call on those that call me son,
> Grandson, or great-grandson,
> On uncles, aunts, great-uncles or great-aunts,
> To judge what I have done.
> Have I, that put it into words,
> Spoilt what old loins have sent?
> Eyes spiritualised by death can judge,
> I cannot, but I am not content.
>
> He that in Sligo at Drumcliff
> Set up the old stone Cross,
> That red-headed rector in County Down,
> A good man on a horse,
> Sandymount Corbets, that notable man
> Old William Pollexfen,
> The smuggler Middleton, Butlers far back,
> Half legendary men.
>
> Infirm and aged I might stay
> In some good company,
> I who have always hated work,
> Smiling at the sea,
> Or demonstrate in my own life
> What Robert Browning meant
> By an old hunter talking with the Gods;
> But I am not content.

(*VP* 604–5)

Lough Gill. An enchanted landscape – an earthly paradise – which accompanied the 'lake-nurtured' Yeats into his adult years. Yeats's verse is bathed in an imagery associated with the meeting of water and land. 'I am certain that the water, the water of the seas and of the lakes and of mist and rain, has all but made the Irish after its image' (*CT* 87).

The Lake Isle of Innisfree. One of twenty-eight islands in Lough Gill. His father read him a passage from Thoreau's *Walden* as a child, and this imparted to Yeats the idea that some day he would live in a cottage on Innisfree. 'I thought that having conquered bodily desire and the inclination of my mind towards women and love, I should live, as Thoreau lived, seeking wisdom' (*R* 136).

Glen-Car waterfall beside Lough Gill. 'Where the wandering water gushes/From the hills above Glen-Car,/In pools among the rushes/That scarce could bathe a star,/We seek for slumbering trout/And whispering in their ears/Give them unquiet dreams;/Leaning softly out/From ferns that drop their tears/Over the young streams' (*VP* 88).

Reading books of adventure in his father's library as a boy, Robert Browning was transported into realms of the imagination. But this option is now perceived by Yeats in his old age as escapist and unavailable. As for the third line in the last stanza, 'I who have always hated work,' which has the force of an admission, it is somewhat surprising from someone who produced volumes. Perhaps behind it lies a lifetime's tussle with the puritan strain in his family background. As his prodigal and contented father once remarked, 'We Irish are still what we've always been, a people of leisure.'[67]

イニスフリイの湖島

いざ立ちて行かばやなイニスフリイへ。
黏土括り細枝編み小さき茅舎かしこに建てん。
九畝なる菽豆、蜜蜂の巣をいとほしみ
住まはなむ、蜂うたふ林のなかに。

かくてわれそこばくの靜寧をえん。
靜寧ぞおもむろに滴して、草蟲すだけるところ
あさあけの薄とばり洩りこぼれ、眞夜ほの光り
晝は輝き、紅雀夕を群れ翔ぶ。

いざ立ちて行かばやな、夜晝のけぢめなく
湖際にてかそけく波の聲あれば。
黃塵の街路を歩すも、なほわれは
胸のおくがに沙々と鳴る其聲を聽く。

Japanese translation of 'The Lake Isle of Innisfree'. From Shotaro Oshima, *Shishu: Hakkon Sobi* (Tokyo: Taibun Sha. B. [1928]). The flyleaf to Yeats's copy contains the author's name 'with kind regards' and dated 5 June 1928.

Lissadell House, home of the Gore-Booth family. 'The light of evening, Lissadell,/Great windows open to the south,/Two girls in silk kimonos, both/Beautiful, one a gazelle.' So begins the memorable 1927 elegy to the two Gore-Booth sisters, Eva Gore-Booth and Con Markiewicz, whom Yeats first met in 1894 when he stayed at Lissadell. He was all the time conscious, as he tells us in *Memoirs*, that 'this house would never accept so pennilesss a suitor'. In the same poem he mistakenly describes Lissadell, which was built in 1832, as 'that old Georgian mansion' (*VP* 475). You will also seek in vain for any mention of the Robert Gore-Booth who in the nineteenth century, according to Kilgannon in *Sligo and Its Surroundings* (1926), annexed to his demesne the thickly populated townland of Ballygilgan and proceeded with a policy of wholesale clearance of the people.

What his family could never give him was an Anglo-Irish pedigree. The stories that accumulated around his family's names were comforting, and with the deployment of phrases such as 'A good man on a horse' and 'Half legendary men' he could furnish something that resembled a mythology. But the essential ingredient was missing. For Yeats's family belonged not to the 'Horse-Protestants',[68] as Brendan Behan once called the Anglo-Irish gentry, but to the Protestant middle class, one wing of which in Yeats's case was clerical, the other commercial. The effect of this on Yeats was apparent to those who knew him best. According to Gogarty, Yeats's friendship with Lord Dunsany, for example, never blossomed because Yeats envied his social status: 'Yeats, though his descent was from parsons, dearly loved a lord. He was at heart an aristocrat, and it must have always been a disappointment to him that he was not born one.'[69] George Moore, who came from a Catholic land-owning family in County Mayo, never lost an opportunity of ridiculing Yeats's pretentiousness; there is a telling passage in *Hail and Farewell* (1911–14) when he recalls George Russell's* story about Yeats crooning 'that if he had his rights he would be Duke of Ormonde', and Russell's reply: 'I am afraid, Willie, you are overlooking your father.'[70]

JOHN BUTLER YEATS

John Butler Yeats (1839–1922) came from a northern family of clergymen and was initially destined for the Church. His grandfather, John Butler Yeats (1774–1846), 'Parson John' as he was affectionately known, was Rector of Drumcliff; his father, William Butler Yeats (1806–62), who 'loved Catholics and hated Presbyterians and Orange men',[71] was Episcopalian Rector of Tullyish in County Down. J. B. Yeats recalls with affection his 'sweet-tempered and affectionate' father, the person 'who made me the artist I am, and kindled the sort of ambition I have transmitted to my sons. . . . To be with him was to be caught up into a web of delicious visionary hopefulness'.[72] For his

20

schooling J. B. Yeats was sent to the Atholl Academy on the Isle of Man, where he struck up a lasting friendship with George Pollexfen. Then came six carefree months at Sandymount Castle, the home of his uncle Robert Corbet, 'a man of generous impulses who lived up to his creed of being a gentleman, a worldling and a club man, nor did he forget that he was a citizen of Dublin, of the type that flourished in the eighteenth century'.[73] In 1857 J. B. Yeats enrolled at TCD, where in his final year he read metaphysics and logic. But school had weakened him 'morally by its constant discipline and vigilance', and it blighted his undergraduate career: '(S)elf-abandoned to a complete relaxation . . . I did not think, I did not work, I had no ambition, I dreamed.'[74]

In early September 1862 he was invited by George Pollexfen to the family's summer home at Rosses Point, and later recalled the magic of his first evening walking on the sandhills high above the sea: 'The place was strange to me and very beautiful in the deepening twilight. A little way from us, and far down from where we talked, the Atlantic kept up its ceaseless tumult, foaming around the rocks called Dead Man's Point. Dublin and my uneasy life there & Trinity College, though but a short day's journey, were obliterated, and I was again with my old school friend, the man self-centered and tranquil and on that evening so companionable.'[75] The visit proved a turning-point: in the space of a fortnight he had been introduced to George's sister, Susan,* fallen in love, and become engaged. It was, as he later confessed, 'a surprise no less to the girl than to me, a sort of stumble in the dark – or rather an overruling Providence'.[76] He returned to Dublin to study law at the King's Inns. In November 1862 his father, who had retired to Sandymount to live in a small house next to Sandymount Castle, died suddenly and J. B. Yeats was left to deal with his mother's grief and his father's properties. The following September he travelled to Sligo to be married in St John's Church, and returned to 5 Sandymount Avenue with his new wife.

Marriage to Susan compelled him to reflect on the family he had married into: 'At Sligo, I was the social man where it was the individual man that counted. It is a curious fact that entering this sombre house of stern preoccupation with business I for the first time in my life felt myself to be a free man, and that I was invited by the example of everyone to be my very self, thereby receiving the most important lesson in my life.'[77] He later confided to John Quinn:* 'I would like to say that my wife taught me sincerity, but then sincerity is a gift.'[78] J. B. Yeats's attitude to the Pollexfens was understandably mixed. It was pleasanter, he later wrote, to live among his own people, 'but to live amongst the Pollexfens was good training'.[79] Yeats senior was exercised, as was Willie after him, by the respective merits of the two families: 'Inarticulate as the sea cliffs were the Pollexfen heart and brain, lying buried under mountains of silence. They were released from bondage by contact with the joyous amiability of my family, and of my bringing up, and so all my four children are articulate, and yet with the Pollexfen force.'[80] In conversation with Lady Gregory in 1902, he rehearsed his son's development in terms of family traits:

> He expects you to change very much in old age, you will become much quieter, and your mother's characteristics will come out. I asked what they were, but he said it was hard to say that, but that he often told her he must take her affection for him on trust, for she never showed any sign of it. But you are also very like his father, who used to walk up and down the room when talking as you do, and to rub his hands. You are also very like your sister Lolly, who will never go to bed till Lily sends her there.[81]

At the same time, with sceptical ideas derived from Mill, Darwin, and Comte and with

21

John Butler Yeats in old age. From his *Essays Irish and American* (1918).

impressive skills as an orator, Yeats senior continued to impress his friends and fellow-students, especially Edward and John Dowden and John Todhunter. For this small quartet, enjoyment was the first principle of life; what they lacked, as Yeats senior recognised, was the deep sincerity of the Pollexfens.

Even when pressured by fundamental changes in his immediate circumstances, J. B. Yeats could maintain his equanimity, for he had, as he informed John Quinn, '*an insulated mind*'.[82] Characteristically, any tensions or differences in outlook he may have had with the Pollexfens were not so much negotiated as ignored. 'The Pollexfen house in Union Street', he told his son in April 1915, 'was to me suffocation. When they were all at home, as on Sundays, I always slipped away and spent the day at my uncles, taking care not to get home till they were all in bed. They all hated each other. How could it be otherwise, since they were not permitted by their strange code of morals to like each other. . . . It was puritanism without religious ecstasy or exultation – a dark cave with its one lamp extinguished though still smoking.'[83] In 1863, the Pollexfens were convinced that Susan was marrying a landlord and a barrister; in 1867, the same year William and Elizabeth Pollexfen moved to the big house at Merville, Yeats senior decided to quit the Bar and follow an artistic career. Henceforth, the Pollexfens were openly hostile to the free-thinking dilettante.

In early 1867, J. B. Yeats left his wife and family behind in Sligo, travelled to London, and enrolled as a student in Hatherley's Art School. In July he took out a six-year lease on 23 Fitzroy Road, near Regent's Park, where he was joined by Susan and the two small children, Willie, the eldest child, and Susan Mary* ('Lily'), who was born in 1866. Other children followed at regular intervals: Elizabeth Corbet ('Lollie') in 1868, Robert Corbet ('Bobbie') in 1870 (who died three years later), John Butler ('Jack') in 1871, and Jane Grace in 1875 (who died the following year). The children were artistically gifted and fondly remembered by their father: 'Lily also has this gift of infectious laughter. We are so grateful to anyone who makes us laugh that we are quite ready to laugh at our own expense. Lollie has a strong ethical sense and plenty of courage, yet Jack could always vanquish her by some sudden sally – perhaps only a knickname – which made her laugh.'[84] From July 1872 to October 1874 Susan and the children lived at Merville. In 1874 Yeats senior completed his apprenticeship as a painter and moved to 14 Edith Villas, North End Road (West Kensington), where his family joined him again.

If Edmund Gosse had not used *Father and Son* for his 1907 autobiography, Yeats might have been tempted to deploy the title for the first volume of his autobiography. Indeed, the severity of Gosse's relation with his father, a member of the Plymouth Brethren, perhaps played a part in Yeats's view of his own father.[85] Whatever the case, in *Reveries* Yeats deliberately emphasises the struggle with his father as a basic theme, and in consequence his father emerges as something of an ogre. He recalls an incident at Sligo when Yeats senior offered to teach him to read instead of going to church: 'I think now that he wanted to make me go for my grandmother's sake and could think of no other way. He was an angry and impatient teacher and flung the reading book at my head, and next Sunday I decided to go to church' (*R* 39–40). The image is memorable but not an adequate description of the father's relation with his eldest son.[86] J. B. Yeats's impatience sprang from a mixture of possessiveness and equality: he wanted a son who would share his intellectual conversation and maintain his distance from the Pollexfens.

Yeats was nine before he began reading, and throughout his life he remained a poor speller. His summer report for 1878 suggested that his writing had improved but his spelling was 'bad'.[87] And so was his handwriting. However, he showed few signs of inferiority on any of these scores. In his letters he employed any number of excuses for his spelling. Writing to Hugh Lane in December 1904, he gets hopelessly confused about Constance Markiewicz's* name: 'I hear from Madam Marcovitch – how the devil do you spell that name –' (*L [K]* 3, 680). In July 1915, he told Lady Gregory the hot weather had interfered with his spelling.[88] In 1924, after seeing Dorothy Pound and Olivia Shakespear,* Yeats told George that Dorothy had left Omar in Paris because he had measles, a word Yeats attempted to spell three times without success.[89] Then in April 1929 he confessed to Sturge Moore:* 'I cannot spell today. I find I do not know what words contain repeated letters and what words do not. It is a matter of nerves with me. If I get out a dictionary I will have to look up too many words' (*Y & TSM* 154).

Being a poor speller also had certain poetic advantages, for it increased the chances of stumbling across an unusual word or collocation. 'He Wishes for the Cloths of Heaven' was originally entitled 'The Clothes of Heaven'. The second line of 'Under Ben Bulben' reads 'Round the Mareotic Lake'. According to George Yeats in a letter to Thomas Mark in April 1939, 'That "c", instead of "d", was a subject of much discussion between WB and myself, he wanted it for sound, and I finally discovered a respectable authority for it!'[90] In his 1954 edition of Yeats's *Letters*, Wade protected Yeats by silently correcting errors, but later editors and scholars have preferred to give today's reader a more direct access to the poet's mind. Of course, it could be argued that with such a poor grasp of spelling (and punctuation) his reputation as a poet should suffer accordingly.

According to Lily Yeats, her father 'hated to see any stranger, even the nurse, touching Willie'.[91] Clearly, there was a tension while at Merville between Yeats senior and the Pollexfens, a tension that Willie as a child both recognised and perhaps also subconsciously displaced. 'It was pleasant in Merville merely because the house was big and the grounds ample, so that one could enjoy nature and had room to get away from human nature.'[92] *Reveries* shows Yeats caught between two father figures, his grandfather and his father, and perhaps it is for this reason that his father is shown in an adverse light.[93] This is complicated by the second reading of experience, which in the Yeats story is defined by 'the decline of the father and the rise of the son'.[94] Equally, as he remarked in a letter to his father in February 1910: 'In the process of writing my third lecture . . . ⟨i⟩t has made me realise with some surprise how fully my philosophy of life has been inherited from you in all but its details and applications' (*L* 549).

23

Even without the Yeatsian associations, landscape and climate conspire to make the area round Sligo one of the most magical in Ireland. As a boy Yeats seems to have missed the underlying romance and mythological significance, enjoying instead the freedom and adventure the countryside offered him. In the Preface to Lady Gregory's *Gods and Fighting Men* (1904) he underlines the intimate association between landscape and childhood:

> Children – or, at any rate, it is so I remember my own childhood – do not understand large design, and they delight in little shut-in places where they can play at houses more than in great expanses where a country-side takes, as it were, the impression of thought. . . . When they imagine a country for themselves, it is always a country where one can wander without aim, and where one can never know from one place what another will be like, or know from the one day's adventure what may meet one with tomorrow's sun. I have wished to become a child again that I might find this book, that not only tells one of such a country, but is fuller than any other book that tells of heroic life, of the childhood that is in all folk-lore, dearer to me than all the books of the western world.[95]

In his Preface to Lady Gregory's *Cuchulain of Muirthemne* (1902), he turns again to childhood, this time to what he missed as a child growing up in Sligo: 'When I was a child I had only to climb the hill behind the house to see the long, blue, ragged hills flowing along the southern horizon. What beauty was lost to me, what depth of emotion is still perhaps lacking in me, because nobody told me, not even the merchant captains who knew everything, that Cruachan of the Enchantments lay behind those long, blue, ragged hills!'[96] The exclamation mark possibly conveys a degree of scepticism on Yeats's part, though more likely it represents his disappointment. How much difference such knowledge would have made to a child is an open question. In Wordsworth's *Prelude* (1805), which affords a key example of autobiography as a romantic spiral, childhood is bathed in often inchoate experiences which accumulate meaning and a higher form of unity only through time and on reflection.[97] The image of childhood recurs throughout Yeats's writings, but when he imagines childhood, he occasionally conveys the impression that he did not have one.

In Yeats, landscape invariably bears a symbolic charge, a conviction that ' "all things are made double one above another" ' and that the forms of nature may be temporal shadows of realities'.[98] In a letter to Bowra in May 1934, Yeats revealed: 'My symbolism came from actual experiments in vision, made by my friends or by myself, in the society which called itself "The Hermetic Students." '[99] 'He approached life', according to Fadiman, 'not as a philosopher, as he fondly believed, but as a sorcerer to whom reality is an infinite stream of interchangeable symbols.'[100] The twin peaks which overshadow Sligo – Ben Bulben, where ended the tragic story of Diarmuid and Grainne, and Knocknarea, under whose cairn lies buried passionate Maeve – never appear in Yeats's work 'unpeopled', without, that is, a mythological aura and resonance.[101] 'Into the Twilight' suggests another characteristic approach:

> Come, heart, where hill is heaped upon hill:
> For there the mystical brotherhood
> Of sun and moon and hollow and wood
> And river and stream work out their will;
>
> And God stands winding His lonely horn,

And time and the world are ever in flight;
And love is less kind than the grey twilight,
And hope is less dear than the dew of the morn.

(VP 148)

Yeats's choice of words here is unusual. 'Hill *heaped* upon hill' is reminiscent of a Van Gogh painting, a consciously worked image to convey energy and to arrest the mind. This is not so much the detailed reconstruction of an Irish scene, or even an 'attempt to penetrate the inner soul of the landscape itself,' which Palgrave in 1897 thought characteristic of the modern attitude.[102] Rather, it attempts to construct a rhythm and a mood about Ireland and the 'mystical brotherhood' of the occult, and shapes itself as symbol rather than as allegory. What is missing in the post-Romantic Yeats, it needs little insisting on, is Blake's forceful attachment to a twin reality: '⟨T⟩o the Eyes of the Man of Imagination, Nature is Imagination itself.'[103]

In a challenging comment, Paul de Man suggests that Yeats's emblematic landscape differs fundamentally from Wordsworth's transcendental vision. Both lead from material to spiritual insights, but 'whereas Wordsworth's imagination remains patterned throughout on the physical process of sight, Yeats's frame of reference . . . originates from experiences without earthly equivalence'. It is true that a Yeats poem rarely ends on a note of tranquillity, but when he insists that 'Yeats's landscapes have a symbolic meaning prior to their natural appearance, and act as predetermined emblems embedded in a more or less fixed symbolic system which is not derived from the observation of nature',[104] de Man overstates his case.

The relation between perception and landscape in Yeats is more varied and complicated than this. Firstly, a landscape observed every day during childhood can grow, almost imperceptibly, into a symbolic landscape in adulthood. Gogarty, defending Yeats against the charge that he did not notice scenery, observed: 'I know that he rarely remarked on scenery. His eyesight precluded that; but when he was a youth he took it all in.'[105] And, as Yeats told Lady Gregory in his sixties, his memory was visual and alert: 'I never forget anything which forms a picture in my mind but I cannot remember the most important details which are abstract in form for even a few weeks.'[106]

Secondly, there is the issue of gender, for Sligo was his mother's land, and in writing about Sligo he was inevitably writing about his mother. Yeats buried almost beyond recovery the cradle that rocked his feminine soul, so it is difficult to assess how much his symbolic landscapes are compensation for her absence from Sligo after the family's removal to London and her subsequent stroke in 1887. What is clear is that his landscapes are invariably accompanied by a sense of longing or by a recognition that there is more to landscape than realistic depiction. As Harold Bloom reminds us, Walter Pater bequeathed to Yeats's generation an impossible aesthetic ideal and the conviction that 'the fruit of experience is an intense consciousness or passion that cannot accommodate itself to experience again'.[107]

Thirdly, and this too constitutes part of the complexity, Yeats's landscapes are located in a physical, identifiable region. His Sligo is not interchangeable with Thoor Ballylee, the tower on the border of Clare and Galway he purchased in 1917. 'The Lake Isle of Innisfree' was composed in London, but generations of readers have not been wrong in wishing to inspect not the occasion that gave rise to the poem (the shop in Fleet Street) but the poet's dream (the island in Lough Gill).[108] Equally, the mistake sometimes made is to confuse 'The Lake Isle of Innisfree' with the island of that name and to forget that Yeats is 'without analogue'.[109]

25

John S. Sargent
1908

'The trees are in their autumn beauty,/The woodland paths are dry,/Under the October twilight the water/Mirrors a still sky' (*VP 322*). The woods at Coole, looking towards the lake. Taken in October.

Facing page: John Sargent's charcoal drawing of Yeats in 1908. According to Gogarty in his memoir of Yeats, Yeats looked exactly like this when they first met in 1902. He was 'a gaunt young man very upright with a shock of dark hair falling over the left brow. Sargent had caught a gesture of Yeats's body-making itself, bolt upright as if posing for a picture. The jaw is clear-cut and firm. The mouth is beautifully modelled. The nose is aquiline with great breadth between the eyes, one of which, the right, is noticeably lower than the other. Round the long white throat he wears a soft collar and one of those flowing silk ties which have become the uniform of the artists and poets.' Yeats thought the sketch 'a charming, aerial sort of thing, very flattering as I think' (*L 509*).

Yeats has altered the landscape of modern Ireland, but in the process he too has been altered. The poet who condemned those who 'fumble in a greasy till' is now an icon who until recently adorned notes issued by the Bank of Ireland.

Fourthly, whereas Joyce gives shape to a landscape already there, Yeats is an inventor of landscape: so 'real' is Innisfree that no map of Lough Gill today would be complete without it. As George Russell understood: 'It is the function of the poet to name woods, stars, mountains, people, actions, thoughts and emotions, so that by those names they will be remembered, and the name shall recall the transfiguring mood and we, too, come into the magic circle.'[110] What de Man does not allow for is the way Yeats's insistence on otherworldliness in his landscapes helped him avoid Victorian genre pictures and the frequent condescension of travelogues, a condescension that often was accompanied, as for example in the case of Charles Kingsley, by a form of incipient racism.[111]

Finally, landscape served different functions at different periods in Yeats's career. In early poems such as 'The Ballad of John O'Hart', or 'The Fiddler of Dooney', a folk attitude to landscape, especially evident in the use of place-names, is on display:

> When I play on my fiddle in Dooney,
> Folk dance like a wave of the sea;
> My cousin is priest in Kilvarnet,
> My brother in Mocharabuiee.
> (*VP* 178)

In a poem from the middle of his poetic career, such as 'The Wild Swans at Coole', where the birds signify intellect when connected with water and emotion when connected with air (see *YVP* 1, 251), landscape is inseparable from memory. In his final poems, the visual art of landscape, as Elizabeth Bergmann Loizeaux suggests,[112] gives way to the plastic art of sculpture or, as in 'An Acre of Grass', to a pared-down, intellectual statement:

> Picture and book remain,
> An acre of green grass
> For air and exercise,
> Now strength of body goes;
> Midnight, an old house
> Where nothing stirs but a mouse.
> (*VP* 575)

The watery landscape and ever-changing seascape were associated in the boy's mind with adventure, not the painter's easel. As a child, the impressionable Yeats climbed mountains, fished for trout in mountain streams, and went herring-fishing at night. '(O)ne never knew a countryside till one knew it at night,' he told his uncle George, who approved of his walking round Lough Gill and sleeping in a wood at night (*R* 135). In such ways, his natural curiosity was aroused: he wanted to discover, for example, which sea birds began to stir before dawn, so he 'called upon a cousin towards midnight and asked him to get his yacht out' (*R* 138). Only someone at home on the sea, or rather someone whose imagination was thoroughly immersed in Shelley and enchanted by the sea, could have written *The Shadowy Waters* (1906). In this dramatic poem the plight of Forgael and Dectora, the male mind and the female will, is lovingly captured by Yeats in the drifting motion and the otherworldliness of the sea. At the end of *The Shadowy Waters*, Forgael's persistence has been rewarded, but his mind continues to wander:

> *Dectora*: Why are you looking at the sea?
> *Forgael*:   Look there!
> *Dectora*: What is there but a troop of ash-grey birds
> That fly into the west?
> *Forgael*:   But listen, listen!
> *Dectora*: What is there but the crying of birds?
> *Forgael*: If you'll but listen closely to that crying
> You'll hear them calling out to one another
> With human voices.
> *Dectora*:   O, I can hear them now.
> What are they? Unto what country do they fly?
> *Forgael*: To unimaginable happiness.
> They have been circling over our heads in the air,
> But now they have taken to the road
> We have to follow, for they are our pilots;
> And though they're but the colour of grey ash,
> They're crying out, could you but hear their words,
> 'There is a country at the end of the world
> Where no child's born but to outlive the moon.'
>
>   (*VP* 246–7)

   In his depiction of landscape Yeats lacks Seamus Heaney's 'possessive' imagination, Ted Hughes's disturbing commitment to Otherness, or Wordsworth's 'depth', but in his evocation of mood and atmosphere Yeats has few rivals. Landscape is part of a larger perception, never an end in itself. '⟨F⟩ill your mind with natural images of slow contemplative nature' was the advice given Yeats through the control Thomas (*YVP* 2, 124).[113] 'It is a natural conviction for a painter's son to believe that there may be a landscape symbolical of some spiritual condition that awakens a hunger such as cats feel for valerian' (*R* 140–41). As he writes (with Edwin Ellis) in the Preface to *The Works of William Blake* (1893), 'Art and poetry, by constantly using symbolism, continually remind us that nature itself is a symbol. To remember this, is to be redeemed from nature's death and destruction.'[114]

   Yeats's Anglo-Irish imagination was haunted by the image of the empty house, by the subconscious fear of eviction from the land, but if you listen closely enough, Yeats says, you will hear human voices. If you stand and look, you will see somebody in that house. There is no value, he would argue, in holding the mirror up to nature: alter the field of vision, capture a mood, seal it with a statement that is both enigmatic and 'subtle, sweet, and beguiling'.[115] It is not 'There is a country at the end of the world where children live for ever' but 'There is a country at the end of the world/Where no child's born but to outlive the moon.' Yeats's landscapes are pointers to a world of '*unimaginable* happiness'. The phrase is precisely weighted: not 'unlimited happiness' but 'unimaginable happiness', where 'unimaginable' means both 'impossible to imagine' (an irreverent thought for a poet in the Romantic tradition) and 'unbelievable' (a loose adjective in common usage given a new lease of life by Yeats). As he told an audience at Wellesley College in November 1903: 'Dreamers are the realists, they see the light at the end; theorists see light along the way, but the end lies in darkness.'[116]

Lean Townsend's 'The Host of the Air'. 'But he heard high up in the air/A piper piping away,/And never was piping so sad,/And never was piping so gay' (*VP* 145). In his copy of Raphael's *Familiar Astrologer* (1911), Yeats underlined the date of his birthday in 1865. Compton Mackenzie recalls a conversation with Yeats in the 1920s in the billiards room at the Savile Club: ' "As a student of astrology," he said in his most hieratic voice, "you'll be interested to know that I was born at an exact sext between the planet Venus and the planet Mercury". Then, lowering his voice in reverence, he added "Indicating the birth of a major poet".'

2

Yeats's Female Daimon

EARLY INTEREST IN THE OCCULT

'There is no subject', remarked Yeats's first biographer, 'on which he "lets himself go" with more audacity and seeming conviction in conversation.'[1] 'The mystical life', he told O'Leary in July 1892, 'is the centre of all that I do & all that I think & all that I write' (*L [K]* 303). When it came to mediums, his obsession sometimes got the better of him, as happened in Chicago in March 1914 when he wanted to visit a certain medium he had heard of. 'I managed with great difficulty', recalls Harriet Monroe, 'to elude reporters who had received some hint and were hot on his trail, and to start him off ahead of them to the lady's Edgewater residence.'[2] In 1899, Nevinson remembered his first meeting with Yeats at the house of Frank Podmore, a founder of the Fabian Society and the sceptical Secretary of the Society for Psychical Research. Yeats spoke chiefly of himself, his spiritual experiences, trances, visions, and apparitions: '⟨S⟩ometimes, he said, the spirit forbids him to say what was in his mind, and then his tongue becomes like a stone; calls himself a Cabbalist, but a sceptic too.'[3] Wilfrid Scawen Blunt* records in his diary for 1 April 1898 Lady Gregory bringing to his estate in Sussex 'the poet Yeats, an Irish mystic of an interesting type', who proceeded to conduct a magical experiment on him:

> He first took out a notebook and made what he called a pyramid in it which was a square of figures, then he bade me think of and see a square of yellow as it might be a door, and walk through it and tell him what I saw beyond. All that I could see at all clearly was that I seemed to be standing on a piece of green, rushy grass, in front of me a small pool from which issued two streams of very blue water to right and to left of me. He then bade me turn and go back through the door, and told me I should see either a man or a woman who would give me something. I failed to see anything but darkness, but at last with some effort I made out the indistinct figure of a child, which offered me with its left hand some withered flowers. I could not see its face. Lastly he bade me thank the person to whose intervention the vision was due, and read from his notebook some vague sentences prefiguring the vision. The performance was very imperfect, not to say null.[4]

According to *Reveries*, Yeats's interest in the occult originated with visits to his Middleton cousins in Ballysodare and progressed through contact with George Pollexfen and his servant Mary Battle. As a child Yeats was superstitious, obsessed with correspondences, his imagination held by 'unaccountable things' (*A* 264). He possessed a strong sense of the uncanny, what Freud defined as 'the old, animistic conception of the universe', 'the idea that the world was peopled with the spirits of human beings', and characterised as 'the subject's narcissistic overvaluation of his own mental processes'.[5]

'Fairy Struck; Or The Dying Child' by F. Goodall. Reproduced in *The People's Journal*, 9 January 1847. Mrs S. C. Hall explained: 'You frequently in Ireland hear the observation, "That child's *not right*; it will come to no good – it's so crabbed." People seldom like to say directly that "the child is fairy struck", but the words "It's not right", signify as much.'

Yeats could never walk in a wood 'without feeling that at any moment I might find before me somebody or something I had looked for without knowing what I looked for' (*CT* 107). Perhaps not surprisingly, he was alarmed by George Eliot, who 'seemed to have a distrust or a distaste for all in life that gives one a springing foot' (*R* 168). He believed that in any dialogue between two people, 'there is always a third, and in every council there is one for whom no chair is set'.[6] The adult who wrote a poem entitled 'The Man Who Dreamed of Faeryland' was the kind of boy for whom the paranormal was not only normal but an 'ungovernable craving' (*A* 264). 'I did not believe with my intellect that you could be carried away body and soul, but I believed with my emotions and the belief of the country people made that easy' (*R* 148). He took to wandering round raths and fairy forts, questioning old people on their experiences of the occult, and listening intently to stories about the little people. Unlike most individuals, however, with the onset of early manhood, Yeats never relinquished what he later termed his 'secret fanaticism' (*R* 149).

Ironically, his father's unbelief had the converse effect and made Yeats more curious about what the Belgian dramatist Maurice Maeterlinck called 'the Great Secret'.[7] Indeed, 'It was only when I began to study psychical research and mystical philosophy that I broke away from my father's influence' (R 170–71). The occult acted as a counter not only against religious doubts but also against a Church emptied of religious feeling. When he began mixing in Olivia Shakespear's occult circles of West Kensington, Yeats must have encountered a scene not unlike that described by his fellow-countryman Shane Leslie in 1916:

> The Church of England reigns chiefly as a social club, with which are deposited the moral standards of society. There are more people in London society today who believe in their family ghosts than in the resurrection of Christ. Superstition has thrived oddly in London, as it throve in the latter Roman Empire, to the disregard of old-fashioned deities. I have known an outgoing governor consult a clairvoyant rather than a bishop. And I recently attended a *séance* in Grosvenor Square, where the recently deceased wife of an Irish viceroy sent messages to her friends in society.[8]

The (female/Irish) occult provided Yeats with a protected environment where he was also safe from Mill, Darwin, and (male/English) Victorian ideas of faith and doubt. As he and Ellis wrote of Blake, 'Self-doubt, the terrible destroyer that would "put out the sun and moon" if they yielded to it, was the one thing of which he was afraid.'[9] It was a high-risk strategy, for the occult demanded from the neophyte a total commitment, so that once inside the circle of belief the impartial intellect was largely abandoned and the self exposed to periodic bouts of loneliness or helplessness. The danger was heightened in Yeats's case by a psychological compulsion to authenticate his beliefs in some tangible form, a compulsion that predisposed him to crystal-gazing and the practice of ceremonial magic. J. B. Yeats, as a letter written in 1921 reminds us, always regretted his son's swerve away from concrete life:

> When is your poetry at its best? I challenge all the critics if it is not when its wild spirit of your imagination is wedded to concrete fact. Had you stayed with me and not left me for Lady Gregory, and her friends and associations, you would have loved and adored concrete life for which as I know you have a real affection. What would have resulted? Realistic and poetical plays – poetry in closest and most intimate union with the positive realities and complexities of life. And that is the world that waits, so far in vain, its poet. I have always hoped and do still hope that your wife may do for you what I would have done. Not idea but the game of life should have been your preoccupation, as it was Shakespeare's and the old English writers', notably the kinglike Fielding. The moment you touch however lightly on concrete fact, how alert you are! and how attentive we your readers become!
>
> (LS 280–81)[10]

Fortunately for readers of modern verse, Yeats senior's fears were only half realised, for Yeats remained his father's son, not least in always carrying with him into his middle and later career as a poet a slight doubt about his otherworldly beliefs.[11] Even in his youth it was there. He hesitated for a year, for example, before joining Madame Blavatsky's Theosophical Society, and when he did so privately expressed reservations in his 'Occult Notes':

J. B. Yeats's portrait of George Pollexfen.

About Xmas 1888 I joined the Esoteric Section of TS ⟨Theosophical Society⟩. The pledges gave me no trouble except two – promise to work for theosophy and promise of obedience to HPB ⟨Helena Petrovna Blavatsky⟩ in all theosophical matters. . . . Last Sunday (this is Oct 24 1889) at a private meeting of members of London Esotericists we passed a resolution that amounts to this (1) we believe in HPB (2) we believe in her teachers (3) we will defend her, subject to our own consciences. I had some doubt as to whether I could sign this second clause.

(*Mem* 281)[12]

'Never give all the heart' (*VP* 202) was how he described his feelings on learning of Maud Gonne's* marriage to John MacBride in 1903, and it is an appropriate sentiment to recollect in this context also. Or we might recall Yeats's famous Blakean declaration of belief in a passage from 'The Tower', where faith and doubt are confidently juxtaposed and held in balance:

> And I declare my faith:
> I mock Plotinus' thought
> And cry in Plato's teeth,
> Death and life were not
> Till man made up the whole,
> Made lock, stock and barrel
> Out of his bitter soul,
> Aye, sun and moon and star, all,
> And further add to that
> That, being dead, we rise,
> Dream and so create
> Translunar Paradise.
>
> (*VP* 414–15)

34

The poet's declaration of faith is initially couched in the form of an attack on the Platonic concept of Ideal Forms, which holds that reality is but an imperfect reflection of a world elsewhere. But then the argument switches, not towards the concreteness of life, which we might legitimately expect, but towards a celebration of the factitiousness of reality. Yeats delights in the ambiguity of 'man made up the whole', a phrase which at this point in the poem seems to release a new surge of energy. For the (w)hole of reality, the poet implies, including the heavens, is a human invention, but 'being dead' (that is, living without imagination) we come alive again through our dreams, and so create the world anew. Thus, Francis Stuart is only half right to claim that 'in spite of his interest in philosophy and mysticism . . . his work was not the expression of a deep, personal faith as it was say, for Rilke, Wordsworth or Blake'.[13] For the keynote of Yeats's work is not the Romantic 'expression of' but the Nietzschean 'triumph over'.

George Pollexfen (1839–1910)

If Yeats reacted against the negative influence of his father, he encountered ready support for his occult ideas in his uncle, whose mind was 'full of pictures' (R 131). George was a hypochondriac and took great care of his appearance (his sensitive skin meant it took him an hour to shave). He was a lover of racehorses (and one-time jockey), popular with his work-force, and a keen astrologer. He impressed Yeats from the outset, being different from his father, and he 'always had faith in my talent' (Mem 77). In his youth Yeats often stayed at Thornhill. After the deaths of his grandparents in 1892, it was Yeats's only home in Sligo: when George died in September 1910, his link with Sligo was effectively broken. But, during the 1890s in particular, George and his Sligo base supplied Yeats with continuing source material for his Irish and occult studies, as well as an ever-renewable badge of identity that he could display to his London and Irish friends alike.

George was 'pleasant and companionable' (L 304), and after lunch and dinner he and Yeats took their constitutional walk together often to the same gate on the road to Knocknarea. They had their disagreements, as in November 1898, when George, a staunch Unionist, took Yeats to a Masonic concert where someone recited a stage-Irishman song. Yeats was so incensed that instead of applauding he insisted on hissing. 'My uncle defends me, but admits that he makes but a poor hand of it and gets beaten' (L 304). Three years later, in 1901, when George was appointed High Sheriff, he was warned against bringing his republican nephew near the Constitutional Club in Sligo. 'Between my politics and my mysticism I shall hardly have my head turned with popularity' (L 351). But politics did not cloud their relationship, and neither did his uncle's illnesses: 'My uncle', he told Lady Gregory in November 1898, 'has been busy since I began this letter in developing the most wonderful series of symptoms of ill health and his depression grows' (L 305).

In October 1892, accompanied by his uncle and a cousin, Yeats visited a cave by the Rosses sands well known as 'a great fairy locality'. In a letter at the time to Richard Le Gallienne, a prominent young critic in London circles, he described what happened next:

I made a magical circle & invoked the fairys. My uncle – a hard headed man of about 47 – heard presently voices like those of boys shouting & distant music but saw nothing. My cousin however saw a bright light & multitudes of little forms clad in crimson as well as hearing the music & the(n) the far voices. Once their was a great sound as of little people cheering & stamping with their feet away in the heart of the rock. The queen of the troop came then – I could see her – & held a long conversation with us & finally wrote in the sand 'be careful & do not seek to know too much about us.'

(L [K] 321)[14]

George and Yeats spent a considerable time together indulging their occult interests. When Mary Battle had gone to bed, their experiments would commence. One night they saw an allegorical marriage of Heaven and Earth. In the morning they were fascinated to discover Mary Battle's dream echo their vision, a dream in which the Catholic bishop of Sligo had married a rich woman no longer young: 'Now all the clergy will get married, and it will be no use going to confession' (A 260). Yeats seems to have taken a lead in their experiments, introducing George to images he had learned from 'MacGregor' Mathers* and showing him how to handle cabbalistic symbols. Yeats's fame spread, and in time, he tells us, he found he had the reputation of being a magician.[15]

The night before George died in 1910, the banshee that accompanied his mother's people was heard. 'I am glad the Banshee cried', he told Lily, 'it seems a fitting thing. He had one of those instinctive natures that are close to the supernatural' (L 552). Eight years later, George was assigned a place of honour in Yeats's poem 'In Memory of Major Robert Gregory'* as one of the 'friends that cannot sup with us':

> And then I think of old George Pollexfen,
> In muscular youth well known to Mayo men
> For horsemanship at meets or at racecourses,
> That could have shown how pure-bred horses
> And solid men, for all their passion, live
> But as the outrageous stars incline
> By opposition, square and trine;
> Having grown sluggish and contemplative.

(VP 325)

In its own way, this too is 'outrageous', but in deploying this particular adjective Yeats seems to incorporate such a response into the poem, half-aware in its insistence on his masculinity that George followed a female pursuit.[16] Ironically, but, again, in keeping, the poet's concern here is not so much with George the astrologer as George the individual. Indeed, explaining human behaviour by reference to the stars is given a further twist through the ungrammatical use of a semicolon in the penultimate line: no amount of astrology can halt the change in the astrologer from the solidity and fitness of youth to the sluggishness of old age.

The Celtic Twilight

Yeats's female-centred interest in the occult stemmed also in part from his mother and in part from contact with Catholic servants. As he remarks in 'The Queen and the Fool', '(W)omen come more easily than men to that wisdom which ancient peoples, and all wild peoples even now, think the only wisdom' (CT 192). His mother 'would spend hours listening to stories or telling stories of the pilots and fishing people of Rosses Point,

Jean Townsend's 'The Song of Wandering Aengus'. 'I went out to the hazel wood,/Because a fire was in my head,/And cut and peeled a hazel wand,/And hooked a berry to a thread;/And when white moths were on the wing,/And moth-like stars were flickering out,/I dropped the berry in a stream/And caught a little silver trout' (*VP* 149).

The ruins of Biddy Early's cottage at Feakle, County Clare. Biddy Early (1798–1874) possessed healing powers and her magic bottle became famous throughout Clare and Galway. 'She is dead some twenty years,' wrote Yeats in 'Ireland Bewitched' (1899), 'but her cottage is pointed out at Feakle in Clare. It is a little rough-built cottage by the roadside, and is always full of turf-smoke, like many others of the cottages, but once it was sought out by the sick and the troubled of all the south-west of Ireland. My friend (Lady Gregory) went to Feakle for me a while back, and found it full of memories of Biddy Early's greatness.' Many years before his own destiny was linked with Thoor Ballylee, in 'Dust Hath Closed Helen's Eye', Yeats refers to a saying of Biddy Early: 'There is a cure for all evil between the two mill-wheels of Ballylee' (*CT* 35).

or of her own Sligo girlhood' (*R* 54). When they lived in Howth from 1881 to 1887, a favourite activity of his mother was listening to stories:

> When I think of her, I almost always see her talking over a cup of tea in the kitchen with our servant, the fisherman's wife, on the only themes outside our house that seemed of interest – the fishing people of Howth, or the pilots and fishing people of Rosses Point. She read no books, but she and the fisherman's wife would tell each other stories that Homer might have told pleased with any moment of sudden intensity and laughing together over any point of satire. There is an essay called 'Village Ghosts' in my *Celtic Twilight* which is but a record of one such afternoon, and many a fine tale has been lost because it had not occurred to me soon enough to keep notes.
>
> (*R* 114–15)

In Sligo his grandmother used to take him as a child to see an old gentlewoman. 'I would sit up upon my chair, very bored, while my elders ate their seed-cake and drank their sherry' (*R* 26). In contrast, the stories of the servants proved enthralling. He was absorbing a more general lesson which would eventually lead through his Notes to Lady Gregory's *Visions and Beliefs in the West of Ireland* (1920) to the system of thought as outlined in *A Vision*: 'Ever since I began to write I have awaited with impatience a linking, all Europe over, of the hereditary knowledge of the country-side, now becoming known to us through the work of wanderers and men of learning, with our old lyricism so full of ancient frenzies and hereditary wisdom, a yoking of antiquities, a Marriage of Heaven and Hell.'[17]

Mary Battle was especially influential. In 1898, Yeats described her to Lady Gregory, fellow-collector of stories and soon to become, after the death of his own mother in 1900, a mother substitute: 'He has a wonderful old servant who is a mine of fairy lore. I have taken down quantities. She is really a kind of saint and is supremely happy. She sees fairies and angels continually. She foretold I was to get a present. She said "there is a drop of drink for you" some days before the port came. She saw it in a tea cup' (*L* 305). Mary Battle had been with George since he was a young man and, indeed, according to Yeats, may have inclined him to 'strange studies' (*R* 133). Yeats himself took down 'quantities' of her stories, and he confesses in *Reveries*, in a phrase reminiscent of the one he used in describing his mother and 'Village Ghosts,' that 'Much of my *Celtic Twilight* is but her daily speech' (*R* 134).

The Celtic Twilight, first published in 1893, gave its name, perhaps inaccurately, to a whole movement.[18] Equally inaccurate is the impression given by Yeats that he went round the country collecting stories from all and sundry, for, as Mary Thuente argues, he employed the same informants, namely Biddy Hart, her husband Paddy Flynn, and Mary Battle.[19] Unlike his contemporaries or near-contemporaries in the field, such as Canon John O'Hanlon or the Irish-American folklorist Jeremiah Curtin, Yeats is less than forthcoming about his informants.[20] However, in his defence, this seems to form part of his intention, to prevent his work from being universalised, or read as a science or as evidence of what anthropologists following Tylor might have termed the 'primitive religion of mankind'.[21]

The note of enjoyment in offending folklorists and systematisers everywhere is struck on the very first page: 'I have therefore written down accurately and candidly much that I have heard and seen, and, except by way of commentary, nothing that I have merely imagined. I have, however, been at no pains to separate my own beliefs from those of the peasantry, but have rather let my men and women, dhouls and faeries, go their way

Cheating the fairies. It was a tradition in Connemara for boys up to the age of twelve to be dressed as girls, for it was thought that girls would not be taken by the fairies. From Donn Byrne, *Ireland: The Rock Whence I was Hewn* (1927).

unoffended or defended by any argument of mine' (*CT* 1). T. W. Rolleston endorsed the 'frankly irresponsible imagination' at work in the tales.[22] 'We want the romance', agreed the anonymous reviewer in the *National Observer*, 'not the classification, and we care not where the stories came from, if only they have phantasy and delight.'[23] *The Celtic Twilight* is arguably the most playful text in the Yeatsian canon, especially apparent in its tongue-in-cheek attitude. In 'A Remonstrance with Scotsmen for Having Soured the Disposition of Their Ghosts and Faeries', Yeats sketches in a sociology of ghosts and at one point slips into a different register and mode of address: 'In Scotland you are too theological, too gloomy. You have made even the Devil religious. . . . You have burnt all the witches. In Ireland we have left them alone. . . . You have discovered the faeries to be pagan and wicked. You would like to have them all up before the magistrate. . . . The Catholic religion likes to keep on good terms with its neighbours' (*CT* 178–9).

Yeats delights in the freedom of the oral tradition of story-telling and almost casually criss-crosses the lines between collector and narrator, and between formal and informal registers.[24] 'A Visionary' is not so much a story as an anecdote about his friend George Russell, who had come to his lodgings 'to talk of the making of the earth and the heavens and much else' (*CT* 15).[25] 'Belief and Unbelief' begins: 'There are some doubters even in the western villages' (*CT* 8), where the word *even* conveys an element of Yeatsian fun. 'The Devil' opens with a deliberate blurring of the notion of impartiality and with a refusal to turn the informant's garrulous voice into the abstract language of masculine scholarship: 'My old Mayo woman told me one day that something very bad had come down the road and gone into the house opposite, and though she would not say what it was, I knew quite well' (*CT* 69). In terms of narratology, such openings are unconventional, and their orientation closer to an oral than to a literary tradition. Sometimes, as

39

An advertising campaign against cot deaths in Ireland in 1992 used the perhaps misplaced lines from Yeats's poem 'The Stolen Child'.

with 'Happy and Unhappy Theologians', the opening is reminiscent of an experienced shanachie: 'A Mayo woman once said to me, "I knew a servant girl who hung herself for the love of God"' (*CT* 71). At other times, as with the opening of 'Village Ghosts', Yeats throws out a general observation closer to his own Nineties, more settled prose style: 'In the great cities we see so little of the world, we drift into our minority' (*CT* 23). In *The Celtic Twilight*, in the half-light at sunrise and sunset, when 'heaven and earth so mingle that each seems to have taken upon itself some shadow of the other's beauty',[26] Yeats

Arthur Hughes's depiction of 'The Fairies' in William Allingham's *Music Master* (1855) accompanies the famous lines once known to every child in Britain: 'Up the airy mountain,/Down the rushy glen,/We daren't go a hunting/For fear of little men;/Wee folk, good folk,/Trooping all together;/Green jacket, red cap,/And white owl's feather!'

'Chin-angles' or 'How the Poets Passed', a caricature by 'Mac' of Dublin (Isa MacNie). According to the story, Yeats, who was then living at 82 Merrion Square, set out to visit George Russell at 84, at the same time as Russell set out to visit Yeats. They missed each other, and the cartoon shows how it happened.

was finding support for his own beliefs by reference to the country people. He was availing himself of what one Victorian commentator defined as 'graceful superstitions', 'infinite material', and 'food for fancy'.[27] In faithfully recording their stories, he was also learning how to write 'in the Irish way'.[28] When he came to deliver a lecture in Cardiff in 1903 on 'The Irish Fairy Kingdom', Yeats proudly proclaimed the two gifts of Ireland to the world: new legends and new attitudes to the supernatural.[29]

The revised, expanded second edition of 1902 betrays the influence of two other women who from the 1890s onwards played a key role in Yeats's life, Maud Gonne and Lady Gregory. Maud Gonne's presence in the second edition of *The Celtic Twilight* can be discerned in the repeated references to Helen of Troy, impossible love, and the emotional life. At the close of 'An Enduring Heart', a story about a man's lifelong attachment to a woman who had emigrated to America, Yeats confesses that he has loved Helen 'and all the lovely and fickle women of the world' (*CT* 60). In the love story of the blind poet Raftery and Mary Hynes, a beautiful woman who lived at Ballylee, Yeats could see his own relationship with Maud Gonne vainly mirrored. The story ends: 'It may be that in a few years Fable, who changes mortalities to immortalities in her cauldron, will have changed Mary Hynes and Raftery to perfect symbols of the sorrow of beauty and of the magnificence and penury of dreams' (*CT* 48).

After reading the first edition of *The Celtic Twilight*, Lady Gregory was keen to meet Yeats and embark on a similar project making use of the local parish of Kiltartan adjoining her estate at Coole.[30] She, however, was interested less in the occult world lying behind the stories, more in 'the beautiful rhythmic sentences in which they were told'.[31] Not unlike Synge,* she was 'moved by the strange contrast between the poverty of the tellers and the splendours of the tales'.[32] Yeats's second edition contained several

41

stories collected while staying with Lady Gregory, including 'Enchanted Woods', 'Dust Hath Closed Helen's Eye', and 'By the Roadside', but, again, there is a question mark about the extent of Yeats's involvement in collecting stories round Coole. On one occasion, Lady Gregory records, the two made an outing to a parish in County Clare.

> Mr Yeats at that time wore black clothes and a soft black hat, but gave them up later, because he was so often saluted as a priest. But this time another view was taken, and I was told after a while that the curate of the Clare parish had written to the curate of a Connacht parish that Lady Gregory had come over the border with 'a Scripture Reader' to try and buy children for proselytising purposes.[33]

Yeats may have given the impression of aloofness, but his attitude towards folk material was highly charged, for, as Eglinton once humorously quipped: 'Yeats had this advantage over Shakespeare, that he believed in the fairies.'[34] The *sidhe* (the shee, or gods, of Irish mythology) were grouped by Oscar Wilde's mother in *Ancient Legends* (1887) under fallen angels, but for Yeats they were heaven's refugees.[35] Even the *lamia* motif, the false face that smiles, which was a dominant motif in nineteenth-century Irish folklore, is drained of much of its malice in Yeats's hands. When the faeries kidnap the living and swing behind them the door of faeryland on the southern face of Ben Bulben, the note sounded by Yeats is never tragic, for the new-born or the newly-wed henceforth move 'in the bloodless land of Faery' (*CT* 118). Yeats sought from the country people cures for both the mind and the body. On one occasion he accompanied Lady Gregory into Connemara in search of a man called Fagan, who had healing powers. Unfortunately, Fagan could do nothing about Yeats's uncertain eyesight, but he did indicate that the harm did not come from 'them'. In a footnote to the story, in a remark that characterises his approach to collecting folk material, Yeats later admitted: 'I was the patient; it seemed to be the only way of coming to intimate speech with the knowledgeable man.'[36]

THE SPECKLED BIRD

The Speckled Bird is a highly revealing portrait of Yeats's emotional and spiritual life in the 1890s, and constitutes, in the words of William O'Donnell, 'a spiritual autobiography . . . in the guise of a naturalistic novel'.[37] Yeats composed four versions of the novel from 1896 to 1902, but, from 726 pages of manuscript and more than a hundred and fifty thousand words, he managed to salvage nothing for publication in his lifetime. In some respects the material seems to have been too close to him: he needed a buffer between reality and imagination, and in this particular case he seems not to have found one. The major characters are based on himself, his father, Maud Gonne, 'MacGregor' Mathers, and Olivia Shakespear. For his settings in Ireland, Yeats uses Edward Martyn's* Tulira Castle, Count Florimond de Basterot's Parkmore (now Duras House, near Kinvara), and Lady Gregory's estate at Coole.

Yeats, or Michael Hearne in the final version, is the speckled bird of Jeremiah: 'Mine inheritance is as the speckled bird, all the birds of heaven are against it' (*Jeremiah* 12:9). The novel begins with Michael, dressed as a gentleman's son, digging in the sand for a pot of gold seen in a dream. On returning home he is cautioned against such dreams by

An Edwardian postcard showing Castle Rock in Lough Key, which Yeats visited in 1895 while staying with Douglas Hyde in County Roscommon (the last person to live in the castle was Hyde's father). With Maude Gonne and Castle Rock in mind, Yeats planned a 'mystical Order which should buy or hire the castle, and keep it as a place where its members could retire for a while for contemplation, and where we might establish mysteries like those of Eleusis and Samothrace; and for ten years to come my most impassioned thought was a vain attempt to find philosophy and to create ritual for that Order' (*A* 253–4). Mathers was to supply the ritual, Maud Gonne the beauty.

his father. John Hearne is an artist but, preoccupied with landlord-tenant problems and with thoughts of his dead wife, has not painted for years. Michael is left to grow up as he likes, a childhood defined by rambles, studio discussion, talks with peasants, and appreciation of nature. He reads the *Mabinogion* and *Morte d'Arthur*, but finds 'continual disappointment with the world he lived in' (*SB* 10). He fasts, has visions of a great bird, faints at dinner, and on doctor's advice is sent away to Paris. There he meets Samuel Maclagan ('MacGregor' Mathers) and deepens his understanding of visions and secret lore. In Paris Michael falls in love with Margaret Henderson (based on Maud Gonne), and they discuss poetry, make-believe, the future, nuns, heaven, and Maclagan's secret order.

On returning to Ireland Michael openly attacks his Catholic upbringing: 'My mass is the daily rising and setting of the sun' (*SB* 34). Life had begun: he would marry Margaret. When they meet again, Margaret notices Michael's agitated state and declares: 'If you do not become more like other people you will have no rest in your life' (*SB* 50). When he suggests marriage she is forced to disappoint him because of a promise to her mother to marry only a Catholic. Book 1 ends with Michael's departure from Ireland. A year later Michael meets Maclagan again and is invited to see his collection of books on alchemy. Introduced to various occult circles in North London, Michael finds himself arbitrating between quarrelsome members. Book 2 ends with the discovery that Margaret is married to Captain Peters (John MacBride was a military man) and that her marriage is unhappy. In book 3 Margaret offers Michael a sister's love, which

Samuel Liddell 'MacGregor' Mathers, dressed in the uniform of an artillery lieutenant, *c.* 1882. When Yeats stayed with him in Paris, Mathers would come down to breakfast with a copy of Macpherson's *Ossian* ready to recite, and at night 'he would dress himself in Highland dress, and dance the sword dance' (*A* 335).

he learns to accept. They plan to go away together, but this proves impossible, since she is pregnant.

Ten years later Michael meets the Maclagans in Montmartre, and he tells them of his love for Margaret and his friendship for another woman (not named, but presumably Olivia Shakespear): 'This woman seemed so friendly and unexacting that he thought she would understand and demand nothing that he could not give and besides she had ⟨blank⟩. Gradually they became closer and closer to one another, and after a time she became his mistress. This went on for two or three years, then they began to gradually drift apart. She began to seem unhappy, and he found it more and more difficult to reconcile this new relationship with the old unaltered feeling' (*SB* 105).[38] As for his mystical beliefs, Michael, unlike Maclagan, is convinced that the symbols of Christianity must be the central expression of any mystical order. The novel ends with Maclagan boarding a train for the East and watching Michael 'with those heroic eyes' (*SB* 107).

The Speckled Bird is Yeats's *apologia pro vita sua* in the 1890s. If Hone had read *The Speckled Bird*, he would have found answers to some of the queries he posed in 1915: 'We would like to know more of Mr Yeats's psychical experiences, his habit of magical practices, his belief in alchemy, and what the astrologers call "true science" than is told us in *Ideas of Good and Evil*.'[39] With it, we have a more complete picture of his relationship with Olivia Shakespear, the concept of a spiritual marriage with Maud Gonne (a sister's love), and the tension between friendship with one and passion towards the other. It also highlights the nature of visionary experience, the isolation of the visionary from those around him, and the relation between institutional Christianity, mysticism, and the East. Further, what emerges from his depiction of occult circles in London is not the 'war of spiritual with natural order'[40] on display in the stories of *The Secret Rose* (1897) but a less spiritual outcome – namely, that metaphysics is shaped by people, and that spiritualists themselves through their own disputes secure for would-be believers and sceptics alike perhaps the best view of the occult.

Yeats was initiated into the 'Order of the Golden Door', as Moore impishly called it, on 7 March 1890.[41] The event took place in Charlotte Street in London, and Yeats, purified by water and sworn to secrecy, assumed the Blakean motto of '*Demon Est Deus Inversus*' (DEDI, the devil is God inverted). In charge of the new Order, which was founded in 1887 were 'MacGregor' Mathers, William Woodman, and William Westcott, all former members of the Rosicrucian Society of England.[42] At the end of March 1888, the first month of recruiting in England, there were nine members, including Henri Bergson's sister, Moina, who became Mathers's wife, and the Reverend William Ayton, who became Yeats's alchemist; by the end of 1890 the total membership in the Isis-Urania Temple in London numbered fifty.[43] Among the fourteen initiations that year were the actress Florence Farr*[44] and Annie Horniman,* who became the leading financial supporter of the Abbey Theatre. Maud Gonne was initiated in November 1891 and took for her motto '*Per Ignem ad Lucem*' (through fire to light). George Pollexfen joined in December 1893 with the aptly chosen motto '*Festina Lente*' (make haste slowly).

Members were required to study, pass examinations, and so progress through the various stages from Neophyte to Philosophus.[45] From the outset they also learnt forms of ceremonial magic.[46] Yeats was involved in the composition of rituals for the Order.[47] However, disputes over principle and clashes over personality were never far from the surface. After moving to Paris in 1892 to found a new Temple, Mathers still insisted on controlling the London Temple, and in 1896 sent a manifesto to this effect. Yeats was slow to distance himself from Mathers, and as late as April 1898 visited him in Paris seeking help in the composition of rituals for his Celtic religious movement. But in April 1900 the conciliatory Yeats was forced to take sides when Aleister Crowley, 'a quite unspeakable person' (*L* 340), was sent by Mathers to seize the headquarters at 36 Blythe

Cecil French's 'Dreamer and the World' appeared in *Green Sheaf*, a magazine edited by Pamela Coleman Smith in 1903 and 1904.

Self-portrait by Yeats with sun and moon in place.

Road. In 'the Battle of Blythe Road' Yeats changed the locks on the house and the police were called, though they refused to intervene. Yeats was expelled by Mathers but then emerged as the leader of a reformed organisation, the Imperator of the Outer Order's Isis-Urania Temple, responsible for instruction in Mystical Philosophy.[48]

In 'All Souls' Night', a poem written in Oxford in 1920, Yeats recalls his continuing affection for Mathers:

> And I call up MacGregor from his grave,
> For in my first hard springtime we were friends,
> Although of late estranged.
> I thought him half a lunatic, half knave,
> And told him so, but friendship never ends.
>
> (*VP* 473)

In 1920 he could 'call up' Mathers with a degree of theatrical and humorous equanimity, but in 1900 he was uneasy about expelling Mathers, and the trouble did not stop there, for, as a leading member on the Executive Council, he was soon embroiled in a long-standing enmity between Farr and Horniman over the issue of secret groups. Yeats argued that such groups create suspicion among those outside, but at a General Meeting on 26 February 1901 he lost the argument and resigned from the Executive. After his defeat he wrote an essay entitled 'Is the Order of R.R. and A.C. to remain a Magical Order?', in which he stressed the Christian foundation of the Order, the need for a system and discipline, and that it should be a Magical Order, not a society for experiment and research.[49]

The Order continued to fragment, especially after the Horos rape trial in 1901 and 1902.[50] Yeats's commitment also cooled, apparently, but he continued to advance through the various levels of adeptship. His future wife joined the Stella Matutina Temple in London, probably in 1914; after their marriage in 1917, she and Yeats were active members of Amoun, the Mother Temple. Yeats remained a member of the Golden Dawn until 1922, by which time he was consigning his visionary beliefs to *A Vision* and the 1890s to the 'tragic generation'. But it would be interesting to know the full history

William Horton's ink caricature of Yeats in 1899. Horton* believed that sexual abstinence was the mystic way: 'Yeats, our way is not down here, our way is the upward one, from height to height beyond the stars to the very foot of God's throne upon whose steps we mount eternally, eternally. . . . All this Spiritism & Spiritistic investigation leads to nothing. It is just turning round & round in a circle & is never a spiral.'

of Yeats's involvement with the Golden Dawn after 1902. In October 1914, Yeats took the role of Postulant in a somewhat unusual ceremony conducted at the Stella Matutina, where he lay down in a coffin to hear the ringing of the thirty-six bells: 'At the Thirteenth Bell he is faint; at the Fourteenth he is very cold; at the Sixteenth he again emerges into a further higher plane; at the Seventeenth he is like a transparent rainbow. The Colours of the Planets play upon him. Then they merge into brilliant Light and for the rest of the Bells he shone with it. The Rising from the Tomb and the Sprinkling appear to involve a very great and serious effort on the part of both Postulant and Officers.'[51] As late as December 1919, as a letter to George Yeats from Christina Mary Stoddart suggests, Yeats's name was proposed for Ruling Chief in the Golden Dawn: 'By January I hope to have heard from F. R. ⟨Robert Felkin⟩ in answer to my proposal to ask D.E.D.I. to be Ruling Chief in place of Mr Reason who wishes to resign. . . . Then I firmly believe F. R. will leave us to ourselves.'[52]

The presence of the Golden Dawn can be felt throughout Yeats's verse. Indeed, reading Yeats is not unlike being at a seance where a chair is left empty for the reader to occupy. Images and symbols often come clothed with the aura of the occult, whose power can be sensed if not fully understood; in this regard Yeats is his own best reader: 'The half-read wisdom of daemonic images,/Suffice the ageing man as once the growing boy' (VP 427). The natural world, too, undergoes a profound transformation in his poetry. Swans 'paddle in the cold/Companionable streams' or 'drift on the still water' (VP 323), but we half-recognise that 'The Wild Swans at Coole' is more than a description of an autumnal scene, more even than an analogous reflection on the poet's autobiography or his declining sexual powers. Like an Instructor, Yeats uses his poetry

Ricketts's motif graced the endpapers of the collected edition of Yeats's work published by Macmillan in the 1920s. 'The little design of the unicorn is a masterpiece in that difficult design' (*L* 691).

to illustrate the passage from the known to the unknown, and, because it is a starting-point not the destination, the physical world is therefore simplified and often bare.

On his table in the Tower in the 1920s he is surrounded by the necessary implements in an occult rite:

> Two heavy trestles, and a board
> Where Sato's gift, a changeless sword,
> By pen and paper lies
> That it may moralise
> My days out of their aimlessness.
>
> (*VP* 421)

'Around me the images of thirty years' (*VP* 601): thus begins his late processional meditation on the paintings in 'The Municipal Gallery Revisited'. With his feet planted firmly in the here and now the Instructor can proceed with authority. Never far away from any such discussion is the topic of Yeats and liturgy. Often the opening to a Yeats poem is reminiscent of the unfolding of the cloth at an occult ceremony, designed to settle the assembled gathering, empty their minds, and prepare them for the service to come. And the widespread use of performative utterances in his verse suggests a mage at work: 'I summon to the winding ancient stair' (*VP* 477); 'I write it out in a verse' (*VP* 394); 'I declare this tower is my symbol' (*VP* 480).

With its stress on spiritual revelation, the Golden Dawn also contributed to Yeats's depiction of Christianity.[53] In a disturbing poem such as 'The Second Coming' Yeats

48

draws on and then undermines the Christian version of salvation history that runs from Bethlehem to the Apocalypse. 'Homer is my example and his unchristened heart' (*VP* 503) is how Yeats once summed up his position, but this comes in a poem where he expresses fascination with the preserved body of the sixteenth-century Spanish mystic St Teresa of Avila. Ironically, Yeats the Protestant – and this is further confirmation that his daimon was female – devoted considerable thought to the Virgin Mary and the significance of the Annunciation in world history, but, as the savage opening lines from *The Resurrection* (1931) suggest, his stance was almost completely devoid of the devotional, his mind closer to astrology than Christianity:

> I saw a staring virgin stand
> Where holy Dionysus died,
> And tear the heart out of his side,
> And lay the heart upon her hand
> And bear that beating heart away;
> And then did all the Muses sing
> Of Magnus Annus at the spring,
> As though God's death were but a play.
> ....
> The Roman Empire stood appalled:
> It dropped the reins of peace and war
> When that fierce virgin and her Star
> Out of the fabulous darkness called.
>
> (*VPl* 903)

Hanrahan, Robartes, and Aherne

The Speckled Bird, *The Secret Rose* (1897), and *The Tables of the Law and The Adoration of the Magi* (1904) were all written within a few years of each other, and there is value in seeing them together. Indeed, a knowledge of *The Speckled Bird* adds considerably to an understanding of the other two. *The Secret Rose* builds on the stories of *The Celtic Twilight* to create a highly symbolic, chronological structure that skilfully embraces ancient Irish myth, the emergence of medieval Ireland, the decline of feudalism and the breakup of monasticism, and the hedge-school culture of Ireland in the eighteenth century (embodied in the invented figure of Hanrahan). Running through the stories are several themes at once personal, historical, and social: the fall of the Old Order, whether medieval, monastic, or Gaelic aristocracy; the need for devotion to a cause, linked to heroism and saintliness; the outcast from society.[54] The title poem, 'The Secret Rose', which serves as an epigraph, strikes an appropriately messianic note:

> *Surely thine hour has come, thy great wind blows,*
> *Far off, most secret, and inviolate Rose?*
>
> (*SR* 10)

With *The Speckled Bird* as background, the Hanrahan stories in *The Secret Rose* carry a much bolder autobiographical imprint. Hanrahan, the wandering hedge-schoolmaster, is the outcast from society. In 'The Book of the Great Dhoul and Hanrahan the Red', he longs to see the shee and 'had really spent half a night on the Grey Rath in great fear,

49

'Minute by minute they live: / The stone's in the midst of all' (*VP* 393). View of Ennistymon, County Clare, the houses sandwiched between the falls and the cemetery.

A statue of St Patrick on which someone has humorously daubed 'RM', Resident Magistrate. In old age Yeats wondered if the sole theme was 'Usheen and Patrick', the swordsman's rebuke of the saint (*L* 798). From Donn Byrne, *Ireland* (1927).

but quite without avail, and, now that a sight of them seemed really possible, he began to tremble all over' (*SR* 132–3). He has a vision of Cleena of the Waves, the queen of the Southern fairies. She is, like Maud Gonne, tall and dressed in saffron: 'Then suddenly he felt rather than saw, and more as an intellectual presence than as a substantial form, a tall woman, dressed in saffron, like the women of ancient Ireland, who stood a little above the floor, her dark hair falling from under a silver fillet. Then from the shadow of her hair shone eyes of a faint blue, very clear and soft, giving to her whole being a look of unearthly mildness, as though she had never known trouble nor met with any affront' (*SR* 134).[55] Yeats/Hanrahan suffers on her behalf, and he imagines Maud/Cleena whispering to him: 'You have always loved me better than your own soul, and you have sought for me everywhere and in everything, though without knowing what you sought, and now I have come to you and taken on mortality that I may share your sorrow' (*SR* 137–8). Love, however, brings more suffering, for in the next story, 'The Twisting of the Rope and Hanrahan the Red', Hanrahan's attempts to win the heart of a 'soft dreamy-looking young girl who sat by the fire' (*SR* 146) are rebuffed by her family, and Hanrahan learns to his cost that the rope he is asked to twist is the Rope of Human Sorrows.

'Rosa Alchemica' (the alchemical rose), a story that stems directly from the Golden Dawn initiation ceremonies, makes us appreciate the inner turmoil the occult occasioned in Yeats.[56] When the narrator, who has written a book on alchemy, is asked by Michael Robartes to join the Order of the Alchemical Rose, he is filled with terror: 'I command you to leave me at once, for your ideas and phantasies are but the illusions that creep like maggots into civilisations when they begin to decline, and into minds when they begin to decay' (*SR* 236). Michael Robartes, who is not unlike Mathers, triumphs, and Yeats/the narrator is escorted to a Temple in the west of Ireland where he hears 'the clash of unknown armies' (*SR* 243). In the initiation ceremony that follows, the narrator is swept into ecstasy dancing with 'an immortal august woman, who had black lilies in her hair' (*SR* 260). On awaking, however, he discovers a chill dawn. Robartes cannot be roused, and he hears angry voices of local people who are against the paganism of the Alchemical Order. The narrator flees for his life, and in the coda to the story we learn that he now wears a rosary – another female emblem – about his neck.

Both Hanrahan and Robartes embark on a journey westward, one because 'Gaelic Ireland was still alive, and the Gaelic poets were still honoured in the West' (*SR* 142), the other because that was where the Temple of the Alchemical Rose was located. Both characters suffer at the hands of the Catholic people, and their identity is shaken. Yeats's involvement with the occult in the 1890s always had repercussions on his Irish identity, and he found himself entangled in a triangular net whose three points were London, Paris, and the West of Ireland. Yeats suffered more than his spiritualist friends in London in this respect, for he had always to take into account these other dimensions, especially Ireland's traditional beliefs, and these stories reveal the extent of his isolation from rural Ireland, whose beliefs he had championed in *The Celtic Twilight*.[57]

The figure of Owen Aherne is the subject of 'The Tables of the Law'. More orthodox than Robartes, Aherne refused to take the biretta and become a cleric. For him, the arts were sent into the world 'to overthrow nations, and finally life herself, by sowing everywhere unlimited desires, like torches thrown into a burning city' (*M* 294). As in 'Rosa Alchemica', the narrator is troubled by Aherne's Joachite beliefs that for some there is a secret law which acknowledges the authority not of the Commandments but of the Holy Spirit. Ten years later, walking along the quayside in Dublin, the narrator catches sight of Aherne. 'I have lost my soul', confesses Aherne, 'because I have looked out of the eyes of the angels' (*M* 306). It is a cautionary tale and reveals some of the pitfalls that troubled Yeats the spiritualist in the 1890s. Like Blake, he felt keenly 'the trance-like absorption of his whole nature that accompanied his finest writing, a mood from which he returned to the ordinary conversation of life as a man from another land.'[58] Aherne represents those who are buffeted by extremes, those who are drawn initially to mystical experiences that threaten all spiritual and social order, to a kind of divine ecstasy embodied in the phrase 'Where There is Nothing There is God'.[59] But then they face a counter-movement, in Aherne's case back to Catholicism and the realisation that the Heart of God can only be touched by separation and sin – in other words, through an acceptance of salvation history.

'The Adoration of the Magi' continues the movement back to the poor chapels of Ireland, where the narrator prays best, 'where frieze coats brush against me as I kneel' (*M* 315). He is visited by three old men (the Magi figures) who had been told by Robartes of the coming again of the gods. After Robartes's death they hear a voice bidding them embark for Paris, 'where a dying woman would give them secret names and thereby so transform the world that another Leda would open her knees to the swan, another Achilles beleaguer Troy' (*M* 310). In Paris, their initial scepticism gives way to problematic belief and an uncertainty as to what they have experienced. The narrator too is unsure if the three men were Immortals or immortal demons: 'Whatever they were, I have turned into a pathway which will lead me from them and from the Order of the Alchemical Rose' (*M* 315).

As it happened, Yeats did not turn away from the mystical Order. What he explores in such stories is the tension between his esoteric beliefs and his identity with the country people of Ireland. He was pulled in opposite directions, one towards 'the secret rose', the other towards beliefs that were sanctioned by the Church. His occult beliefs raised fears in his mind about being an outcast from society. Yeats knew that without the people certain objects, such as a National Theatre, could not be achieved.[60] He was also troubled about the disposition of his work and about losing 'my old country emotion':

> My new work would not help in that spiritualisation of Irish imagination I had set before me. I did not know what to do. Perhaps after all I was to write an elaborate mysticism without any special birthplace. . . . I sought the advice of Diana Vernon. She obtained these sentences, unintelligible to herself: 'He is too much under solar influence. He is to live near water and to avoid woods, which concentrate the solar power.'
>
> (*Mem* 100)

Yeats questioned 'Diana Vernon' (Olivia Shakespear) in London in August 1896, just before his trip to Ireland with Arthur Symons and his visit to Martyn at Tulira Castle, County Galway. At Tulira, after evoking the lunar power, he had the famous Archer Vision: 'I evoked for nine evenings with no great result, but on the ninth night as I was going to sleep I saw first a centaur and then a marvellous naked woman shooting an arrow at a star.'[61] On a visit to Coole while staying at Tulira, he was moved both by the Archer Vision and by Olivia Shakespear's remark: 'When I saw her great woods on the edge of a lake, I remembered the saying about avoiding woods and living near the water. Had this new friend come because of my invocation, or had the saying been but prevision and my invocation no act of will, but prevision also?' (*A* 376). He was anxious about his work 'getting too full of those little jewelled thoughts that come from the sun and have no nation', and it was at this point that Lady Gregory, taking him round the cottages of the poor and collecting stories, 'taught me to understand again, and much more perfectly than before, the true countenance of country life'.[62]

Yeats's occult life never stood still, and in the years leading up to his marriage, his interest in automatic writing and mediumship was extended through contact with 'Leo Africanus' and Elizabeth Radcliffe. In April 1910, Yeats attended a seance given by Mrs Etta Wriedt at William T. Stead's home in Wimbledon, where Leo, a Frustrator rather than a Control, made his first appearance:

> We sat round room not holding hands or touching, but were told to put our feet flat on the floor. There was the usual trumpet and Mrs ⟨Wriedt⟩ was two off to my right. It was perfectly dark. We were seated a very few minutes when we were sprinkled with some liquid – I felt it on my head and hands, a few drops. The medium said it was a baptism. Then there came a very loud voice through the trumpet. It had come for 'Mr Gates'. Or so the medium heard the voice. I said that was me. Then the voice said, 'I have been with you from childhood. We want to use your hand and brain.' 'You possess key,' or, 'you are a key mind', I forget which. 'I am Leo, the writer – writer and explorer.' I tried by questions to get more. 'When did he live; in eighteenth century?' He then said, 'Why man,' or such expression implying impatience, 'I am Leo, the writer. You know Leo, the writer.'

An Edwardian postcard showing another kind of magician at work. In *Memoirs* Yeats confessed: 'I was always longing for evidence, but ashamed to admit my longing, and having read in Sibly's *Astrology* that if you burned a flower to ashes, and then put the ashes under a bellglass in the moonlight, the phantom of the flower would rise before you I persuaded members of the Section who lived more alone than I and so could experiment undisturbed to burn flowers without cease' (*Mem* 23–4).

Here in Harry Furniss's cartoon of 'Punch among the Planets' from the 1890 Christmas number of *Punch*, there is a sketch of Leo Africanus – not the arcane figure of Yeats's occult pursuits but the sad imperialist in military uniform, clutching his profits and transforming the Continent into a Barnum and Bailey circus and menagerie.

When I said I did not, I thought he added, 'You will hear of me at Rome.' He then went. After him came a feeble voice of which we could get little that was clear. This voice was suddenly interrupted by the very loud voice again, telling me 'to sit up straight in my chair'. I was leaning forward. At this point the influence was broken.

(*Mem* 264–5)

This first encounter with Leo was not especially auspicious, because of Leo's Irish accent, which Yeats felt was 'not quite true', being the 'kind of accent an Irishman some years out of Ireland, or an Englishman who had a fair knowledge of Ireland, might assume in telling a story'.[63] Later, however, asked by Leo to record an account of their relationship, Yeats did so in the first person as Leo.

The spookiness of such experimentation obviously attracted Yeats. When his occult sessions in 1913 with Elizabeth Radcliffe yielded a name they did not recognise, Yeats would immediately begin investigations, which sometimes took him to the Home Office. On one occasion, the name of Thomas Emmerson was uncovered, and Yeats and Radcliffe were requested to keep the matter private, since it concerned the character of a dead man.[64] But Yeats also turned explicitly to the occult for personal and emotional direction. In December 1913, he wrote to Radcliffe, the most powerful medium he used before George, seeking her advice. It was Radcliffe's spirits which a year previously had saved him from serious errors at a critical juncture in his life. He wanted her to contact them again.[65] On another occasion he sought her advice about the evil eye:

> Twenty years ago certain things were going very badly with me. I said going to bed 'I will find out before I wake what is wrong.' I meant to find out in dreams or vision about the mind and circumstances of a girl I was in love with who was acting rather strange as I thought. I had no sooner closed my eyes than I seemed shaken (?) out my head. I stood in the drawing-room below mine and before me was a woman, quite unknown to me, who rushed at me in a furious passion. I then seem thrown (?) back into my own room. The vision had vanished. It remains always a mystery to me but I remember it when the controls spoke of the 'evil eye'. I cannot understand.[66]

Then in August 1916, rejected by Maud and excited by Iseult Gonne,* he wrote from Paris: 'Will you please without saying anything to any body ask your controls if they have a message for me.'[67]

What George brought to Yeats by way of an unexpected dowry was the immediate fusing and systematising of all these various strands and approaches to the occult. But there was more, for it was perhaps not her being a medium that took him by surprise but her facility with automatic writing, a practice he had attempted himself and had examined in others. With Radcliffe, the channels of communication were occasionally muddied, but with George he had a captive audience and an immediate answering machine. Between 20 October 1917 and 28 March 1920 Yeats and George ('Georgie, her traditional name is not to be endured')[68] devoted part of nearly every day to automatic writing, filling over 3,600 pages in 450 sittings. They sat at a table, normally at night, alone, with the lights on. In the period at the beginning (5–20 November 1917) and at the end (16 June 1919 to 29 March 1920), George jotted down both questions and answers, a method which, according to Harper, 'does not suggest full automatism'.[69] The word *trance* is not mentioned, but there is a reference on one occasion to the 'glass globe', or crystal ball. On another occasion we learn of a 'golden cloth round medium and a scarlet cloth for you' (that is, Yeats) (*YVP* 2, 133).[70] They regularly burned incense, found towns not conducive to their experiments, and were told to avoid 'Martha', the term the Yeatses used for George's periods.

The Controls were particular and ensured compliance from him, for Yeats was the patient again. 'When you criticize arrangement why not ask that just before possibly making more complications in mistakes' (*YVP* 2, 159).[71] Once, Thomas of Dorlowicz gave him an elaborate timetable to be followed:

> Work five mornings a week – idle one morning – potter over paper one morning
> afternoon & evening go out as much as possible & sleep
> codify evening 5.30 to 7 & nights
> I will come 2 nights a week for system & two evenings when you codify to help now
> I am not nearly done
> You must codify from the very beginning of system & then medium can sort out each division & make a summary of each
> When all is satisfactorily done the writing will begin again regularly for some time . . .
> You are not to write any more poems on system for 2 or 3 weeks because I want you to

finish all this work
You are to go to bed earlier & get up earlier – much better for you

(*YVP* 1, 443)[72]

Evidently, George was determined to get Yeats into shape. According to Elizabeth Cullingford, 'for both partners sexual and occult interests had always been indistinguishable'.[73] This is especially evident in the records of their automatic writing sessions. Indeed, in September 1919 Yeats was congratulated for being a 'good husband – good lover' (*YVP* 2, 414). She reassured him that he could retain his youth 'through theory', telling him not to 'forget your youth now that you have past it' (*YVP* 1, 246).[74] At times Yeats was puzzled and insisted on knowing why when 'you are giving a profound philosophy' he was warned against philosophy: 'I warn you against the philosophy that is bred in stagnation – it is a bitter philosophy a philosophy which destroys – I give you one which leads – I give you one which is from outside – a light which you follow not one which will burn you' (*YVP* 1, 252).[75] At the session on 27 June 1919, he was advised against political involvement in Ireland: 'you may be tempted to join in political schemes if there is trouble & you must not' (*YVP* 2, 320). Occasionally, George lost concentration and asked him to repeat questions; when she was not familiar with details well known to Yeats, as with Parnell's life, she would tell him to choose another person. Yeats – at least to an outsider – seems to have suspected nothing. So present was the third person to his imagination that he would ask the Controls 'why the medium is so tired & ⟨not⟩ sleeping well', and the medium would reply: 'It will work itself off' (*YVP* 1, 245).[76]

The early sessions took place while they were on honeymoon at Stone Cottage, Coleman's Hatch, on the edge of Ashdown Forest in Sussex. At a theoretical level, Yeats was concerned with two questions, questions also explored at some length in *Per Amica Silentia Lunae*: the relation between the Anima Mundi and the Antithetical Self, and the quality in the Anima Mundi that compels that relationship. At a personal level, Yeats was initially preoccupied with Iseult Gonne and her mother, and he wanted the Communicators to reassure him about his choice of marriage partner, or, as he put it, the problem of balance in the personalities of George and Iseult.[77] He was also intrigued by the concept of Initiatory Moment and requested the 'control' to tell him 'dates of my flash', to which the reply came: 1896, 1910, 1913, 1917 (*YVP* 2, 222). These were important years in Yeats's relationships with four women: Olivia Shakespear, Maud Gonne, Mabel Dickinson, and George herself.[78] We learn elsewhere that May 1913 was a significant month, perhaps for both of them, when 'The emotion of paternity was begun', as was his 'hatred of being self deceived' (*YVP* 2, 376).[79] In the same month there is a reference to the medium being a victim, but this is left unexplored.[80] In July 1919, George through the Control Ameritus shows Yeats 'the curious Astrological concurrence with initiatory moments':

In October 1910	♂	♂	♀	
In July 1913	♂	♂	♀	
In May 1913	♂	♂	♀	
In July 1914	♂	♂	♀	
In November 1914	♂	♂	♀	
In November 1915	♂	♂	♀	Date right
In March	♂	♂	♀	1917[81]

The romantic setting of Stone Cottage where love and the occult intertwined.

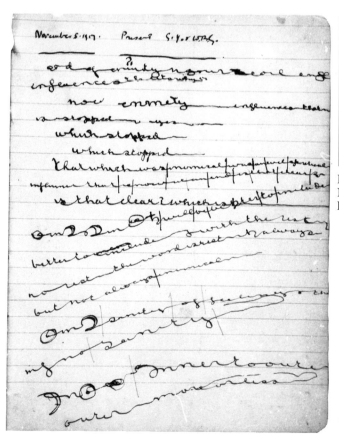

November 5 1917   Present G.Y. + W.B.Y.

end of enmity in your evil influences thats why
now enmity – influences that is stopped – yes
which stopped
which stopped
that which was inimical was an evil spiritual influence that is now at an
end is that clear?
is that clear? which is – ☉ in ☽ & ☽ in ☉ ♄ will be better to include –
better to include it with the rest – no rest – the word is rest – ♄ always
but not always inimical
☉ in ☽ sanity of feeling & thinking – no sanity[2]
☽ in ☉ Inner to outer – outer more or less

First page of Automatic Script by George Yeats, dated 5 November 1917 and conducted at the Ashdown Forest Hotel while on honeymoon.

Immediately after this, there is an intriguing reference to 1910 being date of 'First sight', an allusion perhaps to their first sighting of each other, or to George's initiatory moment, when a new emotion or conviction was initiated.

On 25 August 1919, we learn that no conception took place, so presumably the Yeatses were using the sessions to align astrological birth signs with the births of their children.[82] There is a curious letter from George to Yeats written from Oxford on 4 August 1920, the month she suffered a miscarriage, in which she tells him the baby may not be a reality. On Sunday night she undertook a horary. She had received no communication from Yeats and was anxious. Her horary showed she was in Vth house ⟨☿☉⛢♀□♂+☍☽⟩. Unaware that she might be pregnant, she learnt from the medium of deception especially when it came to Vth house matters. On account of her ill-health, she wondered if she could have been mistaken about the pregnancy. She trusted Yeats had told Solomons, their pediatrician in Dublin, to be discreet since she did not want Lady Gregory to know.[83]

What also emerges from the automatic writing sessions is the extraordinary conviction that he and George, seer and medium, had been 'selected to give birth to the New Master or Avatar of the historical cycle soon to begin'.[84] On 20 March 1919, there appears this entry: 'We gave you Anne – is not that horary remarkable enough?????' (*YVP* 2, 201). Yeats might also have recalled a comment George Russell made to him in June 1896 about the gods returning to Ireland: 'I believe profoundly that a new Avatar is about to appear. . . . It will be one of the kingly Avatars, who is at once ruler of men and magic sage.'[85] In the light of all this, 'The Second Coming' becomes an even stranger poem. Fortunately for the reader, there is also room for humour, as when Thomas, the Control who shows most concern for Yeats's well-being, suggests he drink more and take more exercise: 'no use having a theory if it tires you'.[86] On another occasion he tells the medium to 'take a hot bath then write' (*YVP* 2, 270).

The automatic writing sessions, begun in 1917, and the 164 sleep sessions conducted between March 1920 and March 1924, constitute the seven-year quest for visionary truth, later codified in *A Vision*, the book that George was anxious Yeats finish on 24 October 1924. Then it would be exactly seven years since 'we' started it. She felt it might otherwise go on for another seven years.[87] Interestingly, the use of 'we' strikes a note of exclusion from a process that was initially as much hers as his. All kinds of material float to the surface: the Cuchulain cycle of plays and their relevance to Yeats's life; Iseult's use of incense ('no she has not used it unless perhaps from curiosity' [*YVP* 1, 91]); the twenty-eight stages of the human cycle and the place of specific individuals in that cycle; George's health; the explanation of the symbol of the swan and of the speckled bird (the latter symbolises Phase 14 and represents 'daimon of MG' [*YVP* 2, 280]);[88] the concept of dreaming back; the meaning of the hour-glass; the use and significance of colour symbolism ('Can you give me a colour scale?' he asks the Control Aymor [*YVP* 1, 212]);[89] the difference between critical and initiatory moments ('critical produce events Initiatory produce changes of the mind & heart & will' [*YVP* 2, 213]); the contrast between nations which are pure and those which are mixed ('England and America were especially mixed but my country was resisting mixture' [*YVP* 3, 63]).

In February 1918, the medium announced that Germany, France, and Italy could not go on after March because Neptune and Saturn were in Leo, implying famine and poverty. She could not give a world horoscope for 1919 because the various countries would be busy reconstructing and she needed to find out the exact degrees for ruling capital towns, but peace was imminent, as was the restoration of the Czar (*YVP* 2, 362–5).[90] Several sequences are quite bizarre:

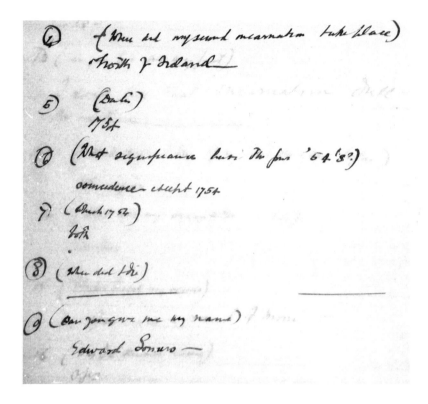

4   Where did my second incarnation take place
    North of Ireland
5   Date
    1754
6   What significance have the four '54s?
    coincidence except 1754
7   Which 1754
    both
8   When did I die

9   Can you give me my name
    Edward Somers
10 any connection with my present family
    Ask your sister
11 Is it a known name
    No
12 Can you tell me any fact
    I dont like that incarnation – dull – go back
13 What did I die of in incarnation before
    Smallpox
14 What was my occupation in life
    Courtier

(YVP 2, 390–91)[91]

According to Anne Yeats, her mother almost never referred to the occult after Yeats's
death; yet Anne felt her mother was more psychic than her father.[92] As for institutional

religion, George was in her youth a rebel and in later life a non-joiner. In the summer of 1954, Grace Jaffe had a long discussion with her cousin George on the subject of religion: 'Georgie never made up her mind to commit herself to Roman Catholicism. I never fully understood her decision to remain outside the church. It was not a question of doctrine or dogma. She said jokingly that she could even accept the idea that the Blessed Virgin Mary "went up to Heaven with all her clothes on"'.[93] Certainly in their correspondence George pays more attention to psychic events than does Yeats. In August 1920 she confessed that she had recently experienced a sense of freedom and had, the previous night, heard a voice saying that the third element should begin its course.[94] In a letter of 29 January 1936, she disclosed she was a little worried about Yeats, who was then in Majorca. A week before she had suddenly awoken with his voice in her ears, groaning. She ran into his bedroom, forgetting that he was away, only to discover Michael fast asleep. Immediately she thought his lung congestion had flared up again.[95] On 2 February George was sent for, as Yeats had suffered a major collapse, with kidney and heart problems.

Equally, George's attitude to the occult seems to have been more knowledgeable and genuine than is sometimes allowed. Asked to edit Russell's letters in 1936, she knew exactly what she wanted. She would include very few of the vague passages which she felt were poorly written.[96] If one adopts a sceptical reading of the automatic writing sessions, then George ceases to be ancillary to Yeats's thought and becomes the shaper of his system. If she plays the part of the various Controls, colluding in her husband's delusions, then she is the source of much that Yeats imagined came from the Spirits. In this light, she deserves credit not only for initiating and maintaining the ruse but also for laying the foundations of *A Vision* and much of his later verse. Her grasp of details and the coherence of her argument are quite astonishing. After dinner, for example, on 4 January 1918, she is asked: 'What is the CG ⟨Creative Genius⟩ of ⟨Phase⟩ 18?' She replied at once: 'The creative genius is of the nature of the phase – thus 12 constructive imagination in philosophic thought – 13 creative imagination in subjective emotion – 14 the moulding of intuitive emotional thought – 16 the wielding of passionate thought – 17 the absorption of artistic creation into subjective thought – Thus 12 is EG ⟨Evil Genius⟩ of 18 – 13 of 17 and 17 of 13 – reverse 14 & 16' (*YVP* 1, 200). Yeats then asked her to illustrate from 'Nietsche' and, shrewdly, she replied: 'It is not mystical it is a system of the intellect.'

In 1931, *The Words upon the Window Pane* prompted a revealing difference of opinion between Yeats and George over the issue of mediumship. In his Notes to the play Yeats confidently asserted:

> It seems to me that after reading many books and meeting many phenomena, some in my own house, some when alone in my room, I can see clearly at last. I consider it certain that every voice that speaks, every form that appears, whether to the medium's eyes and ears alone or to someone or two others or to all present, whether it remains a sight or sound or affects the sense of touch, whether it is confined to the room or can make itself apparent at some distant place, whether it can or cannot alter the position of material objects, is first of all a secondary personality or dramatisation created by, in, or through the medium.
>
> (*VPl* 967)

George was less convinced:

I think the reason I did not very much like Part II Windowpane is that your argument – the dramatisation of the secondary and tertiary personalities of the medium, seem so close to the old pysichical ⟨sic⟩ research theory of the subconscious or at least that I cannot personally understand what you mean except in those terms. If I had to interpret that 'commentary' I could not say that any 'spirit' were present at any seance, that spirits were present at a seance only as impersonations created by a medium out of material in a world record just as wireless photography or television are created; that all communicating spirits are mere dramatisations of that record; that all spirits in fact are not, as far as psychic communications are concerned, spirits at all, are only memory. I say 'memory' deliberately, because 'memory' is so large a part of all psychic phenomena. I dont remember any case in which a spirit (communicating through a medium) had during the latter part of his life been cut off from that every day faculty of memory. Those people who were wounded in the head during war – they dont come – the insane dont come??? ⟨sic⟩ – the spirits who tell us about their houses, their horse racing, their whiskeys and sodas, their children, their autnts ⟨sic⟩ and God knows whatnots, their suicides, were all mainly preoccupied during their lives with those things. Have we any record of a spirit communicating who had been at any period of his life been so physically or mentally incapacitated that memory, even 'subconscious memory', had been obliterated?

Apologies for this diatribe – it all comes out of an idea I had lately that small nations have long memories, big nations have short memories, small nations make Empires.[97]

A recent commentator, K. P. S. Jochum, citing part of this letter, claims that 'Mrs Yeats's move from spiritism to psychology is remarkable and casts further doubt on the automatism of her writing.'[98] The full letter reveals nearly precisely the opposite – namely, a concern to keep spiritual matters separate from psychological explanation. According to George, Yeats's view of mediumship is indistinguishable from a theory of the subconscious: that what happens at a seance is nothing more than a dramatisation of the secondary and tertiary personalities of the medium. For George, spirits are present at a seance not as impersonations of the medium but as impersonations created by the medium out of material in the world, in the same way as the wireless or photography record (physical) events in the world. Her argument is complicated by the claim that spirits are 'only memory' and that the spirits who have come in their sessions have always had a memory. But the burden of her argument is to steer clear of psychological explanations of occult experience. Those spirits who come with memory intact support the view that more is present at a seance than the impersonation of secondary personalities of the medium.

Yeats certainly recognised her powers and, as a letter to 'Dobbs' (as she was called) from the Savile Club in London suggests, he enjoyed putting them on display. The previous night he had been to the College of Psychic Science, and he asks George if he can arrange a seance with their trumpet medium.[99] Anything she spoke in her sleep had potential meaning for Yeats, not just during the so-called sleep sessions but also later when she corrected mistakes. Once in June 1930 Yeats arrived for lunch with Lady Gregory 'a good deal upset by words, occult, connected with his work, correcting some mistake in it – spoken by George in her sleep – she unconscious of it' (LGJ 2, 442).[100] The irony is that, while quick to acknowledge that his own daimon was female, Yeats needed the filter of the occult to recognise George's voice.[101] The further irony is that Yeats took most notice of George's voice when it was not her voice, when she was asleep, for example, ignorant of the communicator's message, and given to 'tricks of speech' (*AV [B]* 22). George's name in the Golden Dawn was 'Nemo', no one (which, rearranged and minus the first letter, can be subsumed into 'Demon', the first word of Yeats's motto); her given name 'Georgina' he translated into its masculine form. He then rewrote her character and personality to suit: 'My wife's interests are musical, literary, practical, she seldom comments upon what I dictate except upon the turn of phrase; she can no more correct it than she could her automatic script at a time when a slight error brought her new fatigue' (*AV [B]* 21). As if this were not enough, in the draft, the issue of authorship/attribution/voice is further compounded: '⟨S⟩he can no more correct it than she could her automatic script, at a time when . . . my errors necessitated endless writing and re-dictating.'[102]

Yeats was an occultist rather than a mystic: he was perhaps more concerned with knowledge than an inner urge God-ward.[103] In May 1914 he went to Mirebeau near Poitiers in France to investigate the so-called miracle of the bleeding oleographs of the Sacred Heart, but was disappointed by the results.[104] In *A Vision*, he conceded: 'I can discover no apparent difference between a natural and a supernatural smell, except that the natural smell comes and goes gradually while the other is suddenly there and then as suddenly gone' (*AV [B]* 16). Not surprisingly, his experimentalism extended to taking drugs. He told Harold Speakman in the 1920s that he had never smoked opium but had tried mescal and hasheesh: 'With hasheesh, after he had looked into the shadow of a curtain, he could see colours *taking form* there.'[105] He was invariably intrigued by coincidence, prevision, and the issue of scientific proof. Reading Spengler's *Decline of the West* in July 1926, as he told Force Stead, he was astonished to discover a similarity between his own thoughts and dates recorded in Galway in 1918 and material in Spengler's book, which was being printed in Germany at the same time. Spengler's version of world history resembled his own in 'Dove or Swan' in *A Vision*. They had arrived at their conclusions from different positions but the result was identical. Disregarding coincidence, Yeats was convinced that his mind and Spengler's had been in contact through intermediaries. But whereas Spengler could prove his theory, Yeats could only suggest.[106]

Yeats always seemed conscious that his beliefs were unorthodox and theatrical. *A Vision*, he confessed to Edith Shackleton Heald* in May 1937, 'is the skeleton in my cupboard. I do not know whether I want my friends to see it or not to see it. I think "Will so-and-so think me a crazed fanatic?" But one goes on in blind faith' (*L* 888). 'You're probably wondering how much of this I believe,' he told a 'spellbound audience' at Wellesley College in May 1920. 'All I can say is what the peasants answer "there is no man mowing the meadow but what sees the little people one time or another." '[107] He accepted that 'mediumship is dramatisation' and that in consequence 'almost always truth and lies are mixed together' (*VPl* 968). Accompanying all his beliefs, as he once confessed to Lady Gregory, was an element of doubt: 'I am like a man looking for the philosopher's stone, or like a man who has found it but doubts if any will believe his chemical gold is anything but brass or copper.'[108] In searching for the will of Hugh Lane, he employed a clairvoyant but conceded: 'The greatest difficulty in judging communications through mediums or clairvoyants is to separate the communication that one seeks from what is merely dramatic. Only the most literal-minded spiritualist thinks there is no dramatic element and one school of investigators thinks that all except the underlying thought itself, is dramatic.'[109] The Frustrators had rightly warned him: 'Remember we will deceive you if we can' (*AV [B]* 13).

3

Yeats and Cultural Nationalism

INTRODUCTION

The significance of Yeats in the development of cultural nationalism in Ireland was well understood by those who knew him best. When Yeats received the Nobel Prize for Literature in 1923, Russell generously observed:

> Yeats has made the name of his country shine in imagination to the rest of the world a hundred times more than any of the political notorieties whose names are on every lip here, but who have rarely uttered a sentence which could be taken up and echoed by people in other lands and made part of their thought. It was by the literary movement of which Yeats was the foremost figure that Ireland for the first time for long centuries came to any high international repute.[1]

Reflecting on his achievement after his death in 1939, Maud Gonne, not without some justification, claimed 'Without Yeats there would have been no Literary Revival in Ireland. Without the inspiration of that Revival and the glorification of beauty and heroic virtue, I doubt if there would have been an Easter Week.'[2]

Cultural nationalism in the nineteenth century afforded a space where – in principle at least – the right to differ about Ireland could be advanced without conceding ground to the later conception of different traditions or separate communities.[3] But, as the observations above suggest, in the emergence of modern Ireland culture and politics were interwoven. Indeed, earlier than he anticipated, the political Yeats, conscious that 'we tear each others character in peices for things that dont matter to anybody',[4] discovered the limits of cultural nationalism. In some respects his personal tragedy was that he could not abandon his hopes for Ireland or accept his place in history. His will was stronger than his intellect, for at root he knew that culture was both opposed to politics and part of it. The lessons were there to be learnt from the outset. As a boy, for example, he spent many afternoons with a village shoemaker who was a great reader:

> I asked him once what Irish novels he liked, and he told me there were none he could read, 'they sentimentalised the people', he said angrily; and it was against Kickham that he complained most. 'I want to see the people', he said 'shown up in their naked hideousness.' That is the peasant mind as I know it, delight in strong sensations whether of beauty or ugliness, in bare facts, and quite without sentimentality. The sentimental mind is the bourgeois mind, and it was this mind which came into Irish literature with Gerald Griffin and later on with Kickham.[5]

A REAL IRISH COTTAGE

It shines thro' the bog thro' the brake & the mireland
And he called it the dear little Shamrock of Ireland.
The dear little Shamrock
The sweet little Shamrock of Ireland.

Moore.

These were some of the conventional images of Ireland writers like Yeats were forced to confront or ignore. All are postcards from the turn of the century.

2767.2. Roadside Butter Market.

Charles Lamb's 'Dancing at a Northern Crossroads'. For the Nineties aesthete, the dancer was a detached, erotic symbol; Yeats was also in touch with the rapturous tradition of Irish dancing. 'O body swayed to music, O brightening glance,/How can we know the dancer from the dance?' (*VP* 446).

'The Exile from Erin'. In their direct statement, narrative outline, and separation of human figures from their background, these early works by Jack B. Yeats are not unlike pictorial ballads.

In everything he touched Yeats was arguing or obscuring a particular case. In the 1890s he ambitiously claimed a place in Irish literature alongside 'Davis, Mangan, Ferguson' but thereafter was unwilling to accept the mantle of poet of national liberation. It was a role that Maud Gonne constantly urged upon him, and, more recently, Edward Said has argued along similar lines that Yeats is 'the indisputably great *national* poet who articulates the experiences, the aspirations, and the vision of a people suffering under the dominion of an off-shore power'.[6] In terms of existentialist philosophy, there was a gulf inside Yeats between *in himself* and *for others*, a tension reproduced at every level of his character and personality: between involvement and detachment in politics, between a generalised hatred of London and the comforting mental picture of Sligo, between dreams of escape and an imaginative redrawing of reality, between championing a national theatre for the Irish people at the turn of the century and retreating a decade later to the private theatre of London drawing-rooms. Such tensions made him acutely conscious of his own role in Irish culture, and they lent a passion as well as a certain tendentiousness and an inevitable blindness to his reconstruction of an Irish nineteenth-century tradition.

In this chapter Yeats is positioned against a select group of nineteenth-century poets, writers, and thinkers who helped shape both the development of cultural nationalism in Ireland and Yeats's view of that development.[7] Run your finger over the intellectual map of Ireland in the past century, and certain features recur or overlap: Ireland as a nation, the need for national regeneration, the language question, the stress on the past and historical continuity, the role of literature, the problem of an audience, the unionist position. Yeats understood this history both as an insider and as an outsider – an insider because of the colonial encounter between Britain and Ireland, an outsider partly by choice, partly by temperament, and partly by circumstance. But it would be wrong to assume that because he was a Protestant he was, or felt himself to be, like Louis MacNeice, 'banned for ever from the candles of the Irish poor'.[8] Rather, he was both 'isolated in the tradition',[9] as Thomas Kinsella suggests, and also the poet who affirmed in the last year of his life the naturalness of the collocation 'We Irish' (*VP* 611).

THE BALLAD POETRY OF IRELAND

As a young man reviewing, collecting, anthologising the work of Irish writers, Yeats embarked, like a self-appointed ambassador, on a dutiful campaign of scrutinising the records of cultural nationalism, putting on one side accounts which needed to be settled and on the other side those which needed to be queried. One thing he recognised above all others: 'From that great candle of the past we must all light our little tapers.'[10] The emphasis on the past was crucial. Firstly, there was no better key to naturalising his intervention in Irish culture than through the nationalist ritual of remembering, honouring, and refashioning the past. In ideological terms, he was thereby simultaneously establishing his own agenda and advancing his own position to speak in the tradition that ran from the United Irishmen in the 1790s, through the Young Ireland movement in the 1840s, to the present. As he boasted in 'To Ireland in the Coming Times':

> *Know that I would accounted be*
> *True brother of a company*

66

That sang, to sweeten Ireland's wrong,
Ballad and story, rann and song;

....

Nor may I less be counted one
With Davis, Mangan, Ferguson,
Because to him who ponders well,
My rhymes more than their rhyming tell
Of things discovered in the deep,
Where only body's laid asleep.

(*VP* 137–8)

It was more than this (ambivalent) solidarity he sought, for as he suggests in *Reveries*: 'I thought we might bring the halves together ⟨Protestant and Catholic⟩ if we had a national literature that made Ireland beautiful in the memory, and yet had been freed from provincialism by an exacting criticism, an European pose' (*R* 200).

Secondly, the past for Yeats was only relevant, as it was for Standish James O'Grady,* when made contiguous with the present. Surprisingly, neither Yeats nor O'Grady grieved for 'the world we have lost'.[11] For them, ancient myths can be evoked again; the past can live in the present; the heroic age can be revived; the present generation can relive the transgression of a former generation. Perhaps only the demise of the Ascendancy provoked in Yeats the sense of irrevocable loss. Thirdly, Yeats was especially interested in the past which existed outside the academy, and which remained uncodified or unexplored. He sought to trace Irish history through ballads, literature, myths and legends, fairy-tales and folk-tales, the records of the people, an approach scorned in fashionable academic circles as being either too subjective or beneath contempt.

Nineteenth-century Ireland constantly renewed itself via songs, music, and ballads. The late nineteenth-century British imperialist was in no doubt as to how politics, ballads, and propaganda connected: 'Fenianism has no more active propagandists than the Irish schoolmasters, as the records of 1867 prove! The literature of that period and of today had and has much to do in disseminating treason among the masses. Of course every Irish child is born a rebel, just as every English one is born a "little Liberal or Conservative", but while the English lad, grown to manhood, sometimes changes sides, the little Irish rebel remains a rebel to the last. The "Spirit of the Nation" ballads, in which Davis and Duffy, Mangan and Lady Wilde blew the trumpet of revolution, are the favourite poetry of the people today, just as they were in Forty-eight.'[12] The Irish song tradition often expressed itself in such overtly propagandist terms, and also in more reflective strains.

A writer such as Tom Moore (1779–1852), when not openly political, cherished the memories and dreams of nationhood, keeping the channels open for direct political intervention at some future date. 'The Light of Other Days', the title of one of Moore's *Irish Melodies* (1808–34), crystallises the relevance of late eighteenth-century antiquarian interests in uncovering a hidden Ireland. Indeed, in Moore the Irish Romantic we witness the transformation of Herder's stress on cultural difference into the fond memory or recuperation of a tradition.[13] In her anthology of eighteenth- and nineteenth-century Anglo-Irish poetry, entitled *Irish Love-Songs* (1892), Katharine Tynan stresses throughout the juxtaposition and influence of the Gaelic on the English, the oral on the literary tradition, and inevitably, because the Gaelic poets were all Jacobites in the eighteenth century, the political on the personal. In her Preface she suggests that 'Poetry in Ireland has a way of rising and falling with revolutions.'[14] The nineteenth century is

67

perhaps in this sense best imagined as a series of interlocking rises and falls, with the United Irishmen and Moore at one end, Yeats and the Revival at the other, and Thomas Davis and Young Ireland in the middle.

As for the more explicit propagandist tradition, the United Irishmen established a pattern followed by the Young Irelanders in the 1840s and the Fenians in the 1860s.[15] After the failure of the 1798 Rising, nationalist sentiment more often than not accompanied the writing of ballads.[16] In a ballad such as 'Wake of William Orr' by William Drennan (1754–1820), which concerns the fate of a Presbyterian farmer from Antrim executed for administering the United Irishmen's oath, the opening anticipates not acquiescence but the poem's final word and clarion call to the nineteenth century, 'arise!':

> Here our murdered brother lies –
> Wake him not with women's cries;
> Mourn the way that manhood ought;
> Sit in silent trance of thought.

The 1820s prompted ballads associated with Daniel O'Connell and Catholic Emancipation; in the 1840s came the *Nation* ballads; in the 1850s ballads about tenant farmers; in the 1860s ballads about the Fenians; in the 1880s ballads about Parnell and the Land League. Yeats understood the strengths and weaknesses of this tradition, and in his 1889 article entitled 'Popular Ballad Poetry of Ireland', he is careful to substitute for the word *nationalist* the more neutral *patriotic*: 'Behind Ireland fierce and militant, is Ireland poetic, passionate, remembering, idyllic, fanciful, and always patriotic' (*UP* 1, 147).[17]

Thomas Davis (1814–45)

Davis is a key figure here. 'One carries on the traditions of Thomas Davis,' affirmed Yeats in 1899, 'towards whom our eyes must always turn, not less than the traditions of good literature, which are the morality of the man of letters, when one is content, like A. E. with fewer readers that one may follow a more hidden beauty; or when one endeavours, as I have endeavoured in this book, to separate what has literary value from what has only a patriotic and political value, no matter how sacred it has become to us.'[18] Taking his cue from the work of the antiquarian scholar, Davis stressed Ireland's antiquity, which was 'honoured in the archives of civilisation, traceable into antiquity by its piety, its valour, and its sufferings'.[19] The inspired propagandist appreciated that 'art is a regenerator as well as a copyist', that 'the ideal has resources beyond the actual'.[20] Moreover, as if he half-knew a poet like Yeats would one day emerge, Davis added the essential ingredient of landscape: 'A man who has not raced on our hills, panted on our mountains, waded our rivers in drought and flood, pierced our passes, skirted our coast, noted our old towns, and learned the shape and colour of ground and tree and sky, is not master of all a Balladist's art.'[21]

Ballads and story-telling were the forms of literature closest to the country people. For Yeats, this represented an opportunity, not available to English writers, to address a popular audience, but it was also a potential pitfall, as Davis illustrated:

When he sat down to write he had so great a desire to make the peasantry courageous and powerful that he half believed them already 'the finest peasantry upon the earth', and wrote not a few such verses as –

> 'Lead them to fight for native land
> His is no courage cold and wary;
> The troops live not that could withstand
> The headlong charge of Tipperary' –

and today we are paying the reckoning with much bombast.[22]

In 'What is "Popular Poetry"'' (1901), Yeats scotches another idea, that the people need everything spelt out to them. On the contrary, he suggests, they are fond of words and verses that keep half the secret to themselves: 'Indeed, it is certain that before the counting-house had created a new class and a new art without breeding and without ancestry, and set this art and this class between the hut and the castle, and between the hut and the cloister, the art of the people was as closely mingled with the art of coteries as was the speech of the people that delighted in rhythmical animation, in idiom, in images, in words full of far-off suggestion, with the unchanging speech of the poets' (*E & I* 10–11).

In contrast to the situation of Irish fiction in the first half of the nineteenth century, which 'in one of its aspects can be termed a kind of advocacy before the bar of English public opinion',[23] the *Nation* poets assumed they belonged to a movement reaching out to and embracing the Irish people. In the confident words of Davis in 'The Ballad Poetry of Ireland':

> Such nationality as merits a good man's help, and wakens a true man's ambition – such nationality as could stand against internal faction and foreign intrigue – such nationality as would make the Irish hearth happy and the Irish name illustrious, is becoming understood. It must contain and represent the races of Ireland. It must not be Celtic, it must not be Saxon – it must be Irish. The Brehon law, and the maxims of Westminster, the cloudy and lightning genius of the Gael, the placid strength of the Sasanach, the marshalling insight of the Norman – a literature which shall exhibit in combination the passions and idioms of all, and which shall equally express our mind in its romantic, its religious, its forensic, and its practical tendencies – finally, a native government, which shall know and rule by the might and right of all; yet yield to the arrogance of none – these are components of *such* a nationality.[24]

For Yeats, as for Davis, 'There is no great literature without nationality, no great nationality without literature.'[25] But his attitude to Davis was coloured by a belief that culture should not be equivalent to politics. He also recognised that the 'leisured classes' could not be moved from 'an apathy, come from their separation from the land they live in, by writing about politics or about Gaelic, but we may move them by becoming men of letters and expressing primary emotions and truths in ways appropriate to this country'.[26] Moreover, after the fall of Parnell in 1890, culture to Yeats represented the freedom – though he would not have expressed it thus – to make politics more political. In this regard, he sought to make the young men 'think of Ireland herself' and thereby broaden the scope for politics not in the moral but in the aesthetic sense. As he told an audience in New York in February 1904:

> To you Irishmen in America what followed ⟨the fall of Parnell⟩ must have seemed a time of sheer desolation, of mere ignoble quarrelling. To us it was the transformation of the whole country. We saw that the imaginations of our young men would be directed away

69

Thomas Davis (1814–45), son of a British Army surgeon, was born in Mallow, County Cork. In 1842 he founded the *Nation*, a newspaper which influenced a generation of Young Ireland balladeers and poets. Davis himself wrote such stirring songs as 'A Nation Once Again' (the unofficial national anthem of nineteenth-century Ireland), 'A Plea for the Bog-Trotters', and 'The West's Asleep'.

from the politics of the hour; that a time had come when we could talk to them of Davis and of Emmet, when we could talk to them of Irish history and Irish culture, when we could make them think of Ireland herself. We would take up the work of Young Ireland, and direct the imaginations of our young men towards Irish nationality, as Thomas Davis and the Young Irelanders understood Irish nationality.[27]

Yeats's objection to Young Ireland was not only that it gave itself up to 'apologetics'[28] but also that it wrecked the historical instinct: 'Young Ireland had taught a study of our history with the glory of Ireland for event. . . . The man who doubted, let us say, our fabulous ancient kings running up to Adam, or found but mythology in some old tale, was as hated as if he had doubted the authority of Scripture.'[29] Young Ireland could also wreck a poet's career, but did not do so in the case of James Clarence Mangan (1803–49), for, as Yeats suggested, 'his style was formed before their movement began, and for this reason perhaps he was always able to give sincere expression to the mood which he had chosen, the only sincerity literature knows of'.[30] Mangan, who was 'kept out of public life by a passion for opium and rum', remained true to himself: '⟨H⟩e was the slave of life, for he had nothing of the self-knowledge, the power of selection, the harmony of mind, which enables the poet to be its master, and to mould the phantasmagoria of the world as he pleases.'

Mangan forms part of an argument Yeats was conducting with the Young Ireland legacy. What is missing from Yeats's discussion, we might note in passing, is any reference to the Great Famine in the 1840s or to Mangan's verse in that context. It is as if that nineteenth-century holocaust never happened, replaced on the one hand by an attack on contemporary newspapers and politics and the ensuing 'incoherence,

70

vulgarity, and triviality', and on the other hand by a Goldsmith-inspired view of the eighteenth century: 'The poor peasant of the eighteenth century could make fine ballads by abandoning himself to the joy or sorrow of the moment, as the reeds abandon themselves to the wind which sighs through them, because he has about him a world where all was old enough to be steeped in emotion.'[31]

The Famine is the Great Unsaid in Yeats, and yet its impact on Ireland's bilingual culture was profound. Until the spread of English, especially in the second half of the nineteenth century, the country people of Ireland sang their own songs in Gaelic. William Carleton (1794–1869) tells us that his mother, who was 'acquainted with the English tongue', sang in Gaelic:

⟨S⟩he had a prejudice against singing the Irish airs to English words; an old custom of the country was thereby invaded, and an association disturbed which habit had rendered dear to her. I remember on one occasion, when she was asked to sing the English version of that touching melody 'The Red-haired Man's Wife', she replied, 'I will sing it to you; but the English words and the air are like a quarrelling man and wife: *the Irish melts into the tune, but the English doesn't*' – an expression scarcely less remarkable for its beauty than its truth. She spake the words in Irish.[32]

Because he never learnt Irish, Yeats perhaps never thought deeply about the loss of language. When he constructs his tradition of Irish literature, the Gaelic culture is there, but his stress falls on continuity. For someone who made so much of sincerity as a benchmark, he crossed certain fault lines with consummate ease. It is extraordinary – but in keeping – that in his Hanrahan stories in *The Secret Rose* (1897) he sought to identify himself with Eoghan Rua O'Sullivan, the red-haired Gaelic poet of the eighteenth century, and no less extraordinary that he should imagine himself as the Gaelic folk-poet Raftery and Maud Gonne as his Mary Hynes, 'A peasant girl commended by a song' (*VP* 410).

Yeats continued his dispute with Young Ireland in a celebrated attack from 1891 to 1893 on the old Young Irelander Sir Charles Gavan Duffy (1816–1903). Yeats objected to his proposed list of titles for an Irish publishing venture because it was narrowly conceived and had a palpable design on the reader.[33] 'All fine literature is the disinterested contemplation or expression of life, but hardly any Irish writer can liberate his mind sufficiently from questions of practical reform for this contemplation.'[34] He was against rhetoric, and for beauty: 'I believe that all men will more and more reject the opinion that poetry is "a criticism of life", and be more and more convinced that it is a revelation of a hidden life, and that they may even come to think "painting, poetry, and music" "the only means of conversing with eternity left to man on earth".'[35] In the context of Ireland at the time and since, Yeats's view of propaganda has been persuasive – but not entirely, for, as Hone in 1915 cautioned:

Again and again Mr Yeats has recorded his conviction that a man should 'find his holy land where he first crept upon the floor'; but we do not find anything inconsistent with this view in his endeavour to rid Irish literature of its propagandist tendencies, and of what he has called 'the obsession of public life'. He was largely successful. Nowadays few patriots assert that a poem, or story, or play must have some rhymed lesson in national politics if it is to be Irish. What could not meet with much appreciation in Ireland was a philosophy based on a mystical conception of the primacy of poetry. The nationalist public encountered the aesthetic passion for the first time, and all its hostility was aroused as if by something unfamiliar and even depraved.[36]

71

In a speech delivered at the Davis Centenary in Dublin in November 1914, Yeats, by now conscious of his marginalised position within the nationalist movement, reviewed his once less than merciful attitude towards Davis: 'Today I have no thought but for his virtue and his service. He was not, indeed, a great poet, but his power of expression was a finer thing than I thought. . . . During the thirty years that have passed since my boyhood I have seen five or six movements founded by young men who might have changed their generation had they copied his magnanimity.'[37]

Sir Samuel Ferguson (1810–86)

Central to the concern over the ballad tradition is what Yeats later defined as Unity of Culture. In his reading of nineteenth-century Irish fiction, he noticed 'two different accents – the accent of the gentry, and the less polished accent of the peasantry and those near them; a division roughly into the voice of those who lived lightly and gayly, and those who took man and his fortunes with much seriousness and even at times mournfully. The one has found its most typical embodiment in the tales and novels of Croker, Lover, and Lever, and the other in the ruder but deeper work of Carleton, Kickham, and the two Banims.'[38] Yeats was opposed to the separation of a literary from a popular culture. It was their closeness to the people that impressed him about nineteenth-century poets like Ferguson or novelists like Carleton. As he emphasises in his Introduction to *Stories from Carleton* (1889): 'William Carleton was a great Irish historian. The history of a nation is not in parliaments and battle-fields, but in what the people say to each other on fair-days and high days, and in how they farm, and quarrel, and go on pilgrimage. These things has Carleton recorded.'[39]

The case of Ferguson is instructive in this regard. In the 1830s thinking Protestants such as Ferguson, fearing that their country was becoming a provincial backwater after the Act of Union, sought a more interventionist – and in consequence nationalist – role for culture:

> This feeling was strongest among the middle classes, which had always been the backbone of the Anglo-Irish tradition. The nobility and the greater landowners were, generally speaking, as much at home in England as in Ireland; but for the minor gentry, the professional classes, the bankers and the well-to-do merchants, Dublin was the centre of social and intellectual life. . . . A determination to assert and strengthen Dublin's position in this respect lay behind the repeated attempts, during the first generation after the Union, to establish in the city something that Ireland had hitherto lacked, a literary periodical of high quality. The task proved a difficult one; but at last, in 1833, the *Dublin University Magazine* began its long and distinguished career.[40]

Ferguson's work in the 1830s and 1840s reflects his interest in advancing a national culture. In translations from the Gaelic, such as 'The Fair Hills of Ireland' and 'Cashel of Munster', he quickly established a distinctive voice. But it was a voice caught in its own making. In a Romantic ballad such as 'The Pretty Girl of Loch Dan', for example, he provides a revealing symbolic encounter in pre-Famine Ireland between the educated, literary, Protestant male stranger and the sensuous, uneducated, native Catholic woman living in a remote glen, who is innocently described in terms shot through with ideology: 'fluttering courtesy', 'startled virgin', and 'lips reluctantly apart'. By contrast, in 'Willy Gilliland' Ferguson returned to his roots with 'An Ulster Ballad' about a rebel – a lover

Samuel Ferguson (1810–86). His poetry was 'truly bardic, appealing to all natures alike, to the great concourse of the people, for it has gone deeper than knowledge or fancy, deeper than the intelligence which knows of difference – of the good and evil, of the foolish and the wise, of this one and of that – to the universal emotions that have not heard of aristocracies, down to where Brahman and Sudra are not even names' (*UP* 1, 100).

of freedom – on the run, Willy Gilliland being one of Ferguson's ancestors who fled from Scotland to Ireland during the Covenanting times, and who managed to survive by fishing in the Glenwhirry River. When his horse was taken by a Covenanter, Gilliland, 'a caverned outlaw lone', recaptured it: 'and still from him descendants not a few/Draw birth and lands, and, let me trust, draw love of Freedom too.'[41]

In his patriotic selection *The Ballad Poetry of Ireland* (1846), Duffy omitted street ballads in favour of 'Anglo-Irish' ballads by such writers as Ferguson, Griffin, Banim, Callanan, Lover, Walsh, and Davis, 'the production of educated men, with English tongues but Irish hearts'.[42] Again, it was Yeats who was closer to the people in this respect, for he appreciated the real significance and achievement of 'Celtic' Ferguson, who in the 1830s wrote of an island 'full of touching recollections and inspiring hopes', and who in the 1880s still cherished the hope that Ireland 'will have her own literature yet'.[43] In his first published piece of prose, written in 1886, Yeats proclaimed his Celtic ancestry:

Sir Samuel Ferguson, I contend, is the greatest Irish poet, because in his poems and the legends, they embody more completely than in any other man's writings, the Irish character. Its unflinching devotion to some single aim. Its passion. 'The food of the passions is bitter, the food of the spirit is sweet,' say the wise Indians. And this faithfulness to things tragic and bitter, to thoughts that wear one's life out and scatter one's joy, the Celt has above all others.

(*UP* 1, 87)

Yeats's choice of thirty titles for a library of Irish books. Published in the *Daily Express* (Dublin) on 27 February 1895.

Yeats's version of 'Down by the Salley Gardens' quickly established itself as part of the Irish song tradition. When it first appeared in *The Wanderings of Oisin and Other Poems* (1889), Yeats explained in a footnote: 'This is an attempt to reconstruct an old song from three lines imperfectly remembered by an old peasant woman in the village of Ballysodare, Sligo, who often sings them to herself.'

NO. 1 (NEW SERIES) JANUARY 1937.

A BROADSIDE

EDITORS: DOROTHY WELLESLEY AND W. B. YEATS.
PUBLISHED MONTHLY AT THE CUALA PRESS, ONE HUNDRED
AND THIRTY THREE LOWER BAGGOT STREET, DUBLIN.

COME GATHER ROUND ME PARNELLITES

Come gather round me Parnellites
And praise our chosen man;
Stand upright on your legs awhile;
Stand upright while you can
For soon we lie where he is laid
And he is underground.
Come fill up all those glasses
And pass the bottle round.

300 copies only.

'Come Gather Round Me Parnellites'. In the 1930s Yeats returned to the ballad form, and wrote with a venom absent from his early ballads. His renewed passion for an uncomplicated nationalism paid off, for when *Last Poems and Plays* was reviewed in the *Irish Book Lover* in July 1940, his name was linked not with Davis, Mangan, and Ferguson but with Parnell: 'He was to English letters what Parnell was to English politics, and both men were of true aristocratic mould of mind.'

THE CASE OF WILLIAM ALLINGHAM RE-EXAMINED

When Yeats spoke before an audience at Wellesley College in May 1920, he opened with an account of his boyhood in Sligo, 'spent in the companionship of William Allingham'.[44] In 1905, he selected sixteen poems by Allingham for publication by his sister's Dun Emer Press, beginning with 'Let Me Sing of What I Know':

> A wild west Coast, a little Town,
> Where little Folk go up and down,
> Tides flow and winds blow:
> Night and Tempest and the Sea,
> Human Will and Human Fate:
> What is little, what is great?
> Howso'er the answer be,
> Let me sing of what I know.[45]

Yeats's affection for Allingham grew out of their similar backgrounds on the north-west coast of Ireland: 'To feel the entire fascination of his poetry, it is perhaps necessary to have spent one's childhood, like the present writer, in one of those little seaboard

William Allingham in 1857. He was the son of a merchant who imported timber, slates, coal, and iron, and who also owned at various times five or six ships. Unlike Yeats, however, Allingham was forced into conventional employment, working for seven years at a bank before becoming a Customs Officer in 1846. He moved between England and Ireland before settling in 1863 in Lymington, on the Hampshire coast overlooking the Isle of Wight. A close friend of Leigh Hunt, Robert Browning, and Alfred Tennyson, his *Diary* contains a revealing portrait of his age.

Connacht towns. He has expressed that curious devotion of the people for the earth under their feet, a devotion that is not national, but local, a thing at once more narrow and more idyllic' (*UP* 1, 260).

Yeats warms to Allingham's homely attachment to his native Ballyshannon and the winding banks of the Erne; equally, he criticises him for separating the local from the national: 'He sang Ballyshannon and not Ireland.... He was the poet of little things and little moments, and of that vague melancholy Lord Palmerston considered peculiar to the peasantry of the wild seaboard where he lived.... The charm of his work is everywhere the charm of stray moments and detached scenes that have moved him' (*UP* 1, 260). It was the same message he wrote for the *Providence Sunday Journal* in September 1888:

> They are so beautiful, these poems, I have hardly the heart to go back again to their nationalism or non-nationalism; and yet I must, for it is the most central notion I have about them. Yes, they are not national. The people of Ireland seem to Mr Allingham graceful, witty, picturesque, benevolent, everything but a people to be taken seriously. This want of sympathy with the national life and history has limited his vision, has driven away from his poetry much beauty and power – has thinned his blood.[46]

The Allingham poems Yeats values are not the longer pieces, such as 'The Music Master' (1855), a story of blighted love, or the condition-of-Ireland poem *Laurence Bloomfield in Ireland* (1864), but the occasional verse wherein 'a rubble of old memories and impressions ⟨are⟩ made beautiful by pensive feeling' (*UP* 1, 260). To Yeats, Allingham is 'the poet of the melancholy peasantry of the West',[47] a child of the spirit world, whose imagination dwells best in the land of dreams and fairies. He is the

Rossetti's illustration to accompany 'The Maids of Elfen-Mere' appeared in Allingham's *Music Master* (1855). The woodcut is by Dalziel. In the first issue of the *Oxford and Cambridge Magazine* (1856), it was described by the young Burne-Jones as 'the most beautiful drawing for an illustration I have ever seen'. The Pastor's Son looks not unlike the youthful Yeats, his heart turned by three beautiful, slightly archaic women gently singing, spinning to a pulsing cadence, while his thoughts are carried away by the wind among the reeds.

composer of ballads such as 'Kate O'Belashanny', emigrant songs such as the bitter-sweet 'The Winding Banks of Erne', poems about knights and abbots and ruined chapels, Aeolian harps and twilight voices. Allingham, author of 'The Maids of Elfen-Mere', represents the mid-Victorian Irish imagination closest to London and the Pre-Raphaelites, yet still in touch with the Irish country people and their fairies:

> 'Twas when the spinning-room was here,
> There came Three Damsels clothed in white,
> With their spindles every night;
> Two and one, and Three fair Maidens,
> Spinning to a pulsing cadence,
> Singing songs of Elfen-Mere;
> Till the eleventh hour was toll'd,
> Then departed through the wold.
>   *Years ago, and years ago;*
>   *And the tall reeds sigh as the wind doth blow.*[48]

Allingham, however, was not quite the figure that Yeats made him out to be. Even as an anthologist of ballads, as his advice to editors suggests, Allingham betrays a modern and scholarly approach to his material: 'He is to give it in *one* form – the best according to his judgment and feeling – in firm black and white, for critics, and for readers cultivated and simple; the ballad itself is multiform, and even shifting, vapourlike, as one examines it; the conditions of his task are therefore by no means easy; and when the work is done with his utmost care and skill, nothing can be easier than to pull it to pieces and prove it "a thing of nought" '.[49] Allingham was also an original collector of ballads, with Ireland his principal field, even if he was mistaken in his belief that 'Ireland would certainly have contributed her full share to our general store of ballads, but for one sufficient reason – her tongue was Keltic; her native popular songs and ballads lie hid in that little-known and expiring language.'[50]

Yeats was also less than just regarding Allingham's social eye, as a passage from Allingham's *Diary* can serve to illustrate:

> In these remote and wild parts Erin is the most characteristically herself, and the most unlike to Saxon England. Her strange antiquities, visible in gray mouldering fragments; her ancient language, still spoken by some, and everywhere present in place-names, as well as phrases and turns of speech; her native genius for music; her character – reckless, variable, pertinacious, enthusiastic; her manners – reconciling delicate respect with easy familiarity; her mental movements – quick, humorous, imaginative, impassioned; her habits of thought as to property, social intercourse, happiness; her religious awe and reverence; all these, surviving to the present day, under whatever difficulties, have come down from times long before any England existed, and cling to their refuge on the extreme verge of the Old World, among lonely green hills, purple mountains, and rocky bays, bemurmured day and night by the Western Ocean.[51]

Nothing here is exaggerated or strident: the poetic turn of phrase, as in 'cling to their refuge on the extreme verge of the Old World', is allowed to stand, without any primitivist overtones, alongside the other observations and reflections. The point is effectively made; the writer is sure of his (English) audience and of his subject matter; the people exist independent of the observer.

In every way, the contrast with Yeats could not be more pronounced. In his Introduction to the November 1905 issue of *Samhain*, the same year he made the Allingham selection, Yeats stressed the gulf between observation and experience: 'The greatest art symbolises not those things that we have observed so much as those things that we have experienced, and when the imaginary saint or lover or hero moves us most deeply, it is the moment when he awakens within us for an instant our own heroism, our own sanctity, our own desire.'[52] Restraint, a readiness to connect experience with observation, is the quality that shines through Allingham's work. Yeats, on the other hand, dismissed observation: 'All good art is extravagant, vehement, impetuous, shaking the dust of time from its feet, as it were, and beating against the walls of the world.'[53] According to Yeats, observation in Ireland in the nineteenth century meant 'the accepted type', 'caricaturing', 'the stage Irishman', a deprivation of freedom, timid imagination, a lack of sincerity, 'impersonal types and images'. Moreover, unlike science, there are no discoveries in literature, 'and it is always the old that returns'. Yeats favoured the 'misrepresentation of the average life of a nation' because in this way the energy of a people is enlarged by the spectacle of energy.

No amount of softening from the beguiling prose can quite compensate for the singular nature of Yeats's beliefs and opinions. He enjoyed quoting Goethe's phrase that 'art is art because it is not nature' (A 279), and gave the impression that it answered complicated arguments about realism or neo-classical ideas of art complementing nature or the positivist or Marxist emphasis on determination. Ironically, history has caught up with him, for, in redrawing the map of what constitutes the aesthetic demesne, Yeats reveals he is but part of an age obsessed with subjective experience and the revolt against positivism.[54] In retrospect, it is clear that Yeats's strength as a writer derives in no small measure from his attempt to shrink the size of that demesne. In reality, the two aspects belong together and constitute in Yeats a form of literary Parnellism: load the scales in favour of individual experience and then wait for the hero-figure (in this case, the cynic might argue, Yeats himself) to emerge: 'In the long run, it is the great writer of a nation that becomes its image in the minds of posterity, and even though he represent, like Aristophanes, no man of worth in his art, the worth of his own mind becomes the inheritance of his people. He takes nothing away that he does not give back in greater volume.'[55]

Yeats played down the serious aspect of Allingham's work and hence failed to recognise, for example, the significance of *Laurence Bloomfield in Ireland*. This long poem is a mid-Victorian version of Maria Edgeworth's *The Absentee* (1812). Like Colambre, Laurence Bloomfield is the young absentee landlord returning to his estate in Ireland:

> A younger son (the better lot at first),
> And by a Celtic peasant fondly nurst,
> Bloomfield is Irish born and English bred,
> Surviving heir of both his parents dead;
> One who has studied, travell'd, lived, and thought,
> Is brave, and modest, as a young man ought;
> Calm – sympathetic; hasty – full of tact;
> Poetic; but insisting much on fact;
> A complex character and various mind,
> Where all, like some rich landscape, lies combined.[56]

Three years before Matthew Arnold's *On the Study of Celtic Literature* (1867), Allingham had answered the charge that the Celt is 'sentimental, – *always ready to react against the despotism of fact*'.[57] Bloomfield is 'poetic', a word associated in Arnold with ineffectual, both in the political and artistic sense, for the Celt, according to Arnold, is unable to produce great poetical works, only 'poetry with an air of greatness investing it all'.[58] Allingham, intent on forestalling the familiar line of argument, quickly adds 'but insisting much on fact'.[59] Allingham keeps an Augustan sense of proportion, that not everything can be made to fit, and if it can it is through the exigency of language and imagery. Arnold refers to a 'commingling' of two temperaments,[60] but Bloomfield has a 'complex character and various mind', well suited to recognise difference, to challenge prejudice, and to sift fact from fiction.

At school in England, Bloomfield undergoes experiences not unlike those that Yeats endured at the Godolphin School in London:

> From school to Ireland, Laurence first return'd
> A patriot vow'd; his soul for Ireland burn'd.
> Oft did his schoolmates' taunts in combat end,
> And high his plans with one Hibernian friend,
> Who long'd like him for manhood, to set free
> Their emerald Inisfail from sea to sea,
> With army, senate, all a nation's life,
> Copartner in the great world's glorious strife,
> Peer in all arts, gay rival in each race,
> Illustrious, firm, in her peculiar place.
> The glories and the griefs of Erin fill'd
> Heart and imagination.[61]

79

Exposed to English prejudice, Bloomfield becomes a nationalist: he returns from school to Ireland not more English but more Irish. Like Colambre, Bloomfield is educated through experience, is temporarily held by 'irresolution's sickness', that moment when he wavers before the immensity of the reformer's task, and then proceeds to philosophise in words that stay close to a moral rather than a Yeatsian metaphysical universe:

> Man's life is double: hard its dues to give
> Within, Without, and thus completely live.[62]

Bloomfield quickly learns the connection between rural poverty and Ribbonism, how evictions and the threat of evictions turn the country people to violence, secret organisations to resist unscrupulous landlords, and nationalism.

Chapter 7 contains a moving portrait of an eviction scene, which Allingham, an uncomfortable witness for civilised values, records from the viewpoint of the rural poor. He wastes no time sketching in the familiar details: three-score well-arm'd police, six crow-bar-men, the child without a stitch, an old man's last kiss upon his doorpost, the thwack of iron bar on stone, the shatter'd walls, doors with useless latch, and firesides buried under fallen thatch. He then adds:

> So was the little Hamlet's crowd at last
> Whirl'd off like leaves before misfortune's blast.
> Some from a seaport, and their lot the best,
> On Neptune's Highway follow'd, east or west,
> The myriads of their kindred gone before, –
> If Irish still, yet Ireland's nevermore.[63]

The touch of Victorian sentimentality is here kept in check by that arresting last line. Allingham does not dwell on it, but he is haunted by the sense of irremediable loss: 'If Irish still, yet Ireland's nevermore.'

Yeats's misreading of Allingham highlights the limitations in his version of cultural nationalism. Yeats's attack on the Arnoldian conception of poetry as a criticism of life meant that a poet like Allingham was effectively relegated to painting pretty pictures in a provincial setting.[64] *Laurence Bloomfield in Ireland* could not be allowed into the Yeatsian canon because it dwelt on the material conditions of the country people and not on their spiritual imagination. In countering the material with the spiritual Yeats effectively abandoned middle earth for what he imagined the higher goals of symbolism, the occult, and visions of Ireland.

STANDISH JAMES O'GRADY, THE FENIAN UNIONIST

No one in the nineteenth century did more to bring out the excitement of ancient Irish mythology than O'Grady.[65] His lofty, bardic style stimulated the imagination of a whole generation:

> On the plain of Tara, beside the little stream Nemna, itself famous as that which first turned a mill-wheel in Ireland, there lies a barrow, not itself very conspicuous in the midst

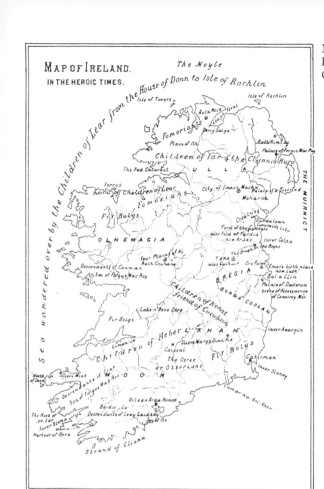

Map of Ireland in the Heroic Times, showing Cuchulain's city, Emer's birthplace, and Tara of the Kings. From Standish O'Grady's *History of Ireland*.

Standish James O'Grady (1846–1928) was described by Nevinson, who met him at Woburn Buildings, as 'moderately exuberant; grey hair all on end, ruddy, and very Irish'. According to Yeats, O'Grady was 'a man whose rage was a swan-song over all that he held dear, and to whom for that very reason every Irish imaginative writer owed a portion of his soul' (*A* 220).

of others, all named and illustrious in the ancient literature of the country. The ancient hero there interred is to the student of the Irish bardic literature a figure as familiar and clearly seen as any personage in the Biographia Britannica. We know the name he bore as a boy and the name he bore as a man. We know the names of his father and his grandfather. . . . We know all the striking events of his boyhood and manhood . . . his battles . . . his physical and spiritual characteristics, the device upon his shield, and how that was originated, carved, and painted, and by whom. We know the colour of his hair, the date of his birth and of his death, and his relations, in time and otherwise, with the remainder of the princes and warriors with whom, in that mound-raising period of our history, he was connected, in hostility or friendship; and all this enshrined in ancient song, the transmitted traditions of the people who raised that barrow, and who laid within it sorrowing their brave ruler and defender. That mound is the tomb of Cuculain, once king of the district in which Dundalk stands today, and the ruins of whose earthen fortification may still be seen two miles from that town.[66]

It was O'Grady who ensured that Cuchulain became the central figure not only of Yeats's work as a writer but also of the Revival as a whole.[67] Yeats was enchanted by O'Grady's ability to transform what might otherwise be a dry antiquarian pursuit into 'the wonder-world of Irish heroic and romantic literature'.[68] O'Grady was, as Russell imagines him in his prose fantasy *The Interpreters* (1922), a modern-day Brehon, a seer and elder statesman.[69] He was more, for in his hands a landscape and a history returned to life, revealing in the process further justification for a separate national identity.

Against Arnold's attempt to colonise the Celt for English culture, O'Grady insisted on Ireland's autonomy: 'Ireland not only escaped subjugation at the hands of Rome, but accomplished such unity of thought and feeling as impressed upon the traditions a large national complexion, so that her history, like that of Greece, blends imperceptibly with her mythology.'[70] In a move that anticipates the Telemachus episode of *Ulysses*, O'Grady outflanked Arnold by suggesting that because of their 'regular progression of thought' a stronger link existed between Ireland and Greece than between England and Greece. The estrangement that Arnold was taught to feel as a young man towards the Celt – an estrangement 'immense, incurable, fatal'[71] – is properly reversed, for it is England that has become estranged from itself. As Gerald Pierce de Lacy laments in O'Grady's unpublished dystopian novel *The Queen of the World or Under the Tyranny* (1900): 'I recalled the England of my experience, the feverish greed of money, the sordid aims, the general low level of thought. Was this the punishment of that? Had the English race been doomed to pursue material wealth for ever, and therefore to fall under the yoke of people with higher ideals and thoughts not quite so grovelling?'[72]

England's greatness is behind her, Ireland's in the future. At each point O'Grady carefully and effectively answered Arnold. Against Arnold's charge of sentimentality, O'Grady argued that to express the whole nature of a race or nation 'the artist needs that absolute freedom which is only supplied by a complete escape from positive history and unyielding despotic fact'.[73] Arnold insisted on the need for scientific, 'disinterested' inquiry into Celtic antiquity.[74] O'Grady, on the other hand, everywhere discerned 'the purple light of imagination', a light which properly blurred the distinction between history and fiction: 'The weird, the supernatural, the heroic, surround characters as certain as Brian Borom – events as trustworthy as the Norman Invasion. The bards never relinquished their right to view their history with the eyes of poets, to convert their kings into heroes and adorn battles and events with hues drawn from mythology; hence the great stumbling-block.'[75]

Until the 1890s, O'Grady was politically an ardent Southern Unionist. His cultural nationalism, however, an extension in its own way of a Unionist cultural tradition dating from the *Dublin University Review* in the 1830s, pre-dated and post-dated his more direct involvement in politics. Indeed, Russell claimed that, while the outer O'Grady was unionist and imperialist, 'the inner O'Grady was passionately national'.[76] During the Land War of 1879 to 1882 he sided with the landlords and urged them in a political pamphlet to organise as a class against the 'wolf of democracy'. He was acutely conscious that to the mass of the people the Irish aristocracy appeared as the deadly foe of the Irish nation: 'They hate us because anti-national, and despise because anti-national for such mean rewards. The day of absolute democratic power in Ireland draws nigh – the day of reckoning and vengeance; while through half-shut eyes we look out and murmur, "It is all well; England is bound to protect us." '[77] With the Land War, in a phrase that foreshadows the vocabulary of Yeats after 1919, 'all traditional and customary conceptions as to the nature of property have been disturbed, and have lost their solidity and definiteness.'[78] In *Toryism and Tory Democracy* (1886), in a passage which anticipates the image at the end of *Reveries* and the mood of *Purgatory* (1938), O'Grady articulates the fears those in the Big House had of servants taking over:

In this old, respectable, and well-built house there is much treasure, much plate; there are many good and desirable things; the larder well-stocked, and the cellars filled with wine. In this house those who were once servants only, and kept in their place and to their work by a strong hand, are now admitted to be the chief authority. . . . I write for those who with me see the dangers thickening within, around, above, and under this ancient fabric, which is our home, endeared by a thousand associations, which is our house sheltering us against storm and rain.[79]

In the 1880s O'Grady elevated class above Ireland; after that decade he elevated Ireland above class. In *Toryism and the Tory Democracy*, he urged on landlords Randolph Churchill's brand of conservatism. If revolution was to be avoided, the labour question had to be tackled. Following Carlyle, O'Grady warned that with the absence of charm from labour relations, a crucial element in controlling labour had disappeared:

Between the landlord and the tenant, the factory owner and his men, the farmer and his labourers, the shop-keeper and his assistant, the producer and the general public, the holders of the National Debt and the nation, the pecuniary view of their mutual relations seems the only one recognised. Thus, when the proletariate, urged from within and from without to assail property, elect, as eventually they must and will, to enter on that fatal course, there is no moral bond or influence that one can see capable of restraining them.[80]

Tories had to care more for men than machinery, go further than the Radicals and assert the principle that 'unemployed labour has a *right* to be employed'.[81] They needed to re-establish between master and men 'the feudal feeling', which is, according to O'Grady, 'one of the most natural and instinctive in the heart of man'.[82]

The Story of Ireland (1894) marked a change in the political attitudes of the 'Fenian Unionist'.[83] The landlords had missed their chance; 'the future of Ireland is with the people'.[84] O'Grady even ends his history with a hymn of praise to Parnell and with the judgement, echoed by Yeats in his 1936 poem 'Come Gather Round Me, Parnellites', that 'posterity will easily forgive Parnell and like him probably all the better for his weakness'.[85] In a subsequent collection of political essays, *All Ireland* (1898), O'Grady

83

argued for unity of purpose among aristocrats, democrats, and plutocrats, for 'Ireland united is Ireland irresistible'.[86] Once an All-Ireland Convention had settled the land question there would be no real causes of dissension, only the prospect of a united Ireland, and 'when Ulster comes into this movement, things will begin to hum'.[87]

O'Grady, however, remained exercised by the inaction on the part of Irish landed interests to their demise as a class. In the fourth issue of his journal *All Ireland Review*, he wrote the first in a series of articles on 'The Great Enchantment':

> Enchantment is a fact of nature. Through suggestion or self-suggestion, a man may be flung into such a condition that his senses will cease to discharge their normal functions; in a stone he will see a flashing diamond, and in a flashing diamond a stone; in discord he will hear music, and in the sweetest music a jarring discord. Nations, too, like individuals, may, as the punishment of their crimes and follies, find themselves flung into such an enchanted condition, and suffer that worst loss of all, the loss of reason.
> THE POLITICAL UNDERSTANDING OF IRELAND TODAY IS UNDER A SPELL, AND ITS WILL PARALYSED.[88]

In a subsequent issue O'Grady claimed that spells and enchantments are not to be shaken off through the use of language: 'They will and can only be removed by shocks!'[89] But the Anglo-Irish aristocracy, which once owned all Ireland from the centre to the sea, 'is rotting from the land in the most dismal farce-tragedy of all time, without one brave deed, without one brave word'.[90] In a later article, in the *Irish Review*, O'Grady went on to advocate that Ireland become a Land of Destiny and lead the fight against modern materialism.[91]

Yeats and O'Grady breathed the same air. Both shared an apocalyptic sensibility which is given dramatic force by O'Grady in *The Crisis in Ireland* (1882) and by Yeats nearly forty years later in 'The Second Coming'.[92] Neither owned a Big House, yet both saw themselves as apologists for that particular class in decline. O'Grady began as a Southern Unionist and moved to the left politically; Yeats in his youth began as a nationalist and moved progressively to the right. At the turn of the century, O'Grady came to advocate an all-Ireland view of politics, a union of all forces in Ireland against the common enemy of England; two decades later, Yeats, as part of a movement to aestheticise politics, formulated the idea of Unity of Culture. For O'Grady, Ireland in the new century was under a spell which could be broken only by force, an idea which resurfaces with particular force in Yeats's poem 'Easter 1916'. In later life, both Yeats and O'Grady urged Ireland to become a Land of Destiny and stop 'this filthy modern tide' (*VP* 611) from reaching her shores.

But there is more to their relationship than simply sharing a similar class position or structure of feeling. Yeats was initially impressed by O'Grady the story-teller.[93] Later, he was attracted to O'Grady's passionate oratory, with its appeal to a muscular form of cultural nationalism different from that of Young Ireland and the '98 tradition. The zigzag paths in O'Grady's intellectual development were forceful reminders of subterranean forces at work in Ireland, but O'Grady never acted as a warning for Yeats. Surprisingly, Yeats failed to appreciate O'Grady's Anglo-Irish predicament, the tension between what was lost and what could be recovered from Irish history, the inevitable solitude arising from their class's displacement in the later stages of the colonial encounter between Britain and Ireland. Indeed, Yeats continued to pursue in his drama and poetry themes and ideas that the restless O'Grady had, years previously, wisely abandoned or transformed. In O'Grady's scheme of things, for example, there was no room

Photograph of John O'Leary taken in 1894. ' "There are things a man must not do to save a nation", he had once told me, and when I asked what things, had said, "To cry in public", and I think it probable that he would have added, if pressed, "To write oratorical or insincere verse" ' (*A* 213).

for the Southern Unionists after 1900, but even into the 1930s Yeats entertained a place for them.[94] Perhaps the relationship between the two can be defined even more closely, for Yeats's career as a writer in part illustrates a remark made by O'Grady in his discussion of early Irish history and bardic literature: how 'the history of one generation became the poetry of the next'.[95] Or as Yeats told the *Daily Chronicle* in 1904: 'Now the centre of the Irish movement has shifted. It was then ⟨at the time of Parnell⟩ agrarian; it is now literary.'[96]

JOHN O'LEARY AND THE FENIAN TRADITION

Yeats first met the old Fenian in 1885. Yeats was an impressionable twenty years of age, O'Leary fifty-five. In 1865, the year of Yeats's birth, O'Leary had been charged with treason-felony on account of his work for the Fenian paper the *Irish People* and been sentenced to twenty years' penal servitude. In 1871 he was freed from Portland Prison

William Strang's woodcut of Katharine Tynan.

T. W. Rolleston at the zither.

on condition that he spent the remaining years of his sentence abroad. In 1885 he returned to Dublin as 'the recognised head of the National Fenians',[97] and gathered around him a group of young people, including Tynan, Maud Gonne, and Douglas Hyde,* who were prepared to dedicate their lives to cultural nationalism.

For Yeats, O'Leary's cultural politics were inseparable from his physical appearance, strength of character, and memorable sayings: 'There are things that a man must not do to save a nation' (*R* 186); 'Davitt wants followers by the thousand . . . I only want half-a-dozen' (*R* 187); and 'Never has there been a cause so bad . . . that it has not been defended by good men for good reasons' (*R* 184). Towards the end of his life, Yeats still maintained that he was 'a nationalist of the school of John O'Leary' (and therefore never touched international politics) (*L* 920–21).[98] When composing 'the terrible beauty' of 'Easter 1916', perhaps Yeats could hear a passage from the closing remarks of O'Leary's *Recollections*: 'Times change and men change with them, but there is a terrible continuity in things Irish, and certain Irishmen, like myself, for example, while undergoing many mental and moral metamorphoses, as the years roll on, still remain very much the same in opinion as regards things English and Irish, and very nearly altogether the same in feeling.'[99]

O'Leary was against socialism, suspicious of Parnell, and advocated changes that would bring lasting dignity to Ireland: 'Better wait another century for the right sort of Home Rule than take an altogether wrong sort in a much shorter period.'[100] Like his fellow-Fenian Charles Kickham (and 'Mr Casey' in Joyce's *Portrait of the Artist as a*

86

Young Man), O'Leary was opposed to the intervention of priests in politics and to the coupling of 'Catholicity and Nationality'.[101] He took care to distinguish Fenianism from the activities of the Land League, but he was equally certain that 'a people who are not prepared to fight in the last resort rather than remain slaves will never be made free by any sort of Parliamentary legerdemain whatsoever'.[102] He stressed a form of moral inwardness for both the individual citizen and the public representative. 'I have seen a lot of those fellows take the Fenian oath,' he is reported as saying about members of Parnell's Parliamentary Party. 'They are now ready to take the Parliamentary oath. Parnell will soon find that they will be faithful to nothing but their interest.'[103]

In the 1890s it hardly amounted to a political platform, and the enigmatic remarks often sounded like well-worn formulas. 'But here was something as spontaneous as the life of an artist. Sometimes he would say things that would have sounded well in some heroic Elizabethan play. It became my delight to rouse him to these outbursts for I was the poet in the presence of his theme' (*R* 186). O'Leary represented unswerving disaffection, historical continuity, and a romantic view of Ireland and the Young Ireland movement: 'The Young Irelanders taught us, not only *not* to fear to speak of the men of '98, but to think and feel that the right thing to do was to imitate them and their methods. '98, '48, and '65 failed, in the literal sense of the word, but in spirit they have none of them failed. To them, and not to any intervening constitutional windbagism, is it due that Ireland is still at its heart's core firm to be free.'[104]

On 18 June 1898, the *Dublin Figaro* carried a report linking the names and images of Yeats and Maud Gonne.

personality or the work of

MR. W. B. YEATS,

the moving spirit in the new Irish Literary Society, and the most promising of all our young authors? Although a Dublin man born and bred, I am afraid Mr. Yeats is practically still a *scriptor ignotus* in his native land, if not in his native city, notwithstanding that his work mainly relates to Ireland and things Irish. He is a son of Mr. J. B. Yeats, the Royal Hibernian Academician, whose mystical and Rosetti-like portrait—drawn by himself—formed the frontispiece of the FIGARO'S Academy Number some time ago.

☀ ☀ ☀

Mr. Yeats is the author of "Mosada," "The Wanderings of Oisin," and other poems (Keegan Paul), and of the best novel of Mr. Fisher Unwin's Pseudonym Library, "John Sherman and Dhoya," written by Mr. Yeats under the pseudonym of Ganconagh. This latter work is our author's first effort at fiction, and a most successful one. "John Sherman" has decidedly made its mark, even the *Review of Reviews* admits that this is so, and says kind things about it. Mr. Yeats is the editor of "Fairy and Folk Tales of the Irish Peasantry," in Mr. Scott's Camelot Series, and of "Irish Fairy Stories," in Mr. Unwin's Children's Library, besides contributing to the *National Observer*, and numerous other high-class journals and magazines. This is not a bad record for a very young man; and if the new National Literary Society goes on and prospers, as it is likely too, Mr. Yeats will probably be amongst the earliest to contribute fresh poems and legends of Ireland "redolent of turf smoke"—as he knows how to make them— to the proposed lending library to be established in connection with the society, and so strike a good blow for the longed for intellectual revival of the inhabitants of this beautiful land, who might, indeed, be termed, for their poetical feeling and warmheartedness, dwellers in *Tir-na-n-Og*.

☀ ☀ ☀

I also with sincere pleasure print a thumb-nail sketch of

MISS MAUD GONNE,

who took a prominent part in conjunction with Mr. Yeats in the formation of this new society.

Blake's 'Paolo and Francesca' (Whirlwind of Lovers). Yeats had this particular print when he was living at Woburn Buildings.

Maud Gonne

'He came towards me. I felt very shy, but taking my courage in both hands, I said in a low voice: "Mr O'Leary, I have heard so much about you; you are the leader of revolutionary Ireland, I want to work for Ireland, I want you to show me how." '[105] This is Maud Gonne recalling her first meeting with O'Leary. She had come to the right person, for O'Leary wanted new recruits for Ireland, 'especially from the Unionist element from which he wanted to form an intellectual backing for the Separatist movement'.[106] Maud Gonne and O'Leary shared a common outlook, differing only on the link between the agrarian and the political struggle. She had been converted to nationalism by witnessing an eviction in rural Ireland, and retained a strong belief in the unity of the two struggles. O'Leary thought this would distract the people's minds from the freeing of Ireland, 'alienate the landed aristocracy and the people of the towns and provoke class war'.[107]

Maud Gonne, the daughter of a Captain in the British Army, and Yeats first met as disciples of O'Leary. Yeats was a 'tall lanky boy with deep-set dark eyes behind glasses', and she was 'a tall girl with masses of gold-brown hair and a beauty which made her

Paris clothes equally unnoticeable'.[108] Yeats knew where to place her almost at once – that is, against an Irish background – for somehow he sensed that she belonged to his version of cultural nationalism, she having 'received the political tradition of Davis with an added touch of hardness and heroism from the hand of O'Leary' (*Mem* 41). They met when

> she drove up to our house in Bedford park with an introduction from John O'Leary to my father. I had never thought to see in a living woman so great beauty. It belonged to famous pictures, to poetry, to some legendary past. A complexion like the blossom of apples, and yet face and body had the beauty of lineaments which Blake calls the highest beauty because it changes least from youth to age, and a stature so great that she seemed of a divine race. Her movements were worthy of her form, and I understood at last why the poet of antiquity, where we would but speak of face and form, sings, loving some lady, that she paces like a goddess. I remember nothing of her speech that day except that she vexed my father by praise of war, for she too was of the Romantic movement and found those uncontrovertible Victorian reasons, that seemed to announce so prosperous a future, a little grey. As I look backward, it seems to me that she brought into my life in those days – for as yet I saw only what lay upon the surface – the middle of the tint, a sound as of a Burmese gong, an overpowering tumult that had yet many pleasant secondary notes.
>
> (*Mem* 40)

If O'Leary symbolised a form of political and intellectual separatism, Maud Gonne represented overwhelming beauty and the tantalising prospect of emotional involvement. However, nearly ten years after their first meeting, Yeats confessed to Lady Gregory that he could not tell if she was more than just kind and friendly.[109] What Yeats failed to allow for was the strength and character of her Fenian aspirations: 'I believe the Celtic literary movement is most important in fact, absolutely essential for the carrying out of our scheme for the liberation of Ireland' (*MGY* 75).[110] Yeats was part of *that* scheme: 'You have a higher work to do – With me it is different I was born to be in the midst of a crowd' (*MGY* 73).[111]

When she told him in December 1898 they could never marry, Yeats was in despair. As he admitted to Lady Gregory in language that is both genuine and psychologically revealing, he was 'unnerved':

> The fact is that MG has told me with every circumstance of deep emotion that she has loved me for years that my love is the only beautiful thing in her life, but that for certain reasons which I cannot tell you, reasons of a generous kind & of a tragic origin, she can never marry. She is full of remorse because she thinks that she has in the same breath bound me to her & taken away all hope of marriage. For years she kept 'a wall of glass between us' as she puts it & the very day she gave way she begged me to see her no more. She has changed altogether since she spoke of her love & is gentler & tender & I am now much happier than I have been for years for I am trying to see things more unselfishly & to make her life happier, content with just that manner of love which she will give me abundantly. . . . My nerves are still feeling the effects; and a restless night has given me a rather bad cold & a little asthma so that I feel like a very battered ship with the mast broken off at the stump. She has gone to Loughrea about some evicted tenants but returns I think tomorrow.[112]

Front cover of the *Gael* (New York), February 1903.

Adam's Curse.

WE sat together at one Summer's end
    That beautiful mild woman your close friend
    And you and I, and talked of poetry.

I said: "A line will take us hours maybe,
Yet if it does not seem a moment's thought
Our stitching and unstitching has been naught.
Better go down upon your marrow bones
And scrub a kitchen pavement or break stones
Like an old pauper in all kinds of weather;
For to articulate sweet sounds together
Is to work harder than all these and yet
Be thought an idler by the noisy set
Of bankers, schoolmasters, and clergymen
The martyrs call the world."

                        That woman then
Murmured with her young voice for whose mild sake
There's many a one shall find out all heartache
In finding that it's young and mild and low.
"There is one thing that all we women know
Although we never heard of it at school.
That we must labor to be beautiful."
I said: "It's certain there is no fine thing
Since Adam's fall but needs much laboring.
There have been lovers who thought love should be
So much compounded of high courtesy
That they would sigh and quote with learned looks
Precedents out of beautiful old books;
Yet now it seems an idle trade enough."

We sat grown quiet at the name of love.
We saw the last embers of daylight die
And in the trembling blue-green of the sky
A moon—moon worn as if it had been a shell,
Washed by time's waters as they rose and fell
About the starn and broke in days and years.

I had a thought for no one but your ears,
That you were beautiful and that I strove
To love you in the old highway of love;
That it had all seemed happy and yet we'd grown
As weary hearted as that hollow moon.

                            W. B. YEATS.

'Adam's Curse', written before 20 November 1902, was printed, along with typos, in the *Gael* (New York) in February 1903, and tells of Yeats's yearning for Maud Gonne 'in the old highway of love'.

Throughout their turbulent relationship Maud Gonne insisted on Yeats's 'higher work'. When he became depressed in June 1908 with theatre business, she took care to encourage him: 'I understand how you feel about the responsibility towards the players who depend on you – it is that recognition of responsibility which I always admire in you & which is such a rare quality in our country but for the sake of Ireland, you *must* keep your writing before all else – A great poet or a great writer, can give nobler & more precious gifts to his country than the greatest philanthropist ever can give' (*MGY* 255).[113] Some things clearly shocked him. 'She spoke of her desire for power, apparently for its own sake, and when we talked of politics spoke much of mere effectiveness, or the mere winning of this or that election' (*Mem* 41). Some opinions he did not share. She was repelled, for example, by the Semitic tendency in the teaching of the Golden Dawn; in July 1909 in Aix-les-Bains she complained about 'the proximity of jew bankers & enterprising fair ladies & fat vulgar creatures'; in April 1909, after being invited by Yeats to a Shakespeare festival, she felt impelled to comment on it being an *English* festival: 'I know that you say that it is a celebration of an England of the past which was not as horrid as the England of today, but even that England was the enemy & destroyer of our country.'[114]

In all the years she spent in France from 1890 to 1918, the year she bought 73 St Stephen's Green, she remained faithful to an image of a fearless Ireland, separate from continental Europe and from the old enemy of England. Not even MacBride's indecent behaviour towards Iseult, Maud Gonne's ten-year-old daughter by Lucien Millevoye, could undermine her support for Ireland, and when his memory was vilified after his execution in May 1916, she wrote to the newspapers in his defence and thereafter called herself Maud Gonne MacBride.[115]

Maud Gonne, like O'Leary, insisted on sacrificing her life to a higher cause. She exercised great influence in addressing crowds at political rallies and Amnesty meetings in the west of Ireland, and had, according to Yeats, 'absolute courage and no strong general grasp of policy'.[116] In 1897 all three found themselves members of the Executive of the '98 Centenary Commemoration Committee, with O'Leary as President and with Yeats sitting next to Maud Gonne at meetings. On 23 May 1897, Jubilee Day, they all marched in procession through the streets of Dublin behind a coffin representing the British Empire. Afterwards, Yeats and Maud Gonne returned to the National Club, locked the doors, and were having tea when they heard a commotion outside. Policemen were waving batons, a woman was lying on the ground still, possibly dead. Maud rushed downstairs, but the door was locked, and Yeats was shouting: 'Don't let her out.'[117] The scene is a vignette of their relationship: Yeats is overcome by a sense of protectiveness towards Maud Gonne; she, however, is determined to play an active role in political struggle. Yeats insisted on imagining her as a Cathleen ni Houlihan figure; she insisted on deflecting such attention onto Ireland itself, onto another symbol – 'the all-protecting mother, who had to be released from the bondage of the foreigner'.[118]

The impasse in their relationship meant years of frustration for Yeats, memorable verse for posterity, and a spiritual marriage that was once consummated at some cost to Maud:

You asked me yesterday if I am not a little sad that things are as they are between us – I am sorry & I am glad. It is hard being away from each other so much there are moments when I am dreadfully lonely & long to be with you, – one of these moments is on me now – but beloved I am glad & proud beyond measure of your love, & that is strong enough & high enough to accept the spiritual love & union I offer –

I have prayed so hard to have all earthly desire taken from my love for you & dearest, loving you as I do, I have prayed & I am praying still that the bodily desire for me may be taken from you too. I know how hard & rare a thing it is for a man to hold spiritual love when the bodily desire is gone & I have not made these prayers without a terrible struggle a struggle that shook my life though I do not speak much of it & generally manage to laugh.

(*MGY* 258–9)[119]

In the aftermath of the Easter Rising, Yeats travelled to Normandy to be with Maud, and in a letter dated 13 July 1916 told Lady Gregory that there was little news. She had again declined his proposal of marriage on account of her age (she was ten years his senior) and because it would have an adverse effect on their work. The following day she wanted to know if Yeats were not relieved by her refusal, and at the same time wondered if it would not be better for the children if they did marry. Yeats thought she might have been hesitating, but he did not return to the topic; he assumed her commitment to politics had something to do with her decision.[120]

In August 1919, nearly two years after his marriage to George, Yeats still cannot let go, as the following transcript of an automatic writing session suggests:

Ballylee   8.15 pm   August 26 1919
Ameritus
Well are you not more vigorous tonight
Yes
Yes but short script is very tiring for medium & interpreter

1   (Why had I that crazy passion for MG)
Those who belong *to image* get these from *past* & past phase – in your case 16 – Those
to idea to future & future phase – interpreter 17
Your passion for 16 was the reaction from your 16

2   (Had I not met 16 in either of the two lives described)
 – No –

3   (What quality in my past lives did she represent.)
Montanism – not as modern meaning – as religious meanings

                                                      (*VYP* 2, 390)[121]

PALL MALL BUDGET

No. 1150.—22nd YEAR.　　　THURSDAY, OCTOBER 9, 1890.　　　*Weekly.* PRICE ... 3d.
BY POST..4½d.

THE "PALL MALL" PICTURE GALLERY.

No. 35.—MR. WILLIAM MORRIS.

Pall Mall Budget, 9 October 1890. *The Sundering Flood* and *News from Nowhere*, extracts of which appeared in Morris's *Commonweal* in 1890, were the only books Yeats 'ever read slowly so that I might not come quickly to the end'.

94

4

Yeats and 1890s London

WILLIAM MORRIS

Together with Madame Blavatsky and W. E. Henley, Morris was one of the three people who most impressed Yeats.[1] For his epigraph to *Responsibilities* (1914) Yeats the practical visionary chose a comment that would have been crystal clear to the English Romantic turned revolutionary-socialist: '*In dreams begins responsibility*'. When Gogarty rehearsed the course of Yeats's life in the *Evening Standard* on 30 January 1939, he did so by reference to Morris: 'He ⟨Yeats⟩ was the last of the Pre-Raphaelites. This did not spring to the eye at once, simply because it is shrouded in Celtic twilight. And yet his master was William Morris.'

Yeats first met Morris in 1886 at the Contemporary Club in Dublin; the following year Yeats moved to Bedford Park in London:

I cannot remember who first brought me to the old stable beside Kelmscott House, William Morris's house at Hammersmith, and to the debates held there upon Sunday evenings by the Socialist League. I was soon of the little group who had supper with Morris afterwards. I met at these suppers very constantly Walter Crane, Emery Walker, in association with Cobden-Sanderson, the printer of many fine books, and less constantly Bernard Shaw and Cockerell, now of the Fitzwilliam Museum, Cambridge, and perhaps once or twice Hyndman the Socialist and the Anarchist Prince Kropotkin. There, too, one always met certain more or less educated workmen, rough of speech and manner, with a conviction to meet every turn.

(*A* 139–40)

Throughout his life the work of Morris was a constant companion:

I had read as a boy, in books belonging to my father, the third volume of *The Earthly Paradise*, and *The Defence of Guenevere*, which pleases me less, but had not opened either for a long time. *The Man Who Never Laughed Again* had seemed the most wonderful of tales till my father had accused me of preferring Morris to Keats, got angry about it, and put me altogether out of countenance. He had spoiled my pleasure, for now I questioned while I read and at last ceased to read; nor had Morris written as yet those prose romances that became after his death so great a joy that they were the only books I was ever to read slowly that I might not come too quickly to the end. It was now Morris himself that stirred my interest, and I took to him first because of some little tricks of speech and body that reminded me of my old grandfather in Sligo, but soon discovered his spontaneity and joy and made him my chief of men. Today I do not set his poetry very high, but for an odd

95

altogether wonderful line, or thought; and yet, if some angel offered me the choice, I would choose to live his life, poetry and all, rather than my own or any other man's.

(*A* 141)

Hanging over his mantelpiece was a portrait of Morris by G. F. Watts; in his library dating from the 1920s, there were copies of: *Useless Work Versus Useless Toil* (1886); Morris's post-revolutionary utopia, *News from Nowhere* (1891), given to Yeats by Masefield; *Art and the Beauty of the Earth* (1899); *Art and Its Producers and the Arts and Crafts of Today* (1901), an example of Morris's pamphleteering and of his attempt to intervene directly in the culture; *The Well at the World's End* (1896), a heroic fantasy; *The Defence of Guenevere* (1904), an early collection of verse; and the twenty-four volumes of *The Collected Works* (1910–15), which was George and Yeats's Christmas gift to each other in 1919. On his fortieth birthday his friends thought it appropriate to present him a copy of *The Works of Geoffrey Chaucer* printed by Morris's Kelmscott Press.

'I owe to him many truths' (*Ex* 221) Yeats once insisted, not least his ideological disposition towards hope: 'Hope is our life', declared Morris in *The Earthly Paradise* (1868–70). 'Hope will not give us up to certainty,/But still must bide with us.'[2] The influence was profound and lasting, and echoes of Morris can be heard in passage after passage of Yeats's prose and in line after line of his verse:

> *Dreamer of dreams, born out of my due time,*
> *Why should I strive to set the crooked straight?*
> *Let it suffice me that my murmuring rhyme*
> *Beats with light wing against the ivory gate,*
> *Telling a tale not too importunate*
> *To those who in the sleepy region stay,*
> *Lulled by the singer of an empty day.*[3]

A singer-poet, born out of his due time, Yeats too, as *John Sherman* suggests, is a John O'Dreams figure, 'more like a haunting Isle of Voices than a comprehensible world'.[4] His incantatory verse is full of 'clamorous wings' and scored with 'half-forgotten things', meanings that hover at the periphery of the mind. In the face of cold destiny he too, as in 'Easter 1916', murmurs 'name upon name', recalling an exotic tale for those who have been lulled into sleep thinking that they but lived 'where motley is worn':

> O when may it suffice?
> That is Heaven's part, our part
> To murmur name upon name,
> As a mother names her child
> When sleep at last has come
> On limbs that had run wild.
>
> (*VP* 394)

Reading the first volume of *The Earthly Paradise* with Yeats in mind underlines the extent of the influence. The quest romance, an example in its own way for Yeats's attempts in *The Island of Statues* (1886), *The Wanderings of Oisin*, and *The Shadowy Waters*, is punctuated throughout with phrases that resurface in Yeats's verse:[5]

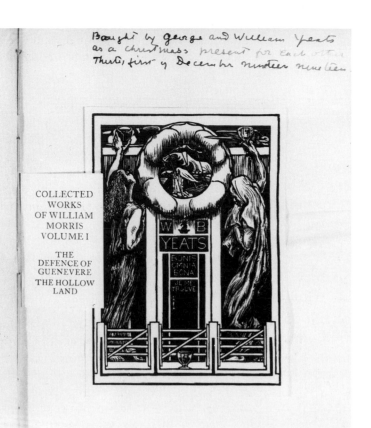

Bought by George and William Yeats as a christmass present for each other. Thirty first of December nineteen nineteen.

These bookplates of George and W. B. Yeats were pasted inside a copy of the first volume of Morris's *Collected Works* (1910–15).

- ○ pierce the woods (*The Earthly Paradise*, 49)
- • and pierce the deep wood's woven shade (*VP* 125)

- ○ souls outworn (page 67)
- • Out-worn heart, in a time out-worn (*VP* 147)

- ○ a land where many a lovely thing has birth (page 70)
- • Many ingenious lovely things are gone (*VP* 428)

- ○ Houses we had, noble with walls and towers,/Lovely with gardens, cooled with running streams (page 71)
- • Surely among a rich man's flowering lawns,/Amid the rustle of his planted hills,/Life overflows without ambitious pains (*VP* 417)

- ○ They taught us their law,/The muster of men-at-arms we saw (page 71)
- • Rough men-at-arms . . . climbed the narrow stairs (*VP* 412)

- ○ and all things for delight (page 71)
- • all things the delighted eye now sees (*VP* 326)

- ○ poets' vain imaginings/And memories vague of half-forgotten things (page 105)
- • Helmets, and swords, and half-forgotten things/That were like memories of you (*VP* 257)

- ○ That still in place of dreamy, youthful hope,/With slow decay and certain death could cope (page 305)
- • Though hope fall from you and love decay (*VP* 148)

The rooms of Yeats's mind, as several critics rightly suggest, were stocked with the ideas of the man who dominated part of his youth.[6] And not just his mental furniture, for in decorating his flat at Woburn Buildings in the mid-1890s, he betrayed Morris's influence. Morris's ideas on simple interior design were for Yeats a benchmark.[7] When he first visited Coole in 1897, 'I was so full of the mediaevalism of William Morris that I did not like the gold frames, some deep and full of ornament, round the pictures in the drawing-room; years were to pass before I came to understand the earlier nineteenth and later eighteenth century, and to love that house more than all other houses' (*A* 389). Thereafter several of the rooms at Coole were decorated with William Morris wallpaper.[8]

Yeats followed Morris in judging an age according to its art, in characterising the nineteenth century as 'the Century of Commerce',[9] and in advocating a simplicity of life, a 'love for sweet and lofty things',[10] and 'a return to the people' (*Ex* 96). Like Morris, Yeats believed civilisation meant not 'more stuffed chairs and cushions, and more carpets and gas, and more dainty meat and drink'.[11] As for the past, he shared Morris's belief that in the fifteenth century there existed 'the completeness of art in the heyday of life'; 'men attained to personality in great numbers, "Unity of Being", and became like a "perfectly proportioned human body", and as men so fashioned held places of power, their nations had it too, prince and ploughman sharing that thought and feeling' (*A* 291). Yeats's Byzantium is but a version of Morris's vision of unity between artist and craftsman, a return to that civilisation when, according to Morris, 'Nothing more beautiful than its best works has ever been produced by man': 'Its characteristics are simplicity of structure and outline of mass; amazing delicacy of ornament combined with abhorrence of vagueness . . . redundant, but not florid, the very opposite of Roman architecture in spirit, though it took many of its forms and revivified them.'[12]

Ironically, some phrases in Morris's *Earthly Paradise*, such as 'the deathless country of your thought' (64), sound Yeatsian. Of course, Morris went beyond 'youth's dreamy load', but then, as Cullingford reminds us, so too did Yeats.[13] The difficulty lies in determining the extent of the influence and the shape of the transformation. When discussing Morris in *Memoirs*, Yeats confesses: 'There were moments when I thought myself a Socialist' (*Mem* 20). Of course, he was not, and was upset by socialist attacks on religion he heard at Morris's. But at precisely the point where the socialist historian E. P. Thompson might have fine-tuned his analysis, he holds back: 'It must have been sad to Morris to have so many pass through the movement, like Yeats, as birds of passage'.[14]

Consider the word *labour*. Labour was part of a complex argument in Morris that derived from his contact with the Pre-Raphaelites and from his reading of Ruskin, Marx, and the Middle Ages. Labour is 'useful work' as opposed to 'useless toil'. It is not 'the reckless waste of life in pursuit of the means of life'.[15] It belongs to the craft-making capacity of human beings, most in evidence in the Middle Ages, and constituted an ideal worth emulating. When Yeats uses the word *labour* he never quite abandons the Morrisian undertow. In 'Adam's Curse', the poet comments on his craft of verse:

A line will take us hours maybe;
Yet if it does not seem a moment's thought,
Our stitching and unstitching has been naught.

(*VP* 204)

Yeats learnt from Morris the patience of commitment, how art is part of Adam's curse, a 'trade', as he insists, from 'The Grey Rock' (1912) to 'Under Ben Bulben' (1938). Even beauty in a woman has to be worked at; 'we must labour to be beautiful' (*VP* 205). From his family background among employers of labour, Yeats understood the value of labour, even when that meant toil, for 'the chief temptation of the artist' was 'creation without toil' (*A* 202). As one of his early critics Robert Lynd once remarked: 'Mr Yeats has laboured his verse into perfect music with a deliberateness like that of Flaubert in writing prose.'[16] Appropriately, when Yeats casts an image of utopia in 'Among School Children', he does so by reference to labour:

Labour is blossoming or dancing where
The body is not bruised to pleasure soul,
Nor beauty born of its own despair,
Nor blear-eyed wisdom out of midnight oil.

(*VP* 445–6)

In listening to Morris, Yeats's thoughts must have turned to Ireland, for what was Ireland but a proving ground for Morris's ideas? His sisters thought likewise. According to their father, the chief enjoyment Lily and Lollie had in running the Dun Emer Industries lay in 'the girls they employ, they know all these *individually*, lend them books, advise them, putting new ideas into their heads. 100 years ago they would have wanted to make them loyal & protestant, now they only seek to make them happy & rational & healthy, sleeping with their windows open & not knuckling down to their brothers or anybody else or anything else – this marks the "Progress of the ages"'.[17] If you overlook the special place of London and the Thames in Morris and stress the 'great tapestry' (*E & I* 513) hanging behind Irish history, the living traditions of Irish popular culture, that art in Ireland is not tribeless, you can quickly discern how Morris's ideas might be adapted to Ireland. Instead of the Arthurian legends and Icelandic sagas there was Oisin, the Red Branch Cycle of stories, and Ireland's folk imagination; for medieval cathedrals there were ancient wells; for Fleet Street there was Innisfree; for 'a speech, exhausted from abstraction' (*A* 142) there were the songs of the Irish country people; for a reading public and 'writing for the reader', as he admonished Morris (*Ex* 220), there was a story-telling tradition and 'Hearers and hearteners of the work' (*VP* 266); for Keatsian 'picture-making' there was the 'imagination of personality' (*Ex* 163); for class war, the union of hut and castle; for international socialism there was a separate nation to establish; for the Firm substitute the Dun Emer Industries; for the Kelmscott Press, the Dun Emer (later, in 1908, the Cuala) Press.[18]

Of course, their differences were also quite marked – not least the spin that Yeats put on Morris's vocabulary after the 1920s. In the 1880s Morris grew increasingly conscious of the 'miserable inequalities produced by the robbery of the system of Capital and Wages'.[19] From this perspective the medieval romance was not so much an escape as a starting-point, a whetstone for social change. Morris understood enough of the deformities of medieval social relations, where towns were 'fortresses for the feudal army',[20] to recognise that any return to the days of 'prince and ploughman' was not so much

Lollie Yeats at the Dun Emer Press, standing centre right. According to their father, writing in May 1906, Lollie is 'the enterprising member of the firm, Lily, the most persistently hopeful'.

fanciful as politically backward. Yeats lacked the spur of social injustice and mistook a metaphor for reality. As is apparent in *News from Nowhere*, Morris objected to the metropolitan *idea* of 'country-looking people' and sought the abolition of the difference between town and country.[21] By contrast, Yeats's image of the Irish country people fed off 'a bitter hatred of London' (*E & I* 98), a knee-jerk reaction Yeats was incapable of overcoming.

Ireland, therefore, was an escape from London, the privileged side across the binary divide, but a divide seen by Yeats in absolute, not relational, terms. He would have been shocked if it were suggested that his ideas of Ireland were inextricably linked with his position in metropolitan culture or that his attempt to establish an earthly paradise in Ireland was a turning-away from Morris's generosity of spirit. But, as Osbert Burdett recognised in 1925, Yeats is in this respect simply part of his age: 'Mr Yeats turned from London to Dublin, and from Dublin to the cabins of the peasants as hungrily as Beardsley turned to watch the crowd around *petits chevaux* in the casino, Dowson to cabmen's shelters, Johnson to a library, or Wilde to Mayfair.'[22]

At the beginning of *The Earthly Paradise*, the wanderers from Norway, in pursuit of an earthly paradise, arrive at a 'nameless city' where they are greeted by the elder of the city:

> From what unheard-of world, in what strange keel,
> Have ye come hither to our commonweal?
> No barbarous race, as these our peasants say,
> But learned in memories of a long-past day,
> Speaking, some few at least, the ancient tongue

100

> That through the lapse of ages still has clung
> To us, the seed of the Ionian race.[23]

In his wanderings in the Land of Youth, Oisin encounters a demon 'crooning to himself an unknown tongue' (*VP* 39); in his invocation 'To the Rose upon the Rood of Time', the poet seeks to '*learn to chaunt a tongue men do not know*' (*VP* 101). In 'The Fisherman', the poet calls up the fisherman's face and wonders if he could 'write for my own race' (*VP* 347). Later, in a bitter exchange with Maud Gonne, Yeats regrets speaking a 'barbarous tongue' (*VP* 313). As for 'commonweal', this was later deployed by Morris for his campaigning journal, but in Yeats's verse it is never easy to predict how the word *common* (or its derivatives) will be used. In a phrase such as 'Tara uprooted, and new commonness/Upon the throne' (*VP* 198), Yeats reveals a complex form of snobbery. But the word also has its Morrisian populist connotations, as in the line from 'At the Abbey Theatre' where Yeats links his project with Hyde's: '⟨W⟩e have made our art of common things.' In 'The Municipal Gallery Revisited' there is the famous parenthetical line full of positive connotation: '(An image out of Spenser and the common tongue)' (*VP* 603). But such words as 'race' and 'tongue', which in Morris belong to the world of medieval romance, acquire an increasingly sinister ring in Yeats under the impact of right-wing, eugenist ideas. What in Morris is a 'nameless city in a distant sea' is converted in the 1938 poem 'Under Ben Bulben', for example, into a defiant sectarian stance:

> Many times man lives and dies
> Between his two eternities,
> That of race and that of soul,
> And ancient Ireland knew it all.
>
> ....
> Scorn the sort now growing up
> All out of shape from toe to top,
> Their unremembering hearts and heads
> Base-born products of base beds.
>
> ....
> Cast your minds on other days
> That we in coming days may be
> Still the indomitable Irishry.
>
> > (*VP* 637–40)

LONDON CLUBLAND

Bedford Park

In March 1888, the Yeats family took up residence again at Bedford Park, this time at 3 Blenheim Road, 'a fine roomy house which by good luck we have got very cheep' (*L [K]* 56). Bedford Park, as Ian Fletcher reminds us, was an artistic enclave for the professional middle class, its beginnings coinciding with the rise of the Aesthetic Movement in the 1870s.[24] Among those who lived there in the early years were the playwright

Aubrey Beardsley's *Avenue Theatre poster for Yeats's play *The Land of Heart's Desire* with Florence Farr in the leading role. Wilde wondered: 'Who has ever managed to suggest such colour in masses of black deftly composed?' Owen Seaman, on the other hand, in *Punch* mocked at 'Aubrey Beer de Beers's Japanee-Rossetti girl'. As for the play itself, G. K. Chesterton thought there was only one thing wrong with it: 'The heart does not desire it.'

Arthur Pinero, the Irish physician, poet, and playwright John Todhunter, York Powell, Regius Professor of Modern History at Oxford, and in the later years the artist H. M. Paget, the historian Oliver Elton, Sydney Cockerell, and Elkin Mathews, the publisher. For Yeats, Bedford Park was 'a romantic excitement': 'We went to live in a house like those we had seen in pictures and even met people dressed like people in the story-books' (*R* 78). Among the many local societies, the two that stood out were the Calumet Club, a discussion group which met every other Sunday evening, and the Amateur Dramatic Club, where in May 1890 Yeats was overwhelmed by Farr's performance in Todhunter's *Sicilian Idyll*.

Family and financial problems emptied Bedford Park of much of its romance.[25] The sale of his father's Irish properties at Thomastown added to the family's gloom, for these yielded just over £7,000, £500 less than he was expecting. Fortunately, in December 1888 Lily found work embroidering at May Morris's and received a much-needed weekly sum of ten shillings. Lollie taught painting; Jack found work with a Manchester newspaper; and Willie was contributing small amounts from journalistic writings. But in April 1888 Yeats's mother, after suffering a second stroke, arrived from relatives in Denby, Yorkshire, spent the next twelve years confined to the house, and found, 'liberated at last from financial worry, perfect happiness feeding the birds at a London window' (*R* 116). Yeats's memories of his mother were perhaps permanently damaged by this illness. In the typescript of the manuscript for *Reveries* there is a revealing deletion: 'My memory of what she was like in those days *has been blurred by years of illness before her death*.'[26] In the final text the italicised phrase has been changed to the more neutral 'has grown very dim' (*R* 54). There is another telling passage in the same manuscript which has also been deleted from the published version. Section VII begins: 'Two pictures come into my memory' (*R* 75). In an earlier draft there were three pictures, the third one associated with Bedford Park and the unexpected appearance of an unwanted relative: 'My sister had opened the door one morning before breakfast and found upon the doorstep a relation who had escaped after being shut up for some temporary fit of madness. When we looked at her, we were ashamed. We knew that we must telegraph to her keeper and send her away (for her madness made her refuse all food). He ⟨she⟩ had put his ⟨her⟩ trust in us, and we were going to betray him ⟨her⟩.'[27]

Thirty minutes from central London, Bedford Park proved a useful base. Kelmscott House was only a mile or so away. Through Tynan Yeats gained access to Lady Wilde's Saturday afternoons at 146 Oakley Street, Chelsea. Henley lived at 1 Merton Place, Chiswick, a short walk from Bedford Park. In 1888 and 1889 Johnson was living in Charlotte Street, Wilde in Tite Street (it was there that Yeats spent Christmas Day 1888). Across the river, meetings of the Southwark Irish Literary Club could be readily attended and addressed. Every six weeks he used to visit Madame Blavatsky at Holland Park (later, Avenue Road) – so regularly that Chesterton thought he might have been bewitched, though not deceived, by the 'coarse, witty, vigorous, scandalous old scallywag'.[28]

The 1890s proved a turning-point in Yeats's career. In the late 1880s, he was still dependent on contacts made through his father. It was through York Powell, for example, that in August 1888 he obtained some free-lance copying work to do at the Bodleian Library, Oxford. In March 1889, he began his collaboration with Ellis on what emerged in 1893 as an edition of Blake's work. Another of J. B. Yeats's friends was less encouraging about his prospects: 'Todhunter says my bad writing and worse spelling will be much against me but thinks I may get some thing to do in the way of an assistant librarianship' (*L [K]* 56). By his thirty-fifth birthday in 1900, however, Yeats was so well

Florence Farr as she appeared in the *Pall Mall Budget*, 26 February 1891. In looks She was not unlike Olivia Shakespear. 'She was the only person to whom I could tell *everything*.' This is what Yeats once told George, his wife.

known that in the calendar of the *Literary Yearbook, 1897* his birthday is mentioned, while at Eton, as Shane Leslie recalls, pupils were translating his verse into Latin elegiacs: 'The only English poetry we learned was in the guise of Latin exercises. My acquaintance with the Celtic School dates from a feverish night turning Yeats into Latin elegiacs. To clothe lines like – "My brother is priest in Kilvarnet,/My cousin in Makarabuie" – into Ovidian measure is like Dr Haig Brown's *tour de force* in putting Euclid (Prop. I) into Latin verse.'[29] As the following list suggests, Yeats had established in London a remarkable circle of friends and associates, nearly all of whom have left some record of their impressions of the London Celt.

London Addresses of Yeats's Friends and Associates

Information from the *Literary Yearbook* for 1897 and 1900.

Beerbohm, Max. 48 Upper Berkeley Street, W.
Besant, Mrs Annie. 43 Tavistock Square, W.C.
Binyon, Laurence. British Museum, W.C.
Blunt, Wilfrid Scawen. 104F Mount Street, Berkeley Square, W.
Davidson, John. St Winifred's, Streatham, S.W.
Davitt, Michael M.P. (South Mayo). House of Commons, S.W.
Ellis, Edwin John. 40 Milsom Road, West Kensington Park.
Farr, Florence. 123 Dalling Road, Ravenscourt Park, W.

Yeats with Edward Dowden, possibly taken at 3 Blenheim Road, Bedford Park, physically close but worlds apart. Professor of English Literature at Trinity College, Dublin, from 1867 until his death in 1913, Dowden had an antipathy for things Irish and, according to Yeats, would say that he 'knew an Irish book by its smell, because he had once seen some books whose binding had been fastened together by rotten glue' (*A* 200).

Field, Michael (Katherine Bradley and Edith Cooper). The Vale Press, 17 Craven Street, Strand, W.C.

Garnett, Edward. Froghole, Limpsfield, Surrey.

Gosse, Edmund. Board of Trade, Whitehall. (In 1900, 29 Delamere Terrace, W.)

Graves, Alfred Perceval. Red Branch House, Wimbledon; The Athenaeum.

Hinkson, Mrs Tynan. 107 Blenheim Crescent, W.

Hopper, Nora. 36 Royal Crescent, Notting Hill, W.

Image, Selwyn. 6 Southampton Street, Bloomsbury, W.C.

Johnson, Lionel. 7 Gray's Inn Square, W.C. (In 1900, 8 New Square, Lincoln's Inn, W.C.)

Le Gallienne, Richard. c/o John Lane, The Bodley Head, Vigo Street, W.

Moore, George. King's Bench Walk, Temple.

Moore, Thomas Sturge. 39 South Grove, Highgate, N.

Plarr, Victor. c/o John Lane, The Bodley Head, Vigo Street, W.

Rhys, Ernest. Hunt Cottage, Hampstead.

Shakespear, Mrs O. 18 Porchester Square, Hyde Park, W.

Shannon, Charles. 2 The Vale, King's Road, Chelsea, S.W.

Shaw, G. Bernard. 29 Fitzroy Square, W.

Shorter, Dora Sigerson. 16 Marlborough Place, N.W.

Symons, Arthur. Fountain Court, The Temple.

Todhunter, Dr J. Orchardcroft, Bedford Park, W.

The Rhymers' Club

In or about May 1890, Yeats, Ernest Rhys, and T. W. Rolleston founded a club for younger poets to read and discuss each other's work. In the first year they met after work in the Cheshire Cheese off Fleet Street, their numbers including Ernest Dowson, Johnson, Le Gallienne, Victor Plarr, Symons, Todhunter, Herbert Horne, and Selwyn Image. Yeats 'intoned his verse with a musical voice and very haunting cadence'; the others read aloud in hushed voices.[30] In retrospect, according to *Autobiographies*, Yeats tells us he felt slightly out of place and provincial, for most of the Rhymers had been educated at Oxbridge, and, as Le Gallienne once remarked in Wildean fashion: 'A critic is any undergraduate of Oxford or Cambridge'.[31] Yeats, who insisted on wearing a brown velveteen coat, a loose tie, and a very old Inverness cape, was probably more in control than he let on, for as he told Heald at the end of his life, he established the Rhymers' Club to overcome his jealousy of other writers.[32]

The tangible result of all these meetings was the publication of two small volumes of verse, *The Book of the Rhymers' Club* (1892) and *The Second Book of the Rhymers' Club* (1894), which were well received and included Dowson's 'Non Sum Qualis Eram Bonae Sub Regno Cynarae', a poem that came to represent the decadent 1890s, Johnson's 'By the Statue of King Charles at Charing Cross', and Yeats's 'Lake Isle of Innisfree'. Interestingly, Dowson was, according to Rhys, 'the one Rhymer we believed to be the most potential in the group'.[33] The Rhymers were a collection of individuals, and they never managed to formulate a programme or manifesto. What united them was 'a passion for things French'[34] and an 'opposition to all ideas, all generalizations that can be explained and debated' (*A* 167) – or, in the folksy lines from Johnson's 'At the Cheshire Cheese':

When nobody bothers us, critic or creditor,
Client, constituent, contributor, editor;
When we're done for awhile with all worry and work,
Free and easy as any unspeakable *Turk*:
When for winter's worst weather we care not a jot,
But the fogs and the winds and the rains are forgot
In the pipe-bowl so ruddy, the punch-bowl so hot:
When the firelight goes dancing around the old wall,
And glows on our glances and us, one and all,
And our feast is the bravest for miles round *Saint Paul!*[35]

As it happened, the Rhymers formed the nucleus of the literary magazines and books of the 1890s. Le Gallienne became the most promising critic of the decade and went on to write its history under the title *The Romantic Nineties* (1926). Symons, Yeats's friend and early champion of Joyce, became editor of the *Savoy* and wrote a key work of criticism, *The Symbolist Movement in Literature* (1899). Rhys, regular contributor to the *Pall Mall Gazette*, was the prime mover behind Dent's 'Everyman's Library'. Plarr was Librarian for many years at the Royal College of Surgeons and author of *In the Dorian Mood* (1896). What all of them sought was an audience, a publisher, the bubble reputation, or, given that they met in the vicinity of Fleet Street, a press baron. The Irishness, or rather Celticness, of the group did not go unnoticed:

They were all very Celtic too, for it was the days of the Celtic Fringe. John Todhunter, as you will gather from the name, was a Celt; and Plarr, whose father was an Alsatian, was a Celt; and Johnson, again the Celtic name, was a Celt – at one time he assumed a brogue and addressed me as 'me dearr'; and Mr Symons, a Dravidian Welshman, was a Celt; and Dowson, who was probably of as pure Norman London descent as you could find, was inclined to believe there was a Celtic strain in him; and Yeats, who was plainly a Firbolg, was the most Celtic of all, and they all declared that there was a Celtic Renaissance.[36]

Johnson, a cousin of Olivia Shakespear, played a short-lived role in this renaissance. The son of a Welsh army officer, he discovered under the influence of Yeats and other Rhymers his Irish antecedents, and then proceeded to write himself into the Revival with a series of poems and a famous article on 'Poetry and Patriotism', later published by the Cuala Press in 1908.[37] Johnson's tribute to Parnell, with its image of Mother Ireland hearing the heavy bells as 'she tells/A rosary of death,' appeared in the *United Irishman* on 7 October 1893, the second anniversary of Parnell's death. In 'Ireland', a poem written in 1894, Johnson traces the male protagonists of Irish history such as Grattan, Davis, and Mangan, acting on behalf of female Ireland. At one point, in a move that provides a suggestive contrast with Yeats's use of the Rose symbol, he addresses the Virgin Mary as 'O Rose': '*O Rose! O Lily! O Lady full of grace!/O Mary Mother! O Mary Maid! hear thou.*' His apocalyptic sensibility was attracted towards themes of death and revenge. In 'The Coming of War', written in 1889, some seven years before Yeats's 'Valley of the Black Pig', he announced that 'An hundred peaceful years are over'; in 'Ninety-Eight' he takes up the opening line of John Kells Ingram's *Nation* ballad 'The Memory of the Dead'; and in 'To the Dead of '98' he anticipates the sacrifice of Pearse and the leaders of the Easter Rising:

from His altar fires you took your flame,
    Hailing His Holy Name.
Triumphantly you gave yourselves to death:
    And your last breath
Was one last sigh for Ireland, sigh to Him,
    As the loved land grew dim.[38]

Yeats was attracted to the disorder of Johnson's life, and Johnson features prominently in *Autobiographies* as a key figure of the tragic generation: 'Two men are always at my side, Lionel Johnson and John Synge whom I was to meet a little later; but Johnson is to me the more vivid in memory, possibly because of the external finish, the clearly-marked lineaments of his body, which seemed but to express the clarity of his mind' (*A* 312). In listening to his imaginary conversations, 'it never seemed very difficult to murmur Villiers de l'Isle Adam's proud words, "As for living, our servants will do that for us"' (*A* 305). But from 1895 onwards Yeats observed his friend's slide into alcoholism – though not without interest to his 'theory' of the 1890s: 'Did the austerity, the melancholy of his thoughts, that spiritual ecstasy which he touched at times, heighten, as complementary colours heighten one another, not only the Vision of Evil, but its fascination?' (*A* 310). When he came to compose 'In Memory of Major Robert Gregory' in 1918, Yeats delighted in the phrase 'much falling', now pressed into a schema of oppositions:

Lionel Johnson comes first to mind,
That loved his learning better than mankind,
Though courteous to the worst; much falling he
Brooded upon sanctity
Till all his Greek and Latin learning seemed
A long blast upon the horn that brought
A little nearer to his thought
A measureless consummation that he dreamed.

                    (*VP* 324)

London provided Yeats not just with an audience for his Irish voice but also, paradoxically, with the contexts which enabled him to retain a 'deep devotion to an inward ideal'.[39] The Rhymers taught him never to make '*a poorer song/That you might have a heavier purse*' (*VP* 273). Equally, it was because he was so far removed from Innisfree and the cabins of Ballysodare that he could allow Ireland to dominate his imagination. He was doubly rewarded, for with his ability to drift in and out of things, Yeats must have been half-conscious he would survive the London Nineties and come to write its epitaph, clinching in prose and verse that reassuringly tragic image of the group with whom he learned his trade: 'I had now met all those who were to make the nineties of the last century tragic in the history of literature, but as yet we were all seemingly equal, whether in talent or in luck, and scarce even personalities to one another. I remember saying one night at the Cheshire Cheese, when more poets than usual had come, "None of us can say who will succeed, or even who has or has not talent. The only thing certain about us is that we are too many"' (*A* 170–71).

Extremes meet, as *Ulysses* reminds us, for the Nineties was a movement that crossed national boundaries, not only between Ireland and England but also between England and France. Yeats's London looked to Paris for its aesthetic ideas and role-models. It was natural for Symons, the English Verlaine as he was once known, to dedicate *The Symbolist Movement in Literature* (1899) to Yeats as 'the chief representative of that movement in our country'.[40] It was natural for Yeats, not to be outdone by Moore's account of artistic life in Paris in *Confessions of a Young Man* (1888), to end his account of 'The Tragic Generation' also with Paris. Indeed, after witnessing a performance of Alfred Jarry's *Ubu Roi* in Paris, Yeats sought to characterise his generation as a whole: 'I say, "After Stéphane Mallarmé, after Paul Verlaine, after Gustave Moreau, after Puvis de Chavannes, after our own verse, after all our subtle colour and nervous rhythm, after the faint mixed tints of Conder, what more is possible? After us the Savage God"' (*A* 348–9).

Oscar Wilde (1854–1900)

In the opening episode of *Ulysses*, the usurper 'Buck' Mulligan taunts Stephen Dedalus: 'We have grown out of Wilde and paradoxes.'[41] Not quite, since in the courtroom scene in 'Circe' when Bloom is arraigned, more than an echo of Wilde's trial can be heard. Wilde, 'the wild rose ⟨that⟩ blossoms/On the little green place', was a warning for Joyce.[42] To Shaw and to Frank Harris, 'Mr Wilde is almost as acutely Irish an Irishman as the Iron Duke of Wellington. . . . He plays with everything: with wit, with philosophy, with drama, with actors and audience, with the whole theatre. Such a feat scandalizes the Englishman, who can no more play with wit and philosophy than he can with a football or a cricket bat.'[43] For Yeats, on the other hand, Wilde was part of the tragic generation but never a warning, or even a rival.

Wilde, according to Yeats, attributed 'characteristics like his own to his country: "We Irish are too poetical to be poets; we are a nation of brilliant failures, but we are the greatest talkers since the Greeks"' (*A* 135). Yeats was troubled by this phenomenon who was 'the greatest talker of his time' (*A* 139) and got his sincerity by contact with events – and 'the dinner-table was Wilde's event'. He tried to explain Wilde to himself by his family history, by an upbringing in a household where his mother 'received her friends with blinds drawn and shutters closed that none might see her withered face' (*A* 138), and where his surgeon father became the subject of Dublin riddles and alarming stories. Shaw, a rival for Farr's attention, merely 'carried his street-corner Socialist eloquence on to the stage', but Wilde was a more complex figure: 'He understood his weakness, true personality was impossible, for that is born in solitude, and at his moon one is not solitary; he must project himself before the eyes of others, and, having great ambition, before some great crowd of eyes; but there is no longer any great crowd that cares for his true thought' (*A* 293–4).

Ellmann suggests that the historical chapter of Yeats's *Vision* is an illustration of Wilde's thesis that, *pace* Taine, the age does not shape art; it is art which gives an age its character.[44] To my mind, Wilde remained fascinating to Yeats, as he was to Harris, largely because he shared his delight in the flourish of one-liners, in axiomatic expressions. 'My first meeting with Oscar Wilde was an astonishment. I never before heard a man talking with perfect sentences, as if he had written them overnight with labour and yet all spontaneous' (*A* 130). Consider the following remarks from *De Profundis*[45] juxtaposed alongside phrases scattered through Yeats's writings:

o I treated art as the supreme reality and life as a mere mode of fiction (*De Profundis*, 33–4).

• For those that love the world serve it in action . . . art/Is but a vision of reality (*VP* 369).

A Peep into the Past
(for the 1st No. of the
"Yellow Book")

Oscar Wilde! I wonder to how many of my readers the jingle of this name suggests anything at all? Yet, at one time, it was familiar to many and if we search back among the old volumes of our Punch, we shall find many a quip and crank cut out at its owner's expense. But time is a quick mover and many of us are fated to outlive our reputations and thus, though at one time Mr Wilde, the old gentleman, of whom we are going to give our readers a brief account, was in his way quite a celebrity, to-day his star is set, his fame obscured in this busy, changeful city.

Once a welcome guest in many of our Bohemian haunts, he lives now a life of quiet retirement in his little house in Tite Street with his wife and his two sons, his prop and mainstay, solacing himself with many a reminiscence of the friends of his youth, whilst he leaves his better-known brother, William, to perpetuate the social name of the family. Always noted for his tenacious memory, it is one of the old gentleman's keenest pleasures to regale a visitor from the outer world with stories of the late, Frank Miles, or Godwin the architect, or Robert Browning or the Earl of Lytton, who were not the only members of the upper Ten Thousand and to honour Mr Wilde with their personal friendships. "All, all are gone, the old familiar faces" and with the quiet resignation of one who knows that he is the survivor of a bygone day, Mr Wilde tends more & more to exist in its memory or to solace himself with the old classics of which he was ever so earnest a student, with his Keats and his Shakespeare, his Joseph Miller and the literal translations of the Greek Dramatists. Not that he is a mere laudator temporis acti, or a bibliophile and nothing more. He still keeps up his writing, is still the glutton for work that he always was. He has not yet abandoned his old intention of dramatising Salomé and the amount of journalistic matter that he quietly produces and contributes anonymously to various periodicals is surprising. Only last year an undergraduate journal called the Spirit Lamp accepted a poem of his in which there were evidences that he has lost little of his old talent for versification.

Mr Wilde is an early riser. Every morning, winter & summer, at 4.30 A.M. his portly form —(he is in appearance not unlike Sir William Harcourt and still stands six-foot three in his slippers)— may be seen bending over the little spirit-kettle, at which he boils himself his cup of hot cocoa. Donning his work-a-day clothes, he proceeds at once to stir his study and commences work, continuing steadily till breakfast, which he takes in company with his wife and sons. Himself most regular in his habits, he is something of a martinet about punctuality in his household and this accounts for the constant succession of page-boys, Breakfast over, the master of the house enjoys his modest cigarette —no costly cigar nor precious meerschaum ever passes his lips — he is a but strict believer in simplicity of life as the handmaiden of hard work. He never nowadays even looks at the morning papers, so wholly

- Art only begins where Imitation ends (100).
- Art is art because it is not nature (*A* 279).

- Between my art and the world there is now a wide gulf, but between art and myself there is none (101).
- I want to create for myself an unpopular theatre and an audience like a secret society where admission is by favour and never to many (*Ex* 254).

- We think in eternity, but we move slowly through time (57).
- *Like a long-legged fly upon the stream/His mind moves upon silence* (*VP* 617).

- But to recognise that the soul of a man is unknowable, is the ultimate achievement of wisdom (95).
- Man can embody truth but he cannot know it (*L* 922).

- Nor could I understand how Dante, who says that 'sorrow re-marries us to God', could have been so harsh to those who were enamoured of melancholy (49).
- Out of cavern comes a voice,/And all it knows is that one word 'Rejoice!' (*VP* 564).

Yeats remained faithful to Wilde throughout his trial, taking trouble to collect supportive letters from leading Irish writers and critics. Wilde was urged by some of his friends to escape to the Continent, but Yeats 'never doubted, even for an instant, that he made the right decision, and that he owes to that decision half of his renown' (*A* 289). Yeats saw Wilde not as another Parnell, the Irishman felled by the British. Rather, he concentrates on the more mundane responses of friends and relatives. Johnson, for example, thought Wilde would produce, when it was all over, 'some comedy exactly like

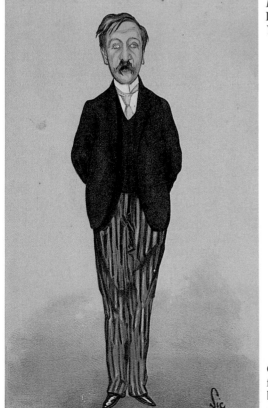

Facing page: First page of Max Beerbohm's manuscript of 'A Peep into the Past', orginally intended for the first number of the *Yellow Book*.

George Moore's 1894 naturalist novel *Esther Waters* contained a frank description of the wet-nurse situation and was consequently banned by W. H. Smith from its bookstalls. This is how Moore appeared in *Vanity Fair* in 1894 under the Caption 'Esther Waters'.

the others, writing from an art where events could leave no trace' (*A* 290). Significantly, the section in *Autobiographies* following Wilde's sentence concerns the Unity of Being that existed 'somewhere about 1450'.

JOURNALS AND JOURNALISM

The *Yellow Book*, the *Savoy*, the *Pageant*, and the *Dome*

The opportunity presented itself in the 1890s of creating an audience across the arts to include poetry, fiction, music, design, craftsmanship. Press barons such as the Harmsworths, Newnes, and Pearson were intent on carving up a new mass market, but there seemed to be room for smaller, more artistic ventures – at least until the Wilde trial in 1895 and the burial of the Aesthetic Movement in the Boer War. Yeats arrived in London just at the time when publishing outlets, as the table below suggests, were about to flourish. The *National Observer* moved south to London in 1890; the *Bookman* started up the following year; in the mid-1890s came the artistic journals, such as the *Yellow Book*, the *Savoy*, the *Pageant*, and the *Dome*. In 1887, John Lane and Mathews opened the Bodley Head in Vigo Street, and two years later began publishing.

The Victorian Age was ripe for dismantling; elder statesmen in the arts, such as Tennyson and Swinburne in poetry or Ruskin and Rossetti in criticism, had made their mark, and the way was clear for a younger generation to tie beauty to a 'strangeness of proportion'.[46] There was a nervous tension in the air, as if something dramatic, some 'trembling of the veil' at Yeats puts it, was about to happen. In a suggestive if neglected essay written in 1891, Edmund Gosse anticipated the critique later espoused by Yeats, Symons, and fully fledged Modernists such as Pound and Eliot:

> Poetry, if it exist at all, will deal . . . with those more frail and ephemeral shades of emotion which prose scarcely ventures to describe. In the future, lyrical poetry will probably grow less trivial and less conventional, at the risk of being less popular. . . . The modern interest in drama, and the ever-growing desire to see literature once more wedded to the stage, will, it can hardly be doubted, lead to a revival of dramatic poetry. . . . The next development of poetry is likely to be very bare and direct, unembroidered, perhaps even arid, in character. It will be experimental rather than descriptive, human rather than animal.[47]

The inaugural dinner of the *Yellow Book*, the Bible of the 1890s, was held at the Hotel d'Italia in Soho on 16 April 1894. The fifty people present included Johnson, Harland, George Moore, and Aubrey Beardsley. Olivia Shakespear sat directly opposite Yeats. Holbrook Jackson suggests that the first number 'was in the nature of a bomb-shell thrown into the world of letters. . . . People were puzzled and shocked and delighted, and yellow became the colour of the hour, the symbol of the time-spirit. It was associated with all that was *bizarre* and queer in art and life, and with all that was outrageously modern.'[48] Burdett defined Beardsley's as an art 'without prejudices', an attempt to 'give outline and definition to the sense of corruption, to recover the vision of evil'[49] but when Wilde, who ironically never wrote for it, carried into court on the day of his trial a copy of what the newspapers assumed was the *Yellow Book*, the magazine's – or rather Beardsley's – fate was sealed.[50]

· ARTHVR · SYMONS ·

Robert Bryden's woodcut of Arthur Symons. Symons once remarked: 'I have imagined more than I have thought. That is to say that imagination, the life of the senses, my sensations, have meant more to me than most things in one's life.' He was a 'solitary soul', incapable of excess, and, according to Yeats, the best listener he ever had.

Throughout the middle years of the 1890s, Yeats, who enjoyed being an Irish rebel and 'delighted in enemies and in everything that had an heroic air' (*A* 323), was nevertheless concerned about the company he kept. Perhaps it was for this reason that he contributed to the *Yellow Book* only one piece, 'The Blessed', a short story, which appeared in April 1897, long after the Wilde trial and the subsequent dismissal of Beardsley as art editor. Yeats placed Beardsley in the thirteenth phase of his lunar cycle, 'his nature on the edge of Unity of Being, the understanding of that Unity by the intellect his one overmastering purpose' (*A* 331). For a time, he thought his work was inspired 'by rage against iniquity', but then decided that Beardsley represented the 'virginity of the intellect', the images of his mind held in a kind of frozen passion.

Beardsley was subsequently recruited by Symons as art editor for the *Savoy*. It was a brave move, but in his Editorial Note to the first issue in January 1896, Symons took care to distance the magazine from the *Yellow Book* by declaring that 'We are not Realists, or Romanticists, or Decadents.'[51] Yeats defended his friend's choice but still felt the popular pressure against Beardsley: 'Yet, even apart from Beardsley, we were a sufficiently distinguished body: Max Beerbohm, Bernard Shaw, Ernest Dowson, Lionel Johnson, Arthur Symons, Charles Conder, Charles Shannon, Havelock Ellis, Selwyn Image, Joseph Conrad; but nothing counted but the one hated name' (*A* 325). Yeats was initially hostile to the *Savoy*'s 'scandalous' owner, for Smithers had a reputation for publishing risqué material, and he was warned against association with the magazine by his Irish associates Rolleston and Russell.[52]

The *Pageant* was a short-lived spectacle, but it brought together inside its covers the leading players on the Nineties stage: Beerbohm, John Gray (the supposed model for

Althea Gyles's design for *The Wind among the Reeds* shows on the front cover the reeds woven into the net of Breasal the fisherman and on the back a torn net and the catch gone. In 'The Fish', which was originally entitled 'Breasal the Fisherman', Yeats dramatises his relationship with Maud Gonne and perhaps with the craft of writing: 'Although you hide in the ebb and flow/ Of the pale tide when the moon has set,/The people of coming days will know/About the casting out of my net,/And how you have leaped times out of mind/Over the little silver cords,/ And think that you were hard and unkind,/And blame you with many bitter words' (*VP* 146).

Henry Fell's striking if slackly decorative cover design for *Poems* (1895). Shannon was Yeats's first choice to do the cover but was unable to do it. Inside Quinn's copy Yeats wrote: 'When he (Fell) did this the spirit had gone out of him.'

Wilde's Dorian Gray), Johnson, Verlaine, Maeterlinck, William Rothenstein,* Charles Conder. Image designed the title page, Lucien Pissarro the end-papers, and Charles Ricketts* the cover. Yeats learnt much from his contact with Ricketts and Shannon, who were 'in certain matters my chief instructors' (*A* 169). Ricketts was responsible for some of the most striking cover designs in the 1890s, including Wilde's *House of Pomegranates* (1891) and *The Sphinx* (1894), Gray's *Silverpoints* (1893), and J. A. Symonds's *In the Key of Blue* (1893). The cover design for the Uniform Yeats Edition which Macmillan published from 1922 to 1926, stamped blind on green cloth and reminiscent of the Vale Press Shakespeare, was also by Ricketts.[53] His disciple, Sturge Moore,* designed the covers for more than twelve of Yeats's volumes for Macmillan, many of which are reproduced in this book. In *A Defence of the Revival of Printing* (1899), Ricketts outlined his guiding principles on typeface and book decoration. His influence – at least on Yeats – paid off. Turn to a page of the first edition of *The Tower* (1928) (see page 214) and you will see the importance of visual setting to Yeats's work: words allowed to breathe on a page dominated by margins – a narrow inner margin, top margin somewhat wider, outside margin wider still, and bottom margin widest of all.[54] Yeats understood well the principles of cover design and the physical authority of black marks on white spaces; what he lacked was Mallarmé's sense of the 'visual unity' of the page.[55]

The first issue of the *Dome: A Quarterly Containing Examples of All the Arts* was divided into four sections: Architecture; Literature; Drawing, Painting and Engraving; and Music. It carried no manifesto and included a tongue-in-cheek review of itself in the Reviews section. Yeats contributed a number of poems, an essay on Althea Gyles entitled 'A Symbolic Artist and the Coming of Symbolic Art', and then a series of benchmark essays on 'The Irish Literary Theatre', 'The Symbolism of Poetry', and 'The Philosophy of Shelley's Poetry'. The confidence with which Yeats expressed himself in these essays reflects a mind stepping clear of the Nineties and intent on the practical establishment of a literary theatre in Ireland. As Laurence Binyon commented in 1923 in a review of the privately printed *Trembling of the Veil*: 'Like Rossetti, but unlike most English artists and men of letters, he has had a sort of political instinct or craving to create a movement, to carry others with him, to make a force against the forces of the time. And it was in Ireland, not in England, that he was to find his apt material.'[56]

Newspaper Journalism

By 1897 Yeats had spent some ten years reviewing for various newspapers and journals, and after some seventy-five book reviews, five in 1894 and eight in 1895, he was justifiably weary of Davidson's 'Seven hundred paces of tesselated road/From Ludgate Circus west to Chancery Lane'.[57] Between 1888 and 1895, he contributed some twenty-one reviews or articles for the Dublin-based *United Ireland*. He wrote regularly for the *Boston Pilot*, the Catholic weekly, and the *Providence Sunday Journal*. But it was for the newly established *Bookman* that he wrote most of his reviews – some forty-five from 1892 to 1903. His peak year was 1895, when he filed twelve reviews and articles. All these years were an object lesson in playing to an audience, for in William O'Brien's Parnellite *United Ireland* Yeats was establishing his credentials to speak on behalf of Ireland to his fellow-countrymen and women, while in the *Bookman* he was trumpeting his role as the London Celt.

Of all the editors Yeats worked for, W. E. Henley at the *New Review*, the *Scots*

Observer, and the *National Observer* exerted the most influence. Yeats's first encounter with him in 1888 was not auspicious: 'I hate journalists. There is nothing in them but tittering, jeering emptiness. . . . The other night I sat there without a word out of me, trying to pluck up resolution to go, but Henley wanted to see me about something and so I waited. The shallowest people on the ridge of the world!' (*L* 83).[58] Henley's star soon ascended. In *Autobiographies*, without the slightest hint of *déjà vu*, Yeats announces that his education began under Henley (*A* 124). The year is 1888; Yeats is twenty-three; O'Leary, 'MacGregor Mathers', and Morris are behind him, as is his father and his uncle George. But the dispossessed son, in many ways the closest spiritual model for Joyce's Stephen Dedalus, is still searching for a father figure. Henley possessed 'what Wilde lacked, even in his ruin, passion, was maybe as passionate as some great man of action, as Parnell, let us say' (*A* 296). With one leg amputated and the other saved only by the skill of Joseph Lister, Henley was a figure, in the words of Wilde, 'never forgotten by his enemies, and often forgiven by his friends'.[59] There is an equally memorable sentence in Yeats, written in the 1930s: 'Henley lay upon the sofa, crippled by his incautious youth, dragged his body, crutch-supported, between two rooms, imagining imperial might.'[60]

In November 1890 Henley returned to London from Edinburgh with a paper that had changed name and widened its appeal, and he proceeded to gather round him a group of young writers, among them Yeats, Andrew Lang, Hugh Haliburton, James Barrie, David Hannay, Francis Watt, Cosmo Monkhouse, Alice Meynell.[61] 'Barrack-Room Ballads. I – Danny Deever' appeared in February 1890, and Kipling became a regular contributor. In turn Kipling was introduced to other members of Henley's club, the Savile: Hardy, Walter Besant, Saintsbury, Gosse. If it seems strange that Yeats should have written for an imperialist paper that in March 1893 published a Special Supplement attacking the Home Rule Bill, his response would have been immediate: 'I disagreed with him ⟨Henley⟩ about everything, but I admired him beyond words' (*A* 124).

Yeats's work as a London reviewer was matched, as the following table suggests, by an equally impressive output as poet and writer of fiction.[62]

Editor	Literary Magazine	Contribution	Date
W. E. Henley	*Scots Observer* (1888–90) *National Observer* (1890–97)	⟨Father Gilligan⟩ (V) The Lake Isle of Innisfree (V) ⟨Rosa Mundi⟩ (V) The White Birds (V) The Twisting of the Rope (S) ⟨The Celtic Twilight⟩ (V) ⟨Cap and Bell⟩ (V) The Crucifixion of Outcast (S) ⟨Kathleen-Ni-Houlihan⟩ (S and V) *More than 12 poems and 8 stories*	5 July 1890 13 December 1890 2 January 1892 7 May 1892 24 December 1892 29 July 1893 17 March 1894 24 March 1894 4 August 1894
William Robertson Nicholl (1891–1923)	*Bookman* (1891–1934)	⟨A Mystical prayer to the Masters of the Elements, Michael, Gabriel and Raphael⟩ (V) The Fiddler of Dooney (V) The Moods (V)	October 1892 December 1892 August 1893

Editor	Literary Magazine	Contribution	Date
		The Host of the Air (V)	November 1893
		The Song of the Old Mother (V)	April 1894
		To Some I Have Talked by the Fire (V)	May 1895
Arthur Symons	*Savoy* (1896)	The Binding of the Hair (S)	January 1896
		The Shadowy Horses (V)	" "
		The Travail of Passion (V)	" "
		Rosa Alchemica (S)	April 1896
		⟨The Cradle Song⟩ (V)	" "
		The Valley of the Black Pig (V)	" "
		⟨O'Sullivan Rua to Mary Lavelle⟩ (V)	July 1896
		⟨O'Sullivan Rua to the Secret Rose⟩ (V)	September 1896
		The Tables of Law (S)	November 1896
		⟨Windle-Straws⟩ (V)	" "
W. E. Henley (1895>)	*New Review* (1889–97)	⟨Wisdom⟩ (S)	September 1895
		⟨The Vision of O'Sullivan the Red⟩ (S)	April 1896
		⟨Everlasting Voices⟩	January 1896
		Death of O'Sullivan ... (S)	December 1896
		⟨O'Sullivan the Red Upon his Wan-derings⟩ (V)	August 1897
		⟨The Tribes of Danu⟩ (S)	November 1897
White, Ricketts, and Shannon	*Pageant* (1896–7)	Costello the Proud ... ⟨S⟩	1896 (annual)
E. J. Oldmeadow	*Dome* (1897–1900)	⟨The Desire of Man and of Woman⟩ (V)	June 1897
		⟨Aodh to Dectora⟩ (V)	May 1898
		⟨Song of Mongan⟩ (V)	October 1898
		⟨Aedh Pleads with the Elemental Powers⟩ (V)	December 1898
		A Symbolic Artist and the Coming of Symbolic Art (E)	December 1898
		The Theatre (E)	April 1899
		Dust hath Closed Helen's Eye (S)	October 1899
		The Irish Literary Theatre (E)	January 1900
		The Symbolism of Poetry (E)	April 1900
		The Philosophy of Shelley's Poetry (E)	July 1900
Frank Harris (1894–8)	*Saturday Review* (1855–1938)	⟨The Twilight of Forgiveness⟩ (V)	2 November 1895
		⟨The Valley of Lovers⟩ (V)	9 January 1897
		⟨Song⟩ (V)	24 July 1897
Henry Harland	*Yellow Book* (1894–7)	The Blessed (V)	April 1897

It has been estimated that between 1887 and 1900 Yeats placed more than 250 poems, articles, and reviews in dozens of journals.[63] Far from being a remote aesthete, Yeats was actively involved in the whole process of what today might be called 'networking'. In the 1890s he quickly acquired the basic skills needed to advance his career and become in the words of St John Ervine 'one of the best advertising agents in the world'.[64] From the viewpoint of the 1920s, Yeats fondly imagined that the 1890s was the 'tragic generation', but for the aspiring writer, oppressed by office work and the garret, this was arguably as good a decade as any since the mid-eighteenth century to be a would-be writer. According to *The Literary Year-Book and Bookman's Directory, 1900*, in the years 1893 to 1899 the number of books published on poetry and drama was: 197 in 1893, 160 in 1894, 231 in 1895, 284 in 1896, 298 in 1897, 290 in 1898, and 317 in 1899.[65]

The Nineties Poet as Lover

Surprisingly, it was in the impersonal columns of newspapers that Yeats expressed his most cherished feelings for women. 'An Epitaph' (later 'A Dream of Death') first appeared in the *National Observer* on 12 December 1891, and was occasioned by a remark Sarah Purser had made to Yeats: 'So Maud Gonne is dying in the South of France, and her portrait is on sale' (*Mem* 44). (As it happened, Maud Gonne was recovering from an illness.) The poem is squeezed in at the bottom of a page dominated by an article about 'The Currency Proposals':

ROSA MUNDI

WHO dreamed that beauty passes like a dream?
  For these red lips with all their mournful pride—
Mournful that no new wonder may betide—
Troy passed away in one high funeral gleam,
  And Usna's children died.

We and the labouring world are passing by:
  Amid men's souls that day by day give place,
  More fleeting than the sea's foam-fickle face,
Under the passing stars, foam of the sky,
  Lives on this lonely face.

Bow down, archangels, in your dim abode;
  Before ye were, or any hearts to beat,
  Weary and kind one stood beside His seat:
He made the worlds to be a grassy road
  Before her wandering feet.

W. B. YEATS.

AN EPITAPH

I DREAMED that one had died in a strange place
  Near no accustomed hand,
And they had nailed the boards above her face,
  The peasants of that land,

And wondering planted by her solitude
  A cypress and a yew.
I came and wrote upon a cross of wood—
  Man had no more to do—

'She was more beautiful than thy first love,
  This lady by the trees';
And gazed upon the mournful stars above,
  And heard the mournful breeze.

W. B. YEATS.

CORRESPONDENCE
RURAL DISCONTENT

[To the Editor of *The National Observer*]
London, *30th Dec.* 1891.

SIR,—Will you permit me to say that although Dr. Emerson's reply to my examination of his statements is exceedingly courteous, it does not in any way alter my opinion of them?

1. I am glad to know that he does not advocate 'wages "rigged" high' as a cure for rural immigration. All the same,

'*Rosa Mundi*' ('The Rose of the World' in *VP*), a poem that initiated a series of Rose poems, first appeared in the *National Observer* on 2 January 1892, above an item of correspondence on rural discontent. The image of Maud Gonne as a modern Helen of Troy was one Yeats frequently drew in his verse. 'The White Birds' was first published in the *National Observer* on 7 May 1892, just above an item from the correspondence column on 'Why Women May Not Vote', and stems from Maud Gonne's refusal of marriage. As they walked along some sea-cliffs, she idly remarked that if she were a bird she would like to be a seagull:

THE WHITE BIRDS

(The birds of fairyland are said to be white as snow.   The Danaan Islands are the islands of the fairies.)

O WOULD that we were, my beloved, white birds on the
    foam of the sea,
For we tire of the flame of the meteor before it can pass by and
    flee ;
And the flame of the blue star of twilight hung low on the rim
    of the sky
Has awaked in our hearts, my beloved, a sadness that never may
    die.

And a weariness comes from those dreamers dew-dabbled, the
    lily and rose ;
Ah ! dream not of them, my beloved, the flame of the meteor
    that goes,
Or the flame of the blue star that lingers hung low in the fall of
    the dew,
For I would we were changed to white birds on the wandering
    foam—I and you.

I am haunted by numberless islands and many a Danaan shore,
Where surely Time would forget us and Sorrow come near us
    no more :
Soon far from the rose and the lily and fret of the flames would
    we be,
Were we only white birds, my beloved, buoyed out on the foam
    of the sea.   W. B. YEATS.

CORRESPONDENCE

'WHY WOMEN MAY NOT VOTE'

[To the Editor of *The National Observer*]

Glasgow, 2nd May 1892.

SIR,—As a reader and admirer of your esteemed paper, I was much surprised that such an article as the one under the above heading should appear in a periodical of so much 'light and leading.' Not only does your contributor affect to regard

---

'The Rose in My Heart', which appeared in the *National Observer* on 12 November 1892, followed a report about bi-metallism and Lancashire operatives. The poem was later anthologised under the title 'The Lover Tells of the Rose in His Heart' in *The Wind among the Reeds*, Yeats's most complete symbolist volume of verse. Yeats imagines

119

himself as Aedh, one of the three figures, or personae, who dominate *The Wind among the Reeds*, the other two being Hanrahan and Michael Robartes. 'Hanrahan is the simplicity of an imagination too changeable to gather permanent possessions, or the adoration of the shepherds; and Michael Robartes is the pride of the imagination brooding upon the greatness of its possessions, or the adoration of the Magi; while Aedh is the myrrh and frankincense that the imagination offers continually before all that it loves' (*VP* 803). The reference in the poem to 'a green knoll apart' is to Yeats's plan to establish an Order of Celtic Mysteries with Maud Gonne:

> ### THE ROSE IN MY HEART
>
> ALL things uncomely and broken, all things worn out and
>   old,
>   The cry of a child by the roadway, the creak of a lumbering
>   cart,
> The heavy steps of the plowman splashing the winter mould,
>   Are wronging your image that blossoms a rose in the deeps
>   of my heart.
>
> The wrong of the things misshapen is wrong too great to be
>   told ;
>   I hunger to build them anew, and sit on a green knoll apart,
> With the earth and the sky and the water remade, like a casket
>   of gold
>   For my dreams of your image that blossoms a rose in the
>   deeps of my heart.
>
> *Sligo, November* 1892.   W. B. YEATS.

The other woman in Yeats's life and verse of the 1890s was Olivia Shakespear. In 'The Travail of Passion', which appeared in the first issue of the *Savoy* in January 1896, and which he composed in November 1895, Yeats addressed her as a member of a chorus of immortal passions where sexual consummation is associated with Christ's crucifixion:

> ### THE TRAVAIL OF PASSION
>
> WHEN the flaming, lute-thronged angelic door is wide;
>   When an immortal passion breathes in mortal clay,
> Our hearts endure the plaited thorn, the crowded way,
> The knotted scourge, the nail-pierced hands, the wounded side,
> The hissop-heavy sponge, the flowers by Kidron stream :
> We will bend down, and loosen our hair over you
> That it may drop faint perfume and be heavy with dew,
> Lilies of death-pale hope, roses of passionate dream.
>
>   W. B. YEATS.

According to John Harwood, *The Wind among the Reeds* is 'fully intelligible in biographical terms,' and the poems, taken chronologically, 'form a history of the paralysed inner self during the 1890s'.[66] Yeats's disguised candour in discussing his relations with Maud Gonne and Olivia Shakespear is especially apparent in 'Aedh to

120

Aodh to Dectora

Three Songs

1

I wander by the edge
  Of this desolate lake,
  Where wind cries in the sedge,
  Until the axle break
That keeps the stars in their round,
And hands hurl in the deep
The banners of East and West,
And the girdle of light is unbound,
Your breast will not lie on the breast
Of your beloved in sleep.

2

Pale brow, still hands, and dim hair,
I had a beautiful friend,
And dreamed that the old despair
Might fade in love in the end:
She looked in my heart one day,
And saw your image was there,
She has gone weeping away.

3

Half close your eyelids, loosen your hair,
And dream about the great and their pride,
They have spoken against you everywhere,
But weigh this song with the great and their pride;
I made it out of a mouthful of air;
Their children's children shall say they have lied.

W. B. Yeats.

Dectora', a sequence of poems published in the *Dome* in May 1898. When he came to arrange the order of *The Wind among the Reeds*, Yeats, as if to obscure a biographical reading, retitled the sequence and split it into three separate poems: 'He Hears the Cry of the Sedge', 'The Lover Mourns for the Loss of Love', and 'He Thinks of Those Who Have Spoken Evil of His Beloved'. The first poem evokes Yeats's despair at being for ever excluded from his lover's breast. The second, where the biographical pressure is keenest, concerns Olivia Shakespear's awareness in spring 1897, after their having been together for twelve months, that Yeats's real love was still Maud Gonne. '"There is someone else in your heart," she said' (*Mem* 89). The third poem is a defence of Maud Gonne against those 'who have spoken against you'.

121

Right: Loie Fuller Skirt Dancing at the Folies-Bergère. From *Picture Magazine* in January–June 1893. Yeats remembered her in 'Nineteen Hundred and Nineteen': 'When Loie Fuller's Chinese dancers enwound/A shining web, a floating ribbon of cloth,/ It seemed that a dragon of air/Had fallen among the dancers, had whirled them round/Or hurried them off on its own furious pace' (*VP* 430).

THE CELT IN LONDON

The Irish Literary Society

In the 1880s Yeats looked to Irish outlets for his poems, but from 1887 until the establishment of the Dun Emer Press in 1903, as the following table underlines, he used London journals to further his career as a writer. Nationalists might have regretted that an Irish poet should surround himself with coterie life in London, but Yeats had an answer: '⟨T⟩he poetry of coteries did not differ in kind from the true folk poetry. Both presupposed a tradition, as so called popular poetry, the verses of the rhetoricians, did not.'[67]

List of Yeats's London Publishers in the 1890s

Kegan Paul, Trench, 20 and 22 Charing Cross Road, W.C.	*The Wanderings of Oisin* (1889)
T. Fisher Unwin, 11 Paternoster Buildings, E.C.	*John Sherman and Dhoya* (1891)
	The Countess Kathleen (1892)

Lawrence & Bullen, 16 Henrietta Street,
Covent Garden, W.C.
Elkin Mathews, Vigo Street, W.
Hodder & Stoughton, 27 Paternoster Row

The Land of Heart's Desire (1894)
Poems (1895)
The Celtic Twilight (1893)
The Secret Rose (1897)
The Wind among the Reeds (1899)
The Shadowy Waters (1900)

In his early study of the Irish Literary Revival, W. P. Ryan remarked: 'In the early eighties, Irish literature was an uncertain or a local quality.'[68] By 1900, London had helped to change all this. According to Ryan, the Irish literary movement began not in Ireland but in Southwark.[69] The Southwark Irish Literary Club held its meetings in the Bath Street Hall, London Road. Its founding President, and a key player in Irish circles in the early 1880s, was Francis Fahy. Yeats went along to his first meeting in March 1888, and on 13 June delivered his first lecture, 'Folk Lore of the West of Ireland'; the following May he lectured on Mangan. In early 1891, at a time when Yeats clashed with Duffy, the Club reorganised itself under the name the Irish Literary Society, London, and moved to Clapham. By that stage, as Ryan reminds us, Yeats was already a force to be reckoned with:

Mr Yeats, who was as much drawn to the Southwark circle as if it were a novel race of *sheogues*, discussed various questions connected with the Irish Literary Society with Mr D. J. O'Donoghue in the congenial shadow of the British Museum. Mr Yeats was decidedly of the opinion that the work might be attempted on a more ambitious scale. He offered to induce Mr T. W. Rolleston and others to throw themselves into the Irish literary movement, and to summon a meeting of sympathisers and willing workers for an early date. The proposal was cordially approved of, and the meeting awaited with interest. It came off at Mr Yeats's house in Chiswick on the 28th of December, 1891.[70]

In March 1893 the inaugural lecture of the Irish Literary Society was delivered by Stopford Brooke at Bloomsbury Mansion on 'The Need and Use of Getting Irish Literature into the English Tongue':

Poetry has always wanted, along with the present, an imaginative world in the past into which to dip for subjects; and we have here in English poetry pretty well exhausted the old realms of human story. The tale of Arthur will have to lie fallow for a time. We have had enough of the Greek stories of late; enough of Italian Mediaevalism. . . . But the Irish stories are as yet untouched; and they have imagination, colour, romance of war and love, terrible and graceful supernaturalism, a passionate humanity, and a vivid love of natural beauty and sublimity.[71]

Brooke's lecture articulates a reading of the Revival different from later versions. Through its language and culture, Ireland could throw off its backward image and become at once an adjunct to the Muse and a revitaliser of the whole of English literature. Indeed, before the Literary Revival came into existence there was a Language Revival. In 1893, the Gaelic League was established; in 1901, Fahy, now President of the Gaelic League of London, took the argument further in a lecture on 'The Irish Language Movement' to the Irish Literary Society: 'No literature can be truly Irish that is not in the Irish language; this alone can treat of any subject, and in any style, mode, or manner, and be by any writer, it will still be, and it only, Irish literature.'[72]

123

· W · B · YEATS ·

Robert Bryden's woodcut of Yeats, who was, according to William Archer, 'the incarnation of the Irish Kelt'. From *Poets of the Younger Generation* (1902).

The Society thrived; in 1894 it attracted four hundred members, in 1898 five hundred. It was strictly non-political, non-sectarian, and, with its club-like atmosphere, catered for a middle- and lower-middle-class clientele: 'The Society has comfortable rooms (reading, writing and smoking), at 8, Adelphi Terrace, Strand, W.C., a central and quiet situation overlooking the Embankment Gardens and the river, and within a few minutes' walk of Charing Cross and Waterloo Stations.' Several of the 'House Dinners' (price 2s. 6d.) were held at St James's Restaurant, organised by gentlemen members of the Society. 'At Homes' were given by lady members.[73] '*Objects*: to afford a centre of social and literary intercourse for persons of Irish nationality, and to promote the study of the Irish language, Irish history, literature, music, and art. *Membership*: Members (town and country) of Irish nationality; Associates and Honorary Members of other nationality. *Lectures*: monthly. *Honorary Secretary*: A. P. Graves.' In *The Literary Year Book, 1897* there is a list of British or Irish authors who gave their address as the Irish Literary Society:

Ashe-King, R.	Hoey, Mrs Cashel.
Brooke, Rev. Stopford.	Hull, Miss Eleanor.
Bryant, Mrs Sophie.	Hull, Professor.
Connell, F. Norreys.	Hyde, Douglas.
Crook, W. M.	Keeling, Miss E. D'Esterre.
Duffy, Sir Charles Gavan.	Lynch, Miss Hannah.
Eccles, Miss O'Connor.	McCarthy, Justin.
Fahy, F. A.	O'Donoghue, D. J.
Ferguson, Lady.	O'Grady, Standish.
Frederick, Harold.	O'Grady, Standish Hayes.
Greene, George A.	O'Leary, John.
Harmsworth, Alfred.	Powell, York.
Hart, Mrs Ernest.	Rolleston, T. W.
Hickey, Miss Emily P.	

When Yeats joined the Irish Literary Society of London he was an outsider often exposed to ridicule. In the first issue of the *Irish Literary Society Gazette* in November 1898, in a section entitled 'About Our Members', the ineffectual Yeats is contemptuously dismissed in a single remark: 'Mr W. B. Yeats is engaged on the preparation of an exhaustive study of the fairy beliefs of the Irish peasantry.'[74] Another caustic remark followed in the January 1899 issue: 'Mr W. B. Yeats' forthcoming volume of poems is to bear the title of *The Wind Among the Reeds*. This (says *The Academy*) is running Mrs. Hinkson's recent poetry book, *The Wind Among the Trees*, rather close.'[75] At Fahy's lecture on 'The Jacobite Songs of Ireland' in February 1899, Yeats's contribution from the floor received a mixed reception. Yeats remarked that

During a recent visit to north-east Galway – the lecturer's native place – he had heard a good deal about Mr Fahy and his songs. Dr. Douglas Hyde, who was with him, found it easier to get particulars about Mr. Fahy, the poet who had gone to London, than about Rafferty, a Gaelic song-writer who lived at the opening of the century, of whom he wanted information. (Laughter.) He did not at all agree with Miss D'Esterre Keeling's opinion of Davis's 'Battle of Fontenoy'. It was a clever imitation of Macaulay, and was very useful in its way; but after all it was mere journalistic and rhetorical poetry. (Laughter and cries of 'No.')

THE CHAIRMAN, in putting the vote of thanks to the meeting, said he was ready to join issue with Mr. Yeats in regard to the ballads of Thomas Davis. (Applause.)

MR. YEATS, interposing, said he had a great admiration for a certain amount of Davis's poetry, but not all.

THE CHAIRMAN said it was the first time that Mr. Yeats had expressed these opinions at the lectures of the society. It was, no doubt, true that Davis hastily wrote many of his ballads for the Dublin journals. He had not had, perhaps, the leisure which Mr. Yeats enjoyed to polish his golden numbers. (Hear, hear.) But few could read these ballads without being deeply stirred – (hear, hear) – and he was perfectly certain that if 'The Ballad of Fontenoy' had been recited it would have evoked as much enthusiasm as any of the songs that were sung that night. (Applause.) Mr. Yeats was extremely eclectic in his views about Irish poetry; – (laughter) – and perhaps they ought to be thankful in having a man of so fine a discrimination and delicate a taste as to be able to see, and the great courage to proclaim it to an Irish audience, that Davis's splendid ballad 'The Battle of Fontenoy', was a piece of mere journalism. (Laughter and applause.)[76]

Yeats's remarks were more graciously received on 11 March when Michael MacDonagh lectured on 'In an Irish Cabin'. A disagreement was registered between Yeats's father and Graves over the Irish peasantry. Yeats senior characterised them as 'harsh, violent, aggressive and revengeful . . . and not . . . childlike, irresponsible, or loving, as they were commonly described by the English'. Graves thought this might apply to the peasantry of Ulster but not to the Kingdom of Kerry. The real issue raised by the lecture for Graves was how to 'get at the Irish people with Irish literature'. W. B. Yeats, no doubt remembering the February lecture, took up the challenge:

MR. W. B. YEATS said his father was not speaking about Ulster . . . but of Tipperary, Queen's County and Sligo – in fact, rebel Ireland; and with that view of the Irish character he substantially agreed. . . . He was not quite sure that he was as anxious as Mr. Graves to make the peasantry read. What he was anxious to do was to make the upper classes read. (Laughter and hear, hear.) As a critic recently said: 'They chiefly put their trust in horses.' (Laughter.) If the Irish educated classes could be induced to study Irish books, Irish interests, Irish economics, the influence would spread down through the social scale to the peasantry. (Hear, hear.)[77]

Yeats was asked to give the April lecture, and he spoke on 'Ideal Theatre', with Gosse in the chair. He began by reminding his audience of the plays to be staged in the Antient Concert Rooms in Dublin in May, and continued by declaring the theatre of Scandinavia to be 'the nearest approach to an ideal theatre in modern Europe. . . . He knew well that neither Mr. Martyn nor himself could claim to be Ibsens or Bjornsons, but they might follow in the way those great men had gone, and in all humility.'[78] His audience was sceptical. Mr Norreys Connell thought Yeats's idea of the theatre could never successfully appeal to the people for support, and as a modern imitation of the old theatre he thought that seemed impossible. Mr Clement Shorter sympathised with Yeats but was against the idea of a limited audience. Mr Gosse thought there was an element of the fairy tale in Yeats's 'picturesque and charming account of the birth of Norwegian Theatre. (Laughter.)'

On 29 March 1899 Yeats was co-opted on to the Committee of the Society; in the first year he attended four Committee Meetings, in the second ten. Yeats's sister Lollie was

Yeats's note, dictated to Lady Gregory and signed by himself, formed the preface to *The Tables of the Law and The Adoration of the Magi*, published by Elkin Mathews in 1904. Ellmann claims Joyce was the young man in question.

also on the Committee and attended regularly. By December 1900 Lady Gregory, Hyde, O'Grady are listed as Vice Presidents of the Society, but Yeats's name appears merely as a Committee member. In the 'Souvenir Programme of the Coming of Age of the Irish Literary Society of London 1892–1913', Eleanor Hull recalls: 'It is pleasant to reflect that the success attained by the ILS of London since its first beginnings on a stormy December night of 1891, in Mr W. B. Yeats' home in Bedford Park, has been due to its fidelity to an ideal.' By 1913 everyone wanted to be associated with Yeats.

18 Woburn Buildings

From 1896 to 1918 Yeats lived at 18 Woburn Buildings at the back of St Pancras Church, next door to a lapidary's shop. A workman occupied the first floor, a shoemaker the ground floor, a pedlar the attic, and he himself, 'the toff what lives in the Buildings',[79] as he was affectionately known to his neighbours, occupied the two rooms on the second floor. On Monday evenings he kept open house:

> On a good evening the sitting-room would be full, with perhaps a dozen men and women. All manner of things were discussed; some of the cleverest read their new poems, or favourite poems; new methods of speaking verse were practised; occultists told of strange

Sketch of 18 Woburn Buildings by R. Schurabe.
Yeats moved here in February 1896 and began his
year-long affair with Olivia Shakespear.

things done by magicians in simpler lands than this, or here, in simpler times; then, there
were the new books; new plays; new paintings to talk of; or some gathered exhibition of
paintings that then meant most to us. When these were our subject, we were happy. We
were, in the main, the last of the Pre-Raphaelite followers.[80]

The windows were permanently closed, and he suffered from bedbugs, but his living-
room, complete with a blue wooden lectern bearing a copy of the Kelmscott Press
Chaucer, a leather armchair given him by Lady Gregory, the bed bought in the company
of Olivia Shakespear from a shop in Tottenham Court Road, and dark-brown wall-
paper, was visually exciting, full of striking 'real works of art on the wall', some of
which are reproduced in this book:

'Memory Harbour' by Jack Yeats.
John Butler Yeats's sketch of Yeats.
John Butler Yeats's illustration of Blake's ballad 'I thought love lived in the hot sunshine'.
A print of Blake's 'The Whirlwind of Lovers'.
An engraving of Blake's head.
A print of Blake's 'Ancient of Days'.
An engraving from Blake's *Job*.
His own pastels of the lake and hills near Coole.

128

This photo of Yeats appeared in the *Tatler* in June 1904.

Elliott and Fry's photograph of John Masefield. From the *Bookman*, April 1909.

Pencil drawing by Cecil French of a woman holding a rose between her lips.
Beardsley's poster for *The Land of Heart's Desire*.
Blake's seventh Dante engraving.[81]

For an artist like Robert Gregory, who stayed in the rooms in 1903 and 1904 when Yeats was on tour in America, they were not ideal, being dark, 'ninetyish', and without electric light.[82] But Masefield was captivated by his master's Monday evenings:

> The writers and the painters and the speakers,
> The occultists, the visionary women,
> Astrologers with Saturn on their moons,
> And contemplative men who lived on herbs
> And uttered gentleness and sanctity,
> The poets of the half-a-dozen schools,
> Young men in cloaks, velvet, or evening dress;
> Publishers, publicists and journalists,
> Parliament men, who served the Irish cause,
> And every Irish writer, painter and thinker.[83]

Maud Gonne also recalled with affection the 'strange talks that room had listened to':

Men of the IRB had met there. William Sharpe had told us of his spirit love, Fiona Macleod. MacGregor had talked of his Rosicrucian mysteries. Sarojini Naidu, the beautiful Hindu Nationalist, 'the little Indian princess', as Willie called her, had read her poems there. The American poetess, Agnes Tobin, had spoken of her determination to save Arthur Symons and had by her strong magnetism brought him back to life from an asylum, only to find the walls of another asylum close on herself. Lionel Johnson had recited his poems and talked of Ireland there and Mrs Emery had chanted her strange chants to a musical instrument invented by Dr Elgar.[84]

* * *

Curiously, the 1890s seemed, even at the time, to possess a retrospective aspect. Had he indulged his backward look in 1900, Yeats might have wondered if he had not lived through a whole period and not just a decade of literature. Equally, so many and varied had been his contacts in literary and artistic circles that he must have genuinely wondered how he could recover a sense of himself from all this heterogeneous activity. The temptation must have been to continue playing the London Celt, a role that carried both status and approbation among his English friends. But, as Masefield reminds us, Yeats in 1900 was moving away from what remained of the English groups in which he had figured, joining other groups in Ireland:

In 1900, Yeats was passing from his first manner, that was at its best in romantic narrative, and from his first maturity, that was at its best in romantic lyric, to new ways and methods. The Irish Literary Movement, which owed most of its life to him, was beginning to turn to the theatre and some of its attendant arts. It was also drawing him from what remained of the English groups in which he had figured, to other groups in Ireland. . . . His mind at the time was full of the interests and enthusiasms that had moved England in the nineties, when London had been the intellectual capital of the world, and of those hopes that had made all Ireland mentally alive in her remotest glens. He was the man then best informed about these two streams of inspiration, and certainly the voice best able to talk about them.[85]

'The Abbey Theatre': embroidery by Lily Yeats.

5

Yeats and the Abbey Theatre

IN THE MAKING

A Theatre of Art in Ireland

In 1889, J. T. Grein, the Dutch founder of the Independent Theatre, posed the question: 'Is a British *Théâtre Libre* – a theatre free from the shackles of the censor, free from the fetters of convention, unhampered by financial consideration – is not such a theatre possible?'[1] When the British Association visited Dublin in September 1908, four years after the official opening of the Abbey Theatre, Yeats supplied an answer:

> We are the first subsidised theatre in any English-speaking country, the only theatre that is free for a certain number of years to play what it thinks worth playing, and to whistle at the timid. . . . Our Patent . . . confines us to plays by Irishmen and upon Irish subjects or to foreign masterpieces (and among those we may not include anything English). This limitation was put in at the request of the other theatres that we might not be their rival, the counsel for one of them being particularly anxious to keep us from playing Goldsmith and Sheridan, who were, he believed, English. . . . We are trying to put upon the stage . . . the life of this country, not a slavish copy of it as in a photograph, but a joyous, extravagant, imaginative image as in an impressionist painting.[2]

The Irish Literary Theatre began life in July 1897 at the home of Count Florimond de Basterot in Duras, County Galway, when Yeats, Lady Gregory, O'Grady, Martyn, and 'Fiona Macleod' made a proposal which simultaneously sought funds and a place for culture above politics:

> We propose to have performed in Dublin in the spring of every year certain Celtic and Irish plays. . . . We hope to find in Ireland an uncorrupted and imaginative audience trained to listen by its passion for oratory, and believe that our desire to bring upon the stage the deeper thoughts and emotions of Ireland will ensure for us a tolerant welcome, and that freedom to experiment which is not found in theatres of England, and without which no new movement in art or literature can succeed. We will show that Ireland is not the home of buffoonery and of easy sentiment, as it has been represented, but the home of an ancient idealism. We are confident of the support of all Irish people, who are weary of misrepresentation, in carrying out a work that is outside all the political questions that divide us.[3]

In April 1899, the month before the first performance of Yeats's *Countess Cathleen* and Martyn's *Heather Field* at the Antient Concert Rooms in Dublin, Yeats spoke to the Irish Literary Society in London about his 'Ideal Theatre':

The theatre of Scandinavia was the nearest approach to an ideal theatre in modern Europe. It was the only theatre whose plays were at once literary and popular. . . . Between 1840 and 1860 there arose a national literary movement in Norway founded like ours upon the old legends and the folk songs and the folk traditions of the country. Like ours, too, it had to conquer the opposition of a cosmopolitan and denationalised class. . . . Heroic ideas and interest in great passions spread abroad among the mass of the people, and the only condition of the drama was at once literary and popular. The ordinary man disliked to take trouble, disliked having to think and feel in new ways. . . . But let a whole people be touched by an intensity, and they would share in the creative impulse of the poets, and every kind of great drama would spring up. Civilisation unchecked by this rare and exceptional enthusiasm killed great drama by teaching people to live upon the surface, to seek easy pleasures, and to meditate little. The actor who spoke his lines like something out of the newspaper drove out that art of oratory which the stage inherited from the rhapsodists. If we were to restore drama to the stage – poetic drama, at any rate – our actors must become rhapsodists again, and keep the rhythm of the verse as the first of their endeavours. The music of a voice should seem more important than the expression of face or the movement of hands. . . . They would, therefore, do their part, according to their limited power, in building up in Ireland a dramatic tradition that would remember the purpose of drama in the world, and they threw themselves upon the national literary movement that they might have an audience. (Applause.)[4]

A materialistic England was the spur for Yeats's ambition in the theatre. 'Ireland is virgin soil, yielding endless inspiration to the artist; and her people, uncontaminated by false ideals, are ready to receive the new art.'[5] In August 1909, with hindsight, Yeats was even more convinced that 'the national characteristics differ in nothing more profoundly than in the attitude towards the stage. The English audience is made up of well-to-do people, who do not want to be disturbed in their composure. They resent any unexpected claim upon their intellects. They listen badly. They do not take the trouble to relate passages to their context – in other words, they resent being expected to understand. An Irish audience, on the other hand, resents not understanding.'[6]

The opposition was of course an exaggeration, for English audiences were especially interested in the new Irish drama. On 15 April 1910, for example, the *Leeds Mercury* noted: 'Ireland is a sealed book to most of us on this side of St George's Channel, and hence we may well seek to welcome the Abbey Theatre Company from Dublin, whose members last evening opened a three days' sojourn before a large gathering in the Albert Hall.' The *Yorkshire Evening News* on the same day enthused: 'Mr Yeats's symbolistic embodiment of Irish nationhood in "Kathleen ni Houlihan" held the audience till you could hear the clock tick in front of the gallery.' Many liked what they were hearing and were appreciative of Yeats's pro-Irish stance. According to Augustine Birrell, Chief Secretary to Ireland from 1907 to 1916, the Revival changed the image of Ireland at Westminster: 'The intelligence of England . . . at last took cognisance of the change, and the Sister Island began no longer to be regarded as a dreary, dingy, disreputable politico-religious problem but a land with a literary and poetical tradition of her own, a "point of view" all her own, and a genius of expression not confined to stale jokes and specimens of "so-called" Irish humour invented to gratify the crude tastes of the English traveller.'[7] Even the *Daily Telegraph*, noting the 1911 visit of the Irish Players to the

Three studio photographs of Yeats taken by Alice Boughton in 1904 convey three different moods.

Yeats's notes for a lecture which he wrote on the inside cover of Lady Gregory's *Poets and Dreamers* (1903). He begins 'I do not underrate new or overrate Ireland' and ends with 'Tradition to help us'. In between come familiar references to 'cultured populace', the spoken not written, printed work as aristocratic, 'The Tramp', and the applied arts of literature and design.

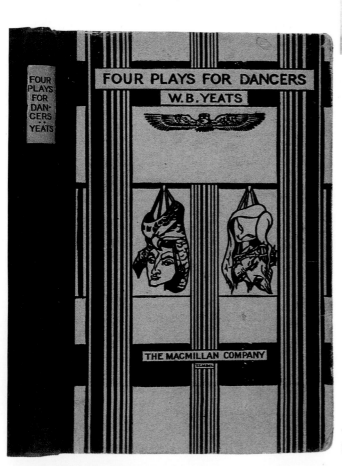

Yeats's *Four Plays for Dancers* (1921). Cover design by Sturge Moore.

Royal Court Theatre, could discern the Revival's importance: 'They have given us a real Ireland instead of a farce posing for a nation, real people instead of a series of incarnations of practical jokes.'[8] It was a time for accommodating difference, as a report in the *Saturday Review* on 18 June 1910 suggests: 'A visit to the Court Theatre would convince anyone that Ireland is a foreign country. An English audience at "The Playboy of the Western World" feels in the presence of a national spirit more conclusively alien to its own than while watching, for instance, the frantic agitations of the Sicilian players.' And as Masefield recognised, Irish exoticism could also fertilise English culture: 'Listening to Synge's plays . . . made me feel what a wealth of fable lay still in the lonely places in England.'[9]

Like Moore, Yeats detected that at the turn of the century 'something was going on in Ireland for sure'.[10] It was Ireland's turn for the spotlight in the history of civilisation, and artists had the responsibility to become 'Artificers of the Great Moment' (*E & I* 260). But Yeats underestimated the gathering strength of Catholic nationalism. The 'de-anglicising' project begun in 1893 also made room for a language of separatism that threatened Yeats's position. Hyde was constantly made aware of the shifting ground of Irish politics, even within the ranks of the Gaelic League. In 1905, for example, Protestants in the Gaelic League complained about bias in the organisation, 'evident, they said, in attitudes toward the Craobh na gCuig Cuigi, or "branch of the five provinces", which some leaguers had dubbed the "branch of the five Protestants", since it was this branch that most Protestants joined.'[11] Synge, too, was disturbed by the direction Irish politics might take. In a letter to Lady Gregory on 11 September 1904, he criticised Frank Fay for having Brian Boru on the brain: 'I do not know whether all this is his own feeling only . . . or whether there is a Neo-patriotic-Catholic clique growing which might be serious. Colum finds my play ⟨The Well of the Saints⟩ unsatisfactory because the Saint is really a Protestant!'[12]

Yeats blamed the lower middle class, the 'new class which had begun to rise into power under the shadow of Parnell' (*E & I* 259), but enemies were there for the making. Martyn, a devout Catholic landowner, emptied the idealism out of Yeats's vocabulary: 'The best thing that could happen to the intellect of Ireland would be if England were blotted out of Ireland's sphere. . . . No two countries, as no two languages, blend worse together than these. . . . Our foreign influences should come from the Continent, not from England. They come more naturally from the Continent; for Dublin has more of the character of a Continental than an English city.'[13] Martyn was joined by F. Hugh O'Donnell in deriding *The Countess Cathleen*:

Mr W. B. Yeats's notion of what is Celtic is everywhere illustrated by his harpings on his pet 'Celtic idea,' that the Gaels of Erin have and had only the thinnest veneer of Christian religion and civilisation, and really reserve their deepest beliefs for demons, fairies, leprechauns, sowlths, thivishes, etc., whom he loves to describe in the stilted occultism of a Mrs Besant or a Madame Blavatsky, and that 'Catholic shrines,' and 'Catholic priests' and Catholic prayers and places are little more than sport for the pranks of the devil's own.[14]

Yeats was not to be deflected. He anticipated it would take 'a generation, and perhaps generations, to restore the theatre of art' (*E & I* 170).[15] The Abbey Theatre was conceived by him along the lines of an arts theatre, perhaps not unlike the clubhouse theatre in Bedford Park, or Antoine's *Théâtre Libre* in Paris, or Grein's Independent Theatre, or the Avenue Theatre in 1894.[16] It was to be 'the theatre of art', not for the ordinary person but 'for ourselves and our friends, and for a few simple people who understand from sheer simplicity what we understand from scholarship and thought' (*E & I* 166). Yeats was so passionate about this that at the Calaroga Club Rooms in Dublin in February 1905 he was forced to modify his 1890s' ambitions: 'Mr Yeats, who was received with applause, replied in some detail to the criticisms that were made ⟨by the speaker Mr Bacon⟩. He said that the phrase "Art for Art's Sake", which was one of the mottoes of the Irish National Theatre Society, had been widely misunderstood. He was not opposed to propagandist plays, as some seemed to think. But he believed that unless the ideal of true art, the sincere expression of emotions, was kept steadily in view, they could not have a drama that would live and take its place among the things that were immortal.'[17] Horniman had no such inhibitions, and would have committed no money to the Abbey Theatre in 1904 if she thought it was for anything but a theatre of Art. On 18 August 1918 there appeared a review of Boyd's *Irish Literary Theatre* in the *Observer*, and one sentence in particular caught her eye: 'The Irish theatre, says Mr Boyd, was intended only for the encouragement of Irish authors.' 'Nonsense,' she inserted in her copy, 'I made it for Art.'[18]

Yeats looked to the European theatre for models, and especially to Ibsen. Curiously, although he had limited enthusiasm for Ibsen's drawing-room dramas (though more than often supposed), in *Where There Is Nothing* (1902) he came close to writing an Ibsenesque play. This play's theme is familiar 1890s Yeats – the visionary who becomes the outcast from society because of his vision – but this theme is now given a stronger social framework. In this respect, Paul Ruttledge is not unlike Brand in the play of that name or Dr Stockmann in *An Enemy of the People*. Ruttledge's hostility to bourgeois society leads him to conclude that people have become like farmyard creatures: '⟨T⟩hey have forgotten their freedom, their human bodies are a disguise, a pretence to keep up to deceive one another' (*VPl* 1069). He joins a group of 'tinkers' and searches for a 'wild beast . . . that can root up spires and towers' (*VPl* 1098–9). Paul's journey, however, unlike Dr Stockmann's, is towards the discovery that 'The Christian's business is not reformation but revelation, and the only labours he can put his hand to can never be accomplished in Time. He must so live that all things shall pass away' (*VPl* 1139).

Perhaps not surprisingly, as Joseph Holloway recorded in his diary, the audience for *The Unicorn from the Stars* (1908), the sequel to *Where There Is Nothing*, found it tough going: ' "Where there is nothing, there is God" – that's the sum total of the knowledge picked up by "Martin Hearne" in his adventures in the Land of Trance in W. B. Yeats's and Lady Gregory's strange and dramatically ineffective three-act play *The Unicorn from the Stars*, produced at the Abbey tonight. . . . It is a mystical and unsatisfying piece . . . presented before a thin house (mostly of friends of the dramatists), and greeted with laughter in the wrong places.'[19]

The European theatre helped Yeats recognise what he did not want: 'English provincialism shouts through the lips of Irish patriots who have no knowledge of other countries to give them a standard of comparison' (*Ex* 232). In Paris he had been duly impressed with *Ubu Roi*, where the actors' faces were hidden by cardboard masks, the scenery was painted to represent indoors and outdoors simultaneously, with a bed, bare tree, and falling snow, and where a placard announced scene changes. According to Symons (who anticipated Yeats's response), Jarry's Symbolist farce is 'the gesticulation of a young savage . . . the brutality out of which we have achieved civilization, and those painted, massacring puppets the destroying elements which are as old as the world.'[20] In June 1902, Yeats attended an unlicensed performance of Maeterlinck's *Monna Vanna* at the Victoria Hall in London, anxious to see not so much the play as 'the method of

Beltaine: Lady Gregory's copy with original sketches by George Russell and Jack B. Yeats.

performance' (*L [K]* 3, 200). He was especially interested in techniques of stage presentation, and in February 1910 during rehearsals for Goldoni's *Mirandolina* Yeats saw for the first time how Gordon Craig's 'screens' – a series of monochromatic folding screens for producing scenic effects – might work in practice.[21] The following January, a set of Craig's screens was first used at the Abbey for a performance of *The Hour-Glass*, an event promoted by Yeats in the Dublin *Evening Telegraph*: 'The primary value of Mr Craig's invention is that it enables one to use light in a more natural and beautiful way than ever before. . . . It is now possible to substitute in the shading of one scene real light and shadow for painted light and shadow' (*UP* 2, 394).

Yeats was a poet before he was a dramatist: 'Like every other poet, I spoke verses in a kind of chant when I was making them, and sometimes, when I was alone on a country road, I would speak them in a loud chanting voice, and feel that if I dared I would speak them in that way to other people' (*E & I* 14). Arnold Dolmetsch, a musician who had settled in London from Europe, made Yeats and Farr 'a beautiful instrument, half psaltery, half lyre, which contains, I understand, all the chromatic intervals within the range of the speaking voice' (*E & I* 16).[22] The tone-deaf Yeats put it to immediate dramatic use, but only Sara Allgood and Farr managed to achieve in the combination of speech and music the effect that Yeats sought.

Contemporary black-and-white photographs give little idea of the lavishness of Yeats's early theatre productions. His theatre of beauty was especially apparent in the

139

colour and design of costumes. In its fashion-like report of *The King's Threshold*, which opened on 8 October 1903 at the Molesworth Hall, the *Freeman's Journal* devoted considerable space to the costumes. The red, green, and purple colours of the court; pale mauve and shot-grey silks for the courtly ladies; the King dressed in a robe of fine brocade in different hues of purple, toning from deepest wine colour to palest silver and with a crown of silver studded with gems; the poet in grey, with a beautifully wrought device of a harp in gold and jewels. As for its meaning: 'One can see in the delicate irony that plays through the poem, that a modern application of the old story has not been far from the poet's thought and that Seanchan, like Cathleen na ⟨sic⟩ Houlihan, stands for a symbol of Ireland unreconciled; but the satire is not insisted upon, only one catches glimpses of it here and there.'[23] In an interview in the *Cambridge Daily News* on 25 November 1905, Yeats illustrated his theory about set designs by reference to Lady Gregory's *Spreading the News*, then being staged at the Victoria Assembly Rooms: 'Mr Yeats pointed to the back curtain that was used last night in Lady Gregory's play, in which the scene was laid "Near a Fair". It was of green and black, with a recurring pattern of a conventional tree. This, he claimed, suggested the open air, without detracting attention from the actors, or attempting to produce an impossible illusion. As far as possible, Mr Yeats explained, they dressed their plays so as to form a consistent colour scheme.'

Cathleen ni Houlihan

It is ironic that someone whose dramatic imagination eschewed direct channels to a modern audience, and who preferred instead to communicate by means that were allusive and indirect, could almost single-handedly establish a national theatre.[24] Shakespeare's Hamlet and Shelley's Alastor are the figures of solitude who haunt Yeats's dramatic imagination. He admired what he took to be Shakespeare's sympathic view of Richard II: '⟨T⟩he defeat that awaits us all, whether they be artist or saint, who find in themselves where men ask of them a rough energy and have nothing to give but some contemplative virtue, whether lyrical fantasy, or sweetness of temper, or dreamy dignity, or love of God, or love of His creatures' (*E & I* 106). Withdrawal from the world is a constant theme of his early plays, yet he sought through the theatre an engagement with an audience. In *The Island of Statues*, his earliest foray into writing plays, enchantment on the island can be purchased only at the cost of transformation into a moon-white stone. In his dramatic poem *The Wanderings of Oisin*, Oisin, after spending three hundred years in the Land of Youth, never manages to negotiate a successful return to Ireland. *The Land of Heart's Desire*, with its Sligo setting and intercourse with the faeries, resembles a story from *The Celtic Twilight*. Its Blakean epigraph – 'O Rose, thou art sick' – reminds us of a social critique that somehow got lost in Yeats's imagination.[25] Mary is caught between two worlds, that of religious orthodoxy and faery land. In *The Countess Cathleen*, the Countess, weighed down with care for her subjects, finds even the path to heaven obstructed.

After the fall of Parnell, Yeats sought a space for culture and for his own dramatic imagination independent of politics. The controversy over *The Countess Cathleen* revealed that his Dublin audiences were highly politicised and ready to convert a play based on a fairly remote theme into their own immediate terms. In 1901, Frank Fay, writing as drama critic for the *United Irishman*, saw what was needed: 'Let Mr Yeats give us a play in verse or prose that will rouse this sleeping land.'[26] In April 1902, with

'Cathleen ni Houlihan' by Sir John Lavery. A watermark and a copy of this painting used to grace Irish banknotes. Lavery's model was his wife, the Chicago-born Hazel Lavery, whose services to Ireland especially during the Treaty negotiations in London did not go unnoticed.

The tall figure of Maud Gonne entering as the Old Woman in Yeats's play. When Bridget asks her what put her to wandering, the disguised Cathleen ni Houlihan replies: 'Too many strangers in the house' (*VPl* 222).

the production of *Cathleen ni Houlihan* by Willie Fay's Irish National Dramatic Society at St Theresa's Hall, Clarendon Street, Yeats did precisely that.[27] The events of 1798, the frequent subject of *Nation* ballads, were fresh in people's minds on account of the 1798 Centennial celebrations. The atmosphere was highly charged, especially as the leading role was played by Maud Gonne, a member of a women's republican group Inghinidhe na hEireann (Daughters of Erin), and herself the inspiration of the whole revolutionary movement.[28] One reviewer thought Maud Gonne was addressing the actors as a well-known nationalist agitator, 'speaking to them just as she might in Beresford Place or Phoenix Park, the only difference was that the words were not her own'.[29]

If *The Land of Heart's Desire* was 'the call of the heart', *Cathleen ni Houlihan* represented 'the call of country'.[30] '⟨M⟩y subject is Ireland and its struggle for independence,' Yeats confidently asserted in the *United Irishman* on 5 May 1902. More generally, what Yeats sought was to 'bring the imagination and speech of the country . . . to the people of the town' (*A* 570); what he effected was something quite different. For with its emphasis on blood sacrifice, *Cathleen ni Houlihan* sent shock waves through Ireland. Stephen Gwynn* wondered if it was right to perform such plays 'unless one was prepared for people to go out to shoot and be shot'.[31] In a letter to Yeats in May 1916, it seemed natural for Maud Gonne to link the beautiful deaths of the leaders with the end of Yeats's play: 'They will be speaking forever, the people shall hear them forever' (*MGY* 377). At the end of his life, in a poem entitled 'The Man and the

142

Echo', Yeats too pondered the part *Cathleen ni Houlihan* played in the events leading up to Easter 1916:

> Did that play of mine send out
> Certain men the English shot?
> (*VP* 632)

He was right to do so, because *Cathleen ni Houlihan* marked a fusion of the mystical and the political without which, as Eglinton speculates, there would have been no Easter 1916: 'And indeed it was this mystical Ireland, beheld clairvoyantly, an Ireland sunk in ancient memories, which turned out to be the real one! Yeats, and the literary movement in which he was the commanding figure, may be said to have conjured up the armed bands of 1916.'[32]

But, as ever, this is only half the truth. During the Application for Letters Patent for the Abbey Theatre in August 1904, Yeats was asked if there was a political tendency in *Cathleen ni Houlihan*, and his reply was appropriately more circumspect: 'I can quite understand people saying that it was written with political intent. It was not. I simply took passionate human material. . . . We have no propaganda except that of good art.'[33] With the passage of time, the context for the play's reception changed. After the announcement that Yeats had been awarded a Civil List Pension, D. P. Moran in the *Leader* on 14 September 1911 was characteristically scornful: 'The author of "Cathleen ni Houlihan", Mr Yeats, is an able-bodied man and stout of limb; if he is past his work as an opal hush poet at least he could dig. But our Irish Bunthorne is now a British Government pensioner. How many foolish and feather-headed youths, we wonder, did he inspire with "extreme" politics?'

Outside Ireland, *Cathleen ni Houlihan*'s revolutionary potential was often not perceived. In November 1903, for example, while Yeats was at Wellesley College, Massachusetts, to give a reading, members of the Phi Sigma Society gave a 'charming presentation' of the play, an event recalled in April 1920 by Miss Bates: 'Mr Yeats first came to Wellesley through the Indian Summer haze of a Saturday afternoon, November 28 1903. President Hazard had invited the Authors Club of Boston out to welcome him, but he eluded the committee sent to meet him at the train, lost his happy way in the woods and wandered into the Browning Room of College Hall just at the end of his party. The reading, his first in America, was given in our old College Chapel – one of those gleaming memories now not inappropriately written in flame.'[34]

EARLY YEARS AT THE ABBEY

Annie Horniman

In November 1909, Yeats and Lady Gregory advised the Abbey Theatre Company that at the end of 1910 Horniman's subsidy of £3,800 would cease, as would the free use of the theatre, amounting to £200 in rent and rates. Now they would be responsible for paying their authors, purchasing patents, and appointing a permanent manager and possibly a third director.[35] In 1904, when she had purchased the Mechanics' Institute in Abbey Street, the outlook for a co-operative venture seemed brighter; indeed, it was

Annie Horniman with teddy bear. Taken c. August 1910.

Sarah Allgood paying homage to Yeats. Standing beside Yeats is his brother Jack; in front of them is Jack's wife Cottie. Taken on 20 July 1911 when Willie, with his natural instinct for pomp and ceremony, gave away his cousin Ruth Pollexfen at her wedding to Charles Lane-Poole in St Columba's College Chapel, Rathfarnham, Dublin. Yeats's clothes were designed by Hugh Lane and made by the best tailor in London.

widely reported in the Irish press that, for her, 'money was no object'. Some conditions, such as the stipulation that seat prices could be increased but not lowered, raised a few eyebrows, but her intention was to make the theatre respectable, a place for serious entertainment, and she knew the value of bourgeois patronage even as she sought to undermine it. The members of the Company, including Yeats, Lady Gregory, the Fay brothers, James Starkey, George Roberts, Hyde, Russell, Synge, Sara Allgood, Fred Ryan, and Padraic Colum, accepted her terms, and on 27 December 1904, the Abbey Theatre, with its 566 seats and its intimate stage some sixteen foot in width and nineteen foot, six inches in depth, opened to great acclaim with a performance of Yeats's verse play *On Baile's Strand* and Lady Gregory's comedy *Spreading the News*, described by the *Irish Times* as a 'tripping little piece founded on a simple idea of modern Irish life'.[36]

In retrospect, the most striking feature about the Abbey Theatre was that it drew together people with similar interests but fundamentally conflicting ideals. Maire Nic Shiubhlaigh (Walker), for example, never conceived of the National Theatre Society as a purely theatrical enterprise: 'It was merely a part of the larger national movement in which most of us were then participating.'[37] Willie Fay thought of the Abbey as *first and foremost a theatrical, not a literary movement*.[38] Lady Gregory desired a 'theatre with a base of realism and an apex of beauty'.[39] The more dilettante Moore, scenting an Irish Renaissance, was 'deliciously excited' at the idea of an Irish Literary Theatre.[40] Martyn in a play such as *The Heather Field* betrayed his debt to Ibsen and his unconscious proximity to Yeatsian parody.[41] The un-Yeatsian Synge, who was, according to Lennox Robinson,* 'not a "man of the theatre"', agreed with MacKenna, after seeing a performance of *The Shadowy Waters*, on the need to resist 'a purely fantastic, unmodern, ideal, breezy, springdayish, Cuchulainoid National Theatre'.[42] Ever since her resignation from the Golden Dawn in February 1903, Horniman's 'search for perfection had become increasingly identified with the theatre',[43] and, in that it made everything else possible, her role in the early years of the Abbey Theatre proved pivotal. As Yeats recognised, 'without her help . . . the Irish Dramatic Movement would not exist today'.[44]

Horniman insisted the Company adopt a professional image, and in June 1905 she made available £500 for salaries, an offer that met with resistance, since many in the Company wanted to retain their amateur status. In autumn 1905, further acrimony ensued when the Irish National Theatre Society became the National Theatre Society, Ltd, with Synge, Yeats, and Lady Gregory appointed Directors. On receiving an anonymous letter from one of the Company (possibly the actor James Connolly) complaining of Yeats's usurpation, the *United Irishman* with some relish observed: 'Everybody will be sorry for the conversion of our best lyric poet into a limited liability company.'[45] Some members, including Maire Nic Shiubhlaigh, her brother Frank Walker, Russell, and Colum, left to form the Theatre of Ireland. Frank Fay and Sara Allgood were given salaries, but the issue of control remained unresolved. As Frank Walker remarked to Holloway:

'All the unpopular people remain at the Abbey – Synge, Yeats.'
'But', I interposed, 'you must remember that only for Yeats the theatre would not exist.'
'That is so, but is it an unmixed blessing?' queried Walker. Ah, there's the rub![46]

Horniman insisted that 'the whole power of the purse . . . be in the Directors' hands'.[47] An opportunity presented itself during the British tour in April 1906 when she had reason to complain about the behaviour of the players, as Yeats relayed to Lady Gregory in July 1906. The O'Dempsey sisters were 'tom-boys', one of whom could not

AJAX YEATS DEFIES THE CENSOR.

Much excitement has been caused in Dublin owing to the determination on the part of the Abbey Theatre, of "Playboy of the West" notoriety, to produce a play of Bernard Shaw's in defiance of the warning of the Viceroy.

Shaw's play *The Shewing-up of Blanco Posnet* caused a stir in the Dublin press when it was staged at the Abbey in August 1909.

be kept on since she was wild and flirtatious. But for Miss Horniman's intervention through Synge, the company, trumpets in hand, would have taken to the streets in Leeds. Yeats added that when she was ill during the tour, she requested reasonable silence after 11 p.m., but had little effect. Indeed, when the train stopped at Edinburgh between Aberdeen and Newcastle, the company wound down the carriage windows and started calling out to people on the platform. The humourless Yeats continued: 'Miss Horniman is indignant because Synge sat with a young woman upon his knee in a public room at Leeds where a stranger might have entered at any moment and in her presence. I need not labour the carelessness of the stage management.'[48] In August 1906, in a move aimed at curtailing Willie Fay's powers over casting, she encouraged Yeats to import Florence Darragh, an Irish actress working in England.[49] She felt now that Willie Fay and Synge were her enemies, Yeats and Lady Gregory her only friends.

In January 1907, Ben Iden Payne, a young enthusiastic English producer who had worked for F. R. Benson, was drafted in to broaden the Abbey's appeal. He arrived in time to witness the *Playboy* riots and left the Company six months later. During 1907 the policy difference between Willie Fay and Horniman sharpened, and in January 1908

SHAW PLAY AT THE ABBEY.

LADY GREGORY. W.B. YEATS. G BERNARD SHAW.

The much-discussed Shaw play, "The Shewing Up of Blanco Posnet," was produced at the Abbey Theatre last night, and created no great impression one way or the other. Lady Gregory and Mr. W. B. Yeats are directors and guiding lights of the Abbey.

he and his brother Frank resigned. The final battle occurred in May 1910 when the Abbey remained open on the day of King Edward VII's funeral. 'Subsidy ceases now' she wired to Lady Gregory, 'unless Directors and Robinson express regret in Dublin press that decent example was not followed'.[50] Yeats was away in France, so Lady Gregory sent a letter to the press indicating that the theatre had stayed open 'owing to accident'. Convinced this was intentionally ambiguous, Horniman stopped the June and December instalments.

   Partly because of a lack of information (his letters to her have not survived), partly because the disputes involved personality clashes, it is not easy to assess Yeats's attitude to Horniman. In September 1906 Yeats sent a curious letter to Lady Gregory about an incident which caused such concern that he came close to resigning. He had just received a letter from Horniman and thought when Lady Gregory had read it she would understand at once that he had no choice but to resign his position as Managing Director. He asked her to contact Synge, adding that the unnamed woman's conduct was disgraceful.[51] Although he never composed poems to Horniman, Yeats seems to have been genuinely concerned for her welfare. In a letter to Lady Gregory dated 6 November 1905, he noticed that her nerves seem to be all right and surmised she lacked strength but there might be other causes.[52] For a time Horniman acted as his amanuensis, and he would often ask her to undertake familiar tasks such as retrieving books from his flat at Woburn Buildings when he was in Dublin.[53] The intimacy was returned: 'There are some moths in your curtains & the books on the top shelf are absolutely filthy.'[54] And when George Pollexfen died in September 1910, he wrote to her immediately with the news.[55]

147

Horniman recoiled from any manifestation of 'national feeling', precisely the quality she recognised as part of Yeats's nature: 'If anyone thinks that "Irish" or "National" are anything to me beyond mere empty words to distinguish a Society, merely a title for convenience, they are much mistaken. . . . The theatre was given for the carrying out of Mr Yeats artistic dramatic schemes and for no other reason.'[56] For the sake of the Abbey, however, Yeats could not afford to fall out with her. To some extent he was hoist on his own petard, for in pursuing a nationalist theatre of Art he ran the constant risk of alienating his chief benefactor. At the same time, he constantly felt the pressure of Lady Gregory's antagonism towards the English intruder. He was called upon to smooth things with Horniman over the musician and arranger Herbert Hughes, who was active in republican circles. Yeats liked him personally but was a little wary of his music because of his politics. On the other hand, if his music were acceptable his contact with republican groups would prove an asset.[57] I have come across one letter Yeats sent to Lady Gregory written in Horniman's hand, in which the grandson of the one-time chief employer in Sligo strikes an uncharacteristically crude note, as if under Horniman's influence. Yeats was keen to proceed with prosecuting Miss Walker, but 'your "goodness of heart" etc stands in the way. . . . We must get these people afraid of us. I am really rather enjoying the game.'[58]

As for Horniman herself, she thought the Irish could not take her seriously 'because I am a cheerful person and dont need any League or Society to back me. When I say that I have spent some thousands of pounds in Dublin the answer is – how you must love Ireland!'[59] It would be wrong to assume that she was universally disliked in Ireland.

Programme of Irish plays at Horniman's Gaiety Theatre, Manchester, February 1909.

IRISH PLAYS

Will be presented by

The Abbey Theatre Company,

From

The Abbey Theatre, Dublin,

At the

Gaiety Theatre, Manchester,

For One Week,

Commencing Monday, Feb. 15th, 1909

Matinees on Wednesday & Saturday, at 2 o'clock.

Evening Performances at 7-30 o'clock.

PRICES AS USUAL.

Directors National Theatre Society: { W. B. Yeats. J. M. Synge. Lady Gregory.

W. A. Henderson, *Secretary.*

MONDAY and **WEDNESDAY.**	**DERVORGILLA.** By Lady Gregory.
	IN THE SHADOW OF THE GLEN. By J. M. Synge.
	THE GAOL GATE. By Lady Gregory.
	THE RISING OF THE MOON. By Lady Gregory.
TUESDAY and **SATURDAY MATINEE.**	**THE WELL OF THE SAINTS.** By J. M. Synge.
	THE JACKDAW. By Lady Gregory.
WEDNESDAY MATINEE and **FRIDAY.**	**THE HOUR GLASS.** By W. B. Yeats.
	THE WORKHOUSE WARD. By Lady Gregory.
	RIDERS TO THE SEA. By J. M. Synge.
	SPREADING THE NEWS. By Lady Gregory.
THURSDAY and **SATURDAY.**	**THE PIEDISH.** By George Fitzmaurice.
	KATHLEEN NI HOULIHAN. By W. B. Yeats.
	HYACINTH HALVEY. By Lady Gregory.
	THE PIPER. By Norreys Connell.

James Hannay ('George Birmingham') wrote to her at Easter 1906: 'I suppose it is being an Englishwoman that makes you able to be sane. We, none of us, appear to be able to laugh because, I suppose, we're all a little mad, driven beside ourselves with self esteem.'[60] Nor should it be assumed that Yeats was not a target for her famous wit. He enjoyed playing with Craig's model for the theatre, 'moving hither and thither little figures of cardboard through gay or solemn light and shade, allowing the scene to give the words and the words the scene' (UP 2, 392). In a letter to Marjorie Garrod in May 1917, Horniman writes: 'Mr W. B. Yeats got an idea for monologues to be spoken in quaint dresses, hence these sketches. The scheme was unworkable with the human material.'[61]

One recent commentator, no doubt reflecting a wider opinion, is genuinely puzzled by Yeats's friendship with Horniman: 'It is difficult to understand why Yeats stood by Horniman in the Golden Dawn quarrels, why he kept up a friendship with her, or how he got through hours, days, and years sitting in a parlor with this wealthy, but unbeautiful and unwitty, woman. . . . One can see that she loved him; one cannot easily see what he saw in her if it were not that bright shilling at the bottom of the electrified tub.'[62] The answer must be that our view of her needs adjusting.

In an interview in May 1914, Horniman declined to speak about her politics except to say she was 'an unenfranchised helot, and that when women were enfranchised she thought they would go sober to the polls'.[63] About trade unionism for actors, she was more enlightened than many of her contemporaries. A trade union for actors 'would force the residential managements to have clean, decent, and safe theatres, and to ensure that everyone under a certain salary should be paid for rehearsals; in fact that the men owners of theatres should see after their property as I look after mine. Is that unreasonable?' The interviewer described Horniman as 'an embodied paradox': in speech, looks, and dress she appeared like a Puritan, yet she was the owner of a theatre in Manchester 'which bears the oddly unpuritan name of "The Gaiety" '.

In taking a strong line against the Abbey's involvement in anything political, Horniman betrays a certain insecurity. Perhaps at root she wanted to prevent the Abbey from being condemned by the English establishment as a seed-bed of disaffection. The plays staged at the Gaiety in Manchester indicate that she was more radical than commentators have allowed, and suffragettes such as Emmeline Pankhurst congratulated her on her pioneering role in the theatre.[64] In later life, Robinson was also magnanimous about the woman who wanted his head on a salver for not closing the Abbey on the death of Edward VII: 'But our theatre owes her so much. She had wealth, but was not a millionairess. Coming from a rather conventional English, midland, mercantile family . . . she slightly shocked her family by falling in love with the arts, particularly the art of the theatre and Mr Yeats's poetic plays. . . . The English midlands and Clare-Galway did not very happily mix.'[65]

The Example of Synge

If Annie Horniman's intention was to create a them-and-us attitude in the Abbey Theatre, she almost succeeded. She underestimated, however, human foibles. Willie Fay married Brigit O'Dempsey (they were forced to travel to Scotland for the ceremony because she was under age). More shockingly, Synge fell in love with another actress, Molly Allgood, and signed his letters to her by identifying with the outcast: 'Your old Tramp'. In May 1907, Synge confided in Molly: 'I feel indescribably sick of the continual

"I Don t Care a Rap.

Cartoon of Synge from *The Abbey Row Not Edited by W. B. Yeats*.

worries of this company, worries with F. J. F ⟨Frank Fay⟩, Miss Horniman, Lady G, Yeats, you never know where it will break out next.'[66] With Horniman, he felt he had to wear 'a sort of masque'.[67] He was against the Abbey becoming either a 'Municipal Theatre' or an executive undertaking for the production of foreign plays.[68] He was suspicious of the 'Yeats-Gregory show',[69] never complimented them on their plays, resisted responsibility as a director, and thought that if the Abbey folded he would take Molly with him to Paris.

'Yeats felt comfortable with Synge only after his death', writes Ann Saddlemyer, 'when despite the genuineness of his sense of loss, he was able to engrave an image more nearly fitting his own pantheon.'[70] During the *Playboy* riots, Yeats defended Synge, 'fighting', as Eglinton recalls, 'in a cause which was not really his own'.[71] But, as is made clear in a comment of Lady Gregory in August 1909 when the Castle attempted to ban Shaw's *Shewing-up of Blanco Posnet*, this was precisely Yeats's territory: 'We did not give in one quarter of an inch to Nationalist Ireland at *The Playboy* time, and we certainly cannot give in one quarter of an inch to the Castle.'[72]

Synge was an awkward reminder of a governing principle of the Revival, that: 'Our movement is a return to the people, like the Russian movement of the early seventies. . . . Plays about drawing-rooms are written for the middle classes of great cities, for the classes who live in drawing-rooms, but if you would uplift the man of the roads you must write about the roads, or about the people of romance, or about great historical people.'[73] Yeats was haunted by the idea of knowing 'all classes of men', and he even thought of disguising himself as a peasant and wandering through the West, boarding a ship as a sailor (*A* 470). For Synge, knowledge was closely allied with experience. He had studied Irish and Celtic civilisation at the Sorbonne under Henri d'Arbois de Jubainville, but he made it his business to assimilate at first hand the life-style of the country people, wishing 'to do for the peasantry of Western Ireland what Loti had done for the Breton fisher folk'.[74] The summers with his family at Castle Kevin in County Wicklow roused his interest in rural Ireland. After relinquishing the Kingdom of God in his teens, he began to take 'a real interest in the Kingdom of Ireland'.[75] In turn, contact with the West became 'the great magnet of my soul'[76] and produced all his plays.

In the nine years from 1898 to the *Playboy* riots of 1907 Synge spent approximately one whole year in the West of Ireland. In each of the five years between 1898 and 1902 he spent a month and more on the Aran Islands, listening to stories and playing his fiddle at house dances. In 1903 and 1904 he lodged for a month with Philly Harris in Glenbeigh, County Kerry. Then in June 1905, he and Jack Yeats were commissioned by the *Manchester Guardian* to spend a month touring the Congested Districts of the West and filing reports. In a speech at the Plymouth Theatre in Boston in September 1911, Yeats blithely declared that Synge 'had nothing of the humanitarian; he had no interest in economics, no interest in social forces, and he had little of the Irish politician . . . nothing interested him but the individual man, in fact I think his own ill health and poverty had made individual destiny momentous to him'.[77] But the twelve articles in the *Manchester Guardian* give the lie to Yeats's belief that Synge was apolitical or uninterested in 'men in the mass' (*E & I* 319).

Like Jack Yeats, Synge was drawn to the elemental, but his social eye was also interested in details which define. He, properly, never speaks of 'the peasantry' but of 'the country people'. Sometimes, as at Swinford, County Mayo, he encounters 'primitive

Cover for Program of Abbey Theatre plays at the Grand Opera House, Chicago, February 1912, in which Synge's play had top billing. The *Playboy* row, however, followed Synge across the Atlantic as his notes suggest.

people', but even here he notices 'the women mostly in bare feet with white handker-chiefs over their heads'.[78] In Carraroe, he discovers 'families' weeding in small green fields of oats, and he engages an old man in conversation about exporting turf to Clare and Aran, the scarcity of potatoes, the price of pigs, emigration. Beyond Carraroe he encounters men and women working on improvements to the road. Again, he takes care to define what each of them is doing and to imagine what they are feeling ('a sort of hang-dog dejection'), to note the wages they receive ('a shilling a day'), and to assess the place of the work in the rural economy ('one person only, generally the head of the family, is taken from each house'). Individuals are rendered socially, not, as in Yeats, metaphysically. Appropriately, too, his articles are complemented by sketches of people engaged in work: a carpenter caulking the bottom of a boat, a ferryman, roadbuilders, kelpmakers.[79]

In Connemara, while overtaking people on their way home from market-day in Galway, Synge shows awareness of a dilemma that never seems to have taxed Yeats:

> One's first feeling as one comes back among these people and takes a place, so to speak, in this noisy procession of fishermen, farmers, and women, where nearly everyone is interesting and attractive, is a dread of any reform that would tend to lessen their individuality rather than any very real hope of improving their well-being. One feels then, perhaps a little later, that it is a part of the misfortune of Ireland that nearly all the characteristics which give colour and attractiveness to Irish life are bound up with a social condition that is near to penury, while in countries like Brittany the best external features of the local life – the rich embroidered dresses, for instance, or the carved furniture – are connected with a decent and comfortable social condition.[80]

Synge understood both the isolation of the West and the way the West fitted into a larger world economy, providing labour in the United States and Britain and spending power at home. Unlike Synge, Yeats was never exercised by the distinction of *in themselves* and *for others*. The country people in Yeats are invariably there for symbolic purposes, whereas in Synge there is also a sense that they exist in themselves. Outside Swinford in Mayo, the young women spend six years or more working in America, then they 'do grow weary of that fixed kind of life' and return with their chains and rings to marry. The young men, meanwhile, go harvesting in England and return with a taste for ale and 'never do a hand's turn the rest of the year, but they will be sitting around in each other's houses playing cards through the night'.[81]

Jack Yeats the painter and Synge the journalist could observe and celebrate with impunity. The problem arose when the subject matter was converted into material for the stage, for then the director-dramatist not only opened himself up, as Horniman shrewdly observed, to the disturbing nature of his imaginative faculty but also took on the contentious role of a spokesperson.[82] He might have guessed as much from the brief notice his first play received in the *Freeman's Journal* in October 1903: 'Mr Synge's "Shadow of the Glen" is a study of modern peasant life in Co. Wicklow by a man who has lived amongst the people and who writes about them, not from the outside, but as one of themselves.'[83] Protests against the play grew, and Yeats was forced to defend his playwright in the *United Irishman*: 'To me it seems that ideas, and beauty and knowl-edge are precisely those sacred things, an Ark of the Covenant as it were, that a nation must value even more than victory.'[84] In the same issue, Maud Gonne MacBride (as she signed herself) took a different view: 'Mr Yeats asks for freedom for the Theatre, freedom even from patriotic captivity. I would ask for freedom for it from one thing

H. Oakley's sketch of Yeats fishing with George Russell and Synge.

more deadly than all else – freedom from the insidious and destructive tyranny of foreign influence.' The argument continued into January 1904, when Yeats himself became the target: 'Mr Yeats values the criticism of his country's oppressors. We do not. We care as little about what Englishmen think about Irish writers as the writers of Hungary did about the opinions of the literary critics of Vienna.'[85]

Whatever he intended by his plays, the Dublin audiences reminded Synge of certain unavoidable implications in his representation of rural Ireland, as the Dublin *Evening Herald* made typographically plain in its opinion of his next play:

If there is one term more than another which
CANNOT be Applied to Mr Synge's Work,
that adjective is satisfying.[86]

The *Freeman's Journal* was no more supportive: 'This is the third of Mr Synge's contributions to the repertoire of the Irish national Theatre; and his point of view as a dramatist is pretty clearly defined. The point of view is not that of a writer in sympathetic touch with the people from whom he purports to draw his characters.'[87] Whatever the conventional view, the hostility towards Synge did not begin with *Playboy*.

The Dublin press came out screaming when *Playboy* hit the stage in the final week of January 1907. The *Dublin Evening Mail* of 28 January was outraged:

A DRAMATIC FREAK

FIRST NIGHT AT THE ABBEY THEATRE

PARIS IDEAS AND PARRICIDES

The article that followed was interspersed with subheadings which would not be out of place in the 'Aeolus' episode of *Ulysses*:

Entirely   Unconvincing

Grips   Your   Throat

The   Slanderously   Improbable

Opulent   n   Flashing   Phrases

A   Five-Pound   Note

Corner-boy   and   Publichouse   Sort

The farce continued the following day in the *Dublin Evening Herald*:

THE PLAYBOY AT THE ABBEY

'KILL THE AUTHOR'

Indignant   Audience

DISORDERLY SCENES

Management   Resolute

Synge so lost himself in his plays that he must have thought he was 'above his handiwork, invisible, refined out of existence, indifferent, paring his fingernails'.[88] Under attack, his first recourse was not thoughts of (Joycean) exile but increased self-absorption and what the *Evening Telegraph* on 29 January 1907 interpreted as the 'cynical sneer of the decadent'. 'I don't care a rap how the people take it,' he told a journalist on the *Dublin Daily Mail* on 29 January 1907. He flew by the nets and escaped through language that was 'as fully flavoured as a nut or apple', and through appeals to artistic integrity, that the play presented what the playwright with the imperceptible accent heard.[89] Synge was ill for two months at the time of the *Playboy* riots, but he still managed, as a letter to MacKenna on 9 April 1907 testifies, to find humour in the row: 'I wonder did you hear that Dublin and *The Freeman* were chiefly outraged because I used the word "shift", instead of "chemise" for an article of fine linen, or perhaps named it at all. Lady G. asked our charwoman – the Theatre charwoman what she thought of it. The charwoman said she wouldn't mention the garment at all if it could be helped, but if she did she hoped she would always say "chemise", even if she was alone! Then she went down on the stage and met the stage carpenter. "Ah" *says she*, "isn't Mr Synge a bloody old snot to write such a play!" There's Dublin delicasy!'[90]

The bitterness of the Dublin press against the Abbey triumvirate needed little to fan it. 'By the Way', the *Freeman's Journal* revealed on 1 February 1907, Lady Gregory's husband was 'the son or grandson of another William Gregory, an Under-Secretary for Ireland, and an enemy of Catholic rights and liberties'. The Dublin *Evening Telegraph* spoke of the 'Yeats regime' and went on to ridicule the debate Yeats staged at the Abbey on Monday evening, 4 February:

"THE PARRICIDE AND THE PEOPLE."

DISCUSSION IN "THE ABBEY."

MR YEATS'S DEFENCE.

A Series of Scenes.

Noisy, Farcical & Disgusting.

Mr J. B. Yeats's Sneer.

"An Island of Plaster Saints"

Although he had not read the play, Yeats's father had seen two performances and felt justified in coming to Synge's defence:

He knew Mr Synge. He knew he had an affection for these people (loud laughter and cat-calls) he had described in 'Riders to the Sea'. His affection for them ('Oh' and laughter) was based on a real knowledge ('No, no', and groans). He lived amongst them, and was their friend (disorder), and intimate with their households (cries and groans). He knew this was an Island of Saints – plaster saints (disorder and groaning). He (Mr Yeats) was no great believer in saints, but he enjoyed the thought that this was a land of sinners (cries of 'Police, police', and laughter). The speaker went on to compare Mr Synge's peasants and Carleton's peasants, amid much interruption. Carleton's peasants were a real insult and degradation (noise) and Mr Synge's peasant was a real, vigorous, vital man, though a sinner (loud laughter and hisses). The speaker could not proceed with the noise.[91]

Yeats could have been distracted by the criticism, but he rode the storm. A year later, in the *Dublin Evening Herald* on 11 February 1908, he was attacking the 'Immoral Irish Bourgeoisie'. In May 1909, after Synge's death, he deliberately revived *The Playboy* and refused to be brow-beaten by the Dublin press.[92] In an interview reported in the *Northern Whig* on 25 August 1909, Yeats was not slow to draw conclusions: 'Synge's work . . . is precisely the work that is dangerous with an Irish audience. It is very hard

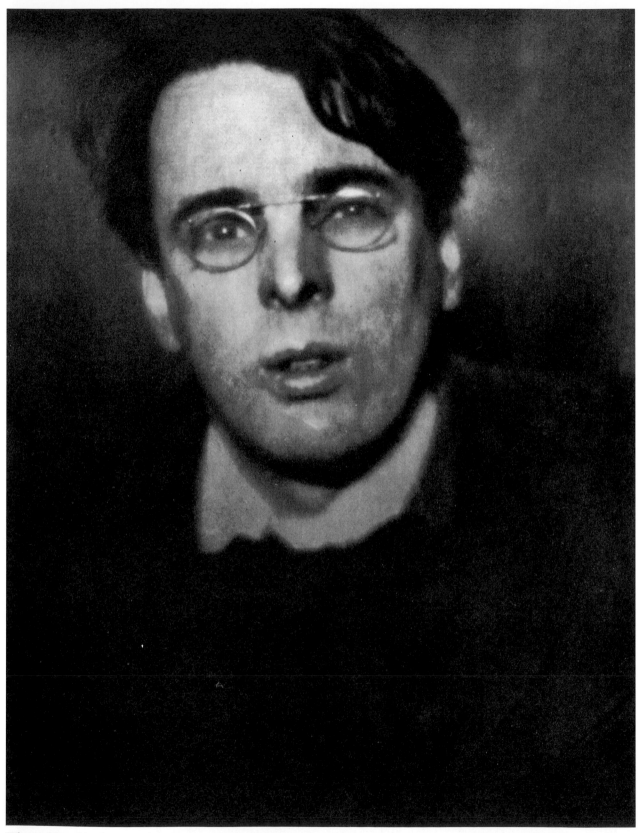

When taking this photograph in January 1908, Alvin Langdon Coburn asked Yeats to recite poetry, and 'without hesitation he began on some beautiful lines, while I flared a magnesium flash-light at intervals'.

to understand, and, therefore, the very desire to do so makes them impatient with it. They have gradually come to know what he means, and to accept his work without resentment. But it has been a long fight. To him everything was capricious and temperamental, and he could not tell his secret quickly.'

It was not the press, however, but Synge and Lady Gregory, especially in their use of language, who made Yeats appreciate what was at stake in a return to the people. *The Pot of Broth*, Yeats admitted, was 'the first comedy in dialect of our movement', but 'the first use of Irish dialect, rich, abundant, and correct, for the purposes of creative art was in J. M. Synge's *Riders to the Sea*, and Lady Gregory's *Spreading the News*' (*VPl* 254). In 'The Tragic Generation', no doubt with his own failure in this direction in mind, Yeats shrewdly observed that it was 'only through dialect could he ⟨Synge⟩ escape self-expression' (*A* 345).[93] Yeats struggled to write dramatic prose. To achieve a more natural rendering of Hiberno-English, he relied on Lady Gregory, who had developed her own brand of dialect known as Kiltartanese, after the village of Kiltartan adjacent to Coole Park. She helped him with *Cathleen ni Houlihan*, for 'One has to live among the people, like you . . . before one can think the thoughts of the people and speak with their tongue' (*VPl* 232). When revising *Where There Is Nothing*, Yeats again needed Lady Gregory: 'I found myself . . . with an old difficulty, that my words flow freely alone when my people speak in verse, or in words that are like those we put into verse; and so after an attempt to work alone I gave my scheme to her' (*VPl* 712).

Lady Gregory's ear was attuned to the speech of her servants and tradespeople, and, whereas Yeats's drama embodies 'the war of the spiritual with the natural order' (*SR* vii), her one-act plays honour the more homely aspects of Irish country life. *Spreading the News* (1904) celebrates small-town gossip, *The Gaol Gate* (1906) Irish keening, *The Rising of the Moon* (1907) the protection afforded the rebel or law-breaker. As a playwright she was closer to Synge than to Yeats. Writing comedies was her forte, but Yeats lived for tragedies, and tragedy, he thought in language foreign to Lady Gregory, 'must always be a drowning and breaking of the dykes that separate man from man, and it is upon these dykes comedy keeps house' (*E & I* 241).

Synge's death triggered a reordering of feelings on Yeats's part. As 'The Death of Synge' (*A* 499–527) suggests, 1909 was a year when Yeats was reflecting more and more on the Mask. Synge, therefore, became part of this tapestry. According to the nurse, Synge on his deathbed 'would have no fuss'. At his funeral Yeats notices mourners who, while he was alive, 'spoke his name, though but to slander'. A remark of Synge's in Paris came to mind: 'We should unite stoicism, asceticism and ecstasy.' He recalls Synge's adverse qualities, envying his self-absorption. Throughout these deliberations on what he comes to identify as Synge's 'self-conquest', Yeats is busy formulating his theory of the anti-self, a concept more fully explored in *Per Amica Silentia Lunae* (1918).

In *A Vision* Synge is positioned at Phase 23. The Will is the Receptive Man; the Mask when true is Wisdom, when false is Self-pity; the Creative Mind when true is Creation through pity, when false Self-driven desire; the Body of Fate is Success. Synge, like Rembrandt, was 'ready to sacrifice every convention, perhaps all that men have agreed to reverence, for a startling theme, or a model one delights in painting; and yet all the while, because of the nature of his *Mask*, there is another summary working through bone and nerve' (*AV [B]* 165). By 1937, Synge – but significantly not Horniman or the Fay brothers – had been incorporated into Yeats's history of modern Ireland:

John Synge, I and Augusta Gregory, thought
All that we did, all that we said or sang

Must come from contact with the soil, from that
Contact everything Antaeus-like grew strong.
We three alone in modern times had brought
Everything down to that sole test again,
Dream of the noble and the beggar-man.

(*VP* 603)

It is doubtful if Molly Allgood's 'Tramp' ever dreamed of the noble, and he would have been less than pleased at history reserving for him a place in the 'Yeats-Gregory show'.

AN UNPOPULAR THEATRE

The Poet Outside the Theatre

Charting Yeats's attitude towards Ireland in the period from 1900 to 1910 is especially difficult, partly because of the overlap between his attitude towards Ireland and his feelings for Maud Gonne. Her marriage to MacBride in February 1903 coincided with Yeats's growing detachment from nationalist politics and an increasing commitment to the theatre. But even before that, in May 1901, Yeats confided in a letter to Lady Gregory: 'I imagine that as I withdraw from politics my friends among the Nationalists will grow less, at first at any rate, & my foes more numerous' (*L [K]* 3, 71). When the Abbey Theatre did not close on the death of Edward VII, the Dublin *Evening Telegraph*, far from supporting Yeats, deliberately twisted the knife: 'We understand that during the last week, and up to the present, Mr Yeats has not been in Dublin. It is understood that he has been residing in France for some time.'[94] Looking back from October 1915 Yeats could afford to be more sanguine and see, for example, Rabindranath Tagore's* position with Indian nationalists mirrored in his own: 'I wonder if your informant is right about Tagore. At half a dozen times in the last twenty years my own fellow countrymen would have said (and always when I was most right) that I had lost their confidence. The position of a man of letters in a patriotic movement is always very difficult.'[95]

Involvement with the theatre, on the other hand, might have proved a counterweight, but in fact it merely stirred his disillusionment with the present, frustration with colleagues, anger with audiences. In a letter to Lady Gregory in 1908, he identified part of his problems with Ireland. He felt he needed time away every year from Ireland, away from everything that moved him to criticism. He was still living on thoughts from their Italian trip the year before, and on letters from Normandy. His imagination was full of Ireland when he no longer saw it, and was adversely affected by every contact with Dublin. He thought that his work was undergoing a change, and that all his recent output had a grotesque almost comic quality to it.[96]

But at the same time, as the Preface to a 1906 two-volume edition of his work indicates, he was preoccupied with widening his audience in Ireland: 'I am no longer writing for a few friends here and there, but am asking my own people to listen, as many as can find their way into the Abbey Theatre in Dublin or some provincial one when our company is on tour. Perhaps one can explain in plays, where one has much more room than in songs and ballads, even those intricate thoughts, those elaborate emotions, that are one's self.'[97] In a lecture on 'The Theatre and Ireland' in March 1910, held under the

Gordon Craig's designs for poster and postcard. The Nineties dome resurfaced in Yeats's 'Byzantium' poems three decades later.

auspices of the Gaelic League, with Hyde in the chair and Pearse in the audience, Yeats delivered a late reminder of the need to keep separate the development of Irish drama and Irish nationalism:

> Mr Yeats, in the course of the lecture, said that if they in Ireland could get down to the rich soil beneath the surface of things they could succeed in creating a great popular and artistic movement. One difficulty in the way of that development was the progress of the Irish national movement, which had stood in the way of the development of Irish drama. They in Ireland had got into an unnatural way of seeing things. They must distrust all organised thought in the effort to create an Irish Theatre, and substitute for it a deeper form of thought. The beginning of all success in literature was distrust in journalism. . . . On the motion of P. H. Pearse a vote of thanks was passed to Mr Yeats for his lecture.[98]

Yeats wrote some sixty poems in the 1890s, and nearly a hundred in the 1910s. But in the first decade of the new century he managed to complete only thirty poems or so, nearly half of which came in 1909 and 1910.[99] Eight of his plays received their first performance in these years, but for the lyric poet the period was so dry that in 1904 and 1906 he wrote no poems he wished to preserve for posterity. Indeed, one contemporary commentator concluded that 'Mr Yeats was thirty-four when he practically gave up lyrical poetry for dramatic poetry.'[100] In turn, the theatre, unlike the Controls in 1917, brought him few metaphors for poetry. It is not the full picture, for his plays contain verse and he rewrote his prose play *The Hour-Glass* as verse, and his involvement in the theatre also produced dividends for his verse.[101] But as Director, Producer, Playwright, Employer, Editor, Censor, Fund-raiser, Impresario, Upbraider, Yeats was so consumed by the theatre in these years that in his diary for 1909 he wondered if 'my talent will ever recover from the heterogeneous labour of these last few years' (*A* 484).

Year	Approximate Number of Poems Written	First Performance of Plays
1899	1	*The Countess Cathleen*
1900	1	
1901	1	*Diarmid and Grania*
1902	3 (+ 'Baile and Aillinn')	*Cathleen ni Houlihan/Pot of Broth*
1903	4 (+ 'Old Age of Queen Maeve')	*The Hour-Glass/The King's Threshold*
1904		*The Shadowy Waters/Where There Is Nothing/On Baile's Strand*
1905	2	
1906		*Deirdre*
1907	1	
1908	5	*The Golden Helmet*
1909	8	
1910	7	
1911	1	*The Countess Cathleen* (revised version)
1912	14	
1913	15	

It might be thought that while the theatre consumed his public attention, in his verse Yeats indulged his private thoughts. But the real autobiography of these years is to be found elsewhere than in his poetry – in his letters, journals, and memoirs.[102] In his verse he gives the *impression* of an embattled private self, but he rarely strikes a personal note. Mention of individuals by name is restricted to Hyde (in 'At the Abbey Theatre') and Lady Gregory (in poems about her illness and her house at Coole). Maud Gonne is referred to in nine of the fourteen poems from *In the Seven Woods* and seven of the twenty-one poems in *The Golden Helmet*, but there is little pressure behind the writing. In a 1909 journal entry a personal note is struck: 'How much of the best I have done and still do is but the attempt to explain myself to her? If she understood, I should lack a reason for writing, and one never can have too many reasons for doing what is so laborious' (*Mem* 142). When such a thought is translated into verse, the personal note is obscured in the syntax and imagery:

> I had this thought a while ago,
> 'My darling cannot understand
> What I have done, or what would do
> In this blind bitter land.'

And I grew weary of the sun
Until my thoughts cleared up again,
Remembering that the best I have done
Was done to make it plain;

That every year I have cried, 'At length
My darling understands it all,
Because I have come into my strength,
And words obey my call';

That she had done so who can say
What would have shaken from the sieve?
I might have thrown poor words away
And been content to live.

(VP 255–6)

In such poems as 'Adam's Curse' and 'The Folly of Being Comforted', both written in 1902, or 'Never Give all the Heart' and 'O Do Not Love Too Long', written in 1905, he did not so much explore the intimacy of his feelings for his 'darling' as reflect on his emblematic position as rejected lover.

But O, in a minute she changed –
O do not love too long,
Or you will grow out of fashion
Like an old song.

(VP 212)

The writing here has none of the enactment of trauma to be found in, say, Hardy's poems of 1912 and 1913. It is as if Yeats wants his lines to carry some representative weight with his reader, to impart advice but, ironically, not to report on first-hand experience.[103] Something similar occurs in his revisions of earlier poems, as Edward Thomas noted in a review of *Poems* (1912): 'He seems to have been revising in cold blood what was written in a mood now inaccessible.'[104]

If *The Wind among the Reeds* is engaged with the articulation of desire, *In the Seven Woods* and *The Golden Helmet* dwell on the theme of wisdom and 'withering into truth'. When he thinks of the Abbey Theatre, Yeats focuses not on achievements but on what he writes best about – setbacks, unfulfilment.[105] In 'The Fascination of What's Difficult' he applies the classical image of Pegasus to his own imagination, in 'At the Abbey Theatre' the image of Proteus to the audiences. There were setbacks, too, for his poetry. He was not only writing less but also finding it more difficult, a theme he took up into his verse and insisted on, as 'Adam's Curse' reminds us:

I said: 'It's certain there is no fine thing
Since Adam's fall but must needs much labouring.'

(VP 204)

In 'All Things Can Tempt Me' he suggests – ironically without irony, considering how few poems he was writing – that nothing now comes more easily than 'this accustomed toil' of writing verse. He was unsure of his audience, and in 'At Galway Races' contrasts the 'timid breath' of the present with a past when the crowd closed in behind and he had 'horsemen for companions'. In 'The Fascination of What's Difficult', written between September 1909 and March 1910, he gives vent to his frustration with the theatre:

> The fascination of what's difficult
> Has dried the sap out of my veins, and rent
> Spontaneous joy and natural content
> Out of my heart. There's something ails our colt
> That must, as if it had not holy blood
> Nor on Olympus leaped from cloud to cloud,
> Shiver under the lash, strain, sweat and jolt
> As though it dragged road-metal. My curse on plays
> That have to be set up in fifty ways,
> On the day's war with every knave and dolt,
> Theatre business, management of men.
> I swear before the dawn comes round again
> I'll find the stable and pull out the bolt.
>
> (*VP* 260)

There is a struggle here to find a voice, part of which can be identified in the powerful combination of rhyme and unstressed final syllable: 'rent' and 'content', where 'content' is both *con*tent and contentment; 'colt' retroactively makes 'difficult' a problem word to pronounce. The half-rhyme of 'blood' and 'cloud' is further evidence of struggle, as is the interwoven rhyme of 'difficult', 'colt', 'jolt', 'dolt', and 'bolt'. But, again, this is not a private voice struggling to get heard but a public voice seeking its customary declamatory mode.

The Dramatic Mask

The setbacks underlined for Yeats the need not for an audience but for distance. His reading of Castiglione's *Book of the Courtier* and his trip to Northern Italy in May 1907 with Lady Gregory and Robert Gregory persuaded him to imagine Ireland in similar terms. While Synge's anti-bourgeois stance led to an identification with the 'Tramp', Cuchulain-inspired Yeats drew an analogy between the long-established life of the well-born and the artist's life: 'We come from the permanent things and create them, and instead of old blood we have old emotions and we carry in our head that form of society which aristocracies create now and again for some brief moment at Urbino or Versailles. We too despise the mob and suffer at its hands' (*Mem* 156). Without anyone to question him, he gave succour to such patrician thoughts and by February 1909, having suffered ten years of what he thought were reversals, confided in his journal: 'To oppose the new ill-breeding of Ireland, which may in a few years destroy all that has given Ireland a distinguished name in the world . . . I can only set up a secondary or interior personality created by me out of the tradition of myself, and this personality (alas, to me only possible in my writings) must be always gracious and simple. It must have that slight separation from immediate interests which makes charm possible, while remaining near enough for fire' (*Mem* 142). Ideology, aesthetics, and economics here overlap. When Horniman withdrew her subsidy, Yeats and Lady Gregory turned immediately to fashionable London society:

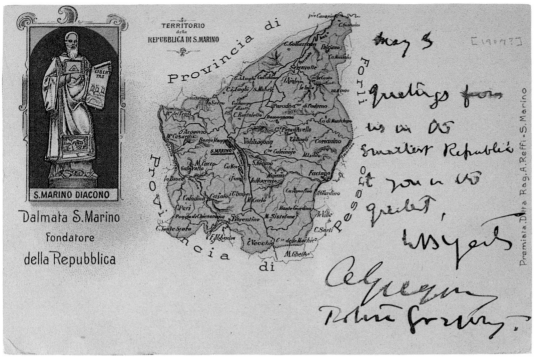

Postcard to John Quinn in New York, signed by Yeats, Lady Gregory, and her son Robert, and sent from San Marino, 5 May 1907.

Programme of *At the Hawk's Well*. With note to say Queen is unwell.

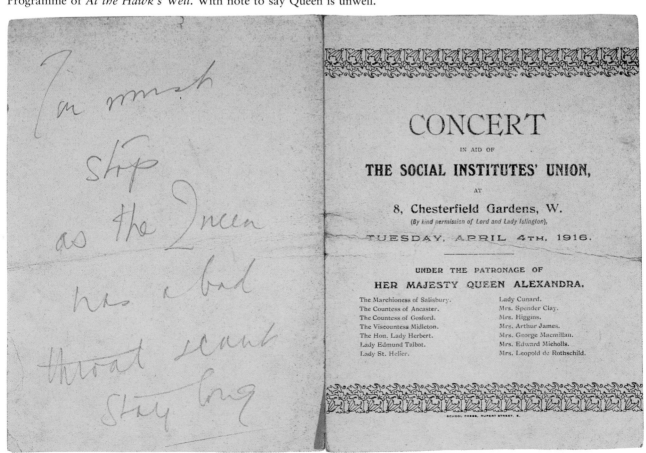

In connection with the appeal for funds for the Irish National Theatre, Dublin, recently published, a drawingroom meeting was held yesterday by Lady Gregory at the house of Sir Hugh P. Lane, 100 Cheyne Walk, Chelsea. Among those present were Lady Falmouth, Lady Wantage, Lady Alice Shaw Stewart, the Hon. Mrs Norman Grosvenor, Lady Mond, Lady Lindley, Lady Lewis, Mrs George Cornwallis West, Mrs Winston Churchill, Mrs Colefax, Mrs John Leslie, Mrs Leverton Harris, Mrs McGlyn, Mrs Belloc Lowndes, Miss Una Birch, Sir Ian Hamilton, Sir Edward Ward, Sir Hugh Lane, General Lawson, Mr Henry Tonks M.P., Mr P. Wilson Steer, Mr G. Bernard Shaw, and Mr Austin Harrison. During the afternoon Mrs Sara Allgood, Miss Maire O'Neill, and Mr O'Rourke, of the Abbey Theatre Company, played 'The Gaol Gate' on a stage erected in the hall, and after the play the guests were addressed by Mr Ford Madox Hueffer, Mr W. B. Yeats, and Mr Bernard Shaw, who appealed for subscriptions towards the endowment fund of the Abbey Theatre.[106]

In 1909 'the doctrine of the Mask', a phrase used in his journal on 13 December 1908, was in place, drawn from his fear of 'the representatives of collective opinion', from his membership of the Golden Dawn, and from his work in the theatre.[107] The theory was amplified in letters to his father in the distinction he drew between character and personality: 'Juliet has personality, her Nurse has character. I look upon personality as the individual form of our passions. . . . Character belongs I think to Comedy. . . . I probably get the distinction from the stage, where we say a man is a "character actor" meaning that he builds up a part out of observation, or we say that he is "an emotional actor" meaning that he builds it up out of himself, and in this last case – we always add, if he is not commonplace – that he has personality' (*L* 548–9).

At his Monday evenings in Woburn Buildings, Yeats theorised at length about drama, masks, and in particular his debt to Craig: 'He was then interested in the more esoteric forms of drama, and was eager to put masks on the actors' faces. He wished to eliminate the personality of the player from the play, and had borrowed some foolish notions from Mr Gordon Craig about lighting and scenery and dehumanised actors.'[108] Unfortunately, the success of Craig's screens was dependent on smooth-running, total productions – and on an appreciative audience, not on unreconstructed theatre-goers like Holloway:

Thursday, January 12. With a great flourish of egotistical trumpets on the part of the management and Yeats in dress clothes with crush opera hat in hand, the Gordon Craig freak scenery and lighting were tried at the Abbey in Lady Gregory's Hiberno-Egyptian one-act tragic comedy *The Deliverer*, and also in Yeats's morality *The Hour Glass*. And while most voted the innovation an affected failure with possibilities for effective stage pictures, none considered it in any way an improvement on the old methods. . . . The dresses designed or carried out from sketches supplied by Craig were most unsightly and ungainly, especially in *The Deliverer*. . . . *The Deliverer* as a piece of dramatic writing is beneath contempt. 'Tripe' was the name applied to it by Miss Allgood when referring to it the other night at the Irish Literary Society. . . . The audience looked on in wonder during the progress of *The Deliverer*, all wondering what it was about and why all the Egyptians spoke Kiltartan, like the natives of the region of Lady Gregory's brain.[109]

In autumn 1911, Nugent Monck was drafted in to experiment with Craig's screens, and his production of *The Countess Cathleen* in London in July 1912 delighted among others Dorothy Shakespear: 'It was very very lovely; against a plain, folded curtain: with no footlights but lantern-light thrown from the back of the dress-circle.'[110] Monck's stay at the Abbey was brief, but he managed to establish a School of Acting and to provide with Craig perhaps the best example of Yeats's idea of a theatre 'that will please the poet and the player and the painter'.[111] In March 1913 a proposal was made by Florence Darragh for a theatre in London devoted to poetic drama with Yeats as Adviser and Craig as Producer and Designer, but this came to nothing.[112] Thereafter, Yeats and Craig went separate ways, Craig back to Italy and more experimentation, Yeats to Japanese Noh, another form of theatre in which masks also played a prominent role but where there was 'no need of scenery that runs away with money nor of a theatre-building' (*E & I* 236).

In 1915 and 1916, under the influence of Pound, Yeats immersed himself in Ernest Fenollosa's translations of Japanese plays, and he surfaced with the Noh-inspired Cuchulain play *At the Hawk's Well*, which received its first 'public' performance on 4 April 1916:

MASKS ON THE STAGE.

NEW W. B. YEATS PLAY FOR A CHARITY.

Lady Cunard has organised a performance at Lady Islington's, 8, Chesterfield-gardens, W., to be given on Tuesday next, at 3.30, for the Social Institutes' Union for Women and Girls, of which the Countess of Ancaster is the President. It provides dinners for many thousand factory girls and munition workers. There will be a play of an unusual kind, given for the first time. It is called "The Hawk's Well, or The Water of Immortality," and it is written by Mr. W. B. Yeats. Mr. Henry Ainley will act the hero, and Ito, the Japanese dancer, will take the part of the hawk's spirit. Masks will be used for the first time in serious drama in the modern world. The masks and costumes have been designed and executed by Mr. Edmund Dulac. Mr. Henry Ainley will wear a mask resembling an archaic Greek sculptured face. Instead of scenery, there will be a chorus of singers and musicians, who describe the scene as well as commenting on the action.

The performance is under the patronage of Queen Alexandra, who will be present. A limited number of tickets at a guinea may be obtained from the Countess of Ancaster, 95, Lancaster-gate, W.; Lady Edmund Talbot, 1, Buckingham Palace-gardens, S.W.; Lady Cunard, 20, Cavendish-square, W.; and Mrs. Arthur James, 3, Grafton-street, W.

How extraordinary that the Irish writer who in 1899 had declared his allegiance to establishing an Irish national theatre should find himself three weeks before the Easter Rising of 1916 staging for a war charity the first performance of a new Irish play, complete with Dulac's masks resembling Greek sculptured faces and a Japanese dancer in the costume of a hawk's spirit, in Lady Islington's drawing-room in front of the Queen! As they looked and listened, it is difficult to imagine what the audience made of the ritualistic unfolding of the cloth, the symbolic figures, the bare scenery, the pared-down imagery, and the anti-bourgeois Beckettian message from Yeats's Druidic Ireland:

> Folly alone I cherish,
> I choose it for my share;
> Being but a mouthful of air,
> I am content to perish;
> I am but a mouthful of sweet air.
> (*VPl* 413)

6

Yeats during the First World War

SEPTEMBER 1913

'September 1913' was first published in the *Irish Times* on 8 September 1913 under the title 'Romance in Ireland (On reading much of the correspondence against the Art Gallery)' and dated '7 September 1913'. It was above a letter by Lady Gregory about American money promised for the Gallery and adjacent to a report on 'DUBLIN LABOUR TROUBLES'. The original context for the poem concerned the collection of mainly impressionist paintings Lady Gregory's nephew, the art collector Hugh Lane, had promised the city of Dublin if a suitable gallery across the Liffey were built.[1] Yeats was so incensed by the negative attitude of the Dublin Corporation that in a speech about the issue he needed to tone down a particular passage which read: 'if the intellectual movement is defeated Ireland will become for our time a little huxtering nation groping in a greasy till for halfpence by the light of a holy candle'.[2] The scorn remained, and a month later, although he omitted from the poem the inflammatory and sectarian references to 'a little huxtering nation' and 'the light of a holy candle', he retained the memorable image of fumbling in a greasy till.

There is another context to the poem which the new title signalled. In July and August 1913, when Yeats was drafting the poem, the struggle between employers led by William Murphy and workers led by James Larkin intensified, culminating on 2 September in the Dublin Lock-Out. The following month, concerned for the welfare of the families, Larkin arranged for the children of the locked-out workers to be sent to England for the duration of the dispute. Murphy retaliated by rousing the Catholic clergy to protest against Catholic children being sent to English (Protestant) homes. Yeats, who had clashed publicly with Murphy before and was later to call him 'an old foul mouth' (*VP* 292), rushed into print again, this time taking his cue from Russell's open letter 'To the Masters of Dublin' in the *Irish Times* on 7 October.[3] In a letter to Larkin's paper the *Irish Worker* under the heading 'Dublin Fanaticism', Yeats accused the press and the police of hounding the workers that 'they might turn the religion of Him who thought it hard for a rich man to enter into the Kingdom of Heaven into an oppression of the poor' (*UP* 2, 407).

In choosing the title 'September 1913' Yeats enlarged the context for the poem, for now not only art but also Romantic Ireland needed defending. Ellmann reads it as a retreat into the privacy of his family, but on the contrary, as is evident from its placing in the *Irish Times*, Yeats was writing himself into a public history.[4] The tone is sharp and uncompromising, the rhymes and half-rhymes characteristically interventionist, the refrain mocking and persuasive. Ironically, we have forgotten its origins in the Lane dispute and now read the poem in the wider terms of Ireland and as part of a sequence of occasional poems which deal with the spirit of the age.[5]

ROMANCE IN IRELAND.

(On reading much of the correspondence
against the Art Gallery.)

What need you, being come to sense,
  But fumble in a greasy till
And add the ha'pence to the pence,
  And prayer to shivering prayer, until
You have dried the marrow from the bone,
  For men were born to pray and save?
Romantic Ireland's dead and gone—
  It's with O'Leary in the grave.

Yet they were of a different kind,
  The names that stilled your childish play;
They have gone about the world like wind.
  But little time had they to pray
For whom the hangman's rope was spun;
  And what, God help us, could they save?
Romantic Ireland's dead and gone—
  It's with O'Leary in the grave.

Was it for this the wild geese spread
  The grey wing upon every tide?
For this that all that blood was shed?
  For this Edward Fitzgerald died?
And Robert Emmet and Wolfe Tone,
  All that delirium of the brave?
Romantic Ireland's dead and gone—
  It's with O'Leary in the grave.

Yet could we turn the years again,
  And call those exiles as they were,
In all their loneliness and pain,
  You'd cry—" Some woman's yellow hair
Has maddened every mother's son "—
  They weighed so lightly what they gave.
But let them be, they're dead and gone:
  They're with O'Leary in the grave.
                              W. B. YEATS.
Dublin, September 7th, 1913.

Above left: 'September 1913' as it appeared in the *Irish Times*, 8 September 1913. *Above right*: Sturge Moore's cover design for *Responsibilities*, published by Macmillan in October 1916. The volume reflects Yeats's continuing determination to intervene in Irish life, albeit from the opposition benches.

National Executive, Irish Trade Union Congress and Labour Party, 1914. James Connolly is standing at the left, Larkin is seated second from right.

Winters in London were detrimental to Yeats's health, so in November 1913 he and Pound rented Stone Cottage in Sussex. 'It is a pretty place,' Dorothy Shakespear had told Pound, ' – common, heather, & woods – Georgie says the latter are haunted'.[6] Yeats took no time in settling into writing and on 23 November, two months after his intervention in Dublin, composed out loud 'The Peacock', a poem nourished in solitude and defiance:

> What's riches to him
> That has made a great peacock
> With the pride of his eye?
> The wind-beaten, stone-grey,
> And desolate Three Rock
> Would nourish his whim.
>
> (*VP* 310)

Yeats and Pound enjoyed each other's company, fenced, took walks in Ashdown Forest, and, in the first winter, read together Joseph Ennemoser's *History of Magic*. 'Yeats is much finer *intime* than seen spasmodically in the midst of the whirl,' Pound confided to William Carlos Williams in December 1913. 'We are both, I think, very contented in Sussex. He returned $200 of that award with orders that it be sent to me – and it has been. Hence the sculptural outburst and a new typewriter of great delicacy.'[7] From 1909, when he witnessed Yeats withdraw the last five pounds from his bank account, Pound was also intimate with his friend's financial position: 'Yeats didn't begin to get an appreciable income from his work till a year or so after he recd. his government pension, he must have been betweeen 46 and 50, nearer the latter.'[8] If Yeats's poem 'His Phoenix' is anything to go by, they also discussed the appeal of women and swapped stories of amorous encounters, for included in the poem is a list of women thought by some commentators to be Pound's girlfriends:

> There's Margaret and Marjorie and Dorothy and Nan,
> A Daphne and a Mary who live in privacy;
> One's had her fill of lovers, another's had but one,
> Another boasts, 'I pick and choose and have but two or three.'
>
> (*VP* 354)[9]

At one level, Pound's befriending of Yeats is easy to explain. The brash American was sizing up the culture industry in Europe, getting the saleable or readable parts ready for dispatch to Harriet Monroe, editor of *Poetry* in Chicago, or to John Quinn*, the New York collector, or wherever he could find a suitable outlet. He entered the leading Irish writer's life intent on transforming it, 'Bill But Yeats', as he later called him, being 'the only poet worthy of serious study', 'so assuredly an immortal that there is no need for him to recast his style to suit our winds of doctrine'.[10] So rapid was his conquest that within a short space he had taken over Yeats's Monday evenings, as Douglas Goldring remembers:

I shall never forget my surprise, when Ezra took me for the first time to one of Yeats's 'Mondays', at the way in which he dominated the room, distributed Yeats's cigarettes and

"STONE COTTAGE"

Postcard of Stone Cottage 'by the waste moore' Yeats sent to Pound in November 1913. 'Very dreamy he was', recounted the housekeeper Miss Welfare. 'One morning, when Mr Pound was away visiting friends I think, he came back from the post office and said, "Why, there's nothing doing, all shut up." "But Mr Yeats," I said, "Didn't you know, it's Christmas Day!"'

Photograph of Ezra Pound. In January 1913, Pound told his American audience in *Poetry* (Chicago) that Yeats 'is the greatest of living poets who use English'.

Pre–First World War Ordnance Survey Map of mid-Sussex. Coleman's Hatch is south-east of Forest Row; Ashdown Hotel, where the Yeatses spent part of their honeymoon, is east of Forest Row; Penns in the Rocks is south-east of Withyam, which is due east of Hartfield and Forest Row. Upper right is Penshurst, the country house eulogised by Ben Jonson.

Chianti, and laid down the law about poetry. Poor golden-bearded Sturge Moore, who sat in a corner with a large musical instrument by his side (on which he was never given a chance of performing) endeavoured to join in the discussion on prosody, a subject on which he believed himself not entirely ignorant, but Ezra promptly reduced him to a glum silence. My own emotions on this particular evening, since I did not possess Ezra's transatlantic brio, were an equal blend of reverence and a desire to giggle.[11]

Why Yeats chose to enjoy the company of this essentially rootless Midwesterner is less easy to explain. Partly because he did not recognise it, partly because he enjoyed it, Yeats could allow for Pound's bad behaviour and what Aldington called 'the uncleanness of his language'.[12] Yeats knew he needed Pound's incisiveness to prevent him from backsliding, as happened later in 1928 when, together again in Rapallo, Yeats made a complimentary remark about Tennyson, which Pound immediately seized on: 'Wm, so excited last evening he even maintained that Lwn Tennyson had written poesy. The Oirish are wonders for argymint.'[13] In 1912, Yeats gave Pound some poems for inclusion in *Poetry* (Chicago) but then discovered he had secretly edited them. A furious Yeats quickly relented, for he accepted that, though Pound frequently hurt people's feelings, 'he has I think some genius and great good will'.[14]

What is clear is that Pound's entry could not have been better timed. By 1913 Yeats was approaching fifty, unmarried, perhaps haunted by the thought, as Lawrence Lipking suggests, that his poetic career was at an end, his daimon in need of renewal.[15] In the persona of Hic in 'Ego Dominus Tuus' can be overheard the Poundian charge:

Pound's sketch of Yeats with intriguing accompaniment.

At Blunt's for his seventy-fifth birthday. From left to right: Victor Plarr, Sturge Moore, Yeats, Blunt, Pound, Richard Aldington, F. S. Flint.

> And, though you have passed the best of life, still trace,
> Enthralled by the unconquerable delusion,
> Magical shapes.
>
> (*VP* 367)

But when Hic declares that a style is found 'by the imitation of great masters', there is an implied criticism of Pound's 'collecting', plagiarist sensibility. Ille, or 'Willie', seeks the personal, 'an image, not a book', indeed 'my anti-self'. For Yeats, inspiration was 'as cold/And passionate as the dawn' (*VP* 348), at once emotional and like ice. In confronting the Imagist-turned-Vorticist, Yeats was forced to raise both the theory and practice of his game, and he clearly relished the challenge, responding, as he did with Joyce, to the tough realism of youth.

Of the two, Yeats was 'the dominant force' (at least this is Longenbach's view), but he needed Pound to admire him during this period of insecurity as a poet.[16] In letters to Dorothy Shakespear, Pound called Yeats 'the Eagle',[17] an image of aristocratic pretensions that fitted in with Pound's own rewriting of the Rhymers' Club and with the quality he admired in Yeats's verse, namely, nobility. Not surprisingly, they fuelled each other's anti-democratic prejudices. In 'September 1913' Yeats took care to distinguish his enemies, but Stone Cottage marked a return to the image of a common enemy in literary audience and general public alike, Pound and Yeats constituting a secret society of Modernism whose unofficial slogan became 'NO compromise with the public'.[18]

172

For both of them, it was a period of reflection. Pound's understanding of Imagism and the esoteric aspect of symbols was greatly enriched by contact with Yeats. With his expert ear, Pound had the confidence to construct his own tradition of English literature, but Yeats was more self-absorbed and preoccupied with retracing the genealogy of his family and his immediate aesthetic roots. In 'The Grey Rock', a poem which he was composing in October 1912[19] and which anticipates Pound's history-cutting exercise in 'Hugh Selwyn Mauberley', Yeats reviewed his work with the Rhymers' Club, taking care to insist, unlike Pound, on continuity:

> I have kept my faith, though faith was tried,
> To that rock-born, rock-wandering foot,
> And the world's altered since you died,
> And I am in no good repute
> With the loud host before the sea,
> That think sword-strokes were better meant
> Than lover's music – let that be,
> So that the wandering foot's content.
>
> (VP 276)

Mutual respect expressed itself in banter. Yeats's letters, typed by Pound, often sparkled into lightheadedness, as happened on the eve of their trip to Newbuildings Place, Southover, Horsham, for Blunt's seventy-fifth birthday: 'Ezra has spent the morning trying to revive his knowledge of Elizabethan english, he says poems of salutation are obsolete but he is doing his best.' They wrote to Harrods about the price of a 'motor'. Yeats thought they should present Blunt with a little alabaster box made by Henri Gaudier-Brzeska and containing a manuscript of a poem by each of them, with Pound's commendatory poem on top.[20] It was a private occasion, and only poets Pound admired were invited, but Yeats's speech was broadcast in the next issue of the *Egoist*:

We are now at the end of Victorian romance – completely at an end. One may admire Tennyson, but one cannot read him. . . . If I take up today some of the things that interested me in the past, I find that I can no longer use them. Every year some part of my poetical machinery suddenly becomes of no use. . . . We represent different schools and interests. To Sturge Moore, for instance, the world is impersonal. . . . Ezra Pound has a desire personally to insult the world. He has a volume of manuscript at present in which his insults to the world are so deadly that it is rather a complicated publishing problem.[21]

The good humour between Yeats and Pound continued into their second winter, and in April 1915 Pound finished his skit on 'The Lake Isle of Inisfree', substituting for Yeats's small cabin a little tobacco-shop and for nostalgia, brains:

> O God, O Venus, O Mercury, patron of thieves,
> Lend me a little tobacco-shop,
>   or install me in any profession
> Save this damn'd profession of writing,
>   where one needs one's brains all the time.[22]

The First World War, however, caught up with them during the third winter, when Yeats returned one evening in February 1916 to find his 'household disturbed'.[23] The

Sturge Moore's cover design for *Reveries over Childhood and Youth*. Printed in gold on mid-blue cloth, it depicts the hand of God tickling the infant into life. At the bottom of the stairwell the infant emerges as a young man on the threshold of life. The first word of the title is given, as is the name of the author, and the initials of the designer. Of all Moore's designs for Yeats, this is perhaps his most engaging. The coyness of the theme is held in check by the panel motif and geometric space. The poetic cover design, however, stands in marked contrast with the book's contents.

two writers, not realising they were in a prohibited area, had created suspicion among the authorities. Pound was requested to obtain a passport, and Yeats asked Robert Bridges* to write something to convince the authorities of Pound's identity. With Jamesian circumlocution, the poet laureate replied: 'Assuming that you are W. B. Yeats, then the man with you is unquestionably the Ezra Pound, who is your secretary, and whom I know, and with whom I have had correspondence. . . . If the Chief Constable thinks you may be two people impersonating W. B. Yeats and Ezra Pound, then there may be some difficulty; but if he is satisfied about you, I feel fully able to reassure him about your companion.'[24]

In 1946, Pound, awaiting possible death in Pisa for treason, looked back on this period of his life at Stone Cottage with affection and humour, and, with 'The Peacock' still ringing in his ears, he stamped out, almost sans corrections, on the prison camp's big office Remington typewriter Canto 83:

174

```
          so that I recalled the noise in the chimney
    as it were the wind in the chimney

              but was in reality Uncle William
    upstairs composing
    that had made a great Peeeeacock
          in the proide ov his oiye
          had made a great peeeeeecock in the
    made a great peacock
            in the proide of his oyye

    proide ov his oy-ee
    as indeed he had, and perdurable

    a great peacock aere perennius
          or as in the advice to the young man to
    breed and get married (or not)
                  as you choose to regard it

    at Stone Cottage in Sussex by the waste moore
    (or whatever)  and the holly bush
          who would not eat ham for dinner
    because peasants eat ham for dinner
          despite the excellent quality
    and the pleasure of having it hot

    well those days are gone forever
          and the traveling rug with the coon-skin tabs
      and his hearing nearly all Wordsworth
          for the sake of his conscience  but
    preferring Ennomosor on Witches
```

Typescript of part of Canto 83 composed by Pound in the compound at Pisa in 1946.

Conventional wisdom has it that Yeats was indifferent to the First World War, and for proof there is 'On Being Asked for a War Poem' (*VP* 359) and the *Oxford Book of Modern Verse* (1936), where Yeats famously declared that 'passive suffering is not a theme for poetry'.[25] For Ellmann, Yeats 'had little to say about the first World War, its issues being too abstract and international for his mind.'[26] In Wade's *Letters*, no letters between 11 June 1914 and 12 September 1914 are reproduced. The letter of 12 September, with its reference to a Zeppelin raid in London, is in fact from 1915, a mistake overlooked by subsequent commentators, including Jeffares in his 1988 biography.[27] The first reference to the war, then, occurs on 24 June 1915 when Yeats, in connection with the Abbey Theatre's London programme, confesses to Quinn that 'the war has hit us hard' (*L* 594). As for how much money Yeats raised for the war effort, this is never gone into, yet there must have been other occasions similar to the one a few weeks before the Easter Rising when he read at Baroness D'Erlanger's house in London in aid of the Star and Garter Fund.[28]

On 31 August 1914, in a letter to Lady Gregory, which included a reference to Prime Minister Asquith's German governess being arrested as a spy, Yeats confessed that outside his own little world people spent their time reading newspapers and talking themselves into a fright. He felt he now understood Stephen Gwynn's frame of mind better as well as the tension at Westminster. He recalled Sir John Moore going into battle reading Gray's 'Elegy', and how he needed tranquillity so that his mind might be ready for swift action. Yeats also told her about Aldington's difficulty in enlisting, his longing to get away from hateful London, and how much material he had for a book about fairies.[29] Overnight, the war marginalised Yeats's position in London; as Pound was quick to urge, '⟨T⟩wo-penny poets, be still! . . . give the soldiers their turn.'[30] No one wanted to listen to talk about an Irish fairy book when Europe was going up in flames. Yet Yeats manages to express genuine concern in this letter and comes close to identifying with British politicians, an intriguing reminder of what might have happened if he had continued with this vein of sympathetic imagination. The need for tranquillity, for example, is a thought that resurfaces in 'Long-legged Fly', a poem that captures in its opening stanza an image of Caesar before battle, maps spread out before him, in need of absolute quiet:

> *Like a long-legged fly upon the stream*
> *His mind moves upon silence.*
>
> (*VP* 617)

The reference to Gwynn is explained in a previous letter to Lady Gregory from the Royal Societies Club in London. Yeats and Gwynn, M. P. for Galway and a member of Redmond's Irish Party, had lunched together, and Gwynn was gloomy about the future. Churchill and Grey had persuaded Asquith to postpone Home Rule. Yeats writes that the Liberals are so angry they might engineer a coalition government with Churchill as premier. A coalition government would suspend until after the war all bills under the Parliament Act. This would exacerbate the position in Ireland, but it would be worse if an anti-Home Rule Conservative government were elected following a 'cataclasm'. If that transpired, Ireland would be betrayed by the Liberals, and the Irish Party ('in Redmond position' in Gwynn's phrase) would be finished. In passing, Yeats says the people in London are letting the war get on their nerves, and 'unless a sufficient number of people read the history of China steadily they will not know what to do if there is real disaster'.[31]

Here, at the beginning of the war, Yeats, in common with many Irish observers since the Home Rule crisis of the 1880s, immediately looked to the larger historical frame and the war's possible outcome. For some, such as James Connolly and a section of the Irish Volunteers, England's difficulty was Ireland's opportunity, but such a view was far from Yeats's thoughts, and he would not have known that in September 1914 the Irish Republican Brotherhood had appointed a military committee to launch a military rising.[32] He still believed that Home Rule could be achieved constitutionally:

> For England may keep faith
> For all that is said and done.
>
> (*VP* 394)

Gwynn was more sanguine and realised how a change of government could jeopardise not only Home Rule (suspended for the duration of the war) but the whole future of the Irish Party.

From her homes in Normandy and Paris, Maud Gonne was closer to the conflict and responded immediately: 'You seemed to have escaped the obsession of this war – I cannot; night & day I think about it *uselessly*. . . . I am torn in two, my love of France on one side, my love of Ireland on the other. . . . This war is an inconceivable madness which has taken hold of Europe. . . . Could the women, who are after all the guardians of the race, end it?' (*MGY* 347–8).[33] In January 1915 while at Stone Cottage Yeats completed 'Her Praise', a poem about Maud in what had then become 'the long war', where Yeats's desolate landscapes seemed to chime with news from the front:

> I will talk no more of books or the long war
> But walk by the dry thorn until I have found
> Some beggar sheltering from the wind, and there
> Manage the talk until her name come round.
>
> (*VP* 351)

The following autumn, Yeats received a series of letters from Maud Gonne about her nursing experiences, and central to them all was the sheer horror of war. She expressed sorrow on hearing that Robert Gregory had enlisted: 'It seems so outside his life & duty, but one cannot tell how others feel things. It must be a terrible anxiety to Lady Gregory' (*MGY* 359).[34] None of this was lost on Yeats, who told a nationalist audience in Dublin in November 1914: 'I have friends fighting in Flanders, I had one in the trenches at Antwerp, and I have a very dear friend nursing the wounded in a French hospital. How can I help but feeling as they feel and desiring a German defeat?'[35]

Yeats spent the war years largely in London. On Sundays, until her death from cancer, he visited Mabel Beardsley;* Friday evenings were spent at Ricketts's; and on Mondays he still held his open evenings at Woburn Buildings (see *L* 595). His social engagements continued much as before. He was still Director of the Abbey, even if the theatre was in the doldrums, and still a member of the Golden Dawn. On 14 October 1914, he attended the Irish Literary Society dinner at Anderton's Hotel in Fleet Street to mark the centenary of Thomas Davis's birth.[36] In November 1915 he dined with Lady Cunard and met Arthur Balfour, and learned at the same time he was to be offered a knighthood in the New Year's Honours List.[37] In January 1917 he was elected to the male-only Savile Club on Piccadilly, and the following month in a letter to Lady Gregory expressed his satisfaction: unlike his previous club, it had good fires, and he enjoyed the silence.[38]

He continued his unofficial ambassadorial functions on Ireland's behalf. In her *Journals*, Lady Gregory records an extraordinary moment in December 1916 while she and Yeats were lunching at 10 Downing Street. Yeats told Asquith about a series of lectures to be held at the Abbey and how he had 'given leave to the young men to discuss an Irish Republic, but that they were not to fix the date for it without consulting him ⟨Yeats⟩ and me ⟨Lady Gregory⟩' (*LGJ* 1, 17).[39] Lady Gregory was furious, not with Yeats, for she was accustomed to making allowances for him, but with Asquith's reply: '⟨T⟩hat is right, keep them out of time and space'. There was clearly tension in the air, because she adds that Asquith 'parted from me with particular cordiality, hoping to see me again'. Lady Gregory had presumably let her feelings be known, but in the intimate setting of Downing Street Yeats seemed over-awed and ill at ease, perhaps imagining that political intrigue, an upper-class guffaw and a patronising view of his fellow countrymen could somehow establish reciprocity with the British Prime Minister. In the period from 1916 to 1923, Yeats saw himself as a potential intermediary between nationalist Ireland and the British government, but if this moment is typical of his achievements as a negotiator, the Irish would leave the table having given away more than they had gained.

With Gosse Yeats was on a more equal footing, especially over Joyce's pension. Gosse declared: 'I would not have let him have one penny if I had believed that he was in sympathy with the Austrian enemy. But I felt you had taken the responsibility in this matter. I have communicated Joyce's name to the Foreign Office, in case they can give him any employment in Switzerland.'[40] Never slow to react when his position was maligned, Yeats replied on 28 August 1915 with some relish, adressing his letter by mistake to Shorter rather than to Gosse.

His altercation with Gosse over Joyce rumbled on, as is evident from a letter he sent George in late 1922. He had been sitting in the Savile Club reading and had overheard Gosse denigrating *Ulysses* for obscenity. Yeats walked over to him and reminded Gosse that he (Gosse) had secured financial support for Joyce from the Royal Literary Fund in 1915. Gosse replied that *Portrait* was a different book from *Ulysses*, to which Yeats suggested that it was hardly less obscene in places. Yeats then strayed to the other end of the room, where he heard Gosse, unaware that he was still there, ask if Yeats was embarrassed. Another voice indicated that he had been but that he had not lost out in the encounter. Not wishing to overhear any more, Yeats went downstairs.[41]

Blocks of time during the war were devoted to other matters: October to December 1916 with the Lane paintings, summer 1916 with marriage proposals to Maud Gonne, August 1917 with a marriage proposal to Iseult Gonne, and October 1917 with marriage to George. During the war he passed his fiftieth birthday, and gave more thought to both the dynastic theme and where to live. In March 1917, weary of town life and wanting to be back in Ireland, he acquired for £35 from the Congested District Board a run-down tower at Ballylee, County Galway, with a derelict cottage attached.[42] In 1918 he moved out of London, spending three months in Oxford, before travelling to Ireland with his new wife.

The war, however, was not without its attendant dangers. In October 1915, Yeats witnessed a Zeppelin raid while dictating in Miss Jacob's office opposite the British Museum.[43] In November 1916, he and Lady Gregory were at the House of Commons in connection with the Lane paintings when a secretary rushed out with the news that a German seaplane had dropped bombs on Eaton Square, the Palace Theatre, Victoria Station, and Brompton Road (*LGJ* 1, 15).[44] The day before his marriage to George in October 1917, Yeats set out to tell Ricketts of his decision but an air raid forced him back to the Gonnes' house, where he was dining, and he had to remain there overnight.[45] In December 1917 he apologised to Augustine Birrell for not staying in town for a dinner party on account of an air raid. The risk was no doubt small, but 'neither of us can do any work with that racket going on, and they are very fond of our neighbourhood, and much of our work is done in the evenings. Or to put it in plain words without any further excuses we are panic-stricken refugees.'[46]

The war obtruded and needed, as was later the case with the War of Independence and the Civil War, to be distanced somehow. In a letter to Farr in October 1914, Yeats observed that out of sheer exasperation with all the talk of war it was now easy to concentrate. In Ireland, by contrast, the war was more distant, and people talked about war out of a sense of duty. Yeats then asked Farr if she remembered the old Golden Dawn prophecies. He remembered Mrs Paget having 'a very stirring one'. Blunt always knew it would come, and as for a German invasion, he had locked his front door and put up a notice that combatants should go round to the kitchen.[47] To Quinn in New York Yeats wrote on 31 October 1914: 'I envy you your distance from the war for here people talk war all day & tell each other endless untrue stories. We are given so little news by the censor that we are devoted to rumour as an Irish village.'[48] His first 'war' poem, composed on 9 November 1914 and entitled 'A Meditation in Time of War', took up this theme of the unreality of war and mankind beside the oneness of life:

> For one throb of the artery,
> While on that old grey stone I sat
> Under the old wind-broken tree,

I know that One is animate,
Mankind inanimate phantasy.
(*VP* 406)

Another way of countering the war was by fashioning his 'habitual memories'.[49] *Reveries* was completed on Christmas Day 1914, its focus less on the much-vaunted Yeatsian dynastic theme than on Yeats's education in isolation. Unlike Kettle with his experience of camaraderie in the trenches, Francis Ledwidge in his more inward, bittersweet understanding of a soldier's heart, or Tynan with her devotion to those who suffered in 'the holy war', Yeats could not shake off his childhood inheritance of solitude and remoteness.[50] In a section deleted from the final version, Yeats discusses memories of Sligo's landscape that have never changed, adding somewhat vacantly: 'Even today I sometimes wonder what takes (?) me so far from these places that I love and then remember that there is not one of my name and house (?) where we were once so many and not one friend of my childhood.'[51] In Yeats, memory is full of such elisions, serving at once to promise the past and close it off, for, as Russell remarked about *Reveries*, 'His memories of his childhood are the most vacant things man ever wrote, pure externalities, well written in a dead kind of way, but quite dull except for the odd flashes. The boy in the book might have become a grocer as well as a poet.'[52]

Pound once declared that after August 1914 almost any poem became a war poem when it entered the demesne of the reader. With this in mind we might construct the following list of Yeats's 'First World War' poems:[53]

1914
November:	'A Meditation in Time of War'

1915
January:	'Her Praise'; 'The People'; 'His Phoenix'
February:	'On Being Asked for a War Poem'
April (?):	'The Scholars'
May:	'To a Young Girl'
October:	'Broken Dreams'; 'A Deep-sworn Vow'; 'Ego Dominus Tuus'; 'Lines Written in Dejection' (probably written in this month)
November:	'Presences'; 'A Thought from Propertius' (probably before) 'A Song' (1915)

1916
July:	'Men Improve with the Years'; 'The Collar Bone of a Hare'
August:	'In Memory of Alfred Pollexfen'
May/Sept.:	'Easter 1916'
October:	'The Wild Swans at Coole'
December:	'Sixteen Dead Men' (possibly December 1917) 'The Hawk' (first published February 1916) 'Memory' (?1915–16)

1917
April:	'The Rose Tree'
October:	'Owen Aherne and His Dancers' 'The Living Beauty' (1917)

180

The Morning Room at the Savile Club. The Club's motto was '*Sodalitas – Convivium*' (sodality and conviviality): there was a tradition of supplying tobacco and notepaper to members, and their low entrance fee remained constant at ten guineas from 1876 until events caught up with them in the new century. In 1927 the club moved to its present location, 69 Brook Street.

'The Balloon of the Mind' (written before 1917)
'The Cat and Moon' (1917)

1918

February:	'Tom O'Roughley'
February/March:	'Shepherd and Goatherd'
March:	'Under the Round Tower'; ?'Solomon to Sheba'
April:	'The Double Vision of Michael Robartes'
May/July:	'To Be Carved on a Stone at Thoor Ballylee'
June:	'In Memory of Major Robert Gregory'
July:	'The Phases of the Moon'
July/Sept.:	'Two Songs of a Fool'
?September:	'A Prayer on Going into My House' (published October)
November 23:	'Demon and Beast'
	'An Irish Airman Foresees His Death' (1918)
	'To a Young Beauty' (probably autumn)

181

'The Saint and the Hunchback' (1918)
'Solomon and the Witch' (1918)
'The Leaders of the Crowd' (1918)

The task that faced Yeats was to obtain a specifically Irish purchase on the war. Wyndham Lewis thought that 'the War has stopped Art dead'; after the war, he declared: 'You will be astonished to find how like art is to war, I mean "modernist" art.'[54] Ricketts conceived of the war as an attack on Art, a War of Vandalism, an expression of 'hatred and envy of the past and for all art in most human beings – latent somewhere'.[55] Yeats resisted all such pressures, and he remained relatively unaffected by the war until it touched his closest friend, Lady Gregory, with the death of her son Robert, shot down in error by an Italian pilot in January 1918.

In his obituary in the *Observer* on 17 February 1918, Yeats dwelt on Robert Gregory's self-absorption as an artist (unlike the draft, which was largely factual).[56] At the same time, he told Quinn that Gregory was the most accomplished man he had ever known. He was a courageous airman and had been particularly successful in single combat with German planes. As for the cause of his death, he apparently fainted while flying at a great height, returning from a reconnaissance expedition. 'Lady Gregory writes me grief-stricken but courageous letters.' He planned to go to Coole at Easter.[57] 'In Memory of Major Robert Gregory', completed in June 1918, took up the idea of Gregory's accomplishment, focusing not on his military prowess and bravery but on his artistic promise and personality. Yeats felt for Gregory through his mother; there is little evidence to suggest the two men were especially close. Indeed, the elegiac form affords a mask that can be used to strike a heartfelt note to conclude the poem: 'but a thought/ Of that late death took all my heart for speech' (*VP* 328). Yeats's other tribute to Gregory, 'An Irish Airman Foresees His Death', is told from the airman's Marinetti-like perspective 'somewhere among the clouds above', but it too is written with Lady Gregory in mind:

> My country is Kiltartan Cross,
> My countrymen Kiltartan's poor.
> (*VP* 328)

The stillness of both these poems reflects Yeats's distaste for the kerfuffle of war poetry,[58] though the tactful avoidance of details surrounding Gregory's death perhaps stems from Yeats's desire not to intrude upon Lady Gregory's grief.

The need for detachment from events informs most of Yeats's writings on the war, a reflection of his own marginalised position inside both Britain and Ireland. But it also dovetailed with an argument he had been conducting with his father about writing, the self, and happiness. According to J. B. Yeats, Gregory was happy because he managed to forget himself in the war, 'seeing nothing but its vastness':

Yet there is another way of self-forgetting which does not require any enormous machinery such as sanguinary war. It is of course that of art and Beauty. The triumph it aims at establishing for ever is to lose yourself while remaining within the vast of your own personality – which is what I understand by Beauty. . . . Now you see the antagonism between a state of war and the practice of art and literature. ⟨War⟩ offers an easier way of forgetting yourself and willing to be happy we grasp at it with eagerness, and all the poets desert the difficult paths they have been climbing; it is so much easier to carry a rifle and a knapsack than to try to write poetry. . . . In everything except art and poetry the loss of self – the oblivion – is not complete.

(LS 247–8)[59]

In 'Ego Dominus Tuus', the philosophical poem written in the second year of the war, Hic argues that men of action have produced art:

> Yet surely there are men who have made their art
> Out of no tragic war, lovers of life,
> Impulsive men that look for happiness,
> And sing when they have found it.

Ille denies such a possibility:

> No, not sing,
> For those that love the world serve it in action,
> Grow rich, popular, and full of influence,
> And should they paint or write still it is action:
> The struggle of the fly in marmalade.
> The rhetorician would deceive his neighbours,
> The sentimentalist himself; while art
> Is but a vision of reality.
> What portion in the world can the artist have
> Who has awakened from the common dream
> But dissipation and despair?

(VP 369)

For Yeats, art is a vision, not a reflection, of reality. After the war, he thanked Sassoon for his little book with its delicate rhythms and its complex irony, but the message was the same. He thought Sassoon had greatly improved on his war work, 'though lacking so popular a theme may not be reason for it. Your "Grandeur of Ghosts" is itself grand in its exact modern fashion; and my own memory of a lunch at Blenheim proves how close you can keep to the facts and yet make it alive.'[60] With its Decadent countering of art to the world, of poetry to rhetoric, 'Ego Dominus Tuus' would have been strained or precious before August 1914, but after that date the imagery does not seem overdone. Indeed, it is the context of a 'tragic war' that gives it added authority. 'The struggle of the fly in marmalade', preceded by references to serving the world 'in action', quickly conjures up the stalemate along the Maginot Line. Waking from a dream also acquires greater urgency because of the war. The one word out of place is the Nineties word *dissipation*.[61]

EASTER 1916

The most famous war poem almost never to appear in First World War poetry anthologies is 'Easter 1916'. Yet for everyone at the time, insurgents, soldiers, politicians, journalists alike, the Easter Rising and the Great War were theatres of the same war. Only later did the poem become detached from one of its historical orbits. Pearse, for

183

example, believed 'the last sixteen months have been the most glorious in the history of Europe. Heroism has come back to the earth.'[62] On the issue of the executions, Shaw insisted that they were prisoners of war, that the relation of Ireland to Dublin Castle was precisely that of Belgium to the Kaiser.[63] Yeats, surveying the incompetence of British generals in France, saw 'no reason to believe that the delicate instrument of Justice is being worked with precision in Dublin' (*L* 613). Maud Gonne had a vision which directly linked the two: 'At the beginning of the war I had a horrible vision which affected me for days. I saw Dublin, in darkness & figures lying on the quays by O'Connell Bridge, they were either wounded or dying of hunger – It was so terribly clear it has haunted me ever since. There must have been scenes like that in the streets of Dublin during the last days' (*MGY* 373).[64] Maud's view intrigued Yeats, not least because it carried visionary weight, and he returned to it immediately in a letter to Lady Gregory on 11 May, at the same time expressing the hope that Maud would continue nursing the French wounded till the trials were over: 'Maud Gonne reminds me that she saw the ruined houses about O'Connell Street and the wounded and dying lying about the streets, in the first few days of the war. I perfectly remember the vision and my making light of it and saying that if a true vision at all it could only have a symbolised meaning' (*L* 613).

Yeats's poem rehearses the mood of 'September 1913'.[65] The colour is grey, the words polite and meaningless, the dress motley. Romantic Ireland is dead and gone. O'Grady's Great Enchantment holds the will of Ireland paralysed. In common with Pearse, Yeats recognised that 'shock is necessary to achievement'.[66] But while the Rising had been planned by the insurgents since the beginning of the war, it came as a profound shock to Yeats, who was visiting Rothenstein in Gloucestershire at the time:

> Yeats was staying with us when the news came, and was much upset. These men, poets and schoolmasters, he explained, are idealists, unfit for practical affairs; they are seers, pointing to what should be, who had been goaded into action against their better judgment.
>
> I hoped that James Stephens was not among them; no, he was too wise, said Yeats; Pearce ⟨sic⟩ and his friends were good men, selfless but rash, throwing their lives away in a forlorn hope.
>
> The future Senator foresaw neither the dark days ahead nor the brighter to come.[67]

On returning to London, Yeats sat down and wrote to Lady Gregory in a vein half-mocking, half-aware that something significant was under way. He did not know if his letter would arrive, now that Arthur Griffith was acting as censor at the General Post Office and 'Starkie' perhaps in charge of the sorting room. He thought the Rising 'a tragic business' that would change Ireland and have important consequences for their work. In London, because of the government's news restriction, they knew little. He had just returned from Rothenstein's, where he had stayed up late and sat for a series of portraits.[68]

On 6 May Yeats thanked Rothenstein for his hospitality, a task he should have completed earlier, 'but this terrible Irish news put letter writing out of my head'.[69] His mood now changed, he wrote again to Lady Gregory on 11 May: 'I had no idea that any public event could so deeply move me – and I am very despondent about the future' (*L* 613). On 23 May he told Quinn that he was 'planning a group of poems on the Dublin rising but cannot write til I first enter (?) the country'.[70] He was absorbing the event from a distance, turning over phrases in his head, picking up others from Maud Gonne's

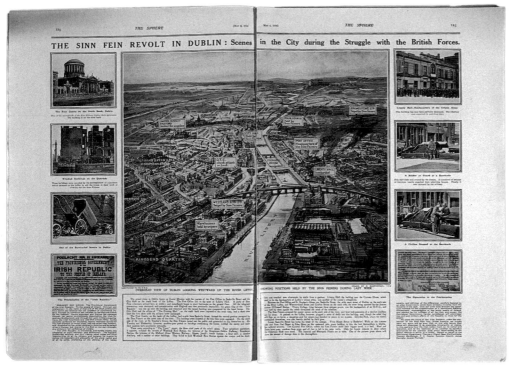

Easter 1916, as it was relayed to readers of the *Sphere*.

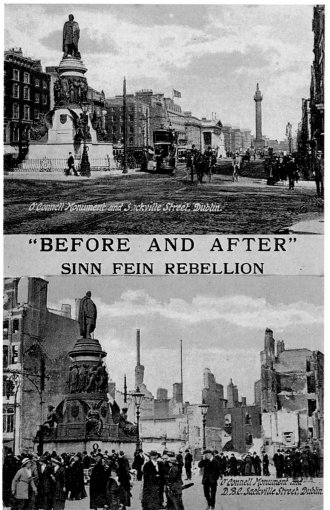

Before and After Sinn Fein Rebellion, a hand-coloured postcard from the period.

Inside the General Post Office, British soldiers survey the damage. 'Transformed utterly:/A terrible beauty is born' (*VP* 393).

letters: 'tragic dignity' (*MGY* 372); 'I do not think their heroique sacrifice has been in vain' (373); the deaths of the leaders are 'full of beauty & romance' (377). In his 11 May letter to Lady Gregory, he downplayed the idea of 'symbolised meaning', but this is precisely what he was pursuing: 'I am trying to write a poem on the men executed – "terrible beauty has been born again"' (*L* 613).

Yeats had enough time between May and 25 September 1916, the date he added to the end of 'Easter 1916', to rid his thoughts of indecision.[71] In a letter to Bridges on 13 June, he mentioned he had just returned from Dublin, where he had dined at Bailey's with Lady Gregory and St John Ervine. Information on this visit is limited, and Yeats chose not to write about it in his *Autobiographies*, but he must have been shocked by the destruction. Lady Gregory was watching his every mood. In August, the month when Casement was executed, she wrote to him: 'I had been a little puzzled by your apparent indifference to Ireland after your excitement about the Rising.' She followed this in September: 'I cannot but be glad all this trouble turns you back to Ireland.'[72] If Yeats was indecisive, the same could not be said of Maud Gonne, who told him on 4 June that she now intended to live in Ireland (*MGY* 380). Meanwhile, his father was at first in two minds about the Rising: 'I am not sure that this absurd "rising" will not in the end help home rule and make it more substantial. I say this chiefly because I remember that York Powell said that the first thing that made English people take Ireland seriously was the assassination of Lord Frederick Cavendish – The English carry on their dealings with Ireland by managing to forget that it exists.'[73] But the executions in early May resolved the issue:

C. Jones's advertisement in the *Irish Independent* on 14 June 1916.

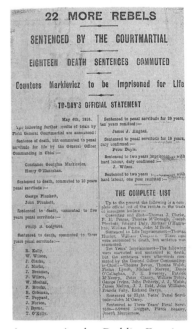

A report in the *Dublin Evening Mail* on 6 May 1916.

Tylers's humorous advertisement appeared in the Dublin *Evening Mail* on 22 May 1916.

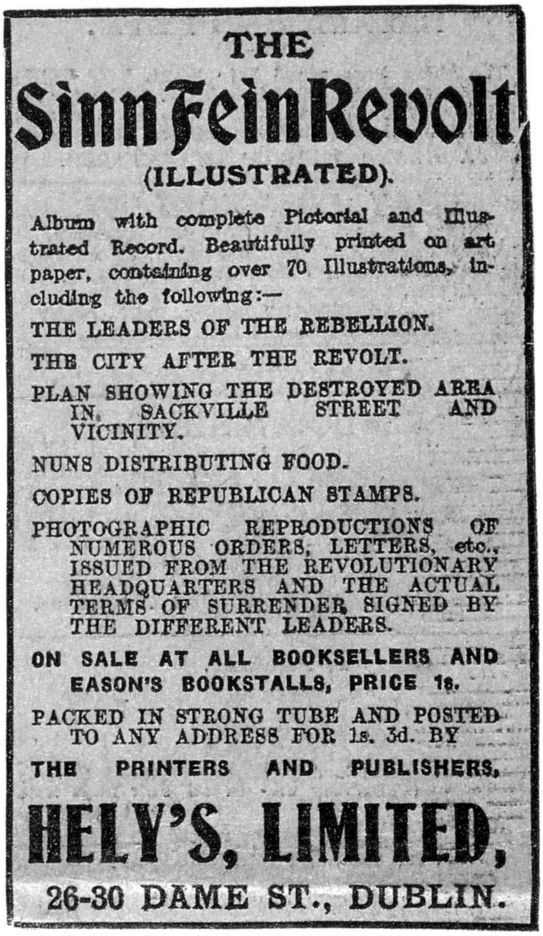

THE
Sinn Fein Revolt
(ILLUSTRATED).

Album with complete Pictorial and Illustrated Record. Beautifully printed on art paper, containing over 70 Illustrations, including the following:—

THE LEADERS OF THE REBELLION.

THE CITY AFTER THE REVOLT.

PLAN SHOWING THE DESTROYED AREA IN SACKVILLE STREET AND VICINITY.

NUNS DISTRIBUTING FOOD.

COPIES OF REPUBLICAN STAMPS.

PHOTOGRAPHIC REPRODUCTIONS OF NUMEROUS ORDERS, LETTERS, etc., ISSUED FROM THE REVOLUTIONARY HEADQUARTERS AND THE ACTUAL TERMS OF SURRENDER SIGNED BY THE DIFFERENT LEADERS.

ON SALE AT ALL BOOKSELLERS AND EASON'S BOOKSTALLS, PRICE 1s.

PACKED IN STRONG TUBE AND POSTED TO ANY ADDRESS FOR 1s. 3d. BY

THE PRINTERS AND PUBLISHERS,

HELY'S, LIMITED,
26-30 DAME ST., DUBLIN.

The *Irish Independent* on 14 June 1916 advertised an illustrated booklet of the Sinn Fein Revolt. The booklets sold well, and, according to the August/September 1916 issue of the *Irish Book Lover*, quickly became a collector's item. Although it was fought by the Irish Volunteers and the Irish Citizen Army, it soon became known as the Sinn Fein Rising.

The English government by cruelly killing these fifteen and putting their name on the role of martyrdom and these lads themselves by their mad ideality and death may or may not have injured the cause of home rule. Nevertheless the national education of Ireland will go on much faster and much further. In the heart of a Protestant people are always materialism and the grim rules that enforce it. In the heart of a Catholic people is ideality with no rules except those that spring spontaneously from the quest for beauty. This ideality the church for its own ends 'manages' and yet it keeps it alive although mostly lying under the mesmeric sleep of the church. Yet it is still there, and so you have an outbreak like the Irish rebellion, which would be impossible in England where there is too much common sense, and yet quite possible in France or in any Catholic country. . . . This Irish rebellion and the fate of these young men make the world richer, yet I do not love the Judas Iscariots who sent them to their fate.[74]

Normally, when he felt strongly about an issue, the courageous, shrewd, or foolhardy Yeats rushed into print. But there is no record of a letter to the press or to the government protesting about the executions, nothing to compare with Shaw's fearless protest.[75] Perhaps, with the line that he had no gift to set a statesman right ringing in his ears, Yeats took the view that it was wrong to meddle, for after all England may keep faith. Perhaps he was anxious about his application for membership to the Savile Club, which he set in motion on 25 May 1916, or about transferring all his copyright to

188

Oliver Sheppard's statue 'The Death of Cuchulain', executed in 1911 and 1912, was placed in the General Post Office in the 1930s as a memorial to those who died in the Easter Rising. The inscription is taken from the Proclamation of the Republic. In 'The Statues', composed in 1938, Yeats wondered: 'When Pearse summoned Cuchulain to his side,/What stalked through the Post Office?' (*VP* 611).

Above right: Pearse statue at St Enda's, Rathfarnham. 'This man had kept a school/ And rode our wingèd horse' (*VP* 392).

Pearse's cottage, Rosmuc, in Connemara.

Macmillan.[76] Perhaps he would have agreed with Russell: 'I asked my own soul about all this trouble and got, not opinions, but a direction of feeling, and what I wrote under that inspiration I do not intend to make public simply because I am in a movement which is non-political and I am an important figure in it and any statement made by me might create a split and cause intense anger in a movement hitherto free from political passions, and in my opinion the only hope for Ireland.'[77] More suspiciously, Conor Cruise O'Brien assumes that the decision to delay was 'calculated'.[78] Such a line seems even less convincing in the light of Yeats's letter to Gwynn in October 1918 concerning the publication of *The Dreaming of the Bones*, his play about the Rising, written for the most part in May and June 1917:

> It is one of my best things but may be thought dangerous by your editor because of its relation to the rising of 1916. My own thought is that it might be published with editorial note either repudiating its apparent point of view or stressing this point of view. England once, the point of view is, treated Ireland as Germany – Belgium. I doubt if a long poem or verse play is worth anything to a popular paper unless they make a feature of it or relate it to current interests.
>
> > (*L* 654)[79]

It is interesting to speculate if, when he was composing 'Easter 1916', Yeats knew he would delay its publication. His name at the time was linked, at least by some, with the causes of the Rising. A correspondent, for example, writing from the west of Ireland in the *Daily Chronicle* on 9 May 1916, observed:

> When W. B. Yeats created the Irish theatre it was with an almost uncanny knowledge of the needs and capacities of the Irish. He having given the lead, Irish theatres sprang up everywhere. . . . Has not this revolution in some sense a genesis in the Irish Theatre? Where out of Paris would you find the Countess Markievicz? That kissing of the revolver now before she handed it up! The terms in which the main body of the insurgents surrendered, 'the members of the Provisional Government', 'the units of the Republican Forces', the sounding titles of such men as P. H. Pearse and James Connolly, it is all of the stuff of drama – the heady wine of the French Revolution in new bottles.[80]

There is merit in the argument that Yeats delayed for fear of fuelling the situation. His historic task since the fall of Parnell was to free 'Irish literature and criticism from politics', and he felt the Rising had overturned 'all the work of years' (*L* 613). Equally, he kept going over in his mind and wondering 'if I could have done anything to turn those young men in some other direction' (*L* 614). But all this remains speculation. A more likely and less spectacular explanation for Yeats's silence and for the delayed publication of the poem until 1920 can be found in a letter to Clement Shorter in March 1917 in which was enclosed a copy of 'the Rebellion poem' for private printing: 'Please be very careful with the Rebellion poem. Lady Gregory asked me not to send it you until we had finished our dispute with the authorities about the Lane pictures. She was afraid of it getting about and damaging us & she is thus (?) timid.'[81]

Pound defined literature as 'journalism that *stays* news', and perhaps the best example of this in modern literature is 'Easter 1916'.[82] For in spite of the delay in publication, and in spite of the work of revisionist historians, the poem will not lie quietly down but still acts – or has the potential to act – like a time bomb in modern Irish culture.[83] *Cathleen ni Houlihan* no longer inspires in quite the same way as it did those first audiences in

1902, but 'Easter 1916', 'perhaps the most remarkable poem of our time upon a public event', continues to impress.[84] As Russell recognised: 'Nothing is more important to a nation than the images which haunt the minds of its people, for it is by these they are led to act.'[85] In a strange way, every time the poem is read aloud there is an act of shaman-like consecration, a summoning of 'the great symbolic beings . . . into the imaginations of entranced subjects',[86] and it is as if not the event but the poem itself is the trans-forming agency:

> I write it out in a verse –
> MacDonagh and MacBride
> And Connolly and Pearse
> Now and in time to be,
> Wherever green is worn,
> Are changed, changed utterly:
> A terrible beauty is born.
>
> (*VP* 394)

Yeats, who was often wise after the event, also recognised that 'shock is necessary to achievement', for, as he once confessed, his inspiration was always unforeseen and sudden. Janet Framer speaks of André Malraux's 'Cassandra-like sense of how and where history was getting ready to be made. What he wrote was, to an unhappily large extent, what history turned out to be.'[87] By contrast, when the most important event in modern Irish history was unfolding, Yeats was in Gloucestershire, but instinctively or by good fortune he managed to hit the appropriately ambivalent long note. So much so that virtually no one any longer thinks of the apprentices, bakers, barmen, bookbinders, brush-makers, carpenters, chauffeurs, coach-builders, coopers, electricians, farriers, goods-checkers, hairdressers, insurance agents, labourers, librarians, locksmiths, night watchmen, porters, printers, riveters, shirt-cutters, shunters, waiters, wax-bleachers, weavers, who went out to break the English connection.[88]

The Dreaming of the Bones

The power of 'Easter 1916' is also apparent in *The Dreaming of the Bones*, a Noh play set not in Dublin but amid the unaccommodated landscape of County Clare. The play is in part an attempt to 'explain' the forces behind the Rising in the light of Yeats's interests in the occult and Irish mythology. Characteristically, from the opening scene there is something that disturbs, something that resists rational incorporation, a reminder that his work is 'not drama but the ritual of a lost faith' (*Y & TSM* 156):

> Have not old writers said
> That dizzy dreams can spring
> From the dry bones of the dead?
> And many a night it seems
> That all the valley fills
> With those fantastic dreams.
> They overflow the hills,
> So passionate is a shade,

> Like wine that fills to the top
> A grey-green cup of jade,
> Or maybe an agate cup.
>
> *(VPl* 762–3)

'Easter 1916' provides a direct discourse on the Rising, but in this play Yeats chooses an indirect route. With references to 'dizzy dreams' and 'dry bones' Yeats tempts the audience to make appropriate political (and sexual) associations. Metaphors in this opening song work not by fusing but by switching between literal and figurative meanings. The grey-green is both descriptive of the cup and evocative of the new Ireland transformed from grey to green. Yeats's version of the historic destiny of the West is embodied in the dreams that overflow the hills and carry into the towns, for Dublin shopkeepers like Thomas Clarke, fumbling in a greasy till, could not themselves construct a vision of Ireland that was anything but materialistic. Something similar happens with a word like 'fantastic'. As with the words *delirium* in 'September 1913' and *bewildered* in 'Easter 1916', 'fantastic' is here used by Yeats in a double sense: the dreams of the insurgents are both deluded and transformative. 'So passionate is a shade' affords a further jolt, but in this case Yeats's interest in the occult is allowed because this seems but another way of imagining the hold the past has on the present. Yeats believes these things are literally true; most people believe they are metaphoric.

The Dreaming of the Bones turns on the encounter between political passion and historical forgiveness. A young man – the *Waki*, or Traveller, in Noh theatre – who fought in the General Post Office and is now on the run from the authorities, meets a stranger and his girlfriend, who are the ghosts of Diarmuid and Dervorgilla, the guilty pair responsible for inviting Henry II into Ireland, for selling the country into slavery, and beginning the seven-hundred-year oppression by Britain. The young man has eyes only for politics. There would be more hiding-places had the trees not been cut down by 'English robbers'; as they pass the ruins of the Abbey of Corcomroe, it is not their religious but their political significance that interests him:

> Is there no house
> Famous for sanctity or architectural beauty
> In Clare or Kerry, or in all wide Connacht,
> The enemy has not unroofed?
>
> *(VPl* 769)

The conversation between the stranger and the young girl returns to the torment of ghosts and to their own predicament as lovers who are now unable to meet with their lips, for ever sundered by the memory of their crime. If someone would forgive them, the curse would be lifted. The young man's response is predictably blunt:

> O, never, never
> Shall Diarmuid and Dervorgilla be forgiven.
>   . . .
> The horizon to the east is growing bright.
>
> *(VPl* 773)

Diarmuid and Dervorgilla, the ghost lovers, drift in a dance from rock to rock, leaving the young man to declare:

NO. 5 (NEW SERIES) MAY 1935.

A BROADSIDE

EDITORS: W. B. YEATS AND F. R. HIGGINS; MUSICAL EDITOR, ARTHUR DUFF. PUBLISHED MONTHLY AT THE CUALA PRESS, ONE HUNDRED AND THIRTY THREE LOWER BAGGOT STREET, DUBLIN.

THE ROSE TREE
"O words are lightly spoken,"
Said Pearse to Connolly,
"Some politicians idle words
Have withered our Rose Tree;
Or maybe but a wind that blows
Across the bitter sea."

300 copies only.

Front page of the May 1935 edition of *Broadsides*. Illustration by Harry Kernoff; music by Arthur Duff.

> I had almost yielded and forgiven it all –
> Terrible the temptation and the place.
> (*VPl* 775)

The play ends with the musicians singing as they unfold and fold the cloth:

> I
> At the grey round of the hill
> Music of a lost kingdom
> Runs, runs and is suddenly still.
> The winds out of Clare-Galway
> Carry it: suddenly it is still.
> . . .
>
> II
> My heart ran wild when it heard
> The curlew cry before dawn
> And the eddying cat-headed bird;
> But now the night is gone.

193

I have heard from far below
The strong March birds a-crow.
Stretch neck and clap the wing,
Red cocks, and crow!
(*VPl* 775–6)

Yeats left Pound in no doubt that 'the Dervorgilla play' was openly nationalist: 'England has no business whatever (as I think you put it) to obtrude his affairs on Ireland.'[89] But the play's enigmatic ending is troubling, though perhaps deliberately so. On the one hand, Yeats recognised that political passion left little room for forgiveness. If the young man were to forgive Diarmuid and Dervorgilla, his passion for Ireland's independence would suffer accordingly. Better to hear 'the strong March birds' (*VPl* 776) – the Easter Rising, that is – than the subjective, wild night which produces bitter dreams. On the other hand, Yeats seems to be saying, the cause of Irish nationalism is somehow bound up with the dry bones that betrayed Ireland in the past. The question he seems to be posing is how to integrate the two sides, how to 'hold in a single thought reality and justice' (*AV [B]* 25). Perhaps the young man, inheriting the bitterness of the past, refusing to participate in the act of dreaming back, turns his heart into a stone. Perhaps there is something unnerving in the way modern Ireland deliberately turns its back on its guilty past and crows for the bright new dawn. Along with the many occult interpretations, *The Dreaming of the Bones* allows such meanings to gather. The 'music of the lost kingdom' is sufficiently broad to encompass a lament for Diarmuid who lost his kingdom of Leinster or the revolutionary nostalgia that fuels modern revolutions. The play is so internal to Ireland that it threatens to make Yeats's interpretation merely external: 'England once . . . treated Ireland as Germany – Belgium.'[90]

OCTOBER 1917

On 20 October 1917, a year before the end of the war, Yeats married Georgina Hyde-Lees at Harrow Road Registry Office, and almost immediately they began their automatic writing sessions. As is evident from chapter 2, so entwined were marriage and the occult with the Yeatses that it is difficult to construct an adequate account or even a chronology of this period. Yet such an account or narrative is clearly as crucial to the Yeats story as was their emphasis on initiatory moments in the life of a believer. Yeats would not have been the first bachelor over fifty approaching married life to have suffered anxieties, but there is a murkiness about the contexts and origins of their relationship which is rightly troubling. This is partly because some correspondence remains unpublished, partly because I suspect both parties were anxious to conceal feelings from each other.

In his Introduction to 'The Great Wheel', Yeats originally wrote:

On the afternoon of October 24th 1917, four days after my marriage my wife said she would attempt automatic writing. She told me afterwards that she had meant to make up messages and having amused me for an afternoon say what she had done. She did invent a few lines, some imaginary name, some imaginary address, some vague greeting, and then it was as if her hand were grabbed by another hand, and then came disjointed sentences

194

The Yeatses' marriage certificate.

in an almost illegible writing. What came was so exciting, sometimes so profound that I persuaded her to give day after day an hour or perhaps hours to the unknown writer, and after some half dozen hours offered to spend what remained to me of life explaining and piecing together those scattered sentences.

This was then shortened: 'On the afternoon of October 27th 1917, four days after my marriage my wife surprised me by attempting automatic writing but didnt suppose she would succeed.'[91] The word *amused* was subsequently changed to 'distracted'. In the 1937 version of *A Vision* Yeats omits any reference to George inventing things or her design to amuse or distract him.

The conventional view is that on getting married George wanted to lift Yeats out of his listlessness and depression and presumably gain his attention. She knew he was impressed by psychic phenomena, and what could be more 'distracting' than an afternoon of automatic writing? As it happened, what was an afternoon's ruse on George's part became a seven-year project for Yeats, 'my wife bored and fatigued by her almost daily task and I thinking and talking of little else' (*AV [B]* 9). Ellmann, perhaps a little disingenuously, writes: 'In the excitement of marriage Mrs Yeats discovered that she possessed this ability to suspend her conscious faculties.'[92] On the contrary, the first days of her marriage were very trying, and, as Ellmann notes in his second edition, she contemplated leaving him (xvi). And neither is Ellmann trustworthy when he states: 'Marriage was a humanizing and normalizing experience, but in no sense a prosaic one' (221). There was nothing normal about Yeats's semi-detached marriage, unless Yeats's leaving George to bring up the children in Ireland and leading a bachelor's life in London and elsewhere is normal. It is difficult to see how it was in any way a humanising experience for George – no matter what she said to Ellmann in the 1940s. When Wade was preparing an edition of Yeats's letters in the early 1950s, he wrote to George about Yeats's letter to Lady Gregory on 19 September 1917 (see *L* 632–3): 'About that letter to Lady Gregory: I had the same idea about it as you have, and that was why I partly

195

asked your advice. How do you think it would do just to cut out the three lines referring to Maud & her "strange conviction", put three dots, and print the rest of the letter? . . . I rather feel that the rest of the letter forms an important bridge; the letters immediately before it are unhappy and about Iseult – and the next letter after it comes from a W. B. married and happy. This letter marks the transition.'[93]

Yeats first met George at Olivia Shakespear's salon at 12 Brunswick Gardens, Kensington.[94] The year was 1911, the same year Olivia's daughter Dorothy and Ezra Pound announced their engagement. Between their first meeting and their marriage in 1917, Yeats and George led relatively separate lives, but it is difficult to believe that in the small circle of occultists and West End salons their paths did not cross quite frequently.[95] On 30 September 1917, less than three weeks before the marriage, Nelly Tucker (Edith Ellen Tucker, George's mother) wrote to Lady Gregory in a vain attempt to have everything called off:

> I am very much afraid that Mr Yeats meant to propose to my daughter in November ⟨19⟩15. I did not consider him free to do so then. But it was only a mutual interest in astrology, which is, so Mr Yeats tells me 'a very flirtatious business'! The war and its interest helped to keep us apart for some time, but unluckily, last March, having no idea that Mr Yeats's life was in any way changed, and feeling a little unkind at my long neglect of him I asked him to come & see me, never supposing there was any question of his marrying my daughter.
>
> Other . . . misconceptions arose, a mutual friend interested him in my daughter, the idea occurred to him that as he wanted to marry, she might do. Fortunately she has no idea of all this unpleasant background, she thinks he has wanted her since the time of the astrological experiments, and when he proposed to come & see us here, I told her he was now free. But it has dawned upon her that there is something amiss, after a long talk with Mr Yeats yesterday. . . . She is under the glamour of a great man 30 years older than herself & with a talent for love-making. But she has a strong and vivid character and I can honestly assure you that nothing could be worse for her than to be married in this manner, so there will be no harm done and a rather unpleasant episode can be closed. She has told no one of the affair, and only a few intimate friends of Mr Yeats (who we do not know) are aware of the matter. Mr Yeats has the kindest heart and I feel that only you can convince him of the entire undesirability of this engagement. George is only 24 and is to begin work at the F.O. in October of a very interesting nature. I am not trying to keep her from marrying, but the present idea seems to me impracticable. . . .
>
> Yours sincerely,
> E. E. Tucker
>
> P.S. . . . If George had an inkling of the real state of affairs she would never consent to see him again, if she realised it after her marriage to him she would leave him at once.[96]

Lady Gregory's reply is not known, but it seems to have reassured George's mother: 'As long as George has no idea of what I told you I think all will be well now. I am much reassured by your opinion of Mr Yeats's feelings.'[97]

On the eve of his marriage Yeats sent an anxious letter to his father in which he commented in turn on George's appearance and personality, the length of time he had known her, her financial status, the longstanding interest of a close friend in the match, and the discovery that George's mother had no objection to the marriage (clearly a distortion on Yeats's part of Nelly Tucker's concerns and the chronology of events). Yeats's letter forms the basis for the family's interpretation. In a chatty letter to her father on 17 October, Lily Yeats writes: 'Willy will have told you, I suppose, just what he told us. She is 24, clever, speaks several languages, and has some money and will have more . . . He says she is comely, so this may mean not good-looking . . . He has known her for some years, but they only settled all this a week ago and are telling very intimate friends so as to keep the Press off.'[98] Interestingly, in a letter, dated 6 November 1917, to his increasingly reluctant financial support Quinn, this is given a different spin by Yeats senior: 'He was married on the 20th. I know nothing further except that she is much too young, yet clever, speaking several languages, and that her father was educated at Eton and Oxford, and that her family own Gainsboroughs and Romneys; which all means money.'[99]

At issue for Nelly Tucker was not only the age gap but also Yeats's affairs with other women.[100] In November 1915, she suggested, Yeats was not free to marry George, a reference perhaps to his affection for Iseult Gonne.[101] When MacBride was executed in May 1916 for his part in the Easter Rising, Yeats travelled to Normandy to propose once again to Maud Gonne. When she declined, Yeats asked Iseult, who enjoyed 'flirting with her mother's rejected admirer'.[102] In September 1916 Yeats escorted mother and daughter back to London, where he introduced Iseult to his London friends, including the Pounds and George. Iseult also seems to have been in his thoughts in spring 1917 when he was purchasing Thoor Ballylee. He told Lady Gregory that a quarrel with Olivia Shakespear had thrown into doubt plans to stay in London and had thus made Ballylee more important than ever.[103] On 1 April 1917 he wondered if he could get a photograph made from Robert Gregory's drawing of Ballylee interest to Iseult.[104]

Yeats's friends differed about his choice of marriage partner, Lady Gregory preferring Iseult, Olivia Shakespear George. In July 1917, but three months before his wedding to George, Yeats, while staying with Maud Gonne in Normandy, continued to be fascinated by Iseult. He was not attracted to her sexually, but was delighted by her youthfulness and found it difficult to decide what he felt. If his feeling towards Iseult became sexual he would immediately leave, for he thought their age difference stood in the way of her happiness.[105] The choice did not in fact materialise, for Iseult refused him, an outcome Yeats half-knew from the start:

> How could she mate with fifty years that was so wildly bred?
> Let the cage bird and the cage bird mate and the wild bird mate in the wild.
>
> (*VP* 450)[106]

On 19 September 1917, Yeats notified Lady Gregory of his intention to marry George: 'Perhaps she is tired of the idea. I shall however make it clear that I will still be friend and guardian to Iseult' (*L* 633). Yeats seems to have been desperate to marry in 1917, perhaps, Harwood suggests, as 'a consequence of astrological advice'.[107] But as late as 13 October, as he confided in Lady Gregory, doubts persisted. Anxious about the future, fearful that the marriage would not take place, constantly preoccupied with Iseult, he felt desperate and emotionally drained. Some calm was restored at a meeting with Iseult from which George deliberately excluded herself. Iseult's kindness to him and her concern for the happiness of George convinced Yeats that his own motives were disinterested and that he could make George happy. The new equanimity allowed Yeats to come to terms with Lady Gregory's accusation that he would be marrying in the clothes he had bought for courting Iseult. All was to be resolved: Iseult was gracious, George was noble, and Yeats was above reproach.[108]

197

Iseult Gonne as a teenager.

Marriage did not at first abolish his doubts or the feeling that he had betrayed three women, Maud Gonne, Iseult, and George herself, but then 'something very like a miraculous intervention' occurred, and his mood, as he told Lady Gregory, altered:

Two days ago I was in great gloom, (of which I hope, and believe, George knew nothing). I was saying to myself 'I have betrayed three people'; then I thought 'I have lived all through this before.' Then George spoke of the sensation of having lived through something before (she knew nothing of my thought). Then she said she felt that something was to be written through her. She got a piece of paper, and talking to me all the while so that her thoughts would not affect what she wrote, wrote these words (which she did not understand) 'with the bird' (Iseult) 'all is well at heart. Your action was right for both but in London you mistook its meaning'. . . . The strange thing was that within half an hour after writing of this message my rheumatic pains and my neuralgia and my fatigue had gone and I was very happy. From being more miserable than I ever remember being since Maud Gonne's marriage I became extremely happy. That sense of happiness has lasted ever since. The misery produced two poems which I will send you presently to hide away for me – they are among the best I have done.

(*L* 633)[109]

The war years were among the most productive of Yeats's career as a writer. He wrote some forty-three poems he wished to preserve for posterity, including a fine elegy 'In

198

Memory of Major Robert Gregory', a tantalising, dialectical study of the Self and Anti-Self in 'Ego Dominus Tuus', and the sweet-tempered 'Wild Swans at Coole'. Three intensely personal yet curiously impersonal plays were composed in this Noh-inspired period: *At the Hawk's Well, The Dreaming of the Bones*, and *The Only Jealousy of Emer*. In *Per Amica Silentia Lunae* he began the construction of a philosophical system that he hoped would comprehend Anima Hominis (the soul of man) and Anima Mundi (the soul of the world). He had championed the cause of Joyce, discovered new interests in Japanese Noh drama, and written introductions to Tagore's Bengali play *The Post Office* (published in July 1914) and Pound's edition of *Certain Noble Plays of Japan*.[110] He had published the first volume of his autobiography, renewed contact with his fictional personae Robartes and Aherne, and embarked on an intense period of occult experimentation with his wife, experimentation which, according to a recent commentator, 'has its place within the resurgence of spiritualism caused by the terrible losses at the front'.[111] Pound had come and was soon to go, and Middleton Murry had dismissed *The Wild Swans at Coole* as Yeats's 'swan song'.[112] Indeed, according to an editorial in the *London Mercury* in January 1920, 'From Mr Yeats and Mr Kipling we do not now expect the unexpected.' But his most authoritative work in poetry and philosophy was still to come. When the war began, Yeats the man was unmarried, approaching fifty, living in London, and under the assumption that Romantic Ireland was dead and gone; when it ended, he was married, middle-aged, and contemplating a return to Ireland, where a terrible beauty had been born and where the terrible wars of 1919 to 1921 and 1922 to 1923 were about to commence. His return to Ireland was anything but an Odyssean *nostos*, and it was not long before he was thinking of leaving again.

Studio portraits of the Yeatses by Underwood and Underwood, taken in New York in 1920. The same year Yeats had been nominated by *Vanity Fair* for the Hall of Fame 'because he is the greatest poet writing English today'.

7

Yeats in the 1920s

FAMILY MAN

Oxford

During the first four years of their marriage, the Yeatses lived in Oxford.[1] London was still detrimental to the poet's health, and, besides, the Controls 'cannot send you images when your mind is restless' (*YVP* 1, 311).[2] They both dreaded Oxford women famous for their lack of clothes sense,[3] but Yeats was determined to make a splash among 'Old, respectable bald heads' where 'All shuffle . . . all cough in ink' (*VP* 337). He bought himself a faun-coloured corduroy jacket, which George commented on favourably in a letter to Lollie. She thought the jacket slightly eccentric but appropriate for Oxford. Their visit to the university city proved a success; they spent their time, happily – reading, writing letters, and visiting the Bodleian.[4]

Yeats instituted his Monday evenings and kept open house for undergraduates and other visitors, such as F. P. Sturm, L. A. G. Strong, and fellow-spiritualist William Force Stead.[5] On Sunday afternoons he was invited out to Garsington Manor, home of Lady Ottoline and Philip Morrell, where he would enter the drawing-room 'flushed and ruffled like an eagle that had been to sleep and omitted to preen its feathers'.[6] In a letter to Yeats in June 1938, Force Stead recalle 'Lady Ottoline with her peacocks and clipped yew hedges – Welbeck Abbey in the background – and her mind full of the Yellow Book and Thomas a Kempis – and so much more.'[7] Yeats was at home in her 'unclassifiably wicked'[8] company, and when she moved to Gower Street in London in 1927 Yeats was again among her regular visitors, along with Eliot, Huxley, and Sassoon.

Oxford was a place to stir memories, and prompted 'All Souls' Night', an elegy on his British occult friends Horton, Farr (Emery), and Mathers. The poem returns us to postwar Oxford where bells ring, ghosts come, and the prospect of peace is disturbed by the (remote) possibility of hearing 'the cannon sound/From every quarter of the world' (*VP* 471). It is not the post-war world that fills the canvas of Eliot's 'unreal city' in *The Waste Land* (1922), and there is no echo in Yeats's poem of the returning soldiers who, according to Aldington, had but one topic of conversation – 'the war, which they refused to discuss with anyone who had not been in it'.[9] Yet somehow it seems appropriate that 'All Souls' Night' should constitute a bookend for a volume about war and violence, most of which was still to be written when this poem was composed in 1920.[10]

> Horton's the first I call. He loved strange thought
> And knew that sweet extremity of pride
> That's called platonic love,

Yeats talking to Lytton Strachey at Garsington Manor.

> And that to such a pitch of passion wrought
> Nothing could bring him, when his lady died,
> Anodyne for his love.
>
> On Florence Emery I call the next,
> Who finding the first wrinkles on a face
> Admired and beautiful,
> And knowing that the future would be vexed
> With 'minished beauty, multiplied commonplace,
> Preferred to teach a school
> Away from neighbour or friend,
> Among dark skins, and there
> Permit foul years to wear
> Hidden from eyesight to the unnoticed end.
>   (*VP* 471–2)

As always, Yeats layers the poem with alternative sources of meaning, for the focus is on friends whose lives were in many ways unsuccessful or had petered out. Because he was a Catholic, Horton could not entertain divorce, and so he was unable to marry 'his lady', Audrey Locke. Yet he could not protect his 'strange thought' from the entanglement of desire, from 'that sweet extremity of pride/That's called platonic love' (*VP*

202

471).[11] With her emigration to Ceylon in 1912, Farr, the New Woman, started life again, discarding the body's "'minished beauty' for the discourse on 'the soul's journey'. The presence of Mathers in the poem reminds us of an unresolved aspect to Yeats's relationship with all three. Farr never returned to England, and died a Hindu in April 1917. After Yeats moved to Oxford, his friendship with Horton became less intimate, and in early 1918 Horton was knocked down by a car, his health deteriorated, and he died in February 1919. After his ejection from the Golden Dawn in April 1900, Mathers, according to Yeats, was driven mad with loneliness for 'meditations upon unknown thought/Make human intercourse grow less and less', and he died in 1918.[12] There is another unresolved aspect in the poem. 'All Souls' Night' was selected as an epilogue to *A Vision*, and in this context the poem reveals a different complexion, for while Yeats 'wished for some system of thought which would never leave my imagination free to create as it would', his occult friends were 'looking for spiritual happiness & without any practical aim for some form of unknown power'.[13]

Events in Yeats's Life in the 1920s

Date	Address	Personal or Historical Event
1918		
January–March	45 Broad Steet, Oxford	
March–April	County Wicklow	
April	Coole Park	
May–September	Ballinamantane House, Gort	'The Phases of the Moon' (July)
Late September	Ballylee, County Galway*	
October	73 St Stephen's Green, Dublin	
November		End of First World War; George contracts pneumonia
December		Sinn Fein election victory
1919		
January	96 St Stephen's Green	Dáil Eireann established; War of Independence begins; 'The Second Coming'
February	96 St Stephen's Green	Birth of daughter Anne; death of Horton
June–August	Intermittently at Ballylee	Relinquishes Woburn Buildings
October	4 Broad Street, Oxford*	
1920		
January–May	USA/Canada Lecture Tour	
June–August	Holland Place, London	
August–December		Actively considers a two-year appointment as professor of English literature in Japan
August		George has miscarriage; Yeats in Glenmalure to counsel Iseult
October		MacSwiney dies on hunger strike; Yeats's tonsils removed by Gogarty
November		'All Souls' Night'; 'To Major Gregory, airman'
1921		
February		Speech at Oxford Union; *Michael Robartes and the Dancer*
April–June	Minchin's Cottage, Shillingford	'Nineteen Hundred and Nineteen'
June	Cuttlebrook House, Thame	

Date	Address	Personal or Historical Event
July		Truce in Anglo-Irish War
August		Birth of son Michael
September		Michael operated on in London
October		*Four Plays for Dancers*
December		Anglo-Irish Treaty signed
1922		
January		At Irish Race Conference in Paris
February		Joyce's *Ulysses*; death of J. B. Yeats
March	82 Merrion Square, Dublin*	
March–September	Ballylee	'Meditations in Time of Civil War'
April		First shots in Civil War
June		Four Courts shelled
August		Death of Griffith; Collins murdered; Republicans blow up bridge at Ballylee
October		Eliot's *Waste Land* published in the *Criterion*; Mussolini's march on Rome
November	Garsington Manor	Childers executed
December	Savile Club/Dublin	Joins Senate
1923		
January	Savile Club/Dublin	Campaigns in London for modification of Treaty and for return of Lane pictures; Gogarty kidnapped by Republicans; perhaps needs persuasion to return to Dublin
April		O'Casey's *Shadow of a Gunman*
May		End of Civil War
September		'Leda and the Swan'
November		Awarded Nobel Prize
1924		
July		Death of John Quinn
August		Tailteann Games
October	Coole	
November	Savile Club	
1925		
January–February	In Sicily and Rome	
May	Savile Club/Coole	
June		Speech on divorce in Senate
October		*The Tower*
1926		
January		*A Vision*
February		O'Casey's *Plough and the Stars* causes controversy at Abbey
March		Visits St Otteran's School, Waterford
May/June	Ballylee	
June		'Among School Children'
July		Reads Spengler's *Decline of the West*
September		'Sailing to Byzantium'
November		*Autobiographies*
1927		
February		Lady Gregory stays whole month
July	Ballylee	O'Higgins assassinated
August		'Blood and the Moon'
November–January	Algeciras, Seville, Cannes	'A Dialogue of Self and Soul' (Dec.)

Date	Address	Personal or Historical Event
1928		
February–April	Rapallo	*The Tower* (February)
June		Sophocles' *King Oedipus*; row after Abbey rejects O'Casey's *Silver Tassie*
July	42 Fitzwilliam Square, Dublin*	
August		*A Packet for Ezra Pound*
September		'Coole Park'; resigns from Senate
November–May	Rapallo	
1929		
January	Rome	
July	Coole	
October		Wall Street Crash
November–March	Rapallo	Makes will (29 December)
December		Nazis win Bavarian municipal elections

* First time occupied by Yeats.

In 1914 Yeats publicly apologised to his ancestors for having nothing but a book 'to prove your blood and mine' (*VP* 270). Marriage to George in 1917 was fraught with difficulty, since Yeats was taken with the idea of family but perhaps not with the responsibility of family life. Moreover, for a man who had experienced many affairs with women, it is surprising that he knew very little about a woman's menstrual cycle and that he needed a medium's prompting in the area of love-making.[14] At the automatic writing session on 31 July 1919, Yeats was told: 'Sexual health unaccustomed for some time to twice – therefore *gradually* try twice as always once will increase fatigue – But you must accustom yourself to gradually declining power & rest assured your power will always be amply sufficient.' Yeats wanted to know why once will increase fatigue: 'Because you cease to be able to do more – it is like not taking enough exercise & a long walk exhausts you.' He thought he should do it twice a month: 'No only when the configurations I told you & *never* more than once for every three times of *once*' (*YVP* 2, 349). In his enthusiasm for the occult, Yeats also needed reminding not to forget love-making, that 'both the desire of the medium and her desire for your desire should be satisfied – that is to say her desire & you as the image of her desire must be kept identical' (*YVP* 2, 487).

He needed little reminding about responsibility for his Yeats family. His father was a constant source of worry, as were his consumptive sister Lily and his impecunious sister Lollie at the Cuala Press, and financially he supported all three. As for his father, Quinn never succeeded in returning him to Ireland, and, unwearied by life, he died in New York in February 1922. On 6 February 1922 the *New York Times* printed Jeanne Robert Foster's elegy, which included lines reminiscent in their thought of the son:

> 'The artist is the only happy man,' he told us.
> 'Art springs from a mood of divine unreason.
> Unreason is when a man cannot be at peace with eternal conditions.'

Yeats himself was less eloquent, but he was no less moved by his father's death. 'He has died as the Antarctic explorers died', he wrote to Lily, 'in the midst of his work and the middle of his thought, convinced that he was about to paint as never before' (*L* 676).

In March 1918, the Yeatses left Oxford for a visit to Ireland that included County Wicklow, Coole Park, and Ballylee. In Dublin, Yeats introduced his new wife to his family, a moment vividly captured in a letter Lollie wrote to her father at the time. Yeats had wired ahead from Chester, so the sisters had time to substitute the plebeian corned beef for a joint of beef and to get Maria to polish the floor again. 'This is my wife, Maria,' announced Yeats on the doorstep. George immediately shook hands, which elicited from Maria the comment 'hasn't she nice manners'. What struck Lollie were George's beautiful blue eyes and something less tangible:

> <Y>ou feel she has plenty of personality but that her disposition is so amiable that she does not often assert herself – not from inertness but because she is happiest in agreement with the people around her – this is the impression she gave us – she has gaiety and is I am sure intuitive – she would fit in anywhere.[15]

The last comment was both an accurate assessment and prediction, for indeed the outwardly placid George went out of her way to fit in with Yeats's lifestyle and Dublin was indeed the 'anywhere' she would call home for the rest of her life.

The following year, Anne was born in Dublin just when the War of Independence began, the month after Yeats had composed 'The Second Coming'. On their return to Oxford in June 1919, Yeats again indulged his dynastic fantasies and imagined fatherhood prolonging his life. He thought of himself living to 1970, perhaps to the year 2000 (when Anne would be 91). His past family stretched before him ennobled by the passage of time like a Chinese emperor.[16] He was delighted with Anne's cradle, her energy, and her theology: 'When she says the Lord's Prayer she makes such interjections as "Father not in heaven – father in the study," or "Dada gone to Coole"' (*L* 684). But, as a letter to Quinn in October 1920 suggests, his children seem to have bored him. When recovering from an operation to remove his tonsils, Yeats would look out of the window at Anne strapped into her perambulator in the garden twisting about and wonder which was more boring, convalescence or infancy.[17]

It comes as a shock to read in Yeats's correspondence of his asking George to tell Anne, if she were old enough to understand, of his love for her.[18] Occasionally, George could barely disguise her exasperation, as when she reminded him to buy a mechanical toy for Michael's birthday; Michael had spent the previous day playing with a toy car given him by their domestic.[19] George was a very private person, not given to display, but she must have been repeatedly hurt by being patronised and made to feel small among his circle of loud friends. She must have been perplexed by a letter he wrote from Coole (the rival for his affections) comparing love to being idle together.[20] In April 1924, when George was ill in Dublin, Yeats could not decide if he should come up from Coole. He thought she had been working too hard and not looking after herself. If he did come to see her he would stay at the Club, because he did not want her thinking he might be uncomfortable.[21] On the other hand, as in May 1928, Yeats was conscious of neglecting her, and contemplated composing a long poem to her, about the length of the Byzantium poem, to compensate for his lack of attention.[22] And we should not forget that 'Under Saturn', written in November 1919, is addressed to George:

> Do not because this day I have grown saturnine
> Imagine that lost love, inseparable from my thought
> Because I have no other youth, can make me pine;
> For how should I forget the wisdom that you brought,
> The comfort that you made?
>
> (*VP* 390–91)

At Oxford, as later elsewhere, George was at the mercy of visitors, most of them intent on seeing her more famous husband.[23] August 1920, when Yeats was in Ireland attempting to resolve Iseult's marital problems and when Lily was staying in the house, was especially taxing.[24] George was anxious about her pregnancy, and the horary was not good. She felt that if Yeats had not returned within a fortnight she would get him to write to her to join him. The following day she was going to the Bodleian not to read, for her eyes were sore, but to be by herself.[25] Yeats, who was a conscientious letter-writer, replied at once, as did George. His last letter made her cry with relief. She was longing for intellectual stimulus. But domestic duties called, and she now had to put Anne to bed.[26] That month George suffered a miscarriage.

For her part, George respected confidences and saw her own role as the wife of a famous poet, but this did not prevent her from being irreverent or even devious in her relations with him. In February 1927 she replied to yet another request from Pound for new poems: 'Non poss! In other words since William was ill & convalesced here we have had Lady G staying here . . . for a month . . . and all has been held up in consequence. There IS a mass of verse bad and goodish . . . but it has to be sorted . . . and until there is once more solitude in the house it seems impossible to get this done.'[27] In September 1927 she urged Pound to reply at once if he wanted 'certain poems' as 'WB doesnt know the bloody moon is gone to you & is imagining I am serialising it with Dial.'[28]

Her letters to McGreevy are peppered with injunctions for him to be discrete or to burn the letter. She was especially frank about her husband's writing, as in 1925:

> I have been reading nothing but poetry just lately *not* his!! and it has made me realise how damnably national he is becoming. Nationality throws out personality and there's nothing in his verse worth preserving but the personal. All the pseudo-mystico-intellecto-nationalistico stuff of the last fifteen years isnt worth a trouser-button. . . . As long as there was any gesture in it, as long as there was a war on and so on and so on, it was worth it, but really now to spend hours listening to rubbish in and out of the Senate and going to committees and being visited by fishermen's associations, and Freddie Ryans' and nincompoops and miaows and bow-wows of all sorts mostly mongrels is a bit too much. However.[29]

In March 1926 she told McGreevy she had 'bit Willy's head off' after a disagreement about a Shaw play: 'Chiefly because he was exalting Abbey acting against "the English Stage Cliché" and I'd been very cock-a-hoop on Saturday night that Ireland hadnt won the triple crown. . . . Anyhow he was most abusive and he was being really very cross and unpleasant coming home from the Abbey and going on like a thorough paced Irish-anti-Englishman.'[30] In his letters to her, McGreevy seems to pick up on George's irreverence towards Yeats. In 1926, in a passage berating the comical way Irish Protestants were attempting to maintain a link with Catholic Ireland, he called Yeats 'the last live Irish Protestant'.[31]

Ballylee

In a lecture to an audience in Boston in September 1911, Yeats revealed the force the 'little picturesque village' of Ballylee exerted on his imagination: 'In Ireland the country life has for us the further fascination that it is the only thoroughly Irish life.'[32] For Yeats, Ballylee was within motoring distance of Cork and 'very far from Oxford education'.[33]

Robert Gregory's Vision of the Tower at Ballylee.

Facing page: Yeats with Michael and Anne in the 1920s. When Yeats was staying at Mount Stewart in County Down with Lady Londonderry, he told her that he always knew if any of his children were taken ill, by a strong smell of burning feathers in his nose.

It was 'a setting for my old age, a place to influence lawless youth' (*L* 651), and when reading *Ulysses* in spring 1922, he wondered if he had had 'this tower when Joyce began I might have been of use, have got him to meet those who might have helped him' (*L* 651). But, for George, the Tower was less romantic, being in need of repair and a drain on their resources, and the American lecture tour in spring 1920 could not have come at a better time, for, as Pound quipped: '⟨H⟩e'll have made enough to buy a few shingles for his phallic symbol on the Bogs. Ballyphallus or whatever he calls it with the river on the first floor.'[34]

There was also the issue of security. During the War of Independence, it was not always safe to visit Ballylee.[35] In 1922, during the Civil War, they spent many months there, perhaps not always aware of possible danger. The Civil War intensified in June 1922 with the defeat of the Republicans in the Four Courts in Dublin. Before that, there were sporadic skirmishes between Free Staters and Republicans, not all of it serious, and in April Yeats could write that they were now comfortably settled, away from newspapers, unaware if civil war was raging elsewhere in Ireland.[36] By October 1922 the situation had deteriorated, and they had an unlucky flight from Ballylee. The adjacent bridge was blown up, the river was blocked, and the ground floor flooded. They were pleased to leave: George and the servants had become nervous at night, as had Anne.[37]

In May 1923, at the end of the Civil War, Yeats returned to Ballylee and relayed the bad news to George. The door to the Tower had been damaged, and they could not get in. The following day he returned with Raftery, only to find nothing stolen. As to the

209

motives of the intruder, Raftery, with a touch of Irish humour, surmised that perhaps it was somebody who wanted a job as a caretaker.[38] The following April, the Tower was beginning to look habitable, and, as Yeats told George, he was delighted with the top room and its fireplace.[39] In May 1924, he told her the whole castle was nearing completion including the new room which had been plastered by Raftery.[40] But no sooner was the Tower complete than they were thinking of leaving it, partly as a result of learning in January 1927 that Lady Gregory was to relinquish Coole. The myth of the Tower proved irresistible. According to Yeats's obituary notice in the *New York Times* on 30 January 1939, the Yeatses 'lived for many years with their two children in an ancient tower on the outermost coast of Ireland'.

THE WIDENING GYRE

The War of Independence (1919–21)

The War of Independence touched Yeats's exposed nationalist nerve, especially in November 1920 when Ellen Quinn, her child in her arms, was murdered in Kiltartan by the Black and Tans. Lady Gregory knew the Quinns personally: 'Poor Malachi Quinn; he had trouble enough to bear, and was sad last week when he came to see me. . . . When I pray "God save Ireland" the words come thrusting through "Gott strafe England" in spite of my desire not to give in to hatred' (*LGJ* 1, 197).[41] Yeats internalised the strength of his substitute mother's feelings, and in 'Reprisals', a poem originally entitled 'To Major Robert Gregory, airman', he contrasted British Army atrocities with the actions of the First World War hero who 'had brought down some nineteen planes':

> Flit to Kiltartan Cross and stay
> Till certain second thoughts have come
> Upon the cause you served, that we
> Imagined such a fine affair;
> Half-drunk or whole-mad soldiery
> Are murdering your tenants there;
> Men that revere your father yet
> Are shot at on the open plain;
> Where can new-married women sit
> To suckle children now? Armed men
> May murder them in passing by
> Nor parliament, nor law take heed; –
> Then stop your ears with dust and lie
> Among the other cheated dead.
>
> (*VP* 791)

On 23 November 1920, Yeats forwarded it to Lady Gregory. He had not asked her permission but he intended sending it to *The Times*. He was happy with the poem, which he felt was good for its purpose. A note on the envelope in Lady Gregory's hand put a stop to this: 'I did not like this and asked not to have it published.'[42] As she confided in her *Journals*: 'I cannot bear the dragging of R., from his grave to make what I think a not very sincere poem – for Yeats only knows by hearsay while our troubles go on – and he quoted words G.B.S. told him and did not mean him to repeat – and which will give pain' (*LGJ* 1, 207).[43] Yeats's last First World War poem was therefore withdrawn, and not published until after both their deaths.

Apparently, in his softer moods, Yeats would declare: 'The English mean well by the Irish, but they don't mean it much.'[44] He lacked the passion of young IRA men like Sean O'Faolain whose experience of revolution brought them into contact with 'men and women at their best, transformed beyond all mortal frailty'.[45] In a debate at the Oxford Union in February 1921, however, Yeats came out fighting:

> Mr W. B. Yeats said the law had never broken down in Ireland. English law had broken down, but though he was not a Sinn Feiner he would say that Sinn Fein justice was real justice. . . . The causes which made the Germans act so in Belgium were the same precisely as those which were making officers – the Black and Tans – act madly and brutally in Ireland today, and those causes were drink and hysteria. . . . The verdict of the military enquiry was that the woman was struck by a descending bullet fired from the lorry 'as a precautionary measure' . . . 'I do not know' declared Mr Yeats 'which lies heaviest on my heart – the tragedy of Ireland or the tragedy of England.'[46]

In April 1921, while Yeats was drafting 'Thoughts Upon the Present State of the World' (later retitled 'Nineteen Hundred and Nineteen'), the phrase about Ellen Quinn resurfaced:

Thoor Ballylee today with the farmhouse sheltered by its wall.

Yeats, George, Anne, and Michael, Summer 1929.

> Now days are dragon-ridden, the nightmare
> Rides upon sleep: a drunken soldiery
> Can leave the mother, murdered at her door,
> To crawl in her own blood, and go scot-free.
> (*VP* 429)[47]

The same month, he wondered in a letter to Lady Gregory if any of his letters arrived with the seal broken. George's seals had been, but he was certain Dublin Castle knew that he and Lady Gregory were not essentially interested in politics.[48] Nowhere in 1921 could be safer to write about the troubles in Ireland than Oxford. Yet, somehow, Yeats would have enjoyed being the centre of a disturbance, as might have happened in November 1921 at Aberdeen when he was forced to abandon a lecture. After his Dublin experience, he found interruptions by an audience rather pleasantly exciting, but it was impossible to prevail against the singing of the National Anthem. He had also detected beneath a friendly surface a certain hostility, not to him personally but towards Ireland.[49] The following November, however, the hostility caught up with him, and he was forced to pay an increased fee at the Savile Club, 'as Ireland is no longer a friend of Greta Britian' ⟨*sic*⟩.[50]

The Tower

The Anglo-Irish Treaty was signed in December 1921, the Yeatses moved to Dublin in March 1922, and the Civil War spread in June 1922. From March to September 1922 they were in Ballylee, for the first time in two and a half years (*L* 680), and it was here that Yeats composed most of the sequence 'Meditations in Time of Civil War'. In August 1922, he informed Sturge Moore he was working on 'a series of poems about this Tower and on the civil war at which I look (so remote one is here from all political excitement)

212

'Benighted travellers/From markets and from fairs/Have seen his midnight candle glimmering' (*VP* 419–20). Samuel Palmer's illustration for *Il Penseroso* appeared in *The Shorter Poems of John Milton* (1889). It was reversed by mistake, the tower appearing on the right.

as if it were some phenomenon of nature' (*Y & TSM* 46).[51] The poem consciously alights on the immediate world at Ballylee: Yeats's writing-table with Sato's sword on it, the acre of stony ground, the torn petals in his garden, the road outside his door, the stream, the moorhens, the bees in the stare's nest. But no image is allowed to stand outside history; each image is taken up into the poet's thought and set rustling. Sato's gift becomes a symbol for art that is changeless, but Yeats quickly adds: 'only an aching heart/Conceives a changeless work of art.' The acre of stony ground is also 'Where the symbolic rose can break in flower'. The road outside is the meeting-place for the poet's direct encounter with what the participants imagined were the opposing forces of history, the Irregulars (or Republicans) and the Free State soldiers 'half dressed in national uniform':

> An affable Irregular,
> A heavily-built Falstaffian man,
> Comes cracking jokes of civil war
> As though to die by gunshot were
> The finest play under the sun.

213

Right: a Japanese
ceremonial sword
given to Yeats in
March 1920 by
Junzo Sato Japanese
consul in Portland,
Oregon. *Far right*:
Sturge Moore's cover
design in gold leaf
for *The Tower*
(1928).

Below: an example
of the layout and
typography from the
Macmillan edition of
The Tower (1928).

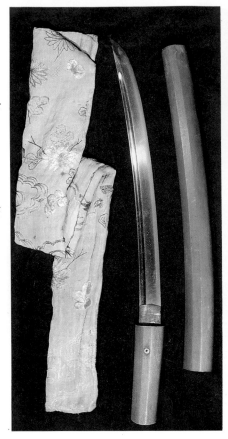

26   MEDITATIONS

I count those feathered balls of soot
The moor-hen guides upon the stream,
To silence the envy in my thought ;
And turn towards my chamber, caught
In the cold snows of a dream.

VI

THE STARE'S NEST BY MY WINDOW

The bees build in the crevices
Of loosening masonry, and there
The mother birds bring grubs and flies.
My wall is loosening ; honey-bees
Come build in the empty house of the
    stare.

We are closed in, and the key is turned
On our uncertainty ; somewhere
A man is killed, or a house burned,
Yet no clear fact to be discerned :
Come build in the empty house of the
    stare.

MEDITATIONS   27

A barricade of stone or of wood ;
Some fourteen days of civil war ;
Last night they trundled down the road
That dead young soldier in his blood :
Come build in the empty house of the
    stare.

We had fed the heart on fantasies,
The heart's grown brutal from the fare,
More substance in our enmities
Than in our love ; oh, honey-bees
Come build in the empty house of the
    stare.

VII

I SEE PHANTOMS OF HATRED AND OF
    THE HEART'S FULLNESS AND OF
    THE COMING EMPTINESS

I climb to the tower top and lean upon
    broken stone,
A mist that is like blown snow is
    sweeping over all,

A brown Lieutenant and his men,
Half dressed in national uniform,
Stand at my door, and I complain
Of the foul weather, hail and rain,
A pear-tree broken by the storm.

I count those feathered balls of soot
The moor-hen guides upon the stream,
To silence the envy in my thought;
And turn towards my chamber, caught
In the cold snows of a dream.

                                    (*VP* 423–4)

In 'Easter 1916' Yeats sought to transform history into symbol; here in 'Meditations in Time of Civil War' he seeks symbols or systems that will somehow resist the encroachment of history. These are no longer soldiers of destiny but warring factions, and there is no terrible beauty to be born. 'Perhaps there is nothing so dangerous to a modern state, when politics takes the place of theology, as a bunch of martyrs. A bunch of martyrs (1916) were the bomb and we are living in the explosion' (*L* 690). Ironically, the months he spent at Ballylee in 1922 were in fact 'a great pleasure': 'George makes at every moment a fourteenth century picture. And out of doors, with the hawthorn all in blossom all along the river banks, everything is so beautiful that to go elsewhere is to leave beauty behind' (*L* 683). But in this poem, Yeats, making effective use of the pause at the ends of lines, evokes the sheer terror of living through such a war.

In May 1927 Yeats asked Sturge Moore to design a cover in gold for *The Tower*: 'The frontispiece I want is a drawing of the castle, something of the nature of a woodcut. If you consent I will send you a bundle of photographs. It is a most impressive building and what I want is an imaginative impression' (*Y & TSM* 109).[52] In November 1927 Moore completed the design and returned the photo to Yeats, adding tongue-in-cheek: 'I think the Tower is recognisably your Tower and not anyone else's' (*Y & TSM* 114).[53] Yeats specified that the Tower 'should not be too unlike the real object, or rather that it should suggest the real object. I like to think of that building as a permanent symbol of my work plainly visible to the passer-by. As you know, all my art theories depend upon just this – rooting of mythology in the earth' (*Y & TSM* 114).[54] In one respect Yeats got what he wanted, for the resemblance of Moore's design to Thoor Ballylee is more apparent than real: the reflection, for example, is strictly speaking impossible, for on this side of the Tower there is no water. Moore's cover design, however, insists on a certain reading of the poems which follow. The solidity of the Tower in the upper half of the central panel is humanised by its reflection in the lower half. If it is to be a 'permanent symbol', then it is also a medium for reflection. Moore might have depicted the Tower as a central object with no water, no reflection, no problematic join between upper and lower halves of the panel. In his Notes to *The Winding Stair* published by the Fountain Press in 1929, Yeats imagined the Tower a 'watch tower or pharos', but there seems no hint of this in Moore's design. Instead, he chose a 'troubled mirror' (*VP* 430), a design that is suggestive and inviting rather than aloof and symbolic. The leaves and branches add a botanical perspective, deflect us from thoughts about 'rooting mythology in the earth', and enforce the human quality.

For Denis Donoghue, '*The Wild Swans at Coole* is history, consistent with symbolism; *The Tower* is symbolism, glancing ruefully at history.'[55] The tension between history and

Dáil Eireann, 10 April 1919. Here are the key players in the emergence of modern Ireland, held together by their opposition to Westminster rule. Many of them, including Kevin O'Higgins and de Valera, were to feature in the Yeats story in the 1920s and 1930s.

This Astrological Judgement upon the Four Quarterly Ingresses of the Present Year appeared in Moore's *Almanack* for 1870. Yeats's poem 'The Second Coming' owes as much to the *Almanack* as to contemporary history, for when he came to read the signs of the times, he consulted the stars and found in them the eye of God.

symbolism is heralded in *The Tower*'s opening poem, 'Sailing to Byzantium', where the protagonist calls to the sages standing in God's holy fire to gather him into the 'artifice of eternity'. The word *artifice* is deliberately ambivalent, being something both beautifully crafted, a work of art, and also something false and artificial. The volume begins with the line 'That is no country for old men', with a journey to the East, to a country other than Ireland. After all, Ireland in the 1920s was indeed in one respect 'no country for old men': the new Free State was governed for the most part by people in their late twenties and early thirties. Kevin O'Higgins, Minister of Home Affairs, was born in 1892; Ernest Blythe, Minister of Local Government, in 1889; Michael Collins, Commander-in-Chief of the Government Forces, in 1890.

But the movement of *The Tower* is towards an affirmation of humanity, the return to the West, to history, to the Civil War, to the inability to escape from time either through philosophy or through art. Not even Moore could have suspected the degree of vulnerability the volume contained, but he had done enough to suggest a tension between image and reality. Moore, who had known Yeats for more than a quarter of a century, did not need to have all the poems in front of him, and the intensity of their correspondence provided the groundwork for a design which was more than adequate to introduce the poems to posterity. It was as if George in one of the automatic writing sessions in March 1918 had planned it, when in reply to his question 'Is tower symbol of PB?' (Passionate Body) she answered: 'Yes but no connection with after death states – it is a symbol only in life – abundant flowing life – never after life' (*YVP* 1, 394).

THE IRISH SENATOR

In October 1922 the Yeatses left Ballylee for Dublin in optimistic mood. He told Force Stead he was unfazed by the postal strike, it being an example of the general state of disorder against which his government was fighting. He had started his Monday evenings again, and extended an invitation to Stead to stay in his pleasant large house, with a great drawing-room, a house built in 1740 for a crowded social life, which had long since passed away. In the eighteenth century a score would have been entertained to dinner or dancing, but George would receive at tea a dozen guests. To reassure Stead, Yeats added – in his unreassuring way – that Dublin was quiet, even though most nights bursts of gunfire could be heard and the newspapers still carried reports of ambushes.[56] In late November 1922, however, while Yeats was at Garsington Manor,[57] the situation dramatically worsened – at least for George. The previous night there was an explosion nearby. George was anxious that Maud Gonne and her associates would be looking to 'Senator' Yeats for his help. (Yeats's name had been publicly linked with the Senate in November 1922.) She listed the circumstances then uppermost in her mind: her unease that the parading of placards had ceased; the possible consequences arising from the execution of Childers and other Republicans; the vehement opposition to the executions especially among the working class.[58]

The following day George sent him another letter, informing him that the Taoiseach had had no knowledge of the four executions the previous week, and that there had been a delay of eleven hours before the relatives of those executed had been informed. She thought no-one cared about the MacSwineys but there was widespread unease about the unauthorised executions. The previous night there was firing again. She went to

217

'Byzantium' by David Finn. 'O sages standing in God's holy fire/As in the gold mosaic of a wall,/Come from the holy fire, perne in a gyre,/And be the singing-masters of my soul' (*VP* 408).

the pictures with McGreevy, and they were greeted on their way out with machine gun fire.[59]

Unlike Yeats, who welcomed the fact that 'We are preparing here, behind our screen of bombs and smoke, a return to conservative politics as elsewhere in Europe' (*L* 693), George, with her political roots in England, could not be so cavalier about the rights and sufferings of individuals. In spite of her 'English sub-soil' and her 'sound anti-Gaelic instinct',[60] she also seems to have developed in a remarkably short time her pro-Irish political sensibilities. She understood, for example, the significance of the unauthorised shootings (they were followed in January 1923 by a renewed upsurge in Republican house-burning). Moreover, as Secretary of the Dublin Drama League, she mixed in circles denied her more famous and reactionary husband. George complained about what she saw as disinformation circulating about Yeats: that he had refused to help Mrs MacSwiney, that he was a supporter of the English Government, that he was opposed to the Free State. George believed that the pro-English accusation came from Helene Malone rather than Maud Gonne. She tried to counter this accusation among pro-de Valera Republican women, and then discovered the accusation had currency only among the Despard group.[61]

While Yeats was in London in early December 1922, lunching with Eliot and talking

218

Joyce, poetry, and recent dreams,[62] he had two officials from the Provisional Government knocked on the door with an invitation to join the Senate.[63] According to fellow-Senator Gogarty, Yeats's appointment was not because of his poetry or his work at the Abbey but because he had been a member of the IRB.[64] Whatever the case, for Yeats an upper chamber meant more autocracy, less democracy. At the first session, according to the *New York Times* on 12 December 1922, 'Mr W. B. Yeats, the poet, dropped into a seat apart from the rest', but, once ensconced in the Senate, he joined the landlords' club in Kildare Street, voted with the Protestant and Unionist group led by Andrew Jameson, and forsook a de-Anglicised Ireland of the Gael for Georgian Ireland, another imagined symbol of cultural superiority, only now, a generation after O'Grady, almost entirely without a social base.

Almost at once Yeats began to make something of his position, and on 5 January 1923 he told George in a letter from the Savile Club that he was attempting to get a modification to the treaty that would advance the cause of peace. He had spoken with Grannard and Southborough, and Grannard was trying to make an appointment for Yeats with an unnamed person who might negotiate both with the Irish Government, the Republicans, and the English cabinet. Southborough was initially unreceptive but was won over by Yeats.[65] In early January 1923 Yeats thought peace was imminent, and he was unimpressed by violence: 'I have two bullet holes in my windows but one gets used to anything' (*L* 696), he told Olivia Shakespear in December 1922.[66] But a letter written by George on 1 February 1923 suggests that Yeats had either suffered a complete loss of nerve about the prospects of remaining in Ireland or come to a realistic assessment of his chances of being assassinated.

In the letter, George's overriding concern is that events have reached a significant juncture and that Yeats should not contemplate, at this key moment, severing links permanently with Ireland. She tried to rally Yeats by telling him that Mrs Humphreys had visited Mrs Gogarty (referred to as Mrs 'Buck Mulligan' – testimony to the rapid influence and power of Joyce's *Ulysses*) to apologise for Oliver Gogarty's kidnapping. George sounds hopeful yet doubtful that de Valera had distanced himself from the more extreme Republican forces. What is remarkable about the letter is the way George identifies with Ireland's and Yeats's needs above those of her daughter and herself.

It is unclear what Yeats had told George, but presumably Said's 'poet of national liberation' had seriously discussed with George the advisability of living outside Ireland. Perhaps events had confirmed certain differences between them about living in Dublin; after all, as he told Olivia Shakespear in December 1922, it was George who was 'very urgent' about living in Dublin (*L* 675). Perhaps in a missing letter, presumably written in the last week of January 1923, Yeats had announced his intention of leaving Ireland for good. There is no mention of this in the biographies, or in Wade's *Letters*, so one is left to speculate. Hone maintains that there was 'no reason to think that Yeats would be molested', the horoscope being favourable.[67] But perhaps Yeats discovered or, worse, imagined his name on a hit list.

On 4 February 1923 the headlines in the *Sunday Independent* ran 'Bombs and Petrol: Senator Mrs Wyse Power the Latest Victim', and under the heading 'The Trail of the Torch' was printed a list of some twenty-four premises destroyed between 8 January and 2 February, which included President Cosgrave's house, Moore Hall – George Moore's family home, Horace Plunkett's house and Stephen Gwynn's. Yeats had been in Plunkett's house shortly before it was burned down and, smelling the presence of an 'elemental', informed Lady Fingall her house would most certainly be destroyed.[68] The headlines in the *Sunday Independent* on 14 January 1923 must have been particularly unnerving, since they concerned 'Buck Mulligan', who was kidnapped while taking a bath at home, and who only managed to escape his captors by plunging at night into the swollen river Liffey.[69]

SPIRITED AWAY

....

Exciting   Experience   of   Eminent   City   Surgeon

....

Dash   for   Liberty

....

Although he never got 'quite used to explosions' (*L* 692), Yeats rarely lacked courage, but George's letter seems to be a response to Yeats's fear for his own life. Certainly, as he told Olivia Shakespear in June 1923, he thought the strain of the Civil War while it continued affected his health (*L* 699). Unfortunately, without more evidence it is difficult to decide if it was George's efforts that persuaded him to return to Dublin.[70] If he had cut his ties permanently with Ireland, it is doubtful if he would have been awarded the Nobel Prize for Literature that November, and his standing as an Irish poet would have been permanently damaged.[71]

His work as a Senator from 1922 until 1928 was as demanding as he chose it to be. 'The Senate amuses me', he wrote to Quinn, '& I think I am quite a useful politician having an inventive mind & no ambition.'[72] He spoke as little as possible on politics and kept his remarks for things he understood. Dublin's social life was picking up, and various classes were wanting to mix together but did not know how.[73] In July 1924 he told George he was having an enjoyable day: writing verse from 10 a.m. until 11.30; 11.30 to 1.30 p.m. subverting Colonel Moore's attempt in a Senate Committee to form a new party; 2 p.m. to 3 p.m. dealing with correspondence; 3 p.m. to 6 p.m. in the Senate. He was in good form but he found he missed her when evening came.[74] The Senate also took its toll. In July 1928 a short speech in the Senate 'upset him very much, a violent pain down from the back of his neck' (*LGJ* 2, 305).[75] When the lecture circuit and the Irish Senate proved burdensome, however, he could retreat to the obscurity of his Club in London.[76]

In the Biographical Notice for the Royal Academy of Sweden, Yeats made much of his work as a Senator. He chaired three Senate Committees: the Irish Manuscript Committee (1923–4), the Coinage Committee (1926–8), and the Committee for the Federation of the Arts. He was appointed to advise the Free State Government on matters concerning education, literature, and the arts, but claimed the right to speak on other matters as well, most famously in the debate on divorce in June 1925:

> I think it is tragic that within three years of this country gaining its independence we should be discussing a measure which a minority of this nation considers to be grossly oppressive. I am proud to consider myself a typical man of that minority. We against whom you have done this thing are no petty people. We are one of the great stocks of Europe. We are the people of Burke; we are the people of Grattan; we are the people of Swift, the people of Emmet, the people of Parnell. We have created the most of the modern literature of this country. We have created the best of its political intelligence. [77]

He condemned the Censorship of Publications Bill in 1928, so loudly that he could be heard in Rapallo: 'Unc. Wm. blazing away over Oirish censorship, Aquinas, etc, in all the Brish and Mick weeklies.'[78] But nothing could stop the five-man Censorship Board banning in the 1930s 1,200 books and some 140 periodicals, including the *News of the World*, *London Life*, Huxley's *Point Counter Point*, Marie Stopes's *Wise Parenthood*, Faulkner's *Soldier's Pay* and *Sanctuary*, all English versions of Colette's *Recaptured*, O'Flaherty's *House of Gold*, O'Faolain's *Midsummer Night Madness*, and Austin Clarke's *Bright Temptation*.

Yeats's defence of freedom coexisted, however, with pro-fascist views, a theme I explore more fully in the following chapter. In an interview on 16 February 1924 with the *Irish Times* under the heading 'From Democracy to Authority: Paul Claudel and Mussolini – A New School of Thought', Yeats was in pugnacious mood:

> Authoritative government is certainly coming, if for no other reason than that the modern State is so complex that it must find some kind of expert government – a government firm enough, tyrannical enough, if you will, to spend years in carrying out its plans. The Marxian Socialist wants to recreate the world according to a scientific theory, while men like Peguy, Claudel and Maurras – whom one can admire as a thinker without admiring his practical politics – see the nation as something like a growing child or an old man, as the case may be, and not an automaton, as Socialists would make it.
>
> I see the same tendency here in Ireland towards authoritative government. What else can chaos produce, even though our chaos has been a very small thing compared with the chaos in Central Europe? The question in Ireland, as elsewhere in Europe, is whether the authoritative Government which we see emerging is the short reaction that comes at the end of every disturbance, lasting ten or fifteen years, or whether it is, as I think, a part of a reaction that will last one hundred or one hundred and fifty years. Not always of the same intensity, it is, still, a steady movement towards the creation of a nation controlled by highly trained intellects. Asked what effect the new movement would have on the social fabric generally, and what weapons it would use to enthrone authority, Dr Yeats shook his head, 'I am afraid', he said, 'it will be busy with very crude things during my lifetime. I shall be a very old man if I live to see it capable of taking up the tasks for which I care and of which I dream.'

Three months earlier, in November 1923, *Life and Letters*, a little-known magazine published in Manchester, warned about a fascist movement being organised in London: 'The increase in anti-Semitic feeling in Germany during the last two years has scarcely attracted sufficient attention abroad. . . . Anti-Semitic diatribes form most of the stock-in-trade of Hitler, the "Bavarian Mussolini". . . . Völkische ideals have become a new gospel to thousands of middle-class Germans.'[79] The 1920s did not alter Yeats's views. On 17 April 1929, 'Völkische' Yeats told Moore that it was Frobenius who 'freed me from British liberalism and all its dreams. The one heroic sanction is that of the last battle of the Norse Gods, of a gay struggle without hope. Long ago I used to puzzle Maud Gonne by always avowing ultimate defeat as a test' (*Y & TSM* 154).

On education Senator Yeats articulated two guiding *secular* principles: the education of the poor should be as good as the education of the rich, and 'the child itself must be the end in education'.[80] In a speech on 'The Child and the State' on 30 November 1925, he bypassed the religious view and argued that 'Berkeley proved the world was a vision, and Burke that the State was a tree, no mechanism to be pulled in pieces and put again, but an oak tree that has grown through centuries'.[81] All this seemed a rehearsal for 'Among School Children', a poem whose achievement is especially marked when set

221

against the actual circumstances of Yeats's visit in March 1926 to a school run by nuns on Montessori principles:

Willy has been in the thick of – I *wont* use an epithet – Education Bills. . . . We lunched with Mother De Sales on Sunday . . . terrible O terrible . . . pale green washed walls and sacred pictures of the late eighteenth century, a dreadful plaster – very whitened plaster – Christ in the centre of the mantelpiece draped in red push with tassels flanked on either side by two oriental and purely mundane figures, one of each sex, very markedly so and these in turn flanked by two of the worst vases I have ever seen. . . . Then we were conducted into another room for lunch. . . . But O Tom – the lunch . . . soup, half sherry . . . chicken with brandy sauce . . . already my head reeled, but though I refused port the brazen William drank two large glasses after refusing whiskey and brandy that were urged upon him. . . . Then we went down to the schools, very empty and freezing of a Sunday afternoon. . . . spent near two hours over curriculums, Montessori apparatus, P.N.E.U. (otherwise known and ⟨as⟩ Parents National Educational Union . . . it invaded Ireland about the time we chucked you over!) Willy asking blushing nuns how often the floors were washed . . . asides to me from Sister Mary Ellen 'O DEAR! I wouldn't mind saying ANYTHING to you . . . but a man . . . o DEAR . . .' 'Do the children come clean?' Or do you have to wash them? More blushes. Then at last back to the Convent where the Reverend Mother awaited us with hot milk. . . . They make one feel ashamed, ashamed of life and drinking and smoking And caring for nothing not even husband and children or relations (*who* really does?) or anything but a line written in a book and a particular person that is but part of one's own supreme egotism.[82]

The opening stanza of 'Among School Children' sets the scene: Yeats is 'questioning', the children learn to 'be neat in everything', he imagines he appears to them in the guise of a 'sixty-year-old smiling public man'. One recent commentator claims that the poet is being contemptuous of 'a form of education that teaches the children to be "neat in everything" while true labour in its multiple levels of meaning is ignored'.[83] But Yeats is probably mocking his own stiffly formal questions which embarrassed George and nuns alike. The poem also seems to constitute in part an intertextual reply to a conversation he may have had with George. Yeats takes issue with her view that the nuns are devoid of care, and he transforms their 'dreadful' religious plasters into an image of religious experience:

> Both nuns and mothers worship images,
> But those the candles light are not as those
> That animate a mother's reveries,
> But keep a marble or a bronze repose.
> And yet they too break hearts –
>
> (*VP* 445)

This, however, is the limit of George's presence in the poem, for it is not her image but the changes in Maud Gonne's which drive his heart wild; and when he thinks of maternity, again it is not his wife's but his own youthful mother's experience that he invokes.

By the time we reach the end of the poem, the sherry in the soup has been forgotten, replaced by a profound meditation on the soul's Porphyrian descent into matter. Once noticed, it is less easy, however, to keep on one side the fascist undertones of the

222

Corporate State and loss of individuality in this poem.[84] But if the interference is not too strong, 'Among School Children' can be enjoyed as a hymn to the Burkeian unity of life and a forceful illustration of one of Yeats's last remarks, how, in opposition to Plotinus, 'Man can embody truth but he cannot know it' (*L* 922):[85]

> O chestnut-tree, great-rooted blossomer,
> Are you the leaf, the blossom or the bole?
> O body swayed to music, O brightening glance,
> How can we know the dancer from the dance?
>
> (*VP* 446)

Yeats's engagement with the Senate did not last, and after his two terms he publicly declared to Pound: 'Do not be elected to the Senate of any country. . . . Neither you nor I, nor any other of our excitable profession, can match those old lawyers, old bankers, old business men, who, because all habit and memory, have begun to govern the world' (*AV [B]* 26).[86] It was a decision endorsed by George. As she told McGreevy, Yeats appeared pleased at resigning from all responsibilities.[87]

A VISION

In July 1923 Yeats was anxious to discuss with Sturge Moore 'the big design for the philosophy book' which 'must have a Unicorn in the middle' (*Y & TSM* 47–8). Moore's 'Monoceros de Astris' (the Unicorn from the Stars) was used in the Cuala Press edition of *Reveries* (1915), but the motif is perhaps best explained in the context of *The Unicorn from the Stars* (1908). In a dream Martin Hearne finds himself on a horse that was transformed into a unicorn which began trampling grapes in a vineyard. The dream is cut short, and Martin is unhappy at the prospect of living another fifty years and not knowing its end. He is advised by his troubled companion, the religiously orthodox Father John, that the 'life of vision, of contemplation, is a terrible life, for it has more temptation in it than the common life' (*VPl* 661). The dream reappears, and Martin recognises its (Nietzschean) meaning: 'To destroy, to overthrow all that comes between us and God' (*VPl* 670). 'We are the army of the Unicorn from the Stars!' (*VPl* 686). 'We will destroy all that can perish! It is only the soul that can suffer no injury. The soul of man is of the imperishable substance of the stars!' (*VPl* 691). Martin's 'madness' is too much for his companions, the police are called, and in a scuffle Martin is shot dead.

Yeats, conscious that his 'book of books' was strange, embeds *A Vision* in several narratives.[88] Opposite the title page there is a portrait by Edmund Dulac* of Giraldus 'from the Speculum Angelorum et Hominorum'. This is a ruse on Yeats's part, for the portrait is in fact none other than Yeats himself.[89] The subtitle is also part of this elaborate disguise: 'An Explanation of Life Founded Upon the Writings of Giraldus and Upon Certain Doctrines Attributed to Kusta Ben Luka'. Also on the title page we read that it was 'Privately Printed for Subscribers Only by T. Werner Laurie'. Owen Aherne writes the Introduction, and he recalls a meeting at the National Gallery in 1917 with his fictional companion, the antithetical Michael Robartes, who asks: 'Where is Yeats? I want his address. I am lost in this town and I don't know where to find anybody or anything' (xvi). Robartes tells Aherne that after the village riot in 'Rosa Alchemica' he found himself in Cracow and there discovered a book entitled 'Speculum Angelorum et Hominorum' (1594), which contained a portrait of Giraldus and various diagrams of gyres and circles. Seeking further understanding of the book's esoteric meaning, Robartes travelled via Damascus towards Mecca. Now in London, he wants to communicate his findings to Yeats. 'This bundle ⟨of notes⟩', he explains to Aherne, 'described the mathematical law of history, that bundle the adventure of the soul after death, that other the interaction between the living and the dead and so on' (*AV [A]* xx). Yeats agrees to write the exposition.

Aherne's Introduction is followed by Yeats's poem 'The Wheel and the Phases of the Moon' in which Robartes sets out the twenty-and-eight phases of the moon, after which comes 'The Dance of the Four Royal Persons'. In the Dance marks are made in the sand and interpreted by Kusta ben Luka; the Caliph is satisfied, and human nature is explained. *A Vision* proper begins at this point, with an explanation of 'the Great Wheel' itself.

The elaborate approach-work is then abandoned, replaced by the confident language of science and definition. *A Vision* is not a dream such as Martin Aherne experiences in *The Unicorn from the Stars*. Nor is it a discourse on religious ecstasy or the Celestial Body. If it is Christian, it is so by adoption: there is little emphasis on salvation history and little room for morality. *A Vision* is 'a perception of the eternal symbols'[90] or, to use the phrase from the book itself, 'desert geometry', marks in the sand. According to Yeats in that intriguing line from 'Under Ben Bulben', 'Measurement began our might' (*VP* 638), and the two dominant mathematical symbols which underlie human nature and explain human history are the wheel and the gyre. Without the gyre Yeats's system would be one-dimensional; without the wheel it would lack deliberation and direction. Blake's 'Mental Traveller' belongs to the gyre where 'The woman and the man are two competing gyres growing at one another's expense' (*AV [A]* 134); Yeats's wheel is a development on from this, an attempt to explain the course of history, types of personality according to the Four Faculties, and even interaction with the dead, especially through a process of dreaming back. The wheel allows for large historical generalisations; the gyre fixes the source of energy in a ceaseless double movement of primary and antithetical phases and forms.

A Vision is the work of a believer, his poetry that of a sceptic.[91] The diagrammatic character of *A Vision* cannot conceal a tension between gyre and wheel, between what I take to be a dialectical and a cyclical view of history. A gyre is, strictly speaking, part of the symbol of the wheel, in that it traces the movement between two cones moving in and out of each other. But it also belongs to a process that has a dialectical character, whereby 'An age is the reversal of an age' (*VP* 541), or, as expressed in *A Vision*, where 'Each age unwinds the thread another age had wound . . . all things dying each other's life, living each other's death' (*AV [A]* 183). Yeats's concept of dialectic stems from his reaction against Victorian ideas of progress. However, its radical edge is used to blunt his sense of apocalypse, for violence and destruction belong to a pattern of one civilisation succeeding another. Yeats would have found nothing wrong with writing 'The Second Coming' one month, followed the next by 'A Prayer for My Daughter'.[92] Tellingly, in his copy of Bergson's *Matter and Memory* (1919), Yeats pencilled in after a diagram of the wheel 'repetition' and after the gyre 'creation'.

Equally, the emphasis on origins and patterns does not completely eclipse questions of meaning and purpose. In 'Sailing to Byzantium', the protagonist seeks 'Monuments of unageing intellect' but his heart lies with 'Whatever is begotten, born, and dies'. What could be more uninspiring than 'set upon a golden bough to sing/To lords and ladies of Byzantium/Of what is past, or passing, or to come' (*VP* 407–8)? Indeed, as Moore pointed out, 'such a goldsmith's bird is as much nature as a man's body' (*Y & TSM* 162).[93] In *A Vision*, Yeats fondly imagines living in Byzantium 'a little before Justinian opened St Sophia and closed the Academy of Plato', for 'in early Byzantium, and maybe never before or since in recorded history, religious, aesthetic and practical life were one'. (*AV [A]* 191). The awkward rhyming of 'Byzantium' and 'come' tells a different story. For the unreconstructed Yeats knew that

> Man is in love and loves what vanishes,
> What more is there to say?
> (*VP* 429–30)

There is a curious mixture in Yeats of contradictory impulses. In spite of his search for patterns, Yeats was ever expecting the unexpected, and he was much taken with scenes of annunciation, with the unrepeatability of sudden action, such as the terrible beauty of Easter 1916 or Zeus's coupling with Leda:

> A shudder in the loins engenders there
> The broken wall, the burning roof and tower
> And Agamemnon dead.
> (*VP* 441)

From his work on gyres, he confidently declared in his Notes to *Resurrection* (1931), 'All our thought seems to lead by antithesis to some new affirmation of the supernatural', adding in Nietzschean fashion: 'It has seemed to me of late that the sense of spiritual reality comes whether to the individual or to crowds from some violent shock' (*VPl* 934–5).

That *A Vision* meant much to Yeats should not, however, be doubted: the 'stylistic arrangements of experience' (*AV [B]* 25) were the culmination of seven years' collaboration with George Yeats.

Some will ask if I believe all that this book contains and I will not know how to answer. Does the word belief, used as they will use it, belong to our age, can I think of the world as there and I standing here to judge it. I will never think any thoughts but these, or some modification or extension of these; when I write prose or verse they must be somewhere present though not it maybe in the words; they must affect my judgment of friends and of events; but then there are many symbolisms and none exactly resembles mine. What Leopardi in Ezra Pound's translation calls that 'concord' wherein 'The arcane spirit of the whole mankind turns hardy pilot' – how much better it would be without that word 'hardy' which slackens speed and adds nothing – persuades me that he has best imagined reality who has best imagined justice.[94]

The sessions for George and the writing for Yeats were exhausting: 'My life has been too exciting it seems and I must now pay for it'(*Y & TSM* 55).[95] But, equally, like Blake he felt that 'Inspiration & Vision was then, & now is, & I hope will always Remain, my Element, my Eternal Dwelling place'.[96] And from his Controls he had learned the Blakean lesson:

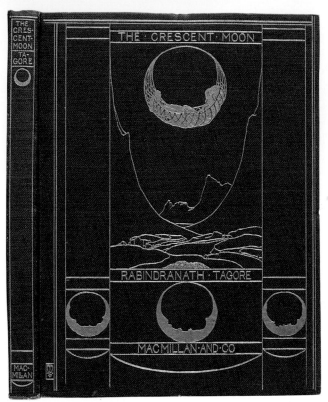

Moore's *Monoceros de astris*. 'The truth is that it is a private symbol belonging to my mystical order and nobody knows what it comes from. It is the soul' (*L* 662).

'Leda and the Swan', a sculpture in bronze by Jean Townsend.

> What they undertook to do
> They brought to pass;
> All things hang like a drop of dew
> Upon a blade of grass.
>
> (*VP* 505)

A *Vision* was also part of a larger intervention. In February 1923 Yeats told George that there was a common ground in every intellectual inquiry.[97] The idea had been with him since his twenties, when he heard a voice in his head saying 'Hammer your thoughts into unity' (*Ex* 263). Gwynn, who in his survey of Ireland in 1924 made much of Yeats's achievement, unconsciously touched on the ideological nature of Yeats's concept of Unity of Being:

Looking back on it now after forty years, I should say that the Ireland of the Free State possesses a strong central culture for which there was no equivalent in my undergraduate days. . . . In 1884 an Irish play in Dublin meant one of Boucicault's melodramas; an Irish poet meant Aubrey de Vere, or T. C. Irwin, or George Savage Armstrong. In 1924, we have all the best work of the Abbey Theatre to point to: Yeats is awarded the Nobel Prize and George Russell ranks by consent with the leading poets. . . . In short, literature which in the Ireland of my boyhood did little more than accentuate party cries, has become a central and uniting culture.[98]

In the context of Ireland in the 1920s any talk of Unity of Culture or Unity of Being must have rung especially hollow, for where Yeats was intent on making connections, many were set on breaking them. Defeated in the Civil War, O'Faolain was licking his wounds and 'far from seeing any improvement in the quality of Irish life now that we had swapped British administrators for Irish administrators, I felt a strong sense of moral decay.'[99] To Stuart, 'the romantic, the inspiring, the lyrical, will always be a lost cause in this dark age which is organised for business men and commerce'.[100] Peadar O'Donnell speaks of 'the minds that were bruised in the prisons of 1922' and the 'black vengeance', especially following the executions of 8 December, that continued into the 1930s.[101] In an article entitled 'Lessons of Revolution' published in the *Freeman* on 25 July 1923 a dejected Russell noted: 'The champions of physical force have, I am sure without intent, poisoned the soul of Ireland.' Then in March 1926, O'Casey's* *Plough and the Stars* produced a scene at the Abbey reminiscent of the *Playboy* riots, followed from April to June 1928 with the Abbey's much-publicised rejection of O'Casey's *Silver Tassie*, which led to Yeats being confined to bed for two days on account of the O'Casey affair.[102]

While working on *A Vision*, Yeats was told by his Controls not to read philosophy till it was finished, since 'they feared, I think, that if I did do so I would split up experience till it ceased to exist' (*Y & TSM* 83). After it was written, he told Moore in March 1926, 'I read for months every day Plato and Plotinus. Then I started in Berkeley and Croce and Gentile. You introduced me to your brother's ⟨the philosopher G. E. Moore⟩ work and to Russell' (*Y & TSM* 83).[103] Yeats and Moore conducted an intense correspondence about the nature of experience and psychical phenomena, and the example they kept returning to was Ruskin's cat. Once, in a conversation with Frank Harris, Ruskin suddenly ran to the other end of the room, picked up, or seemed to pick up, some object which he threw out of the window. Ruskin explained that it was a tempting demon in the shape of a cat. Yeats argued that 'if the house cat had come in both cats would have looked alike to Ruskin. . . . Neither your brother nor Russell gives any criterion by which Ruskin could have told one cat from the other' (*Y & TSM* 63).[104]

It is clear that *A Vision* forms part of Yeats's polemic against modern rationalist and realist thought, a polemic he carried over, often whimsically, into his verse:

I

Locke sank into a swoon;
The Garden died;
God took the spinning-jenny
Out of his side.

II

Where got I that truth?
Out of a medium's mouth,
Out of nothing it came,
Out of the forest loam,
Out of the dark night where lay
The crowns of Nineveh.

(*VP* 439)

Yeats believed that 'psychical research has undermined every current statement of the realist position' (*Y & TSM* 80).[105] From his subsequent career, it becomes clear that in

A Vision he was marshalling his troops, gaining the confidence, especially in the area of epistemology, to tackle both English and Continental philosophy. Against English empiricism he invoked the Irish philosopher Berkeley and added Blake: 'The essential sentence is of course "things only exist in being perceived", and I can only call that perception God's when I add Blake's "God only acts or is in existing beings or men" '(*Y & TSM* 80).[106] In 'Blood and Moon', Yeats cannot resist a swagger across the line:

> And God-appointed Berkeley that proved all things a dream,
> That this pragmatical, preposterous pig of a world, its farrow that so solid seem,
> Must vanish on the instant if the mind but change its theme.
>
> (*VP* 481)

Against rationalism he summoned the esoteric tradition of Western thinking from the pre-Socratics through the *Kabbalah*, Boehme, and Swedenborg to Blake and Yeats. To counter the claims of naturalism in art he produced Calvert and Palmer. *A Vision* also gave his ensuing poetry a startling authority and a lightness of touch, the effort of having overcome a 'mountain' of thought (as in the lines from 'Meru'):

> Civilisation is hooped together, brought
> Under a rule, under the semblance of peace
> By manifold illusion; but man's life is thought,
> And he, despite his terror, cannot cease
> Ravening through century after century,
> Ravening, raging, and uprooting that he may come
> Into the desolation of reality:
> Egypt and Greece, good-bye, and good-bye, Rome!
>
> (*VP* 563)

As is evident from the books in his library at Dalkey, Yeats constantly made notes on his reading in philosophy during the 1920s. Inside the back cover of A. N. Whitehead's *Science and the Modern World* (1926), Yeats pencilled in queries and objections:

'events' = souls
Aspects of other 'events' = visible world.
Aspects are seen in patterns which can be analysed into 'eternal objects' (scents, colours etc) & 'enduring' objects (mountains etc)
The 'eternal objects' are not localized in space.
What is the relation between 'an event' & the aspect it shows of another event? What is its relation to the colour 'scent' etc which it shows as? Swedenborg makes spiritual beings define themselves by 'colours' etc to which they are related by correspondence. Whiteheads thought is hardly the same but what is it? Do we not get very close to Berkeley, if as Whitehead advises we accept 'naive experience'. Do we not get a visible world which is the least common denominator of the imagined worlds of all individuals? Mohini Chatergi ⟨Chatterjee⟩ taught (?) this from which (?) I assume it Brahmanism.

Against Bergson's *Matter and Memory* (1919), he argued:

A state of existence where all express their nature would be free & without change. There would be no code so no change, no limit & so no compulsion. Bergson confines freedom to constancy of creation – to partial freedom – that is he sees 'the intelligible' not as Leibnitz a free monad, but as world of 'pure perception' where all is bound to all. This 'pure perception' is a consciousness which neutralises itself. This I do not understand. He does not explain 'neutralise' in this book. We are in the present 'pure perception' also in past and future. May it not be that we forget.[107]

He made short work of Russell's *Outline of Philosophy* (1927):

My mind follows abstraction with difficulty but I think this is a fair summary. Events are ultimate reality & from this time & space, spirit & matter are all emergent. What are to the 'observer' side by side in space, are to another one after another in time. But if this be so surely we must go further & say what is present to one is mental to another (time = sensation of mind (?)). Mental & physical are as interchangeable as time & space.

The idea of this book & all books of this school is that though they say events are neutral between mind & matter they think in terms of matter. Event, radiation, stuff, brain (?) are all material terms. In substituting 'neutral stuff' for the union of subject & object they are therefore by implication materialists.[108]

He was less than happy with Saurat's portrait of Blake in *Blake and Modern Thought* (1929):

To sum. Blake did not think England the place of primitive humanity, or of the original wisdom because these were before the flood of time & space. The historical druids he thought degenerate man – 'rocky druidism'. He speaks of England & its past because he lived there. In the same way the folklore of the Echte hills in Galway says the last judgement will be among those hills. Blake seeks the near & the particular always. Saurat, like Blakes other critics, never recognises Blakes humour his love of bewildering, his art student tricks.

Some of the notes reveal drafts of poems. Facing the last flyleaf of Swedenborg's *Principia* (1912), opposite a diagram of two interlocking gyres, Yeats sketched out a draft of 'A Needle's Eye', a supernatural poem first published in *Poetry* in 1934, which carried for its original title 'A Crowded Cross':

> All the stream that's roaring by
> Came out of a needle's eye;
> Things unborn, things that are gone,
> From needle's eye still goad it on.
> (*VP* 562)

As to his friends' perception of *A Vision*, Olivia Shakespear probably spoke for many:

I have been struggling with your book & find a good deal of it quite intelligible & interesting! But it wd take weeks of study to make out the system as a whole, & I am afraid I shall never accomplish it. . . . I think it is rather terrible – all so unending & no rest or peace till one attains an unattainable goal. I am really thankful not to find anything about Love in it. (I don't mean sexual love.) I believe men are so made that they naturally hate one another & all this talk about Love is Bunkum.

For heaven's sake don't send me any more Harris. I shall get rid of him somehow, as I shouldn't like Harry to discover him after my death![109]

8

Yeats in the 1930s

RAPALLO

In November 1927, George Yeats took her ailing husband south to the sun, first to Algeciras, then to Seville, and on to Cannes. In February 1928, they arrived in Rapallo, where George left Yeats with Dorothy Pound for a welcome break in Switzerland: 'William is much better. Dont think he is likely to "give trouble" while I'm Swissing. . . . W requires . . . four detections ⟨detective novels⟩ a week! Apart from them he has histories of Indian philosophy & various english parasites in that line . . . to say nothing of the works of St Theresa. . . . Quite horrid, the latter, *I* think!'[1]

Pound was pleased to see his old friend again:

Facing page: the lake at Coole in the fading October twilight.

Yeats and George at Algeciras, November 1927.

Yeats soon recovered his health: 'Unc. Wm. manages the stairs OK., now talking of settling in the Vicinanza & starting a Monday SOIReeeeeee.'[2] For his part, Pound was reassured to discover nothing new about his friend's ideas: 'Unc. Wm. still floundering in theological era.'[3]

Life for George did not get easier. Michael, at school in Switzerland, continued to lose weight and, on medical advice, they had gone to winter in Rapallo. In one of her frankest disclosures, she told McGreevy in March 1928 that Yeats had been ill on and off since February 1927 with what she thought was a breakdown. She even admitted that if she could have anticipated the severity of his condition, she would never have had children.[4]

In April 1928 the Yeatses went to Dublin to dispose of 82 Merrion Square, and again George was left to cope with arrangements. She again confided in McGreevy. The combination of domestic duties, arranging the sale of the house and removal of furniture, and most of all having Lady Gregory as a house guest, was becoming trying in the extreme. That summer she could not contemplate opening Ballylee, preferring instead a furnished cottage in England.[5]

The following November, after seeing all 'the usual people' in London (Dulac, Ricketts, Sturge Moore, Lady Lavery), the Yeatses returned to Rapallo for an extended stay.[6] Aldington was in Rapallo at the time, and he sometimes saw Yeats 'taking his daily constitutional, so wrapped in contemplation that he ought to have been as invisible as Aeneas in the golden cloud of Venus'.[7] One night the Yeatses dined with Aldington at his hotel:

Yeats used to worry himself a lot about Ezra, who seemed to support one of Yeats's numerous fads, the theory of the antithetical self. . . . It was a cold night, and Yeats arrived with his hands thrust into a pair of grey woolen socks, because he had lost his gloves. Recovering from this shock, we went to dinner. But with the spaghetti a long thin lock of Yeats's hair got into the corner of his mouth, and the rest of us watched with silent awe his efforts to swallow his hair with a strand of spaghetti. Giving this up in dudgeon, he suddenly turned to me and said to me in portentous tones: 'How do you account for

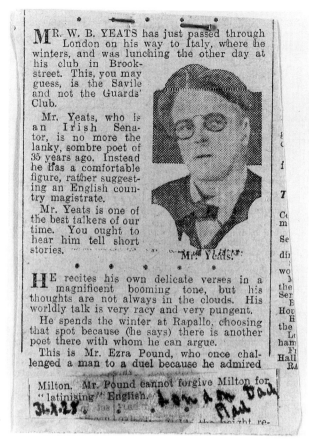

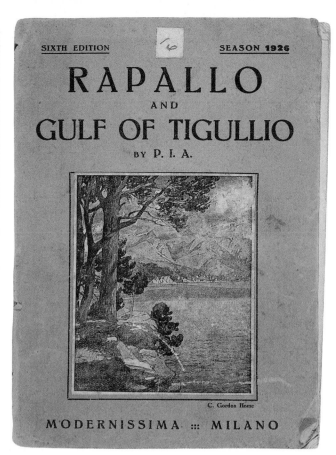

The *Daily Mail* on 31 October 1928 carried an article about Yeats on his way to Italy.

Guide to Rapallo used by Yeats.

Ezra? . . . Here is a man who produces the most distinguished work and yet in his behaviour is the least distinguished of men. It is the antithetical self.'[8]

Pound was watching Yeats too: 'Unc. Wm. has a large pair of very Camel pyjamas. no other onuzual sights.'[9] And he was enjoying Yeats's attempts at verse: 'Unc. Wm. has writ a pome each strophe ends with: Devil take Kink George.'[10]

In December 1928, Aldington, Pound, and Yeats were concerned about the imminent publication of 'Possum's book of Christian essays'[11] (T. S. Eliot's *For Lancelot Andrewes*), but Eliot sent Pound an amusing pre-emptive strike:

Dear Rabbit, No I hope you Wont see the Book, whatever Unc. Wm. says about It. Anyway, you wouldnt like it, but it may satisfy You to Know that in Bloomsbury it is regarded like our youngest daughters Bastard: it is not Spoken Of, like the Bargee's daughter. Our Embly, she's in the fambly way but were keeping of it Quiet.[12]

In March 1929 Pound arranged for Yeats to meet the German dramatist Gerhard Hauptmann, a ceremony which 'passed off calmly last evening with sacrifice of two pheasants. No other bloodshed.'[13] Pound felt Rapallo was 'getting ter BBB that bhloody central wot with all these licheray blokes; and Unc. Wm. fraternizing with Jawg ⟨George Antheil⟩ and trying to produce a celtic Oedipus etc. and another murkn publisher etc. and the Hauptmann = Yeats formalities etc. . . .'[14] But he enjoyed 'convarsation with W. B. Y', and rarely lacked entertainment, especially when 'Unc. Wm. came to lunch to express profound impression produced by effort to comprehend cantos. etc.'[15]

On his next stay in Rapallo, in November 1929, Yeats's health again caused concern: 'Pore ole Willum is confined to his bed, and trustin' to the scotch lady doctor because she charges more than the natives. I suppose I'd better not tell him about how she thinned down the population of the Verdi.'[16] In December 1929 Yeats made his will, witnessed by Pound and the English poet Basil Bunting. In early January 1930, Pound thought Yeats had typhoid, but it proved a 'False allarrum. Unc. W. has NOT typhus but paratyphoid ozzi ze sole.'[17]

Ill-health notwithstanding, Yeats managed to find Rapallo highly conducive to imaginative work. 'This is an indescribably lovely place, some little Greek town one imagines. . . . Here I shall put off the bitterness of Irish quarrels and write my most amiable verses', he told Lady Gregory in February 1928 (*LGJ* 2, 235). Several poems in *Words for Music Perhaps* (1932), including the bawdy Crazy Jane sequence, were composed here. In November 1929 he finished a curious love poem to Olivia Shakespear (if it is to her, that is), for he realised (if this constitutes an explanation) that 'When Lady Gregory goes, and she is now very frail, I too shall have but one old friend left. (MG has been estranged by politics this long while)' (*L* 769):

> Speech after long silence; it is right,
> All other lovers being estranged or dead,
> Unfriendly lamplight hid under its shade,
> The curtains drawn upon unfriendly night,
> That we descant and yet again descant
> Upon the supreme theme of Art and Song:
> Bodily decrepitude is wisdom; young
> We loved each other and were ignorant.
>
>   (*VP* 523)

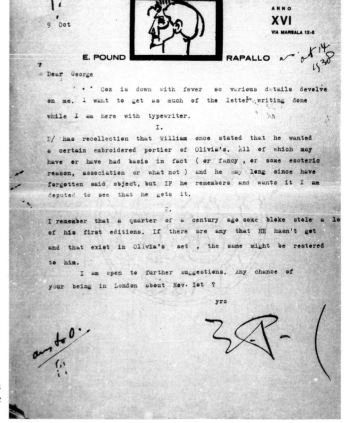

Pound's letter to George on 14 October 1938. Olivia Shakespear died on 3 October, and the irresponsible Pound was responsible for disposing of her effects.

On 4 February 1909, Yeats received a letter from Robert Gregory with news of his mother's illness. At first, he thought his own mother was ill and that his sister was asking him to come at once: '⟨T⟩hen I remembered that my mother died years ago, and that more than kin was at stake. She has been to me mother, friend, sister and brother. I cannot realise the world without her – she brought to my wavering thoughts steadfast nobility' (*Mem* 160). In June 1910 when Yeats, looking 'fatter and rosier than formerly', visited his estate in Sussex, Blunt recognised an essential truth about Yeats: 'Lady Gregory has been the making of him.'[18] As a writer, she took an active, and often unacknowledged, part in editing and collaborating with him on his work. She was central to the formation of the Abbey Theatre, acted as his secretary, plied him with soup when he was enervated, and, perhaps most importantly for posterity, as a member of the Anglo-Irish, she provided Yeats with an emblem that was at once dignified, secure, and in decline.[19]

Coole, where 'passion and precision have been one/Time out of mind' (*VP* 264), where poetry, friendship, and the historical imagination could compensate for his lack of a birthright, was Yeats's 'home for nearly forty years' (*L* 799). Whenever he invited himself down – and he spent at least twenty summers there – he was given the room above the library in the centre of the west of the house, looking down to the lake. He played the part with ease. There is a photograph of him posing with Corly the Piper (see page 238), as if he were a patron welcoming the blind eighteenth-century harper Carolan. When Austin Clarke furtively caught sight of him at Coole in the 1920s, Yeats was 'stalking across the lawn to Lady Gregory's mansion with fishing rod, basket and net, looking like one of the gentry'.[20] On his first visit to Coole, George Moore was shown the table at which Yeats wrote: he admired the clean pens, the fresh ink, and the spotless blotter, caustically adding that 'these were her special care every morning'.[21]

There was 'a strangeness and romance about Coole'.[22] Lady Gregory recalled the 1870s when parties of shooting guests descended: a Dillon from Clonbrock, a Crofton from Moate, a Persse from Roxborough, a Gough from Lough Cutra, maybe a Gregory from Stychale, a Greville from Warwick, once even a Duke of Marlborough from the Phoenix Park. Just after her marriage in 1880 the land war intensified, and by 1890 the landscape of rural Ireland was altered for ever: 'Some of the county families had shut up their houses, some had grown poor; dinners such as had gathered neighbours from many miles around during our big Roxborough shooting parties had ceased, for the roads were not safe after dark; hunting was meddled with here and there, the days of easy and idle hospitality had passed away.'[23]

Coole Park did not escape these changes, but Lady Gregory managed to delay their impact until the 1920s. Contemporary history enhanced the house's tragic possibilities and strengthened in Yeats's eyes the value of the accumulated objects and the sense of historical continuity: 'Old marble heads, old pictures everywhere' (*VP* 491). The house was full of an auctioneer's collectables: silver, glass, porcelain, a suite of mahogany furniture, a pair of Dresden fluted bowls, with flat handles, pierced and chased with flowers, a pair of silvered figures of dancing boys nine inches high, a large oval salver, with gadroon border, and handles chased with lions' masks and foliage, on claw feet, thirty inches long.[24] The breakfast room was decorated with Morris wallpaper of dim golden leaves; prints included ones of William Pitt (1766) and Burke (1775). Elsewhere in the house there was a portrait of Gladstone, letters from American writers and British

Above left: Mr William Gregory, the Liberal M. P. and Governor of Ceylon, as he appeared in *Vanity Fair* in 1871, under the caption 'An Art Critic'. 'Nature has given him a clear head, and culture has provided him with special qualifications, while the circumstances of his having long represented an Irish county has invested him with a peculiar importance to the generation that has been brought to deal with Irish difficulties. . . . Mr Gregory has a keen natural appreciation of the beauties of form and colour, and besides being a Trustee of the National Gallery, is listened to on questions of pictures and statues with all the respect due to an Art critic.'

Above right: the autograph tree at Coole, now numbered and ringed. Number 13 is Sean O'Casey, 11 W. B. Yeats, 4 is the large descending initial GBS, 7 is Augusta Gregory, 10 is the graceful AE with accompanying triangle.

Lady Gregory sitting under the catalpa tree at Coole. In an obituary notice in *Everyman* in June 1932, Austin Clarke surmised: 'But for the literary stirrings of the time, Lady Gregory might have remained living quietly, the widow of an eminent British official, in her manor in County Galway, an old Georgian place hidden among thin green woods, seven in number, and wild privet hedges.'

The library at Coole, with armchair covered in a Morris design.

Prime Ministers. In the library, where Yeats could pick up the *Life of Swift* in a fine old edition, as he did on 14 October 1928, he could further his interest in eighteenth-century Ireland and mount his attack on Whiggery. On a shelf in the drawing-room were Blunt's volumes, a touching reminder of Lady Gregory's secret affair in the aftermath of her marriage. Outside, there were Yeats's beloved Seven Woods, and on the copper beech the initials of famous contemporaries who were her guests. It was a house to add things to as if, like Yeats's volumes, in homage:

> Some of the books are dedicated to me; many of the poems and plays were dedicated to me in this room, I, never a very expert typist, sitting in a window recess, blackening my fingers as I changed the ribbon of my Remington . . . he suggesting changes to the last as he walked up and down the room. For all but a score of summers he spent here brought a good harvest in the quiet of the lake and the shadows of the woods . . . his peace not broken, as was often mine, by angers against the clambering ambition of ivy and the wantonness of twig-breaking squirrels, and the greediness of rabbits nibbling the living bark from the trees.[25]

There was a pattern to his life at Coole. While there in July and August 1930, he worked in the morning at his philosophy, and in the evening they read together Trollope's *American Senator*. Visitors provided good company, a break in routine, and a source for gossip:[26]

> They came like swallows and like swallows went,
> And yet a woman's powerful character
> Could keep a swallow to its first intent.
>
> (*VP* 489)

237

The romantic-looking Wilfrid Scawen Blunt as a young man.

Yeats, Lady Gregory, and possibly Robert Gregory. With Corly the Piper.

One August, he was taken out for a drive by Gogarty in his Ford. Gogarty insisted on overtaking everything in sight, including a Rolls Royce. Yeats was not amused: his head had hit the top of the car twice, and he ended up with a headache.[27]

More significantly, as he stressed in 'Coole Park and Ballylee, 1931', Coole was only a few miles from Ballylee, its physical proximity a symbol of the cultural continuity he sought for himself among the Anglo-Irish:

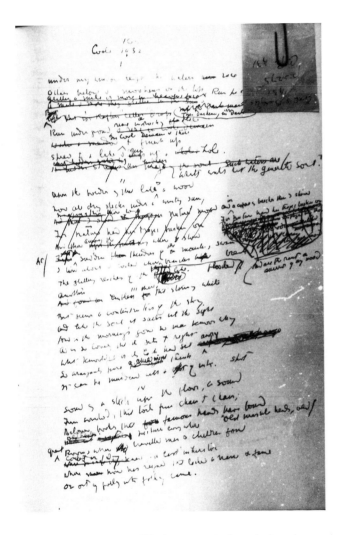
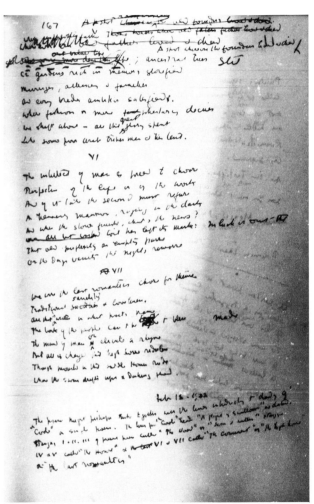

Under my window-ledge the waters race,
Otters below and moor-hens on the top,
Run for a mile undimmed in Heaven's face
Then darkening through 'dark' Raftery's 'cellar' drop,
Run underground, rise in a rocky place
In Coole demesne, and there to finish up
Spread to a lake and drop into a hole.
What's water but the generated soul?

(*VP* 490)

Such a poem could only be written when the historical moment had passed, and Coole

239

and Ballylee were being consigned to history. At Coole Yeats found quiet and a stilling of emotions, but to write verse he needed the energy of inspiration. As soon as the scene in the opening stanza of this poem is established, the observer-narrator dramatically shifts the focus and compels us to make sense of the connection between Coole and Ballylee in terms other than landscape, transforming a flat statement in the draft into an inviting rhetorical question: 'What's water but the generated soul?' The energy in the poem, in evidence from the draft to completed version, derives not from nostalgia or courtly *sprezzatura* but from the juxtapositioning of emblems and reality. In the wood he is startled by the sudden thunder of the mounting swan; the sky is 'So arrogantly pure a child might think/It can be murdered with a spot of ink.'

In the hands of Elizabeth Bowen, such images would prove threatening, as are the woods, for example, in *The Last September* (1923), which harbour those bent on the destruction of the Big House in Ireland. But Yeats deliberately avoids the local interpretation and goes for a wider sense of disturbance, drawing the reader ever inwards into the poem. Yeats even manages the trick of energising such unpoetic words as 'glittering', 'lovely', 'reigned', 'glorified', 'sanctity', 'bless', and 'fantasy' (which he misspells). More tellingly, in spite of its parochial address in the West of Ireland, the power and authority of this poem derives from its passionate syntax, its invigorating use of the eight-line stanza *ottava rima*,[28] its curiously detached yet seductive awareness of modernity:

> Where fashion or mere fantasy decrees
> We shift about – all that great glory spent –
> Like some poor Arab tribesman and his tent.
>
> We were the last romantics – chose for theme
> Traditional sanctity and loveliness;
> Whatever's written in what poets name
> The book of the people; whatever most can bless
> The mind of man or elevate a rhyme;
> But all is changed, that high horse riderless,
> Though mounted in that saddle Homer rode
> Where the swan drifts upon a darkening flood.
>
> (*VP* 491–2)

Yeats is at his most persuasive when least able to do damage, and here in this poem his reactionary sentiments can be allowed to stand as tributes to a dream that if implemented would have returned Ireland with a vengeance to the eighteenth century. Yeats no doubt composed it with Lady Gregory in mind, but, ironically, as an entry in her journal for 5 January 1930 reveals, her thoughts were less patrician than his: 'Coole no longer ours. But the days of landed property have passed. It is better so' (*LGJ* 2, 485–6).[29]

George was less happy with Yeats's dependence on Lady Gregory, especially towards the end, as she told Dorothy Pound in August 1931: 'She wants W. to go down to Coole for most of September, & I hope he will – he doesnt seem to mind the re-iterations. Personally they send me nearer lunacy than anything I ever met.'[30] But nothing could shake Yeats's devotion towards her, and he kept George informed: in May 1930, a lump in Lady Gregory's breast; on 10 January 1931, a great deal of pain; the end of July 1931, violent pains from rheumatism. Yeats felt something of the pressure from George, for on 13 September 1931, in response to Lady Gregory's request for him to stay as long as

Photo of Yeats taken in 1932 by Martin Voss. 'I study hatred with great diligence,/For that's a passion in my own control,/A sort of besom that can clear the soul/Of everything that is not mind or sense' (*VP* 558).

Pirie MacDonald's photograph of Yeats taken in New York in 1932.

possible, he added that he would have to set a time limit.[31] Lady Gregory thought well of him to the end: 'He is so kind, & makes his tea, & talks pleasantly – carries his kindness through the day' (*LGJ* 2, 630).[32] To Yeats, she was 'indomitable to the last, seeing to all her household duties and weekly charities' (*L* 796).

THE FASCIST CHARGE

The issue of Yeats and fascism seems destined to remain unresolved, condemned for ever to speculation. Clifton Fadiman in his review of Hone's biography in the *New Yorker* on 6 February 1943 was partly right in his assessment:

> He died at the right time, with his magnificent poetic gift still in flower and before the war could make painfully evident the growing mystical-Fascist bent of his political 'philosophy'. An aristocrat like Yeats could never have conducted himself, of course, with the paranoid vulgarity of his great friend, the American traitor Ezra Pound. But towards the end his views grew increasingly anti-democratic, and it is hard to forget that his sympathy for General O'Duffy's Blueshirt Party even induced him to write three songs for the Irish Fascist movement. He later, it is true, revised them, 'increasing their fantasy, their extravagance', Mr Hone writes, 'so that no party could sing them'.

O'Brien went further and suggested that if a collaborationist regime was established in Dublin, 'one would have expected to see ⟨Yeats⟩ at least a cautious participant, or ornament'.[33] Frank O'Connor* recalls Yeats referring to Mussolini as his hero, Mussolini also taking little but fruit and milk for his diet.[34] Bowra, on the other hand, maintained that the accusation of fascism was 'not preposterous, but it is wrong. His interest in politics was of a cosmic kind.'[35]

Stack the cards one way and Yeats is a pro-fascist, a one-time supporter of the Blueshirt movement in Ireland, as close to being a fascist as makes no difference; stack them another way and Yeats is part of his time, an authoritarian, an anti-capitalist, a nationalist of the school of O'Leary, a cultivator of hatred, hopelessly deluded, a political failure, or, as he told Heald in August 1938, freer than a bird.[36] Evidence can be produced to support any of these positions. As part of his age, there is the *Irish Times* hailing Hitler on 4 March 1933 as 'Europe's standard bearer against Muscovite terrorism'. When he opened his correspondence from intimate friends like Sturge Moore he found support for Hitler: 'Wyndham Lewis, who has been to Germany, tells me that the Hitlerites will certainly come in to power soon. . . . The enthusiasm of the Hitlerites is unbelievable and they celebrate their martyrs in war songs which they sing with delirious gusto' (*Y & TSM* 167).[37]

Those more suspicious by nature can with equal justification list a number of charges against Yeats. In the *Manchester Guardian* on 24 February 1932, on the same page as an article on Yeats's protest against the Irish ban on O'Flaherty's *Puritan*, a report appeared on British Aid for Refugees which contained a reference to 'the orderly migration of "involuntary migrants" from Germany'. The same day the paper carried an editorial on 'Hitler's Campaign' during the German presidential elections: 'The violence of Herr Goebbels, the Nazi leader, in the Reichstag yesterday and the pandemonium which ensued give an indication of the turbulent passions that will be aroused. . . . If

Hitler comes into power there will be a new situation created full of dangerous possibilities.' On 14 February 1934, Yeats was awarded the financially lucrative Goethe Prize in Frankfurt, a city once the heart of liberal Germany but in 1934 dominated by the Nazis, and to mark the occasion *The Countess Cathleen* was performed. The previous year the prestigious award went to Thomas Mann, in 1931 to Freud, but from 1934 to 1939 Yeats was the only foreigner to receive it. Yeats's eye was not a camera, but even he must have been aware of the new brutalism issuing from Nazi Germany and fascist Italy. He was a friend of the pacifist and Communist sympathiser Ethel Mannin, but, when approached by her and Ernst Toller in 1935 on behalf of the imprisoned German writer Carl Ossietsky, he refused to lift a finger.[38]

Odon Por's *Fascism* appeared in English translation in 1923. The author quoted extensively from George Russell's *National Being* (1916) to show the need for a more spiritual underpinning of fascism: 'A. E.'s vision and method . . . liberates us . . . from the habit of making everything in society depend chiefly on economic factors and motives . . . and convinces us that not through class struggles but through a co-ordination of function in obedience to a high national ideal – may true social life be created.'[39] Such a perception of a link between Italian fascism and the thinking of Yeats's one-time closest friend reminds us of a worrying overlap in the 1910s and 1920s between political positions on the (Guild Socialist or Co-operative) left and the (fascist) right.[40]

In the same volume, O. Zuccarini declared: 'Fascism is not merely a reaction; it marks the end of an epoch.'[41] The language is too programmatic or limiting to be Yeats's: for him, the end of an era is marked by the 'Second Coming' and is not confined to fascism. But Yeats, too, sought a movement that united the citizen and the individual: 'For the first time the State has become for Italians a living and present reality, developing a national character of its own, and casting aside all those hindrances, legislative and bureaucratic, which had served to divide the citizen from the man, the Government from the country, and Rome from the districts and provinces where the most genuine and valuable characteristics of our Italian people are still preserved intact.'[42] Across Europe a strong State appealed to those on the right who had witnessed civil war or who had been defeated in war. On 12 January 1923, at a time when the property of Irish Senators was being torched, Dino Grandi in *Popolo d'Italia* enthused: 'Higher than the right of man stands the right of the life of the State. And the right of the Nation over the individual.'[43] Por expanded: 'Fascism is revolutionary, not because it seized power by illegal means, but because by means of its dictatorship, it is constructing a functional democracy. . . . The term "functional democracy" and all that it implies is well understood in England, but it is unknown in Italy. . . . Until the forms of functional democracy have been worked out a dictatorship seems to be the only possible form in which Fascism can rule the State.'[44]

The Irish people had arguably more sense than Yeats imagined and ensured the survival of their new State institutions through the period of the Civil War and its aftermath. Ten years after Por's *Fascism*, and five years after leaving the Senate, Yeats in summer 1933 tried his hand again at direct political involvement, this time with the Irish Blueshirts under General O'Duffy, one-time Head of Police in the Free State. It was perhaps, as Cullingford, following Michael Yeats, suggests – or rather claims – 'a temporary outburst of fanaticism',[45] brought about in part through his friend Captain MacManus (who thought Yeats might prove the philosopher of the movement), and resulted in Yeats's three marching songs. Three years later the Blueshirts sent men to Spain to fight alongside Franco's fascist forces, but Yeats soon discovered some home truths. Christian Action, he realised in December 1936, was 'gathering all the bigots together. We have all been threatened with what can only mean mob violence by a Catholic preacher' (*DWL* 110). By February 1937 Yeats and MacManus were convinced that 'neither of us wanted to see General O'Duffy back in Ireland with enhanced fame helping "the Catholic front"' (*L* 881). The following month, the fascist alarm bells were ringing even louder in Yeats's ears: 'I am convinced that if the Spanish war goes on, or if ⟨it⟩ ceases and O'Duffy's volunteers return heroes, my "pagan" institutions, the Theatre, the Academy, will be fighting for their lives against combined Catholic and Gaelic bigotry' (*L* 885).

In some respects, the nearest Yeats got to writing a fascist poem of merit, and this shows his real distance from fascism, is 'Beautiful Lofty Things', a poem which Jeffares dates as 1937 and which Yeats sketched out on the back flyleaf and cover of his copy of Sacheverell Sitwell's *Canons of Giant Art*: *Twenty Torsos in Heroic Landscapes* (1933). Yeats's poem, in its own way a case study of how he planned a poem as a whole, can be read as a reply to Sitwell's overlong, tiresome celebration of the heroes of history. Sitwell traces a journey from 'The Farnese Hercules', where 'In the dun twilight other shadows creep,/While this first giant art is born out of rolling high speeches', through 'Krishna with the Milkmaids', where 'Dawn dawn dawn/The beating of the drum:/O give us back our gods again', and eventually to 'Grande Adagio – The Enchanted Palace':

> Italian talents make a Roman peace,
> The Pax Romana, mother of the arts,
> Bears another Italy, born in our day,
> To save mankind and build him all his pleasures.
> Look! Look! the fleet of Aeneas, the white, white sails;
> His men are aeronauts, are Roman airmen.
> Italy, the land of death, is land of birth;
> The Enchanted Palace wakens into life,
> The morning is Italian, it lives again.[46]

According to Sitwell, 'In so far as any poem can have a political intention, it is true of this final passage of the whole book. It is in praise of Fascist Italy.'[47]

Yeats was sufficiently impressed by *Giants of Modern Art* to include the section entitled 'Agamemnon's Tomb' in *The Oxford Book of Modern Verse, 1892–1935* (1936). However, by way of intertextual reply to the owner of Renishaw Hall, Yeats assembled his own quirky pantheon of gods and effectively shifted the discussion away from politics to personal memories, now appropriately mythologised.

> ⟨?⟩ beautiful sight ⟨cancelled⟩ lofty things, O'Learys noble head
> Standish O'Grady standing drunk between the tables & speaking
> ⟨?⟩ to that drunken audience sweet ⟨cancelled⟩ high non-sensical words
> My father on the Abbey stage before him a raging crowd
> This land of saints & then as the applause died out
> Of plaster saints, his old beautiful mischievous head thrown back
> ⟨next two lines cancelled⟩
> Augusta Gregory seated at her great ormolu table
> aproaching her eightieth year ⟨cancelled⟩
> Her eightieth winter approaching; yesterday (?) he threatened my life

But I ⟨cancelled⟩ I told him that nightly
But I said that I wrote at this from six to seven night after night ⟨cancelled⟩
With the blinds pulled up. Maud Gonne waiting a train at Howth Station
Pallas Athene in that straight (?) back & arrogant head
All the Olympians, a sight no longer ⟨?⟩

⟨on opposite page: further revisions⟩

> Beautiful lofty things: O'Leary's noble head;
> My father upon the Abbey stage, before him a raging crowd:
> 'This Land of Saints', and then as the applause died out,
> 'Of plaster Saints'; his beautiful mischievous head thrown back.
> Standish O'Grady supporting himself between the tables
> Speaking to a drunken audience high nonsensical words;
> Augusta Gregory seated at her great ormolu table,
> Her eightieth winter approaching: 'Yesterday he threatened my life.
> I told him that nightly from six to seven I sat at this table,
> The blinds drawn up'; Maud Gonne at Howth station waiting a train,
> Pallas Athene in that straight back and arrogant head:
> All the Olympians; a thing never known again.
>
> (VP 577–8)

245

Penns in the Rocks, near Groombridge in Sussex. A plaque in the grounds is dedicated to Yeats, de la Mare, W. J. Turner, Ruth Pitter, Vita Sackville West, Dorothy Wellesley, with inscription: 'They Learn In Suffering What They Teach In Song'. Another plaque carries Yeats's epitaph from 'Under Ben Bulben'. One of the rooms in the house, used as a nursery, was known until the 1960s as 'The Yeats Room'. In 'To Dorothy Wellesley' Yeats speaks of 'the sensuous silence of the night' and adds in parentheses: '(For since the horizon's bought strange dogs are still)' (*VP* 579), a reference to Wellesley saving 'this little corner of Sussex from a town of scarlet bungalows' (*DWL* 53).

Yeats's choice of heroes and heroines is as personal and idiosyncratic as the remembered moments or vignettes which adorn their haloes. We can even allow Yeats a degree of poetic licence with his memory, for, as noted in chapter 5, his father was not applauded at the Abbey Open Evening to discuss Synge's *Playboy*. Indeed, the pause before 'plaster saints' was greeted by groans, and, eventually, because of the noise, he was forced to sit down. By contrast, in 1937 O'Grady is no longer cast in the role of father of the Revival but has become a figure who utters 'high nonsensical words': without the adjective *high* Yeats would have difficulty persuading us that here was someone of significance. Lady Gregory, 'seated at her great ormolu table', is suitably indifferent to her fate, while Maud Gonne has in her height and gait the arrogance of a Pallas Athene. The poem ends with an act of enclosure, their stature secured as beyond argument: 'All the Olympians; a thing never known again.'

The difficulty for Yeats the lyric poet, as opposed to Yeats the political thinker, was that his subject matter did not lend itself to fascism. Deane claims that 'fascism was the political form of occultism',[48] but even here Yeats shifts the ground or obscures the argument. He told McGreevy that mediumship was akin to democracy and that every truth had its opposite.[49] None of the four figures Yeats admired in 'Beautiful Lofty Things' was a fascist. Neither for that matter was Pearse, who is associated in 'The

Statues' with the chief hero of Yeats's life, Cuchulain. J. B. Yeats was a Liberal Home Ruler; O'Grady was a Fenian Unionist and therefore full of contradictions; Lady Gregory in the 1920s sided with the Republicans; and Maud Gonne was above all a hater of England and an Irish nationalist. All four were engaged in confronting the public, and their heroic stature, as Yeats conceives of it, arose in part from this encounter. What none of them found or, with the possible exception of O'Grady, sought was an identity between citizen and individual. Equally, the stance Yeats adopts in the poem is one of regret or nostalgia, 'a thing never known again', far removed from Sitwell's hymn to fascist Italy. In Ireland during the 1930s, Yeats had nowhere else to turn but to a mythologised past, for, although 'Fianna Fáil possessed the type of charismatic leader cherished by fascist ideologists',[50] de Valera was treated with suspicion by Yeats and his circle.[51]

Dorothy Wellesley

Lady Gerald Wellesley, whom he first met through Lady Ottoline Morrell in May 1935, further complicated the political picture for Yeats. After Lady Gregory's death, 'Dottie' or 'Dotz', as she was known to Vita Sackville-West, took over the role of upper-class country-house hostess, providing at Penns in the Rocks near Groombridge in Sussex beautiful gardens and good conversation.[52] But her Englishness meant Yeats had to be more circumspect than he might otherwise have been. He did not send her 'The Ghost of Roger Casement' because of her English sympathies.[53] And he insisted: 'How can I hate England, owing what I do to Shakespeare, Blake & Morris. England is the only country I cannot hate' (*DWL* 111).[54] In February 1937, he felt obliged to tone down the significance of his ballad on Parnell, 'Come Gather Round Me, Parnellites' (see page 75), disingenuously calling it a 'song about a personality far removed from politics of the day', and suggesting that its theme was 'ancient history' (*DWL* 130).[55] Within a short

Rothenstein's sketch of Dorothy Wellesley appeared opposite the title page of her *Selections from the Poems of Dorothy Wellesley* (1936). Yeats thought her 'Matrix' 'perhaps the most moving philosophic poem of our time . . . moving precisely because its wisdom, like that of the sphinx, was animal below the waist.'

time, however, the ground clearing, they arrived at an 'intimate understanding', and the turned-on Yeats began composing extraordinary lines such as 'For the womb the seed sighs' (*DWL* 99, 102).[56] Their intimacy deepened with 'The Three Bushes', a poem jointly composed by exchange of correspondence in July 1936, at the end of which Yeats disclosed: 'Ah my dear how it added to my excitement when I re-made that poem of yours to know it was your poem. I re-made you and myself into a single being. We triumphed over each other and I thought of *The Turtle and the Phoenix*' (*DWL* 82).[57]

Wellesley's political position is never made fully explicit in her letters. In her private life she was intense, unconventional and given to taking risks; in her friendship with Yeats she consciously espoused a country and a cause not always popular among the English ruling class in the 1930s; in her anxiety over the Abdication Crisis in 1936 she perhaps confused royalist sentiment with her own deeply felt concern about the public revelation of private life. Her poetry in a volume such as *Lost Planet* (1942) seems to suggest her politics were more cosmic than anything else. Whatever Yeats was, she was not pro-fascist. In January 1937 she told Yeats: 'I see small difference between Communism and Fascism, both being tyrannical. On the whole Hitler a better human being perhaps than Mussolini' (*DWL* 122). Yeats's reply was suitably cavalier: 'Here are three poems that give the essence of my politics' (*DWL* 123).[58] The poems in question were 'The Great Day', 'Parnell', and 'What Was Lost' (*VP* 590–91). The tone of 'The Great Day' is scornful, detached, and, if this constituted the essence of his politics, surprisingly hollow:

> Hurrah for revolution and more cannon shot!
> A beggar upon horseback lashes a beggar on foot.
> Hurrah for revolution and cannon come again!
> The beggars have changed places, but the lash goes on.

'Parnell', a disillusioned two-liner, continues the theme in the Irish context:

> Parnell came down the road, he said to a cheering man:
> 'Ireland shall get her freedom and you still break stone.'

'What Was Lost' is yet more sobering:

> I sing what was lost and dread what was won,
> I walk in a battle fought over again,
> My king a lost king, and lost soldiers my men;
> Feet to the Rising and Setting may run,
> They always beat on the same small stone.

While staying with her in September 1938, Yeats wrote to Heald that it was pointless writing to Wellesley until after Hitler's speech, since she was preoccupied with whether or not she could go to her villa in the south of France.[59] When Chamberlain returned from Munich in 1938, Yeats wrote again, expressing his great relief.[60] While at Heald's in October 1938, Yeats told George that billeting the refugees had been mismanaged and caused quite a stir in Steyning.[61] Not far away, at Rodmell in Sussex, Virginia and Leonard Woolf, with their fingers closer on the national pulse, were making plans for a joint suicide pact in case Britain was overrun by the Nazis. But there is a curious letter from Wellesley which appeared in *The Times* on 9 February 1939 under the heading 'Mr W. B. Yeats: Problems of the Future':

Those who have been privileged to discuss with him ⟨Yeats⟩ in recent years the questions of poetry and life which have occupied his mind will bear witness to his passionate interest in the new ideas now at work in Europe. He had latterly been studying eugenic authorities, and had embodied his ideas on the vital importance of quality as distinct from quantity of population in an informal prose essay, shortly to be published by the Cuala Press. . . . Little more than a fortnight ago he was eagerly discussing with Austrian and German acquaintances the philosophy of the poets Stefan Georg and Rilke. He was following with sympathetic interest and shrewd practical advice the plans of a group of English friends for giving concrete expression to ideas of a constructive democracy in Great Britain.[62]

The phrase 'constructive democracy' seems to echo Por's 'functional democracy', but Wellesley almost certainly did not intend this. However, she must have been politically naive if she thought it would enhance Yeats's reputation as a practical thinker to tell the world in February 1939 about his 'constructive democracy', his studying 'eugenic authorities', and his 'shrewd practical advice' (examples of which she fortunately does not provide).

MEMORY AND IMAGINATION

This Absurdity

On arriving at the age of sixty, Yeats asked, not unreasonably in his case,

> What shall I do with this absurdity –
> O heart, O troubled heart – this caricature,
> Decrepit age that has been tied to me
> As to a dog's tail?
>
> (VP 409)

In any dialectical or materialist account of Yeats there has to be room for the contradiction or tension between the otherworldliness of his thoughts and the materiality of his body, the 'crock' that he became. The 1930s were ushered in and overshadowed by the will he made in Rapallo on 29 December 1929. In February 1930, George disclosed to Lady Gregory that Yeats had lost twenty-three and a half pounds (*LGJ* 2, 505). From February to May 1935 he suffered a serious bout of congestion of the lungs; while he was in Majorca with Shri Purohit Swami in January 1936, his heart and kidneys gave cause for concern, and George had to rush to his bedside.[63] In spite of the Steinach operation in April 1934, which Yeats imagined rejuvenated his sex life even though it was only a vasectomy, his health continued to deteriorate. The image of Yeats as 'the Wild Old Wicked Man' (*VP* 587) was, as Harwood rightly maintains, a mask, for by the mid-1930s Yeats was suffering from high blood pressure, heart disease, kidney disease, rheumatism, poor circulation, and chronic respiratory infections.[64] Even climbing stairs proved difficult. Some could see the humorous side. V. S. Pritchett recalls an amusing conversation between Yeats and H. G. Wells at the Savile Club in 1938:

Yeats in Rapallo, April 1930. 'I have had the further entertainment of growing a beard and had for a time a magnificent appearance with the beard and hair of St Peter out of a Raphael cartoon, and after that the local barber called every week and after several weeks produced a masterpiece, and I have now hair brushed upward and a small beard running down into a point' (Y & TSM 160).

Wells: Isn't it Yeats?

Yeats: Ah. Good morning, Wells.

Wells: You're looking very old, Yeats.

Yeats (*goes slightly grey*):   None of us gets younger, Wells.

Wells: Ah, the days we had when we were young. Do you remember how we used to walk on Hampstead Heath with X and Y?

Yeats: Yes. I wonder what they're doing nowadays?

Wells (*eating noisily*):   Dead.

Yeats (*greys further*):   Both of them?

Wells: Yes. And when we went to the Bedford to see Dan Leno with young Z?

Yeats: How is Z now?

Wells: Dead. (*Pause.*) And Yeats do you remember the time we went boating at Richmond and took those girls with us? One of them wore a pink dress and had beautiful long blond hair?

Yeats (*moved, puts down his knife and fork*):   Yes, I remember her. She was very beautiful. What's happened to – surely she can't be dead? She was much younger than us.

Wells: No, she isn't dead.

Yeats: Thank heavens for that.

Wells (*illustrating, graphically*):   Paralysed, all down one side. (*To waiter.*) I'll have the steak.[65]

George Moore, Edmund Gosse, and Edmund Dulac as they appeared in the *Bookman*, May 1931.

S. S. Koteliansky, James Stephens, and Lady Ottoline Morrel, taken at 10 Gower Street, London, 1935. Koteliansky thought Yeats the epitome of the Irish people, meaning something false and fabricated; Stephens was the one original writing talent that had come out of Ireland.

Shri Purohit Swami with Yeats on balcony in Majorca, 1935. Yeats was working with Shri Purohit on a translation of the *Upanishads*. In 1934 Yeats's potency revived after the Steinach operation, so much so that in 1937 he refused an invitation to visit India because, as he told the Swami, he feared weeks of sexual abstinence: 'I believe that if I repressed this for any long period I would break down under the strain as did the great Ruskin.'

On the other hand, as he announced to Heald in August 1938, Yeats was living like a butterfly and writing poetry, his only healthy life.[66] Convalescing also gave him new bursts of life and, indeed, strengthened his writing. In January 1938, while staying at the Hotel Terminus in Monte Carlo, he informed George he was working on 'On the Old Boiler'; he was writing in bed, the windows open, the wind gently blowing, and his breathing normal.[67] A week later, from the Carlton Hotel in Menton, he inadvertently put his finger on a distinctive feature of his last poems – his dependence on the spectacle of his own mind.[68] Or, as he put it in 'The Circus Animals' Desertion': 'What can I but enumerate old themes?' (*VP* 629). Inevitably, the idea of death, 'the soul and body embracing' (*L* 917), was rarely out of his thoughts. Like Ribh, the imaginary hermit and critic of St Patrick, he found Christian love insufficient: 'At stroke of midnight soul cannot endure/A bodily or mental furniture' (*VP* 558).

His poor health helped Yeats put his life in final order. He told Lady Gregory in 1931 that he was entirely occupied with what he hoped would be the final revision of his work for Macmillan. It was a pleasant task, since it meant envisioning his work as a whole and discovering that it was just that.[69] After finishing 'Under Ben Bulben' in September 1938, he turned to writing a play about Cuchulain's death. It was necessary, he told Heald, to

252

end his plays on this theme.[70] The last word in *The Death of Cuchulain* (1939) is given to a hot-blooded harlot remembering 'that most ancient race', and coursing through the beautifully subtle on-running lines are Yeats's vivid memories of love-making and the ineluctable modality of the body:

> I adore those clever eyes,
> Those muscular bodies, but can get
> No grip upon their thighs.
> I meet those long pale faces,
> Hear their great horses, then
> Recall what centuries have passed
> Since they were living men.
> That there are still some living
> That do my limbs unclothe,
> But that the flesh my flesh has gripped
> I both adore and loathe.
>
> (*VPl* 1062)

Illness, however, did not diminish Yeats's desire to organise the world. In September 1930 Lady Gregory noted in her journal: 'Yeats so full of life and fire sprung from the ashes of his illness – will found an Academy of Letters' (*LGJ* 2, 553).[71] In February 1932 George called on him to initiate a new intellectual movement: 'I really do believe that this is the moment to start things off, & the few people I have seen since you went away all say the same thing – we are tired of politics, we want an intellectual movement politics are the death of passion & passion is the food of the intellect.'[72] At the Abbey, the accession to power of Fianna Fáil in 1932 threatened changes, especially over appointments to the Board of Directors. But Yeats held out against an attempt by de Valera to interfere in the choice of plays to tour the United States in 1933: 'We refuse such a demand ⟨to drop Synge's *Playboy* and O'Casey's *Juno and the Paycock*⟩; your Minister may have it in his power to bring our theatre to an end, but as long as it exists it will retain its freedom.'[73] Yeats was also keen to bring young talent into the Abbey, and in April 1933 F. R. Higgins* was appointed to the Board, followed by O'Connor in October.[74] In January 1935, to further his ambitions for a poetic theatre, he formed a Dramatic Committee in London consisting of Dulac, the ballet master and producer Rupert Doone, Eliot, Ashton, and Margot Collis's secretary.[75] His writing also involved him in organisation, not only in assembling material for *The Oxford Book of Modern Verse, 1892–1935*, but also in editing from 1935 to 1937 the second series of *Broadsides*, a venture which he undertook with Higgins, W. J. Turner,* and Wellesley: 'We can do little, but we can sing, or persuade our friends to sing, traditional songs, or songs by new poets set in the traditional way.'[76]

In a Fenian's Bones

In the 1930s, if events had turned out differently, Yeats could have secured his future as a poet within an English tradition, and he might even have identified himself more openly with the English Establishment. In late spring 1930, for example, there was considerable support in the English press for Yeats to succeed Bridges as Poet Laureate.[77] Later that year Yeats told Lady Gregory that the Athenaeum in London wanted to elect

Yeats and Joyce repeatedly returned to the significance of the fall of Parnell for modern Irish history. Here is the scene of the famous meeting in Committee Room 15 of the House of Commons when Parnell's party turned against him. Mr Sexton turns to the arms-folded Parnell in accusation: 'We are your colleagues not your slaves.' From *Pall Mall Budget*, 4 December 1890.

Fishermen in Curraghs (1934), by Harry Kernoff. Yeats's romantic Ireland had a continuing appeal.

A *Picture Post* view of Ireland in July 1940, the generations united by poverty and the rosary.

PICTURE
POST

THE FAITH OF EIRE
An old Irish peasant with a child

HULTON'S NATIONAL WEEKLY

In this issue:
THE STORY OF IRELAND 3D

JULY 27, 1940   Vol. 8. No. 4

Sligo in the 1930s, a hand-coloured postcard. Talk of 'seven heroic centuries', 'coming days', or 'the indomitable Irishry' (*VP* 640) seemed strangely out of place in de Valera's Ireland of the small farmer.

O'CONNELL STREET, SLIGO.   R.668

Yeats positioned uncertainly on a garden seat.

Maud Gonne in old age, looking magnificent,
according to Yeats.

him a member; as Rothenstein recognised, it was 'a greater honour than a knighthood and less expensive than a peerage' (*LGJ* 2, 561).[78] To celebrate his seventieth birthday in 1935, a Presentation Committee was formed in London consisting of leading figures in the arts: Binyon, De la Mare, Dulac, Eliot, Augustus John, Gilbert Murray, Rothenstein, Sturge Moore, and Vaughan Williams. When he toured North America in late 1932 he must have been especially pleased that Ford provided him with a Lincoln car in all the major cities, with the same drivers who acted as chauffeurs to Churchill.[79] In 1937 the BBC set the seal on his achievement by inviting him to give a series of broadcasts, which went out on 2 April, 22 April, 3 July, and 29 October 1937, and for which he received fifteen guineas (£15.75) per programme.[80]

It was probably as well that he was not appointed Poet Laureate, for Yeats was 'an old Fenian and I think the old Fenian in me would rejoice if a Fascist nation or government controlled Spain, because that would weaken the British empire, force England to be civil to Indians, perhaps to set them free. . . . But this is mere instinct' (*L* 881). On the subject of the Abdication Crisis in December 1936, the modern Seanchan found himself composing 'A Model for the Laureate', a poem whose last stanza was designed to deceive no-one:

> The Muse is mute when public men
> Applaud a modern throne:
> Those cheers that can be bought and sold,
> That office fools have run,
> That waxen seal, that signature,
> For things like these what decent man
> Would keep his lover waiting,
>   Keep his lover waiting?
>   (*VP* 597–8)[81]

The theme of return to old themes is especially marked in his Fenian-inspired ballads of the *Broadsides*, two of which – 'The Rose Tree' and 'The Curse of Cromwell' – were broadcast by the BBC on 3 July 1937. In November 1936 William Maloney's *Forged Casement Diaries* (1936), a book detailing evidence to prove the diaries were forged, revived his bitterness against the British Establishment:

> I say that Roger Casement
> Did what he had to do.
> He died upon the gallows,
> But that is nothing new.
>   (*VP* 581)

Yeats was determined not to be misunderstood: 'I feel that one's verse must be as direct & natural as spoken words' (*DWL* 109).[82] He relished attacking the Old Enemy, and irreverently imagined 'The Ghost of Roger Casement' being sung to the tune of 'The Church's One Foundation':

> John Bull has stood for Parliament,
> A dog must have his day,
> The country thinks no end of him,
> For he knows how to say,

257

At a beanfeast or a banquet,
That all must hang their trust
Upon the British Empire,
Upon the Church of Christ.
The ghost of Roger Casement
Is beating on the door.

(VP 583)

Inspiration

In June 1930 a delighted Yeats told George that, having left a great pile of manuscript on Macmillan's floor, he felt he had been set free.[83] The late harvest had in fact only just begun, for the 1930s proved to be Yeats's most productive decade as a lyric poet. In the 1920s he composed just over seventy poems, but in the last decade of his life he produced more than a hundred. The three best-ever years together were 1936 to 1938, which saw eighteen, fifteen, and seventeen, respectively. At no other time in his life was his output greater: of the 386 poems in the *Variorum Edition, The Winding Stair* (1933) contains sixty-three poems, *A Full Moon in March* (1935) seventeen, and *Last Poems* (1940) fifty-six. His letters to George convey a less confident picture. In October 1937, while staying with Heald, he wrote that since coming to England he had been upset because, though he tried every day, he could not find a theme for poetry. He thought he was finished and was for blaming the diet, but then quite suddenly he found a theme which in turn led to another.[84] In July 1938, also while staying at Steyning, he found an idea for a new Crazy Jane poem, a figure he had almost forgotten.[85] And, as is clear from a letter to Margot Ruddock in April 1936, he never relinquished the view expressed in 'Adam's Curse': 'When your technic is sloppy your matter grows second-hand – there is no difficulty to force you down under the surface – difficulty is our plough.'[86] As for the quality of his own late verse, he was especially reassured in 1938 by Pound's cautious approval.[87]

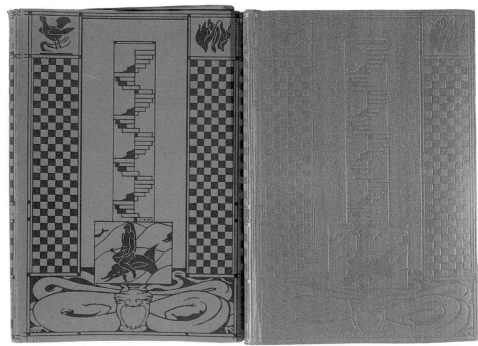

The Winding Stair, a companion volume to *The Tower*, was originally entitled *Byzantium*. Moore's cover design, stamped blind, includes reference to 'the winding path,' the 'cocks of Hades', 'an agony of flame', 'astraddle on the dolphin's mire and blood', and a 'gong-tormented sea'. The central panel is dominated by the Tower's gyre-like winding stair, below which there is a figure astraddle a dolphin, and at the bottom there is an art-nouveau swirling motif, possibly there to suggest 'marbles of the dancing floor'.

After his several visits to Penns in the Rocks from July to October 1937, Dorothy Wellesley concluded that 'Sex, Philosophy, and the Occult preoccupy him' (*DWL* 174). In his Notes to *The Words upon the Window Pane* (1931), he stressed his Irish roots: 'I divine an Irish hatred of abstration likewise expressed by that fable of Gulliver among the inventors and men of science, by Berkeley in his *Commonplace Book*, by Goldsmith in the satire of *The Good-Natured Man*, in the picturesque, minute observation of *The Deserted Village*, and by Burke in his attack upon mathematical democracy' (*VPl* 961). He knew what he liked. 'I hate Gerard Manley Hopkins', he told Ruddock, 'but people quite as good as I am admire him. He belongs to the movement immediately before mine. . . . His poetry and Meredith's . . . belong to each other; and my movement – I gave it its formula "the natural words in the natural order" – was the escape from artificial diction.'[88] He enjoyed Lawrence's *Women in Love*, which he finished reading in November 1932 at Waterville, Maine, and felt closer to him than to Virginia Woolf. He admired Lawrence's courage and the vividness of his thought, but felt his language too romantic and his metaphors often jaded.[89] In an interview with Louise Morgan in 1931, Yeats confessed: 'I love Jane Austen and her perilous pursuit of good breeding. . . . I love Henry James also. With him the perilous pursuit of good breeding begins once more!'[90]

In the 1930s Yeats completed a behaviourist 'Questionnaire on Creative Effort' under the direction of William McDougall at the Psychological Laboratory in Cambridge.[91] He was asked about the nature of his inspiration, the issue of voluntary control over his imagination and how he extended the passive moment, writer's block and how he dealt with it, the relation between creative and critical faculties, the satisfaction or otherwise with the finished product. During the period of general productive inclination, he never passively waited for inspiration, and usually, as we have seen, absorbed himself in detective stories. After half a century of writing verse, Yeats knew he knew more than the social scientists. He remained, however, a swimmer under water, rarely on top of things, always subject to the process, where 'all the time I seem thinking of something else . . . where every thought is like a bell with many echoes' (*VPl* 957). Yeats recognised that poetry arose from a play of forces between the unconscious and the conscious mind. On 26 January 1938, he wrote to Wellesley: 'I am finishing my belated pamphlet ⟨"On the Boiler"⟩ and will watch with amusement the emergence of the philosophy of my own poetry, the unconscious becoming conscious. It seems to increase the force of my poetry' (*DWL* 153).

In the late great phase of Yeats's verse nothing got in the way. Doubts about his inspiration, or his health, visits to galleries, presentations of carvings – all are incorporated into the process of composition. As James Stephens suggested in 1943, 'He did not winter to decay, he died in a spring-time, and younger than he was born.'[92] In July 1935, on the occasion of his seventieth birthday, he was given a piece of lapis lazuli by Harry Clifton, and he at once communicated his pleasure to Wellesley: 'I notice that you have much lapis lazuli; someone has sent me a present of a great piece carved by some Chinese sculptor into the semblance of a mountain with temple, trees, paths and an ascetic and pupil about to climb the mountain. Ascetic, pupil, hard stone, eternal theme of the sensual east. The heroic cry in the midst of despair. But no, I am wrong, the east has its solutions always and therefore knows nothing of tragedy. It is we, not the east, that must raise the heroic cry' (*DWL* 8). A year later, on 25 July 1936, 'Lapis Lazuli', 'almost the best I have made of recent years' (*DWL* 83), was finished, the last third of the poem devoted to a close description of the carving:

Two Chinamen, behind them a third,
Are carved in lapis lazuli,
Over them flies a long-legged bird,
A symbol of longevity:
The third, doubtless a serving-man,
Carries a musical instrument.

Every discoloration of the stone,
Every accidental crack or dent,
Seems a water-course or an avalanche,
Or lofty slope where it still snows
Though doubtless plum of cherry-branch
Sweetens the little half-way house
Those Chinamen climb towards, and I
Delight to imagine them seated there;
There, on the mountain and the sky,
On all the tragic scene they stare.
One asks for mournful melodies;
Accomplished fingers begin to play.
Their eyes mid many wrinkles, their eyes,
Their ancient, glittering eyes, are gay.

(*VP* 566–7)

The relaxed style shows no strain: the heroic cry in the midst of despair is no longer heard, muffled by the silence of the description and the ice of the inspiration. The ekphrasis, greatly enhanced when read alongside the carving itself, has no difficulty coping with the aggressive Nietzschean idea of tragic joy, the complex series of subtle pararhymes, or the positioning of the 'return' ('and I'), which is held back for six and a half lines, awkwardly attached to the end of a line, and momentarily arrested again before the verb *delight*. Here inspiration and accomplishment seem as one, though in fact Yeats, not unlike the Chinese sculptor with the original piece of lapis lazuli, worked on and transformed the original set of ideas contained in the 1935 letter. It was left to Joyce in *Finnegans Wake* to mock 'the lazily eye of his lapis' (293. 11).

LAST AFFAIR IN SUSSEX AND DEATH IN FRANCE

Edith Shackleton Heald

In 1937, when their relationship became intimate, Heald was fifty-three and Yeats in his early seventies. A strong supporter of women's rights, Heald was a professional journalist, had been Special Correspondent in the 1920s on the London *Evening Standard*, and in the 1930s was responsible for a weekly book page in the *Lady*, then edited by her sister Nora.[93] In an article for the *Daily Express* on 10 August 1929 she listed the men who interested her: the King, Einstein, Dulac, Shaw, Wells, and Yeats, 'whose grave manners and melodious conversation seem to take one back to a more spacious ancient world, who can be as practical as any other Irishman (which is saying a lot) and yet sees

Above: Lapis Lazuli Mountain (Ch'ien Lung Period, 1739–95). This was given to Yeats on his seventieth birthday by Harry Clifton.

Delphi, Greece. Yeats's news for the Oracle at Delphi was that the body has a sensuous life of its own: 'Down the mountain walls/ From where Pan's cavern is/Intolerable music falls./ Foul goat-head, brutal arm appear,/Belly, shoulder, bum,/Flash fishlike; nymphs and satyrs/Copulate in the foam' (*VP* 612).

Last Poems and Two Plays. Moore's cover design, at once simple to the eye and tantalising to the intellect, refers not to any particular line or stanza but symbolises the underlying theme of the book. In a covering note, Moore explained: 'Nut, the Egyptian goddess of the heavens is shown planted on and dominant over the lion while she lifts the starry sphere. Thus the royalty and ferocity of brute fact supports the intellect that projects a complete plan: or taken in an aspect that returns again and again in these poems, the goddess and the "noble animal" are symbols for the fascination and ruthlessness of generations that raise above themselves the mind that "Michael Angelo knew".'

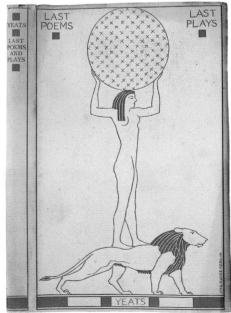

Above: Yeats with Edith Shackleton Heald and her sister Nora, taken at Steyning.
Gilbert Spencer's strikingly un-Yeatsian illustration of 'Three Things' (Ariel Poems no 18, 1929).

The Chantry House, Steyning, with plaque on wall.

the fairies and has dealings with spirits'.[94] In 1934 she moved with her sister to the Chantry House in Steyning, Sussex, and it was there in 1936 that she welcomed her hero.[95]

There is an early mention of Steyning in a letter from Yeats to George in October 1936. He told her about his diary for the coming week: lunch with Rothenstein, followed by a studio portrait session; Wednesday: BBC lecture; Thursday: the Shackletons, then Oxford, he thought, then Penns in the Rocks, then a broadcast, then home.[96] By May 1937 his friendship with Heald had strengthened.[97] A little later, the issue of names cropped up, reminiscent of earlier affairs, and he asked her not to call him by his first name.[98] On 10 June 1937 he informed George that on Sunday he was motoring to somewhere in Sussex with Dulac and Helen Beauclerck, to spend the remainder of the weekend with the person he called Dulac's friend.[99] In her reply George came straight to the point: today was his birthday, and then, after a semi-colon, she wished him well in the company of the Dulacs and Miss Shackleton.[100]

Summer 1937 was spent in part between Steyning and Penns in the Rocks. It was not, however, a bed of roses, for he found the Chantry House – or at least this is what he told George – occasionally tiring. He longed to return to London where he could be by himself until 3.30 p.m. when he went to his club.[101] In July 1937 Wellesley suffered a mental collapse, and Yeats was on hand to give advice and feel the strain along with Hilda Matheson.[102] In September, he told George that his uneventful life meant he had nothing to record.[103] But in fact intrigue was in the air, as is evident from his letter to Heald from Dublin in early August in which he planned a trip abroad with her.[104] From December 1937 onwards, his letters to Edith became more passionate and suggestive.[105]

George's attitude to this relationship is curious. She must have known of his amorous feelings for Heald, and yet she seemed prepared to collude with his fantasies or was indeed disposed to sharing her husband with another woman. After receiving a letter from Yeats in May 1938, she wrote to Heald highlighting the balance in their relationship: Heald was familiar with the way he would overload the last week with seeing visitors, and George was familiar with his arriving home utterly exhausted.[106] A week later she wrote again about his medicine and played on the contrasts between intellectual stimulation and coronary stimulation, and between Sussex countryside and the bleakness of Ireland.[107]

Steyning was also where the incorrigibly romantic Yeats wrote his epitaph, 'Under Ben Bulben', and there can be few more incongruous settings in which to boast emptily about being Irish than a village nestling in the South Downs:

> Irish poets, learn your trade,
> Sing whatever is well made,
> Scorn the sort now growing up
> All out of shape from toe to top,
> Their unremembering hearts and heads
> Base-born products of base beds.
> Sing the peasantry, and then
> Hard-riding country gentlemen,
> The holiness of monks, and after
> Porter-drinkers' randy laughter;
> Sing the lords and ladies gay
> That were beaten into the clay
> Through seven heroic centuries;

'The Bay, Monte Carlo' by Sir John Lavery. It was here amid the splendour and light of the south of France that Yeats wrote his last poem, 'The Black Tower', in January 1939: *'There in the tomb the dark grows blacker,/But wind comes up from the shore:/They shake when the winds roar,/Old bones upon the mountain shake'* (VP 636).

Cast your mind on other days
That we in coming days may be
Still the indomitable Irishry.
(VP 639–40)

On St Patrick's Day 1943, just a few years after Yeats wrote these lines, de Valera broadcast his dreams of Ireland, and one would be hard put to say which was the more unappealing: 'A land whose countryside would be bright with cosy homesteads, whose fields and villages would be joyous with the sounds of industry, with the romping of sturdy children, the contests of athletic youths and the laughter of comely maidens, whose firesides would be the forum for the wisdom of serene old age.'[108]

Final Weeks

Probably the last exchange of correspondence between the Yeatses occurred in November 1938 and concerned the London arrangements before their departure for the south of France. George wondered if he intended staying the Friday night (25 November) at his club and meeting at Victoria Station, or alternatively spending the night with her at the Grosvenor Hotel. She needed to know, she told him. If these arrangements were not suitable she intended staying at a small hotel near Victoria. In his reply Yeats wondered if the Grosvenor was suitable for lunch or if she was lunching with someone else.[109] As Tolstoy recognised, people die as they live, but in this case it is appropriate that George, the protector of his later reputation, was with Yeats when his end came on 28 January 1939. It is also not without significance that he was surrounded not by Irish friends but by Hilda Matheson, the first Director of Talks at the BBC, fellow Savilian, the Australian poet and music critic W. J. Turner, and Wellesley, minor poet and member of the English landed classes, who wrote to Rothenstein:

Hilda, W. J. Turner & I went to see him on the Saturday before he died. I had never seen him in better health, wits, charm or vitality. He was wearing his light brown suit, blue shirt & handkerchief. Under the lamp his hair seemed a pale sapphire blue. I thought during the talk: 'What a beautiful man.' He read aloud his last poem. A fine affair as I remember it. He asked Hilda to make a tune for it. His last projective thought seems to be this wish for 'Words for Melody'. . . . Tuesday he could not come to spend the evening here as he seemed tired. Wednesday Turner left for England. Thursday Hilda & I went to see him. I stayed only five minutes, he seemed very ill. In the afternoon we went again. Mrs Y said, 'Come back & light the flame.' I sat on the floor by his bed holding his hand; he struggled to speak: 'Are you writing – are you writing?' 'Yes, yes.' 'Good, good.' He kissed my hand, I his. Soon after he wandered a little in his speech. On Friday he was worse. I saw him for a few minutes. He then passed into what proved to be his last coma. He had much pain from the heart, but morphia helped him. So ended in the material sense this short and beautiful friendship. Mrs Y was there; and only last Monday (a week today) he was buried in a little rock (?) village *Roquebrune*, where his coffin will lie until it is taken back to Sligo.[110]

Tributes poured in from religious and political leaders, old friends, actors and actresses, poets and painters, friends and enemies alike, and on 6 February 1939 a list was sent to the Irish press of telegrams and messages of sympathy the family had received:[111]

The Very Rev. Dr Cregg, Primate of All Ireland.
The Abbey Theatre Board of Directors.
The Abbey Experimental Theatre.
Father Patrick Browne.
Mrs Margaret Clarke.
Mr and Mrs Padraic Colum.
Mrs Erskine Childers.
Mr and Mrs Con Curran.
Dr and Mrs Costello.
The Rt Rev. Dr T. A. Harvey, Bishop of Cashel.
Lord Dunsany.
Miss Lilian Davidson.
Mr Edmund Dulac.
Mr and Mrs Desmond Fitzgerald.
The Friends of the National Collection
Mr James A. Farrell.
Dr T. O. Graham.
Margarete and Gerhardt Hauptmann.
His Excellency the German Minister, Dr Hempel.
Mr Hugh Hunt.

Miss May Craig.
Miss Ann Clery.
Miss Maureen Delaney.
Mr and Mrs Alan Duncan.
Mr Victor Brown.
Mr G. Bottomley.
Mr Hilton Edwards.
Mr and Mrs Peter Judge.
Mr James Joyce.
Mr D. K. Kostal.
Dr Larchet.
John and Constance Masefield.
Dr Patrick Mccartan.
Mrs James MacNeill.
Miss Ria Mooney.
Dr Maxwell.
Mr James Montgomery.
Miss Nora McGuinness.
Mr Ezra Pound.
District Justice Kenneth Reddin and Mrs Reddin.
Mr George Shiels.
Dr Bethel Solomons.

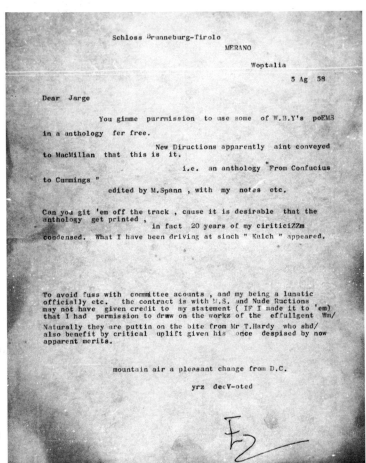

Schloss Brunneburg-Tirolo

MERANO

Woptalia

5 Ag 58

Dear Jarge

You gimme purrmission to use some of W.B.Y's poEMS
in a anthology fer free.

New Diructions apparently aint conveyed
to MacMillan that this is it.

i.e. an anthology "From Confucius
to Cummings "

edited by M.Spann , with my notes etc.

Can you git 'em off the track , cause it is desirable that the
anthology get printed ,
in fact 20 years of my ciriticiZZm
condensed. What I have been driving at sinch " Kulch " appeared.

To avoid fuss with committee acounts , and my being a lunatic
officially etc. the contract is with M.S. and Nude Ructions
may not have given credit to my statement (IF I made it to 'em)
that I had permission to draw on the workz of the effullgent Wm/

Naturally they are puttin on the bite from Mr T.Hardy who shd/
also benefit by critical uplift given his once despised by now
apparent merits.

mountain air a pleasant change from D.C.

yrz decV-oted

Pound's letter to George in 1958 requesting her help with Yeats's publisher. In May 1958 Pound was released from St Elizabeth's Hospital in Washington, D.C., and here humorously refers to 'my being a lunatic officially'. In 1965 he made a fleeting visit to Dublin to see George.

Dr and Mrs Starkie.
Dr Wilbraham Trench.
Mr Weenink, Consul-General for the
  Netherlands.
Mr and Mrs Dudley Figges.
Cauvet Duhamel, French Chargé D'Affaires.
Mr J. J. Hayes.
Mr James A. Healy.
Miss Olive Jackson.
Mr Eugene Kinkead.
Mr Sean T. O'Kelly, An Tanaiṣte.
Madame Maud Gonne Macbride.
Michael Macliamoir.
Mr Thomas McGreevy.
Mr P. S. O'Hegarty.
Mr and Mrs Dermod O'Brien.

Mr and Mrs S. O'Sullivan.
Miss Prollie Mulhern.
Miss Aideen O'Connor.
The Royal Society of Literature.
Mr Arthur Shields.
Mr and Mrs Francis Stuart.
Mr and Mrs Sowby.
Dr Rowlette.
Shelagh Richards.
Irish Literary Society, London.
Royal Hibernian Academy of Arts.
Mr and Mrs T. Sturge Moore.
Dr Robert Collis.
Mr V. C. Clinton Baddeley.
Lady Gerald Wellesley.
Mr George White.

Joyce sent a wreath in honour of the man he considered the greater writer. In a letter of condolence written to George on 30 March 1939, Eliot, who was to deliver the first

Yeats Memorial Lecture in Dublin in 1940, described Yeats as the leading modern poet.[112] Meanwhile, David Garnett in the *New Statesman and Nation* on 4 February 1939 called Yeats 'a great poet, in my opinion the greatest of all Irish poets, and he was unique among the poets not only of his country, but of the world. Posterity may recognise, I think, what has escaped his contemporaries: his enormous influence upon practical affairs.' 'His greatness is such', thought O'Casey, 'that the Ireland which tormented him will be forced to remember him for ever.'[113] Jack Yeats recalled his brother talking about someone and asking, 'What will history say about him?': 'And then, it came to my lips without a conscious thought, I said "men of genius are not in history" and I immediately knew I meant himself.'[114] 'You were silly like us: your gift survived it all,' wrote the English outsider Auden, forging in his original thoughts a connection between Yeats and Kipling, poets born in the same year, both wrong-headed, both to be pardoned by Time that 'Worships language and forgives/Everyone by whom it lives'.[115]

In early March 1939 in a letter to McGreevy, George revealed Yeats's private wishes regarding the funeral arrangements. He told her that if he died in the South of France, he wanted to be buried there and then in a year's time when he was forgotten by the press, his remains, like some tree or plant, were to be transported to Sligo. He had no wish for the kind of funeral Russell had.[116] Because of the war, Yeats's remains were not translated to Sligo until 1948. The Abbey Theatre wanted him to be buried in St Patrick's Cathedral along with Swift,[117] but Yeats's instructions were clear:

> Under bare Ben Bulben's head
> In Drumcliff churchyard Yeats is laid.
> An ancestor was rector there
> Long years ago, a church stands near,

James Malton's eighteenth-century view of St Patrick's, Dublin. 'Swift haunts me: he is always just round the next corner' (*VPl* 958). Yeats admired 'that arrogant intellect free at least from superstition' (*VPl* 955), but sought a permanent dwelling place amid his clerical ancestors in his native County Sligo.

267

'Under bare Ben Bulben's head/In Drumcliff churchyard Yeats is laid.' In that half-rhyme 'head/laid' Yeats characteristically refused to round things off (*VP* 640).

> By the road an ancient cross.
> No marble, no conventional phrase;
> On limestone quarried near the spot
> By his command these words are cut:
>
> > *Cast a cold eye*
> > *On life, on death.*
> > *Horseman, pass by!*
>
> > > *September 4, 1938*
> > > (*VP* 640)

Or, as Pound translated:

> 'Neath Ben Bulben's buttocks lies
> Bill Yeats, a poet twoice the soize
> Of William Shakespear, as they say
>
> Down Ballykillywuchlin way.
> Let saxon roiders break their bones
> Huntin' the fox
>   thru dese gravestones.[118]

    George Yeats was forty-six when her husband died; she still had nearly thirty years of her life to run. With Lollie Yeats's death in 1940 she took charge of the Cuala Press (with Higgins and, later, O'Faolain and O'Connor as Editors) and published a further fifteen titles, including MacNeice's *Last Ditch* (1940), Masefield's *Some Memories of W. B. Yeats* (1940), O'Connor's translation of *A Lament for Art O'Leary* (1940), and an edition of letters between Farr, Shaw, and her husband. With Thomas Mark she prepared the so-called definitive edition of the poems, published in 1949. In the weeks following her husband's death and in response to a letter from Macmillan, she discussed an official biography. She thought Joseph Hone would be the most suitable person: he was Irish, had sufficiently impressed Yeats with his biography of George Moore, and he was someone she could work with, especially given the sensitive nature of much of the material. She would destroy nothing, but was keen to ensure that it was not used in a sensational fashion. As for Macmillan's *edition de luxe*, which Yeats knew would be published only after his death, she wanted to see proofs of the contents for Macmillan's last two volumes. She then referred to the publication of the last two small books of poems published by the Cuala Press, one called 'New Poems' and one called 'Last Poem' (*sic*) which would be published in April.[119]

Other Macmillan volumes followed: *Autobiographies* (1955), *Mythologies* (1959), *Essays and Introductions* (1961), *Explorations* (1962). She watched Yeats's standing among the critics rise: the Yeats issue of the *Southern Review* (1941–2), *The Permanence of Yeats* (1950), the 1965 centennial essays.[120] But she kept her own counsel and lived on in Dublin, rarely leaving her adopted country.

In the aftermath of Yeats's death she assumed immediate and total responsibility for how her husband looked to posterity. In a letter in June 1939, Dorothy Wellesley expressed sympathy with her position: 'I just want to tell you that I quite understand that you really don't want anything published about him at all. To be the wife of a genius must be hard, to be the widow of a genius perhaps impossible.'[121] When discussing possible illustrations with George, Matheson and Wellesley discovered that Yeats 'had a rooted objection to photographs of himself being used in books'.[122] After all, as W. P. Ryan noted in December 1895, Yeats 'walks into our world a Stranger',[123] and it looks as if this is how George intended him to remain after his departure. Even to her last years she was overseeing her husband's reputation. She told Roger McHugh, for example, that she did not want Yeats's correspondence with Margot Ruddock to appear in 1965, the centenary year.[124]

Inevitably, it is her own role that now obtrudes and raises questions. In his Preface to the 1979 edition of *Yeats: The Man and the Masks*, Ellmann records that when he was working on Yeats's material at George's house in Dublin during 1946 and 1947, she was especially anxious about the unpublished first draft of Yeats's autobiography (since published as *Memoirs*). She also told Ellmann they had 'the first and only serious quarrel of their marriage'[125] over the second edition of *A Vision*, when Yeats intended to reveal her part in the automatic writing sessions. I doubt whether anyone reading the correspondence of the Yeatses could agree with George that this was their only serious quarrel. It also raises doubts about the overall direction of Ellmann's biography. Ellmann believed the crucial struggle in Yeats was between father and son; but in meeting George in post-war Dublin he must have realised something was afoot and that the crucial relationship lay elsewhere: 'One quality in her husband never ceased to astonish her . . . his extraordinary sense of the way things would look to people later on. Very possibly he knew that she would be at the centre of his story. If she bore his impress, he also bore hers.' Yet for nearly half a century, this key figure in the Yeats romance has been relegated to the credits or the acknowledgements page; she now deserves to tell her own tale – and in her own words.

Notes

Introduction

1 Henry Nevinson, *Changes and Chances* (London: Nisbet, 1923), 302.
2 David Pierce, *W. B. Yeats: A Guide through the Critical Maze* (Bristol: Bristol Classical Press, 1989), 2.

1 Yeats and Sligo

1 In a letter to Edith Shackleton Heald on 29 May 1937, Yeats specifically asked her not to call him by his first name. Original letter in the Houghton Library, Harvard University.
2 John Partridge, *Merlinus Liberatus: An Almanack for the Year of Our Redemption, 1865* (London: The Company of Stationers), 13.
3 At a lecture given in May 1901, Yeats spoke of 'his own habit of vacillation – how when tortured by this curse he would try to cleanse his mind (I think by fasting and similar means), and when he had reasoned the matter out and made a decision in his best and purest mood, he never allowed any subsequent mood to alter his decision in practice, though his mind would often continue to sway.' Henry Nevinson, *Changes and Chances* (London: Nisbet, 1923), 301.
4 Joseph Hone, *William Butler Yeats: The Poet in Contemporary Ireland* (Dublin and London: Maunsel, 1915), 3. Hone copied this from a paper in the possession of 'Miss Yeats'.
5 'Early Memories of Yeats', *Dublin Magazine*, July–September 1953, 24.
6 Letter from Martin Ross to Edith Somerville, 8 August 1901. In Gifford Lewis (ed.), *The Selected Letters of Somerville and Ross* (London: Faber and Faber, 1989), 252.
7 'Notes on the Celtic Renaissance: The Personality of W. B. Yeats', *Gael*, August 1899, 132.
8 George Moore, *Evelyn Innes* (1898; repr. London: Ernest Benn, 1929), 142.
9 Henry Nevinson, *Changes and Chances*, 209. Yeats 'talked well and incessantly, moving his hands a good deal, and sometimes falling into a natural chant; says "D'ye see?" to every sentence'. G. K. Chesterton, who knew the Yeats family well when they lived at Bedford Park, thought Willie 'perhaps the best talker I ever met, except his old father'. See his *Autobiography* (London: Hutchinson, 1936), 142.
10 W. P. Ryan, *The Irish Literary Revival: Its History, Pioneers and Possibilities* (London: The Author, 1894), 29.
11 See Manwaring Poetry Reading Scrapbook, no. 4 1937–41, 45, in Wellesley College, Special Collections, English Poetry Collection.
12 Lines taken from Wilfrid Gibson's poem 'The Three Poets' in his *Solway Ford* (London: Faber and Faber, 1945), 73–4. The three poets in question were Laurence Binyon, T. Sturge Moore, and Yeats.
13 Francis Byrne Hackett's typescript account of Irish Literary Society Reception, March 1904. MS Vault File, Yale.
14 Maurice Bowra, *Memories, 1898–1939* (London: Weidenfeld and Nicolson, 1966), 237.
15 Max Beerbohm, *Mainly on Air* (London: Heinemann, 1957), 100.
16 Ibid., 101.
17 Horatio Sheafe Krans, *William Butler Yeats and the Irish Literary Revival* (London: William Heinemann, 1905), 101.
18 Robert Lynd, *Home Life in Ireland* (London: Mills and Boon, 1909), 308. In *John O'London's Weekly* on 10 August 1929, Robert Lynd wrote an open letter to Yeats along similar lines outlined in his 1909 book. Yeats remained a puzzle to Lynd, who wondered whether 'there are a minor and a major poet mixed in you'. But he insisted that 'the signal quality of your genius is not vagueness, but energy'. More recently, Joyce Carol Oates took up a similar theme in the *New York Times Book Review* on 7 September 1969: 'Of the modern poets Yeats is the most formidable, most alarming and mad – reading his work, one resists it, resists his personality, fearful of succumbing to something harsh and demonic in it. And yet there is no way into Yeats without succumbing to him, giving up one's will to his.'
19 William Blake in 'Annotations to Sir Joshua Reynolds's Discourses' (*c.* 1808), in *The Complete Writings of William Blake*, ed. Geoffrey Keynes (London: Oxford University Press, 1966), 458.
20 In 1902 John Quinn sent Yeats a copy of

270

Thomas Common's edition of Nietzsche's work. In a letter to Lady Gregory on 26 December 1902, Yeats confesses to his newly discovered enthusiasm: 'Dear Friend . . . you have a rival in Nietzsche, that strong enchanter. . . . Nietzsche completes Blake & has the same roots – I have not read anything with so much excitement since I got to love Morris's stories which have the same curious astringent joy' (*L [K]* 3, 284).

21 What Yeats meant by a powerful and passionate syntax is partly explained by a phrase in the same sentence, 'a complete coincidence between period and stanza'.

22 John Masefield, *Some Memories of W. B. Yeats* (Dublin: Cuala Press, 1940), 29.

23 See the *Gael* (New York), December 1902, 379. The article cites the Irish editor of the *Southern Cross* (Buenos Aires).

24 George Bornstein, *Yeats and Shelley* (Chicago and London: Chicago University Press, 1970), xv.

25 *New Yorker*, 6 February 1943, 53.

26 In his later influence on American poetry, Yeats was himself like a mother country. See, for example, Terence Diggory, *Yeats and American Poetry: The Tradition of the Self* (Princeton: Princeton University Press, 1983).

27 'As the Irish soldiery poured down Broadway and a score of other city highways on the ending of the war, they chanted to the rolling cheers: "We're marching next to Ireland." That was the cradle-song of the Fenian movement.' F. Hugh O'Donnell, *A History of the Irish Parliamentary Party*, vol. 2 (London: Longmans, Green, 1910), 403.

28 According to A. N. Jeffares, Yeats 'never took the oath but always regarded himself as an IRB man'. See *W. B. Yeats: A New Biography* (London: Hutchinson, 1988), 80.

29 In *Finnegans Wake*, the upright Shaun the Post is twinned with the 'low sham', Shem the Penman. Remorselessly compared with Shem, Shaun invariably comes off the worse. 'Shaun! Shaun! Post the post!' (404.7).

30 John Eglinton, *Irish Literary Portraits* (London: Macmillan, 1935), 17.

31 'And there is such a thing as plebian ⟨sic⟩ pride.' Letter to Quinn, 18 January 1918. Copy in QUINN. Yeats was criticising his son's devotion to Lady Gregory.

32 Letters to Mrs Philips, 18 and 27 April 1934. In the Brotherton Collection, University of Leeds.

33 W. B. Yeats, *A Book of Irish Verse: Selected from Modern Writers* (London: Methuen, 1895), xxv.

34 See report in the *Boston Evening Transcript*, 30 November 1903.

35 John Eglinton, *Irish Literary Portraits*, 34.

36 Arland Ussher, *Three Great Irishmen: Shaw, Yeats, Joyce* (New York: Mentor, 1957), 78.

37 Cited in Warre B. Wells and N. Marlowe, *A History of the Irish Rebellion of 1916* (Dublin and London: Maunsel, 1916), 73n.

38 Katharine Tynan, *Peeps at Many Lands: Ireland* (London: Adam and Charles Black, 1909), 27–8.

39 Susan Mitchell, *George Moore* (Dublin and London: Maunsel, 1916), 60–61.

40 See his essay 'Culture and Colonization: A Northern Perspective', in Michael Kenneally (ed.), *Irish Literature and Culture* (Gerrards Cross: Colin Smythe, 1992), 158–72.

41 Cited in E. H. Mikhail, *W. B. Yeats: Interviews and Recollections*, vol. 2 (London: Macmillan; New York: Barnes and Noble, 1977), 309.

42 For a recent discussion of Kipling's views, see Peter Keating's Preface to his *Rudyard Kipling* (London: Martin Secker and Warburg, 1994).

43 Reported by Pound in 'Credit and the Fine Arts', in the *New Age*, 30 March 1922. Reprinted in Ezra Pound, *Ezra Pound and the Visual Arts*, ed. with introduction by Harriet Zinnes (New York: New Directions, 1980), 146.

44 The gate prominently displayed in the bookplate for Yeats (see page 97) could be Sturge Moore's punning reminder of the derivation of Irish Yeats from English Gates.

45 Letter dated 9 March 1889.

46 William M. Murphy, *Prodigal Father: The Life of John Butler Yeats (1839–1922)* (Ithaca and London: Cornell University Press, 1979), 79.

47 Cited in A. Norman Jeffares (ed.), *Yeats the European* (Savage, Maryland: Barnes and Noble, 1989), 190. The cousin in question was Olive Jackson.

48 Jack B. Yeats, *Sligo* (London: Wishart, 1930), 8, 41.

49 The image of 'lake water lapping with low sounds by the shore' is reminiscent of Sir Bedivere's lines in Tennyson's 'Morte D'Arthur': 'I heard the ripple washing in the reeds,/And the wild water lapping on the crag.' It took Yeats longer than he imagined to discover his own music.

50 W. B. Yeats, *John Sherman and Doyha*, ed. Richard Finneran (Detroit: Wayne State University Press, 1969), 46.

51 Ibid., 59. A similar moment is recalled in 'Under Saturn', a poem written in November 1919, when Yeats returned to Sligo with his new wife, George: 'You heard that labouring man who had served my people. He said/Upon the open road, near to the Sligo quay–/No, no, not said, but cried it out – "You have come again,/And surely after twenty years it was time to come."/I am thinking of a child's vow sworn in vain/Never to leave that valley his fathers called their home' (*VP* 391). The old woman's question resurfaces in Yeats's play *The King of the Great Clock Tower* (1934), transformed now from its local colour into powerful sentiment: 'O what is life but a mouthful of air?/*Said the rambling, shambling travelling-man;*/Yet all the lovely things that were/Live, for I saw them dancing there' (*VPl* 1005).

52 W. B. Yeats, John Sherman and Doyha, 78.

53 John Butler Yeats, *Essays Irish and American* (Dublin: Talbot Press; London: T. Fisher Unwin, 1918), 33.

54 W. B. Yeats, *John Sherman and Dhoya*, 103.

271

55 Ibid., 51.
56 Hone, *William Butler Yeats*, 11. Hone was later entrusted with the task of writing Yeats's biography.
57 For a discussion of the play in terms of dreaming back, see F. A. C. Wilson, *Yeats and Tradition* (1958; repr. London: Methuen, 1968), 137–55. Wilson also reads the play as a polemic against democratic Ireland (the boy is sixteen, born therefore in 1922). For a wide-ranging discussion of *Purgatory*, especially in the context of fascism, see W. J. McCormack, *From Burke to Beckett: Ascendancy, Tradition and Betrayal in Literary History* (Cork: Cork University Press, 1994), 302–40.
58 Katharine Tynan, *Memories* (London: Eveleigh Nash and Grayson, 1924), 282.
59 Tadgh Kilgannon, *Sligo and Its Surroundings* (Sligo: Kilgannon, 1926). The Pollexfens owned three extensive mills, one at Sligo and the other two at Ballysodare. Among the Directors there was no Pollexfen.
60 The Silver Swan Hotel today stands on the site of a Pollexfen sawmill.
61 Kilgannon *Sligo and Its Surroundings*, 314.
62 Yeats has an Anglo-Irish love of 'character'. Compare the following passage written in the same period as *Reveries*: 'Ireland in those days was a forcing bed for individuality. Men and women, of the upper classes, were what is usually described as "a law unto themselves", which is another way of saying that they broke those of all other authorities. . . . Equally vigorous . . . was the growth of character.' E. Somerville and Martin Ross, *Irish Memories* (London: Longmans, Green, 1918), 68–9.
63 John Butler Yeats, *Essays Irish and American*, 53.
64 Ibid., 32.
65 'Pol-ex-fen' is George Yeats's pun. See *YVP 2*, 359.
66 'Are You Content?' was first published in April 1938. Yeats's right-wing interest in eugenics was being exercised at this time. In late November 1937 Yeats received a letter from the Eugenics Society in London, informing him that his subscription was overdue. (NLI MS 30583. Letter dated 30 November 1937.) In January 1938 he received a letter from an apologist for eugenics in reply to his inquiry about evidence for a link between superior intelligence and the upper classes. 'I know of no observations as to intelligence quotients among the leisured classes living on unearned incomes. Such persons would be very difficult to get hold of in any organised body. Yours sincerely. C. P. Blacker.' (NLI MS 30583. Letter dated 17 January 1938.) David Bradshaw is less troubled by Yeats's interests in eugenics. See 'The Eugenics Movement and *On the Boiler*', in Deirdre Toomey (ed.), *Yeats and Women: Yeats Annual*, no. 9 (London: Macmillan, 1992), 189–215.
67 John Butler Yeats, *Essays Irish and American*, 54.
68 Brendan Behan, *Brendan Behan's Island: An Irish Sketch-Book* (London: Hutchinson, 1962), 18.
69 From an unpublished essay on Dunsany by Gogarty. Cited in Mark Amory, *Biography of Lord Dunsany* (London: Collins, 1972), 75. Tom Moore also 'dearly loved a lord'.
70 George Moore, *Hail and Farewell: Ave, Salve, Vale* ed. Richard Cave (Gerrards Cross: Colin Smythe, 1976), 540. Douglas Goldring, commenting on this episode, writes: 'Although A.E. [Russell] could not be described as feline in his comments on Yeats, there was a hint that he regarded Yeats's weakness for playing up to social figures as indicating a streak of the charlatan and the poseur. As Irish literary men, like members of a large family, understand each other with a devastating clarity, he was probably right.' *The Nineteen Twenties: A General Survey and Some Personal Memories* (London: Nicholson and Watson, 1945), 118.
71 J. B. Yeats in a letter to Quinn, 27 November 1913. In QUINN. The poet's grandfather 'would rather any day be a papist priest than an Episcopalian minister. . . . He was intensely curious about catholic doctrine'. J. B. Yeats thought if we have the one we must have the other: 'The law is the core of protestantism. "*A passionate humanity is the core of the catholic doctrine*"'.
72 John Butler Yeats, *Early Memories: Some Chapters of Autobiography* (Dundrum: Cuala Press, 1923), 35.
73 Ibid., 54.
74 Ibid., 56. Corbet lived in a castellated house, not a traditional castle. He 'made an accidental fortune through a lucky political appointment'. (See Murphy, *Prodigal Father*, 30).
75 Ibid., 85.
76 J. B. Yeats in his 'Memoirs'. Cited in Murphy, *Prodigal Father*, 42–3.
77 J. B. Yeats, *Early Memories*, 89.
78 Letter to Quinn, 27 April 1916. In QUINN.
79 J. B. Yeats, *Early Memories*, 91.
80 Ibid., 92. In *Reveries*, Yeats delights in what must have been a familiar turn of phrase of his father's: 'Yet it was a Yeats who spoke the only eulogy that turns my head. "We have ideas and no passions, but by marriage with a Pollexfen we have given a tongue to the sea cliffs"' (*R* 37).
81 Lady Gregory to W. B. Yeats, Monday, 21 November ⟨n.y.⟩ (? 1902). In BERG.
82 B. L. Reid, *The Man from New York: John Quinn and His Friends* (New York: Oxford University Press, 1968), 494. Letter dated 21 February 1921.
83 J. B. Yeats to W. B. Yeats, 25 April 1915. In *Letters to W. B. Yeats*, vol. 2, ed. Richard Finneran, George Mills Harper, William M. Murphy (London: Macmillan, 1977), 312.
84 J. B. Yeats to Quinn, 23 November 1918. In QUINN.
85 In a letter to his father on 26 December 1914, where he comments on the newly completed *Reveries*, Yeats noted: 'Some one to whom I read the book said to me the other day "If Gosse had not taken the title you should call it 'Father and Son'"' (*LS* 203). Yeats originally chose for his title 'Memory Harbour, A Revery

on my Childhood and Youth', but he was forced to change this on discovering that Filson Young had used 'Memory Harbour' for a title.

86 It is worth recording here the early faith Yeats senior had in his son. In a letter to Edward Dowden in 1884, he writes: 'That he is a poet I have long believed, where he may reach is another matter.' Cited in Douglas Archibald, *John Butler Yeats* (Lewisburg: Bucknell University Press, 1974), 42.

87 Copy of school report in Box 93, SUNY Stony Brook.

88 Letter postmarked 5 July 1915. Original in BERG.

89 Copy in Box 77, SUNY Stony Brook.

90 Cited in Richard Finneran, *Editing Yeats's Poems: A Reconsideration* (London: Macmillan, 1990), 92.

91 Cited in Murphy, *Prodigal Father*, 45.

92 J. B. Yeats to W. B. Yeats, 25 April 1915. In *Letters to W. B. Yeats*, vol. 2, 312.

93 In a letter to his father dated 26 December 1914, Willie seems oblivious of any potential harm he might cause Yeats senior: 'You need not fear that I am not amiable' (*LS* 203). For his part, Yeats senior was pleased with 'your little autobiography'. See *Letters to W. B. Yeats* vol. 2, 334. In a recent study John Harwood takes a more critical view of what he sees as the destructive influence of Yeats senior on his son. Yeats senior was 'a walking disaster area', the 'boy who never grew up'. See his *Olivia Shakespear and W. B. Yeats: After Long Silence* (London: Macmillan, 1989), 34–5. In a letter to Quinn on 30 September 1921, W. B. Yeats took a dialectical view of his relationship with his father: 'He even hates the sign of will in others. It used to cause quarrels between me and him, for the qualities which I thought necessary to success in art or in life seemed to him "egotism" or "selfishness" or "brutality". I had to escape this family drifting, innocent and helpless, and the need for that drew me to dominating men like Henley and Morris and estranged me from his friends, even from sympathetic unique York Powell. I find even from letters written in the last few months that he has not quite forgiven me.' Cited in Reid, *The Man from New York*, 493–4.

94 With the publication of *The Wanderings of Oisin* in 1889 and 'The Lake Isle of Innisfree' in 1890, the poet had become famous. With a quarter of a century behind him and more than thirty years still in front of him, the painter never achieved widespread fame, and, as if to confirm the transfer of power, it was the son who in the 1890s began to obtain commissions for his father. Yeats senior, writing on 17 May 1906 to Elkin Mathews, hoped for posthumous fame: 'I think I paint very much better and that I have painted portraits which at any rate will confer on me a posthumous fame'. (In the Brotherton Collection, University of Leeds.) Quinn had almost given up the task of persuading Yeats's father to return to Ireland. 'Well, I have done all I can do. I cannot order

you back. The expense of your remaining here is up to W.B.Y. . . . I have not the strength to keep on indefinitely in the role of Cassandra.' Letter dated 13 January 1919. In QUINN.

95 Lady Gregory, *Gods and Fighting Men: The Story of the Tuatha De Danaan and of the Fianna of Ireland* (London: John Murray, 1904), xiv.

96 Lady Gregory, *Cuchulain of Muirthemne* (1902; repr. Gerrards Cross: Colin Smythe, 1976), 16–17.

97 For discussion of the term *romantic spiral*, see M. H. Abrams, *Natural Supernaturalism: Tradition and Revolution in Romantic Literature* (New York: W. W. Norton, 1971), 183–7. In contrast to the Neoplatonic tradition, Romantic writers and philosophers compared life to an ascending circle or spiral. *Reveries* in part resembles a romantic spiral, but Yeats is too captivated by the idea of 'reveries' to articulate a consistent line of development. Indeed, his final sentence has the characteristic look of a throwaway: '⟨W⟩hen I think of all the books I have read, and of the wise words I have heard spoken, and of the anxiety I have given to parents and grandparents, and of the hopes that I have had, all life weighed in the scales of my own life seems to me a preparation for something that never happens.'

98 From Yeats's essay 'The Literary Movement in Ireland', in *Ideals in Ireland*, ed. Lady Gregory (London: At the Unicorn, 1901), 100. The quoted phrase is from Ecclesiasticus.

99 Letter dated 31 May ⟨1934⟩. Cited in C. M. Bowra, *Memories, 1898–1939* (London: Weidenfeld and Nicolson, 1966), 240.

100 Clifton Fadiman, *New Yorker*, 6 February 1943, 54.

101 Yeats uses the word *unpeopled* in his Preface to Lady Gregory, *Gods and Fighting Men*. To Yeats as a boy, Ben Bulben was 'the great mountain that showed itself before me every day through all my childhood and was as yet unpeopled' (xxiv).

102 Francis T. Palgrave, *Landscape in Poetry from Homer to Tennyson* (London: Macmillan, 1897), 8. Palgrave suggests the modern attitude to landscape takes several different forms: the subordination of human interests to nature; penetration to the inner soul of the landscape and drawing from it moral lessons, whether for encouragement or to warn; landscape as a symbol of underlying spiritual truths or idealised by strong emotions; more accurate treatment of nature as a result of the sciences. The deepest aspect of the modern treatment of landscape, according to Palgrave, lies in the recognition of mind by mind, of the unity between the wonders of the world without and the wonders of the world within, the perception of divine purpose. In this light, Yeats both does and does not belong to the late nineteenth century.

103 Letter from William Blake to Dr Trusler, 23 August 1799. In *The Complete Writings of William Blake*, 793. According to Hazard Adams, the most important thing about Blake's vision is that 'it presents basically a

single image or central form of experience into which can be drawn all minute particulars, where what have always been looked upon as contraries are unclothed and shown to be "equally true"'. See *Blake and Yeats: The Contrary Vision* (1955; repr. New York: Russell and Russell, 1968), 66.

104 Paul de Man, *The Rhetoric of Romanticism* (New York: Columbia University Press, 1984), 143, 139. For a recent discussion that takes its cue from de Man's study, see Denis Donoghue, 'Yeats and European Criticism' in A. Norman Jeffares (ed.), *Yeats the European*, 38–48. Donoghue argues that in Yeats's case Nietzsche intervened between symbol and emblem, between European Symbolism and neo-Platonism.

105 Oliver St John Gogarty, *William Butler Yeats: A Memoir* (Dublin: Dolmen, 1963), 25. Gogarty might have been taking Dorothy Wellesley to task: 'Yeats did not himself draw much inspiration from nature. . . . Yeats once said to me in an outburst of irritability: "Why can't you English poets keep flowers out of your poetry?"' See *DWL* 173. It is interesting to contrast Yeats on landscape and childhood with a near contemporary, the journalist and nationalist M.P., T. P. O'Connor (1848–1929), who edited *T. P.'s Weekly* from 1902 onwards and who went on to become in 1924 a Privy Councillor at Westminster: 'As I grew up in Ireland, my imagination was chiefly busy in building the opulent palaces that are the stuff of day dreams rather than in seeing or appreciating what was going on around me. It was some two or three years after I left it before I saw Ireland again; and then neither lake nor sea nor sky existed for me; I had eyes only for the rags of the cabins, the ruined houses, the desolated towns.' See Hamilton Fyfe, *T. P. O'Connor* (London: George Allen and Unwin, 1934), 60.

106 Yeats in a letter quoted in Lady Gregory's *Journals*, 1 January 1929. See *LGJ* 2, 371.

107 Harold Bloom, *Yeats* (New York: Oxford University Press, 1970), 35.

108 Apparently, after their marriage George was especially keen to see Innisfree, but when they got to Lough Gill Yeats had difficulty making out which island was the one of his poem. 'The Lake Isle of Innisfree' quickly degenerates into parody once the visionary landscape is removed. On 28 March 1908 the *Westminster Gazette* printed an imaginary conversation between Tom Moore and Yeats: 'I will arise and go now, and go to Charing Cross,/And a small cabman hire there, of grey and mottled face;/Twelve brown pence will I give him, and one for the poor old hoss,/And drive alone to a fly-blown place.'

109 Richard Ellmann cautions against a simple reading of Yeats's poems on pictorial themes. The sources of 'Leda and the Swan' produced a flurry of interest among critics in the 1960s, but Ellmann argues that Yeats is doing something different from Michelangelo, or Leonardo, or Gustave Moreau, or the person who sculptured the Greek bas-relief in the British Museum. The details Yeats chooses to focus on and the intellectual weight are Yeats's, for he is without analogue. See 'Yeats Without Analogue' in the *Kenyon Review*, vol. 26, Winter 1964, no. 1, 30–53. This essay is reproduced in Ellmann's *a long the riverrun: Selected Essays* (Harmondsworth: Penguin, 1988), 18–32.

110 See Russell's essay 'Yeats and the Nobel Prize' in Monk Gibbon (ed.), *The Living Torch A. E.* (London: Macmillan, 1937), 258.

111 'You cannot conceive to English eyes the first shock of ruined cottages; and when it goes on to whole hamlets, the effect is most depressing.' This is Kingsley writing in July 1860 about his journey from Markree Castle (marked on the County Sligo map near Collooney) in County Sligo to Westport. 'But I am haunted by the human chimpanzees I saw along that hundred miles of horrible country. I don't believe they are our fault. . . . But to see white chimpanzees is dreadful; if they were black, one would not feel it so much, but their skins, except where tanned by exposure, are as white as ours.' *Charles Kingsley: His Letters and Memories of His Life*, vol. 2, ed. F. E. Kingsley (London: C. Kegan Paul, 1878), 107.

112 See the chapter on 'Yeats's Sculptural Poetry' in Elizabeth Bergmann Loizeaux, *Yeats and the Visual Arts* (New Brunswick and London: Rutgers University Press, 1986).

113 Session took place on 13 November 1918.

114 Edwin J. Ellis and W. B. Yeats (eds), *The Works of William Blake: Poetic, Symbolic, and Critical*, vol. 1 (London: Bernard Quaritch, 1893), xiii. Loizeaux makes the valuable additional point: 'In Yeats's finest poems the symbolic landscape never takes precedence over the landscape as experienced.' *Yeats and the Visual Arts*, 82.

115 Horatio Sheafe Krans, *William Butler Yeats and the Irish Literary Revival*, 108.

116 Report in the *Boston Evening Transcript*, 30 November 1903.

2 Yeats's Female Daimon

1 Joseph Hone, *William Butler Yeats: The Poet in Contemporary Ireland* (Dublin and London: Maunsel, 1915), 73.

2 Harriet Monroe, *A Poet's Life: Seventy Years in a Changing World* (New York: Macmillan, 1938), 333.

3 Henry Nevinson, *Changes and Chances* (London: Nisbet, 1923), 209. See also Nevinson's 'W. B. Yeats: The Poet of Vision' in *London Mercury*, March 1939, 485–91.

4 Wilfrid Scawen Blunt, *My Diaries: Being a Personal Narrative of Events 1888–1914* (New York: Alfred Knopf, 1932), 290–91.

5 See Freud's essay 'The Uncanny' (1919) in S. Freud, *Art and Literature*, tr. James Strachey, ed. Albert Dickson (Harmondsworth: Penguin, 1985), 362–3. It is *uncanny* how much of this essay can be applied to Yeats.

6 This was in reply to a question after a lecture

on magic delivered in London on 4 May 1901. See Nevinson, *Changes and Chances*, 301.

7 According to Maeterlinck, the Great Secret, the only secret, is that all things are secret. *The Great Secret*, tr. Bernard Miall (London: Methuen, 1922), 267–8.

8 Shane Leslie, *The End of a Chapter* (London: Constable, 1916), 104–5.

9 E. J. Ellis and W. B. Yeats (eds), *The Works of William Blake: Poetic, Symbolic, and Critical*, vol. 1 (London: Bernard Quaritch, 1893), 21. The Preface to this edition constitutes, it seems to me, part of Yeats's autobiography. Frequently, as in the discussion of the contrast between visionary mood and ordinary life, Yeats could be talking about himself: 'The difference between Blake in his visionary mood and Blake in his ordinary life is that between a man to whom it was the point of duty to yield to no one, and a man who, with old Irish politeness, wished to contradict no one' (91). Here is an early formulation of the contrast later explored in *Per Amica Silentia Lunae* between the Primary Self and the Anti-Self. Yeats also saw his own schooling in terms similar to Blake's and Shelley's, being persecuted by his fellows, 'who were made uneasy by the abstracted gaze and strange manner of one who was marked out for their enmity by the burning ribbon of genius' (9). Yeats believed that Blake's father was an O'Neil, who married Ellen Blake, the keeper of a *shebeen* in Rathmines, Dublin. Yeats imagined his mentor, Blake, was in the same tradition as himself, being both Irish and mystical.

10 Letter dated 30 June 1921. T. W. Rolleston, in a speech delivered to the Press Club in Dublin in 1896, expressed similar concern: 'Yeats's turn for mysticism, though it has produced much beautiful and interesting work, is a very real danger to him. Not that I object to mysticism in itself, for we Irish are all mystics in a sense, and a very real sense. You must either be a mystic or an atheist. But by mysticism in literature I mean the description of the working of spiritual forces in the technical language of a recondite system of philosophy and not in language that goes home to the bosoms and brains of ordinary men and women.' C. H. Rolleston, *Portrait of an Irishman: A Biographical Sketch of T. W. Rolleston* (London: Methuen, 1939), 20–21.

11 Yeats senior worked the other way and did allow for the paranormal. As he wittily put it in a letter to Quinn on 29 October 1912: 'I am as you know an agnostic but a firm believer in certain people being about to know things hidden from ordinary folk.' In QUINN.

12 For a recent study of the rise and fall of Blavatsky, see Peter Washington, *Madame Blavatsky's Baboon: Theosophy and the Emergence of the Western Guru* (London: Secker and Warburg, 1993). Yeats was expelled from the Society in 1890 for conducting experiments which were not approved: occult research needed Madame Blavatsky's approval, and Yeats knew she was fearful of anything which suggested black magic. See

Memoirs, 282.

13 See Francis Stuart's essay in *The Yeats We Knew*, ed. Francis Macmanus (Cork: Cork University Press, 1965), 40.

14 This episode is retold in 'Regina, Regina Pigmeorum, Veni' in *The Celtic Twilight*.

15 See *Memoirs*, 76. This comes in the context of a discussion about his visit to Sligo in November 1894.

16 It is even more outrageous when lines 6 and 7 are juxtaposed with an earlier draft where 'outrageous' qualifies merely 'thing': 'But as the indifferent stars betide,/Many an outrageous thing beside.' See draft of 'In Memory of Major Robert Gregory' dated 24 May 1918, in BERG.

17 See Notes to *The Unicorn from the Stars*, in *VPl* 712–13.

18 In an interview with Sybil Bristowe in *T. P.'s Weekly* on 4 April 1913, Yeats corrected her when she spoke of a Celtic movement: he belonged to an Irish movement.

19 Mary Thuente, *W. B. Yeats and Irish Folklore* (Totowa, New Jersey: Gill and Macmillan and Barnes and Noble, 1980), 131. Yeats maintains his chief informant was Paddy Flynn from Ballysodare, and he makes no reference to Biddy Hart by name (*CT* 4). In *Irish Fairy Tales* (1892) Yeats refers to 'old Biddy Hart'. The 'old Mayo woman' in *The Celtic Twilight* is Mary Battle.

20 For comparison, see Canon J. O'Hanlon, *Irish Folk Lore: Traditions and Superstitions of the Country; with Humorous Tales* (London: Cameron and Ferguson, 1870); Jeremiah Curtin, *Myths and Folklore of Ireland* (London: Sampson and Low, 1890) and *Tales of the Irish Fairies* (London: Nutt, 1895). Curtin never goes beyond the evidence – he stops, therefore, precisely at the point where Yeats would want to begin his investigations. Patrick Kennedy, Yeats's immediate predecessor in the field, anticipated a twentieth-century concern among folklorists, namely, the role of story-tellers themselves in shaping a story, but for the most part Kennedy is a Victorian collector, interested in the comparative study of folktales and in how such tales in Ireland fitted into a European picture. See his *Legendary Fictions of the Irish Celts* (London: Macmillan, 1866) and *The Fireside Stories of Ireland* (Dublin: McGlashan and Gill, 1870).

21 In his Introduction to *Fairy and Folk Tales of Ireland* (1888) Yeats complained of the scientific intrusion into the study of folklore. Irish collectors, however, 'have made their work literature rather than science, and told us of the Irish peasantry rather than of the primitive religion of mankind, or whatever else the folklorists are on the gad about'. Cited in *W. B. Yeats, Fairy and Folktales of the Irish*, ed. Kathleen Raine (Gerrards Cross: Colin Smythe, 1973), 6. E. B. Tylor was the author of the influential work on anthropology *Primitive Culture*, which was first published in 1870.

22 See his review of Yeats's *Irish Fairy Tales* in

the *Library Review*, August 1892, 345.

23 *National Observer*, 3 March 1893, 403.

24 Hence the doubt among critics in classifying *The Celtic Twilight*. To Thuente, it is a series of essays; Frank Kinahan, on the other hand, in 'Hour of Dawn: The Unity of Yeats's *Celtic Twilight* (1893, 1902)', begins by describing the pieces as essays, then switches to 'prose narratives', then 'narratives', and finally ends with 'folktale'. See *Irish University Review*, vol. 13, no. 2, Autumn 1983, 189–205.

25 Russell is part of 'that great Celtic phantasmagoria whose meaning no man has discovered, nor any angel revealed' (*CT* 22). Yeats's relationship with his occult friend Russell was never smooth, especially in their youth. The two had different overall ambitions: Russell burnt all his manuscripts at the time when Yeats's output was increasing significantly (the years 1887 to 1892, when he went to London). Their separate paths became more pronounced in 1890 when Yeats joined the Golden Dawn and Russell the Theosophical Society: Yeats invoked the spirits to enter this world; Russell refused to interrogate the spirits, preferring instead a view of astral light. For further discussion see Peter Kuch, *Yeats and AE* (Gerrards Cross: Colin Smythe, 1986), *passim*.

26 This 1890s phrase can be found in 'The Twisting of the Rope and Hanrahan the Red', one of the stories in *The Secret Rose* (London: Lawrence and Bullen, 1897), 143.

27 See 'Fairy Struck; Or The Dying Child' in the *People's Journal*, 9 January 1847, 17.

28 'When I was a boy I used to wander about at Rosses Point and Ballisodare listening to old songs and stories. I wrote down what I heard and made poems out of the stories or put them into the little chapters of the first edition of "The Celtic Twilight", and that is how I began to write in the Irish way.' See his dedication to Lady Gregory in *Where There Is Nothing: Being Volume One of Plays for an Irish Theatre* (London: A. H. Bullen, 1903), vii.

29 Holograph MS Notes for lecture beginning 'Two Gifts of Ireland to World'. These notes seem to form the outline of a lecture Yeats gave on 19 February 1903 in the Town Hall, Cardiff. Original in Wellesley College, Special Collections, English Poetry Collection.

30 As a child, Lady Gregory's interest in local stories had been aroused by her nurse Mary Sheridan, but it lay dormant until the mid-1890s. See Colin Smythe (ed.), *Lady Gregory, Seventy Years: 1852–1922, Being the Autobiography of Lady Gregory* (Gerrards Cross: Colin Smythe, 1974), 306, 2–3. In *Visions and Beliefs in the West of Ireland*, Lady Gregory devotes a whole section to Mary Sheridan's stories.

31 *Visions and Beliefs in the West of Ireland*, 15.

32 This is the phrase she uses after visiting a workhouse in County Galway in her *Poets and Dreamers: Studies and Translations from the Irish* (1903; repr. Gerrards Cross: Colin Smythe, 1974), 98.

33 *Visions and Beliefs in the West of Ireland*, 63.

34 John Eglinton, *Irish Literary Portraits* (London: Macmillan, 1935), 28.

35 For further discussion of Yeats in the context of Irish folklore in the nineteenth century, see Frank Kinahan, *Yeats, Folklore, and Occultism: Contexts of the Early Work and Thought* (Boston and London: Unwin Hyman, 1988), 41–85.

36 For an account of this episode, see *Visions and Beliefs in the West of Ireland*, 69–73. The footnote can be found on page 358. Yeats's attitude towards Maud Gonne was also like that of a patient awaiting a cure.

37 William Butler Yeats, *The Speckled Bird*, ed. William O'Donnell (Toronto: McClelland and Stewart, 1976), xviii. Yeats wrote four versions of this novel, the 'Island' version (*c.* 1897), 'Leroy' (*c.* 1897–8), 'De Burgh' (*c.* 1900), and the one I concentrate on here, the 'Final' version (*c.* 1902). O'Donnell's edition reprints the variants.

38 The blank is presumably a reference to Olivia Shakespear's husband, Hope Shakespear.

39 Hone, *William Butler Yeats*, 72.

40 In his dedication to *The Secret Rose*, Yeats told Russell that the stories have 'but one subject, the war of spiritual with natural order' (*SR* vii).

41 George Moore, *Hail and Farewell: Ave* (London: William Heinemann, 1911), 66.

42 For information on the Golden Dawn, see in particular Israel Regardie, *The Golden Dawn: An Account of the Teachings, Rites and Ceremonies of the Order of the Golden Dawn* (1937–40; Saint Paul: Llewellyn, 1971); Ellic Howe, *The Magicians of the Golden Dawn: A Documentary History of a Magical Order, 1887–1923* (London: Routledge and Kegan Paul, 1972); and George Mills Harper, *Yeats's Golden Dawn* (London: Macmillan, 1974). The Golden Dawn claimed direct descent from the Rosicrucian Order as outlined by Franz Hartmann in his book *In the Pronaos of the Temple* (1890).

43 According to Regardie, any fair-sized room could be adapted for the exigencies of a Temple. 'All furniture from the centre should be cleared away, leaving a central space in which one may freely move and work. A small table covered with a black cloth will suffice for the Altar, and the two Pillars may be dispensed with but formulated in the imagination as present. He may find it very useful to paint flashing Angelic Tablets...as well as the Banners of the East and West.... If he is able to obtain small plaster-casts of the heads of the Kerubim – the lion, the eagle, bull and man – and place these in the proper stations, they will be found together with the Tablets to impart a considerable amount of magical vitality and atmosphere to the Temple.' *The Golden Dawn*, 90. For further information on Yeats's alchemist, see *L (K) 3*, 149 n.

44 Farr's motto was S.S.D.D. (*Sapientia Sapienti Dono Data*: wisdom is given to the wise as a gift).

45 For an account of the various stages in the Stella Matutina, see Regardie, *The Golden Dawn*, vol. 2. There were three separate orders

– the Order of the Golden Dawn in the Outer, the Second Order of the R.R. and A.C., and the unnamed Third Order of Masters. The clothing ritual included cassock, sash, red and yellow shoes, and admission badges.

46 These practices are described in the third volume of Regardie's *Golden Dawn*.

47 Yeats was also responsible for examining neophytes and others. Maud Gonne once wrote to him: 'If you are not in London perhaps Mrs Emery would kindly examine me for my 3°–8°' (*MGY* 51). The letter is dated 13 ⟨? October 1893⟩.

48 A two-page report, drawn up by the Scribe 'Fortiter et Recte' (Annie Horniman), and entitled 'Statement of Recent Events which have led to the present constitution of the Second Order in London' (1900), describes 'Perdurabo' ⟨Crowley⟩ arriving at Blythe Road 'dressed in Highland dress, a black mask over his face, a plaid thrown over his head and shoulders, an enormous gold or gilt cross on his breast, and a dagger at his side. All this melodramatic nonsense was of course designed in the hope that it would cause members to sign a pledge of allegiance to D.D.C.F. ("MacGregor Mathers"). He was, however, stopped by the landlord, and compelled to leave by Fratres H.E.S. and D.E.D.I. ⟨Yeats⟩ assisted by a policeman.' See *NLI MS* 30086. Mathers had been accused of forging documents relating to the founding authority of the Golden Dawn in England. For more details, see Howe, *The Magicians of the Golden Dawn*, 203–32.

49 This essay is reproduced as Appendix K in Harper, *Yeats's Golden Dawn*, 259–68. Harper provides a detailed discussion of the essay in the same volume. 'R.R. & A.C.' stands for Rubidae Rosae & Aureae Crucis (Of the Red Rose & Golden Cross), a section of the Golden Dawn. For further details, see Yeats's letters in January and February 1901 to the members of the Golden Dawn reproduced in *L (K)* 3.

50 A member of the Golden Dawn, Horos was found guilty of subjecting a young woman named Daisy Adams to a Neophyte initiation ceremony, which the Solicitor-General claimed was blasphemous. The publicity proved extremely damaging to the Golden Dawn, and it was forced to change its name to the Hermetic Society of the Morgenrothe. For details on the Horos case, see Howe, *The Magicians of the Golden Dawn*, 239–40.

51 Cited in Howe, *The Magicians of the Golden Dawn*, 273.

52 Cited in Harper, *Yeats's Golden Dawn* (London: Macmillan, 1974), 129.

53 For a wide-ranging discussion of Yeats and Christianity, see Kathleen Raine, *Yeats the Initiate: Essays on Certain Themes in the Work of W. B. Yeats* (Mountrath, Ireland; London: George Allen and Unwin, 1986), 379–407.

54 For a critical discussion of these stories, see S. Putzel, *Reconstructing Yeats: 'The Secret Rose' and 'The Wind Among the Reeds'* (London: Gill and Macmillan, 1986).

55 In his *Memoirs* Yeats recalls in similar terms his first impressions of Maud Gonne: 'I had never thought to see in a living woman so great a beauty. It belonged to famous pictures, to poetry, to some legendary past. A complexion like the blossom of apples, and yet face and body had the beauty of lineaments which Blake calls the highest beauty because it changes least from age to age, and a stature so great that she seemed of a divine race' (*Mem* 40). Maud Gonne had hazel eyes.

56 In his Notes to *The Wind Among the Reeds*, Yeats conveys the impression that the conflict and fear aroused by the occult have been allayed by being channelled into three distinct personages, Hanrahan, Robartes, and Aedh, who are but principles of the mind (see *VP* 803). Yeats's final ordering of poems in *The Wind Among the Reeds* had the effect of obscuring the biographical dimension. See Harwood, *W. B. Yeats and Olivia Shakespear*, 59–82. For a discussion of the changes in Yeats's portrayal of Michael Robartes, see Michael J. Sidnell's essay 'Mr Yeats, Michael Robartes, and Their Circle' in George Mills Harper (ed.), *Yeats and the Occult* (London: Macmillan, 1975), 225–54. Francis Bickley, in a study which was proof-read by Yeats, claims that in 1897 while in Paris the poet was 'suffering a reaction against the influences of the day, and seeking simpler modes. He, too, had ventured, none more boldly, into the mysterious caves of symbolism, and had returned from his journey with much garnered wisdom, but with a new love for the sun.' *J. M. Synge and the Irish Dramatic Movement* (London: Constable; Boston and New York: Houghton Mifflin, 1912), 11–12.

57 Peter Kuch assumes the narrator of 'Rosa Alchemica' is Russell, and he reads the story as an implicit critique of Russell's view that a return to the pagan gods would not meet strong resistance from the Irish country people. See *Yeats and AE*, 112. He also suggests that Michael Robartes is modelled on Russell. In the 1920s, Russell confessed to Harold Speakman that in Ireland he and Yeats were not read: they were 'anathema because of their beliefs'. See *Here's Ireland* (London: Arrowsmith, 1926), 287. In a review of A. E. Housman's edition of *The Writings of William Blake*, Yeats betrays the clarity of someone arguing against himself: 'The public loves writers that are magnified reflections of itself, but abhors all who claim to belong to some special community, some special cult, some special tribe which is not its kin.' *Bookman*, August 1893, 146.

58 Ellis and Yeats (eds), *The Works of William Blake*, vol. 1, 89.

59 *Where There is Nothing* (Yeats's *Enemy of the People*) is a play that takes up this theme of the tension between visionary experience and social order.

60 It was not only the people he feared but also wealthy Catholics, such as Edward Martyn, who were important in the development of a National Theatre in Ireland. Martyn was a

pious Catholic and in August 1897 took exception to Yeats's invoking the lunar powers, especially since Yeats was sleeping in a room above the chapel (see *Memoirs* 101).

61 According to a recent biography, Symons's experience at Tulira chimed with Yeats's: 'On the following morning, unaware of Yeats's vision, Symons read him a poem inspired by a dream of a beautiful woman, "the Symbolic Diana", fully clothed who had visited him (the same woman, Yeats was convinced, who had appeared to him).' Karl Beckson, *Arthur Symons: A Life* (Oxford: Clarendon Press, 1987), 145–6.

62 W. B. Yeats, *Where There Is Nothing*, viii–ix.

63 For further information about Leo Africanus, see Richard Ellmann, *Yeats: The Man and the Masks* (1949; repr. Oxford: Oxford University Press, 1979), 195ff., and Arnold Goldmann's essay 'Yeats, Spiritualism, and Psychical Research', in *Yeats and the Occult*, 108–29.

64 Yeats to Elizabeth Radcliffe, 17 August ⟨1913⟩. Address: The Prelude, Coleman's Hatch, where he was staying with George and family. Copy in the Bodleian Library, Oxford.

65 Yeats to Elizabeth Radcliffe. Postmark 29 December 1913. Copy in the Bodleian Library, Oxford.

66 Yeats to Elizabeth Radcliffe, 26 October ⟨n.y.⟩. Address: Jury's Hotel, Dublin. Copy in the Bodleian Library, Oxford. Radcliffe is 'Miss X' in Ellmann, *Yeats*, 195.

67 Yeats to Elizabeth Radcliffe, 30 August 1916. Address: Hotel Govarni, Passy, Paris. Original in the Bodleian Library, Oxford. A week after his marriage, Yeats wrote again to her: 'My wife is a friend of Mrs Fowlers and of other friends of yours and she is a close student of all my subjects. I wish you could tell me exactly what information came to you on Oct 4. I have a strong reason, not curiosity for asking this.' 28 October ⟨1917⟩. Ashdown Forest Hotel. Copy in the Bodleian Library, Oxford.

68 Yeats to Quinn, 29 November 1917. In the Rare Book and Manuscripts Division, New York Public Library.

69 George Mills Harper, *The Making of Yeats's 'A Vision': A Study of the Automatic Script*, vol. 1 (London: Macmillan, 1987), xii–xiii.

70 Session on 16 December 1918.

71 Session on 4 January 1919.

72 Session on 12 May 1918.

73 Elizabeth Butler Cullingford, *Gender and History in Yeats's Love Poetry* (Cambridge: Cambridge University Press, 1993), 110.

74 Session on 11 January 1918.

75 Session on 14 January 1918.

76 Session on 11 January 1918. Everything seemed to be grist for the mill. In his 'Introduction to "A Vision"', he writes: 'I have heard my wife in the broken speech of some quite ordinary dream use tricks of speech characteristic of the philosophic voices' (*AV [B]* 22).

77 Given that George was the Medium, the Control's answer was, understandably, evasive: '⟨I⟩n the case of the medium the primary contains certain hereditary faults which are of a nature of limitation rather than active

suppressions – the antithetical contrasts to them are of a nature so opposite as to increase the suppression rather than relieve it.' See Harper, *The Making of Yeats's 'A Vision'*, 25. Yeats, too, was evasive. There is an intriguing sentence in a letter George wrote to Yeats on 1 January 1935, where she says she informed a visiting scholar that Yeats had made Pollock eliminate all references to Maud Gonne in his ⟨1935⟩ biography. See Box 119, SUNY Stony Brook. As for the relationship between George and Iseult, Iseult spent Christmas 1917 with the Yeatses at Stone Cottage. In 1918, George was concerned for 'Maurice', especially over her employment prospects, and in a letter to Pound dated 28 May ⟨1918⟩ expressed the hope that Clement Shorter, who had a sentimental attachment to Ireland, might find work for Iseult on the *Bookman*. Original letter in the Ezra Pound Correspondence at Yale.

78 Yeats must have told George about these relationships. His affair with Olivia Shakespear began in 1896; that with Mabel Dickinson ended in June 1913 after the scare about her pregnancy; the significance of the year 1910 in connection with Maud Gonne is unclear, but Yeats seems to let that go.

79 Session on 14 August 1919. I presume this is George's inference. The affair with Mabel Dickinson ended on 6 June 1913 after she told him about her false pregnancy; 'paternity implies possession MD = Desire'.

80 See session on 29 March 1919. See *YVP* 2, 224.

81 See session on 22 July 1919. See *YVP* 2, 331.

82 Anne was born on 26 February 1919, Michael on 22 August 1921. George suffered a miscarriage in August 1920. In a cancelled passage from 'Introduction to "The Great Wheel"', Yeats wrote: '⟨M⟩y wife saw apparitions especially before the birth of her son.' See NLI MS 30758, p. 11.

83 See Box 118, SUNY Stony Brook.

84 This is Harper's belief in *The Making of Yeats's 'A Vision'*, 5. See also Harper's discussion in *YVP* 3, 226.

85 In Alan Denson (ed.), *Letters from AE* (London, New York, Toronto: Abelard-Schuman, 1961), 17–18. Letter dated 2 June 1896.

86 *The Making of Yeats's 'A Vision'*, 15.

87 Box 118, SUNY Stony Brook. The dates and evolution of the Yeatses' automatic writing sessions bear strong resemblances to those conducted in Paris by André Breton and his friends. These anti-rational (but secular) events began in autumn 1919, continued at the end of 1922 with sleep sessions or hypnotic slumber, and finished in 1924 with the Surrealist Manifesto, when 'Surrealism entered its reasoning phase'. See André Breton, *Conversations: The Autobiography of Surrealism* (New York: Paragon House, 1993), 43–71. It would be interesting to know what Yeats would have made of such a 'coincidence'.

88 'Am I not right in thinking that MGs making apparent to me mask as understood by genius extended over some 20 years.' Answer: 'No only since 1910.' 'How am I to describe in

writing of system her influence during those 20 years.' Answer: 'That of bringing to the surface the conditional memory.'

89 Yeats's interest in colour symbolism is in essence that of an occultist. In his reading, Yeats invariably attended to the meaning of colours. On the back cover of his edition of Jacob Boehme's *High and Deep Searching Out of the Threefold Life of Man Through, or According to, the Three Principles*, tr. John Sparrow (1650; repr. ed. C. J. Barker (London: John Watkins, 1909), Yeats noted Boehme's discussion of colour symbols: 'The cross every where signifieth the Number Three: where then beneath *blue* appeareth, which signifieth the substantiality; in the middle appeareth *red*, which signifieth the Father in the glance of fire; next which appeareth *yellow*, which signifieth the light and lustre of the Majesty of the Son of God; and the *dusky brown*, with the mixture of all forms, signifieth the other kingdom of darkness in the fire (184–5). See Edward O'Shea, *A Descriptive Catalog of W. B. Yeats's Library* (New York and London: Garland, 1985), 38. Surprisingly, there is no colour scale in *A Vision*. In Regardie we read that 'Colours are Forces, the Signatures of Forces', and that 'Hodos Chamelionis' is the 'Path of Mixed Colours'. *The Golden Dawn*, vol. 2, 236.

90 See session on 23 February 1918.

91 Session on 26 August 1919 at Thoor Ballylee.

92 This derives from a conversation I had with Anne Yeats in April 1993.

93 See Grace Jaffe, 'Vignettes' in *Yeats Annual*, no. 5, 151.

94 George to Yeats, 6 August 1920. Box 118, SUNY Stony Brook.

95 George to Yeats, 29 January 1936. Box 119, SUNY Stony Brook.

96 Ibid.

97 George to Yeats, 24 November ⟨1931⟩. Box 119, SUNY Stony Brook. Letter cited by Ann Saddlemyer in *Omnium Gatherum: Essays for Richard Ellmann*, ed. Susan Dick et al. (Gerrards Cross: Colin Smythe, 1989), 291.

98 See K. P. S. Jochum's 'Yeats's *Vision Papers* and the Problem of Automatic Writing: A Review Essay', in *English Literature in Transition, 1880–1920*, vol. 36, no. 3, 1993, 332. Jochum cites a doctoral thesis in which George's letter appears, adding that the letter is undated in the Yeats Archives at SUNY Stony Brook. It is in fact dated 24 November ⟨1931⟩.

99 Yeats to George Yeats, 10 February 1923. Box 77, SUNY Stony Brook. Ellmann, no doubt voicing George's attempt to present a level-headed portrait of her husband, maintains that after his marriage Yeats 'gave up his obsession for going to seances'. See *Yeats*, 221. Yeats's correspondence with George in the 1920s contains more than passing reference to seances. In February 1924 he accompanied George to a seance with Mrs Cooper. (See his letter to George, 13 February 1924, in Box 77, SUNY Stony Brook.) In 1928, he told George that he had been visiting mediums, and learnt about

his son's future intellectual promise. 'Thursday ⟨1928⟩'. In Box 77, SUNY Stony Brook.

100 Journal entry, 2 June 1929.

101 '⟨M⟩y daimon is female' declared Yeats at the session on 13 April 1919. See *YVP* 2, 245.

102 'Introduction to "The Great Wheel"' in NLI 30758, p. 16.

103 For this distinction between occultist and mystic, see Max Heindel, *The Rosicrucian Mysteries* (London: L. N. Fowler, 1916), 16–17.

104 For details, see George Mills Harper's essay '"A Subject of Investigation": Miracle at Mirebeau' in Harper (ed.), *Yeats and the Occult*, 172–89. Yeats was accompanied by Maud Gonne and Everard Fielding. After analysis at the Lister Institute in London, the blood was found to be not human blood, which confirmed Yeats in his belief that 'in the unconscious there is a will to cheat and to be found cheating' (180).

105 Harold Speakman, *Here's Ireland* (London: Arrowsmith, 1926), 305.

106 See Yeats to William Force Stead, 30 July 1926. Original in the Osborne Stead Collection at Yale. See also Yeats's letter to Olivia Shakespear, 2 July ⟨1926⟩ in *L* 716.

107 See 'Ireland's Greatest Poet at Wellesley' in Wellesley College, Special Collections, English Poetry Collection.

108 Yeats to Lady Gregory, 24 February ⟨1921⟩. In BERG.

109 Typescript entitled 'Clairvoyant Search for Will ⟨of Sir Hugh Percy Lane⟩', p. 12, in BERG.

3 *Yeats and Cultural Nationalism*

1 Monk Gibbon (ed.), *The Living Torch A.E.*, (London: Macmillan, 1937), 256–7.

2 See S. Gwynn (ed.), *Scattering Branches: Tributes to the Memory of W.B. Yeats* (London: Macmillan, 1940), 27.

3 According to Charles Gavan Duffy in the *Dublin University Magazine* in February 1847, Davis was invariably surrounded by 'an atmosphere of goodwill, which hostile politicians could not enter without mutually conceding "the right to differ", and agreeing to do something for the common good.' Cited in Lady Ferguson, *Sir Samuel Ferguson in the Ireland of His Day*, vol. 1 (Edinburgh and London: William Blackwood, 1896), 144.

4 Letter to Lady Gregory, 10 February 1897. 'I find the infinite triviality of politics more trying than ever. We tear each others character in peices for things that dont matter to anybody.' NLI MS 30992. Yeats, in Manchester with Maud Gonne, had been exhausted attending political meetings.

5 W. B. Yeats in *Samhain*, November 1905, 6. Charles Kickham's most famous novel, *Knocknagow or the Homes of Tipperary*, appeared in 1879. Gerald Griffin's *Collegians*, a novel dramatised by Boucicault in *The Colleen Bawn* in 1860, was first published in 1829.

6 Edward Said, *Nationalism, Colonialism and Literature: Yeats and Decolonization* (Derry: Field Day, 1988), 5. For revised version, see *Culture and Imperialism* (London: Chatto and Windus, 1993), 265–88. Yeats's relationship with national liberation is more complicated than Said imagines.

7 For more standard recent accounts of Yeats in the context of nineteenth-century Ireland, see, among others, Malcolm Brown, *The Politics of Irish Literature: From Thomas Davis to W. B. Yeats* (London: George Allen and Unwin, 1972); Robert Welch, *Irish Poetry from Moore to Yeats* (Gerrards Cross: Colin Smythe, 1980); W. J. McCormack, *From Burke to Beckett: Ascendancy, Tradition and Betrayal in Literary History* (Cork: Cork University Press, 1994); Seamus Deane's essay 'Poetry and Song, 1800–1890' in *The Field Day Anthology of Irish Writing*, vol. 2 (Derry: Field Day, 1991), 1–9. A useful collection of relevant source essays on culture can be found in Mark Storey (ed.), *Poetry and Ireland Since 1800: A Source Book* (London and New York: Routledge, 1988).

8 This is how Belfast-born Louis MacNeice (1907–63) in his poem 'Carrickfergus' characterised his own predicament as the Rector's son. In an essay entitled 'Traveller's Return', which he wrote after a ten-month stay in the United States in 1940, MacNeice, always trustworthy in such matters, speaks of himself as 'an example of uprootability. Born in Ireland of Irish parents, I have never felt properly "at home" in England, yet I can write here better than in Ireland. In America I feel rather more at home than in England (America has more of Ireland in it), but I am not sure how well I could work if I settled there permanently.' *Horizon*, vol. 3, no. 14, February 1941, 114.

9 See W. B. Yeats and Thomas Kinsella, *Davis, Mangan, Ferguson? Tradition and the Irish Writer* (Dublin: Dolmen Press, 1970), 62.

10 W. B. Yeats, *Letters to the New Island*, ed. Horace Reynolds (Oxford: Oxford University Press, 1934; repr. 1970), 158. The sentence first appeared in the *Boston Pilot* on 19 November 1892.

11 *The World We Have Lost* (London: Methuen, 1965) is the title of Peter Laslett's study in which he compares the structure of British society before and after the Industrial Revolution.

12 'The Irish Schoolmaster' by 'A Master' in the *National Observer*, 6 October 1894.

13 A key idea in Herder is that civilisations have their own specific outlook, to be understood in terms of their own scale of values, not by some universal benchmark. See Isaiah Berlin, *Vico and Herder: Two Studies in the History of Ideas* (London: Hogarth Press, 1976).

14 Katharine Tynan, *Irish Love-Songs* (London: T. Fisher Unwin, 1892), 8. She defends her choice of Mangan's 'Dark Rosaleen' because it is 'the most beautiful poem of our Anglo-Irish literature'. The anthology owes most to Edward Walsh (1805–50) and Ferguson, who, above all others, 'knew how to transfuse the wild simplicity of the Irish songs into English, keeping their strange and lovely flavour as of wild bees' honey – sweet and unsophisticated' (7). Yeats is represented by 'An Old Song Resung' ('Down by the Sally Gardens') and 'To an Isle in the Water'.

15 See, in particular, Mary Helen Thuente's essay 'The Literary Significance of the United Irishmen' in *Irish Literature and Culture*, ed. Michael Kenneally (Gerrards Cross: Colin Smythe, 1992), 35–54. For more information on the songs of the United Irishmen, see Georges-Denis Zimmerman, *Songs of Irish Rebellion: Political Street Ballads and Rebel Songs, 1780–1900* (Dublin: Allen Figgis, 1967), 35–58. For a recent discussion, see Tom Dunne's essay 'Popular Ballads, Revolutionary Rhetoric and Politicisation' in Hugh Gough and David Dickson (eds), *Ireland and the French Revolution* (Blackrock, Dublin: Irish Academic Press, 1990), 156–78.

16 The Protestant Volunteers in the 1780s, according to Thomas Crofton Croker, had their own songs, some of which might have become part of the ballad tradition if the 1798 Rising had not been put down by the British. See his *Popular Songs of Ireland* (1839; repr. London: Routledge and Sons, 1886), 73. Crofton Croker's edition was bitterly attacked by Duffy for presenting *common* ballads as the national minstrelsy of Ireland. See his *Ballad Poetry of Ireland* (1846; repr. Dublin: James Duffy, 1874), 19.

17 The distinction between 'literary nationalist' and 'literary patriot' is well made by D. G. Boyce in *Nationalism in Ireland* (London: Croom Helm; Dublin: Gill and Macmillan, 1982), 230ff. The Burkeian Unionist Ferguson and the middle-class Tory Protestants who ran the *Dublin University Review* were literary patriots, not literary nationalists, and their efforts 'were directed toward establishing and fostering Irish literature for literature's sake, and as a sign to the cultured world that Ireland was no backwater' (230). See also John Hutchinson's distinction between cultural nationalists and political nationalists in *The Dynamics of Cultural Nationalism: The Gaelic Revival and the Creation of the Irish Nation State* (London: Allen and Unwin, 1987): 'Whereas cultural nationalists aspired to revive a distinctive Irish *community*, the goal of political nationalists was Ireland's normalization among the nations of the world by the regaining of her independent *statehood*' (152). In his discussion of *Poems and Ballads of Young Ireland* (1888), an anthology often referred to as marking the starting-point of the Revival, Boyd carefully provides another set of distinctions between patriotic and non-political: '*Poems and Ballads of Young Ireland* is patriotic, but patriotism in the old sense did not inspire these writers. For political history they substituted legends, fairy tales, the spiritism of the Irish countryside'. Ernest Boyd, *Ireland's Literary Renaissance* (New York: Alfred Knopf, 1922), 96. For yet another distinction between 'national' and

'political', see Francis Fahy's address to the Irish Literary Society in London in February 1901: 'His ⟨O'Connell's⟩ mind was wholly centred on political nationality. He hardly understood anything national that was not also political, and nearly all Irish leaders since his day, except Davis and Smith O'Brien, have laboured under that same defect.' *The Irish Language Movement* (London: Gaelic League, 1901), 6.

18 *The Book of Irish Verse* (London: Methuen, 1911), xiv–xv. Yeats's comment was written for the 1899 edition.

19 From 'The Library of Ireland' in *The Prose Writings of Thomas Davis*, ed. T. W. Rolleston (London: Methuen, ⟨1890⟩), 227.

20 From 'National Art', ibid., 146–7.

21 From 'A Ballad History of Ireland', ibid., 207.

22 W. B. Yeats, *A Book of Irish Verse* (1895), xv.

23 Thomas Flanagan, *The Irish Novelists, 1800–1850* (New York: Columbia University Press, 1959), 38.

24 *The Prose Writings of Thomas Davis*, 193.

25 W. B. Yeats, *Letters to the New Island*, 103–4. From Yeats's article on Browning in the *Boston Pilot*, 22 February 1890.

26 W. B. Yeats, *A Book of Irish Verse* (1911), xiv (written for the 1900 revised edition). Yeats was not alone in thinking this. In a letter to Professor Blackie on 5 May 1875 concerning the endowment of a Chair of Celtic Literature at the University of Edinburgh, Ferguson lamented how in Ireland 'our upper classes . . . if they would not see themselves entirely excluded from local power and consideration, must place themselves to some . . . extent in sympathy with the bulk of the people; and it is easier and more probable that this conformity should take place in the direction of literary and intellectual harmony'. Ferguson, *Sir Samuel Ferguson in the Ireland of His Day*, vol. 2, 221–2.

27 TS of speech 'Emmet the Apostle of Irish Liberty' delivered at the New York Academy of Music to the Clan-na-Gael, 28 February 1904 (pages 12–13). Published in the *Gaelic American*, 5 March 1904. In BERG.

28 'Ireland, since the Young Irelanders, has given itself up to apologetics' (A 520). In a Speech Supporting Home Rule, Yeats gave expression to the politics of his cultural nationalism: 'I am an Irish Nationalist because I have believed since I had my first thoughts about it that no country can prosper unless the greater proportion of its intellect is occupied with itself.' NLI 30095.

29 W. B. Yeats, *Synge and the Ireland of His Time* (Dundrum: Cuala Press, 1911), 7–8.

30 W. B. Yeats, *A Book of Irish Verse* (1895), xvi.

31 Ibid., 22.

32 William Carleton, *Traits and Stories of the Irish Peasantry* (1830; repr. London: William Tegg, 1867), x.

33 From 1891 to 1893 Yeats was involved in a public controversy with Duffy over the publication of a series of books for the Irish market. For a discussion of this dispute, see chapter 3 of Philip Marcus, *Yeats and the Beginning of*

the Irish Renaissance (Ithaca, New York: Cornell University Press, 1970).

34 W. B. Yeats, in *Samhain*, November 1905, 12.

35 John Eglinton, W. B. Yeats, A. E., William Larminie, *Literary Ideals in Ireland* (1899; repr. New York: Lemma, 1973), 36.

36 Joseph Hone, *William Butler Yeats: The Poet in Contemporary Ireland* (Dublin and London: Maunsel, 1915), 55.

37 See W. B. Yeats and Thomas Kinsella, *Davis, Mangan, Ferguson? Tradition and the Irish Writer*, 15, 18.

38 W. B. Yeats, *Prefaces and Introductions*, ed. William H. O'Donnell (London: Macmillan, 1988), 29.

39 Ibid., 28.

40 J. C. Beckett, *The Anglo-Irish Tradition* (London: Faber, 1976), 135. Not all middle-class Protestants were as enlightened as Ferguson. When Carleton arrived in Dublin in 1825, cultural life was dominated by the Evangelicals.

41 All these poems can be found in C. Gavan Duffy, *The Ballad Poetry of Ireland* (1846; repr. Dublin: James Duffy, 1874). The biographical details are in Ferguson, *Sir Samuel Ferguson in the Ireland of His Day*, vol. 1, 24–5.

42 Duffy, *The Ballad Poetry of Ireland*, 20.

43 *Sir Samuel Ferguson in the Ireland of His Day*, vol. 1, 101, 354. The first quotation comes from 'Attractions of Ireland', an article Ferguson wrote for the *Dublin University Review*, July–December 1836. The second quotation comes from a letter to William Allingham dated 9 March 1882.

44 See 'Ireland's Greatest Poet at Wellesley' in Wellesley College, Special Collections, English Poetry Collection.

45 *Sixteen Poems by William Allingham: Selected by W. B. Yeats* (Dundrum: Dun Emer Press, 1905). These lines form the opening section to a longer poem entitled 'A Stormy Night: A Story of the Donegal Coast'. Among the poems chosen by Yeats are 'The Winding Banks of Erne' and 'The Maids of Elfen-Mere'.

46 W. B. Yeats, *Letters to the New Island*, 172.

47 This is Yeats's verdict in his Introduction to *A Book of Irish Verse* (1895), xx.

48 For the complete poem, see William Allingham, *The Music Master* (London: G. Routledge, 1855), 202–4.

49 William Allingham (ed.), *The Ballad Book: A Selection of the Choicest British Ballads* (London and Cambridge: Macmillan, 1864), xxix.

50 Ibid., xxxii. The Henry Bradshaw Collection of Irish Ballads in Cambridge University Library is testimony to the wealth of broadside ballads in English that were written in Ireland during the mid-Victorian period. According to the *Irish Book Lover* (May 1910, vol. 1, no. 10, 134), the Bradshaw Collection, which was presented in 1870 and 1886, numbered more than seven thousand titles . In volume 1 of the collection alone, mostly written from 1867 to 1870, there are 209 street ballads on such topics as support for the clergy, sport,

the Fenians and their return, domestic problems, love songs, foreign wars (especially Garibaldi, and including the anti-war song 'Johnny I Hardly Knew Ye'), emigration, and eviction. Henry Bradshaw (1831–86), whose interest in Irish literature and antiquities stemmed from a teaching post he once enjoyed at St Columba's College, near Howth, was University Librarian at Cambridge from 1867 until his death.

51 *William Allingham: A Diary, 1824–1889*, ed. H. Allingham and D. Radford (1907; repr. Harmondsworth: Penguin, 1985), 17.

52 W. B. Yeats, in *Samhain*, November 1905, 11. The contrast with Ferguson is also most pronounced at this point. Ferguson, Deputy Keeper of Records in Ireland and author of numerous articles on antiquarian topics, wrote in the January 1840 issue of the *Dublin University Magazine*: 'It is a most prejudicial error to suppose that matter of fact . . . is necessarily dry or uninteresting; on the contrary, there can be no true romance, no real poetry, nothing, in a word, that will effectually touch either the heart or the imagination, that has not its foundation in experience of existing facts, or in knowledge of facts that have existed in times past.' Cited in Ferguson, *Sir Samuel Ferguson in the Ireland of His Day*, vol. 1, 109.

53 *Samhain*, November 1905, 9.

54 H. Stuart Hughes in *Consciousness and Society: The Reorientation of European Social Thought, 1890–1930* (New York: Random House, 1958) entitles his second chapter 'The Decade of the 1890's: The Revolt Against Positivism'. In attacking the previous generation, Yeats lumped together Allingham, George Eliot, Tyndall, Huxley, and the French School of Realistic Painting.

55 *Samhain*, November 1905, 9.

56 William Allingham, *Laurence Bloomfield in Ireland* (London and Cambridge: Macmillan, 1864), 6.

57 Matthew Arnold, *On the Study of Celtic Literature* (London: Smith, Elder, 1867), 102. The italicised phrase comes from Henri Martin's *Histoire de France*.

58 Ibid., 104.

59 *Laurence Bloomfield in Ireland*, 49.

60 *On the Study of Celtic Literature*, 111. 'Here . . . are two very unlike elements to commingle; the steady-going Saxon temperament and the sentimental Celtic temperament.'

61 *Laurence Bloomfield in Ireland*, 6–7.

62 Ibid., 60.

63 Ibid., 146.

64 Allingham receives no better treatment from Colin Meir in his otherwise reliable survey of the nineteenth-century ballad tradition. *The Ballads and Songs of W. B. Yeats: The Anglo-Irish Heritage in Subject and Style* (London: Macmillan, 1974), 6. Yeats's view of Allingham is the one that prevails in Ernest Boyd's *Ireland's Literary Renaissance*. Allingham is accused by Yeats and Boyd of being both too provincial and not provincial enough; he stands condemned for not being

sufficiently Irish, and 'were it not for his ballads, he would not find a place in the history of Anglo-Irish literature' (82). For a fairer estimate Seamus Deane's discussion of Allingham in *The Field Day Anthology of Irish Writing*, vol. 2 (Derry: Field Day, 1991). See also Antony Coleman, 'The Big House, Yeats and the Irish Context' in Yeats *Annual*, no. 3 (London: Macmillan, 1985), 33–54.

65 O'Grady came from a family of country squires. His conversion to cultural nationalism occurred in 1873 when he read an uncut version of George Petrie's 1833 essay 'The Round Towers of Ireland'. See Hugh Art O'Grady, *Standish James O'Grady: The Man and the Work* (Dublin: Talbot, 1929). For Boyd, O'Grady is 'the father of the Literary Revival in Ireland', who influenced, among others, Russell, Todhunter, Yeats, and Eglinton. See Boyd, *Ireland's Literary Renaissance*, 26–54. Russell was 'intoxicated' by O'Grady's *History of Ireland*, and set about interpreting the Gaelic gods and myths in terms of Eastern mysticism. Pearse, too, drew inspiration from O'Grady. For recent discussions of O'Grady's significance, see Malcolm Brown, *The Politics of Irish Literature: From Thomas Davis to W. B. Yeats* (London: George Allen and Unwin, 1972), 371–90; and W. J. McCormack, *From Burke to Beckett*, 231–9.

66 Standish James O'Grady, *History of Ireland: Cuchulain and His Contemporaries*, vol. 2 (London: Sampson Low; Dublin: Ponsonby, 1880), 4–5.

67 *Poems and Ballads of Young Ireland* (1888) is a striking illustration of the effect of O'Grady on the younger generation of Irish poets.

68 From 'A Wet Day', O'Grady's account of how he became interested in Irish history and myths. See the *Irish Homestead*, Christmas number, December 1899, 9.

69 A.E., *The Interpreters* (London: Macmillan, 1922). In this novel of ideas, the historian Brehon (modelled on O'Grady and Russell himself) is contrasted with the poet Lavelle, (modelled on Yeats). Lavelle, 'the imperialist of idealism' (20), insists on Ireland's distinctiveness. In contrast to Lavelle, who celebrates sacrifice, Brehon insists on the transforming power of love (and hate) and the need for a 'serenity of feeling' (138). Unconvinced, Lavelle protests: 'All distinctions of nationality seem to dissipate in a haze in this transcendentalism' (143). However, it is Brehon's viewpoint which is upheld in the novel.

70 S. J. O'Grady, *History of Ireland: Critical and Philosophical*, vol. 1 (London: Sampson Low; Dublin: Ponsonby, 1881), 64–5.

71 Arnold, *On the Study of Celtic Literature*, 18.

72 Luke Netterville (pseudonym for S. J. O'Grady), *The Queen of the World or Under the Tyranny* (1900), p. 89. Copy in NLI. The novel is set in A.D. 2179 when Gerald Pierce de Lacy wakes to discover that 'great Tyranny' rules the whole world. The watchword 'Remember Ireland' comes about because Ireland had rebelled but was put down. Eventually the King is overthrown, Lenore the

Princess succeeds to the throne, and Gerald is nominated to her council. The novel ends with Gerald waking up on the greensward of a quiet Irish valley.

73 *History of Ireland: Critical and Philosophical*, vol. 1, 57.

74 '(T)he mode of dealing with these documents . . . has hitherto been most unsatisfactory. Those who have dealt with them, have gone to work, in general, either as warm Celt-lovers or as warm Celt-haters, and not as disinterested students of an important matter of science.' Arnold, *On the Study of Celtic Literature*, 31–2.

75 *History of Ireland: Critical and Philosophical*, vol. 1, 64.

76 Gibbon (ed.), *The Living Torch A.E.*, 144.

77 Standish James O'Grady, *The Crisis in Ireland* (Dublin: Ponsonby; London: Simpkin and Marshall, 1882), 30–31. To a House of Commons increasingly dominated by the middle class, there was little sympathy with the plight of Irish landlords. As one commentator expressed it in 1885: 'Landlordism, it is to be feared, however beneficent and picturesque in theory, is practically a failure.' See Goldwin Smith's article entitled 'The Administration of Ireland' in *Contemporary Review*, vol. 48, July–December 1885, 4.

78 O'Grady, *The Crisis in Ireland*, 25. Compare, for example, the use of the words *traditional* and *custom* in the following lines from 'A Prayer for My Daughter' (1919) and 'Coole Park and Ballylee, 1931': 'We were the last romantics – chose for theme/Traditional sanctity and loveliness' (*VP* 491). 'How but in custom and in ceremony/Are innocence and beauty born?' (*VP* 406). Somerville and Ross also fondly believed in the cultural importance of the Big House: ' "Gentry-houses", places that were once disseminators of light, of the humanities; centres of civilisation; places to which the poor people rushed, in any trouble, as to Cities of Refuge. They are now destroyed, become desolate, derelict.' *Irish Memories* (London: Longmans, Green, 1918), 154–5.

79 Standish James O'Grady, *Toryism and Tory Democracy* (London: Chapman and Hall, 1886), 110–11.

80 Ibid., 108. As Quinn once suggested to Russell, O'Grady was not unlike an Irish Carlyle. See B. L. Reid, *The Man from New York: John Quinn and His Friends* (New York: Oxford University Press, 1968), 162.

81 O'Grady, *Toryism and Tory Democracy*, 145.

82 Ibid., 257.

83 For 'Fenian Unionist', see Lady Gregory's letter to editor of *All Ireland Review*, 15 December 1900, 5. Yeats had used the phrase in a letter to Lady Gregory in November 1897: 'O'Grady is writing a little book on the Fenian movement. . . . He is the first Fenian Unionist on record' (*L* 292). The book never materialised. Yeats also called O'Grady 'the Irish Ruskin', because he had a way of 'taking extravagant little points and preaching unexpected truths from them'. See Henry Nevinson, *Changes and Chances* (London: Nisbet, 1923),

303.

84 Standish James O'Grady, *The Story of Ireland* (London: Methuen, 1894), 184.

85 Ibid., 211.

86 Standish O'Grady, *All Ireland* (Dublin: Sealy, Bryers and Walker; London: T. Fisher Unwin, 1898), 150.

87 Ibid., 101.

88 *All Ireland Review*, vol. 1, no. 4, 27 January 1900, 1. Much of 'The Great Enchantment' is reproduced in Lady Gregory (ed.), *Ideals in Ireland* (London: Unicorn, 1901), 77–83.

89 *All Ireland Review*, vol. 1, no. 7, 17 February 1900, 1.

90 Ibid., vol. 1, no. 12, 24 March 1900, 5.

91 *Irish Review*, November 1913, 466. 'And I want you, young men of Ireland, you before the rest, to begin the inevitable war against this brutal all-but Almighty God of the whole earth. . . . I want it begun in Ireland, my own country, land of the Heroes and the Saints: Inis Fail.' The idea of Ireland as a Land of Destiny was common in the nineteenth century. Aubrey de Vere published a chronicle poem entitled 'Inisfail' (Land of Destiny) in 1861, tracing the path of Irish history from the Norman Conquest to the Penal Laws in the eighteenth century. In his *Recollections of Aubrey De Vere*, he returns to the same theme: 'One of the lessons taught to us by Irish history is this: that to the different nations different vocations are assigned by Providence; to one, an imperial vocation, to another, a commercial one; to Greece an artistic one, to Ireland, as to Israel, a spiritual one' (London: Edward Arnold, 1897, 354). Without such views of Ireland as special there would have been no Yeats.

92 Malcolm Brown makes a similar link between O'Grady and Yeats: 'The symbolic structure of "The Second Coming" is a close paraphrase of Standish O'Grady's emotional reaction to the successive phases of the land war.' *The Politics of Irish Literature*, 171n.

93 When O'Grady was composing *The Flight of the Eagle* in 1897, a story about the boyhood of the Elizabethan Irish hero Hugh Roe O'Donnell, he had Yeats partly in mind. See the abridged version of *The Flight of the Eagle* (Dublin and Cork: Mercier, 1980), 82. For more information, compare W. B. Yeats, *Memoirs*, 59.

94 Historically, the decline and fall of Southern Unionism can be charted through different lenses. The long view is that once the Act of Union became law in 1801 the decline was inevitable because the national ideal had thereby passed into Catholic hands. The shorter view argues for any or all the following causes: (i) the Great Famine of 1845–8, which demonstrated the unfitness of Britain to rule in Ireland; (ii) the Encumbered Estates Act of 1849, which resulted in a significant transfer of land from the landed gentry to 'hard-fisted graziers' (F. S. L. Lyons, *Ireland Since the Famine* [London: Fontana, 1973], 26); (iii) the Tenant Right Movement of the 1850s; (iv) the Irish Land Purchase Act of

1870, convincingly argued by E. D. Steele in his *Irish Land and British Politics: Tenant Right and Nationality, 1865–1870* (Cambridge: Cambridge University Press, 1974), where he lends support to the thesis advanced by the nationalist historian P. S. O'Hegarty that this Act marked 'the beginning of the end of the conquest' (2); (v) the Land War of 1879–82; (vi) the Wyndham Act of 1903, which transferred huge tracts of land to tenant farmers; (vii) the split in the ranks of the Unionists in the mid-1880s between Southern and Ulster Unionists; (viii) the First World War, which weakened (primarily through death) Unionist sentiment in Ireland; (ix) the new understanding of nationalism by Southern Unionists at the Irish Convention, 1917–18; (x) the years immediately following the First World War when many Big Houses were burnt to the ground during and after the War of Independence. Both Thompson and Buckland argue for 1922 as the date when Britain and Ireland ceased being countries of a landed aristocracy. See F. M. L. Thompson, *English Landed Society in the Nineteenth Century* (London: Routledge and Kegan Paul, 1963), and Patrick Buckland, *Irish Unionism*, vol. 1, *The Anglo-Irish and the New Ireland, 1885–1922* (Dublin: Gill and Macmillan; New York: Barnes and Noble, 1972).

95 O'Grady, *History of Ireland*, 50.
96 See 'A Poet's Mission' in the *Daily Chronicle*, 18 March 1904.
97 F. Hugh O'Donnell, *A History of the Irish Parliamentary Party*, vol. 2 (London: Longmans, Green, 1910), 313.
98 In a letter to Harold Macmillan on 15 May 1935 concerning a portrait to be used for the *Collected Poems*, Yeats wrote of his father's magnificent portrait of O'Leary and how O'Leary guided his first steps at organising in Ireland. NLI MS 31057.
99 John O'Leary, *Recollections of Fenians and Fenianism*, vol. 2 (London: Downey, 1896), 241.
100 Cited in Marcus Bourke, *John O'Leary: A Study in Irish Separatism* (Tralee: Anvil, 1967), 179.
101 O'Leary, *Recollections of Fenians and Fenianism*, vol. 2, 66.
102 Ibid., 57.
103 O'Donnell, *A History of the Irish Parliamentary Party*, vol. 2, 313.
104 O'Leary, *Recollections of Fenians and Fenianism*, vol. 2, 227.
105 Maud Gonne MacBride, *A Servant of the Queen: Reminiscences* (London: Victor Gollancz, 1938), 89. They first met at the Contemporary Club in Dublin, a debating society which Yeats attended 'to become self-possessed, to be able to play with hostile minds as Hamlet played, to look into the lion's face, as it were, with unquivering eyelash' (*R* 179).
106 Ibid., 90. O'Leary was one of the few contacts this group had with Catholic Ireland. 'Yet, looking back on those days, it is strange to realise how completely this life of young men, almost all of them eagerly Nationalist, was

destitute of contact with Catholic Ireland. Old John O'Leary, the ex-Fenian, afforded a contact with it; but O'Leary was not a devout and perhaps not a practising Catholic; and he was out of sympathy with the Nationalism of the revolution. In fact, for all of us, Catholic Ireland as an active force might have been a great secret society from which we were excluded: though its all-powerful leader was the Protestant landlord, Parnell.' Stephen Gwynn, *Ireland* (London: Ernest Benn, 1924), 106. The young men Gwynn has in mind were those who met at Dowden's house in the late 1880s and early 1890s: Hyde, Yeats, Rolleston, Taylor, and T. W. Lyster.
107 Maud Gonne MacBride, *A Servant of the Queen*, 216–17. In his *Recollections* vol. 2, O'Leary makes the point that the Fenians attracted most support from 'shopmen' in towns: '⟨T⟩he men in the shops, as compared with the men in the workshops, were relatively more important in '65 than in '48' (238).
108 This is how Maud Gonne begins her recollection of Yeats in Gwynn (ed.), *Scattering Branches*, 17.
109 NLI 30992. See letter dated 10 February 1897.
110 Letter dated 24 July 1897.
111 Letter to Yeats, postmark 3 July 1897. Maud Gonne was in fact born near the garrison town of Aldershot on 21 December 1866, at the full moon.
112 Yeats to Lady Gregory, 15 December ⟨1898⟩. Original in BERG. What he could not tell Lady Gregory was that Maud Gonne had Millevoye's child and that she was fearful of physical love.
113 Letter dated 26 June 1908. Both Maud Gonne and Tynan expressed doubts at this time about Yeats's involvement in the theatre. 'Don't think I under rate the value of your theatre but it is as NOTHING in comparison with your poems & while you are absorbed in the business management of the theatre you won't write a line of poetry' (*MGY* 301, June/July 1911). 'Whether he ⟨Yeats⟩ has done Irish poetry and Irish literature a service by directing it towards the drama remains to be seen.' Katharine Tynan, *The Wild Harp: A Selection from Irish Poetry* (London: Sidgwick and Jackson, 1913), xiv.
114 *MGY* 134, 275, 270. E. Fuller Torrey claims that 'W. B. Yeats, A. R. Orage, and D. H. Lawrence were all known for their anti-Semitism'. See *The Roots of Treason: Ezra Pound and the Secret of St. Elizabeths* (New York: McGraw-Hill, 1984), 69. To support his case he cites C. David Heymann's *Ezra Pound: The Last Rower* (New York: Seaver Books, 1976): 'Yeats, Lewis, Eliot, and D. H. Lawrence were all staunch reactionaries in whose writings can be found traces, and in some cases more than traces, of a snide and demeaning anti-Semitism' (76). Yeats was certainly a reactionary, but I have found no traces of anti-Semitism in his writings.
115 In November or December 1905, the year of the Iseult incident and Maud's public wrangling with MacBride, she defended herself in a

letter to Yeats against the charge in English newspapers that she was English and that she only became a Catholic to marry him (see *MGY* 220). In January 1905, Yeats played the role of trusty confidant and was kept apprised of Maud's situation (see *MGY* 183–90). In turn, he kept Lady Gregory informed. On 9 January 1905, he told her about MacBride's drunken behaviour, his advances towards the servants, and about an offence such that the children could not be trusted with him. Maud wished for a divorce, but this was dismissed by the family lawyer, Barry O'Brien. If Maud pressed for a divorce, MacBride, who continued to live on her capital, threatened to go public with the Millevoye story. Yeats thought she should proceed and risk scandal. In the next letter to Lady Gregory, dated 11 January 1905, Yeats had difficulty expressing his horror concerning MacBride's offence. Two days later the innocent Yeats wrote again to Lady Gregory, and told her that MacBride, in conversation with O'Brien, had accused three people of being Maud's lovers, an unnamed person (Yeats thought it was Stead), Chipriani, and himself. O'Brien told him that was groundless in the case of Yeats, since Yeats showed no sign in that direction.

116 Letter to Lady Gregory, dated 23 January 1898. In BERG.
117 The incident is recalled in *A Servant of the Queen*, 275.
118 Maud Gonne, in Gwynn (ed.), *Scattering Branches*, 20.
119 Letter dated December 1908. According to Jeffares, who notes a change of tone in their correspondence, it is likely that Yeats and Maud Gonne slept together in December 1908 (*MGY* 34). Yeats continued to defend Maud from her accusers. On 19 March 1911 he warned Constance Markiewicz: 'I have heard that there is an attempt to black ball Madam Gonne at the arts club "on personal grounds". This would do her great injury in Dublin I am afraid . . . all we who are her friends would resign at once from the club.' In the Houghton Library, Harvard University.
120 Yeats to Lady Gregory, 13 July 1916. In BERG.
121 Montanus was a Phrygian enthusiast of the second century who claimed that the Holy Spirit dwelt in him. George clearly knew how to impress Yeats and deflect his enthusiasm for his former lover.

4 *Yeats and 1890s London*

1 See Wilfrid Scawen Blunt, *My Diaries: Being a Personal Narrative of Events 1888–1914* (1919–20; repr London: Martin Secker, 1932), 724. Diary entry, 5 June 1910. In a letter to May Morris on 27 February 1934, Yeats explained that he did not know her father 'intimately': what he meant was Morris's powerful personality had through time become so vivid as to deceive him into thinking he knew him intimately. Original in the James Augustine Healy Collection at Colby College, Maine.
2 William Morris, *The Earthly Paradise*, vol. 2 (London: Ellis, 1870), 282.
3 Ibid., vol. 1, 2.
4 W. P. Ryan, *Literary London: Its Lights and Comedies* (London: The Author, 1898), 122.
5 When *The Wanderings of Oisin* was first reviewed in the *Scots Observer*, on 9 March 1889, Yeats's name was linked with Morris. With the onset of the 1890s, however, Yeats abandoned the quest romance for 'short-winded' forms of writing: the short story, the lyrical poem, the one-act play. 'This reduction of everything to its climax can be seen in all the art of the period. . . . The age was short-winded and its art . . . could only stay over short distances.' Bernard Muddiman, *The Men of the Nineties* (London: Henry Danielson, 1920), 61–2.
6 See, for example: Peter Faulkner, *William Morris and W. B. Yeats* (Dublin: Dolmen Press, 1962); Dorothy Mackenzie Hoare, *The Works of Morris and Yeats in Relation to Early Saga Literature* (Cambridge: Cambridge University Press, 1939); the chapter on Morris in Elizabeth Cullingford, *Yeats, Ireland and Fascism* (London: Macmillan, 1981). John Masefield, whose first reading of *The Wanderings of Oisin* 'made me Yeats's disciple' (*So Long to Learn: Chapters of an Autobiography* [London: Heinemann, 1952], 127), was also deeply affected by Morris. Masefield found in the sagas 'a reality touched with romance that seemed the perfection of story-telling' (114). Masefield believed that Yeats's method of chanting verse, or 'cantilating', derived from Morris, who had said that 'the verse ought to be chanted' (129).
7 See for example the passage in 'The Beauty of Life' itemising the essential furniture in a home. In G. D. H. Cole (ed.), *William Morris* (1934; New York: Random House, 1974), 561–2.
8 See Lady Gregory's *Coole*, ed. Colin Smythe (Dublin: Dolmen Press, 1971).
9 Cole (ed.), *William Morris*, 547.
10 Asa Briggs (ed.), *William Morris' News from Nowhere and Selected Writings and Designs* (Harmondsworth: Penguin, 1986), 102.
11 Cole (ed.), *William Morris*, 561.
12 Ibid., 482. From 'Gothic Architecture'.
13 The influence of Morris 'was revealed primarily in Yeats's Irish utopianism, and in specific instances such as his support for the workers in the Dublin Lock-Out of 1913, his desire for art galleries and educational facilities for the poor, his attitude to social legislation in the Irish Senate, his conviction that the State should supply the basic necessities and decencies of life for its citizens, and his often repeated approval of the idea of limiting incomes'. Cullingford, *Yeats, Ireland and Fascism*, 26.
14 E. P. Thompson, *William Morris: Romantic to Revolutionary* (1955; London: Merlin, 1977), 555.

15 William Morris, in his Preface to *Arts and Crafts Essays by Members of the Arts Exhibition Society* (1893; London and Bombay: Longmans, Green, 1899), xii.

16 Robert Lynd, *Old and New Masters* (London: T. Fisher Unwin, 1919), 157.

17 Letter to Elkin Mathews, 17 May 1906. Original in the Brotherton Library, University of Leeds.

18 For further discussion of the debt of the Cuala Press to the Kelmscott Press, see Liam Miller, *The Dun Emer, Later the Cuala Press* (Dublin: Dolmen Press, 1973). See also Richard Kuhta's 'On the Breadth of a Half Penny: The Contribution of the Cuala Press to the Irish Literary Renaissance' in *Bookways: A Quarterly for the Book Arts*, no. 6, January 1993, 12–17. Kuhta writes: 'As quintessentially Irish as the Cuala volumes may appear, it is important to recognise that their roots were sown in England, and the look of a Cuala page is not unlike English texts of the period. Indeed, the Caslon Old Face employed at Cuala was a typeface suggested to Elizabeth ⟨Yeats⟩ by her friend and adviser, Emery Walker, co-founder of the Doves Press' (16). For a recent stimulating discussion of Yeats's debt to Morris, especially in the context of the printed word, see Jerome McGann, *Black Riders: The Visible Language of Modernism* (Princeton, New Jersey: Princeton University Press, 1993).

19 In Briggs (ed.), *News from Nowhere*, 127. From 'Useful Work Versus Useless Toil'.

20 Ibid., 245.

21 Ibid., 203. 'What I mean is, that I haven't seen any poor people about.'

22 Osbert Burdett, *The Beardsley Period: An Essay in Perspective* (London: John Lane, The Bodley Head, 1925), 274.

23 Morris, *The Earthly Paradise*, vol. 1, 6.

24 See 'Bedford Park: Aesthete's Elysium' in *W. B. Yeats and His Contemporaries* (Brighton, Sussex: Harvester Press, 1987), 43–82. See also Mark Glazebrook, *Artists and Architecture of Bedford Park, 1875–1900* (Privately printed, 1967).

25 For details of the family's life at Bedford Park, see William Murphy, *Prodigal Father: The Life of John Butler Yeats (1839–1922)* (Ithaca and London: Cornell University Press, 1978), 152–30.

26 NLI MS 30868. Page 25 of TS for *Reveries over Childhood and Youth*. The words in italics have been deleted.

27 TS *Reveries over Childhood and Youth*, 35–6. The changes in gender may be an attempt at concealment, for Yeats was concerned not to betray too many family secrets.

28 G. K. Chesterton, *Autobiography* (London: Hutchinson, 1936), 149.

29 Shane Leslie, *The End of a Chapter* (London: Constable, 1916), 35.

30 Ernest Rhys, *Everyman Remembers* (London and Toronto: J. M. Dent and Sons, 1931), 105. For a readable account of evenings at the Rhymers Club, see Mark Longaker, *Ernest Dowson* (Philadelphia: University of Pennsylvania Press, 1945), 87–110.

31 Richard Le Gallienne, *Retrospective Reviews: A Literary Log, Volume 1, 1891–1893* (London: John Lane, The Bodley Head; New York: Dodd Mead, 1896), xix.

32 Letter to Edith Shackleton Heald, 5 February 1938. Original in the Houghton Library, Harvard University.

33 Rhys, *Everyman Remembers*, 106. It was Dowson's death in February 1900 that was for Rhys a sign of the Rhymers' final breakup.

34 Muddiman, *The Men of the Nineties*, 81.

35 *The Complete Poems of Lionel Johnson*, ed. Iain Fletcher (London: Unicorn Press, 1953), 258. This poem is recalled by Yeats in 'The Grey Rock': 'When cups went round at close of day – /Is not that how good stories run? –' (*VP* 271).

36 Edgar Jepson, *Memories of a Victorian*, vol. 1 (London: Victor Gollancz, 1933), 237.

37 This essay appeared with a companion essay by Yeats in *Poetry and Ireland: Essays by W. B. Yeats and Lionel Johnson* (Dundrum: Cuala Press, 1908). Johnson writes: 'I have a healthy hatred of the West Briton heresy. Further, no Irishman living has a greater love, and a greater admiration, for the splendid poetry of Davis, Mangan, and their fellows. But I dislike coercion in literature' (21).

38 *The Complete Poems of Lionel Johnson*, 193.

39 Compare the *Times* obituary on 31 January 1939: 'It was this deep devotion to an inward ideal which distinguished him from his contemporaries in the nineties, whose revolt against ugliness was rather of the senses than the imagination, and whose cultivation of beauty was often therefore merely mannered.' As it happened, several other 1890s figures, including Wilde, Douglas, Johnson, Dowson, Beardsley, and Gray, possessed an inward ideal, but they turned to Rome.

40 Arthur Symons, *The Symbolist Movement in Literature* (1899; New York: E. P. Dutton, 1958), xix.

41 James Joyce, *Ulysses: The Corrected Text* (Harmondsworth: Penguin, 1986), 1.554.

42 James Joyce, *A Portrait of the Artist as a Young Man* (New York: Viking, 1968), 7. The pun at the beginning of the novel seems to provide a potential yoking together of the fate of Stephen and Wilde. The opening episode of *Ulysses* is more explicit in connecting them to Ireland's history of dispossession.

43 G. B. Shaw, *Our Theatres in the Nineties*, vol. 1 (London: Constable, 1932), 10, 9. From a review of *An Ideal Husband* in January 1895. Similar views can be found in Frank Harris, *Oscar Wilde: His Life and Confessions*, vol. I (New York: The Author, 1918), 89 and *passim*.

44 Richard Ellmann, *Oscar Wilde* (London: Hamish Hamilton, 1987), 285.

45 Oscar Wilde, *De Profundis* (1905; repr. London: Methuen & Co, 1915).

46 'The majority of the work of the movement ⟨of the 1890s⟩ . . . can be described as impressionisms of the abnormal by a group of individualists. For in all their work the predominant keynote will be found to be a

keen sense of that strangeness of proportion which Bacon noted as a characteristic of what he called beauty.' Muddiman, *The Men of the Nineties*, 135. Yeats enjoyed quoting a remark of Beardsley: 'Beauty is so difficult' (*A* 333).

47 Cited in *Review of Reviews*, February 1891, 159.

48 Holbrook Jackson, *The Eighteen Nineties: A Review of Art and Ideas at the Close of the Nineteenth Century* (1913; repr. London: Grant Richards, 1922), 46. For other surveys of the *Yellow Book*, see, among others, Fraser Harrison's Introduction to *The Yellow Book: An Illustrated Quarterly* (London: Sidgwick and Jackson, 1974), 3–48; Richard Le Gallienne, *The Romantic Nineties* (1926; repr. London: Putnam, 1951), 131–40; and J. W. Lambert and Michael Ratfcliffe, *The Bodley Head, 1887–1987* (London: The Bodley Head, 1987), 59–74. For a recent cultural history of the 1890s as a whole, see Karl Beckson, *London in the 1890s: A Cultural History* (New York and London: W. W. Norton, 1992). See also Simon Houfe, *Fin de Siècle: The Illustrators of the Nineties* (London: Barrie & Jenkins, 1992).

49 Burdett, *The Beardsley Period* (1925), 103.

50 The book was in fact a French novel, *Aphrodite*, by Pierre Louys, bound in yellow. When Wilde was arrested on 5 April 1895, hostile crowds gathered outside the Bodley Head. Lane withdrew Wilde's books, and all traces of Beardsley were deleted from the fifth volume of the *Yellow Book*, which was then being set by the printers.

51 In 'The Decadent Movement in Literature', in *Harper's New Monthly Magazine*, November 1893, Symons had written flowingly about decadence: 'It reflects all the moods, all the manners of a sophisticated society; its very artificiality is a way of being true to nature' (859). By 1896, the need for distance was everywhere apparent and the 1890s were already being recast as history. In his retrospective essay 'Be It Cosiness', in the *Pageant*, 1896, Beerbohm remarked: 'I belong to the Beardsley period. . . . *Cedo junioribus*. Indeed, I stand aside with no regret. For to be outmoded is to be a classic, if one has written well' (235).

52 It was Smithers who published Beardsley's eight 'Lysistrata' and the four 'Juvenal' drawings. On his deathbed, Beardsley asked that the 'Lysistrata' and other bawdy drawings be destroyed.

53 'I have chosen – much to Macmillan's avowed disapproval – a fairly sound green of the old Vale Press type. . . . The cover is quite abstract decoration in which you can detect (by the eye of faith alone) roses & sprays of Ewe with their berries. I found your preferences in Fauna, caves, fountains etc beyond the range of an end paper so I have combined most of them in a sort of book plate design which is placed inside the cover.' Letter from Ricketts to Yeats ⟨early autumn 1922⟩. In *Letters to W. B. Yeats*, vol. 2, 430.

54 The comparison with Morris's Kelmscott Press was one often made at the time. See J. G. P. Delaney, *Charles Ricketts: A Biography* (Oxford: Clarendon Press, 1990), 126–7. See page 318 for an account of the Yeats Uniform Edition and Ricketts's preference for blind blocking. Yeats found the design 'serviceable and perfect'.

55 In his comments on Mallarmé's 'Un coup de dés', Paul Valéry writes: 'Toute son invention, déduite d'analyses du langage, du livre, de la musique, poursuivies pendant des années, se fonde sur la considération de la "page", unité visuelle.' In *Variété*, vol. 2 (Paris: Gallimard, 1930), 73.

56 *Bookman*, January 1923, 197. 'We have had books upon "The Nineties", books of facile criticism and impression; but who will want to read such, when here is a book written from within about that "tragic generation", in which Wilde and Henley, Beardsley and Davidson, Dowson and Johnson appear so livingly?'

57 The two lines of verse are from Davidson's poem 'Fleet Street'. Published posthumously in *Fleet Street and Other Poems* (London: Grant Richards, 1909), 9–20. 'The Lake Isle of Innisfree' is Yeats's riposte to those who followed Whistler in celebrating London. Yeats's animosity towards Davidson is barely concealed in *Autobiographies* (see page 318). The feeling was mutual. According to Rhys in *Everyman Remembers*, Yeats was Davidson's 'pet aversion' (109). For more on Davidson's view of Yeats, see J. Benjamin Townsend, *John Davidson: Poet of Armageddon* (New Haven: Yale University Press, 1961), *passim*.

58 Letter to Katharine Tynan, 30 August 1888. Though not a great admirer of Henley's verse, Yeats still found room to include him in *The Oxford Book of Modern Verse, 1892–1935*.

59 Cited in William Rothenstein, *Men and Memories: Recollections of William Rothenstein, 1872–1900* (London: Faber and Faber, 1931), 312.

60 W. B. Yeats, *The Oxford Book of Modern Verse, 1892–1935*, vi.

61 Henley had made a name for himself as a regular contributor in the 1880s to the *Saturday Review*, a weekly paper opposed to Irish nationalism. Irish books were reviewed 'favourably or Saturdayishly' as Yeats remarked to Katharine Tynan in September 1888 (see *L [K]* 97).

62 The titles to the poems or stories are as they appeared in the various journals. ⟨⟩ indicates an original title later changed by Yeats. For details of the changes, see *VP* 100–79 *passim*. (V) indicates the contribution is a poem, (S) a story, (E) an essay.

63 See Allen Richard Grossman, *Poetic Knowledge in the Early Yeats: A Study of 'The Wind Among the Reeds'* (Charlottesville: University Press of Virginia, 1969), 9.

64 St John Ervine, *Some Memories of My Elders* (London: George Allen and Unwin, 1923), 260.

65 *The Literary Year-Book and Bookman's Directory, 1900*, ed. Herbert Morragh

(London: George Allen, 1900). In 1899, 7,567 books were published, with six shillings as the favourite price. Other new journals included the *Windmill Quarterly*, the *Anglo-Saxon Review*, the *Review of the Week*, and the *Sphere* (ed. Clement Shorter). The 1890s also saw the rise of literary agents like A. P. Watt, whose clients included Jane Barlow, Davidson, Hardy, Conan Doyle, and Yeats. In *Elkin Mathews: Publisher to Yeats, Joyce, Pound* (Madison, Wisconsin: University of Wisconsin Press, 1989), James Nelson refers to 'the heyday of the so-called "minor" poets in the early nineties' (125). The demand thereafter declined.

66 John Harwood, *Olivia Shakespear and W. B. Yeats: After Long Silence* (London: Macmillan, 1989), 64, 66. For an illuminating reading of *The Wind Among the Reeds* which stresses the unattainability of wisdom, see Grossman, *Poetic Knowledge in the Early Yeats*.

67 See Joseph Hone, *William Butler Yeats: The Poet in Contemporary Ireland* (Dublin and London: Maunsel, 1915), 51.

68 W. P. Ryan, *The Irish Literary Revival: Its History, Pioneers and Possibilities* (London: The Author, 1894), 11. A similar view is expressed in his land-league novel, *The Heart of Tipperary: A Romance of the Land League* (Dublin: Clery, n.d.): 'We have little to show for the centuries of our nation's life beyond a record of planning and battling' (76–7). Ryan's account of the Revival differs markedly from that in Ernest Boyd's *Ireland's Literary Renaissance* (New York: Alfred Knopf, 1922). Boyd stresses throughout the Irish background, and how the 'same current was working simultaneously in Dublin and London' (86). Ryan, however, felt that 'it was owing to accidental and temporary circumstances that any Irish intellectual movement originates in London or any other foreign centre' (38). As it happened, the Pan-Celtic Society began in Dublin in March 1888. The Irish National Literary Society held its inaugural lecture in August 1892. In deference to its sister organisation in Dublin, the Irish Literary Society of London delayed its own inaugural lecture until March 1893.

69 A similar view was more cavalierly expressed by Shane Leslie: 'As the old Irish tongue died out, there arose a literary compassion in England which took the form of a Celtic movement. A school of writers arose who made literary capital by belauding or belittling, libelling or labelling the Irish. Thanks to an audience of the middle class fleeing English Teutonism and Philistinism, these writers won a cockney fame. Only Yeats deserved laurelled rank, though he is not so much an Irish poet as a Rossetti, lost in what old writers called "a Druidical mist" ' (*The End of a Chapter*, 136).

70 Ryan, *The Irish Literary Revival*, 36. See 61–72 for an insider's view of the dispute between Duffy and Yeats. Pen portraits of the leading figures associated with the Irish Literary Society can be found in chapter 5 of Ryan (77–124).

71 Cited in A. P. Graves, *To Return to All That: An Autobiography* (London: Jonathan Cape, 1930), 261–2. According to Graves, this lecture was given in spring 1891.

72 Francis Fahy, *The Irish Language Movement* (London: Gaelic League, 1901), 14.

73 By 1900, the Society possessed seven hundred library books, and the thriving lecture programme continued. See Graves, *To Return to All That*, 265–8. The *Irish Literary Society Gazette* was launched in November 1898, when the Society had nearly five hundred members.

74 By contrast, Lady Gregory has written 'an interesting article' in the November number of *Nineteenth Century* on 'Ireland, the Real and the Ideal'; 'Mr Stephen Gwynn is bringing out two works this season – *Tennyson, a Critical Study* (Blackie and Sons); and *The Repentance of a Private Secretary* (John Lane)'; 'The Perfect Wagnerite' is the title of Mr G. Bernard Shaw's latest work. It is published by Grant Richards'; 'Mr T. W. Rolleston is preparing *An Anthology of Irish Poetry*, which Smith, Elder will publish. An introduction will be contributed by the Rev. Stopford Brooke'; 'Rev. Stopford Brooke has just completed the first volume of *The History of English Literature*, by various authors, which Macmillan and Co. are to publish.'

75 *Irish Literary Society Gazette*, vol. 1, no. 2, January 1899, 7.

76 Ibid., vol. 1, no. 3, 7. Graves was in the Chair.

77 Ibid., vol. 1., no. 4, June 1899, 4–5. Graves, apparently, did not respond, but the Chairman in his closing remarks suggested that 'unfortunately the Irish peasantry were being swept off the face of the earth despite the fighting qualities for which Mr J. B. Yeats gave them credit. ⟨Hear, hear.⟩'

78 Ibid., vol. 1, no. 4, June 1899, 5–7.

79 Masefield, *So Long to Learn*, 140.

80 Ibid., 143.

81 For further details, see John Masefield, *Some Memories of W. B. Yeats* (Dublin: Cuala Press, 1940). See also *So Long to Learn*, 145–7. Furnishing Woburn Buildings produced considerable anxiety in Yeats: 'She ⟨Olivia Shakespear⟩ came with me to make every purchase, and I remember an embarrassed conversation in the presence of some Tottenham Court ⟨Road⟩ shop upon the width of the bed – every inch increased the expense' (*Mem* 88).

82 Richard Allen Cave's appendix, 'Robert Gregory: Artist and Stage Designer', in Ann Saddlemyer and Colin Smythe (eds), *Lady Gregory, Fifty Years After* (Gerrards Cross: Colin Smythe; Totowa, New Jersey: Barnes and Noble, 1987), 355.

83 Masefield, *Some Memories of W. B. Yeats*, p. 15.

84 Maud Gonne MacBride, *A Servant of the Queen*, 331. She confuses Elgar with Dolmetsch.

85 Masefield, *So Long to Learn*, 141.

5 Yeats and the Abbey Theatre

1 Cited in Michael Orme, *J. T. Grein: The Story of a Pioneer, 1862–1935* (London: John Murray, 1936), 70. For a survey of books on Yeats and drama, see my *W. B. Yeats: A Guide Through the Critical Maze* (Bristol: Bristol Classical Press, 1989), 48–68.

2 'British Association Visit, Abbey Theatre, Special Programme', September 1908.

3 Cited in Lady Gregory, *Our Irish Theatre* (1913; repr. New York: Capricorn, 1972), 8–9.

4 Yeats's lecture on the 'Ideal Theatre' was delivered to the Irish Literary Society of London on 23 April 1899. Report in *Irish Literary Society Gazette*, vol. 1, no. 4, June 1899, 5–6. The meeting was chaired by Gosse, who in his closing comments sought to qualify Yeats's view of the Norwegian theatre, for 'there was an element, if he might put it so, of the fairy tale in Mr Yeats' picturesque and charming account of the birth of the Norwegian Theatre. (Laughter.)' Ibsen produced an enormous number of cosmopolitan plays; the Norwegian national theatre made full use of commercial plays: 'But they all knew exactly what Mr Yeats meant, and they all sympathised with him.' James Flannery in *W. B. Yeats and the Idea of a Theatre: The Early Abbey Theatre in Theory and Practice* (New Haven and London: Yale University Press, 1976) argues that 'Yeats's dramatic theories are more important than his actual practices', and that his basic struggle 'was to reconcile theory with practice'. Unfortunately, in the struggle 'the practical realities of life and the theatre caused his original theories and ideals to be misconstrued, attacked, destroyed, and ultimately forgotten' (xii–xiii).

5 *Beltaine*, no. 2, February 1900.

6 Interview with Yeats reported in the *Northern Whig*, 25 August 1909.

7 Augustine Birrell, *Things Past Redress* (London: Faber and Faber, 1937), 214.

8 *Daily Telegraph*, 6 June 1911.

9 See John Masefield, *So Long to Learn: Chapters of an Autobiography* (London: William Heinemann, 1952), 154.

10 George Moore, *Hail and Farewell: Ave* (London: William Heinemann, 1911), 43. The mocking 'for sure' captures Moore's distance from the events he describes.

11 See Janet Egleson Dunleavy and Gareth W. Dunleavy, *Douglas Hyde: A Maker of Modern Ireland* (Berkeley and Los Angeles: University of California Press, 1991), 244.

12 In *The Collected Letters of John Millington Synge, Volume 1, 1871–1907*, ed. Ann Saddlemyer (London: Methuen, 1983), 94.

13 'A Comparison between Irish and English Theatrical Audiences' in *Beltaine*, no. 2, February 1900, 12.

14 F. Hugh O'Donnell, *Souls for Gold!* (London, 1899), 5. The pamphlet contained the mocking subtitle 'Pseudo-Celtic Drama in Dublin'. The *Freeman's Journal* on 10 May 1899 published a letter signed by Dublin Catholic students of the Royal University in which they declared: 'The subject is not Irish. It has been shown that the plot is founded on a German legend. The characters are ludicrous travesties of the Irish Catholic Celt... slanderous caricature of the Irish peasant.' At the opening night, Joyce clapped vigorously at the end of the performance and refused to sign a letter attacking the play composed by his friends Francis Skeffington and Thomas Kettle. The incident is recalled in James Joyce, *A Portrait of the Artist as a Young Man: Text, Criticism, and Notes*, ed. Chester G. Anderson (New York: Viking Press, 1968), 226. When Yeats read Joyce's 'remarkable book', which gave an accurate picture of their struggle in Ireland, he was struck by its mention of their first performance at the Antient Concert Rooms. See his letter to Lady Gregory, 10 February 1917. In BERG.

15 This quotation is taken from Yeats's benchmark essay 'The Theatre', first published in the *Dome* in April 1899.

16 For Yeats's involvement in London theatre societies in the early 1900s, see Ronald Schuchard, 'W. B. Yeats and the London Theatre Societies, 1901–1904' in *Review of English Studies*, November 1978, 415–46. Yeats was involved in the Masquers Society, whose first formal meeting was held on 6 July 1903 at Clifford's Inn. Among those attending were Sturge Moore, Gilbert Murray, Florence Farr, and Miss Craig. This attempt at an exclusive Theatre of Beauty came to nothing and perhaps pointed Yeats more firmly in the direction of Dublin as his theatre base. See also *L (K)* 3, 721–5.

17 See report in the *Freeman's Journal*, 3 February 1905.

18 See Annie Horniman Newspaper Cuttings, vol. 10, page 73. In the John Rylands University Library of Manchester.

19 See *Joseph Holloway's Abbey Theatre: A Selection from His Unpublished Journal 'Impressions of a Dublin Playgoer'*, ed. Robert Hogan and Michael J. O'Neill (Carbondale and Edwardsville: Southern Illinois University Press, 1967), 96. Entry: 21 November 1907. Martin Hearne is the Paul Ruttledge figure. For a recent discussion of Yeats and Ibsen, see George Watson, 'Yeats, Ibsen and the "New Woman"', in *Yeats the European*, ed. A. Norman Jeffares (Savage, Maryland: Barnes and Noble, 1989), 238–53.

20 Arthur Symons, 'A Symbolist Farce' in *Saturday Review*, 19 December 1896, 646.

21 Craig was at the forefront of European drama, and in 1908 he was invited to Moscow to work with Stanislavsky on a production of *Hamlet* at the Art Theatre (it was eventually staged in January 1912). Yeats's production notebook is discussed by Liam Miller in *The Noble Drama of W. B. Yeats* (Dublin: Dolmen Press; North America: Humanities Press, 1977), 154 ff.

22 Dolmetsch's instrument was made of twelve strings, and Farr spoke to it an octave lower than she sang. See Yeats's letter to Bridges, 20 July 1901, in *L (K)* 3, 91. For a synopsis of

23 The *Freeman's Journal*, Thursday, 8 October 1903.

24 This is a deliberate exaggeration. It was of course 'our Theatre' according to Lady Gregory. Lady Gregory was not only central in establishing the theatre but also wrote plays and collaborated with Yeats in writing his plays, including: *Diarmuid and Grania*, *Cathleen ni Houlihan*, *The Unicorn from the Stars*, *The Pot of Broth*, *The King's Threshold*, and *Deirdre*. See her *Our Irish Theatre*, 78–82.

25 There are equivalents between Blake's 'Sick Rose' and *The Land of Heart's Desire*: the newly married Mary is the Rose; she is unsatisfied with her role, hence sick; enter the faery, the invisible worm; she finds herself questioning her domestic bliss, her crimson joy; Blake's dark secret love is the Land of Heart's Desire, which in turn destroys Mary. But such equivalents seem more formal than real, and at the end of the play we wonder why Mary should have to die.

26 Frank Fay, 'The Irish Literary Theatre', *United Irishman*, 4 May 1901.

27 Yeats had presented the play to Fay's Company because he wanted to hear his work spoken with a Dublin accent, and he had been impressed with their production of Hyde's *Casadh an tSugáin*. Contact between Yeats and the Fay brothers was established in August 1901. Willie Fay became General Manager of the Abbey Theatre and Frank Fay one of its leading actors.

28 'Our cup now ran over, for, as President of Inginidhe na hEireann, Miss Gonne was in fact what Kathleen ni Houlihan was in symbol.' So wrote Willie Fay in William Fay and Catherine Carswell, *The Fays of the Abbey Theatre* (London: Rich and Cowan, 1935), 119. For further details about Inghinidhe na hEireann, see Margaret Ward, *Maud Gonne: Ireland's Joan of Arc* (London: Pandora, 1990), 55–71.

29 Cited in Lennox Robinson, *Ireland's Abbey Theatre: A History, 1899–1951* (London: Sidgwick and Jackson, 1951), 27. The *Freeman's Journal* on 5 April 1902 commented on Maud Gonne's performance: 'Her interpretation of the part was marked by a very high degree of histrionic power.'

30 Yeats's comment in an interview with Arthur Griffith's paper the *United Irishman*, 5 May 1902.

31 Stephen Gwynn, *Irish Literature and Drama in the English Language* (London: Nelson, 1936), 158.

32 John Eglinton, *Irish Literary Portraits* (London: Macmillan, 1935), 26. Beatrice Glenavy was also impressed by Yeats's play and went on to paint an allegorical picture of Kathleen ni Houlihan in Sarah Purser's Stained Glass Works. The picture was bought by Maud Gonne and presented to Pearse's St Edna's College: 'Some time later I met one of the boys from the school and he told me that this picture had inspired him "to die for Ireland"! I was shocked at the thought that my rather banal and sentimental picture might, like Helen's face, launch ships and burn towers!' See Beatrice, Lady Glenavy, *Today We Will Only Gossip* (London: Constable, 1964), 91.

33 See report in the *Freeman's Journal*, 5 August 1904.

34 Wellesley College *News*, 29 April 1920. Copy in Wellesley College, Special Collections, English Poetry Collection.

35 'Paragraph Written in November 1909 with Supplements and Financial Statement.' Horniman spent more than £10,000 on the Abbey, not including the losses on various UK tours. In 1904 and 1905 she spent £2,000 on the building and subsidy, but thereafter her contribution subsided: £932 in 1906, £703 in 1908, £655 in 1908, and £150 in 1909. By 1909 the Abbey Theatre was making the kind of profit to survive independent of her. For details, see Gerard Fay, *The Abbey Theatre: Cradle of Genius* (London: Hollis and Carters, 1958), 103.

36 *Irish Times*, 28 December 1904. The 'simple idea' was the rural post office as hub of local gossip.

37 Maire Nic Shiubhlaigh, *The Splendid Years* (London: James Duffy, 1955), 73.

38 Fay and Carswell, *The Fays of the Abbey Theatre*, 106.

39 Lady Gregory, *The Collected Plays of Lady Gregory*, vol. 1, ed. Anne Saddlemyer (Gerrards Cross: Colin Smythe, 1970), 262.

40 Moore, *Hail and Farewell: Ave*, 45.

41 Carden Tyrrell's final speech in the play betrays not a hint of irony: 'Oh, where is that beauty now – that music of the morning? ⟨Suddenly arrested.⟩ Such strange solemn harmonies – ⟨Listens.⟩ The voices – yes, they are filling the house – those white-stoled children of the morning. ⟨His eyes for a moment wander slowly to the doorway at back.⟩ Oh, the rainbow – ! ⟨To Kit.⟩ Come quick, see the lovely rainbow! ⟨They go to watch it hand in hand.⟩ Oh, the mystic highway of man's speechless longings – ! My heart goes forth upon the rainbow to that horizon of joy!' See Edward Martyn, *The Heather Field* (Dublin: Talbot, n.d.), 91.

42 Lennox Robinson's quotation appears in his *Ireland's Abbey Theatre*, 65. Synge's comment is contained in a letter to Stephen MacKenna, 28 January 1904, in *The Collected Letters of John Millington Synge*, vol. 1, 74. *The Shadowy Waters* was staged in January 1904.

43 Sheila Goodie, *Annie Horniman: A Pioneer in the Theatre* (London: Methuen, 1990), 73. From March to October 1903, Horniman consulted her tarot cards on four separate occasions to determine the right course of action regarding the Irish National Theatre. Sheila Goodie sets the theatre in opposition to the occult, but it is worth remembering that programmes for the Gaiety Theatre carried an astrological sign reminiscent of the Golden Dawn. Equally, there are similarities in the pattern of her behaviour with both groups. Her financial support for the Golden Dawn

was significant: from March 1891 to December 1896 she gave Mathers £1,334. She was also a disciplinarian for the group. But she became uneasy about Mathers's political talk, and she never liked the drinking or growing rowdiness or 'the continual glorification of the Mars forces'. Moreover, 'The money affairs eventually made me unable to express my opinions freely.' Her refusal to submit to Mathers led to her expulsion. After her reinstatement in October 1898, she discovered the existence of Farr's secret group in the Order and in February 1901 fought unsuccessfully alongside Yeats to remove it. See Ellic Howe, *The Magicians of the Golden Dawn: A Documentary History of a Magical Order 1887-1923* (London: Routledge & Kegan Paul, 1972), 112, 234 ff. In retrospect, Horniman's behaviour at the Abbey in the 1900s was not unlike the behaviour of 'Fortiter et Recte' in the Golden Dawn in the 1890s.

44 Corrected TS ⟨Obituary?⟩ Note about A. E. F. Horniman. NLI 30282.

45 *United Irishman*, 10 June 1906.

46 Journal entry dated 13 January 1906. In *Joseph Holloway's Abbey Theatre*, 69.

47 Letter from Horniman to the Directors of the Abbey, 4 July 1906. Original in the Synge Correspondence in TCD. MSS 4424/257.

48 Yeats to Lady Gregory, 4 July 1906. In BERG. Yeats, too, was by now convinced that the Company needed re-organising.

49 'The alternative to this is the giving of my plays to English companies, for if I am to be of any use ever in Ireland I must get good performances. Till I get that I shall be looked on as an amateur.' Letter to Synge, 13 August 1906. Cited in Flannery, *W. B. Yeats and the Idea of a Theatre*, 216.

50 See Joseph Hone, *W. B. Yeats, 1865–1939* (London: Macmillan, 1942), 239.

51 See Yeats to Lady Gregory, undated ⟨September 1906?⟩. In BERG. Unfortunately, the letter is not reproduced in *Theatre Business* (1982). Whose conduct was scandalous is not clear. In September 1906, Willie Fay was in correspondence with Lady Gregory about his plans to marry Brigit O'Dempsey. Her father, a lawyer, warned the Theatre (possibly through Annie Horniman) that she was under age. There is a reference to this in a letter Yeats wrote to Farr on 30 September ⟨1906⟩: 'Fay's enemy says he will attack him next time "before the public on the stage".... It is all about a young woman' (*L* 480). But it is difficult to see this as a resigning matter on the part of a Director. The dating of the letter would help toward clarification.

52 Original in BERG.

53 See his letter to her dated 10 December 1906 in the John Rylands University Library of Manchester.

54 Horniman to Yeats, 7 July 1907. In *Letters to W. B. Yeats*, vol. 1, 184.

55 See his letter to her dated 29 September 1910. Original in the John Rylands University Library of Manchester.

56 Horniman to Synge, 7 January 1906. Original in the Synge Correspondence in TCD. MSS 4424/228.

57 See letter to Lady Gregory, 11 November 1905. In BERG. Herbert Hughes set the Fool's song for the performance of *On Baile's Strand*, and arranged and edited *Irish Country Songs* (London and New York: Boosey, 1909), which included a setting for Yeats's 'Down by the Sally Gardens'.

58 Letter dated 3 January 1906. Original in BERG. The issue seems to have been Maire Walker's (Nic Shiubhlaigh) reneging on her contract after discovering, firstly, that her brother Frank had not signed and, secondly, that Sara Allgood was to be regarded as the leading actress of the Company. For further details, see William Murphy, *Prodigal Father The Life of John Butler Yeats (1839–1922)* (Ithaca and London: Cornell University Press, 1978), 295–8, and Adrian Frazier, *Behind the Scenes: Yeats, Horniman, and the Struggle for the Abbey Theatre* (Berkeley and Los Angeles: University of California Press, 1990), 124–8. In Hone's biography there is a reference to Yeats threatening a young and pretty actress 'to show that the fundamental fact of all business was contract' (207). When Yeats writes about authority in his published work, he never betrays that he himself was high-handed as an employer. 'The Abbey Theatre', he proclaims in 'Estrangement', 'will fail to do its full work because there is no accepted authority to explain why the more difficult pleasure is the nobler pleasure.... We require a new statement of moral doctrine, which shall be accepted by the average man, but be at the same time beyond his power in practice' (*A* 491–2). As late as 8 May 1909, *Sinn Fein* was lamenting the departure of Maire Nic Shiubhlaigh and urging the Abbey and the Theatre of Ireland to sink their differences in their struggle against a commercial theatre: 'Oh Yeats, Yeats!' the paper pleaded.

59 Horniman to Lady Gregory, 17 April 1906. Original in TCD. MSS 3454/284.

60 Copy in the John Rylands University Library, of Manchester.

61 Horniman to Marjorie Garrod, 28 May 1917. In the John Rylands University Library of Manchester.

62 See Frazier, *Behind the Scenes*, 48.

63 *Christian Commonwealth*, 20 May 1914.

64 See her letter in the John Rylands University Library of Manchester.

65 Lennox Robinson, *I Sometimes Think* (Dublin: Talbot Press, 1956), 119.

66 Synge to Molly Allgood, 28 May 1907. In *The Collected Letters of John Millington Synge*, vol. 1, 360.

67 Synge to Molly Allgood, 22 May 1907. In *The Collected Letters of John Millington Synge*, vol. 1, 351. In a letter to Synge dated 26 May 1904, in which she cast his horoscope, Horniman revealed a more human side: 'The study of astrology gives one a beautifully non-libelous means of abusing people I can assure you.' Original in the Synge Correspondence, TCD. MSS 4424/146.

68 See his letter to Lady Gregory and Yeats on 13 December 1906. In *The Collected Letters of John Millington Synge*, vol. 1, 260–61.

69 In March 1907 Synge asked Frank Fay for a list of the number of times *Spreading the News*, *The Shadow of the Glen*, *Kathleen ni Houlihan*, *Riders to the Sea*, and *On Baile's Strand* had been played at the Abbey since its opening. 'I expect their pieces have been done at least three times as often as mine. If that is so there'll be a row. I am tied to the company now by your own good self otherwise I would be inclined to clear away to Paris and let them make it a Yeats-Gregory show in name as well as in deed. However it is best not to do anything rash. They have both been very kind to me at times and I owe them a great deal.' In *The Collected Letters of John Millington Synge*, vol. 1, 318.

70 See her Introduction to *The Collected Letters of John Millington Synge*, vol. 1, xv.

71 John Eglinton, *Irish Literary Portraits* (London: Macmillan, 1935), 29. 'Synge was more than an episode in Yeats's history: he was a disturbing event, which brought Yeats back from the abstract to the personal.' Yeats believed he had 'discovered' Synge in Paris in 1896, and he must have been piqued that Synge never came under his wing. In *Paddy and Mr Punch: Connections in Irish and English History* (Harmondsworth: Allen Lane, 1993), Roy Foster suggests that Yeats's attitude towards Synge was in part dictated by an inferiority complex arising from Synge's superior position on the Irish Protestant middle-class ladder (198–9).

72 Lady Gregory, *Our Irish Theatre*, 155. Yeats and Lady Gregory had been invited to the Castle for talks. The attempted banning of Shaw's play on the grounds of blasphemy created more column inches in the Dublin press than the *Playboy* riots of 1907. In his 1988 biography, Jeffares declares that Horniman was 'decidedly irritated' by the Abbey's decision to stage Shaw's play, 'thinking that this was a political act, the play having been banned in England' (179). I have found no evidence to support such a view. Indeed, according to Goodie, Horniman 'was delighted to see the fight now being taken up on behalf of Bernard Shaw's play'. See her *Annie Horniman*, 134. For a recent, albeit tendentious, discussion of these events, see Lucy McDiarmid, 'Augusta Gregory, Bernard Shaw, and the Shewing-Up of Dublin Castle', in *PMLA*, January 1994, 26–44. McDiarmid argues that the censorship controversy was deliberately provoked by the Abbey Directors and Shaw: 'In the approving presence of the military and economic pillars of the colonial community and their rich, well-dressed friends, Shaw, Gregory, and Yeats produced the spectacle of their resistance to English colonial rule' (27). A 'conspiratorial' reading has, I suspect, little value: it certainly misses, for example, the humorously theatrical moment captured in the headline 'AJAX YEATS DEFIES THE CENSOR' (see page 146).

73 Yeats writing in *Samhain*, October 1902, 9.

74 According to Maurice Bourgeois in a lecture to the National Literary Society in Dublin in January 1912, this is what Synge 'used to say'. See the *Irish Book Lover*, vol. 3, no. 8, March 1912, 132–3.

75 *The Autobiography of J. M. Synge: Constructed from the Manuscripts by Alan Price* (Dublin: Dolmen; London: Oxford University Press, 1965), 26.

76 Cited in David Greene and Edward Stephens, *J. M. Synge, 1871–1909* (New York: Collier, 1961), 96. On leaving Inishmaan in June 1898, Synge asked: 'Am I not leaving in Inishmaan spiritual treasures unexplored whose presence is a great magnet to my soul?'

77 See report in the *Boston Evening Transcript*, 29 September 1911.

78 *Manchester Guardian*, 19 July 1905.

79 J. B. Yeats thought Synge and 'the common people' were 'a strong influence in Jack's life'. See his letter to Quinn, 6 January 1914. Original in QUINN. For a recent discussion of Synge's articles in the *Manchester Guardian*, see Adele M. Dalsimer's essay 'The Irish Peasant Had All His Heart: J. M. Synge in *The Country Shop*', in Adele M. Dalsimer (ed.), *Visualizing Ireland: National Identity and the Pictorial Tradition* (Boston and London: Faber and Faber, 1993), 201–30.

80 *Manchester Guardian*, 10 June 1905.

81 Ibid., 19 July 1905.

82 See Horniman's letter to Synge on 26 May 1904: '(Y)our imaginative faculty is of a disturbing nature to other people $)o^o\delta$ as well as to yourself.' Original in the Synge Correspondence, TCD. MSS 4424/146.

83 *Freeman's Journal*, 8 October 1903.

84 *United Irishman*, 24 October 1903.

85 Ibid., 7 January 1904. The words are almost certainly Griffith's, author of *The Resurrection of Hungary* (1904).

86 *Evening Herald*, 6 February 1905.

87 *Freeman's Journal*, 7 February 1905.

88 This was one of Stephen Dedalus's Flaubertian aesthetic ideals. See Joyce, *A Portrait of the Artist as a Young Man*, 215.

89 There is a reference to Synge's 'imperceptible accent' in Francis Bickley, *J. M. Synge and the Irish Dramatic Movement* (London: Constable; Boston and New York: Houghton Mifflin, 1912), 12n. In his Preface to *The Playboy of the Western World*, Synge advanced the cause of his play by reference to popular speech and imagination. He might have been better advised to argue a case not for verisimilitude but for 'variation', an argument he touched on in his essay 'The Vagrants of Wicklow' (see *Shanachie*, no. 2, 1906–7), a section of which was reproduced in the Abbey Programme for the first performance of *Playboy* (see page 151).

90 *The Collected Letters of John Millington Synge*, vol. 1, 329. Another amusing incident occurred in Court when Patrick Columb, the father of the playwright, was charged with offensive behaviour in the pit of the Abbey. He had been asked by the audience to 'Hush', and

when Police Constable 47 C put his hand on him to desist, replied: 'Who are you, you –.' Under cross-examination, the Police Constable was asked if he heard anything offensive on the stage. 'I heard **One Offensive Word** used.' The headlines ran: **LAST NIGHT'S ROW AT ABBEY/DISTURBERS CHARGED IN THE POLICE COURT/Mr Yeats in the Box/ HIS DEFENCE OF THE PLAY/'THE EXAGGERATION OF ART'/STRONG PROTEST BY ONE OF THE AUDIENCE/Accused Fined Forty Shillings.**

91 Support for *The Playboy* found little expression either at the debate in the Abbey or in the press. Skeffington was alarmed by the disturbances but even more alarmed by Yeats's use of the police. In a letter to the *Evening Telegraph* on 2 February 1907, Gwynn complained that Synge had put his admirers in a difficult position: 'I do not in the least regret that the play was hissed at its first performance, for the very good reason that if it were played with acceptance, word would immediately go out that parricide is a popular exploit in Ireland.'

92 'For some unexplicable reason the management of the Abbey Theatre revived *The Playboy of the Western World* last night. Even if the management consider it the right thing to disregard the decisive verdict of the Dublin public, they ought not, in the interests of the late Mr Synge's repute as a dramatist, present such a worthless piece as a sample of his talents.' *Freeman's Journal*, 28 May 1909. According the Dublin *Daily Express* on 31 May 1909, 'the violent dissent which it provoked on its first production has almost entirely subsided'. Irish-American audiences continued to find *Playboy* problematic. On 26 November 1911, the *New York Times* drama critic confessed: 'But it is still possible to understand why its exposition of a peculiar hero worship should rile an Irishman and leave a rankling feeling in his breast.' In January 1912 the Irish Players were arrested in Philadelphia for staging an immoral play.

93 St John Ervine in a letter to the *Saturday Review* on 8 July 1911 claimed that Synge 'literally could not write about middle-class people at all. It was only when he turned to the West, and wrote of peasants, that he produced literature.'

94 *Evening Telegraph*, 12 May 1910. In a small city like Dublin at the time, everyone knew that France meant Maud Gonne.

95 Yeats to Bridges, 18 October ⟨1915⟩. In Richard Finneran (ed.), *The Correspondence of Robert Bridges and W. B. Yeats* (London: Macmillan, 1977), 45–6.

96 See Yeats to Lady Gregory, n.d. (someone has pencilled in 1907, but the reference to the Italian trip suggests the date is 1908). In BERG.

97 *The Poetical Works of William B. Yeats, volume 1, Lyrical Poems* (New York and London: Macmillan, 1906). The Preface was dated July 1906.

98 Report in *Sinn Fein*, 12 March 1910. An editorial the same day took issue with Yeats.

99 I have relied on A. N. Jeffares, *A New Commentary on the Poems of W. B. Yeats*, and Daniel Albright, *W. B. Yeats: The Poems*, for constructing these statistics and the ensuing chart.

100 Cornelius Weygandt, *Irish Plays and Playwrights* (London: Constable; Boston and New York: Houghton Mifflin, 1913), 43.

101 Thomas Parkinson's thesis is that Yeats's involvement in the Abbey Theatre transformed the nature of his ensuing verse. See his *W. B. Yeats, Self-Critic: A Study of his Early Verse* (Berkeley and Los Angeles: University of California Press, 1951). According to Parkinson, Yeats's verse after *The Golden Helmet* displays a poet responding more vigorously to the demands of the immediate world. Personal speech now has the look of dramatised tension, and the poet seeks a relationship between a daily mood and a moment of exultation.

102 Yeats's *Memoirs*, a draft for his autobiography and a journal he kept between 1908 and 1930, was first published in 1972.

103 Yeats's struggle to find his voice of feeling is especially evident in abandoned poems. See, for example, a letter to Lady Gregory dated 26 November ⟨1911⟩. In BERG. Lady Gregory's (restraining) presence can be felt throughout Yeats's verse in these years. Russell's interpretation of Yeats's poetic career at this time is also worth recalling: 'He began about the time of *The Wind among the Reeds* to do two things consciously, one to create a "style" in literature, the second to create or rather to re-create W. B. Yeats in a style which would harmonise with the literary style. . . . The error in his psychology is, that life creates the form, but he seems to think that the form creates life.' Letter to George Moore, 6 April 1916. In Alan Denson (ed.), *Letters from AE* (London, New York, Toronto: Abelard-Schuman, 1961), 110.

104 In *Poetry and Drama*, March 1913, 56.

105 It was a view that prevailed. In his Preface to the significantly entitled *The Cutting of an Agate*, written in 1918, he describes his work during the ten years after 1902 as being 'busy with a single art, that of a small, unpopular theatre' (*E & I* 219). The Dublin press provided little source of comfort: 'The Abbey Theatre is not popular. Nobody ever said it was. It is a badly-fitted theatre for one, and is amateurishly managed for another. Not many theatre-goers waver in their choice between a shilling seat in the "Abbey" pit and the same in the upper circle of the Theatre Royal. . . . We are driven to the blunt conclusion that there is something radically wrong with the, shall we say, pragmatics of the movement.' *Leader*, 16 May 1908. A sense of unfulfilment never left Yeats, and in answer to a question in the 1930s concerning feelings of dissatisfaction or impersonality about his work, he replied that he found it impossible in a short space to answer such a question.

106 Report in the Dublin *Evening Herald*, 25 June 1910. On 28 October 1910 at the Lord Chancellor's House in Dublin, a call for subsidy was

made by the Chief Secretary to Ireland, Augustine Birrell. By November 1910, the fund had reached £2,800, but Yeats had been advised by his business consultants to ensure that figure reached £5,000. See report in the *Irish Times* on 22 November 1910. When Joyce came to construct his 'lists' in the 'Cyclops' episode of *Ulysses*, he needed to look no further than contemporary press reports for parody.

107 The phrase 'the representatives of collective opinion' is from *Memoirs* (138), and appears immediately before his discussion of the doctrine of the Mask. At this stage the doctrine of the Mask was used by Yeats to distinguish the self as centre, as face, from the self as visionary seeker, as mask. The distinction between person and mask was made by Mathers in a letter to Horniman dated 8 January 1896 and was presumably commonplace among members of the Golden Dawn: 'When you entered the Order, you took the motto of "Fortiter et Recte", that is you left the "Miss Horniman" personality outside the Order. Do not forget that the words "person", "personality" are derived from the Latin word "Persona" which means "a mask"'. Cited in Howe, *The Magicians of the Golden Dawn*, 122. Whereas for Wilde the mask was a form of lying, in occult circles the mask was a way of confronting hidden truth, a point made by Herbert Levine in *Yeats's Daimonic Renewal* (Ann Arbor, Michigan: UMI Research Press, 1983).

108 Ervine, *Some Impressions of My Elders* (London: George Allen and Unwin, 1923), 265.

109 *Joseph Holloway's Abbey Theatre*, 148.

110 Dorothy Shakespear to Pound, 14 July 1912. In *Ezra Pound and Dorothy Shakespear: Their Letters 1909–1914*, ed. Omar Pound and A. Walton Litz (New York: New Directions, 1984), 134.

111 W. B. Yeats, *Plays for an Irish Theatre* (London and Stratford: A. H. Bullen, 1913), xii.

112 See Darragh-Craig proposal (dated *c*. 1911), Box 93, SUNY Stony Brook. 'We propose to establish a theatre for plays which appeal to the sense of beauty and admit of beautiful staging.... We might begin in London, or begin out of London.... We should not open before, at the earliest, the Spring or Autumn of 1914.'

6 Yeats during the First World War

1 Lane was aboard the *Lusitania* when it was sunk by a German submarine in 1915. In his will he donated the collection to the National Gallery in London, but in an unwitnessed codicil he specified Dublin instead. For further discussion, see Lady Gregory, *Hugh Lane's Life and Achievement, with Some Account of the Dublin Galleries* (London: John Murray, 1921).

2 Letter to Lady Gregory, 9 August 1913. In BERG.

3 For further details, see Elizabeth Butler Cullingford, *Yeats, Ireland and Fascism* (London: Macmillan, 1981), 78–82, and A. N. Jeffares, *A New Commentary on the Poems of W. B. Yeats* (London: Macmillan, 1984), 105–14.

4 See Ellmann, *Yeats*, 207. Yeats enjoyed an embattled status, but we should remember that this was partly his own construction. The *Irish Times*, for example, was 'glad to publish a new poem by Mr W. B. Yeats.... We want a prosperous Ireland, but we must not sacrifice to it the sweeter qualities which have formed the character of our people.... ⟨T⟩oday's meeting of the Corporation may be the really decisive one, and that, if the day is lost, the city will deserve the reproach which Mr Yeats makes against those who have grudged the money and the granting of Sir Hugh Lane's conditions.'

5 The age could quickly shift too. 'No other words ⟨Romantic Ireland's dead and gone⟩ would adequately describe the catastrophe which the Southern Irish people have brought upon their country.' So began an article on 'The Tragedy of Ireland' in the *English Review*, December 1923, 683.

6 Dorothy Shakespear to Pound, 4 September 1913. In *Ezra Pound and Dorothy Shakespear: Their Letters 1909–1914*, ed. Omar Pound and A. Walton Litz (New York: New Directions, 1984), 249.

7 Letter dated 19 December 1913. Address: Coleman's Hatch. See Ezra Pound, *Ezra Pound and the Visual Arts*, ed. with intro. Harriet Zinnes (New York: New Directions, 1980), 273.

8 Pound to Henry Allen Moe, 31 March 1925. In Pound, *Ezra Pound and the Visual Arts*, 296.

9 For further details and discussion, see Humphrey Carpenter, *A Serious Character: The Life of Ezra Pound* (London: Faber and Faber, 1988), 334–5.

10 The first quotation comes from Pound's letter to James Laughlin dated 17 May 1934. See *Ezra Pound and James Laughlin: Selected Letters*, ed. David M. Gordon (New York and London: W. W. Norton, 1994), 31. The second is from Pound's essay 'Status Rerum', *Poetry* (Chicago), vol. 1, January 1913, 123. The third appeared in his review of *Responsibilities* in *Poetry* (Chicago), vol. 4, May 1914, 11.

11 Douglas Goldring, *South Lodge: Reminiscences of Violet Hunt, Ford Madox Ford, and the English Review Circle* (London: Constable, 1943), 49. Goldring does not put a date on this particular evening, but Carpenter assumes it must have been the winter of 1911–12. See Carpenter, *A Serious Character*, 171.

12 See Richard Aldington's review of 'Blast' in the *Egoist*, 15 July 1914.

13 Letter to Olga Rudge dated 20? January 1928. See the Olga Rudge Papers at Yale.

14 Letter to William Rothenstein dated 14 November ⟨1913⟩. In the Houghton Library, Harvard University. In 1914, Pound made

extensive revisions to 'The Two Kings'. See the copy of manuscript corrections to *Responsibilities* in the Ezra Pound Papers at Yale.

15 Lawrence Lipking, *The Life of the Poet: Beginning and Ending Poetic Careers* (Chicago: University of Chicago Press, 1981). According to Lipking, who centres his discussion on *Per Amica Silentia Lunae*, 'A Poet who wishes to grow must learn to read his early work' (15). Pound certainly helped Yeats read his early work, but, as with his reading of Nietzsche in 1902, he was probably quite a long way on that journey of renewal before Pound's entry.

16 James Longenbach, *Stone Cottage: Pound, Yeats, and Modernism* (Oxford: Oxford University Press, 1988), 19–20.

17 See *Ezra Pound and Dorothy Shakespear*, *passim*.

18 From Pound's essay 'On Criticism in General' (1923). Cited in Longenbach, *Stone Cottage*, 57.

19 A fifteen-page holograph draft of this poem, dated 21 October 1912, exists in BERG. Albright dates the poem 1913; Jeffares, in *A New Commentary on the Poems of W. B. Yeats*, 102, suggests it was written before 1913.

20 Yeats to Lady Gregory, 15 January 1914. In BERG. See Richard Aldington, *Life for Life's Sake* (London: Cassell, 1968), 153.

21 See Richard Aldington, 'Presentation to Mr W. S. Blunt' in the *Egoist*, 2 February 1914. Aldington was Assistant Editor at the *Egoist*.

22 'The Lake Isle' first appeared in *Lustra* (1915). See Ezra Pound, *Personae* (London: Faber and Faber, 1952), 128. The manuscript of the poem in the Ezra Pound Papers at Yale is dated 30 April 1915.

23 Letter from Yeats to George Mair. Typed by Pound at Stone Cottage. Original in BERG. Longenbach dates it February 1916. 'The trouble is that Ezra Pound is an American and that his wife though she is English born has never been out of Europe in her life has become an American by marrying him.' Yeats then adds – though the humour and accent are Pound's – 'I have cross questioned the two aliens carefully and they seems ⟨sic⟩ to be generally observing the laws, but cannot give me a coherent account of what the police want.' Cited in Longenbach, *Stone Cottage*, 261.

24 Letter from Bridges to Yeats, 5 February ⟨1916⟩. The letter is reproduced in full in Longenbach, *Stone Cottage*, 262.

25 Invited by Edith Wharton in 1915 to contribute to an illustrated book of original verse and prose 'for the benefit of the American Hostels for refugees' Yeats forwarded 'A Reason for Keeping Silent'. See Edith Wharton (ed.), *The Book of the Homeless* (New York: Charles Scribner's Sons, 1916). Placed in the context of other contributions, Yeats's poem strikes one as pusillanimous. For 'passive suffering', see W. B. Yeats (ed.), *The Oxford Book of Modern Verse, 1892–1935*, xxxiv.

26 Ellmann, *Yeats*, 232. 'An Irish Airman Foresees His Death' is discussed by Ellmann in the 'abstract' context of esoteric Yeatsism. There is almost no other mention of the First World War in Ellmann. Elizabeth Cullingford in *Yeats, Ireland and Fascism* suggests that the delicately balanced situation in Ireland in August 1914 (would England keep faith/Redmond recruiting/the IRB making a 'protest in arms') 'helps to explain Yeats's non-committal attitude towards the war in Europe' (86).

27 Jeffares devotes two sentences to Yeats's response to the war: 'In the autumn of 1914 Yeats wrote to his father about the war; he thought that England was paying the price for having despised intellect. The war, he supposed, would end in a draw with everyone too poor to fight for another hundred years "though not too poor to spend what is left of their substance preparing for it".' A. N. Jeffares, *W. B. Yeats: A New Biography* (London: Hutchinson, 1988), 203.

28 See *Lady Cynthia Asquith Diaries, 1915–18* (London: Hutchinson, 1968), 152. Diary entry of 11 April 1916.

29 See Yeats to Lady Gregory, 30 August 1914, from Royal Societies Club, St James's St S.W. In BERG. When Aldington tried to enlist, he was refused because the authorities thought he might be a spy.

30 From Pound's unpublished poem 'War Verse'. Cited in Longenbach, *Stone Cottage*, 115.

31 Yeats to Lady Gregory, dated Friday ⟨1914?⟩. In BERG. If this letter precedes the one dated 30 August 1914, I think the Friday is Friday, 29 August. At the beginning of the war, Asquith brought Grey and Churchill into his Council of War. In July 1914, Grey and Churchill had suggested a 'British decision' be imposed on the Irish; now after the outbreak of war it would be in keeping for them to suggest the Home Rule issue be put on the back-burner. The war 'enabled Asquith to extricate himself from a hopeless Irish policy'. See Patricia Jalland, *The Liberals and Ireland: The Ulster Question in British Politics to 1914* (Brighton, Sussex: Harvester Press, 1980), 259.

32 See Joseph Lee, *Ireland, 1912–1985: Politics and Society* (Cambridge: Cambridge University Press, 1989), 23.

33 Letter dated 26 August 1914.

34 Letter dated 1 October ⟨1915⟩.

35 TS in possession of Michael Yeats. Cited in Cullingford, *Yeats, Ireland and Fascism*, 87. This must have formed part of the speech made in November 1914 to celebrate the centenary of Thomas Davis, part of which is quoted in Warre B. Wells and N. Marlowe, *A History of the Irish Rebellion of 1916* (Dublin and London: Maunsel, 1916), 73.

36 Report in the *Irish Book Lover*, vol. 6, no. 4, November 1914, 57.

37 Letter of W. B. Yeats to Lady Gregory, 1 December 1915 (*LS* 249–50). See also his letter to Lily, 10 December 1915: 'Please keep it to yourself as it would be very ungracious of me to let it get talked about in Dublin' (*L* 604).

38 Yeats to Lady Gregory, 10 February 1917. In BERG. For histories of the Savile, see A. F. B.

Williams/Sir Herbert Stephen, *The Savile Club, 1868–1923* (London: Privately Printed, 1923), and Garrett Anderson, *Hang Your Halo in the Hall: A History of the Savile Club* (London: Savile Club, 1993). The club was noted for its conversation. Fellow-members of the Club while Yeats was there included: Bridges (elected 1872), Gosse (1876), Kipling (1891), Rothenstein (1908), Orpen (1909), A. N. Whitehead (1911), Beerbohm (1918), Elgar (1919), St John Ervine (1922), and Walter Starkie (elected honorary member in July 1926).

39 Journal entry, 1 December 1916. According to Rothenstein, Yeats 'fretted somewhat that he had not been consulted' over the Rising. See Joseph Hone (ed.), *J. B. Yeats: Letters to His Son W. B. Yeats and Others, 1869–1922, 1865–1939* (London: Faber and Faber, 1944), 300.

40 Gosse to Yeats, 25 August 1915. In the Ezra Pound Papers at Yale.

41 Yeats to George Yeats. Box 77, SUNY Stony Brook. Letter filed ⟨January 1923⟩. Probably late November 1922 (see chapter 7, note 61).

42 See Yeats's letter to Quinn on 16 May 1916. In QUINN.

43 Yeats to Lady Gregory, 17 October 1915. Cited in *Seventy Years: Being the Autobiography of Lady Gregory* (Gerrards Cross: Colin Smythe, 1974), 524. Lady Gregory kept a file on 'Folk-lore of the War'.

44 Journal entry, 28 November 1916.

45 See Yeats to Ricketts, 23 December ⟨1917⟩. In the Bodleian Library, Oxford.

46 Yeats to 'Professor' Birrell, 20 December 1917. Address: Ashdown Forest. Copy of letter in NLI 30134.

47 See Yeats to Florence Farr Emery, 14 October 1914. In BERG.

48 Cited in *The Letters of John Quinn to William Butler Yeats*, ed. Alan Himber (Ann Arbor: UMI Research Press, 1983), 147. By the end of the war, Quinn wanted to see 'all those responsible for the German atrocities, those who ordered them as well as those who executed them, tried, all formalities being observed, and shot'. See letter to W. B. Yeats, 14 November 1918, 196.

49 The phrase 'habitual memories' was used by Yeats in the Preface of an early draft of 'A Reverie over Childhood and Youth'. Copy in the James Augustine Healy Collection, Colby College, Maine.

50 Just before his death at the Somme, the Irish critic and politician Thomas Kettle (1880–1916) wrote: 'The bombardment, destruction, and bloodshed are beyond all imagination, nor did I ever think that the valour of simple men could be quite as beautiful as that of my Dublin Fusiliers.' Cited in Robert Lynd, *Old and New Masters* (London: T. Fisher Unwin, 1919), 205. The Irish soldier-poet Francis Ledwidge (1887–1917) came to recognise the complex fate of an Irishman serving in France after the Easter Rising. In one of his poems 'Soliloquy', he writes: 'It is too late now to retrieve/A fallen dream, too late to grieve/A name unmade, but not too late/To thank the gods for what is great;/A keen-edged sword, a soldier's heart,/Is greater than a poet's art.' In *The Complete Poems of Francis Ledwidge*, intro. Lord Dunsany (London: Herbert Jenkins, 1919), 260. Katharine Tynan produced a collection of poems about the war entitled *The Holy War* (London: Sidgwick and Jackson, 1916). 'Lament' was dedicated to 'The Immortal Tenth ⟨Irish⟩ Division', who suffered huge casualties at Suvla: 'Was it for this we gave to die/All our beautiful, our young/Dear dead darlings, sacrificed? (53).

51 'A Reverie over Childhood and Youth', 57. In the James Augustine Healy Collection, Colby College, Maine.

52 Letter to George Moore, 6 April 1916. In Alan Denson (ed.), *Letters from AE* (London, New York, Toronto: Abelard-Schuman, 1961), 110.

53 For Pound's comment, see Longenbach, *Stone Cottage*, 115. Information for this list has been elicited for the most part from Jeffares, *A New Commentary on the Poems of W. B. Yeats*, and Albright, *W. B. Yeats: The Poems*.

54 See W. K. Rose (ed.), *The Letters of Wyndham Lewis* (London: Methuen, 1963), 69, 90. Letters to Kate Lechmere ⟨summer 1915⟩ and Pound ⟨August 1917⟩. For the reference to 'modernist' art, see Wyndham Lewis, *Blasting & Bombardiering* (1937; rep. London: Calder and Boyars, 1967), 4.

55 Ricketts to Robert Ross, September 1914. Cited in J. G. P. Delaney, *Charles Ricketts: A Biography* (Oxford: Clarendon Press, 1990), 278.

56 See NLI 30791. For the obituary in the *Observer*, see UP 2, 429–31.

57 Yeats to Quinn, received 5 March 1918. In QUINN.

58 In a letter to Pound dated 23 November ⟨1919⟩, Yeats expressed impatience with the fuss of war poetry he had seen. In the Ezra Pound Papers at Yale.

59 Letter from J. B. Yeats to W. B. Yeats, 10 June 1918. For related discussion, see Frank Kermode, *Romantic Image* (London: Routledge and Kegan Paul, 1957), 30–42.

60 Yeats to Siegfried Sassoon, 5 May ⟨1925⟩. In the James Augustine Healy Collection, Colby College, Maine.

61 That Yeats had in mind the 1890s is given further confirmation in *Per Amica Silentia Lunae* (London: Macmillan, 1918), 21–2, when he discusses Johnson and Dowson as eponymous poets: 'Johnson and Dowson, friends of my youth, were dissipated men, the one a drunkard, the other a drunkard and mad about women, and yet they had the gravity of men who had found life out and were awakening from the dream.' The prose passage follows (in both senses) the sequence of the poem, a reversal of Yeats's usual practice of composition.

62 From his speech 'Peace and the Gael' in P. H. Pearse, *Political Writings and Speeches* (Dublin: Talbot, 1952), 216. When Mrs Pearse was asked if her sons Pat and Willie thought

they had a chance of winning, she replied: 'No; they knew they would fail, but as Pat said to me, the fight would save Ireland's soul.' See NLI 30612.

63 In a letter to the *Daily News*, 10 May 1916. Reproduced in Bernard Shaw, *The Matter with Ireland*, ed. David H. Greene and Dan H. Laurence (London: Rupert Hart-Davis, 1962), 112.

64 Letter to Yeats ⟨May 1916⟩.

65 With its specific reference to 'Lord Edward and Wolfe Tone', 'Sixteen Dead Men' can also be seen as a reply to 'September 1913'. Similarly with the theme of sacrifice in 'The Rose Tree'. When he spoke at Wellesley College in May 1920 he made a direct connection between the poems: 'Shortly after I wrote *Riding to Paradise* I began to get old and let reflections and morals get into my work instead of emotion. . . . Age came prematurely, bringing with it, as its first lyric, *September 1913*, a ballad whose stirring patriotism lifts it to the level of the finest of national songs. Its power of stirring patriotism is equalled only by *The Red Rose Free*, a noble tribute to Pierce ⟨sic⟩, the man who died in making Ireland ungovernable, the great idealist of the Irish revolution.' See 'Ireland's Greatest Poet at Wellesley' in Special Collections, Wellesley College. *Riding to Paradise* is presumably 'Running to Paradise', written at Coole in September 1913. *The Red Rose Free* is presumably 'The Rose Tree'.

66 A remark of Yeats's recorded by Lord Dunsany in his journal, 23 April 1924. Yeats and George were staying at Dunsany Castle. See Mark Amory, *Biography of Lord Dunsany* (London: Collins, 1972), 196. By 1924, the remark was more sinister, for as Dunsany noted: 'It is often pathetic to find great minds finding the most ingenious excuses for murder; it makes for tolerance no doubt, but also for insincerity.'

67 William Rothenstein, *Men and Memories: Recollections of William Rothenstein, 1900–1922* (London: Faber and Faber, 1932), 321.

68 See letter to Lady Gregory, 27 April 1916. NLI 30992. Yeats's jibe at Griffith stemmed from Yeats's mistaken assumption that the Rising was led by Sinn Fein. Within a matter of weeks, however, it was being referred to as the Sinn Fein Rebellion. The reference to Starkie is presumably to James Starkey ('Seamus O'Sullivan'), a friend of Griffith's.

69 Yeats to William Rothenstein, 6 May ⟨1916⟩. In the Houghton Library, Harvard University.

70 Yeats to Quinn, 23 May 1916. In QUINN. This part of the letter is omitted by Wade from his edition of *Letters*.

71 Hone agrees with Eglinton that 'Easter 1916' was 'composed within a few weeks of the executions'. See Hone, *W. B. Yeats, 1865–1939*, 300–301. Jeffares believes it was written while staying with Maud Gonne in Normandy in July and August 1916. See Jeffares, *A New Commentary on the Poems of W. B. Yeats*, 190. Albright wisely dates it '11 May–25 September'.

72 *Seventy Years*, 548.

73 J. B. Yeats to Quinn, 27 April 1916. In QUINN. 'When March 1916 ended, Ireland was scarcely touched by anti-British feeling. When May began, a wave of it was in motion, and by June it had swept over the country.' Stephen Gwynn in *The Irish Situation* (London: Jonathan Cape, 1921), 47.

74 J. B. Yeats to Quinn, 4 June 1916. In QUINN.

75 See Shaw's letter to the *Daily News*, 10 May 1916. Reproduced in Shaw, *The Matter with Ireland*, 112.

76 Regarding Macmillan's, see the Editor's Gossip in the August/September 1916 issue of the *Irish Book Lover*. 'Now, I am told, he has finally transferred all his copyright to the great firm of Macmillan, who will henceforth be solely responsible for his future works. I should not be a bit surprised but that when normal conditions return the outcome of this might be an additional bay in the chaplet of our bard, viz, a Globe Edition of Yeats!' (13).

77 Russell to Charles Weekes, 25 May 1916. In Denson (ed.), *Letters from AE*, 111. Russell was editor of *Irish Homestead* at this time, and wrote about the economic causes of the Rising, how there would have been no revolt had Murphy and the employers not been so unmerciful during the 1913 Lock-Out.

78 See Conor Cruise O'Brien, 'Passion and Cunning' in *In Excited Reverie*, 240. As it happened, 'Easter 1916' was eventually published in the *New Statesman* on 23 October 1920, two days before Terence MacSwiney died on hunger strike in Brixton Prison. *Pace* O'Brien, Yeats's sense of timing could not have been better to advance the cause of an independent Ireland.

79 Yeats was staying at 73 St Stephen's Green, which Maud Gonne had bought in March 1918. Maud Gonne herself was in Holloway Prison, following the so-called German Plot, an attempt by the authorities to link Sinn Fein to a treasonable conspiracy with the Germans.

80 'Force Behind the Dublin Revolt' in *Daily Chronicle*, 9 May 1916. Warre B. Wells and N. Marlowe in *A History of the Irish Rebellion of 1916* are more cautious about the link between the Rising and the Revival. They cite Lionel Johnson's 'Ways of War' as an example of the 'writer during the last twenty years who came nearest to expressing Irish patriotic emotion in great verse', but add that it was written by 'an Englishman and a recluse'. In a footnote, they admonish those who have 'sought to connect the Anglo-Irish literary movement with the impulse of the rebellion. In fact the leaders of that movement had in recent years detached themselves altogether from the Nationalist agitation, the utilitarian character of which Mr Yeats was fond of deploring' (70–71). But it is also worth remembering that among the first to be killed in the Rising was Sean Connolly, a member of the Abbey Theatre Company. More intriguing is the link between the 1890s aesthetic movement and the Easter Rising, an observation half-made by Arland Ussher in *Three Great Irishmen: Shaw, Yeats, Joyce* (New York, Mentor, 1957).

Ussher refers to the 1890s' 'Declaration of Independence' and to Yeats as the de Valera who linked that decade with Easter 1916 (90).

81 Letter from Yeats to Clement Shorter, 28 March ⟨1917⟩, cited in Tom Paulin, *Minotaur: Poetry and the Nation State* (London: Faber and Faber, 1992), 38. I think Paulin misreads the penultimate word here. He has 'not', which could only make sense if 'she' were emphasised. In other situations (as over 'Reprisals'), Lady Gregory *did* show herself timid when it came to bad publicity; Yeats was typically more cavalier. To my eye the word is either 'this' or, more likely, 'thus'. The original letter is in BERG. As for the draft of the Rebellion poem, although dated 25 September 1916, this is not the final version as published in 1920. Lines 17–27 in the second verse stanza read: 'That woman at whiles would be shrill/In aimless argument/Had ignorant good will,/And all she got she spent,/Her charity had no bounds:/Sweet-voiced and beautiful/She had ridden well to hounds./This man had managed a school/And our winged mettlesome horse.' Shorter confused 'And' for 'On' in the line 'On our winged horse' – other drafts, such as the first typed copy with Yeats's corrections in his own hand, also have 'And' for the first word in this line. See copy in NLI 30216.

82 Cited in Carpenter, *A Serious Character*, 505. Original in E. Pound, *Jefferson and/or Mussolini* (London: Stanley Nott, 1935), 9.

83 See, for example, the many impassioned essays in Máirín Ní Dhonnchadha and Theo Dorgan (eds), *Revising the Rising* (Derry: Field Day, 1991), and Edna Longley's recent collection of essays, *The Living Stream: Literature and Revisionism in Ireland* (Newcastle: Bloodaxe, 1994).

84 A. G. Stock, *W. B. Yeats: His Poetry and Thought* (1961; repr. Cambridge: Cambridge University Press, 1964), 170.

85 From 'Yeats and the Nobel Prize' in Monk Gibbon (ed.), *The Living Torch A. E.* (London: Macmillan, 1937), 259.

86 'The writers of this book have summoned the great symbolic beings – Olohon, Orthona, Orc, and others – not the imaginations of entranced subjects by merely pronouncing and making them pronounce the words.' See *The Works of William Blake*, vol. 1, ed. Edwin John Ellis and William Butler Yeats (London: Bernard Quaritch, 1893), 327.

87 Janet Framer, *Men and Monuments* (London: Hamish Hamilton, 1957), 52.

88 For a full list of the occupations of prisoners removed from the Richmond Barracks on 30 April 1916 to Knutsford Detention Barracks in England, see John Boyle, *The Irish Rebellion* (London: Constable, 1916), 115–16. It was certainly not a poets' or a shopkeepers' rising.

89 Letter from Yeats to Pound, 15 July ⟨1918⟩. Original in Ezra Pound Papers at Yale. In the same letter Yeats expressed the view that by that stage the war might be over and that Quinn would have to take a risk with *The Dreaming of the Bones*, a play Yeats thought

would meet with American resentment. The play was eventually published in *Little Review* in January 1919.

90 Yeats's phrase must have been on the lips of the Anglo-Irish at the time. When Lady Beatrice Glenavy was in a War Depot in Surrey during the last six months of the war, she was forced to listen to fellow workers berating the Irish for their opposition to conscription and the 'stab in the back' of Easter 1916. 'I stood up and made the only speech I ever made in my life. I said, "The Irish people are only doing what you English would do if you had been conquered by Germany."' See her *Today We Will Only Gossip* (London: Constable, 1964), 109.

91 See NLI 30758, page 1.

92 Ellmann, *Yeats*, 222.

93 Allan Wade to George Yeats, 27 February 1952. Box 118, SUNY Stony Brook.

94 'I did not meet WBY until May 1911 but knew EP. quite well from 1910 & my recollection is that he was seeing a good deal of WB.' George Yeats to Allan Wade, 24 November 1953. Cited by Ann Saddlemyer in her essay 'George, Ezra, Dorothy and Friends: Twenty-Six Letters, 1918–59' in *Yeats Annual*, no. 7, ed. Warwick Gould (London: Macmillan, 1990), 4.

95 On 2 December 1911, Dorothy Shakespear informed Pound: '☐comes to Dante ⟨Yeats⟩ on Thursday, after all.' In their letters George is identified by a ☐. *Ezra Pound and Dorothy Shakespear*, 80. (It would be interesting to know what 'after all' means.)

96 Cited in *Olivia Shakespear and W. B. Yeats*, 157–8. The mutual friend is presumably Olivia Shakespear. Grace Jaffe has suggested that her aunt Nelly Tucker may herself have had a flirtatious relationship with Yeats. See her reminiscences 'Vignettes', in *Yeats Annual*, no. 5, 144.

97 *Olivia Shakespear and W. B. Yeats*, 158. Letter dated 9 October. Original in BERG.

98 Yeats's letter is undated but was written on a 'Monday' from Woburn Buildings: copy in QUINN. Lily's letter: copy in QUINN. The use of 'comely' to describe George can be compared with Dorothy Shakespear's description of George in a letter to Pound on 14 September 1911: 'Georgie's face *is* square: but she is very handsome, I think, as well. She is awfully intelligent, & I believe admires yr. poems – what more can be said? Alarmingly intuitive at 18. There is no one I am likely to tell about your rhythmic triumphs.' *Ezra Pound and Dorothy Shakespear*, 58. Dorothy and George enjoyed each other's company. They had common interests (country walks, painting, holidays together) and were free spirits in conventional surroundings. In April and May 1913 they visited Rome together and had hoped that Ezra would accompany them. Letter dated 9 February 1913.

99 Copy in QUINN.

100 Yeats had several relationships, not all of which have been fully documented. While he was at Coole in June 1913, Yeats received a

telegram from Mabel Dickinson, saying she was pregnant: '⟨T⟩he experience alarmed not only Yeats but Lady Gregory, who thought marriage was the answer lest some similar crisis disturb the poet's peace in the future.' Jeffares, *W. B. Yeats: A New Biography*, 195. According to Hone, *W. B. Yeats: 1865–1939*, Lady Gregory 'set her mind on match-making. . . . During one summer of the war . . . she drove down several times to Stone Cottage, each time accompanied by a different young lady with means and looks; with one of these charmers he was often seen in London.' See 301–2. All this is curious, not least because Yeats was not at Stone Cottage in the summers. We should also remember that Yeats destroyed perhaps three quarters of his letters to Olivia Shakespear (who was still known by her pseudonym, 'Diana Vernon', when Jeffares published *W. B. Yeats: Man and Poet* in 1949). On a separate point, Yeats's financial status was not raised by Mrs Tucker. If it had been, Yeats, already in receipt of £150 per annum for his Civil List Pension, could have produced a reasonable defence: his earnings between 1913 and 1917 only once fell below £500. See NLI 30398. This was in contrast to Henry Hope Shakespear when he learned of Pound's proposal of marriage to his daughter Dorothy. See Henry Shakespear's letter to Ezra's father, Homer Pound, on 28 November 1911. In Ezra Pound Papers Family Correspondence, YCAL Mss 43, Box 53, at Yale. A year later, on 13 September 1912, Olivia Shakespear wrote to Pound with the same message: 'She has never mentioned you to me, & I don't know if she still considers herself engaged to you – but as she obviously can't marry you, she must be made ⟨to⟩ realise that she can't go on as though you were her accepted lover – it's hardly *decent*! . . . You ought to go away – Englishmen don't understand yr American ways, & any man who wanted to marry her wd be put off by the fact of yr friendship (or whatever you call it) with her. If you had £500 a year I should be delighted for *you* to marry her (no nonsense about waiting 5 years etc.) but as you haven't, I'm obliged to say all this.' *Ezra Pound and Dorothy Shakespear*, 153–4.

101   As early as August 1913, there is a reference in a letter from Pound to Dorothy Shakespear about Yeats's attention to Iseult. See *Ezra Pound and Dorothy Shakespear*, 238.

102   Jeffares, *W. B. Yeats: A New Biography*, 218.

103   Letter from Yeats to Lady Gregory, 9 March 1917 in NLI MS 30992. What the difference was with Olivia Shakespear is not gone into. Was he anxious about bringing a bride into Woburn Buildings, the scene of his illicit affair with Olivia Shakespear in 1896 and 1897? Did Olivia express her opposition to Yeats's alliance with Iseult? The logic is intriguing and difficult to follow. At the beginning of 1935, George, in seeking to field scholarly questions from a person called 'Edwards', searched in vain for the date of Yeats's move to Woburn Buildings. She was very tempted to open the

contents of his private memoirs to ascertain when he first took up residence at Woburn Buildings, but eventually managed to identify the date from his bundle of 1897–8 letters to Lady Gregory. She reassured Yeats that she had not opened other correspondence. Box 119, SUNY Stony Brook. Letter dated 1 January 1935.

104   NLI MS 30992. It is also worth recalling here that on 11 May 1917 Yeats completed the Prologue to *Per Amica Silentia Lunae*, addressed to 'Maurice', his name for Iseult.

105   Letter to Lady Gregory dated 13 July 1917. In BERG.

106   In a letter to Lady Gregory dated 14 August 1917, Yeats wrote that Iseult had been raised by Maud Gonne is such a strange fashion that she is indifferent to what other girls find shocking. In August the same year, Yeats and George rescued Iseult from the tyrannising behaviour of a young woman where she was lodging. Iseult was frightened by everyone around her, including the young woman, Pound, Yeats himself. George, pleased to be able to express her antipathy to Chelsea, got the furniture van and seized the furniture. In BERG.

107   *Olivia Shakespear and W. B. Yeats*, 156.

108   See Yeats to Lady Gregory, 13 October 1917. Original in BERG.

109   This letter, dated 29 October 1917, was addressed to Lady Gregory. The two poems were later subsumed under the single title 'Owen Aherne and his Dancers' (*VP* 451–2), two lines of which refer directly to George: 'I did not find in any cage the woman at my side./ O but her heart would break to learn my thoughts are far away.' The reference to living all through this before seems to be an allusion to the parallel emotional triangle of 1896–7. At that time, Yeats's affair with Olivia Shakespear came to an end with the reappearance of Maud Gonne. In 1917 it looked as if something similar would await George when she realised that Iseult continued to hold sway over his feelings. For further discussion, see *Olivia Shakespear and W. B. Yeats*, 160ff. *The Only Jealousy of Emer*, one of Yeats's *Plays for Dancers*, was completed in the wake of his marriage, and reflects a continuing obsession with this emotional triangle.

110   Yeats had championed Tagore in the years preceding the war and come to see in him a reflection of his own position within the British Empire: when the War ended, Yeats thought England would adopt a different attitude towards India, whether for good or ill he could not say, but she would recognise that India possessed its own public life. Letter from Yeats to William Rothenstein. Letter no. 28, n.d., from Stone Cottage. Original in the Houghton Library, Harvard University.

111   See Elizabeth Butler Cullingford, *Gender and History in Yeats's Love Poetry* (Cambridge: Cambridge University Press, 1993), 106.

112   Middleton Murry's review appeared in the *Athenæum*, 4 April 1919.

7 Yeats in the 1920s

1 Their original intention was to winter in Oxford, as a letter from George to Miss Bates of 12 May 1920 suggests. They were always in Oxford at 4 Broad St from 1 October to 1 May. Original at Wellesley College.

2 Session on 30 January 1918.

3 Yeats to Quinn, 14 June ⟨1919⟩. In QUINN.

4 George Yeats to Lollie Yeats, 7 February 1918. Box 118, SUNY Stony Brook.

5 For details of their relationship, see George Mills Harper, 'William Force Stead's Friendship with Yeats and Eliot' in *Massachusetts Review*, vol. 21, no. 1, Spring 1980, 9–38.

6 L. A. G. Strong, *Green Memory* (London: Methuen, 1961), 237.

7 NLI MS 30133.

8 Yeats to Quinn, 3 March 1921. In QUINN.

9 Richard Aldington, *Life for Life's Sake* (London: Weidenfeld and Nicolson, 1968), 187.

10 Hugh Kenner persuasively argues in 'The Sacred Book of the Arts' (1955) that Yeats's volumes do not reflect their compositional history, that Yeats 'didn't accumulate poems, he wrote books', where one poem lights up another. In John Unterecker (ed.), *Yeats: A Collection of Critical Essays* (Englewood Cliffs, New Jersey: Prentice Hall, 1963), 10–22.

11 For information on Horton, see George Mills Harper, *W. B. Yeats and W. T. Horton: The Record of an Occult Friendship* (Atlantic Highlands, New Jersey: Humanities Press, 1980). At their automatic writing session on 24 May 1919, they were told to leave a chair for Horton (72). Harper maintains that 'According to Yeats's account, Horton was one of two people directly responsible for the development of the System in *A Vision*.' A Control had indicated a link between Lady Littleton's script and a 'scrap of paper by Horton concerning chariot with black & white horses'. The Control indicated that 'Yeats is a prince with an evil counsellor', while Horton had warned Yeats about the dark horse driving his chariot into the enemy's camp. Black and white winged horses feature again in one of the earliest automatic writing sessions (and again in a Sleep on 11 January 1921). Yeats was so impressed by the original cross-correspondence that, according to Harper and Hood, 'Horton's prophetic warning is central to *A Vision*' (*AV [A]* xvi).

12 Moina MacGregor Mathers was less impressed and in January 1924 complained bitterly of Yeats's portrait of her husband in *The Trembling of the Veil* (1922): 'Now I will quote a few of your words – "*he was to die of melancholia*" – what can you know of the manner of his death?' In *Letters to W. B. Yeats*, ed. Richard Finneran, George Mills Harper and William M. Murphy, vol. 2, 447.

13 From a rejected version of the dedication 'To Vestigia' intended for *A Vision*. Cited in George Mills Harper, *Yeats's Golden Dawn* (London: Macmillan, 1974), 132. 'Vestigia' was Moina Mathers's motto in the Golden Dawn.

14 George reportedly told Ellmann about Yeats's ignorance of menstruation. See Richard Ellmann, *along the riverrun: Selected Essays* (Harmondsworth: Penguin, 1989), 240.

15 Lollie Yeats to John Butler Yeats, 13 March 1918. Cited in Gifford Lewis, *The Yeats Sisters and the Cuala* (Blackrock, Co. Dublin: Irish Academic Press, 1994), 143.

16 Yeats to Quinn, 14 June ⟨1919?⟩. In QUINN. In 2000 AD Anne would be in her eighty-first year.

17 Yeats to Quinn, 30 October 1920. Written in Oxford. In QUINN.

18 See Yeats to George Yeats, 29 November 1922. Address: the Savile Club. Box 77, SUNY Stony Brook.

19 George Yeats to Yeats, 23 August ⟨1924⟩. Address: 82 Merrion Square, Dublin. Box 118, SUNY Stony Brook.

20 Yeats to George Yeats, 3 October ⟨1924?⟩. Box 77, SUNY Stony Brook.

21 Yeats to George Yeats, Monday, ⟨April 1924⟩. Box 77, SUNY Stony Brook. The Club is probably the Arts Club, Upper Merrion Street, Dublin.

22 Yeats to George Yeats, Wednesday ⟨?⟩, 42 Fitzwilliam Square (moved here in July 1928). Box 77, SUNY Stony Brook. I have not come across the poem in question. In another letter from the Savile Club, dated 29 November 1922, Yeats informs George he has received a letter from her mother: 'It seems I have given you "a great and splendid life" – as if I only had.' Box 77, SUNY Stony Brook. George was also conscious of Yeats thinking her neglected. 'Please do not think that I am "feeling neglected" – your own phrase!' 26 October ⟨1931⟩. Cited in *Omnium Gatherum*, 285.

23 For a patronising view of George by one of Yeats's aunts, see George Yeats to McGreevy, July ⟨1926?⟩. Original in the George Yeats Correspondence with Thomas McGreevy in TCD. MS 8104/40.

24 George expressed her sympathy with Iseult, whose marriage to Francis Stuart had proved unhappy. Perhaps with hindsight, she added that no settlement entered into after marriage could be satisfactory. George Yeats to Yeats, July 1920. Box 118, SUNY Stony Brook.

25 George Yeats to Yeats, 4 August 1920. Box 118, SUNY Stony Brook.

26 George Yeats to Yeats, 6 August 1920. Box 118, SUNY Stony Brook. Iseult was living at Glenmalure at this time. George and Yeats were trying to keep secret the state of Iseult's marriage. For details, see Geoffrey Elborn, *Francis Stuart: A Life* (Dublin: Raven Arts Press, 1990), 39–45.

27 George Yeats to Pound, 20 February 1927. Cited by Ann Saddlemyer in her essay 'George, Ezra, Dorothy and Friends: Twenty-Six Letters, 1918–59' in *Yeats Annual*, no. 7, 9–10.

28 8 September 1927. In ibid., 10. Yeats's poem 'Blood and Moon' was written in August 1927. Yeats was anxious not to lose money

from American copyright on his work. On 7 May 1926, he told Marianne Moore at the *Dial* that by an arrangement undertaken some years previously, her magazine had American rights to his work. See YCAL MS 34, Box 8 at Yale.

29 George Yeats to McGreevy, 31 December 1925. Cited in Ann Saddlemyer, 'George Hyde-Lees: More Than a Poet's Wife' in Jeffares (ed.), *Yeats the European*, 192.

30 15 March 1926. TCD MS 8104/36. Cited by Ann Saddlemyer in a lecture at the MLA in 1991. George was especially critical of chauvinistic nationalism, whether English or Irish. She thought patriotism would destroy England in the near future. In spite of winning the last war, England had emerged much the worse, with high unemployment, hated by everyone else, and a royal family preoccupied with their own philistine diversions. Patriotism was therefore being used to explain this state of affairs to the English and to conceal things from the rest of the world. She cautioned McGreevy against living in England; his lyrical description of the English Arnoldian countryside was unappealing to her, but neither did she take to the West of Ireland, with its bleak landscape and ghosts. George Yeats to McGreevy, 26 July 1926. Address: Ballylee. TCD MS 8104/42.

31 Tom McGreevy to George Yeats, 10 June 1926. NLI MS 30859. George accused McGreevy of being hostile to the Anglo-Irish, to which he replied: 'I do think their work is done, and I think they are getting patriotic in the bad sense – Lennox's play ⟨Lennox Robinson's *Big House*⟩ is one of the signs – but I am not animossy.' Letter dated 16 August 1926.

32 Report in the *Boston Evening Transcript*, 29 September 1911.

33 In 1921, Yeats still intended living in Cork. See Yeats's letter to Quinn, 3 March 1921. In QUINN.

34 Pound to Quinn, 1 June 1920. Cited in B. L. Reid, *The Man from New York: John Quinn and His Friends* (New York: Oxford University Press, 1968), 419. According to Anne Yeats, 'The floods could nearly always be counted on. . . . Then she'd come down, sweep out the worms and things and then he'd come down and life would resume as usual. . . . Mother and father lived in the Tower and we lived in the cottages.' See John Unterecker, 'An Interview with Anne Yeats' in *Shenandoah*, vol. 16, no. 4, Summer 1965, 7–20.

35 Writing to Quinn on 30 May 1921, Yeats revealed his disappointment at not going to Ballylee, but he had been advised against it by Lady Gregory. In QUINN.

36 Yeats to William Force Stead, 7 April ⟨n.y.⟩. Address: Ballylee. The year is possibly 1922. Original in the Osborn Stead Collection at Yale.

37 Yeats to Quinn, 19 October 1922. In QUINN.

38 Yeats to George Yeats, 1 May ⟨1923⟩. Box 77, SUNY Stony Brook.

39 See Yeats to George Yeats, Wednesday, ⟨April 1924⟩. Box 77, SUNY Stony Brook.

40 See Yeats to George Yeats, 8 May ⟨1924⟩. Box 77, SUNY Stony Brook.

41 Lady Gregory in her journal, 5 November 1920.

42 Yeats to Lady Gregory, 26 November ⟨1920⟩. In BERG.

43 Journal entry, 28 November 1920.

44 Laurence Housman, *The Unexpected Years* (London: Jonathan Cape, 1937), 320. Housman thinks he learnt the phrase from Yeats.

45 Sean O'Faolain, *Vive Moi!: An Autobiography*, ed. Julia O'Faolain (London: Sinclair-Stevenson, 1993), 145.

46 Speech at Oxford Union, 17 February 1920. Reported in the *Oxford Chronicle*, 18 February 1920. Cited in A. N. Jeffares, *W. B. Yeats: Man and Poet* (London: Routledge, 1962), 328.

47 A. N. Jeffares in *A New Commentary on the Poems of W. B. Yeats* (London: Macmillan, 1975) states that this poem was written in 1919 (229). The date inserted at the end of this poem is '1919', but as Yeats indicated in a letter to Olivia Shakespear in April 1921, he was 'writing a series of poems ("thoughts suggested by the present state of the world" or some such name)' (*L* 668). Albright thinks Yeats's retitling and redating the poem 'may reflect Yeats's sense of the importance of 1919, the year in which Ireland's war of independence took on a new ferocity' (Albright (ed.), *W. B. Yeats: The Poems*, London: J. M. Dent, 1994, 651). There must be another reason for Yeats's decision, for the new ferocity came in May 1920 when the Black and Tans were introduced into Ireland. In another rare error, Albright wrongly dates the start of the Civil War as December 1921 (651). The Anglo-Irish Treaty was signed in December 1921, but the Civil War did not start in earnest until June 1922. It is difficult to see Yeats moving to Dublin in March 1922 if he thought he would be in the middle of a Civil War. As he remarked in a letter to Olivia Shakespear in March 1922, 'No I am not alarmed about Ireland nor are my correspondents there though I expect a few months' more trouble. . . . De Valera is losing' (*L* 679).

48 Yeats to Lady Gregory, 2 April 1921. In BERG.

49 Yeats to George Yeats, 10 November 1921. Box 77, SUNY Stony Brook.

50 Yeats to William Rothenstein, Sunday, 2 November ⟨n.y.⟩. Address: the Savile Club. The new annual fee was £212. Original in the Houghton Library, Harvard University.

51 Letter dated 15 August ⟨1922⟩.

52 Letter dated 23 May 1927.

53 Letter dated 16 November 1927.

54 Letter dated 21 September 1927.

55 Denis Donoghue, *Yeats* (London: Fontana/Collins, 1971), 87.

56 See Yeats to William Force Stead, 4 October ⟨n.y.⟩. Sent from 82 Merrion Square. Original in the Osborn Stead Collection at Yale.

57 In her letter dated 23 November 1922, George told Yeats she was forwarding two clean shirts

to Garsington, and the remainder of his wash to the Savile Club. In the letter she wrote the following day, after her signature she asked him to convey her love to Ottoline. Yeats was at the Savile by the end of November, for it was there that he had his altercation with Gosse over Joyce's *Ulysses*.

58 George Yeats to Yeats, 23 November 1922. Address: 82 Merrion Square. Box 118, SUNY Stony Brook. Yeats woke up at the Savile Club to the sound of two volleys and immediately thought that Childers was dead. See George Yeats's letter to Yeats, 24 November 1931. Box 119, SUNY Stony Brook.

59 George Yeats to Yeats, 24 November 1922. Box 118, SUNY Stony Brook.

60 In an undated letter to Yeats written in 1930, George Yeats referred to getting down to her most English sub-soil after enduring four-and-a-half hours of a visitor's talk. See Box 119, SUNY Stony Brook. McGreevy thought George Yeats had a 'sound anti-Gaelic instinct'. See his letter to George Yeats, 7 January 1925. NLI 30859.

61 George Yeats to Yeats, 28 November 1922. Box 118, SUNY Stony Brook. For a different reading of these events, see Margaret Ward, *Maud Gonne: Ireland's Joan of Arc* (London: Pandora, 1990), 123ff. Helena Moloney was a leading member of the Irish Women Workers' Union; Charlotte Despard, sister of Lord French, Viceroy of Ireland from 1918 to 1921, was founder of the Women's Freedom League and became interested in Irish affairs after staying with Maud Gonne in January 1921. In the postscript to his letter to George the day he received this (presumably 29 or 30 November), Yeats told her to stay indoors in the evening until the crisis abated. He was alarmed by reports in the newspapers and would be relieved when 6 December was over. Box 77, SUNY Stony Brook. This letter is dated simply 'Saturday' and wrongly identified as ⟨January 1923⟩. On 6 December the Irish Free State officially came into existence when the members of the Dáil met for the first time and took the Oath of Allegiance. Republican deputies boycotted the ceremony. Hence Yeats's fears. The date of the letter is I think Saturday, 25 November. In his postscript he refers to receiving George's letter about Maud Gonne and her slander. He might have begun his letter on Saturday and finished it after receiving George's letter written on the 28th. As for George's membership of the Dublin Drama League, little has been written about this. Through her involvement with drama (and through her mixing in republican circles that were under the watchful eye of Dublin Castle), George was (presumably) intent on establishing a degree of independence of her husband. A letter to Yeats on 2 May 1930 about recent Abbey audiences suggests her own distaste for bourgeois theatre, women with diamonds in their hair, white lace caps, and lorgnettes, all having a grand evening. Box 119, SUNY Stony Brook.

62 On 3 December Yeats wrote to George from the Savile Club in London. He told her about the lunch he had just had with Eliot and how he had agreed to contribute an essay on Dante's designs for the *Criterion*. They would have to start reading Dante in the evenings, ensuring that each design as they came to it was displayed on a chair. He found Eliot charming and discovered he quite liked *The Sacred Wood*. Box 77, SUNY Stony Brook. The letter to Dulac on page 693 in Wade's *Letters* (1 December 1922) must be wrongly dated, for I think I am correct in saying that Yeats was in London on 1 December 1922. He dined with Eliot and Dulac on 3 December, and the letter seems to refer to this occasion. The reference to having spoken in the Senate is further proof, for the Senate was not convened until 9 December. Yeats was sworn in on 11 December 1922, and on 12 December 1922 he made his first speech, in support of Lord Glenavy's nomination to chair the Senate.

63 See letter from George to Yeats, 1 December 1922. Box 118, SUNY Stony Brook. George expressed the hope that he would be home in ten days' time.

64 See Hone, *W. B. Yeats: 1865–1939*, 350. Gogarty also played a part in Yeats's nomination.

65 Yeats to George Yeats, 5 January 1923. Box 77, SUNY Stony Brook. The Earl of Granard was a fellow Senator. Southborough was in 1917 elected Secretary to the Irish Convention; in 1919, he offered to act as intermediary between Sinn Fein and the British Government. For more details, see Bernard G. Krimm, *W. B. Yeats and the Emergence of the Irish Free State, 1918–1939: Living in the Explosion* (Troy, New York: Whitston, 1981), 68–9. Krimm cites a letter from Yeats to Granard dated February 1923 as evidence of Yeats's involvement in talks, but this letter to George, which he does not cite, pre-dates that by a month. Yeats spoke again in the Senate on 10 and 24 January, but was at the Savile again some time before 3 February 1923. The letter dated 5 January 1923 in Wade's *Letters* is slightly puzzling, since it carries Yeats's address in Dublin. On 10 February 1923, Yeats sent George another letter from the Savile Club, this time optimistic both about retrieving the Lane pictures and about the progress of the negotiations. Box 77, SUNY Stony Brook.

66 The review of Hone's biography in *Time* on 8 February 1943 expressed a common view of Yeats: 'The Postwar brought Yeats honors: membership in the first Senate of the Irish Free State; and the Nobel Prize. As a Senator Yeats shunned the politterateurs for the men of practical affairs. He was proud of two bullet holes in his window which were a by-product of civil war. . . .' In Hone's biography the letter to Bridges in which he refers to the two bullet holes ('Life here is interesting, but restless and unsafe') is wrongly dated 27 January 1923 – it is given as 4 January by Wade and in Finneran (ed.), *The Correspondence of Robert Bridges*

and W. B. Yeats (London: Macmillan, 1977), 48–9.

67 See Joseph Hone (ed.), *J. B. Yeats: Letters to His Son W. B. Yeats and Others 1865–1939* (London: Faber and Faber, 1944), 351. In an undated letter to McGreevy in 1923, George Yeats comments on Russell's possible nomination. The previous evening she had heard that Russell had refused to give a formal reply to the offer before consulting his wife. Russell, she thought, lacked moral courage. Original in the George Yeats Correspondence with Thomas McGreevy in TCD. The assassination of a Dáil Deputy on 7 December 1922 provoked the summary reprisal execution of four anti-Treaty prisoners, including Rory O'Connor and Liam Mellowes. No more Dáil deputies were murdered, but relatives of Treaty supporters were targeted, including Cosgrave's uncle and the father of O'Higgins. See Joseph Lee, *Ireland, 1912–1985* (Cambridge: Cambridge University Press, 1991), 66–7. The night before the Senate convened, however, Republicans carried out several incendiary raids, adding 'a new terror to the dangers which threaten the members of the Dáil and Senate'. See *New York Times*, 12 December 1922.

68 See Hone, *W. B. Yeats: 1865–1939*, 351. Plunkett had been appointed Senator along with Yeats. Lady Fingall played host to the bachelor Plunkett. See Margaret Digby, *Horace Plunkett: An Anglo-American Irishman* (Oxford: Basil Blackwell, 1949), 156.

69 For a graphic account, see Ulick O'Connor, *Oliver St John Gogarty: A Poet and His Times* (London: Jonathan Cape, 1964), 194ff. O'Connor gets the date wrong.

70 On 8 February 1923 Yeats spoke again in the Senate.

71 George's revealing letter of 1 February 1923 can be found in Box 118, SUNY Stony Brook. In letters to friends, as for example to Rothenstein on 23 November ⟨1923⟩, Yeats acknowledged the Prize was also for the Free State. People in Ireland were grateful for his winning them recognition and, consequently, Yeats felt good about life. Original in the Houghton Library, Harvard University.

72 Yeats to Quinn, 3 November 1923. In the Rare Books and Manuscripts Division, New York Public Library.

73 29 January 1924. In ibid.

74 Yeats to George Yeats, 27 July ⟨1924⟩. Box 77, SUNY Stony Brook.

75 Journal entry, 15 August 1928.

76 See Yeats's letter to George Yeats, 24 May 1923. Box 77, SUNY Stony Brook.

77 'Debate on Divorce' in *The Senate Speeches of W. B. Yeats*, ed. Donald R. Pearce (London: Faber and Faber, 1961), 99.

78 Pound to Olga Rudge, 4 November ⟨1928⟩. Original in the Olga Rudge Papers at Yale. In September 1928 Yeats contributed articles to the *Irish Statesman* and the *Spectator* on 'The Censorship and St Thomas Aquinas' and 'Irish Censorship'.

79 *Life and Letters* (Manchester), November 1923, 72.

80 *The Senate Speeches of W. B. Yeats*, 111.

81 Ibid., 168.

82 George Yeats to McGreevy, 26 March 1926. Letter cited by Ann Saddlemyer in a lecture at the MLA conference in December 1991.

83 Alex Aronson, 'Tagore's Educational Ideals' in Mary Lago and Ronald Warwick (eds), *Rabindranath Tagore: Perspectives in Time* (London: Macmillan, 1989), 87. Tagore makes a point also made by Yeats in his poem: 'The object of education is to give man the unity of truth.' *Personality* (London: Macmillan, 1917), 126.

84 For a different but related reading of 'Yeats's most Utopian poem', see Elizabeth Butler Cullingford, *Gender and History in Yeats's Love Poetry* (Cambridge: Cambridge University Press, 1993), 185–202.

85 In the Third Tractate on Dialectic, Plotinus asserts that 'Dialectic . . . has no knowledge of propositions – collections of words – but it knows the truth and, in that knowledge, knows what the schools call their propositions: it knows above all, the operation of the soul, and, by virtue of this knowing, it knows, too, what is affirmed and what is denied.' *Plotinus: The Ethical Treatises*, vol. 1, tr. Stephen Mackenna (London: Philip Lee Warner, 1917), 54. In June 1926, he composed 'Among School Children'; on 27 May, he recommended Sturge Moore read Mackenna's *Plotinus* (*Y & TSM* 93). Plotinus, Doughty's *Arabia*, some bad detective novels, and a French play were the only books he had with him at Ballylee in June 1926.

86 George Yeats wanted him to leave the Senate after the Education Bill was passed and return to writing verse. With the death of her great-aunt she hoped to get a share of her father's money. She thought he was no longer effective and she was worried about his health. He had discussed the matter with Lady Gregory who told him he ought to stay to keep a worse man out. George was surprised at how McGreevy's enlightened country viewed poets, adding her delightful series of dots to express her mixture of humour, irony, and exasperation. Cited by Ann Saddlemyer in Jeffares (ed.), *Yeats the European*, 192.

87 George Yeats to McGreevy, 15 March 1928. Original in the George Yeats Correspondence with Thomas McGreevy in TCD. MS 8104/57.

88 The reference to his book of books is in a letter by Yeats to T. Werner Laurie, 29 July ⟨1924⟩. Original at Colby College, Maine.

89 Douglas Goldring was less impressed by Yeats's ruses. When renting Woburn Buildings in 1919 he read a treatise on the mystical significance of the phases of the moon which had been published in the United States and which was among Yeats's books: 'Some months later, while on a visit to Dublin, my mother-in-law, Ellie Duncan – a life-long friend of Yeats – gave a party at 16 Ely Place to enable the poet to deliver an informal lecture to such of the *intelligentsia* as cared to attend. The subject, to

my surprise, was the influence on character of the phases of the moon. I listened spellbound while Yeats explained to his audience that the teaching he was about to expound to them had been revealed to him "in a dream" by a Moorish initiate with whom he had made contact on the astral plane. His listeners, mostly elderly women, stared at him goggle-eyed when he made this rather startling opening statement.' Douglas Goldring, *The Nineteen Twenties: A General Survey and Some Personal Memories* (London: Nicholson and Watson, 1945), 118.

90 '"Vision, or imagination", writes Blake, "is a representation of what actually exists, really and unchangeably. Fable, or allegory, is formed by the daughters of memory." A vision is, that is to say, a perception of the eternal symbols, about which the world is formed, while allegory is a memory of some natural event into which we read a spiritual meaning.' *The Works of William Blake*, vol. 1, ed. Edwin John Ellis and William Butler Yeats (London: Bernard Quaritch, 1893), 307.

91 According to Northrop Frye, the key to Yeats's thought lies not in *A Vision* but in his poetry: what such poems as 'News for the Delphic Oracle' and 'Byzantium' reveal is that the image is a product of the imagination and that 'the process of redemption is to be finally understood as an identification with Man and a detachment from the cyclical image he has created'. See his essay 'The Rising of the Moon: A Study of *A Vision*' in D. Donoghue and J. R. Mulryne (eds), *An Honoured Guest: New Essays on W. B. Yeats* (London: Arnold, 1965), 32. The relation between Yeats's poetry and *A Vision* is handled differently by different critics. For a survey, see my *W. B. Yeats: A Guide through the Critical Maze* (Bristol: Bristol Classical Press, 1989), 83–95.

92 For a slightly different reading of Yeats's view of history see Thomas Whitaker, *Swan and Shadow: Yeats's Dialogue with History* (Chapel Hill: University of North Carolina Press, 1964). Whitaker argues that if taken literally or finally 'Dove or Swan' is deterministic, but from inside history it is a romantic, subjective vision dramatising Yeats's 'central belief that acceptance of history is at one with freedom and creativity' (95). In *Blake and Yeats: The Contrary Vision* (1955; repr. New York: Russell and Russell, 1968), Hazard Adams claims that, in contrast to Yeats, the wheel and gyre in Blake represent progression, that Yeats focuses on frustrations, Blake on possibilities, etc. In a later chapter on *A Vision*, Adams argues that Yeats did not transcend 'the problem of duality but he had symbolised the problem and organised his experience in symbolical form' (177).

93 Letter dated 16 April 1930. It was Moore's criticism that prompted Yeats to write 'Byzantium'.

94 MS of 'Introduction to The Great Wheel', NLI MS 30758 (p. 20). MS dated 23 November 1928. In the published version the final sentence reads: 'They have helped me to hold

in a single thought reality and justice' (*AV [B]* 25).

95 Letter dated 21 October 1924.

96 William Blake, 'Annotation to Sir Joshua Reynolds's Discourses' in *The Complete Writings of William Blake*, ed. Geoffrey Keynes (London: Oxford University Press, 1966), 477.

97 See Yeats to George Yeats, 3 February 1923. Box 77, SUNY Stony Brook.

98 Stephen Gwynn, *Ireland* (London: Ernest Benn, 1924), 118–20.

99 Sean O'Faolain, *Vive Moi!: An Autobiography* (London: Sinclair-Stevenson, 1993), 175.

100 Francis Stuart, *Things To Live For: Notes for an Autobiography* (London: Jonathan Cape, 1934), 42–3. Stuart had taken the republican side in the Civil War and was imprisoned. But his Yeatsian rebelliousness continued: 'Once Dublin was a city full of adventure and romance. . . . I walk through those streets that I once fought to defend, feeling a little like a stranger. And it was this spirit of smugness and deadness that we fought against and were defeated by. The spirit of liberal democracy. We fought to stop Ireland falling into the hands of publicans and shop-keepers' (253–4).

101 Peadar O'Donnell, *The Gates Flew Open* (1932; repr. Cork: Mercier Press, 1965), 36.

102 See her letter to MacGreevy, 8 June 1928, in the George Yeats Correspondence with Thomas McGreevy in TCD. MS 8104/60.

103 Letter dated 14 March 1926.

104 Letter dated 16 January ⟨1926⟩.

105 Letter dated 12 March 1926.

106 Ibid.

107 Transcripts of Yeats's notes are provided in Edward O'Shea, *A Descriptive Catalog of W. B. Yeats's Library* (New York and London: Garland, 1985). His transcription of this particular passage is slightly different from mine. His first sentence reads: 'A state of existence which all confines. This nature. . . .'

108 O'Shea has several different readings: (1) 'What are to an "observer" side by side in space are to another one after-existences in time.' (2) '(time equals sensitivity of mind)'. (3) 'The idea of this book and all books of the school is that thought, they say events, are neutral. . . .' (4) 'Event, radiation, stuff, name all material being.' See O'Shea, *A Descriptive Catalog of W. B. Yeats's Library*, 232.

109 Olivia Shakespear to Yeats, 14 February 1926, in *Letters to W. B. Yeats*, vol. 2, 467–8. The reference to his sending her novels by (presumably) Frank Harris provides further insight into how Yeats obtained his sexual pleasures.

8 *Yeats in the 1930s*

1 George Yeats to Dorothy Pound, 2 February 1928. See Ann Saddlemyer, 'George, Ezra, Dorothy and Friends: Twenty-Six Letters, 1918–59' in *Yeats Annual*, no. 7, 13.

2 Pound to Olga Rudge, 19 February ⟨1928⟩. Original in the Olga Rudge Papers at Yale.

3 21 or 22 February 1928. In ibid.

4   15 March 1928. Address: Albergo Rapallo. Original in the George Yeats Correspondence with Thomas McGreevy in TCD. MSS 8104/57.

5   14 May 1928. In ibid., MSS 8104/59.

6   Yeats's letter is quoted in Lady Gregory's journal on 14 November 1928. See *LGJ* 2, 337.

7   Richard Aldington, *Life for Life's Sake* (1941; London: Cassell, 1968), 306. According to Basil Bunting, Yeats was more in touch than he appeared. When they met at Yeats's flat, Yeats astonished Bunting by reciting twenty-eight lines of one of Bunting's poems. See 'Yeats Recollected' in *Agenda*, vol. 12, no. 2, Summer 1974, 40.

8   Aldington, *Life for Life's Sake*, 95.

9   Pound to Olga Rudge, 4 December 1928. Original in the Olga Rudge Papers at Yale.

10   23 February ⟨1929⟩. In ibid.

11   ⟨23 December 1928⟩. In ibid.

12   T. S. Eliot to Pound, 31 December 1928. Original in the Olga Rudge Papers at Yale. Reproduced with permission of Valerie Eliot. What did the serious Yeats make of the word-play of his fellow modernists Eliot, Joyce, and Pound? With his poor command of spelling and foreign languages, much of their humour must have passed him by.

13   Pound to his mother, 3 March 1929. Original in the Ezra Pound Papers at Yale.

14   Pound to Olga Rudge, 8 March 1929. Original in the Olga Rudge Papers at Yale.

15   8 March 1929. In ibid. The 'convarsation' comes in a letter to his father dated 20 January 1929.

16   26 December ⟨1929⟩. In ibid.

17   12 January 1930. In ibid. Until early March 1930, Pound kept away from Yeats during his illness: 'Today I met Ezra for the first time – you know his dread of infections – seeing me in the open air and the sea air, he sat beside me in front of the café and admired my beard' (*L* 772–3).

18   Wilfrid Scawen Blunt, *My Diaries: Being a Personal Narrative of Events 1888–1914* (1919–20; repr. London: Martin Secker, 1932), 725.

19   For an extended critical discussion of Yeats and Coole, see Daniel Harris, *Yeats, Coole Park and Ballylee* (Baltimore: Johns Hopkins University Press, 1974). Harris makes good use of Ben Jonson's 'To Penshurst' and suggests that 'Yeats's country house poems are consequently "about" something quite different from Jonson's: the complex interaction between an individual personality and an ideal, actual world almost lost' (85).

20   Austin Clarke, 'Glimpses of W. B. Yeats' in *Shenandoah*, vol. 16, no. 4, Summer 1965, 30.

21   George Moore, *Hail and Farewell: Ave* (London: William Heinemann, 1911), 271. Yeats had his revenge on Moore in *Dramatis Personae*, completed in 1935: 'He lacked manners, but had manner; he could enter a room so as to draw your attention without seeming to, his French, his knowledge of painting, suggested travel and leisure. Yet nature had denied him the final touch: he had

22   a coarse palate' (*A* 443).

Lady Gregory, *Coole*, ed. Colin Smythe (Dublin: Dolmen Press, 1971), 89. During the *Playboy* riots, the *Pall Mall Gazette* on 31 January 1907 provided an unromantic sketch of Lady Gregory's husband: 'Sir William was born in the Under-Secretary's Lodge in the Phoenix Park in 1817, and he stood for Dublin city as a Conservative in 1842, defeating Lord Morpeth, who had the support of Daniel O'Connell (then Lord Mayor) at his back. The contest cost him £9,000. In later years he became a Palmerstonian Liberal, and later still a Gladstonian of the earlier period. In 1871 he became Governor of Ceylon, and was a successful administrator. After his return from Ceylon he married the present Lady Gregory as his second wife, and their son, Mr William Robert Gregory, is an artist.'

23   Lady Gregory, *Hugh Lane's Life and Achievement, With Some Account of the Dublin Galleries* (London: John Murray, 1921), 30.

24   These are some of the items which went to Sotheby's for auction in the 1920s. Copy in BERG.

25   Lady Gregory, *Coole*, 39. The sale of her books at Sotheby, Wilkinson and Hodge on 15 December 1927 made £112.15s.6d. Copy in BERG.

26   'All the private parts of yr letter re affairs at Coole interested me much, but I daren't comment on it. I don't know how far letters are safe?' Olivia Shakespear to Yeats, 27 September 1931, in *Letters to W. B. Yeats*, ed. Richard Finneran, George Mills Harper and William M. Murphy, vol. 2, 521.

27   See Yeats to George Yeats, Wednesday, 31 August ⟨n.y. 1931?⟩. Address: Coole. Box 78, SUNY Stony Brook.

28   For a full-length study of Yeats's use of metrics, and in particular *ottava rima*, see Robert Beum, *The Poetic Art of William Butler Yeats* (New York: Ungar, 1969). Beum notices that after 1919 Yeats's chief stanzas are octaves and sestets and that *ottava rima* becomes one of his favourites. Of 390 poems in *Collected Poems*, sixty-three are sestets, sixty-two octaves.

29   Stanza 6 was deleted from this poem and now stands on its own under the title 'The Choice', an indication that the poem is not just about Lady Gregory but also takes up the familiar Yeatsian opposition of action versus reflection.

30   George Yeats to Dorothy Pound, 22 August ⟨1931⟩. Cited in Ann Saddlemyer, 'George, Ezra, Dorothy and Friends: Twenty-Six Letters, 1918–59' in *Yeats Annual*, no. 7, 16. I think this letter should be dated 1931, not 1930.

31   See Yeats's correspondence with George, Box 77, SUNY Stony Brook.

32   Journal entry, 27 February 1932.

33   Cruise O'Brien, 'Passion and Cunning', in Jeffares and Cross (eds), *In Excited Reverie: A Centenary Tribute to William Butler Yeats, 1865–1939* (London: Macmillan, 1965), 273.

34   See 'Two Friends: Yeats and A.E.,' in *Yale*

35 Maurice Bowra, *Memories, 1898–1939* (London: Weidenfeld and Nicolson, 1966), 239.

36 Yeats to Heald, 6 August ⟨1938⟩. In the Houghton Library, Harvard University. For a review of studies on Yeats and fascism, see my *W. B. Yeats: A Guide through the Critical Maze* (Bristol: Bristol Classical Press, 1989), 109–15. For a discussion of Yeats as a political failure, see Michael North, *The Political Aesthetic of Yeats, Eliot, and Pound* (Cambridge: Cambridge University Press, 1991).

37 Letter dated 11 January 1931.

38 Ethel Mannin, *Privileged Spectator: A Sequel to 'Confessions and Impressions'* (London: Jarrolds, 1939), 82–4. The situation proved an embarrassment. The Savile Club did not admit women, and they adjourned in the rain to Claridge's nearby. Yeats refused to involve himself in the Ossietsky affair. Yes, he had signed the petition on behalf of Casement, but that was all, and Casement was an Irish affair. 'Yeats was uncomfortable and Toller and I in tears – and elegant ladies and gentlemen in evening dress all round, and waiters and flunkeys moving about, and the orchestra playing and the chandeliers glittering.'

39 Odon Por, *Fascism*, tr. E. Townshend (London: Labour Publishing, 1923), 151.

40 According to his biographer, Russell 'surveyed the modern world from the standpoint of a co-operator, and Irish nationalist, and a Theosophist. . . . Borrowing Hilaire Belloc's vivid phrase "the servile state", he passionately advocated the Co-operative Commonwealth as a more human alternative ⟨to a regimented society⟩.' Henry Summerfield, *That Myriad-Minded Man: A Biography of George William Russell, 'A.E.,' 1867–1935* (Gerrards Cross: Colin Smythe, 1975), 148. For Belloc's argument, see *The Servile State* (London and Edinburgh: T. N. Foulis, 1912). Russell's 'Lessons of Revolution', published in the *Freeman* on 25 July 1923, is unequivocal: 'If politicians refuse the democratic solution of our troubles, if they insist on force, we will have proletarian wars and religious wars. . . . The end of it all would be that the most ruthless militarism would conquer. . . . We can establish Irish nationality only by building in the heart and the imagination' (467). In 1939, Frank O'Connor contrasted Russell with the 'fascist and authoritarian' Yeats: 'Russell was a North-of-Ireland Protestant and proud of it. He was a democrat, with leanings towards communism; pacifist, internationalist, despiser of tradition and class, and, inspite of his mysticism, a thoroughgoing rationalist and humanitarian.' See his 'Two Friends: Yeats and A.E.' in *Yale Review*, vol. 29, no. 1, September 1939, 60–88.

41 Cited in Por, *Fascism*, 169.

42 Ibid., 177.

43 Ibid., 12.

44 Ibid., 160–61.

45 Elizabeth Butler Cullingford, *Yeats, Ireland and Fascism* (London: Macmillan, 1981), 207. In 'Yeats: The Public Man' Michael Yeats had used a similar phrase: 'His authoritarianism and aristocratic leanings, always strong, led him to flirt briefly with the semi-Fascist Blueshirt movement.' See *Southern Review* V, New Series no. 3, July 1969, 883.

46 Sacheverell Sitwell, *Canons of Giant Art: Twenty Torsos in Heroic Landscape* (London: Faber and Faber, 1933), 188.

47 Ibid., 225.

48 Seamus Deane, 'Blueshirt', *London Review of Books*, 4 June 1981, 23–4. In *Celtic Revivals: Essays in Modern Irish Literature, 1880–1980* (London: Faber, 1987), Deane suggests that Yeats's 'so-called fascism is, in fact, an almost pure specimen of the colonialist mentality' (49).

49 W. B. Yeats to Thomas McGreevy, ⟨n.d.⟩. Address: 42 Fitzwilliam Square. Original in the George Yeats Correspondence with Thomas McGreevy in TCD. MS 8104/71a. McGreevy had been reading *The Words upon the Window Pane*.

50 Joseph Lee, *Ireland, 1912–1985* (Cambridge: Cambridge University Press, 1991), 182. Lee argues strongly that despite the trappings 'Fianna Fáil was no more fascist than the Blueshirts'.

51 On 5 May 1932 Lollie Yeats wrote to Anna Russell: 'We are all greatly depressed at the moment. De Valera's Government has upset all the Standing orders . . . over 40 new tariffs proposed – the discussion is today . . . business is at a standstill.' More trouble ensued in March 1935 with the arrest of twenty-five Republicans: '⟨O⟩ne of the ministers Sean (Shawn) Lemass who lives beside us in Dundrum is heavily guarded – guards hidden in the bushes and so on – our maid calmly saying – If they shoot Lemass I hope they will shoot him in town and not out here".' Copies at Colby College, Maine.

52 Yeats to George Yeats, 19 August ⟨1935⟩. Box 78, SUNY Stony Brook.

53 Yeats to Heald, Sunday ⟨n.d.⟩ Sent from Riversdale. Probably October 1936, when he was completing the poem. See his letter to Wellesley on 23 December 1936, in which he enclosed the poem (*DWL* 113).

54 Wellesley replied: 'Of course I do not think you "hate England". I do not suppose you would be friends with me if you did? I (unlike you) hate hate, and love love, and think there is some racial difference here. Now, if hatred grows as it seems to be doing all European culture may be destroyed, and all of us reduced to brutes.'

55 Letter dated 26 February ⟨1937⟩.

56 Letters dated ⟨29 October 1936⟩ and 9 November 1933.

57 'The Ballad of the Serving Maid', as it was originally called by Wellesley, seems to have given offence to George. In a letter to George on 29 June 1939 about the publication of their correspondence, Wellesley refers to 'the long continued row about the Ballad of the Serving Maid'. In the same letter, she writes: 'I just

want to tell you that I quite understand that you really dont want anything published about him at all. To be the wife of a genius must be hard, to be the widow of a genius perhaps impossible.' Box 118, SUNY Stony Brook. As is clear from a letter to Wellesley, Yeats was much taken with a poem by Turner: 'But when a man is old, married and in despair/Has slept with the bodies of many women;/Then if he meets a woman whose loveliness/Is young and yet troubled with power . . ./Terrible is the agony of an old man/The agony of incommunicable power/Holding its potency that is like a rocket/That is full of stars.' It 'rends my heart', he told her ⟨23 June 1936⟩ (*DWL* 65).

58 Letter inside envelope dated 28 January 1937.
59 Yeats to Heald, 12 September ⟨1938⟩. Original in the Houghton Library, Harvard University.
60 2 October ⟨1938⟩. In ibid.
61 Box 79, SUNY Stony Brook.
62 W. J. McCormack takes a suspicious line. See his *Dissolute Characters: Irish Literary History through Balzac, Sheridan Le Fanu, Yeats and Bowen* (Manchester and New York: Manchester University Press, 1993), 203. *Lost Planet*, the volume of verse published by the Hogarth Press in 1942, probably affords a more accurate record of Dorothy Wellesley's politics at this time. She hails the pride of the swan (aristocracy), writes an epitaph for the 'dull' common man, and in 'Fire', an incantation for Yeats, celebrates 'the mystical/Core of life'. The inter-war years she describes as 'locust years'. Hers are the politics of inconsolable loss, as the title suggests. The Austrian acquaintance in Wellesley's letter is probably Turner's friend, the Jewish pianist Arthur Schnabel. See *DWL* 192.
63 See NLI MS 30124 for George's list of his illnesses. When he was ill in Majorca in January 1936, George kept Lily and Lollie Yeats informed. The British Consul and his wife drove up to see Yeats, loaded down with pillows, a bed rest, a wicker table, fifteen detective novels and westerns, three magazines and a bed pan. ⟨Sunday, n.y.⟩ Box 118, SUNY Stony Brook. It was during this illness that Yeats wrote to George from the Hotel Terramar, Palma de Mallorca, asking her to come and look after him. ⟨January 1936⟩. Box 118, SUNY Stony Brook. On 2 March 1936, George wrote again to Yeats's sisters about moving to a small villa which would halve their costs, though she did not know when he could be moved home. Box 118, SUNY Stony Brook. In April 1936, Yeats was convalescing at Casa Pastor, San Agustin, Palma de Mallorca, the summer villa of a Palma stockbroker. See Roger McHugh (ed.), *Ah Sweet Dancer: W. B. Yeats, Margot Ruddock: A Correspondence* (London: Macmillan, 1970), 79–80. In June 1936, he was back at the Savile in London, but the suffering continued. See *DWL* 64. In September 1936, after returning to Dublin, George confided to Wellesley that his coming visit might be the last time he went unaccompanied to England. See *DWL* 99.

64 John Harwood, *Olivia Shakespear and W. B. Yeats* (London: Macmillan, 1989), 191.
65 Cited by Michael Meyer, *Not Prince Hamlet: Literary and Theatrical Memoirs* (London: Secker and Warburg, 1989), 249–50.
66 Yeats to Heald, 6 August ⟨1938⟩. Original in the Houghton Library, Harvard University.
67 Letter dated 17 January 1938. Box 79, SUNY Stony Brook.
68 Letter dated 23 January 1938.
69 Letter dated 5 January 1931. In BERG.
70 Yeats to Heald, 2 October ⟨1938⟩. Original in the Houghton Library, Harvard University.
71 26 September 1930. When he left Coole on 17 October, he was finishing his Swift play. Ill or not, as Yeats confessed, 'Swift haunts me; he is always just round the next corner' (*VPl* 958).
72 Letter from George to Yeats, 29 February ⟨1932⟩. Box 119, SUNY Stony Brook. Cited by Ann Saddlemyer in *Omnium Gatherum*, 300.
73 Letter of Yeats to J. J. McElligott, a civil servant in the Department of Finance, 1 March 1933. Cited in Tim Pat Coogan, *De Valera: Long Fellow, Long Shadow* (London: Hutchinson, 1993), 502. According to Coogan, Yeats was 'one of the few people successfully to stand up to de Valera during this decade of sustained triumph' (501).
74 Rows at the Abbey pepper his correspondence with Heald in 1937 and 1938. On 3 June 1938 he refers to firing Hunt; on 6 June he speaks of the unceasing struggle at the Abbey, O'Connor's resignation, and O'Faolain's hatred for Yeats's pugnacity. Originals in the Houghton Library, Harvard University. A letter dated 6 June ⟨1938⟩ refers to O'Connor's resignation.
75 See Yeats's letter to George, 3 January 1935. Box 78, SUNY Stony Brook. The venture came to nothing. Margot Collis's maiden name was Ruddock.
76 Preface, 'Music and Poetry', to *Broadsides: A Collection of New Irish and English Songs* (1937; repr. Shannon: Irish University Press, 1971). Yeats felt responsible for the Cuala Press and in November 1938 planned a series of *Fors Clavigera* with two issues a year, in the spring and autumn. *On the Boiler* was to form the first issue, in which, as he told Heald on 28 November 1937, he would outline a plan for the youth of Ireland. (Yeats's precedence was Ruskin's *Fors Clavigera: Letters to the Workmen and Labourers of Great Britain*, a series of ninety-six letters published monthly, beginning in 1871.)
77 See Charles Powell in the *Observer* on 27 April 1930; the *New Statesman* on 26 April 1930; the *Church Times* on 2 May 1930; Robert Lynd in the *Daily News* on 26 April 1930; *Week-end Review* on 26 April 1930; *Public Opinion* on 2 May 1930.
78 Letter mentioned on 2 November 1930. Yeats was eventually proposed by Rothenstein and D. S. MacColl in October 1936 and elected in February 1937. He was delighted with his new club, as he told George. He had a telephone at his bedside, not in a cold corridor. He could also get exactly the food he wanted from

the light luncheon room; the library was well-stocked, and there were two large reading rooms. ⟨1937⟩. Box 79, SUNY Stony Brook.

79   Yeats to George from the Book-Cadillac Hotel in Detroit, 12 November 1932. Box 787, SUNY Stony Brook.

80   Yeats mentioned details of the payment in a letter to George on 1 April 1937. Box 79, SUNY Stony Brook. The Director of Talks at the BBC was Hilda Matheson, a friend of Wellesley and former lover of Vita Sackville-West. Margot Ruddock helped with the BBC broadcasts, reading and singing his poems, sometimes to her music. For further information see Wade's *Bibliography* and 'George Barnes's "W. B. Yeats and Broadcasting," 1940', and Jeremy Silver's 'W. B. Yeats and the BBC: a Reassessment' in *Yeats Annual*, no. 5, 181–94. As always, George recognised the importance of these broadcasts, and she wanted him to practise: 'You'll have to keep closely to the fifteen minutes in both cases – you can try the "talk" out on me . . . you wont be able to tiger up and down the room as you usually do when you speak!' See her letter to Yeats from 42 Fitzwilliam Square on 8 September 1931. Cited by Ann Saddlemyer in *Omnium Gatherum*, 282. George and Michael listened in to the 2 April 1937 broadcast, which they found excellent. George was not especially keen on Yeats's choice of poems, but she thought he spoke in his natural-speaking voice and he gave the impression he was enjoying himself. See letter dated 3 March ⟨1937⟩, which should I think read 3 April 1937. Box 119, SUNY Stony Brook.

81   Ironically, in July 1937, Wellesley was in a state of nervous breakdown partly as a result, Yeats thought, of the Coronation strain. See his letters to George in July 1937. Box 79, SUNY Stony Brook. Yeats attempted to persuade her to go into a nursing home, but thought he would be unsuccessful. By 24 September 1937 she had recovered.

82   Letter dated 4 December ⟨1936⟩. In Ireland, Yeats found himself feted after the publication on 2 February 1937 of 'Roger Casement' in de Valera's paper, the *Irish Press*.

83   Yeats to George, June 1930. Box 77, SUNY Stony Brook.

84   Yeats to George, 13 October 1937. Box 79, SUNY Stony Brook.

85   Yeats to George, ⟨13 July 1938⟩. Box 79, SUNY Stony Book.

86   Yeats to Margot Ruddock, ⟨early April 1936⟩. In McHugh (ed.), *Ah Sweet Dancer*, 81.

87   Yeats to George from Penns in the Rocks, 13 November ⟨1938⟩. Box 79, SUNY Stony Brook. After Yeats's death, George wrote to Pound: 'Many thanks for yr letter – WBY wrote to me from London that you had said some of his recent pomes were "quite good. This is very high praise from Ezra" – Glad you said it – He referred to the remark with evident pleasure several times while we were in France.' Letter ⟨February? 1939⟩. In Ann Saddlemyer, 'George, Ezra, Dorothy and Friends: Twenty-Six Letters, 1918–59' in *Yeats*

Annual, no. 7, 19.

88   Letter dated ⟨probably late March 1935⟩. In McHugh (ed.), *Ah Sweet Dancer*, 39.

89   Yeats to George, 4 November 1932. Box 78, SUNY Stony Brook.

90   Cited in Mikhail, *W. B. Yeats: Interviews and Recollections*, vol. 2, 203. The novelist that Yeats regarded above all others was Balzac.

91   The Questionnaire and Yeats's replies can be consulted in NLI MS 30098.

92   James Stephens, ' "He Died Younger than He Was Born" ' in the *Listener*, 17 June 1943.

93   For biographical details see Diana Souhami, *Gluck: 1895–1978* (London: Pandora, 1988), 211 ff. Some sixty letters of Yeats's correspondence with Edith, including passages omitted from Wade's *Letters*, can be consulted in the Houghton Library, Harvard University. On 28 July 1952, Wade reassured Heald: 'I will leave out the parts you have outlined in red.' Original in the Houghton Library, Harvard University.

94   Cited in Souhami, *Gluck, 1895–1978*, 215–16.

95   A special room was prepared for Yeats and called 'The Yeats Room', which it remained until October 1944, when it was cleared to make way for 'Gluck' (Hannah Gluckstein). Among Yeats's last affairs, two were with women who were bisexual.

96   Yeats to George, 2 October 1936. Sent from the Athenaeum. Box 79, SUNY Stony Brook. On 7 October 1936, he told George he was going to Steyning for a few days.

97   Yeats to Heald, 18 May ⟨1937⟩. Passage omitted from Wade's *Letters*. Original in the Houghton Library, Harvard University.

98   Yeats to Heald, 29 May ⟨1937⟩. Original in the Houghton Library, Harvard University.

99   Yeats to George, 10 June 1937. Box 79, SUNY Stony Brook.

100   George to Yeats, 13 June 1937. Box 119, SUNY Stony Brook. In her biography of 'Gluck', Diana Souhami assumes that George 'was unperturbed by his interest in Edith' (217), but, as the irony of this letter suggests, I think such an assumption is mistaken.

101   Yeats to George, 28 June 1937. Box 79, SUNY Stony Brook. Letter written from Steyning. Yeats's London address at this time was 52 Holland Park, W. 11. In September 1937 Yeats voiced a similar complaint: that he had had enough of conversation and outings by car. Letter to George, ⟨September 1937⟩, from Steyning. Box 79, SUNY Stony Brook.

102   Yeats to George, 15 July 1937, from Steyning. Box 79, SUNY Stony Brook.

103   Yeats to George, 24 September 1937, from Penns in the Rocks. Box 79, SUNY Stony Brook.

104   Yeats to Heald, 2 August ⟨1937⟩, from Riversdale. Original in the Houghton Library, Harvard University.

105   See Yeats's correspondence with Heald in the Houghton Library, Harvard University.

106   George Yeats to Heald, 6 May 1938. Original in the Houghton Library, Harvard University.

107   George Yeats to Heald, 12 May 1938, from

Riversdale. Original in the Houghton Library, Harvard University.

108 Cited in Coogan, *De Valera*, 628.

109 Letters dated 20 November 1938 and 21 November 1938. Yeats sent his from Steyning, George hers from Dublin. Boxes 79 and 119, SUNY Stony Brook.

110 Wellesley to Rothenstein, 6 February 1939. Original in the Papers of William Rothenstein in the Houghton Library, Harvard University. In its report of the burial service on 31 January 1939, de Valera's paper, the *Irish Press*, referred to Wellesley simply as 'the poetess': 'Besides Mrs Yeats those present included Mr Dermod O'Brien, President of the Royal Hibernian Academy of Arts, and Lady Gerald Wellesley, the poetess.' And they quickly added: 'From the United States yesterday came inquiries as to the arrangements for the funeral. One message from Dr P. MacCartan guaranteed £100, if it were needed, towards defraying the cost of bringing the remains back to Ireland. Dr MacCartan was the Republican Envoy in New York in the years subsequent to 1916, was one of the first Sinn Fein T.D.'s, and is the author of the book, "With de Valera in America".'

111 A copy of this list is in the Yeats Collection. NLI.

112 T. S. Eliot to George Yeats, 30 March 1939. See NLI MS 30102.

113 Sean O'Casey, *Autobiographies*, vol. 2 (London: Macmillan, 1963), 347. Other tributes included Padraic Colum in the *New York Times Book Review* on 12 February 1939, Stephen Gwynn, Austin Clarke, and St John Ervine in the *Observer* on 5 February 1939, Gogarty in the *Evening Standard* on 30 January 1939.

114 Jack Yeats in a letter to Hone, cited in J. M. Hone, 'Yeats as Political Philosopher', in the *London Mercury*, March 1939, 496.

115 Auden deleted the reference to Kipling in the 1966 edition of his *Collected Shorter Poems*. For a comparison between 'Under Ben Bulben' and Auden's utterly un-Yeatsian 'In Memory of W. B. Yeats', written within six months of each other, see Lawrence Lipking, *The Life of the Poet: Beginning and Ending Poetic Careers* (Chicago: University of Chicago Press, 1981), 152–61.

116 George Yeats to McGreevy, 6 March 1939. Original in the George Yeats Correspondence with Thomas McGreevy in TCD. MS 8104/77.

117 See the *Irish Press* 31 January 1939: 'In an effort to have the remains of Dr Yeats brought to Ireland for burial in St Patrick's Cathedral, Dublin, Mr Lennox Robinson, a director of the Abbey Theatre, accompanied by Master Michael Yeats, had left Ireland for London last night intending to fly from Croydon to Roquebrune today.' In March 1941, David Wilson, the Cathedral Dean, offered St Patrick's as the site for Yeats's final resting-place. See Hone, *Yeats*, 478. See also James Lovic Allen, *Yeats's Epitaph: A Key to Symbolic Unity in his Life and Work* (Wash-ington, D.C.: University Press of America, 1982), 41.

118 Cited in Richard Ellmann, *Eminent Domain: Yeats among Wilde Joyce Pound Eliot and Auden* (New York: Oxford University Press, 1970), 82. This 'Wabash version of Irish dialect' was first published in 1958.

119 George Yeats to Harold Macmillan, 13 February 1939. Box 118, SUNY Stony Brook. The repetition of words used in the original suggests George was still suffering from the effects of her bereavement. The edition de luxe had been first mooted in 1930; in 1931 Yeats got ready volume 1 on poetry, and he corrected the proofs in the summer of 1932; in 1933 *Collected Poems* was published by Macmillan, perhaps instead of the edition de luxe; in November 1939, because of the war, that edition was 'suspended'. The series of dots in George's letter after 'his death' suggests something of Yeats's frustration at the delay. After Yeats's death, George and Thomas Mark, an editor at Macmillan, collaborated on an edition of Yeats's poetry (finally published by Macmillan in 1949 as *The Poems of W. B. Yeats*, 2 vols), and their editorial decisions have been the subject of heated debate among Yeatsians in recent years. Mark departed from the 1933 *Collected Poems* on more than seventy-five occasions, preferring the proofs of the edition de luxe, thus, according to Richard Finneran, ignoring the principle of 'later and correct'. For a summary of the debate, see my *Yeats: A Guide through the Critical Maze*, 22–6. See also Warwick Gould, 'W. B. Yeats and the Resurrection of the Author' in the *Library*, 6th series, vol. 16, no. 2, June 1994, 101–34. For the origins of Yeats's connection with Macmillan, see Charles Morgan, *The House of Macmillan, 1843–1943* (London: Macmillan, 1944).

120 James Hall and Martin Steinmann (eds.), *The Permanence of Yeats* (New York: Macmillan, 1950). Centennial essays included Jeffares and Cross (eds), *In Excited Reverie*, Donoghue and Mulryne (eds), *An Honoured Guest*, D. E. S. Maxwell and S. B. Bushrui (eds), *W. B. Yeats, 1865–1965: Centenary Essays on the Art of W. B. Yeats* (Nigeria: Ibadan University Press; London: Nelson, 1965), and Liam Miller (ed.), *The Dolmen Press Centenary Papers MCMLXV* (Dublin: Dolmen, 1968).

121 Dorothy Wellesley to George Yeats. 29 June 1939. Box 118, SUNY Stony Brook.

122 Wellesley to Rothenstein, 22 July 1939. Original in the Papers of William Rothenstein at the Houghton Library, Harvard University.

123 *Weekly Sun*, Literary Supplement, 1 December 1895.

124 See McHugh (ed.), *Ah Sweet Dancer*, 13.

125 Ellmann, *Yeats: The Man and the Masks*, xxi. On p. xvi, Ellmann also mistakes the date of their marriage – not 17 October, which was George's birthday, but 20 October 1917. Later in the book, on p. 219, the date has changed to 21 October 1917.

APPENDIX 1

Chronology of the Life and Times of William Butler Yeats

1865   April: Lincoln assassinated; end of American Civil War. 13 June: Yeats born at what is now 5 Sandymount Avenue, Dublin. December: John O'Leary sentenced to 20 years' penal servitude for Fenian activities.

1866   December: birth of Maud Gonne.

1867   July: family moves to 23 Fitzroy Road, near Regent's Park, London. Birth of Susan Mary Yeats ('Lily'). Birth of Lionel Johnson. Arnold's *On the Study of Celtic Literature*.

1868   Birth of Elizabeth Corbet Yeats ('Lollie').

1870   Birth of Robert Corbet Yeats ('Bobbie'), who died three years later. Morris's *Earthly Paradise*.

1871   Birth of John Butler Yeats ('Jack').

1872–4   With his grandparents in Sligo.

1875   Birth of Jane Grace Yeats, who died the following year.

1876   Yeats joins his father at Burnham Beeches, London.

1877   January: Yeats enrols (until 1881) at the Godolphin School, Hammersmith.

1878   O'Grady's *History of Ireland: The Heroic Period*.

1879   Land War in Ireland (until 1882). Family moves to 8 Woodstock Road, Bedford Park, London.

1880   March: marriage of Isabella Augusta Persse to Sir William Gregory.

1881   Family moves to Howth. Yeats enrols (until December 1883) at the Erasmus Smith High School, Dublin. May: birth of Robert Gregory.

1882   February: birth of James Joyce. May: Phoenix Park murders. Yeats enamoured of Laura Armstrong.

1884   Early spring: family moves to Terenure, Dublin. May: Yeats enrols at Metropolitan School of Art, Dublin.

1885   'The Island of Statues' published in the *Dublin University Review*, April–July. June: helps found the Dublin Hermetic Society. Meets O'Leary on his return to Ireland from exile in Paris. October: birth of Ezra Pound. Late 1885/early 1886: meets the seductive young Bengali Brahmin Mohini Chatterjee in Dublin.

1886   April: leaves Art School. Hears Morris lecture at the Contemporary Club in Dublin. June: Home Rule Bill defeated in House of Commons. October: *Mosada*.

1887   May: joins father at 58 Eardley Crescent, South Kensington. Visits Madame Blavatsky in Holland Park for first time. June: begins attending evenings at Morris's. August/September: stays at Thornhill, Sligo, with George Pollexfen. Collecting stories. Late summer: Susan Yeats, his mother, suffers two strokes and becomes incapacitated.

1888   January/February: *Poems and Ballads of Young Ireland*. March: family moves to 3 Blenheim Road, Bedford Park. September: edits *Fairy and Folk Tales of the Irish Peasantry*. Birth of T. S. Eliot. Christmas: joins Theosophical Society. Spends Christmas Day with Wilde.

1889   30 January: first meeting with Maud Gonne at Bedford Park, London. *The Wanderings of Oisin*. August: edits *Stories of Carleton*. Death of William Allingham.

1890   March: initiated by 'MacGregor' Mathers into the Order of the Golden Dawn (in Charlotte Street, London). May (probably): with Ernest Rhys, T. W. Rolleston, and others, founds the Rhymers' Club in London. October: death of Morris. December: Parnell's leadership of the Irish Parliamentary Party fatally undermined in Committee Room 15 at the House of Commons.

1891   May: death of Madame Blavatsky. July: proposes to Maud Gonne. October: death of Parnell in Brighton. November: Maud Gonne initiated into the Order of the Golden Dawn. *John Sherman and Dhoya*. J. T. Grein founds Independent Theatre Society. December: with T. W. Rolleston, founds the Irish Literary Society in London.

1892   February: *The Book of the Rhymers' Club*. March: death of Sir William Gregory. June: helps found National Literary Society, Dublin, with John O'Leary as President. September: *The Countess Cathleen*. October/November: attends funerals of his maternal grandparents in Sligo. 17 October: birth of Georgina Hyde-Lees. November: Hyde's lecture on 'The Necessity of De-Anglicising the Irish Nation' delivered to the Irish National Literary Society in Dublin.

1893   February: *The Works of William Blake*. July: formation of the Gaelic League. Summer: serious quarrel with Maud Gonne over his literary plans for the Irish National Literary Society. September: Home Rule Bill passed in House of Commons, defeated in the Lords. December: *The Celtic Twilight*.

1894   February: Wilde's *Salome* published with illustrations by Beardsley. Yeats in Paris accompanies Maud Gonne to a production of *Axel*. March/April: *The Land of Heart's Desire* produced at the Avenue Theatre in London. April: Irish Agricultural Organisation Society founded by Horace Plunkett. Meets Olivia Shakespear. June: first meeting with Lady Gregory. Summer: possible meetings with Gore-Booth sisters in London. August: Iseult Gonne born. October: with George Pollexfen (until following May). Mid-November: visits home of Gore-Booth family at Lissadell, County Sligo.

1895   March: *A Book of Irish Verse*. April: visits Douglas Hyde at Frenchpark, County Roscommon. May: second trial of Wilde ends with sentence of two years' imprisonment. October: *Poems*. Shares rooms with Arthur Symons in Fountain Court, The Temple.

1896   January: first issue of the *Savoy*. February: moves to 18 Woburn Buildings. Begins year-long affair with Olivia Shakespear ('Diana Vernon'). August: with Arthur Symons visits Edward Martyn at Tulira Castle, County Galway. Sees 'Archer Vision'. Trip to the Aran Islands. December: in Paris to discuss a 'Castle of Heroes' with Maud Gonne. Sees performance of Jarry's *Ubu Roi*. Takes hashish. Meets Synge.

1897   April: *The Secret Rose*. May: anti-Diamond Jubilee riots in Dublin. Stays with George Pollexfen. Wilde released from prison. June: *The Tables of the Law and The Adoration of the Magi*. July: proposal to establish the Irish Literary Theatre drawn up by Yeats and Lady Gregory at Duras, County Galway. Spends two months at Coole with Lady Gregory.

1898   February: Wilde's *Ballad of Reading Gaol*. April–May: in Paris to discuss Celtic mysticism with Mathers and Maud Gonne. September: with

311

George Pollexfen (until following January). November: in Dublin Maud Gonne tells a devastated Yeats about Millevoye and her previous sex life. She and Yeats undertake a spiritual marriage. George Moore's *Evelyn Innes* published with dedication to Yeats.

1899 March: Griffith's *United Irishman* and Pearse's *Claidheamh Soluis* (The Sword of Light) launched. April: *The Wind Among the Reeds*. May: *The Countess Cathleen* produced at the Antient Concert Rooms, Dublin. The Irish Literary Theatre established. *Beltaine*, no. 1. May–November: Coole acts as his base. October: collaborates with George Moore on *Diarmuid and Grania*.

1900 January: death of Susan Yeats. February: *Beltaine*, no. 2. April: 'The Battle of Blythe Road' (dispute at Golden Dawn in London). *Beltaine*, no. 3. August: commemoration at Killeenan, County Galway, for the eighteenth-century Gaelic poet Raftery. November: death of Wilde. December: *The Shadowy Waters*.

1901 January: death of Queen Victoria; accession of Edward VII. February: Maud Gonne joins John MacBride on American lecture tour. Yeats meets her in London on return ('Adam's Curse'). Yeats and Horniman resign their offices from the Golden Dawn. May–June: stays with George Pollexfen. July: at Coole. August: attends Pan Celtic Congress in Dublin. October: *Samhain*. *Diarmuid and Grania* produced by Benson at the Gaiety Theatre, Dublin.

1902 April: *Cathleen ni Houlihan* produced at Saint Teresa's Hall, Dublin, with Maud Gonne in title role. Lady Gregory's *Cuchulain of Muirthemne*. October: *The Pot of Broth* produced in the Antient Concert Rooms, Dublin. *Samhain*. November: Dun Emer Press founded. December: meets Joyce (on his way to Paris) in London.

1903 February: Irish Literary Society becomes the Irish National Theatre Society with Yeats as President. Marriage of Maud Gonne to John MacBride. March: *The Hour-Glass* produced at Molesworth Hall, Dublin. The Masquers Society founded in London with Yeats on Committee. May: *Ideas of Good and Evil*. August: *In the Seven Woods*. September: *Samhain*. November–March: lecture tour in the United States and Canada.

1904 January: Sean MacBride born. *The Shadowy Waters* produced at Molesworth Hall, Dublin. April: Horniman buys the Mechanics' Institute, Abbey Street, Dublin, and transforms it into a theatre for the Irish National Theatre Society. June: *Where There Is Nothing* produced at the Royal Court, London. October: Joyce departs for the Continent with Nora. October–November: Yeats entertains his American organiser and financial supporter, John Quinn, on his visit to Ireland. November: sees Shaw's *John Bull's Other Island* produced at the Royal Court, London. December: *Samhain*. 27 December: Abbey Theatre opens with performance of *On Baile's Strand*.

1905 January/February: Maud Gonne thinks of divorcing MacBride. July: fortieth birthday marked by presentation of Kelmscott *Chaucer*. August: Maud Gonne granted legal separation. November: *Samhain*. Abbey company on tour to Oxford, Cambridge, and London.

1906 October: *The Arrow*. November: *On Baile's Strand* at Abbey. Griffith's policy of Sinn Fein outlined. December: *Samhain*.

1907 January: *Playboy* riots. March: death of O'Leary. May: tour of Northern Italy and San Marino with Lady Gregory and Robert Gregory. Joyce's *Chamber Music*. December: John Butler Yeats moves to New York.

1908   January: Fay brothers resign from Abbey. Spring: affair with Mabel Dickinson.

1911   January: Craig's 'screens' used for first time at Abbey in production of *The Hour-Glass*. April: in Paris. September–October: on tour with Abbey in the United States.

1912   January: Irish Players arrested in Philadelphia for staging 'immoral' *Playboy*. March: chairs Pound lecture on Anglo-Saxon verse. June: meets Rabindranath Tagore. July: Nugent Monck's London production of revised *Countess Cathleen*. August: stays with Maud Gonne in Normandy. September: Florence Farr departs for Ceylon.

1913   January: Third Home Rule Bill passed by House of Commons; defeated in the Lords. Lunches with Asquith at 10 Downing Street. February: joins the Society for Psychical Research. June: ends affair with Mabel Dickinson. July: Home Rule Bill suffers similar fate in House of Lords. August: spends two long weekends with Georgina Hyde-Lees and family at Coleman's Hatch, Sussex. September: Dublin Lock-Out of workers. November: Irish Citizen Army formed by Connolly; Irish Volunteers founded under Redmond. November–January: with Pound at Stone Cottage, Coleman's Hatch, Sussex.

1914   January: 'Peacock' dinner at Blunt's estate in Sussex. February–April: American Tour. May: Home Rule Bill passed. Investigates 'miracle' of bleeding heart at Mirebeau with Maud Gonne and Everard Fielding. *Responsibilities*. June: Joyce's *Dubliners*. First issue of Wyndham Lewis's *Blast*. July: attends 'Cinema Supper' organised by J. M. Barrie at the Savoy Restaurant and Theatre (guests include Ricketts, Shaw, and Prime Minister Asquith). 4 August: outbreak of First World War. Georgina Hyde-Lees volunteers with Red Cross as hospital cook, later nurse. September: Home Rule Bill receives royal assent, but its operation is suspended because of the war. Irish Republican Brotherhood secretly appoints committee to launch military rising. November: Davis Centenary lecture in Dublin.

1915   January–February: at Stone Cottage. May: Hugh Lane drowns on board *Lusitania*. First Vorticist Exhibition in London. July–August: helps Joyce obtain pension from Royal Literary Fund. November: possibly proposes to Georgina Hyde-Lees. December: refuses a knighthood.

1916   January–March: at Stone Cottage with the Pounds. March: *Reveries over Childhood and Youth*. April: *At the Hawk's Well* performed at Lady Cunard's house, London. Easter Rising. May: execution of John MacBride. Applies for membership of the Savile Club in London. Summer: transfers whole of copyright to Macmillan. June: fleeting visit to Dublin. Casement on trial for treason. July–August: at Colville, Normandy. August: Casement executed. Death of Alfred Pollexfen. October–December: campaigning for return of Lane pictures to Dublin. December: lunches with Asquith at 10 Downing Street. Joyce's *Portrait of the Artist as a Young Man* published in New York.

1917   January: elected to the Savile Club. March: purchases Thoor Ballylee. April: Florence Farr dies of cancer in Ceylon. August: in Normandy, where he proposes to Iseult. September: escorts Maud Gonne and Iseult back to London. 20 October: marries Georgina Hyde-Lees at Harrow Road Registry Office. Honeymoon at Stone Cottage. Start of automatic writing sessions (continue until March 1920). November: *The Wild Swans at Coole* (Cuala Press). December: Ashdown Cottage in Sussex.

1918   January–early March: in Oxford. *Per Amica Silentia Lunae*. March–April: at Glendalough and Glenmalure. May–September: at Ballinamantane House, near Coole. Late September: moves into Thoor Ballylee. In Dublin, rents 73 St Stephen's Green from Maud Gonne. November: end of First World War. George Yeats ill with pneumonia. Yeats refuses Maud Gonne entry to her house. December: Sinn Fein landslide election victory.

1919   January: Dáil Eireann established; War of Independence begins. February: birth of Anne Butler Yeats. May: returns to England. *The Player Queen* produced at King's Hall, London. June: relinquishes Woburn Buildings. Summer at Ballylee. October: moves to 4 Broad Street, Oxford.

1920   January–May: United States and Canada lecture tour (in part to pay for restoration of Ballylee). March: beginning of sleep sessions while in California (Yeats and his wife conduct 164 sleep sessions between this date and March 1924). April: marriage of Iseult Gonne and Francis Stuart. June: Pound's *Hugh Selwyn Mauberley*. October: Terence MacSwiney dies on hunger strike in Brixton Prison. November: 'Bloody Sunday' in Dublin.

1921   January: the Pounds leave England for the Continent. February: *Michael Robartes and the Dancer*. Denounces British policy in Ireland at the Oxford Union. April–June: at Minchin's Cottage, Shillingford, near Oxford. June: moves to Cuttlebrook House, Thame. August: birth of Michael Butler Yeats (needs operation in September). October: *Four Plays for Dancers*. December: Anglo-Irish Treaty signed.

1922   February: *Ulysses* published in Paris. John Butler Yeats dies in New York. March: moves to 82 Merrion Square, Dublin. Leaves Golden Dawn. March–September: at Ballylee. April:

Vrouwe Emer's Groote Strijd (*The Only Jealousy of Emer*) produced at Hollandsche Schouwburg, Amsterdam. June: Civil War intensifies. August: Michael Collins killed in ambush. Bridge at Ballylee blown up by Republicans. September: Cosgrave elected Head of Provisional Government. October: *The Trembling of the Veil*. November: Erskine Childers executed for possessing revolver, the first of seventy-seven Republicans to be executed. At the Savile, defends Joyce's *Ulysses* against Gosse's charge of obscenity. December: Yeats nominated to Senate and receives honorary degree from Trinity College, Dublin. Over lunch with Eliot discusses Joyce and writing essay on Dante for *The Criterion*.

1923   January: Yeats in London, seeks end to Civil War and resolution of Lane pictures dispute. Gogarty kidnapped by Republicans; escapes by plunging into the river Liffey. Yeats possibly contemplates permanent removal from Ireland. May: end of Civil War. November: awarded Nobel Prize, which he receives in person in December.

1924   May: *Essays*. July: death of Quinn in New York. August: Tailteann Games. Autumn: suffers from high blood pressure.

1925   Christmas: Yeats's daughter Anne catches pneumonia. January–February: in Sicily and Rome. June: Speech on divorce in Irish Senate. August: Abbey receives endowment from the Free State Government.

1926   January: *A Vision*. February: rioting at Abbey over O'Casey's *Plough and the Stars*. March: visits St Otteran's Scool, Waterford. May: *The Only Jealousy of Emer* and *The Cat and the Moon* produced by Dublin Drama League at Abbey. Appointed Chair of Senate Coinage Committee. Fianna Fáil launched as political party by de Valera. November:

Autobiographies. December: *Sophocles' King Oedipus* at Abbey.

1927 January–February: ill with arthritis and influenza. Summer: at Ballylee. July: Kevin O'Higgins, Minister for Justice, assassinated. Joyce's *Pomes Penyeach.* September: *Sophocles' Oedipus at Colonus* at Abbey. November–December: reading Lewis's *Time and Western Man.* November–April: in southern Europe.

1928 February: *The Tower.* Death of Hardy and funeral in Westminster Abbey. June: controversy over rejection of O'Casey's *Silver Tassie.* July: makes last Senate speech. Moves to 42 Fitzwilliam Square, Dublin. October: at Coole. November–May 1929: in Rapallo.

1929 January: visits Rome. May: meets Lewis. July–August: at Coole. Final family visit to Ballylee. November–March: in Rapallo. December: makes will.

1930 February: Censorship Board established. April–May: Yeats's name mentioned to succeed Bridges as Poet Laureate. May: at Coole. November: *The Words upon the Window Pane* at Abbey. November–February: winters in County Dublin on Killiney Hill.

1931 May: receives honorary doctorate from Oxford University. July–September: at Coole. August: George has operation in Dublin. September: BBC broadcast from Belfast. October: death of Ricketts. December: *The Dreaming of the Bones* at Abbey.

1932 Winter and spring: at Coole nursing Lady Gregory. February: de Valera's Fianna Fáil win elections. April: death of Lady Gregory. July: moves to Riversdale, Rathfarnham. September: Irish Academy of Letters formed. October–January 1933: lecture tour of the United States.

1933 February: O'Duffy sacked as Chief Commissioner for Gárda Siochána (Irish Police). March: dispute with de Valera over choice of plays by Abbey for their U.S. tour. July–August: becomes involved in O'Duffy's Blueshirt movement. September: *The Winding Stair.* November: *Collected Poems.*

1934 January: *Letters to the New Island.* February: awarded Goethe Prize by Nazi-dominated Frankfurt. April: Steinach operation (unilateral vasectomy). June: the Yeatses in Rapallo to dispose of their flat. July: *The Resurrection* and *The King of the Great Clock Tower* at Abbey. September: meets and becomes infatuated with Margot Ruddock. October: addresses the Fourth Congress of the Alessandro Volta Foundation in Rome. November: *Collected Plays. Wheels and Butterflies.* December: begins friendship with Ethel Mannin.

1935 Late January and February: at Riversdale with congestion of lungs. June: meets Dorothy Wellesley through Lady Ottoline Morrell. Seventieth birthday dinner at the Royal Hibernian Hotel in Dublin (Francis Hackett proposes toast, seconded by John Masefield). July: death of George Russell in Bournemouth. August: at Penns in the Rocks, Withyam, Sussex, the home of Dorothy Wellesley. October: operation to remove lump on tongue. November: *A Full Moon in March.* December: departs for Palma, Majorca, to spend winter with Shri Purohit Swami. *Dramatis Personae.*

1936 January–April: ill in Majorca; George flies out to be with him. January: death of Kipling. May: Margot Collis (Ruddock) follows Yeats to Majorca, suffers breakdown. June: in London and at Penns in the Rocks. 11 October: BBC broadcast on 'Modern Poetry'. November: *The Oxford Book of Modern Verse, 1892–1935.* O'Duffy forms 'Irish Brigade' to fight alongside Franco in

Spanish Civil War (returns June 1937). December: Abdication crisis.

1937 February: Radio Eireann broadcast of his poems. Elected to the Athenaeum Club. March: contemplates a trip to India with Lady Elizabeth Pelham. April: two broadcasts on poetry for the BBC. May: friendship develops over summer with Edith Shackleton Heald at her home in Steyning, Sussex. June: celebrates his birthday with the Dulacs and Edith Shackleton Heald. 3 July: BBC broadcast on 'My Own Poetry'. October: *A Vision* (second edition). BBC broadcast on 'My Own Poetry Again'.

1938 January–March: South of France. January: *The Herne's Egg*. April: at Steyning and Penns in the Rocks. May: *New Poems*. June: Douglas Hyde appointed first President of Ireland. July–August: in England. August: *Purgatory* at Abbey with sets designed by Anne Yeats. September: Munich accord; distribution of gas-masks. October: death of Olivia Shakespear. December: at Cap Martin in South of France.

1939 28 January: Yeats dies at Roquebrune. Abbey Theatre closed for a week as a mark of respect. May: Joyce's *Finnegans Wake*. July: *Last Poems and Two Plays*. September: outbreak of Second World War; Ireland remains neutral. *On the Boiler*.

1941 January: death of Joyce. Coole Park demolished.

1948 September: Yeats's body returns to Ireland and is buried under Ben Bulben at Drumcliffe Churchyard, County Sligo.

1951 July: Abbey Theatre destroyed by fire (re-opens July 1966).

1953 April: death of Maud Gonne.

1968 23 August: George Yeats dies at her home in Dublin, aged 75. The report of her death in the *New York Times* is overshadowed by the fated Democratic Party Convention in Mayor Daly's Chicago. Civil Rights March from Coalisland to Dungannon, County Tyrone.

APPENDIX 2

Dramatis Personae in Yeats's Life and Work

FAMILY

For material on Yeats's family, see the work of William Murphy, especially *Prodigal Father: The Life of John Butler Yeats (1839–1922)* (Ithaca and London: Cornell University Press, 1978), and *The Yeats Family and the Pollexfens of Sligo* (Dublin: Dolmen, 1971). He is currently writing a study of Yeats's sisters.

George Pollexfen (1839–1910)

George Pollexfen was John Butler Yeats's brother-in-law and Yeats's maternal uncle. George and J. B. Yeats became friends at the Atholl Academy on the Isle of Man. After graduating from Trinity College, Dublin, in the summer of 1862, J. B. Yeats travelled to Sligo to renew his friendship, and immediately fell in love with George's sister Susan. In the 1890s the hypochondriac George, the melancholic Freemason and later member of the Golden Dawn, became W. B. Yeats's favourite uncle, and Yeats often stayed with him at Thornhill, his home on Knappagh Road, Sligo. George never married, but he kept a servant, Mary Battle, who may have been responsible for turning him in the direction of the occult. An accomplished jockey, he rode under the name Paul Hamilton. He was less successful as a businessman, and after William Pollexfen's death in 1892 George's brother-in-law Arthur Jackson was brought in to rescue the Pollexfen Company. George was popular with his workforce, and when he died he was given a large funeral. Thereafter, Yeats's contact with Sligo declined.

Susan Yeats (née Pollexfen) (1841–1900)

Eldest daughter and one of twelve children of William Pollexfen and Elizabeth Middleton. In 1863, after a brief courtship, she married John Butler Yeats and thought she would enjoy a settled life as a barrister's wife. Instead, she suffered constant upheaval, moving back and forth between Ireland and London, had six children, two of whom died in childhood, and spent the last thirteen years of her life after a stroke 'feeding the birds at a London window' (*A* 62). Yeats later wondered if he had inherited his mother's nervous weakness. His mother kept alive his love for Sligo, and 'it was always assumed between her and us that Sligo was more beautiful than other places' (*A* 31). But Yeats rarely refers to her in his work, and she remains a significant absence.

John Butler Yeats (1839–1922)

The 'father of all the Yeatssssss' (Pound's phrase) and in many ways, as his correspondence with his son suggests, the most remarkable of them all. After a history of artistic failure, he became the portrait painter of the Irish Revival, and his work now hangs in the National Gallery of Ireland in tribute both to the figures themselves and to the artist who painted them. His neglect of his family – or rather his absence from them – was legendary, and in 1907 he departed for New York, never to return. In *Reveries*, Yeats is a little unfair to him, as if he needed to stress that he had come out from under his father's shadow. In reality, John Butler Yeats was the chief influence in his life, and he inherited from him a belief in art, a

317

scepticism in religion, and an inability to work alone. See *J. B. Yeats: Letters to His Son W. B. Yeats and Others, 1869–1922*, ed. Joseph Hone (London: Faber and Faber, 1944), and John Butler Yeats, *Early Memories: Some Chapters of an Autobiography* (Dundrum: Cuala Press, 1923). An obituary appeared in the *New York Times Book Review and Magazine* on 19 February 1922 under the title 'Yeats of Petitpas', Petitpas being a little restaurant on West Twenty-ninth Street, a home to painters where the impecunious Yeats held court.

Susan Mary ('Lily') Yeats (1866–1949)

After little formal education, from 1888 to 1894 Lily worked with May Morris as an embroideress at Kelmscott House, Hammersmith. Then in 1902 she was involved with Evelyn Gleeson in the establishment of the Dun Emer Industries. The most psychic of the children, she often had dreams and premonitions, and heard, for example, the banshee cry the night before George Pollexfen died in 1910. She recalled family life in Sligo in similar terms: 'The servants played a big part in our lives. They were so friendly and wise and knew so intimately angels, saints, banshees, and fairies.' George Yeats found Lily quite tiring, especially when she stayed with her in Oxford in August 1920. Lily was her father's favourite. Indeed, 'Never had a brother better sisters than Willie, and I think he knows it now and is glad to help them, as he does copiously and generously; and never had a father better daughters than I have.'

Elizabeth Corbet ('Lollie') Yeats (1868–1940)

Lollie began her career as a teacher of art in a London County Council school. Then in November 1902, under the influence of Morris's Kelmscott Press, she presided over the foundation of the Dun Emer Press, which in 1908 became the Cuala Press. Yeats's *In the Seven Woods*, published in July 1903, 'the year of the big wind', was the first of eleven titles to be printed by Dun Emer Press. Sixty-five titles were published by the Cuala

Press from 1908 to 1945, nearly half of them by or concerning W. B. Yeats. The Cuala Press was housed in Churchtown until August 1923, when it moved to the basement of 82 Merrion Square. In February 1925 it moved again, to 133 Lower Baggot Street in Dublin. Lollie never found it easy (she thought she should have stuck to teaching, at least she would have got a pension), but courage, determination, and her brother's financial support enabled the Cuala Press to survive and add a distinctive arts-and-crafts touch to modern Irish culture. Her father once told her: 'In you are two races – the Yeats and the Pollexfens – the first always makes the best of things – and the second makes the worst of things.' For the work of the two presses, see Liam Miller, *The Dun Emer Press, Later the Cuala Press* (Dublin: Dun Emer Press, 1973). For a defence of her life, see Gifford Lewis, *The Yeats Sisters and the Cuala* (Blackrock, Co. Dublin: Irish Academic Press, 1994).

Jack B. Yeats (1871–1957)

According to Susan Mitchell, Jack was 'whimsical and kindly, most winning of all the Yeatses'. He was born in London, but from 1879 to 1887 he lived with his grandparents in Sligo. After attending art school in London, he found work with the *Vegetarian, Paddock Life*, and then in Manchester as a poster artist. In 1894 he married Mary Cottenham White ('Cottie'), and in 1897 settled in Devon. His watercolour period followed, often centred on the theme 'Life in the West of Ireland', and by 1910 he had completed seventeen exhibitions. In 1902 he collaborated with his brother and Pamela Coleman Smith on *A Broadsheet* (to which his friend Masefield contributed). In the summer of 1905 Jack and Synge were commissioned by the *Manchester Guardian* to provide a series of sketches in words and pictures of the Congested Districts in the West of Ireland. From 1908 to 1915, his illustrations appeared in *A Broadside*, a revival of the earlier venture. In 1910 he relocated to Ireland, eventually settling at Greystones, County Wicklow. His illus-

318

trations appeared in books by Synge, Colum, Masefield, Robert Lynd, and George Birmingham (*Irishmen All*, 1913), but collaboration with his brother was limited. He illustrated Yeats's *Irish Fairy Tales* (1892), supplied the illustration of 'Memory Harbour' opposite the title page of *Reveries over Childhood and Youth* (1916), collaborated on the new series of *A Broadside* (1935–7), and was responsible for the front cover of *On the Boiler* (1939). The unpretentious Jack was a Republican who hated war, and paintings like 'Bachelor's Walk: In Memory' (1915) and 'The Funeral of Harry Boland' (1922) remind us of his distance from his brother. MacGreevy summed up Jack's importance: 'He paints the Ireland that matters.' In 1916 he suffered a bout of depression but came through to produce from the mid-1920s a wholly new abstract style of painting. Jack's imagination was not limited to Ireland, and under the pseudonym W. Bird his work appeared regularly in *Punch* from 1910 to 1941. For his biography, see Hilary Pyle, *Jack B. Yeats: A Biography* (Savage, Maryland: Barnes and Noble, 1989). His early memories can be found in *Sligo* (London: Wishart, 1930). See also Thomas McGreevy, *Jack B. Yeats: An Appreciation and an Interpretation* (Dublin: Victor Waddington, 1945).

George Yeats (née Hyde-Lees) (1892–1968)

Bertha Georgina Hyde-Lees was born on 17 October 1892 at Hartley Wintney, near Odiham in Hampshire. Her father, William Hyde-Lees (c. 1865–1909), who had studied law at Wadham College, Oxford, resigned his commission from the Army after inheriting money from his uncle. His marriage to 'Nelly' Woodmass survived only a few years, and after separation George's parents lived in London. Her father travelled abroad, introduced George's brother Harold to Parisian night-life, and in November 1909 at the age of 45 died of drink. Harold (1890–1963) became an Anglican clergyman and in January 1921 married Ada Gwynne Younghughes. George and her mother lived in South Kensington. In February 1911,

Nelly married Harry Tucker, Olivia Shakespear's brother, and Olivia and her daughter Dorothy acted as witnesses. Dorothy and George became very close friends; they were unorthodox in their beliefs, enjoyed the outdoors and painting, and took many holidays together both in England and on the Continent. Harry and Nelly set up house at 16 Montpelier Square, Knightsbridge. It was Harry who discovered Stone Cottage and The Prelude at Coleman's Hatch in Sussex. George possibly first met Yeats in May 1911. In 1914 he sponsored her admission to the Golden Dawn, and she quickly progressed through the various levels. She was almost certainly in love with Yeats for some years before he took any interest in her. Yeats believed the stars pointed to 1917 as a favourable year for marriage. George was not his first choice, but there is evidence to suggest that he had proposed to her in November 1915. Their marriage in October 1917 produced doubts in Yeats's mind over his choice of partner, but these were allayed when she 'faked' automatic writing as a way of claiming his attention. There followed seven years of automatic writing and sleep sessions. Yeats found security in marriage, she friendship and fulfilment in her children. George was an independent, free spirit when she married and probably shared the medium's belief that 'normality is not normal unless it has excess somewhere' (*YVP* 1, 127): she enrolled briefly in an art school in London and harboured ambitions to write novels. But she sacrificed much, not least her youth, and she needed considerable resources in coping with Yeats's 'Sinbad' life-style, his dependence on Lady Gregory, and his repeated affairs in London and elsewhere. In the 1920s she became secretary of the Dublin Drama League and helped Lollie with the running of the Cuala Press until Lollie's death in 1940, when she took it over until her own death. She was an astute editor of Yeats's verse and was not slow in giving her opinion. But after his death she was determined not to add to the gossip about her husband. She died in Dublin in 1968. Her biography is being written by Ann

Saddlemyer – a report of her work in progress can be found in 'George Hyde-Lees: More Than A Poet's Wife' in A. N. Jeffares (ed.), *Yeats the European* (Savage, Maryland: Barnes and Noble, 1989), 191–200. See also her essay ' "Yours Affly, Dobbs": George Yeats to her Husband' in Susan Dick et al. (eds), *Omnium Gatherum: Essays for Richard Ellmann* (Gerrards Cross: Colin Smythe, 1989), 280–303. For information on George's life, see John Harwood, *Olivia Shakespear and W. B. Yeats: Speech after Long Silence* (London: Macmillan, 1989); *Ezra Pound and Dorothy Shakespear: Their Letters, 1909–1914*, ed. Omar Pound and A. Walton Litz (New York: New Directions, 1984); Richard Ellmann, *along the riverrun: Selected Essays* (Harmondsworth: Penguin, 1989). Her exchange of letters with Yeats can be consulted at SUNY Stony Brook; her correspondence with Tom MacGreevy can be found in Trinity College, Dublin, and in the National Library of Ireland. Those interested in seeing the help George gave Yeats in formulating *A Vision* should also consult the three-volume *Yeats's Vision Papers* (London: Macmillan, 1987). For a recent discussion of her role as medium, see Elizabeth Butler Cullingford, *Gender and History in Yeats's Love Poetry* (Cambridge: Cambridge University Press, 1993).

FRIENDS AND CONTEMPORARIES

Aubrey Beardsley (1872–98)

Born in Brighton, Beardsley made his debut as a book illustrator with *Morte d'Arthur*, published in 1893 by J. M. Dent. The following year he was appointed art editor of the *Yellow Book* and overnight became a celebrity, 'a picture of the age as well as of its epitome', in the words of Holbrook Jackson. His sexually explicit illustrations to Wilde's *Salomé* caused an outcry, and he was forced to resign, but in 1896 he was taken on by Arthur Symons as art editor of the *Savoy*. Never in good health on account of his lungs, Beardsley, according to Beerbohm,

'knew that life was short, and so loved every hour of it with a kind of jealous intensity'. In March 1897, he was received into the Catholic Church and moved to the south of France, where he died the following year. (Yeats thought his death had been hastened by masturbation.) Yeats frequently quoted Beardsley's 'Beauty is so difficult' and, on his lunar cycle, placed him at the thirteenth phase, on the edge of Unity of Being.

Mabel Beardsley (1871–1916)

Sister of Aubrey Beardsley and wife of actor George Bealby Wright. According to Yeats, in reference to the Rhymers' Club, she was 'practically one of us' (*L* 574); later, she used to attend Yeats's Monday evenings at Woburn Buildings. From 1912, when she was diagnosed as suffering from cancer, until her death in 1916, Yeats was a frequent visitor to her bedside and composed a series of poems on her entitled 'Upon a Dying Lady'. On one occasion she told him: 'I wonder who will introduce me in heaven. It should be my brother but then they might not appreciate the introduction. They might not have good taste' (*L* 575).

Wilfrid Scawen Blunt (1840–1922)

According to Pound, Blunt was 'the last of the great Victorians'. (See *Poetry* [Chicago], vol. 1, 1913.) It would be more correct to describe Blunt, the poet, playwright, agitator for the cause of Ireland and Egypt, one-time lover of Lady Gregory, breeder of Arabian horses, as an example of late-Victorian Byronism. His contacts with Ireland were many. His cousin George Wyndham, Irish Chief Secretary and author of the Wyndham Land Act of 1903, was a frequent visitor to New Buildings, Southover, Horsham, Sussex. In 1881, Blunt conducted an affair with Lady Gregory while she was wintering with her husband in Egypt; in 1888, he was imprisoned for making a speech against evictions on an estate adjoining Coole; in April 1907, his Cuchulain-inspired play *Fand* was performed at the Abbey; in 1911, he appointed Fred Ryan, the first secretary of the Abbey Theatre, editor of *Egypt*, a

London journal dedicated to the cause of Egyptian nationalism. Yeats was a frequent visitor to New Buildings, and he helped Blunt celebrate his seventy-fifth birthday with peacock pie. In his *Oxford Anthology of Modern Verse, 1892–1935* (1936), Yeats included seven poems by Blunt. For his autobiography and comments on Yeats, see Wilfrid Scawen Blunt, *My Diaries: Being a Personal Narrative of Events, 1888–1914* (London: Martin Secker, 1932).

Robert Bridges (1844–1930)

Poet, critic, and one-time physician, Bridges was appointed Poet Laureate in 1913, a position he held until his death. He and Yeats first met in March 1897 at Bridges's home at Yattendon, when Yeats produced a pack of magic cards and proceeded to conduct an occult experiment. In 1910, they became founding members of the English Academy of Letters. They corresponded regularly, and when Yeats was living in Oxford from 1918 to 1922 he was often invited to Bridges's home at Chilswell, near Oxford. Yeats greatly admired Bridges's verse: 'It has an emotional purity and rhythmical delicacy no living man can equal' (*L* 707). See Richard Finneran (ed.), *The Correspondence of Robert Bridges and W. B. Yeats* (London: Macmillan, 1977). For a recent biography, see Catherine Philips, *Robert Bridges: A Life* (Oxford: Oxford University Press, 1992). See also *The Selected Letters of Robert Bridges*, 2 vols, ed. Donald E. Stanford (Newark: University of Delaware Press; London and Toronto: Associated University Presses, 1983).

Edmund Dulac (1882–1953)

According to Ethel Mannin, Dulac was probably Yeats's greatest friend in the 1930s. And it was a friendship that could survive assaults, for as George recognised, her husband had a knack of remaining friends with those he had verbally abused. Dulac was a close friend of Edith Shackleton Heald, and he used to drive Yeats down to Sussex to see her. An accomplished artist, illustrator, and stage designer, Dulac designed the masks and costumes for *At the Hawk's Well*, executed the woodcut for Giraldus Cambrensis which forms the frontispiece for *A Vision*, and composed musical settings for some of Yeats's poems. For his views on Yeats, see 'Without the Twilight' in Stephen Gwynn (ed.), *Scattering Branches* (London: Macmillan, 1940), 135–44.

'John Eglinton' (William Kirkpatrick Magee) (1868–1961)

Born in Dublin and educated at the same high school as Yeats. After a successful undergraduate career at Trinity College, Dublin, he worked in the National Library of Ireland from 1898 to 1921, and appropriately appears in the library episode of *Ulysses*, where Joyce mercilessly plays on his pseudonym. Co-editor with Fred Ryan of *Dana*, a short-lived magazine (1904–5) dedicated to freedom of thought, he was also a fine critic, his early essays appearing in *Bards and Saints* (1899) and *Pebbles from a Brook* (1901). After the establishment of the Free State, he moved to England but continued his involvement in Irish letters. See his *Irish Literary Portraits* (London: Macmillan, 1935), which contains an essay on Yeats, and *A Memoir of A. E.* (London: Macmillan, 1937).

Florence Farr (Emery) (1860–1917)

After failing to become a schoolteacher, Farr embarked on a stage career. In 1884 she married another actor, Edward Emery, but the marriage was not a success; he emigrated to the United States in 1888, and they divorced in 1894 (she is sometimes referred to by critics and historians as Florence Farr Emery or Florence Emery). Yeats was captivated by her performance in John Todhunter's *Sicilian Idyll* staged in May 1890 at Bedford Park, and a close friendship ensued, based on the theatre and the occult. She joined the Golden Dawn in 1890 and quickly became a leading member in the Isis-Urania Temple in London. She was for a time Shaw's lover and acted in the Independent Theatre's production of *Widowers' Houses* and *Arms and the Man*, which was first performed in April 1894 at the Avenue Theatre in London. Florence also acted in *The Land of Heart's Desire*, which Yeats wrote with her in mind, played Aleel in the first production of *The Countess Cathleen*, and in 1899 was appointed General Manager for the first season of the Irish Literary Theatre. In July 1905 she played the part of Dectora in the Theosophical Society's production of *The Shadowy Waters*. In the early years of the new century, with the help of Arnold Dolmetsch's psaltery, she and Yeats gave poetry readings making use of the technique of 'cantillating'. In the dispute over secret groups inside the Golden Dawn after Mathers's expulsion, she lined up against Yeats and Annie Horniman. Their friendship survived, and there is evidence that they had an affair in 1903, but there is something secretive about their relationship: in 'Speaking to the Psaltery' in the early editions of *Ideas of Good and Evil*, she is not mentioned by name but only as a friend; in July 1905, writing from Coole, Yeats invites her to join him on a cycling trip to Canterbury, and adds: 'I do not see why we should not go with some harmless person to keep up appearances' (*L* 456). According to George Yeats, their relationship did not last, because 'she got bored'. In 1907 she contributed articles on the 'new woman' in *New Age* and on drama in the *Mint*. In 1912, she suddenly decided to emigrate to Ceylon, where she became principal of a girls' school and dedicated herself to the local Tamil culture until her death from cancer in 1917. For her biography, see Josephine Johnson, *Florence Farr: Bernard Shaw's 'New Woman'* (Gerrards Cross: Colin Smythe, 1975). Her correspondence with Yeats and Shaw can be found in Clifford Bax (ed.), *Florence Farr, Bernard Shaw and W. B. Yeats: Letters* (London: Home and Van Thal, 1946). See also George Watson's essay 'Yeats, Ibsen and the New Woman', in A. Norman Jeffares (ed.), *Yeats the European* (Savage, Maryland: Barnes and Noble, 1989), 238–52. Pound wrote 'Portrait d'une Femme' with Farr in mind. A fictional portrait of Yeats appears in her semi-autobiographical novel, *The Solemnization of Jacklin* (1912).

Oliver St John Gogarty (1878–1957)

Gogarty, one of the models for Joyce's 'Buck' Mulligan, first met Yeats in 1901 at a play-reading given by Lady Gregory at the Nassau Hotel in Dublin. Medicine and writing were his two careers, and these were supplemented by his larger-than-life personality and mischievous wit. A nose and throat surgeon, he was often called on by Yeats for medical advice, and in October 1920, 'with exuberant gaiety' he removed Yeats's tonsils. In December 1922, he was appointed, along with Yeats, to the Senate. The following month, he was kidnapped by Republicans, and only managed to escape by diving into the Liffey and swimming away. Yeats, whose appointment to the Senate was in part secured by Gogarty, was alarmed and perhaps seriously considered a general removal from Ireland. In a letter of George to Yeats in February 1923 there is a reference to 'Buck Mulligan', testimony to Joyce's power over his fictional and role models. Yeats and Gogarty continued to socialise together both in Dublin and in the west of Ireland. In *The Oxford Book of Modern Verse, 1892–1935*, Yeats gave Gogarty, 'one of the great lyric poets of our age', considerable space. For Gogarty on Yeats, see *As I Was Going down Sackville Street* (London: Rich and Cowan, 1937); *Mourning Became Mrs Spendlove and Other Portraits, Grave and Gay* (New York: Creative Age Press, 1948); *William Butler Yeats: A Memoir* (Dublin: Dolmen Press, 1963).

Maud Gonne (MacBride) (1866–1953)

Daughter of a British Army officer (he reached the rank of Colonel), her contact with Ireland began when her father was posted to the Curragh a year after the 1867 Fenian Rising. She was converted to Irish republicanism after witnessing eviction scenes in Donegal in 1888. She first met Yeats on 30 January 1889, when 'a hansom drove up to our door at Bedford Park' and out stepped 'a classical impersonation of the

Spring' (*A* 123). Yeats regularly proposed to her from 1891 until 1916, but all she offered was a spiritual marriage. Her own life was in constant turmoil. Her relationship with Lucien Millevoye, a follower of the 'new Napoleon', General Boulanger, produced two illegitmate children, George, who was born in 1890 and who died the following year of meningitis, and Iseult, born in August 1894. In February 1903 she married John MacBride, the following January Sean their son was born, and in August 1905 she was granted a legal separation. For fear of losing custody of Sean, she was obliged to remain in France (either in Paris or at Coleville in Normandy), and on account of her Catholicism she could not remarry. On 5 May 1916 John MacBride was executed, and Yeats dutifully crossed to Coleville to propose once more, which he did on 1 July. In the aftermath of Easter 1916 Maud Gonne determined to live in Ireland, but she needed a passport from the British authorities. This was secured by Yeats, who in August 1916 travelled to London with Iseult on her behalf. The following month, Yeats left France, his proposals of marriage having been rejected by both mother and daughter. In early 1918 Maud Gonne MacBride, as she now proudly called herself, bought 73 St Stephen's Green, Dublin, a house she rented later that year to the Yeatses. During the so-called German Plot of May 1918, Maud Gonne was arrested and imprisoned in Holloway Prison until October 1918, when she made her way under disguise to Ireland. She thought to stay in her own home in Dublin, but Yeats barred her entry on account of George being seriously ill and seven months pregnant. The breach in their relationship was partly healed in July 1920 when Maud Gonne appealed to Yeats to help Iseult resolve her marital problems with Francis Stuart. During the War of Independence her house became the centre of IRA activity, but in the Civil War she campaigned against the government's repressive measures (her son Sean had been interned for republican activities). Her differences with Senator Yeats were now greater than ever,

but in late summer 1938 she visited him at Riversdale, Rathfarnham. He thought she had never looked better. For her view of Yeats, see 'Yeats and Ireland', in Stephen Gwynn (ed.), *Scattering Branches* (London: Macmillan, 1940). As for her autobiography, *A Servant of the Queen* (London: Victor Gollancz, 1938), Yeats, as he told George in October 1938, was so upset by it that he could not sleep. He thought it was the same old Maud prepared as ever to place her enthusiasm before her reason. For her biography, see Nancy Cardozo, *Maud Gonne: Lucky Eyes and a High Heart* (London: Victor Gollancz, 1979); Margaret Ward, *Maud Gonne: Ireland's Joan of Arc* (London: Pandora, 1990). For her correspondence with Yeats, see *The Gonne-Yeats Letters, 1893–1938*, ed. Anna MacBride White and A. N. Jeffares (London: Pimlico, 1993).

Iseult Gonne (Stuart) (1894–1954)

The illegitimate daughter of Maud Gonne and Lucien Millevoye, Iseult suffered at the hands of her stepfather John MacBride. After declining Yeats's proposals of marriage in 1916–17, in April 1920 she married Francis Stuart, seven years her junior. Yeats continued to see her; indeed, in July 1920, he was encouraged by George to go to her aid when they heard reports of Stuart's 'sadism' towards her. Iseult is the subject of several Yeats poems, including 'To a Child Dancing in the Wind', 'Men Improve with the Years', 'To a Young Girl', 'Owen Aherne and His Dancers'. In *The Only Jealousy of Emer*, Yeats's play which at one level can be read as concerning the three women he proposed to in 1916 and 1917, the character of the Woman of the Sidhe, or Fand, is modelled on Iseult (George is Emer, and Maud Gonne is Eithne). In his autobiography, *Things To Live For* (London: Cape, 1934), Stuart writes in passing about his marriage with Iseult and their time in Glenmalure. See also Geoffrey Elborn, *Francis Stuart: A Life* (Dublin: Raven Arts, 1990). Yeats's poem 'Leda and the Swan' was published in

Stuart's short-lived magazine *Tomorrow* in August 1924.

Eva Gore-Booth (1870–1926)

Sister of Constance Markievicz, Eva left her home at Lissadell, County Sligo, at twenty-two and worked in the trade union and women's movement in Manchester. Between 1904 and 1918 she published ten volumes of verse. When Yeats visited Lissadell in 1894 he thought of becoming her suitor but dismissed it from his mind: '⟨T⟩his house would never accept so penniless a suitor' (*Mem* 78). Yeats thought the Gore-Booth sisters wasted their lives in action, Eva in social work, Constance in revolutionary politics.

Augusta, Lady Gregory (née Persse) (1852–1932)

She was the seventh daughter of Dudley Persse of Roxborough, County Galway. In 1880, after his return from Ceylon where he had been Governor, she married Sir William Gregory of nearby Coole Park, who was then aged sixty-three, his life of public service effectively over. Their only child, Robert Gregory, was born the following year. During the 1880s Lady Gregory travelled widely through Europe, Egypt, and India with her husband. In 1882 and 1883 she conducted a secret love affair with Wilfrid Scawen Blunt, and when it ended she wrote a series of poems, 'A Woman's Sonnets', which were published under Blunt's name in 1892 (the recent release of Blunt's papers shows the extent of his alteration of these poems). After her husband's death in 1892, she took to wearing widow's weeds, as if in atonement for her double life, and devoted herself to service of Ireland and of her tenants. In 1894 she rented a flat in Queen Anne's Mansions, London, and that spring at the home of Lord Morris met 'Yates' for the first time. In August 1896, the two met again, at Edward Martyn's home Tulira Castle. In 1897, Yeats spent the first of some twenty summers at Coole, and while there, on a visit to the Comte de Basterot at Duras, Kinvara, County Galway, they formulated their proposal for an Irish Literary Theatre. In 1898, captivated by Yeats's *Celtic Twilight* (1893), she visited the Aran Islands, collecting folklore, an activity she pursued in the cottages of her own neighbourhood. During the first decade of the new century she was preoccupied with the theatre in Dublin and in 1904 became Patentee and Director with Yeats and Synge of the Abbey Theatre. She perfected a style of rendering Hiberno-English known as 'Kiltartanese' after the name of her local parish, and composed a series of one-act comedies for the Abbey, including *Spreading the News* (1904) and *Hyacinth Halvey* (1906). Her translation of stories from the Red Branch Cycle, *Cuchulain of Muirthemne* (1902), influenced Yeats in the development of his Cuchulain cycle of plays. More translation followed with *Gods and Fighting Men* (1904). She also wrote tragedies, translated Molière, and contributed to the Revival's Parnellite theme in *The Deliverer* (1911), a play in which Parnell is depicted as Moses. Her collaboration with Yeats remains under-appreciated, but she helped him in writing several of his plays, including *Cathleen ni Houlihan*. In 1907 she travelled with 'courtier' Yeats and Robert Gregory to medieval and Renaissance cities in northern Italy. The last two decades of her life were dominated by efforts to secure a Dublin home for the paintings collected by her nephew Hugh Lane, who drowned when the *Lusitania* was torpedoed in the First World War. The war also claimed her son Robert, who was killed in a flying accident over Italy in 1918. In the period after the Civil War, Roxborough was burned down, but Coole remained untouched, a mark of affection for her among Republicans. In the 1920s she championed the work of Sean O'Casey, who thought of her as a blend of Jesus and Puck. For Yeats, Lady Gregory was by turns substitute mother, financial support, encourager, conscience, unacknowledged and acknowledged collaborator, representative of patrician values, subject for verse. When she died he wrote: 'I have lost one who has been to me for nearly forty years my strength and my conscience' (*L* 796). In 1941 her home at Coole Park was demolished. Her work in the theatre she recorded in *Our Irish Theatre: A Chapter of Autobiography* (1913; repr. Gerrards Cross: Colin Smythe, 1972). Her journals, which she kept from 1916 to 1932, convey a vivid impression of a private self caught up in a public history. See *Lady Gregory's Journals, Volume One: Books One to Twenty-nine, 10 October 1916–24 February 1925*, ed. Daniel Murphy (Gerrards Cross: Colin Smythe; New York: Oxford University Press, 1978), and *Lady Gregory's Journals, Volume Two: Books Thirty to Forty-four, 21 February 1925–9 May 1932*, ed. Daniel Murphy (Gerrards Cross: Colin Smythe; New York; Oxford University Press, 1978). See also *Seventy Years: Being the Autobiography of Lady Gregory* (Gerrards Cross: Colin Smythe, 1974). For her life, see Elizabeth Coxhead, *Lady Gregory: A Literary Portrait* (London: Secker and Warburg, 1966); Hazard Adams, *Lady Gregory* (Lewisburg: Bucknell University Press, 1973); Mary Lou Kohfeldt, *Lady Gregory: The Woman behind the Irish Renaissance* (London: André Deutsch, 1985). For a recent survey of her work, see especially Ann Saddlemyer and Colin Smythe (eds), *Lady Gregory, Fifty Years After* (Gerrards Cross: Colin Smythe; Totowa, New Jersey: Barnes and Noble, 1987). Her writings have been collected in the multi-volume Coole Edition published by Colin Smythe.

Robert Gregory (1881–1918)

Only son of Lady Gregory, he was educated at Harrow and Oxford. Thereafter, he studied at the Slade School of Art in London, went to Paris, and returned to Coole. He accompanied his mother and Yeats on their 1907 tour of Italy. An exhibition of his paintings was held in London in October 1914. After enlisting in 1915, he transferred in January 1916 to the Royal Flying Corps. He was awarded the Légion d'Honneur and the Military Cross, but was killed in a flying accident on the North Italian Front on 23 January 1918. Four of Yeats's poems focus on Robert Gregory, one of which, 'Reprisals', was not published until 1948.

Stephen Gwynn (1864–1950)

Born in Dublin, he graduated from Oxford in 1896 and returned to Dublin in 1904 after spending some years as a journalist in London. From 1906 to 1918 he was a nationalist M.P. for Galway City. During the First World War he enlisted, served in France and reached the rank of Captain. In January 1923 his house at Kimmage, Co. Dublin, was torched by Republicans. Gwynn was a prolific writer, a poet, biographer, essayist, and political commentator. See, for example, *The Irish Situation* (1921), *Experiences of a Literary Man* (1926), and *Ireland in Ten Days* (1935). He knew Yeats well, and they met frequently in London, especially during the First World War. After Yeats's death, Gwynn edited the excellent volume of tributes, *Scattering Branches* (London: Macmillan, 1940).

Edith Shackleton Heald (1884–1976)

In 1934, after a successful career in journalism, Edith and her sister Nora moved from their Regency house in St Petersburg Place, near Hyde Park, to the Chantry House, Steyning, Sussex. Nora continued to edit the *Lady* and Edith to write a weekly column, 'With Prejudice', under the name 'Clio'. According to Yeats, Edith was once the best paid woman journalist in the world. Their romance blossomed in 1937, and they exchanged some sixty letters, now housed in the Houghton Library, Harvard University. At Steyning Edith kept 'the Yeats room' especially for his use, and he wrote several poems there as well as parts of *Purgatory*. After he died, the painter Hannah Gluckstein ('Gluck') moved into the Chantry House and became Edith's partner. For further details, see Diana Souhami, *Gluck: 1895–1978* (London: Pandora, 1988).

Frederick Robert Higgins (1896–1941)

Irish poet, founding member of the Irish Academy, Managing Director of the Abbey

Theatre, and co-editor with Yeats of *Broad-sides* (1935–7). His poetry reflects a strong interest in the Irish folk tradition. For his views on Yeats, see 'Yeats as Irish Poet', in Stephen Gwynn (ed.), *Scattering Branches* (London: Macmillan, 1940), 145–55.

Annie Horniman (1860–1937)

Patron of the Abbey Theatre from 1904 to 1910 and a pioneer of repertory theatre in Britain, she used her legacy from her family's tea empire to support such theatre ventures as Shaw's *Arms and the Man* at the Avenue Theatre in 1894 before progressing to full-scale subsidy at the Abbey and the Gaiety Theatre in Manchester from 1908. Before her involvement in the theatre, an interest in the occult led her to join the Golden Dawn in January 1890, and it was there that she met Yeats, Farr, and others connected with a Theatre of Art. She financially supported Mathers but later withdrew her subsidy on account of his heavy drinking and the intrusion of politics into the occult. Mathers reacted by expelling her, an action that led to rebellion among the London members in spring 1900. In the ensuing months she campaigned against secret groups in the Golden Dawn, an issue that Yeats too felt strongly about. In February 1903 she resigned from the Golden Dawn, and the same year, consulting her tarot cards, she decided to throw her support behind Yeats and an Irish theatre in Dublin. Disputes plagued the early years at the Abbey, and she was often at the centre of them. Her notes on yellow cards were so full of complaint that Synge felt he was in danger of losing all feeling for daffodils. 'A puritan in the theatre' who established a theatre that went by the title 'The Gaiety', she was a more complicated and humorous person than is sometimes allowed. She thought a repertory theatre should be professionally managed and the actors and actresses be in a trade union. Ten volumes of newspaper cuttings from the early years of this century, deposited in the John Rylands Library at the University of Manchester, attest to her interest in the Abbey Theatre project. For a recent biography, see Sheila Goodie, *Annie Horniman: A Pioneer in the Theatre* (London: Methuen, 1990). See also Adrian Frazier, *Behind the Scenes: Yeats, Horniman, and the Struggle for the Abbey Theatre* (Berkeley and Los Angeles: University of California Press, 1990).

William Horton (1864–1919)

A mystical painter, Horton was one of Yeats's occult friends. In March 1896 Yeats acted as his sponsor for initiation into the Golden Dawn, but after 1899 their friendship cooled. He continued to seek Yeats's advice over his symbolic drawings but later blamed his inability to create on Yeats. Horton also criticised Yeats for not pursuing a higher visionary path. He considered the Yeatses' automatic writing sessions to be 'unreliable, foolish or dangerous', but they left a chair vacant for him after his death. Yeats wrote an introduction to Horton's *Book of Images* (1898), and, partly because of his cautionary and revealing 'scrap of paper' concerning Plato's Phaedrus myth, thought of dedicating *A Vision* to him. Horton appears in Yeats's 'All Souls' Night' along with other members of the Golden Dawn. For their correspondence, see George Mills Harper, *W. B. Yeats and W. T. Horton: The Record of an Occult Friendship* (Atlantic Highlands, New Jersey: Humanities Press, 1980).

Douglas Hyde (1860–1949)

Hyde was a key figure in the making of modern Ireland. His 'sensational' speech 'On the Necessity of De-Anglicising the Irish Nation' before the National Literary Society, Dublin, in November 1892 was followed in 1893 by the publication of *Love Songs of Connacht*, translations of Gaelic songs into a more natural style of English. The same year he became President of the Gaelic League, a movement dedicated to a language revival in the classrooms of Ireland. In 1901, his Gaelic play *Casadh an tSúgáin* (The Twisting of the Rope) was the first modern play in Gaelic to be staged in Dublin. Where Hyde immersed himself in the folk mind, Yeats, from a similar background, wanted a more interventionist role in the culture: 'He had the folk mind as no modern man has had it, its qualities and its defects' (*A* 439). Reluctant to countenance the politicisation of the Gaelic League, Hyde resigned at the *ard-fheis* in August 1915. In 1925 he was coopted as a Free State Senator; in the early 1930s he became Chairman of the Folklore Institute; and in 1938 he returned to public life with his appointment as the first President of Ireland. For a recent biography, see Janet Egleson Dunleavy and Gareth W. Dunleavy, *Douglas Hyde: A Maker of Modern Ireland* (Berkeley and Los Angeles: University of California Press, 1991).

Lionel Johnson (1867–1902)

Son of an Irish Army Officer, and cousin of Olivia Shakespear, Johnson was educated at Winchester and New College, Oxford. He embarked on a career as a literary critic in London, joined the Rhymers' Club, and published two volumes of verse, including *Ireland and Other Poems* (1897). For a few years, Johnson was Yeats's closest friend in London: ' "I need ten years in the wilderness," he would say to me, "and you ten years in a library" ' (*Mem* 35). But with the alcoholic disorder of his personal life, Johnson soon became associated in Yeats's mind with the tragic generation of the 1890s. Yeats did much to promote Johnson's work after his death: a selection of his verse entitled *Twenty-One Poems* was published in 1905 by the Dun Emer Press, and *Poetry and Ireland: Essays by W. B. Yeats and Lionel Johnson* was published by the Cuala Press in 1908. Johnson is referred to by name in two of Yeats's poems, 'The Grey Rock' and 'In Memory of Robert Gregory'.

James Joyce (1882–1941)

Without Yeats, Joyce would have found it immensely difficult to assume that Dublin was anything other than a provincial city. At first his competitor, Yeats became by the time of *Finnegans Wake* his accomplice, 'a daintical pair of accomplasses', Yeats with his gyres and Joyce with his interlocking circles and female delta. In conversation with Thomas MacGreevy in April 1928, Joyce 'spoke very kindly of W. B. recalled that he met him once at Euston at 9 *a.m.* to bring him to his rooms and talk.' (Joyce was on his way to Paris in December 1902 and needed some reviewing work to subsidise his medical studies; Yeats set his alarm to ensure he got up on time.) After Joyce left Ireland in October 1904, they met perhaps only twice, once in Dublin in 1912 when Joyce called on Yeats for help in securing a publisher for *Dubliners*, and once in Paris in 1922 when they met in a restaurant with the Pounds. But their careers overlapped, and they always showed awareness of each other in their work. Yeats was at first unsure of Joyce and tried to place him by reference to the Royal University, Aquinas, a closed mind, the 'son of a small Parnellite organiser'; then he realised he was someone to be reckoned with. This was followed by a sense of protectiveness (he relished defending *Ulysses* against Edmund Gosse at the Savile Club in 1922), and selective admiration for his writings. In an interview conducted with the *New York Times* in March 1914, Yeats half-recognised that someone like Joyce would emerge: 'The world will have to go through a period of violent realism, of dragging into the light what is hidden, before it can return to a literature of beauty and peace.' Interviewer: 'Has the sex problem figured in the new Irish dramas?' Yeats: 'In Ireland the sex question has hardly arisen. The problems that interest Ireland are all those of public life.'

Constance Markievicz (née Gore-Booth) (1868–1927)

Elder sister of Eva Gore-Booth, Constance studied painting in London and Paris, where she met and married a Polish Count, Casimir Dunin-Markievicz. On returning to Dublin in 1903 she became involved in drama and the arts before turning to nationalist politics. In 1909 she founded Na Fianna, an Irish boy-scout movement. During the Dublin Lock-Out of 1913 she ran a soup kitchen for workers, work described by Yeats in 'Easter

1916' as 'ignorant good-will'. In the Easter Rising she helped capture the College of Surgeons, was imprisoned in England, and released in June 1917. In the general election of 1918 she became the first woman to be elected to the House of Commons, but refused to take her seat. Instead, she was appointed Minister of Labour in the first Dáil Éireann. During the Civil War she took the republican side and went on hunger strike. In 1926 she joined de Valera's newly formed Fianna Fáil party, and was re-elected to the Dáil in 1927. As a boy, Yeats was struck by her beauty and aristocratic bearing as he peered over to the grey wall and roof of Lissadell, home to 'Two girls in silk kimonos, both/Beautiful, one a gazelle' (*VP* 475). For a recent biography, see Diana Norman, *A Life of Constance Markievicz* (Swords, Co. Dublin: Poolbeg, 1988).

Edward Martyn (1859–1923)

Educated at Belvedere, Beaumont, and Oxford, Martyn returned to his family home at Tulira Castle in County Galway. He founded the Palestrina Choir in the Pro-Cathedral in Dublin, the Feis Cheoil, an annual music festival, and Túr Gloine, a co-operative for making stained-glass windows. In 1899, with George Moore and Yeats, he helped establish the Irish Literary Theatre. He wrote several Ibsenesque plays, including *The Heather Field* (1899) and *Maeve* (1899), a play that Yeats thought 'too poetical, too remote from normal life to draw the crowd' (*A* 425). In 1906, with Padraic Colum and others, Martyn broke away from the Abbey Theatre to form the Theatre of Ireland. In *Hail and Farewell* (1911–14), Moore contrasted Yeats's parlour magic with Martyn's cathedral magic; in *Dramatis Personae* (1935), Yeats, who had earlier written about them in his play *The Cat and the Moon* (1926), called Moore a peasant sinner and Martyn a peasant saint; in the 'Scylla and Charybdis' episode of *Ulysses*, Stephen Dedalus imagines them as Don Quixote and Sancho Panza, adding, 'We are becoming important, it seems.' It was while staying at Tulira Castle in August 1896 that Yeats had his Archer Vision of a 'marvellous naked woman shooting an arrow at a star', but Martyn was angry with Yeats for using the room above the chapel to evoke the lunar powers.

John Masefield (1878–1967)

Journalist and writer, Masefield was a friend of Yeats from the autumn of 1900, when they first met, until Yeats's death in 1939. From 1900 to 1907, he often attended Yeats's Monday evenings at Woburn Buildings, and has left vivid accounts in both prose and verse. In 1930 he was appointed Poet Laureate to succeed Robert Bridges. See *Some Memories of W. B. Yeats* (Dublin: Cuala Press, 1940), *So Long to Learn: Chapters of an Autobiography* (London: William Heinemann, 1952), *Letters to Reyna*, ed. William Buchan (London: Buchan and Enright, 1983). For a biography, see Constance Babington Smith, *John Masefield: A Life* (Oxford: Oxford University Press, 1978).

Samuel Liddell 'MacGregor' Mathers (1854–1918)

Son of a commercial clerk, Mathers moved to London from Bournemouth in 1885 after the death of his mother. In 1887 he helped to found with Dr William Woodman and Dr Wynn Westcott, Coroner for North London, the Order of the Golden Dawn, a society dedicated to the practice of ceremonial magic. The same year his book *The Kabbala Unveiled* was published. Under the influence of the Celtic Movement, he took the name MacGregor and asserted his right to the Jacobite title of Earl of Glenstrae. Yeats first met him in the British Museum Reading Room in 1889, almost at once fell under his spell, and was initiated by him into the Golden Dawn on 7 March 1890. After 1891, Mathers lived in Paris with his wife Moina Bergson, sister of the famous philosopher Henri Bergson, and took to wearing full Highland costume. Until 1896 Mathers was supported financially by Horniman (until 1890 he was Curator of the Horniman Museum at Forest Hill), but she withdrew her allowance on account of his drinking habits and neglect of occult duties. His attempt to control the London Temple through Farr led to rebellion in spring 1900. Westcott was accused of forging the correspondence of Fraulein Sprengel and therefore casting doubt on the German origins of the Golden Dawn. This backfired, and Mathers dispatched Aleister Crowley to repossess the London headquarters in Blythe Road. The headquarters were retaken by the London members, led by Yeats, and Mathers was expelled in April 1900. The Temples in Bradford and Edinburgh remained loyal to Mathers, as did Westcott. Yeats's admiration for Mathers can be felt in his 1890s fictional portrait of Maclagan in *The Speckled Bird*, and in the 1920s he returned to Mathers in his verse and *Autobiographies*. For information on Mathers, see Ellic Howe, *The Magicians of the Golden Dawn: A Documentary History of a Magical Order, 1887–1923* (London: Routledge and Kegan Paul, 1972).

George Moore (1852–1933)

Born into a distinguished Catholic landed family in County Mayo, Moore lived through several phases of his life and emerged to tell the story of each: a young man in Paris mixing in artistic circles (*Confessions of a Young Man*, 1888); the Land War in Ireland (*A Drama in Muslin*, 1887); English naturalism (*Esther Waters*, 1894); Irish Catholicism and provincial lifestyle (*The Untilled Field*, 1903, and *The Lake*, 1905); return to Ireland and goodbye again (*Hail and Farewell*, 1911–14). His friendship with Yeats issued in their jointly written play, *Diarmuid and Grania* (1901); Moore had earlier dedicated *Evelyn Innes* (1898) to Yeats. But then they parted. Yeats, often accompanied by the mocking image of a rook, is rarely out of Moore's sights in *Hail and Farewell*, but Yeats took his revenge twenty years later in *Dramatis Personae* (1935): 'He lacked manners, but had manner; he could enter a room so as to draw your attention without seeming to, his French, his knowledge of painting, suggested

travel and leisure. Yet nature had denied him the final touch: he had a coarse palate' (*A* 443). The authorised biography was written by Joseph Hone; see *The Life of George Moore* (London: Victor Gollancz, 1936).

Thomas Sturge Moore (1870–1944)

Poet, wood engraver, art historian, and brother of the Cambridge philosopher G. E. Moore, Sturge Moore began his career as a wood engraver under Ricketts and Shannon at the Vale in 1888. His first work was published in the *Dial* in 1892, and from 1896 to 1903 he was involved in editing books for the Vale Press. He first met Yeats in 1899, and in time they became close friends. Moore was responsible for the cover designs of the following Yeats titles published by Macmillan between 1916 and 1940: *Reveries over Childhood and Youth* (1916), *Responsibilities* (1918), *Per Amica Silentia Lunae* (1918), *The Wild Swans at Coole* (1919), *The Cutting of an Agate* (1919), *Four Plays for Dancers* (1921), *The Tower* (1928), *The Winding Stair* (1933), *Last Poems and Plays* (1940). He was also responsible for the Cuala Press edition of *Four Years* (1921) and for the Harvard University Press edition of *Letters to the New Island* (1934). Their correspondence in the 1920s and 1930s helped Yeats clarify his ideas on the paranormal; in contrast to his friend, the sceptical Moore, in his essay on Yeats in 1939, thought 'extreme complication was the most acceptable character of this psychic Cosmos'. See *W. B. Yeats and T. Sturge Moore: Their Correspondence, 1901–1937*, ed. Ursula Bridge (London: Routledge and Kegan Paul, 1953; repr. Westport, Conn.: Greenwood Press, 1978); 'Yeats', in *English: The Magazine of the English Association*, vol. 2, no. 11, 1939, 273–8. See also Malcolm Easton (ed.), *T. Sturge Moore (1870–1944): Contributions to the Art of the Book and Collaboration with Yeats* (Hull: University of Hull, 1970).

Sean O'Casey (1880–1964)

Dramatist of the Dublin tenements, his early trilogy (*The Shadow of a Gunman*, 1923; *Juno and the Paycock*, 1924; and *The*

Plough and the Stars, 1926) met with both popular acclaim and, for the last play, republican hostility. For Yeats, the Easter Rising showed that romantic Ireland was not dead and gone; for O'Casey, 'Things had changed, but not utterly; and no terrible beauty was to be born. Short Mass was still the favourite service, and Brian Boru's harp still bloomed on the bottles of beer.' His next play, *The Silver Tassie*, was rejected by Yeats and caused a bitter wrangle and exchange of letters in public, as a result of which O'Casey left Ireland and settled permanently in Devon. His affection for Lady Gregory never wavered, and in time, as his six-volume *Autobiographies* (1939–54) suggest, he became reconciled with Yeats.

'Frank O'Connor' (Michael O'Donovan) (1903–66)

Irish novelist, short-story writer, translator, and dramatist, he took the republican side during the Civil War. Appointed a Director of the Abbey in 1935, he was constantly engaged with battles over the Theatre's direction. He resigned soon after Yeats's death, became poetry editor of the *Bell*, had a successful career in the 1950s lecturing in the United States, and returned to Ireland in 1961. In the 1930s O'Connor provided the elderly Yeats with youthful opposition and renewed contact with Gaelic culture. For his memories of Yeats, see 'Two Friends: Yeats and A.E.', *Yale Review*, vol. 29, no. 1, September 1939, 60–88. Cited in E. H. Mikhail, *W. B. Yeats: Interviews and Recollections*, vol. 2 (London: Macmillan; New York: Barnes and Noble, 1977), 260–71. For his life, see James Matthews, *Voices: A Life of Frank O'Connor* (New York: Atheneum, 1987).

John O'Leary (1830–1907)

In 1865, while still a medical student at Trinity College, Dublin, O'Leary was arrested for Fenian activities. He spent five years in prison, and fifteen years in exile in Paris. On returning to Ireland in 1885, he became President of the Young Ireland Society and of the Irish Republican Brotherhood.

Yeats first met him in 1886 and at once recognised that he was 'in the presence of his theme' (*A* 96). Yeats associated O'Leary with a romantic form of Irish nationalism, a form that accompanied Yeats throughout his life. O'Leary assembled his reminiscences in *Recollections of Fenians and Fenianism*, 2 vols (London: Downey, 1896). For Yeats's views of O'Leary, see *Autobiographies*. O'Leary makes a memorable appearance in 'September 1913' ('Romantic Ireland's dead and gone,/It's with O'Leary in the grave') and 'Beautiful Lofty Things' ('O'Leary's noble head').

Ezra Pound (1885–1972)

It was in May 1909 that Olivia and Dorothy Shakespear introduced Pound to Yeats, 'the only living man whose work has anything more than a most temporary interest'. During the winter 1911–12, he took charge of Yeats's Monday evenings, distributing Yeats's cigarettes and Chianti. In November 1913 Yeats and Pound spent the first of three winters at Stone Cottage, Coleman's Hatch, in Sussex, Pound acting as Yeats's secretary. Their professional and personal interests were often entwined at this period. In April 1914, Pound married Dorothy Shakespear. Three years later, Yeats married her cousin, Georgina Hyde-Lees, and Pound was best man. Pound expressed an early interest in Olivia Shakespear, the woman Yeats had lived with in 1896 and 1897; in the summer of 1918 Iseult was his secretary and possibly lost her virginity to him in Yeats's flat at Woburn Buildings. After his abandonment of England in 1920, Pound remained in contact with Yeats, and the two spent several winters together in Rapallo beginning in 1928. They enjoyed each other's company. Yeats wrote *A Packet for Ezra Pound* (1929), warning him against becoming a Senator; in the Cantos written in prison in Pisa in 1946 and 1947, the 'American traitor' affectionately recalled their time together at Stone Cottage. The extent of their influence on each other is the subject of James Longenbach's *Stone Cottage: Pound, Yeats and Modernism* (New York and

Oxford: Oxford University Press, 1988). For Pound's biography, see Humphrey Carpenter, *A Serious Character: The Life of Ezra Pound* (London: Faber and Faber, 1988). For the Pounds' view of the Yeatses, see *Ezra Pound and Dorothy Shakespear: Their Letters, 1909–1914*, ed. Omar Pound and A. Walton Litz (New York: New Directions, 1984). For Pound's early period in London, see Patricia Hutchins, *Ezra Pound's Kensington: An Exploration, 1885–1913* (London: Faber and Faber, 1965).

John Quinn (1870–1924)

Irish-American lawyer and wealthy patron of the arts, Quinn, 'the busiest man in America' according to Pound, played a not insignificant role in the development of the Literary Revival in Ireland. During his first visit to Ireland in the summer of 1902, he met the leading figures of the Revival, including the Yeats family. Yeats's first lecture tour of the United States and Canada in 1903 and 1904 was organised and financed by Quinn. J. B. Yeats's years in New York from 1907 until his death in 1922 were subsidised by Quinn. In 1909, a serious quarrel broke out between W. B. Yeats and Quinn over Quinn's mistress Dorothy Coates (Quinn accused Yeats of loose gossip and of making advances), and it was not until 1914 that they became reconciled. Never slow to express his viewpoint, Quinn told Yeats he was on Britain's side during the First World War, was bored by Crowley and magic, warned him about the drain on his resources that Thoor Ballylee would represent, and thought Irish nationalists had backed the wrong horse in supporting Sinn Fein. Quinn took an active interest in all matters connected with literature and the arts in Ireland. In 1912 he represented the Abbey players when they were arrested in Philadelphia for staging *The Playboy of the Western World*. In 1916, with the publication of *A Portrait of the Artist as a Young Man* by Benjamin Huebsch in New York, he championed Joyce, and in 1920 and 1921 he acted as lawyer in defence of the American editors of the *Little Review* for publishing the

'Nausicaa' episode of *Ulysses*. For his biography, see B. L. Reid, *The Man from New York: John Quinn and His Friends* (New York: Oxford University Press, 1968). For his correspondence, see Alan Himber (ed.), *The Letters of John Quinn to William Butler Yeats* (Ann Arbor, Michigan: UMI Research Press, 1983).

Charles Ricketts (1866–1931) and Charles Shannon (1863–1937)

Yeats's friendship with Ricketts dates from November 1899 when they met at an Arnold Dolmetsch concert. Ricketts at first thought Yeats interestingly provincial, and, later, in 1904, after a dinner party with Rothenstein and Yeats, he confided in his journal: 'Yeats was diffuse, conventional and transcendental, astute, but too partial to the notion of the rule "whereby I shall be saved".' Earlier, in 1896, with the help of Llewellyn Hacon, Ricketts and Shannon established the Vale Press, and published some fifty titles before its demise in 1903. They also edited an occasional magazine, the *Dial*, and ran an art shop, The Sign of the Dial, in Warwick Street in London. Ricketts went on to become a leading authority on Japanese and oriental art. Yeats, along with Wilde and Shaw, used to attend their Friday open evenings at 1 The Vale (off the Chelsea Road). After his schemes in London for a Literary Theatre came to nothing, Yeats still wanted Ricketts to become the designer for the Irish National Theatre Society. Ricketts designed the scenery and costumes for the 1908 Abbey production of Synge's *Well of the Saints*, and the costumes for several of Yeats's plays, including *The King's Threshold*, staged at the Royal Court Theatre in May 1914, and *On Baile's Strand*, performed in London in June 1915. A Ricketts motif appears on the inside covers of the uniform edition of Yeats's work published by Macmillan in the 1920s, the cover design for which, stamped blind on green cloth and reminiscent of the Vale Press Shakespeare, was also by Ricketts. Shannon's oil painting of Yeats, now hanging in the Houghton Library, Harvard University, was executed in 1908. For Ricketts's biography, see J. G. P. Delaney, *Charles Ricketts: A Biography* (Oxford: Clarendon Press, 1990). See also Charles Ricketts, *Self-Portrait: Taken from the Letters and Journals*, collected and compiled by T. Sturge Moore, ed. Cecil Lewis (London: Peter Davies, 1939). For a discussion of Ricketts's designs for Yeats's plays, see Liam Miller, *The Noble Drama of W. B. Yeats* (Dublin: Dolmen Press; New Jersey: Humanities Press, 1977).

Lennox Robinson (1886–1958)

Together with T. C. Murray and R. J. Ray, Robinson was one of the Cork school of 'realist' playwrights, his plays including *The Clancy Name* (1908), *Harvest* (1910), *Patriots* (1912), *The White-Headed Boy* (1916), and *The Big House* (1926). He was Manager of the Abbey Theatre from 1910 to 1914 and from 1919 to 1923, when he was appointed a Director, a post he held until 1956. Robinson was responsible for the Abbey not closing on the death of Edward VII and thereby earned the wrath of Annie Horniman. For his memories of Yeats, see 'The Man, the Dramatist' in Stephen Gwynn (ed.), *Scattering Branches* (London: Macmillan, 1940), 55–114, and *Curtain Up* (London: Michael Joseph, 1942). 'From the day I met him to the day of his death he ⟨Yeats⟩ was the dominant personality in my life.' The official history of the Abbey Theatre, *Ireland's Abbey Theatre: A History, 1899–1951*, was written by Robinson and published in 1951.

William Rothenstein (1872–1945)

Born in Bradford in the same year as Max Beerbohm, Gordon Craig, Aubrey Beardsley, and William Nicholson, Rothenstein went on to become one of the leading painters of his generation. After sharing a studio in Paris with Phil May, he moved to Oxford and then in 1894 to London. He lived near The Vale in Chelsea, and Ricketts and Shannon became his closest friends. His portfolio of prints, *Liber Juniorum* (1899), included portraits of Beardsley, Binyon, Housman,

and Yeats. Rothenstein first met Yeats at York Powell's home in Bedford Park in 1893, and their friendship grew. When the Easter Rising broke out, Yeats was staying with Rothenstein at Iles Farm in Gloucestershire. The following month Rothenstein's brother Albert Rutherston proposed Yeats for membership of the Savile Club. In 1935, on Yeats's seventieth birthday, Rothenstein was responsible for organising a tribute. Rothenstein's sketches of Yeats (ink, pencil, chalk, crayon, lithograph) extend from 1897 to 1935. For illustrations and memories of Yeats, see his *Men and Memories*, 2 vols (London: Faber and Faber, 1931–2), and *Since Fifty* (London: Faber and Faber, 1939). See also his essay 'Yeats as a Painter Saw Him', in Stephen Gwynn (ed.), *Scattering Branches* (London: Macmillan, 1940).

Margot Ruddock (Collis) (1907–1951)

In September 1934, six months after his Steinach operation, Yeats fell under the spell of the poet and actress, Margot Collis. In the London production of *The Player Queen*, she played the role of Queen. He wrote a poem to 'Margot' (unpublished until 1970) in which he expressed the hope that 'The Age of Miracles renew,/Let me be loved as though still young/Or let me fancy that it's true,/When my brief final years are gone/You shall have time to turn away/And cram those open eyes with day.' In 1936 she suffered a breakdown in Barcelona the day after arriving from Majorca, where she had been visiting Yeats. 'A Crazed Girl' and 'Sweet Dancer' were inspired by her. She died in an asylum in 1951 at the age of forty-four. For more details of their relationship, see Roger McHugh (ed.), *Ah, Sweet Dancer: W. B. Yeats, Margot Ruddock: A Correspondence* (London and New York: Macmillan, 1970).

George Russell ('AE') (1867–1935)

Poet, artist, and mystic, Russell was a practical visionary who joined Plunkett's Irish Agricultural Organisation Society, edited their magazine, the *Irish Homestead*, from 1905 to 1923, and became an influential voice as editor of the *Irish Statesman* from 1923 to 1930. In his youth he was an active member in Dublin of the Theosophical Society and the Hermetic Society, and became closely associated with Yeats. Russell is the subject of Yeats's story 'A Visionary' in *The Celtic Twilight* (1893). He was also involved with Yeats in theatre work in the early years of the new century and was appointed Vice-President of the Irish National Theatre Society. But then their ways parted. In the 1920s, Russell held Friday afternoon teas at his house in Rathgar, and he seldom missed Yeats's evenings at Merrion Square, where he and Yeats would argue about politics, Indian philosophy, and poetry. After his death George Yeats told her husband that Russell was the nearest to a saint they would ever meet. She thought Yeats a better poet but no saint. In *The Interpreters* (London: Macmillan, 1922), a novel of ideas about Ireland, Russell used Yeats as his model for the character of Lavelle and described him as 'the imperialist of idealism'. For his views on Yeats, see Monk Gibbon (ed.), *The Living Torch AE* (London: Macmillan, 1937), Alan Denson (ed.), *Letters from AE* (London and New York: Aberlard-Schuman, 1961), and Peter Kuch, *Yeats and AE* (Gerrards Cross: Colin Smythe, 1986). For Yeats on Russell, see among others *The Letters of W. B. Yeats* (1954) and his 1932 essay 'My Friend's Book' in *Essays and Introductions* (1961).

Olivia Shakespear (née Tucker) (1867–1938)

When Olivia Shakespear died in October 1938 Yeats wrote to Dorothy Wellesley: 'For more than forty years she has been the centre of my life in London and during all that time we have never had a quarrel, sadness sometimes but never a difference. When I first met her she was in her late twenties but in looks a lovely young girl. When she died she was a lovely old woman. You would have approved her. She came of a long line of soldiers and during the last war thought it her duty to stay in London through all the air raids. She was not more lovely than distinguished – no matter what happened she never lost her solitude. She was Lionel Johnson's cousin and felt and thought as he did. For the moment I cannot bear the thought of London. I will find her memory everywhere' (*L* 916). Yeats was introduced to Olivia Shakespear in May 1894 by Lionel Johnson. She had an unhappy marriage and in March 1896 began an affair with Yeats that lasted until spring 1897. In *The Wind among the Reeds*, a series of Olivia Shakespear poems can be discerned, where the beloved is mortal and clothed in the imagery of hair (in the Maud Gonne series the beloved is like an immortal and repeatedly referred to by her eyes). His affair with Olivia Shakespear, 'Diana Vernon' as he refers to her in *Memoirs*, ended when his dormant passion for Maud Gonne reawoke, and subsequently Yeats suffered a breakdown, in part because he felt guilty about abandoning her. Contact was renewed in 1900, and in 1909 she introduced Pound to Yeats. Their relationship may have strengthened again after June 1910; in 1911 they were at seances together. Her salon played host to mediums, occultists, and writers alike, and these included Eva Fowler, the Radcliffe sisters, Wyndham Lewis, Henri Gaudier-Brzeska, Richard Aldington, Hilda Doolittle, William Carlos Williams, and T. E. Hulme. Pound's marriage to her daughter and Yeats's marriage to her niece meant that their paths were even more closely entwined. 'After Long Silence', a poem written in 1929, seems to afford a nostalgic glimpse of their 1890s relationship: 'Bodily decrepitude is wisdom; young/We loved each other and were ignorant' (*VP* 523). For an account of their relationship, see John Harwood, *Olivia Shakespear and W. B. Yeats: After Long Silence* (London: Macmillan, 1989). In *The Literary Year-Book, 1897* (London: George Allen, 1897), Olivia Shakespear is described as 'one of the few artists in fine fiction of our generation, who is content to write, or so we imagine, purely for art's sake.' Her novels include *Love on a Mortal Lease* (1894), *The*

False Laurel (1896), and *The Devotees* (1904).

Arthur Symons (1865–1945)

Born in Wales of Cornish parents, Symons played an important part in the Yeats story during the 1890s, replacing Lionel Johnson as his intimate friend. Yeats first met him at the Rhymers' Club. In October 1895 Yeats rented rooms adjacent to Symons in Fountain Court. Their friendship deepened with trips to Ireland in the summer of 1896 and to Paris in November and December 1896. The same year Symons edited the short-lived magazine the *Savoy*, to which Yeats contributed stories and verse. In 1899 there appeared *The Symbolist Movement in Literature*, in which Symons, who was himself known as the English Verlaine, hailed Yeats as 'the chief representative of that movement in our country'. Echoes of Symons's imagery can be heard in Yeats's verse, but after Symons's breakdown in 1908 Yeats distanced himself from his former friend. For his life, see Karl Beckson, *Arthur Symons: A Life* (Oxford: Clarendon Press, 1987). For Yeats's account of his friendship with Symons, one of the figures in 'The Tragic Generation', see *Autobiographies*, 318–29.

John Millington Synge (1871–1909)

The first major playwright the Abbey Theatre produced, Synge (pronounced as in *sing*-song) had been 'a drifting, silent man, full of hidden passion' (*Mem* 203). Yeats believed he had been the making of Synge by persuading him in December 1896 when they met in Paris to go to Ireland: 'I told him of Aran where I had just been – and find expression for a life that lacked it' (*Mem* 105). Having been brought up in a restricted Dublin middle-class Protestant background and losing God, he discovered Ireland, the country people, and his own voice. His plays, from the tragic pathos of *Riders to the Sea* through the black comedy *The Well of Saints* to the ever-fresh *Playboy of the Western World*, capture his love affair with rural Ireland. His unconventional life-style

occasionally shocked Yeats, his Co-Director of the Abbey, not least because he found inspiration in Maire O'Neill, one of the players. Vilified by the Dublin press, especially after the *Playboy* riots in January 1907, Synge remained aloof, nursing the Hodgkins' disease from which he died in March 1909. For Yeats's views on Synge, see 'J. M. Synge and the Ireland of His Time' in *Essays and Introductions*, and 'The Death of Synge' in *Autobiographies*. Synge's opinion of Yeats can be found in *The Collected Letters of John Millington Synge*, vol. 1, 1871–1907, ed. Ann Saddlemyer (Oxford: Clarendon Press, 1983), and Ann Saddlemyer (ed.), *Letters to Molly: John Millington Synge to Maire O'Neill, 1906–1909* (Cambridge, Mass.: Belknap Press of Harvard University, 1971).

Rabindranath Tagore (1861–1941)

Bengali writer and teacher, in 1913 Tagore won the Nobel Prize for Literature, was awarded a doctorate by Calcutta University, and received a knighthood in 1914. On his third visit to England, in 1912 and 1913, he was acclaimed by a group of writers and artists that included Rothenstein and Yeats. In 1913, Tagore's play *The Post Office* was produced at the Abbey Theatre, and the same year there appeared *Gitanjali (Song Offerings)*, published by Macmillan with a foreword by Yeats, and *The Crescent Moon*, also published by Macmillan, with a cover design by Sturge Moore. His feelings of being a stranger in London are recorded in his autobiography *My Reminiscences* (London: Macmillan, 1917). *Personality*, a series of essays on philosophy and education, was published by Macmillan in 1917, a year before Yeats's *Per Amica Silentia Lunae*, a work with which it can be compared. In his study *Rabindranath Tagore: His Life and Work* (Calcutta: Association Press; London: Oxford University Press, 1928), Edward Thompson took Yeats to task for naively assuming that 'the civilisation of Bengal remains unbroken' and for inventing an unbroken unity of the Eastern mind: 'No man ever had such enthusiastic disciples and

334

friends as Rabindranath, but no man ever ploughed his way through such a cloud of detraction' (32). A similar criticism can be found in Mary Lago's essay 'Restoring Rabindranath Tagore', in Mary Lago and Ronald Warwick (eds), *Rabindranath Tagore: Perspectives in Time* (London: Macmillan, 1989). There is evidence in his letters, however, that Yeats was aware of the animosity felt by Indians against Tagore, and he once compared his own embattled position in Ireland with Tagore's in India.

Walter James Turner (1889–1946)

Australian by birth, he came to Europe at an early age and settled in England. He quickly established himself as a poet and music critic, writing for the *New Statesman*, the *Daily Express*, and the *London Mercury*. A friend and disciple of the pianist Arthur Schnabel, in the 1930s he worked with Yeats on bringing together music and verse. He arranged the music for Yeats's second BBC broadcast on 'The Poet's Pub' and also contributed to several issues of *Broadside* (1935–7). Yeats, who used to lunch with Turner at the Savile Club, thought enough of Turner's verse to include twelve of his poems in *The Oxford Book of Modern Verse, 1892–1935*. He also praised his satirical novel *The Aesthetes* (1928), and in so doing gave offence to Lady Ottoline Morrell, the model for Lady Caraway. Yeats was perplexed and wrote, but she was unmoved. At the bottom of his last letter to her in March 1937, she added 'Yeats fini!' Yeats and Turner were apparently the best talkers at the Savile, a club that prided itself on its talk. According to Patric Dickinson, they talked simultaneously and never listened to one another. Turner was with Yeats at Roquebrune the week he died in January 1939. For Turner's memories of Yeats, see *Arrow*, Summer 1939, cited in E. H. Mikhail, *W. B. Yeats: Interviews and Recollections*, vol. 2 (London: Macmillan; New York: Barnes and Noble, 1977), 251–5. For his biography, see Wayne McKenna, *W. J. Turner, Poet and Music Critic* (Gerrards Cross: Colin Smythe, 1990). See also

Anthony Garrett Anderson, *Hang Your Halo in the Hall: A History of the Savile Club* (London: Savile Club, 1993).

Katharine Tynan (Hinkson) (1859–1931)

Yeats first met the aspiring Irish poet Katharine Tynan in June 1885. She took an early interest in his work and encouraged him to write a play on an Irish subject. Both came under the influence of O'Leary, as is evident from her contribution to *Poems and Ballads of Young Ireland* (1888) and from the Irish Catholic sensibility on display in her early volumes of verse, *Shamrocks* (1887) and *Ballads and Poems* (1891). On marrying Henry Hinkson, a barrister and classics scholar, she moved to London and became a regular contributor to magazines and journals. She wrote more than a hundred novels, some eighteen poetry collections, and two biographies. Her memories of Yeats can be found in *Twenty-Five Years: Reminiscences* (London: Smith Elder; New York: Devin-Adair, 1913); *The Middle Years* (London: Constable, 1916); *Memories* (London: Nash and Grayson, 1924). See also *W. B. Yeats: Letters to Katharine Tynan*, ed. Roger McHugh (Dublin: Clonmore and Reynolds; London: Burns, Oates and Washbourne, 1953).

Dorothy Wellesley (née Ashton) (1889–1956)

In early summer 1935 Lady Ottoline Morrell drove Yeats down to see Lady Gerald Wellesley at Penns in the Rocks, her country home at Withyam, near Groombridge, in Sussex. So began an intimate relationship and a correspondence on poetry that proved valuable both to Yeats in his declining years and to students of Yeats ever since. After losing Coole with Lady Gregory's death in 1932, Yeats found compensation and a new pleasure in the wife of the seventh Duke of Wellington. Yeats would send her newly composed poems, such as 'Lapis Lazuli', and make corrections to her own verse, which he rated very highly. She and her partner Hilda Matheson were with Yeats when he died at Roquebrune. See *Letters on Poetry from W.*

B. *Yeats to Dorothy Wellesley* (1940; repr. London: Oxford University Press, 1964). Volumes of her own verse include *Poems* (1920), *Deserted House* (1931), *Lost Planet* (1942), and *Rhymes for Middle Years* (1957). *Lost Planet* contains several tributes to Yeats. See also *Beyond the Grave: Letters on Poetry to W. B. Yeats, From Dorothy Wellesley* (Tunbridge Wells: privately printed by C. Baldwin, n.d.).

Further Reading

YEATS'S TEXTS

Autobiographies (London: Macmillan, 1955).

A Book of Irish Verse Selected from Modern Writers (London: Methuen, 1895).

A Critical Edition of Yeats's A Vision (1925), ed. George Mills Harper and Walter Kelly Hood (London: Macmillan, 1978).

A Vision (London: Macmillan, 1962).

Essays and Introductions (London: Macmillan, 1961).

Explorations, selected by Mrs W. B. Yeats (London: Macmillan, 1962).

Fairy and Folk Tales of the Irish Peasantry (London: Scott, 1888).

John Sherman and Dhoya, ed. Richard J. Finneran (Detroit: Wayne State University Press, 1969).

Letters to the New Island, ed. Horace Reynolds (Cambridge, Mass.: Harvard University Press, 1934).

Memoirs, ed. Denis Donoghue (London: Macmillan, 1972; New York: Macmillan, 1973).

Mythologies (London and New York: Macmillan, 1959).

The Oxford Book of Modern Verse, 1892–1935, chosen by W. B. Yeats (Oxford: Clarendon Press, 1936).

The Secret Rose, Stories by W. B. Yeats: A Variorum Edition, ed. Philip Marcus, Warwick Gould, and Michael J. Sidnell (Ithaca and London: Cornell University Press, 1981).

The Senate Speeches of W. B. Yeats, ed. Donald R. Pearce (Bloomington: Indiana University Press, 1960).

The Speckled Bird, with Variant Versions, ed. William H. O'Donnell (Toronto: McClelland and Stewart, 1976).

Uncollected Prose by W. B. Yeats, vol. 1, ed. John P. Frayne (London: Macmillan; New York: Columbia University Press, 1970).

Uncollected Prose by W. B. Yeats, vol. 2, ed. John P. Frayne and Colton Johnson (London: Macmillan, 1975; New York: Columbia University Press, 1976).

The Variorum Edition of the Poems of W. B. Yeats, ed. Peter Allt and Russell K. Alspach (New York: Macmillan, 1957; repr. 1973).

The Variorum Edition of the Plays of W. B. Yeats, ed. Russell K. Alspach (London and New York, Macmillan, 1966; repr. London: Macmillan, 1979).

The Works of William Blake: Poetic, Symbolic, and Critical, 3 volumes, ed. Edwin J. Ellis and W. B. Yeats (London: Quaritch, 1893).

W. B. Yeats: Prefaces and Introductions, ed. William H. O'Donnell (London: Macmillan, 1988).

Editions of the Poems

The Poems of W. B. Yeats, 2 volumes (London: Macmillan, 1949).

The Collected Poems of W. B. Yeats (London: Macmillan, 1950).

W. B. Yeats: The Poems, A New Edition, ed. Richard Finneran (New York: Macmillan, 1983; London: Macmillan, 1984).

Yeats's Poems, ed. A. Norman Jeffares (London: Macmillan, 1989).

The Book of Yeats's Poems, ed. Hazard Adams (Tallahassee: Florida State University Press, 1990).

W. B. Yeats: Selected Poetry, ed. Timothy Webb (Harmondsworth: Penguin, 1991).

Collected Poems of W. B. Yeats, ed. Augustine Martin (London: Vintage, 1992).

W. B. Yeats: The Poems, ed. Daniel Albright (1990; rev. edn London: J. M. Dent, 1994).

Domville (Oxford: Clarendon Press, 1986).

The Collected Letters of W. B. Yeats, vol. 3, 1901–4, ed. John Kelly and Ronald Schuchard (Oxford: Clarendon Press, 1994).

The Gonne-Yeats Letters, 1893–1938: Always Your Friend, ed. Anna MacBride White and A. Norman Jeffares (London: Pimlico, 1993).

LETTERS

Letters on Poetry from W. B. Yeats to Dorothy Wellesley, intro. Kathleen Raine (1940; London and New York: Oxford University Press, 1964).

J. B. Yeats: Letters to His Son W. B. Yeats and Others, 1869–1922, ed. Joseph Hone (London: Faber and Faber, 1944).

Florence Farr, Bernard Shaw, W. B. Yeats: Letters, ed. Clifford Bax (London: Home and Van Thal, 1946).

W. B. Yeats: Letters to Katharine Tynan, ed. Roger McHugh (Dublin: Clonmore and Reynolds; London: Burns Oates and Washbourne, 1953).

W. B. Yeats and T. Sturge Moore: Their Correspondence, 1901–1937, ed. Ursula Bridge (London: Routledge and Kegan Paul; New York: Oxford University Press, 1953).

The Letters of W. B. Yeats, ed. Allan Wade (London: Rupert Hart-Davis, 1954).

Ah, Sweet Dancer: W. B. Yeats, Margot Ruddock: A Correspondence, ed. Roger McHugh (London and New York: Macmillan, 1970).

The Correspondence of Robert Bridges and W. B. Yeats, ed. Richard Finneran (London: Macmillan, 1977).

Letters to W. B. Yeats, 2 volumes, ed. Richard Finneran, George Mills Harper, and William M. Murphy (London: Macmillan; New York: Columbia University Press, 1977).

The Collected Letters of W. B. Yeats, vol. 1, 1865–95, ed. John Kelly and Eric

BIOGRAPHICAL STUDIES

Ellmann, Richard, *Yeats: The Man and the Masks* (1948; rev. ed. London: Oxford University Press, 1979).

———, *Eminent Domain: Yeats among Wilde, Joyce, Pound, Eliot and Auden* (New York: Oxford University Press, 1967).

Eglinton, John, *Irish Literary Portraits* (London: Macmillan, 1935).

Ervine, St John E., *Some Impressions of My Elders* (London: George Allen and Unwin, 1923).

Gibbon, Monk, *The Masterpiece and the Man: Yeats as I Knew Him* (London: Rupert Hart-Davis, 1959).

Gogarty, Oliver St John, *William Butler Yeats: A Memoir* (Dublin: Dolmen, 1963).

Gwynn, Stephen (ed.), *Scattering Branches: Tributes to the Memory of W. B. Yeats* (London: Macmillan, 1940).

Harper, George Mills, *W. B. Yeats and W. T. Horton: The Record of an Occult Friendship* (Atlantic Highlands, New Jersey: Humanities Press, 1980).

Harwood, John, *Olivia Shakespear and W. B. Yeats: After Long Silence* (London: Macmillan, 1989).

Hone, Joseph, *William Butler Yeats: The Poet in Contemporary Ireland* (Dublin and London: Maunsel, ⟨1915⟩).

———, *W. B. Yeats: 1865–1939* (London: Macmillan, 1942).

Jeffares, A. N., *W. B. Yeats: Man and Poet* (1949; rev. ed. London: Routledge and Kegan Paul, 1962).

338

———, *W. B. Yeats: A New Biography* (London: Hutchinson, 1988).

Kelly, John, '"Friendship is the only house I have": Lady Gregory and W. B. Yeats' in Ann Saddlemyer and Colin Smythe (eds), *Lady Gregory Fifty Years After* (Gerrards Cross: Colin Smythe, 1987).

Lewis, Gifford, *The Yeats Sisters and the Cuala* (Blackrock, Co. Dublin: Irish Academic Press, 1994).

MacBride, Maud Gonne, *A Servant of the Queen* (London: Gollancz, 1938).

Martin, Augustine, *W. B. Yeats* (Dublin: Gill and Macmillan, 1983).

Masefield, John, *Some Memories of W. B. Yeats* (Dundrum: Cuala Press, 1940).

Mikhail, E. H., *W. B. Yeats: Interviews and Recollections*, 2 volumes (London: Macmillan, 1977).

Moore, George, *Hail and Farewell*, 3 volumes (London: Heinemann, 1911–14).

Murphy, William, *Prodigal Father: The Life of John Butler Yeats (1839–1922)* (Ithaca and London: Cornell University Press, 1978).

O'Casey, Sean, *Autobiographies*, 2 volumes (London: Macmillan, 1963).

Pollock, J. H., *William Butler Yeats* (London: Duckworth; Dublin: Talbot Press, 1935).

Tynan, Katherine, *Memories* (London: Eveleigh Nash and Grayson, 1924).

Yeats, Michael, 'Yeats: The Public Man' in *Southern Review* V, New Series, no. 3, July 1969, 872–85.

INTRODUCTIONS

Archibald, Douglas, *Yeats* (Syracuse: Syracuse University Press, 1983).

Donoghue, Denis, *Yeats* (London: Fontana/Collins, 1971).

Faulkner, Peter, *Yeats* (Milton Keynes: Open University Press, 1987).

Peterson, Richard F., *William Butler Yeats* (Boston: Twayne, 1982).

Tuohy, Frank, *Yeats* (London: Macmillan, 1976).

REFERENCE BOOKS AND GUIDES

Balliet, Conrad A., *W. B. Yeats: A Census of the Manuscripts* (New York and London: Garland, 1990).

Bradford, Curtis, *Yeats at Work* (Carbondale: University of Southern Illinois Press, 1965).

Bushrui, Suheil, and Tim Prentki, *An International Companion to the Poetry of W. B. Yeats* (Gerrards Cross: Colin Smythe, 1989).

Clark, David, *Yeats at Songs and Choruses* (Gerrards Cross: Colin Smythe, 1983).

Cross, K. G. W., and R. T. Dunlop, *A Bibliography of Yeats Criticism, 1887–1965* (New York: Macmillan, 1971).

Domville, Eric, *A Concordance to the Plays of W. B. Yeats*, 2 volumes (Ithaca and London: Cornell University Press, 1972).

Finneran, Richard, 'W. B. Yeats' in *Recent Research on Anglo-Irish Writers* (New York: The Modern Language Association of America, 1983).

Gordon, D. J. (ed.), *W. B. Yeats: Images of a Poet* (Manchester: Manchester University Press, 1961).

Jeffares, A. N., *A New Commentary on the Poems of W. B. Yeats* (London: Macmillan, 1984).

Jeffares, A. N., and A. S. Knowland (eds), *A Commentary on the Collected Plays of W. B. Yeats* (London: Macmillan, 1975).

Jochum, K. P. S., *W. B. Yeats: A Classified Bibliography of Criticism*, 2nd ed. (Urbana: University of Illinois Press, 1990).

O'Donnell, William, *A Guide to the Prose Fiction of W. B. Yeats* (Ann Arbor, Michigan: UMI Research Press, 1983).

———, 'Checklist of Portraits of W. B. Yeats,' in *Yeats Annual*, no. 8 (London: Macmillan, 1991), 184–98.

O'Shea, Edward, *A Descriptive Catalog of W. B. Yeats's Library* (New York and London: Garland, 1985).

Parrish, Stephen Maxfield, and James Allan Painter, *A Concordance to the Poems of W. B. Yeats* (Ithaca and London: Cornell University Press, 1963).

Pierce, David, *W. B. Yeats: A Guide through the Critical Maze* (Bristol: Bristol Classical Press, 1989).

Stallworthy, Jon, *Between the Lines: Yeats's Poetry in the Making* (Oxford: Clarendon Press, 1963).

—— , *Vision and Revision in Yeats's 'Last Poems'* (Oxford: Clarendon Press, 1969).

Taylor, Richard, *A Reader's Guide to the Plays of W. B. Yeats* (London: Macmillan, 1984).

Unterecker, John, *A Reader's Guide to W. B. Yeats* (1959; repr. London: Thames and Hudson, 1975).

Ure, Peter, *Yeats the Playwright: A Commentary on Character and Design in the Major Plays* (London: Routledge and Kegan Paul, 1963).

Wade, Allan, *A Bibliography of the Writings of W. B. Yeats*, 3rd ed., rev. Russell K. Alspach (London: Rupert Hart-Davis, 1968).

CRITICAL STUDIES

Adams, Hazard, *Blake and Yeats: The Contrary Vision* (1955; repr. New York: Russell and Russell, 1968).

Bloom, Harold, *Yeats* (New York: Oxford University Press, 1970).

Bohlmann, Otto, *Yeats and Nietzsche: An Exploration of Major Nietzschean Echoes in the Writings of William Butler Yeats* (London: Macmillan; Totowa, New Jersey: Barnes and Noble, 1982).

Bornstein, George, *Yeats and Shelley* (Chicago and London: Chicago University Press, 1970).

Craig, Cairns, *Yeats, Eliot, Pound and the Politics of Poetry* (London: Croom Helm, 1981).

Cullingford, Elizabeth Butler, *Yeats, Ireland and Fascism* (London: Macmillan, 1981).

—— , *Gender and History in Yeats's Love Poetry* (Cambridge: Cambridge University Press, 1993).

Diggory, Terence, *Yeats and American Poetry: The Tradition of the Self* (Princeton: Princeton University Press, 1983).

Donoghue, Denis, and J. R. Mulryne (eds), *An Honoured Guest: New Essays on W. B. Yeats* (London: Edward Arnold, 1965).

Ellmann, Richard, *The Identity of Yeats* (London: Macmillan, 1954).

Engelberg, Edward, *The Vast Design: Patterns in W. B. Yeats's Aesthetic* (London: Oxford University Press, 1965).

Flannery, James W., *W. B. Yeats and the Idea of a Theatre: The Early Abbey Theatre in Theory and Practice* (New Haven and London: Yale University Press, 1976).

Fletcher, Ian, *W. B. Yeats and His Contemporaries* (Brighton, Sussex: Harvester, 1987).

Grossman, Allen Richard, *Poetic Knowledge in the Early Yeats: A Study of 'The Wind among the Reeds'* (Charlottesville: University Press of Virginia, 1969).

Hall, James, and Martin Steinmann (eds), *The Permanence of Yeats: Selected Criticism* (New York: Macmillan, 1950).

Harris, Daniel, *Yeats: Coole Park and Ballylee* (Baltimore: Johns Hopkins University Press, 1974).

Henn, T. R., *The Lonely Tower: Studies in the Poetry of W. B. Yeats* (London: Methuen, 1950).

Jeffares, A. Norman (ed.), *Yeats the European* (Savage, Maryland: Barnes and Noble, 1989).

Jeffares, A. Norman, and K. G. W. Cross (eds), *In Excited Reverie: A Centenary Tribute to William Butler Yeats, 1865–1939* (London: Macmillan, 1965).

Kermode, Frank, *Romantic Image* (London: Routledge and Kegan Paul; New York: Macmillan, 1957).

Kinahan, Frank, *Yeats, Folklore and Occultism: Contexts of the Early Work and Thought* (London: Unwin and Hyman, 1988).

Kline, Gloria, *The Last Courtly Lover: Yeats and the Idea of Woman* (Ann Arbor, Michigan: UMI Research Press, 1983).

Langbaum, Robert, *The Mysteries of Identity: A Theme in Modern Literature*

(Oxford: Oxford University Press, 1977).

Larrissy, Edward, *Yeats the Poet: The Measures of Difference* (Hemel Hempstead: Harvester, 1994).

Levine, Herbert, *Yeats's Daimonic Renewal* (Ann Arbor, Michigan: UMI Research Press, 1983).

Lipking, Lawrence, *The Life of the Poet: Beginning and Ending Poetic Careers* (Chicago and London: University of Chicago Press, 1981).

Loizeaux, Elizabeth Bergmann, *Yeats and the Visual Arts* (New Brunswick and London: Rutgers University Press, 1986).

Longenbach, James, *Stone Cottage: Pound, Yeats, and Modernism* (Oxford: Oxford University Press, 1988).

Lynch, D., *Yeats: The Poetics of the Self* (Chicago and London: Chicago University Press, 1979).

MacNeice, Louis, *The Poetry of W. B. Yeats* (London: Oxford University Press, 1941).

Melchiori, Giorgio, *The Whole Mystery of Art: Pattern into Poetry in the Work of W. B. Yeats* (London: Routledge and Kegan Paul, 1960).

Moore, Virginia, *The Unicorn: William Butler Yeats's Search for Reality* (New York: Macmillan, 1954).

North, Michael, *The Political Aesthetic of Yeats, Eliot, and Pound* (Cambridge: Cambridge University Press, 1991).

O'Hara, Daniel, *Tragic Knowledge: Yeats's Autobiography and Hermeneutics* (New York: Columbia University Press, 1981).

Parkinson, Thomas, *W. B. Yeats, Self-Critic: A Study of his Early Verse* (Berkeley and Los Angeles: University of California Press, 1951).

————, ed., *W. B. Yeats: The Later Poetry* (Berkeley and Los Angeles: University of California Press, 1965).

Perloff, Marjorie, ' "The Tradition of Myself": The Autobiographical Mode of W. B. Yeats', in *Journal of Modern Literature*, vol. 4, 1975, 529–73.

Pritchard, William, ed., *W. B. Yeats: A Critical Anthology* (Harmondsworth: Penguin, 1972).

Putzel, Stephen, *Reconstructing Yeats: 'The Secret Rose' and 'The Wind Among the Reeds'* (Dublin: Gill and Macmillan, 1986).

Raine, Kathleen, *Yeats the Initiate: Essays on Certain Themes in the Work of W. B. Yeats* (Dublin: Dolmen; London: George Allen and Unwin, 1986).

Stead, C. K., *The New Poetic: Yeats to Eliot* (London: Hutchinson University Library, 1964).

————, *Pound, Yeats, Eliot and the Modernist Movement* (London: Macmillan, 1986).

Stock, A. G., *W. B. Yeats: His Poetry and Thought* (1961; repr. Cambridge: Cambridge University Press, 1964).

Torchiana, Donald, *Yeats and Georgian Ireland* (Oxford: Oxford University Press, 1966).

Vendler, Helen, *Yeats's 'Vision' and the Later Plays* (Cambridge, Mass.: Harvard University Press, 1963).

Watson, George, *Irish Identity and the Literary Revival: Synge, Yeats, Joyce and O'Casey* (London: Croom Helm; New York: Barnes and Noble, 1979).

Whitaker, Thomas, *Swan and Shadow: Yeats's Dialogue with History* (Chapel Hill: University of North Carolina Press, 1964).

Wilson, Edmund, *Axel's Castle: A Study in the Imaginative Literature of 1870–1930* (New York and London: Scribner's, 1931).

Wilson, F. A. C., *Yeats and Tradition* (London: Gollancz, 1958).

Young, D., *Troubled Mirror: A Study of Yeats's 'The Tower'* (Iowa: Iowa University Press, 1987).

HISTORICAL STUDIES AND
BACKGROUND INFORMATION

Boyd, Ernest, *Ireland's Literary Renaissance* (New York: Alfred Knopf, 1922).

Brown, Terence, *Ireland: A Social and Cultural History, 1922–1985* (London: Fontana, 1985).

Brown, Malcolm, *The Politics of Irish*

Literature: From Thomas Davis to W. B. Yeats (London: George Allen and Unwin, 1972).

Costello, Peter, The Heart Grown Brutal: The Irish Revolution in Literature, from Parnell to the Death of Yeats, 1891–1939 (Dublin: Gill and Macmillan, 1977).

Deane, Seamus, Celtic Revivals: Essays in Modern Irish Literature 1880–1980 (London: Faber and Faber, 1987).

Freyer, Grattan, W. B. Yeats and the Anti-Democratic Tradition (Dublin: Gill and Macmillan, 1981).

Foster, Roy, Paddy and Mr Punch: Connections in Irish and English History (Harmondsworth: Allen Lane, 1993).

Harper, George Mills, Yeats's Golden Dawn (London: Macmillan, 1974).

———— (ed.), Yeats and the Occult (London: Macmillan, 1976).

Howe, Ellic, The Magicians of the Golden Dawn: A Documentary History of a Magical Order, 1887–1923 (London: Routledge and Kegan Paul, 1972).

Innes, C. L., Woman and Nation in Irish Literature and Society, 1880–1935 (Hemel Hempstead: Harvester Wheatsheaf, 1993).

Kain, Richard, Dublin in the Age of William Butler Yeats and James Joyce (Norman: University of Oklahoma Press, 1962).

Kirby, Sheelah, The Yeats Country: A Guide to Places in the West of Ireland Associated with the Life and Writings of William Butler Yeats (Dublin: Dolmen Press; London: Oxford University Press, 1962).

Lee, Joseph, Ireland, 1912–1985: Politics and Society (Cambridge: Cambridge University Press, 1989).

Lloyd, David, Anomalous States: Irish Writing and the Post-Colonial Moment (Dublin: The Lilliput Press, 1993).

Longley, Edna, The Living Stream: Literature and Revisionism in Ireland (Newcastle: Bloodaxe, 1994).

Lynd, Robert, Home Life in Ireland (London: Mills and Boon, 1909).

Malins, Edward, and John Purkis, A Preface to Yeats (1974; rev. ed. London: Longman, 1994).

Marcus, Philip, Yeats and the Beginning of the Irish Renaissance (Ithaca and London: Cornell University Press, 1970).

McCormack, William J., From Burke to Beckett: Ascendancy, Tradition and Betrayal in Literary History (Cork: Cork University Press, 1994).

Miller, Liam, The Noble Drama of W. B. Yeats (Atlantic Highlands, New Jersey; Dublin: Dolmen Press, 1977).

O'Driscoll, Robert, and Lorna Reynolds (eds), Yeats and the Theatre (London: Macmillan, 1975).

Ó hAodha, Micheál, Theatre in Ireland (Oxford: Blackwell, 1974).

Reid, B. L., The Man from New York: John Quinn and His Friends (New York: Oxford University Press, 1968).

Robinson, Lennox, Ireland's Abbey Theatre: A History, 1899–1951 (London: Sidgwick and Jackson, 1951).

Thuente, Mary, Yeats and Irish Folklore (Dublin: Gill and Macmillan; Totowa, New Jersey: Barnes and Noble, 1981).

Toomey, Deirdre (ed.), Yeats and Women: Yeats Annual, no. 9 (London: Macmillan, 1992).

Welch, Robert, Irish Poetry from Moore to Yeats (Gerrards Cross: Colin Smythe, 1980).

————, Changing States: Transformations in Modern Irish Writing (London and New York: Routledge, 1993).

Worth, Katharine, The Irish Drama of Europe from Yeats to Beckett (London: Athlone Press, 1978).

Yeats, Michael, 'W. B. Yeats and Irish Folk Song', in Southern Folklore Quarterly, vol. 31, no. 2, June 1966, 153–78.

JOURNALS

Yeats: An Annual of Critical and Textual Studies, ed. Richard Finneran (Ann Arbor and London: UMI Research Press, 1983–).

Yeats Annual, ed. Warwick Gould (London: Macmillan, 1982–).

Index

ML